HUMAN INTIMACY:
Marriage, the Family and Its Meaning

Second Edition

Frank D. Cox
Santa Barbara City College, California

West Publishing Company
St. Paul   New York   Los Angeles   San Francisco

Copy editing: Joanne Cuthbertson
Design: Janet Bollow
Illustrations: John Foster, Sue Sellars
Production Coordination: Janet Bollow Associates
Composition: Hansen & Associates Graphics

Library of Congress Cataloging in Publication Data

Cox, Frank D
  Human intimacy.

  Bibliography: p.
  Includes index.
  1. Family—United States. 2. Marriage—United
States. 3. Sex customs—United States. I. Title.
HQ535.C7 1981   306.8'0973   80–24987
ISBN 0–8299–0367–4
2nd Reprint 1981

Acknowledgments

page 13 Figure 1 "Intensity Matrix for the Analysis of an Intimate Relationship" in Carolynee Kieffer, "New Depths in Intimacy" from MARRIAGE AND ALTERNATIVES: EXPLORING INTIMATE RELATIONSHIPS by Roger W. Libby and Robert N. Whitehurst. Copyright © 1977 by Scott, Foresman and Company. Reprinted by permission.

page 16 Copyright 1979 by the National Council on Family Relations. Reprinted by permission.

pages 31-34 Reprinted from "The Family: Is It Obsolete?" by Etzioni, The Journal of Current Social *ISSUES*, Winter 1977.

page 37 Copyright © 1948 by Cole Porter. Copyright Renewed, Assigned to John F. Wharton, as Trustee of the Cole Porter Musical and Literary Property Trusts. Chappell & Co., Inc., owner of publication and allied rights. International Copyright Secured. ALL RIGHTS RESERVED. Used by permission.

pages 37-38 Copyright © 1956 by Alan Jay Lerner and Frederick Loewe. Chappell & Co., Inc., publisher and owner of allied rights throughout the world. International Copyright Secured. ALL RIGHTS RESERVED. Used with permission.

page 41 Reprinted from Social Forces 15 (May 1937): "Comparative Data on Division of Labor by Sex" by George Murdock. Copyright © The University of North Carolina Press.

page 44 Reprinted by permission of the PaperBook Press, Westwood, Mass.

page 44 Human Behavior/The Family by Robert Wernick and the Editors of Time-Life Books © 1974 Time Inc.

page 46 Data from pp. 45-49 in THE SOCIAL CONTEXT OF MARRIAGE, 3rd Edition by J. Richard Udry. Copyright © 1966, 1971, 1974 by J. B. Lippincott Company. Reprinted by permission of Harper & Row, Publishers, Inc.

page 47 Copyright © 1974 Chronicle Publishing Company, reprinted by permission of the author.

page 49 Reprinted by permission from Frieze, Irene H. et al., *Women and Sex Roles*, W. W. Norton, publisher.

page 51 Reprinted with permission from Exploring the Sex Differences by D. Z. Ullian. Copyright by Academic Press, Inc. (London) Ltd.

page 61 Reprinted with permission from *Newsweek*, April 30, 1979.

page 63 Reproduced by permission from Beyond Sex Roles edited by Alice G. Sargent, from Women in organizations: sex roles, group dynamics, and change strategies by Roseabeth Moss Kanter, copyright © 1977, West Publishing Company. All rights reserved.

page 64 From OPEN MARRIAGE: A New Life Style for Couples by Nena O'Neill and George O'Neill. Copyright © 1972 by Nena O'Neill and George O'Neill. Reprinted by permission of the publisher, M. Evans & Co., Inc., New York.

page 71 Reproduced by permission from Beyond Sex Roles edited by Alice G. Sargent, copyright © 1977, West Publishing Company. All rights reserved.

pages 74-75 Reprinted by permission of The Village Voice. Copyright © The Village Voice, Inc., 1971.

page 80 From MARRIAGE: East & West by David and Vera Mace. Copyright © 1959, 1960 by David and Vera Mace. Reprinted by permission of Doubleday & Company, Inc.

page 90 © 1975 United Feature Syndicate, Inc.

pages 92-95 Adaptation of Chapter 5, "The Six Basic Styles" from STYLES OF LIVING by Marcia Lasswell and Norman Lobsenz. Reprinted by permission of Doubleday & Company, Inc.

page 95 From PSYCHOLOGY, Cox, Frank D., 1973, Dubuque, Iowa, Wm. C. Brown Company Publishers.

page 99 Dennis the Menace ® cartoon courtesy of Hank Ketcham and © By Field Enterprises Inc.

page 104 Copyright © 1977 Human Behavior Magazine. Reprinted by permission.

pages 146-147 Source: Adapted from a table compiled by William E. Mariano, THE WORLD ALMANAC AND BOOK OF FACTS, 1975 edition; Copyright © Newspaper Enterprise Association, Inc., New York, 1974.

page 148 Copyright © 1972 by Susan Admiston. First appeared in *Ms. Magazine*. Reprinted with permission of Julian Bach Literary Agency, Inc.

pages 168-170 © 1969 by Claude M. Steiner, 2901 Piedmont Avenue, Berkeley, CA.

page 176 From Shirley J. Gilbert, "Self-Disclosure, Intimacy and Communication in Families," THE FAMILY COORDINATOR, July 1976, pp. 221-232. Copyright © 1976 by the National Council on Family Relations. Reprinted by permission.

page 178 From Richard Hunt and Edward Rydman, CREATIVE MARRIAGE (Boston: Holbrook Press, 1976), pp. 50-51.

page 185 Reproduced by permission from Beyond Sex Roles edited by Alice G. Sargent, from man/woman dynamics: some typical communication patterns by Carol Pierce and Janice Sanfacon, copyright © 1977, West Publishing Company. All rights reserved.

pages 191-193 Reprinted by permission of William Morrow & Co., Inc. from THE INTIMATE ENEMY by Dr. George R. Bach & Peter Wyden. Copyright © 1968 by George R. Bach & Peter Wyden. Also reprinted by permission of Dr. George R. Bach, Distinguished Professor of Psychology, Professional School of the Humanities, San Diego, California.

pages 196-198 Selection is reprinted from THE MIRAGES OF MARRIAGE by William J. Kederer and Dr. Don D. Jackson, with

Contents in Brief

Contents

**Chapter 1
Human Intimacy:
The Family and
Its Meaning**
page 1

**Chapter 2
People Liberation:
Changing Masculine
and Feminine Roles**
page 35

Chapter 12
The Challenge
of Parenthood
page 359

Chapter 13
Family Life Stages:
Mid-Life Crises to
Surviving Spouse
page 391

Preface

The second edition of a textbook is always exciting for an author. First, it means that the book was well enough received that a second edition is warranted. Second, it means that the author has a great deal of new input coming from the many people who have used the book. With such input, a second edition cannot help but be much improved. Third, in a field as complex and rapidly-changing as marriage and the family, the need to update is perhaps more pressing than in many other fields.

For all of these reasons, it was with great joy and anticipation that I undertook to make *Human Intimacy* an even better textbook, more up to date, more thorough, more interesting, more readable, and, above all, more exciting. With the help of the following reviewers and, of course, the many production prople at West Publishing Company, I believe that we have accomplished our goals.

Special thanks for their time and input go to:

Esther Hay, Kansas State University

Lois Mickle, Oklahoma State University

Ed Powers, Stephen Goettsch, Chris Johnson, and Lois Sabol, Iowa State University

George Roleder, Mt. San Antonio College, California

Alexis Walker, University of Oklahoma

Marsha Widdows, Phoenix College

You will find that the second edition is a thorough revision. In addition to the usual updating, there have been substantial additions to the book. Two new chapters highlight these additions.

Chapter 8, "The Subtle Revolution: The Working Woman," examines woman's entry into the world of work, which represents one of the major changes in family life in the past forty years.

Chapter 13, "Family Life Stages: Mid-Life Crises to Surviving Spouse," follows the family through the middle and later years of its existence, thus completing the evolving and changing picture of the family over time.

Human Intimacy remains a positive statement about marriage and the family. It realistically reflects the place of marriage and family in today's American society. But more important, it tries to offer hope for tomorrow's family by emphasizing what the family ideally can become as well as what it currently is. The beauty of the institution called family is that it is adaptable and flexible. Those persons with knowledge of themselves, the family, and their culture have the opportunity in America to build a marriage and a family that will suit their own liking. Families can change for the better; intimate relationships can become more deeply satisfying and fulfilling. It is with these ends in mind that *Human Intimacy* was written.

As was the case with the first edition, many people besides the author are responsible for this book. I already have mentioned those who so generously offered their suggestions for improvement and the many fine production people at West Publishing. I would like to add special mention to Janet Bollow who has again designed an attractive and appealing book and the editorial staff at West who made the project a successful and happy experience.

Frank D. Cox

⌒ Preface to the First Edition

Human Intimacy: Marriage, the Family and Its Meaning was written to stimulate thinking about the meaning and function of marriage and the family in American life. It is now both popular and easy to criticize marriage. Indeed, if one listens to popular commentary, marriage is all but dead in the United States. Yet, this is far from the truth. While the merits of marriage and family are being vigorously debated, as they always have been, and alternate life styles are being tried by some, marriage and family are still a prominent part of the American scene. Most of us participated in families as we grew up. And more than 90 percent of us will be a marriage partner at some time in our life. Of those over 18 years of age, 73 percent of the males and 67 percent of the females are currently married. I believe that the family is functioning better than doomsday critics would have us believe and that intimacy is still most often sought within a family setting.

With criticism of marriage so popular, it is difficult to concentrate on improving the marital relationship. Yet a marriage does not naturally take care of itself nor will "love" alone make a marriage successful. After all, most people who have divorced, married their ex-spouse out of "love." What happened? Why didn't their relationship work?

Human Intimacy stresses the point that every person does have the ability to improve his or her intimate relationships. Marriages tend to get into trouble because people believe that they cannot do much about their marriage and because many of us are unwilling to take the time to nourish and enrich our intimate relationships.

In *Human Intimacy*, I take a positive view of the potentials inherent in the marital relationship and throughout the book emphasize how those potentials may be actualized. In addition, of course, the entire field of family life is examined and discussed, I hope, in a positive and constructive manner (see Inset 1 – 2, page 10 for the basic assumptions upon which the book is based).

One advantage of American society is the wide spectrum of choice it offers individuals in most aspects of life. Although family patterns have been somewhat limited in the past, a wider variety of intimate life styles is becoming acceptable. For example, the loosening of traditional sex roles allows individuals greater freedom to adapt marriage to their own liking, to make their intimate relationships unique and vital, than did past generations. Marriage is seen to involve personal satisfaction rather than just the proper fulfillment of duties and specific roles.

It is my hope that *Human Intimacy* will contribute to your ability to make intelligent, satisfying choices about intimate and meaningful relationships. Individuals who are able to make satisfying choices in their lives are most apt to be fulfilled persons. And fulfilled persons have the best chance of making their marriage relationship exciting and growth-producing.

This book has several features designed to aid your reading. First, each chapter is preceded by a comprehensive outline that gives an overview of the material to follow. The outline also serves as a excellent study guide and tool of review.

Second, "Insets" supply interesting detail, allow hypothesizing, and present controversy. They also add variety to the reading much as an aside adds variety to a lecture.

Because the field of marriage and family is fraught with controversy and divergent opinions, "Scenes from Marriage" appear at the end of each chapter. These are essentially condensed excerpts and discussions from other sources that add new dimensions and/or conflicting viewpoints to each chapter.

To add life and realism, many case studies are scattered throughout the book. They highlight the principles being discussed and help one to see how a principle might be applied in everyday life.

As with all such undertakings, many more people than myself alone have contributed to *Human Intimacy*. The most important contributors are the many family members with whom I have interacted all my life. Grandparents, parents, aunts, uncles, cousins, siblings, and, of course, my immediate family. In addition, there are all the many fine researchers and writers in the field who have influenced and contributed to my thoughts. Then, there are the many production people who under the guidance of West editorial staff and Janet Bollow actually put the book together in a well-edited and attractive manner. Dr. Norman Jacobs must receive a special word of thanks for his contributions to chapters 5 and 6.

Frank D. Cox

HUMAN INTIMACY:
Marriage, the Family and Its Meaning

Chapter 1

Contents

Human Intimacy:
The Family
and Its Meaning

Most Americans are involved in family life. Most of us have been reared in families and over 90 percent of us will marry at some time in our lives, thus creating a new family unit of our own. Because of our close involvement with families, we usually have strong personal feelings about both marriage and family. Such feelings are natural. Yet we must examine our feelings about such an intimate topic in order to understand just how the American family might affect us personally. Thus, to study the research data on marriage and the family is also to study one's own feelings about the institutions. A piece of data may appear simple and clear (one in two American marriages will break up), yet its meaning will vary with the individual according to his or her own feelings. This is why there appears to be so little agreement about how marriages and families are changing and what the changes mean. Each of us interprets the data in a personal manner based on our own experiences.

Lest one take this to mean that there are *only* personal opinions about the family institution, let me hasten to add that there is, indeed, a broad and rich foundation of scientific information about this most personal and intimate of relationships. The person who has knowledge of this information is in a much better position to understand his or her own feelings about marriage and family than is the ignorant person. Those who understand both the scientific information and their own feelings are in the best position to build intimate relationships that are successful and satisfying. It is towards this end that this book has been written.

My purpose in presenting this brief overview (most of the examples are discussed more thoroughly later in the book) is to highlight the changes taking place, not to advocate them. Whether such changes are good or bad for the American family and society is open for debate.

An Overview of Changes in Family Life

Only a few years ago R. M. Rimmer's novel *The Harrad Experiment* (1966) upset a good number of parents. Rimmer advocated experimental cohabitation as part of the college curriculum. Men and women, he said, should live together to learn about intimate relationships which, after all, will be their major mode of living throughout their future lives.

Until recently, American colleges and universities acted as surrogate parents. Dormitory rules were strict, and male and female interaction was controlled. Before World War II, pregnancy and even marriage were often grounds for expulsion. Yet, not many years after *The Harrad Experiment* surprised and shocked many people, more than half the nation's resident college students live in coeducational dorms (*Time*, June 3, 1974). There are even schools where men and women can share the same suite.

Cohabitation has become a popular way of life among a growing segment of the population. Approximately 2.3 percent of all couples living together are cohabiting; that is, living together without the benefit of marriage. However, it is estimated that about 25 percent of undergraduate college students will have cohabited at some time before they graduate (Macklin, 1978) (see Chapter 14).

Another dramatic change in the marriage institution has been the trend toward easier divorce. In 1969, California became the first state to institute "no-fault" divorce. Up until then, divorce laws in the United States were based on ecclesiastical fault-finding doctrines of the seventeenth century. To obtain a divorce, one party had to prove the other at fault or guilty of at least one among several legal grounds for divorce, such as nonsupport, adultery, or mental cruelty. Often the terms of the divorce punished the guilty spouse by granting a disproportionately high property settlement or alimony, or both, to the aggrieved party. Many liberal theorists, realizing that seldom is only one spouse at fault, advocated easier divorce. In the early 1930s, Judge Benjamin Lindsey suggested a "companionate" marriage that could be easily dissolved. Anthropologist Margaret Mead has promoted the idea of a "two-step" marriage. People who did not plan to have children would take part in a marriage that could be easily dissolved. Those desiring children would participate in a marriage that involved greater personal and legal commitment.

California's dissolution of marriage law grants divorce simply and quickly. All a spouse must do is show irreconcilable differences. Lawyers are not even necessary if the couple can agree upon child custody and property settlement. All but three states have now followed California by instituting some form of no-fault divorce legislation (see Chapter 15).

The legal acceptance of abortion is another dramatic recent change that affects marriage and family (see Chapter 10). For years, abortion has been strictly regulated by the states. Even an impregnated rape victim could not have an abortion in most states. Many women died from illegal abortions. Women's groups and groups concerned with personal freedoms began to exert pressure on state legislatures, and gradually the states reformed their abortion laws in the late sixties and early seventies. Then, on January 22, 1973, the U.S. Supreme Court overturned all state abortion laws, making abortion on request a legal reality. Although the conflict over abortion is continuing, the right of a woman to make her own decision about her body had been established legally.

Adoption by a single person, birth control pills for minor girls without parental consent, transsexual operations, marital contracts, reversed sex roles (including maternity leave for fathers), gay liberation, and surrogate sex partners to help solve sexual problems are some of the many changes in sexual mores that affect marriage and the family. And what about the science of biology and attempts to develop and control life itself? Here, too, breakthroughs may drastically affect our sexual mores, marriage, and the family.

Although still in the future, but a distinct possibility, genetic engineering will allow prospective parents to pick sex, eye color, stature, and many other physical characteristics for their future child while avoiding possible genetic defects.

Refinement of freezing techniques has already permitted the establishment of sperm and egg banks. A further step has been the test tube baby, the first of whom was born in England in 1978. The egg is fertilized outside the womb and after a certain amount of development is placed into the woman's uterus where it continues to develop until birth (see Scenes from Marriage, p. 322).

Cloning, on the other hand, is asexual propagation. That is, reproduction is brought about without sexual fertilization. Body cells, which contain all genetic information, have already been successfully used to reproduce plants and, more recently, frogs.

For example, J. B. Gurdon of Oxford University (Rorvik, 1971) takes an unfertilized egg (sex cell) from a frog and destroys its nucleus with ultraviolet radiation. He then removes the nucleus from a body cell of another frog. This nucleus is implanted into the egg cell. Since the egg cell now has a full genetic complement, it acts as if fertilization has taken place. It begins to divide, finally producing a new tadpole. Since all the genetic material has come from one donor, the new tadpole is identical to the body cell donor. Such experiments suggest the possibility that one day it might be possible to produce many identical copies of desired people by using their body cells.

Some feel that such possibilities will mean the end of the family, yet the family is alive and well and is still the institution of choice for the vast majority of Americans (*U.S. News and World Report*, 1975). Surveys of the American population concluded that most people firmly believe that marriage is necessary, and that family forms should be preserved. Four out of five respondents said that a happy family life was their most important personal goal (The Yankelovich Organization, 1974; *Time*, 1977; *Psychology Today*, 1979; Kinsey, 1978).

In general, it is easy and popular to attack marriage and suggest alternatives to current practices. But the attacks tend to imply that marriage is a rigid relationship that has passed relatively unchanged into our modern culture. Actually, "marriage has undergone dramatic change, and is still steadily changing, as it adapts itself to today's world" (Mace & Mace, 1977).

In fact, changes in the family due to modernization have led other critics of marriage to long for "the good old days." This suggests that there was some lost golden age of the family. Study of family history, however, fails to uncover any such golden age. The Skolnicks (1980, p. 16) point out that those condemning modernization may have forgotten the problems of the past. Our current problems inside and outside of the family are genuine, but we should never forget that many of the most vexing issues confronting us as men and women, parents and children, derive from the very benefits of modernization — benefits too easily taken for granted or forgotten in the lately fashionable denunciation of modern times. There was no problem of the aged in the past because most people never aged; they died before they got old. Nor was adolescence a difficult stage of the life cycle when children worked and education was a privilege of the rich. And when most people were hungry illiterates, only aristocrats could worry about sexual satisfaction and self-fulfillment. Modernization surely brings trouble in its wake, but how many would, on balance, really want to trade the troubles of our era for the ills of earlier times?

The Maces note that the family has changed from an institution characterized as "formal," "authoritarian," "rigidly disciplined," and as maintaining "rigid sex roles" to a companionship pattern described as an "interpersonal relationship," with "mutual affection," "sympathetic understanding," and "comradeship" (Mace & Mace, 1977, pp. 393–394):

> Surely the first group of terms represents precisely the values in marriage which the counterculture has deplored, and the second group the very values which it has extolled.
>
> What we are saying is that the monogamous marriage and nuclear family function far better in the companionship mode than they ever did in the institutional pattern; and that they can adapt very easily — much more easily than the more clumsy multilateral structures — to the new emphasis on personal and relational growth and development.

Although we have discussed changes in family life, I believe that it is within a creative, dynamic, and changing marriage that most Americans will find intimacy and satisfaction. Despite the popularity of attacking marriage as an institution, most Americans spend most of their lives within a marriage and family relationship. This indicates to me that we need to expend more energy on making marriage viable and fulfilling than we spend on suggesting alternatives to it. As the Maces (1977, p. 392) point out:

> The possibilities for better marriage are exciting. In what we now call the marriage enrichment movement, we are experimenting with new tools and getting encouraging results. In skillfully led couple groups, we are seeing significant and lasting changes taking place in dull, superficial marriages as they break loose and embark on new growth. We are becoming aware that the majority of marriages in North America are functioning far below their potential. But we now realize that couples need no longer accept this miserable yield. With proper help and guidance they can appropriate the locked-up capacity for depth within the relationship that has been there all the time, but that no one helped them to actualize.
>
> In short, we are at last beginning to provide the services to marriages which should have been available a generation ago, when the new alternative companionship style was emerging to replace traditional marriage.

Marriage, children, forever together, mom, dad, apple pie, love, Sunday softball in the park, grandmother's for Sunday dinner — The American Family.

Cohabitation, childlessness, divorce and remarriage, stepdad, stepmom, junk food, child abuse and wife beating, spectator sports in front of the T.V., Pizza Hut for Sunday dinner — The American Family.

Student: "But these two descriptions can't both be of the American family."
Friend: "Oh, but they are and, indeed, there are infinite other descriptions that would also fit. American families each and every one, are unique, in-dividual, and representative of the individuals and their in-teractions within the family."
Student: "But how then can we study the American family if each is unique?"
Friend: "Because they all have certain things in common. They are all alike in some ways."
Student: "But they can't be. You just said they were all different and unique."
Friend: "They are and they are also always changing."
Student: "But how can you study something that is unique and also always changing?"
Friend: "Because change occurs in the midst of con-tinuity and continuity can remain despite change."

Student: "You are saying then that each family is unique but has things in common with all other families and, in addition, families are always changing but have continuity."
Friend: "Yes."
Student: "It sounds like a riddle."
Friend: "It is a riddle because in order to understand the family one must be able to live with and understand two abstract principles:

1. Change can occur within continuity, and
2. Uniqueness can exist within commonality."

As you try to understand the family and what is happening to it, remember that the American family, like social change, covers a vast territory and at the same time is far from uniform in design. Everyone is highly conscious of many aspects of change in family life, and yet the central core of family life continues very much the same as it has existed for many generations (Glick, 1977, p. 43). Grasping the two ideas *change within continuity* and *uniqueness within commonality* will help you cope with the seeming riddles of the American family.

Change within Continuity and Uniqueness within Commonality

How can we understand the many changes that are taking place in the American family? As we pointed out, there is seldom agreement on what the many changes mean for the family institution or for the individual American. The meaning of these changes often seems incomprehensible.

Some examples of diverse data interpretation will help to clarify what we mean by these two principles. For example, the divorce rate has risen steadily throughout this century. In 1900, there was about one divorce for every twelve marriages. Today there is about one divorce for every two marriages, although the recent dramatic upsurge in divorce (starting about 1965) has slowed in the past three years. Many use this statistic to support their contention that the family in America is in real trouble, the institution is on the rocks, and that the family will soon be dead and buried. Yet many others see these statis-tics as positive. Americans will have better marriages and more fulfilling family lives because they must no longer put up with the dissatis-factions and empty-shell marriages that previous generations accepted. Indeed, remarriage statistics indicate that divorced persons have even higher marriage rates than single, never-married persons. Thus, most divorced persons leave a particular mate but not the institution of marriage.

A second example again illustrates the conflict that statistics about changing family characteristics evoke. America's birth rate has fallen dramatically since 1957, reaching a low of about 14.5 births per 1000 population in 1975.* In 1979 that had risen to 15.8 per 1000 population, still relatively low compared to earlier levels. Many suggest that the decreased birth rate resulted because many young women decided not to have children. "Having children is no longer an important part of marriage." "Careers are more important and children are only troublesome to the pursuit of one's own goals." Yet, although the proportion of women who state they expect to remain childless went up slightly from 1967 to 1974, decreasing again in 1975 (Bane, 1976), if as few women remain childless as say they will, the childless proportion among women born between 1940 and 1955 will be the lowest ever recorded. The birth rate is decreasing not because more women are remaining childless, but because there has been a large decrease in the number of children each mother has. The average mother born between 1846 and 1855 had 5.7 children. Women born between 1931 and 1935 had an average of 3.4 children. This figure has continued to drop.

Thus, the decreasing birth rate may not mean that families are abandoning having children at all. Rather, it seems to mean that families are having fewer children, which is probably positive for the children. Evidence suggests that children do better in smaller families where they receive more adult time and attention. Bane (1976), after reviewing much demographic data about the family and children, concluded:

> In short, the major demographic changes affecting parents and children in the course of this century have not much altered the basic picture of children living with and being cared for by their parents. The patterns of structural change so often cited as evidence of family decline do not seem to be weakening the bonds between parents and children.

These two examples hopefully point out just how confusing and controversial interpretation of marriage and family data can be. Further, they demonstrate both principles that our two friends were discussing.

First, both examples show change within continuity. The divorce rate has increased dramatically in the past few years, which is indicative of change. Yet those divorcing return to marriage rather

*America's birth rate has generally been falling for the past 200 years with the major exception of the baby boom between about 1945 and 1956, which was related to dislocations and the prosperity caused by World War II.

quickly (close to 50 percent are remarried within three years), indicating continuity of the marriage institution.

Families are having fewer children, a change from the past. But they are indeed having and rearing children as families have always done (continuity).

Both examples can also demonstrate uniqueness within commonality. Two married couples share the commonality of being married. Each partner of one marriage is in their first marriage. One partner of the other marriage is in their second marriage. Thus each couple, although sharing the characteristic of being married, is also unique in so far as their previous marriage experience is concerned.

Some couples opt for no children when they marry, others for one or two or three. All couples share the opportunity to have children in their marriage but are unique in the way they utilize the opportunity.

We have commenced our study of marriage and the family by quickly surveying some of the many changes that are occurring. As we think about these changes, keep in mind the continuity. 1979 was the fourth consecutive year that the total number of marriages grew. It was the largest total ever, 2.3 million, or nearly double the 1.17 million divorces recorded. The number of marriages was up about 3 percent over 1978, exceeding by about 26,000 the earlier all-time peak of 2.29 million marriages in 1946. Thus, marriage remains popular and most Americans still spend the greater share of their lives in family units.

Perhaps the biggest change of all is the increasing acceptance of various forms of intimate relationships. We are, after all, a pluralistic society, a society made up of diverse groups. Thus it seems natural that in such a society numerous acceptable family forms might be found. Inset 1-2 presents the basic assumptions on which this book has been written.

Why Is the Family So Important?

Throughout history, people have needed people in order to survive. The physical weakness of the human species as compared with many of the other vertebrates was overcome in early history largely through cooperative efforts in orderly groups. Today, technology protects us from the environment, but people still need the emotional support of other people — especially the family — in order to survive as healthy human beings.

The newborn human is totally dependent on adults for physical survival and this dependency lasts for a much longer period than for most other animals. Without some kind of stable adult unit to provide child care, the human species would have disappeared long ago.

In addition to physical dependence, the newborn must be socialized into the group. *Socialization* is the process of acquiring the skills necessary to survive both as an individual and as a member of society.

Children must also receive emotional nurturance. They need a stable, warm, loving, and touching environment. Children raised

Let me now state clearly the assumptions on which this book is based. You are free to take exception to these, but before doing so I suggest reading the chapters cited after each assumption for a broader discussion of that assumption.

All people, lay and professional alike, hold certain beliefs about marriage and the family, and that includes authors. It is important to recognize and make clear just what these beliefs are, since they color this and most other books on the subject. I urge you to examine and question the following basic suppositions:

1. The family is the basic unit of human organization, although its strength and form vary greatly across cultures and time (Chapter 1).

2. The American family, especially the middle-class family, has certain characteristics that make it somewhat unique when compared to other family systems. Among these characteristics, the following stand out:

a. The relative freedom of choice in mate selection and vocation (Chapters 1, 3, and 4).

b. The extremely private character of the family (Chapter 1).

c. The high economic standard and abundant material possessions (Chapters 7 and 8).

d. The relative individual freedom within the family, fostered by a high standard of living, physical mobility, lack of broader familial responsibilities such as care of the aged, and the pluralistic nature of the American society (Chapters 14 and 17).

3. If defined functionally, the family is essentially universal. The structural form varies according to the social and external environments in which it exists (Chapter 1).

4. A free and creative society is one that offers many structural forms by which family functions, such as child rearing and sexual gratification, may be fulfilled (Chapter 14).

5. The family in modern America is the basic economic unit for the society since it is the primary consuming unit (Chapter 7).

6. The family becomes increasingly important to its individual members as social stability decreases and/or people feel more isolated and alienated (Chapters 1 and 5).

7. The attitudes and reactions of family members toward environmental influences are more important to family functioning than are the environmental influences themselves (Chapters 5 and 6).

8. Each individual can marry any one of a number of persons within the broad limits set by social norms, and build a satisfying and stable relationship, if both partners' expectations for and attitudes about the relationship are realistic (Chapters 3 and 4).

9. Any family relationship can change, just as the individuals within the relationship can and do change. Change does not mean an end to the relationship. Indeed, lack of change over time is probably unhealthy and may ultimately lead to the demise of the relationship (Chapters 5, 6, and 17).

10. The fully functioning family *can* act as a buffer against mental and physical illness (Chapters 1 and 17).

without emotional nurturance are usually troubled as adults and often have great difficulty supplying emotional warmth to their own children.

The Need for Emotional Nurture An ingenious series of studies by H. F. and M. K. Harlow (1962) demonstrated the importance of mothering to successful social and sexual adjustment in monkeys. The infant monkeys were reared with two artificial mothers, one of wire and the other of soft terry cloth. Regardless of which mother fed the infant monkey, all the infants preferred the cloth mother.

Continuing investigation showed that monkeys raised only by contact with an artificial mother, wire or terry cloth, did not develop normal patterns of social or sexual behavior. When a few of the females succeeded in mating and becoming mothers, they did not display normal maternal behavior. Apparently their early social deprivation permanently impaired their ability to form effective relations with other monkeys.

Although in America many believe it is necessary for children to receive emotional nurturing from their parents, there is some question as to whether this nurture has to come from parents. Harlow and others, for example, found that if the motherless infant monkeys were allowed to play for a short time each day with other infant monkeys, there were no symptoms of maladjustment (Jensen and Babbitt, 1968). Also, in many Israeli kibbutz settlements, children are reared in peer groups supervised by professional child care personnel. (They do have contact with their parents, however.) The children are healthy, without signs of emotional disturbance.

Some theorists go further, believing that it is stimulation, not love, that is necessary for development, and that stimulation need not be combined with a warm, personal relationship. According to Laurence Casler, for example, "Love, although not harmful, is superfluous" (1974; for a thorough discussion of this point of view, see Casler's pages 77–116).

Love and intimacy
are an important part of
growing up.

However, this is a minority viewpoint in the United States. Historically the family has been, for better or worse, the major institution through which people reproduced, reared, and socialized their offspring, and through which emotional nurture and security were supplied. Supplying children with warmth, care, and love remains a family function valued by many.

The family is so important because it supplies physical and emotional nurture during the long dependence of the human infant. Since the family serves to socialize the child it also acts as the central organizing unit for the general society.

The Need for Intimacy Seeking closeness with others, whether the closeness is physical, intellectual, or emotional, seems to be a basic need of most people (Fromm, 1956; Maslow, 1971; Morris, 1971; and Murstein, 1974). To feel close to another, to love and feel loved, to experience comradeship, to care and be cared about are all feelings that most of us wish and need to experience. Such feelings can be found in many human relationships. However, it is within the family that such feelings are ideally most easily found and shared. I say "ideally" because it is apparent that there are many families in which such feelings are not found. But families that do not supply much intimacy are usually families in trouble, and often these families disintegrate since members are frustrated in their needs for meaningful intimate relationships. A successful family, then, supplies intimate relationships to its members.

The term *intimacy* is used as a general term to cover all of the kinds of feelings mentioned above, as well as its general use as a euphemism for sexual intercourse. Because of the many meanings, a clear and concise definition is difficult to make. For our purposes, we will use Carolynne Kieffer's (1977) definition: "Intimacy is the experiencing of the essence of one's self in intense intellectual, physical and/or emotional communion with another human being" (p. 267).

Recently, B. J. Biddle (1976) has shed light on the concept of intimacy. Biddle suggests that intimacy must be considered on each of three dimensions — breadth, openness, and depth.

Breadth describes the range of activities shared by two people. Do they spend a great deal of time together? Do they share occupational activities, home activities, leisure time, and so on?

Openness implies that a pair share meaningful self-disclosures with one another. They feel secure enough and close enough to share intellectually, physically, and emotionally. They trust each other enough that they can be honest most of the time and this encourages further trust in one another.

Depth means that partners share really true, central, important, and meaningful aspects of themselves. Self-disclosure leads to deeper levels of interaction. In the ultimate sense, both are able to transcend their own egos and fuse in some spiritual way with the essence or central being of their partner. Such an experience is difficult to attain, yet many believe that it is in the deepest intimate experiences that love and potential for individual growth are found. Abraham Maslow (1968), for example, holds that each individual must find deep intimacy to become a self-actualizing and fulfilled person.

Kieffer (1977) adds to Biddle's three dimensions the age-old idea of intellectual, physical, and emotional *realms of action*. In a totally intimate relationship, there would be breadth, openness, and depth in each activity realm. Table 1-1 describes a highly intimate

Table 1-1 Intensity Matrix for the Analysis of an Intimate Relationship[1]

	Intellectual	Physical	Emotional
Breadth (range of shared activities)	Telling of the meaningful events in one's day Participating in a political rally Years of interaction resulting in the sharing of meanings (phrases, gestures, etc.) understood only by the partners Decision making regarding management of household	Dancing Caressing Swimming Doing laundry Tennis Shopping Gardening Sexual intercourse Other sensual/sexual activities	Phone calls providing emotional support when separated Experiencing grief in a family tragedy Witnessing with pride a daughter's graduation from college Resolving conflict in occasional arguments
Openness (disclosure of self)	Disclosing one's values and goals Discussing controversial aspects of politics, ethics, etc. Using familiar language Not feeling a need to lie to the partner Sharing of secrets with the partner, and discretion regarding the secrets of the partner	Feeling free to wear old clothes Grooming in presence of the other Bathroom behavior (elimination, etc.) in presence of the other Nudity Few limitations placed upon exploration of one's body by the partner Sharing of physical space (area, possessions, etc.) with few signs of territoriality	Describing one's dreams and daydreams Feeling free to call for "time out" or for togetherness Maintaining openness (disclosure) regarding one's emotional involvement with other intimates Telling of daily joys and frustrations Emotional honesty in resolving conflict Expressing anger, resentment, and other positive and negative emotions
Depth (sharing of core aspects of self)	"Knowing" of the partner Having faith in the partner's reliability and love Occasional experiencing of the essence of one's self in transcendental union Working collectively to change certain core characteristics of the self, and of the partner	Physical relaxation, sense of contentment and well-being in the presence of the other	Committing oneself without guarantee, in the hope that one's love will be returned Caring as much about the partner as about oneself Nonjealous supportiveness toward the other intimate relationships of the partner

Source: From *Marriage and Alternatives: Exploring Intimate Relationships* by Roger W. Libby and Robert N. Whitehurst. Copyright © 1977 by Scott, Foresman and Company. Reprinted by permission.
[1]You can use this matrix to analyze your own intimate relationships or to compare levels of involvement or discern patterns among your various relationships.

relationship. Of course, as Kieffer cautions, such a description is simplistic and does not include the numerous psychological processes that characterize the interaction of the partners or that brought them to this level of involvement. In addition, she reminds us that intimacy is a process, not a state of being. Thus this particular description only indicates where this particular couple is at this moment in time.

In the past, intimacy was built into one's life by the social acceptance and support of the family. However, as the economic pattern changed in this country, and as increasing geographical mobility separated people from their families, social emphasis shifted from family closeness to individual self-fulfillment. And many people have found the achievement of intimacy more difficult because of this shift.

But life today offers many different opportunities for fulfilling intimacy needs. Marriage is no longer seen as the *only* avenue to intimacy. If we examine our lives, we will probably find we have a "patchwork intimacy." Kieffer means by this that most people are involved in a multitude of intimate relationships of varying intensity.

We can see this more clearly if we examine the idea of "open marriage" (O'Neill & O'Neill, 1972). The O'Neills propose that the old idea of marriage expected both partners to fill *all* of their intimacy needs from the marriage. In an "open marriage," on the other hand, a partner can limit physical intimacy to the marriage relationship, but share intellectual intimacy with, perhaps, some work colleagues. Also, the partners are free to spend time away from each other, with other companions.

If one is secure in a marital relationship of deep intimacy, then enough trust may develop so that each partner can say to the other, "I love and care for you so much that I encourage you to seek fulfillment through finding intimacy wherever it might exist for you." Of course, such trust must be earned and respected; it is not easy to come by.

If intimacy is as rewarding as suggested and if American society is allowing each person to seek it in other ways than just in marriage, we probably need to develop an ethic for intimates. For example, how do we keep the quest for individual intimacy and fulfillment within acceptable boundaries to our spouse? How do we keep the quest from lapsing into the selfish pursuit of always "doing one's own thing?" Questions like these must be considered by all couples seeking intimacy.

The Family as a Buffer Against Mental and Physical Illness Our tenth basic assumption (p. 10) stated that "the fully functioning family *can* act as a buffer against mental and physical illness." It is important that the word "can" is emphasized. The family can do this if it is well integrated, fully-functioning, and successful (see Chapters 5 and 17). This is an ideal and we realize that few families probably will approach it. Yet ideals are important. They can give us direction, goals toward which to move. In many ways pointing out ideals, what families could be, how families can optimally function, is an important purpose of this book.

WHAT DO YOU THINK?

Is intimacy a goal for you?

Why, if it is, is it difficult for you to be intimate?

In what action realm (intellectual, physical, emotional) do you share intimacy most easily? Why?

Which realm is most difficult? Why?

With whom can you be the most intimate overall?

In what ways is your relationship with your parents intimate? Why?

In what ways can you not be intimate with your parents? Why?

As families have become smaller and more isolated from societal supports because of industrialization and alienation processes, intimate relations within the family have become more intense, more emotional, and more fragile. For example, if a child has no other significant adults with whom to intimately interact besides his or her parents, then this emotional interaction becomes crucial to the child's development. If this interaction is positive and healthy, then the child develops in a healthy manner. On the other hand, if it is not and the child has no other sources of intimate interaction, then the child is apt to develop in an unhealthy manner. The family, in a sense, is a hothouse of intimacy and emotionality because of the close interaction and intensity of relationships. It has the potential to do either great good or great harm for its members. Since it can do the latter, it becomes even more important to understand how it can do the former, i.e., help its members towards health.

As we pointed out earlier, we all will spend a good part, if not all, of our lives within a family unit. It is within this setting that most of us will achieve our closest intimacy with other persons. It is shared human intimacy that leads to security, feelings of self-esteem, and openness and sharing. Such feelings lead to improved communication and good communication both within oneself and with others tends to be therapeutic. According to Carl Rogers (1951) "the emotionally maladjusted person is in difficulty first, because communication within himself has broken down, and second, because, as a result of this, his communication with others has become damaged." To the degree that our family can help us to become good communicators, it can help us towards better life adjustment.

When one compares health statistics on married, single, divorced, separated, and widowed people, it is clear that married people are the healthiest. Verbrugge (1979) surveyed a great deal of data on the following six general health indicators: (1) incidence of acute health conditions, (2) percentage of people limited in activity by a chronic condition, (3) percentage of people with a work disability, (4) rates of restricted activity, bed disability, and work loss, (5) average number of physician (or dental) visits per year, and (6) percentage of people with a hospital stay in past year, average length of stay, and hospital discharge rates.

She adjusted rates for age and found that there were significant differences between the various groups listed. Table 1-2 summarizes the empirical results for each of the six health indicators on a three-level scale: high, intermediate, and low incidence of health problems.

It is clear from these data that divorced and separated people appear least healthy while married people appear overall to be the most healthy. A single dramatic example shows the differences between the groups quite clearly: commitments to mental hospitals in 1970, expressed as rate per 10,000 population, were as follows:

	Total	Single	Married	Widowed	Divorced	Separated
Men	34	213	10	47	101	115
Women	23	116	11	26	48	77

Table 1-2 Marital Differentials in Health: Empirical Results

	Age-Adjusted Rates[1]			
	High	**Intermediate**		**Low**
Acute Conditions				
Incidence rates	Sep, D	(W, S, M)		
Chronic Conditions				
Prevalence rates (health exam. survey)	W	D	Sep, M	S
Short-Term Disability				
Restricted activity rates (all conditions)	Sep	W, D		M, S
Restricted activity rates (acute conditions)	Sep	D, W	M	S
Bed disability rates (acute)	Sep	D, W	M	S
Work loss rates (acute)	D/Sep	W	M	S
Restricted activity days per acute condition	Sep	D, W	M	S
Bed disability days per acute condition	Sep	D, W		M, S
Long-Term Disability				
Limiting chronic condition	Sep	D, W	S	M
Major-activity limitation	Sep	D, W	S	M
Partial work disability	D/Sep	W	S	M
Complete work disability	W	D/Sep	S	M
Duration of work disability	S	(D/Sep, W, M)		
Utilization of Health Services				
Physician visits per year	Sep, D, W		M	S
Dental visits per year, and any visit in past year	S		M	FM
Any hospital stay in past year	Sep, D, W		M	S
Hospital discharge rates	Sep, D	W	M	S
Length of hospital stay	Sep		D, W, S	Low
Institutionalization				
Health institution rates	S		D, Sep, W	M

Source: Lois Verbrugge, "Marital Status and Health." *Journal of Marriage and the Family*, May 1979, p. 280.
[1]Marital groups are abbreviated: M (married), S (single), D (divorced), Sep (separated), W (widowed). Some tabulations combine these: D/Sep (divorced and separated together), FM (formerly married).

You can see dramatic differences between the groups and between men and women. In this particular case, single men and women had the highest institutionalization rates (see p. 427) for suggested explanation), and men's rates were generally higher than women's rates.

It is of great interest to examine rates for other specific health problems. For example, the American Council of Life Insurance reports that divorced white American males under 65 — compared to married men — had a death rate from strokes and lung cancer that was double, seven times greater for cirrhosis of the liver, double for stomach cancer and heart disease, and five times higher for suicide.

Interpretation of such data is complex and controversial.* However, there are substantial enough differences between various marital groups to suggest real rather than simply chance differences. The fact that married persons generally appear most healthy and divorced and separated persons least healthy suggests that the family has

*Such health data can be interpreted in a variety of ways besides the way in which I have interpreted it. See the Verbrugge (1979) reference and read the entire article to better understand the complexity of dealing with these health data.

a strong influence on health. The successful family operates to improve its members' health while the unsuccessful family may do the opposite. If this is true, it becomes a matter of health to work towards improved family functioning.

The term *family* is used here in the broadest possible sense; it is defined as whatever system a society uses to support and control reproduction and human sexual interaction. This broad definition solves many apparent conflicts over the meaning of changes presently taking place in family functions and structure. For example, in this usage Israeli kibbutzim are families, even though major child rearing responsibilities are assumed by persons other than parents.

Most authors give a narrower definition. For example, Robert Winch (1971, pp. 10–11) defines family as: "A set of persons related to each other by blood, marriage, or adoption, and constituting a social system whose structure is specified by familial positions and whose basic societal function is replacement." Lucille Duberman (1977, p. 10) says the family is "an institution found in several variant forms, that provides children with a legitimate position in society and with the nurturance that will enable them to function as fully developed members of society." Narrow definitions like these seem to limit family functions to child rearing.

Part of the reason for the debate over the health of the American family (see Scenes from Marriage, pp. 28–34) is confusion between the functions of the family institution and the structure by which these functions are fulfilled. There are many structures that can fulfill the responsibilities of the family. In modern America, the duties and thus the functions of the family have been reduced. And new structures, or alternative family forms, are being tried to fulfill these functions. Let us take a closer look at these functions.

Family Functions The family serves both the society and the individual. Sometimes, of course, there is a conflict between the social and individual functions, as with recent mandatory sterilization laws in India. Although having more children may benefit a particular family, the Indian government feels that too many children harm the larger society. So we must always consider these two functions if we are to understand the family. For the family to remain a viable social institution, it must meet the needs of society and individuals and hold conflict between these two levels to a minimum.

The family has handled a broad range of functions in different times and societies. In some primitive societies, this institution is synonymous with the society itself, bearing all the powers and responsibilities for societal survival. As societies become more complex, simple and then more elaborate social institutions form and take over many responsibilities that formerly belonged to the family.

Families are primarily responsible for replenishing the population.

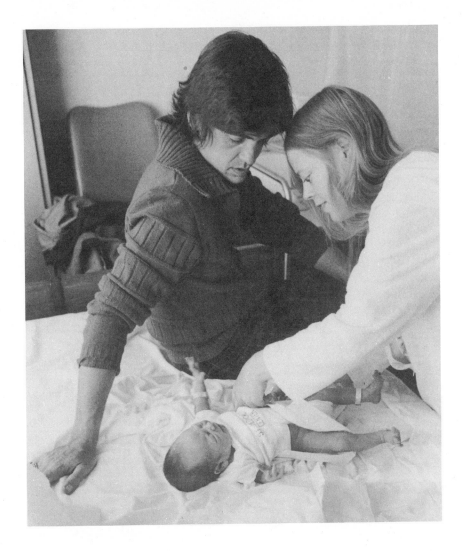

Let us then begin by taking a look at the functions that must be carried out for a society to remain intact. Winch (1971, p. 13) identifies the following as necessary for the maintenance of society:

1. Replacements for dying members of the society must be produced.
2. Goods and services must be produced and distributed.
3. Provision must be made for accommodating conflicts and maintaining order internally and externally.
4. Newborn human replacements must be socialized to become participating members of the society.
5. Individual goals must be harmonized with the values of the society, and there must be procedures for dealing with emotional crises and maintaining a sense of purpose.

Although the American family is still involved with all five of these functions, other social institutions have assumed the primary responsibility for some of them. For example, the family is no longer a production unit per se. Some individuals in the family work to produce goods and services, but this is usually done outside the family setting in a more formalized job situation. The family, however, is still an economic unit in that it demands goods and services and is the major consumption unit in the United States. The courts and police maintain external order, although the family is still primarily responsible for maintaining order within its own structure. Formal education now trains children to become participating members of society, although the family begins and maintains the socialization process.

Thus we find that the contemporary American family is left with one of Winch's primary functions, that of providing a continuing replacement of individuals so that society continues to exist. A second primary function, that of providing emotional gratification and intimacy to members, helping them deal with emotional crises so they grow in the most fulfilling manner possible, also remains.

Since human beings are still being conceived and born in the age-old, time-honored fashion, the family's importance as the means of replenishing the population is obvious. The family is still the most efficient way available to us of nurturing dependent infants. The second function, however, warrants more discussion. In general, as the pace of life quickens, and as people become increasingly alienated from their larger society, the family can become more important as a refuge and source of emotional gratification for its members. The family has been called the "shock absorber" of society — the place where bruised and battered individuals can return after doing battle with the world, the one stable point in an ever-changing environment. If you do not belong to a family, where can you turn for warmth and affection? Who will care for you when you are sick? What other group would tolerate your failures the way a devoted wife, husband, mother, or father would?

The family can serve as "portable roots," anchoring one against the storm of change. Furthermore, the family can provide the security and acceptance that leads to inner strength, the strength to behave individually rather than always in conformity with one's peers. In one husband's words (Rogers, 1972, p. 192),

> The power, the strength, the refuge of our marriage has given us a kind of core to operate from, which has allowed both of us to be very much mavericks in most social terms. My hunch would be, for instance, that if you see a man who is very conventional, very frightened, you know, very unsure of what direction to move and always looking at how his peers evaluate him — my bet is you can predict he doesn't have a very good marriage because if he did, he wouldn't have to do that. He'd find his core, his identity, and his being somewhere else [in his marriage]. And these things would be secondary as they ought to be.

That is, the family can be a source of security, a protective shield against environmental pressures. Thus the way family members react to environmental stresses is far more important than the stresses themselves.

I do not mean to deny the importance of social problems such as depression, inflation, unemployment, and poverty. General social upheaval such as America went through during the Vietnam war in the 1960s and the continuing furor over minority rights affect the family drastically. For example, if my child is to be bused twenty miles into a new neighborhood and school so that racial equality can be achieved, there will certainly be family ramifications. I, as a parent, will lose some control over my child. The distance to school may mean that I cannot participate in many school activities, such as PTA and class parties. I will not know the families of my child's playmates. My child will be exposed to different social mores and expectations, which I may or may not find acceptable.

Yet more important than the political fact of busing will be the family's reaction to it. Will it accept and support it? Will it picket, riot, and protest? Will it transfer children from public into private school? Each family's reaction to busing teaches their children values about minority groups, racial prejudice and/or tolerance, law, and authority. That is, how the family reacts is as important to its members as the social stimulus.

An additional function of the family, then, might be to help family members interpret social influences. Granted, an individual family might teach an interpretation unacceptable to others in the society as a whole.

The more the merrier?

Although consensus has it that the modern family has lost some functions, it may also be true that it has gained new ones. For example, F. I. Nye (1974) suggests that three new roles are now present in the American family:

1. *The recreational role:* Family members spend their leisure time, especially vacation time, together.
2. *The therapeutic role:* Each family member assists the others in solving individual problems that may either originate in the family or be external to it. As we become more isolated from the larger ongoing society, such support becomes more crucial.
3. *Changed sexual roles:* Traditionally it was the woman's role to meet her husband's sexual needs. Now the feminist movement has emphasized the equal importance of the husband meeting his wife's sexual needs, thereby placing a new responsibility on the man, and, of course, changing the female role also.

We have seen the family's functions changing over time. And we can certainly assume that its functions will continue to change. Do changing functions mean that the family will disappear as we know it? Not necessarily. Clark Vincent (1966) has pointed out an additional and overriding family function, the family's high adaptive capability. The family is a system in process rather than a rigid unchanging system. As J. F. Crosby (1975, p. 40) has pointed out:

> No one can yet foresee what the structure of the future family will look like because no one can know with certainty what the functions and needs of the future family will be. It is likely, however, that the needs for primary affection bonds, intimacy, economic subsistence, socialization of the young, and reproduction will not yield to obsolescence. To the extent that human needs do not change drastically, the family structure will not change drastically.

Table 1-3 points out some of the different structures that have arisen over time to handle the various functions of the family.

Sexual Regulation   As we have already noted, each family structure has reproduction as its primary function. Along with this is the regulation of sexual behavior.

In the animal world, sex and reproduction are, for the most part, handled automatically and instinctively. The female indicates that she is in estrus (ready to conceive) and the male responds and impregnates her. Most of the mechanisms and behaviors of sex and reproduction are built into the biology of the animal. There are fixed periods of sexual readiness, and the animal has little choice in its sexual behavior.

Human beings, as we all know, are different. Sexual behavior may be sought and enjoyed at any time, regardless of the stage of the female reproductive cycle. Humans are free to use sex not only for reproduction but also for pleasure. But, as in so many other aspects of human life, freedom of choice is a mixed blessing. Humans must balance their continual sexual receptivity and desire with the needs of

Table 1-3 Different Family Structures

Kind	Composition	Functions
Types of Marriage		
Monogamy	One spouse and children	Procreative, affectional, economic consumption
Serial monogamy	One spouse at a time but several different spouses over time. Married, divorced, remarried.	Same
Common-law	One spouse. Live together for long enough period that state recognizes couple as married even though they have not been formally and legally married. Only a few states recognize this marriage.	Same
Polygamy	Multiple spouses	Same
Polygyny	One husband, multiple wives	Any, power vested in male.
Polyandry	One wife, multiple husbands	Any, power usually vested in female.
Group	Two or more men are collectively married to two or more women at the same time.	Any. Very rare
Types of Families		
Nuclear family	Husband, wife, children	Procreative, affectional, economic consumption
Extended family	One or more nuclear families plus other family positions such as grandparents, uncles, etc.	Historically the extended family might serve all social functions, educational, economic, reproductive, affectional, religious as it did in precommunist China.
Composite family	Two or more nuclear families that share a common spouse	Normally those of the nuclear family
Tribal family	Many families living together as a larger clan or tribe	Usually those of the extended family
Consensual family	Man, woman, and children living together in legally unrecognized relationship	Any
Commune	A group of people living together sharing a common purpose with assigned roles and responsibilities normally associated with the nuclear family	Can provide all functions with leadership vested in an individual, council, or some other organized form to which all families are beholden.
Single-parent family	Usually a mother and child. Only about 10% of American single-parent families consist of father and child.	Same as monogamy without a legally recognized reproductive function
Concubine	Extra female sexual partner recognized as a member of the household but without full status	Usually limited to sex and reproduction
Authority Patterns		
Paternalistic	Any power vested in male	Any
Maternalistic	Any power vested in female	Any
Egalitarian	Powers divided in some fair manner between spouses	Any

other individuals and with the needs of society as a whole. They must find a system that will provide physical and mental satisfaction in a socially acceptable context of time, place, and partner.

No matter what system is worked out to handle sexuality, humans seem to be comfortable only when they can convince themselves that the system is proper, just, and virtuous. When each culture has established a satisfactory and "correct" system, it bolsters it with a complex set of rules accompanied by prescribed punishments for transgressions.

However, our society has evolved to a point where the old rules no longer work well, so we are faced with trying to create new ethics to control sexuality. Western literature on marriage and the family is filled with arguments over the proper sexual system for humans. Were men and women originally promiscuous, polygamous (multiple spouses), or monogamous (sexual exclusiveness and one spouse at a time)? We have even applied Darwin's theory of evolution to the male-female relationship in an effort to demonstrate that the monogamy of Western cultures is the highest and therefore the only proper form of relationship. Yet close and objective study of the multiple methods devised by humans to work out their sexual and family life tends to destroy most of the historical arguments for any straight-line evolutionary theory of family development. In their book *The Family in Various Cultures* (1974, pp. 3–5), S. A. Queen and R. W. Habenstein conclude that since there is such variance among family patterns and the way in which sexuality is controlled, "no single form need be regarded as inevitable nor more 'natural' than any other." They further state "We assume that all forms of the domestic institution are in process, having grown out of something different and tending to become something still different. But there is no acceptable evidence of a single, uniform series of stages through which the developing family must pass."

In recent years, people have started to study the effect that government policies and laws have on the family. The family, after all, exists within a society and that society is governed by laws. The family is therefore affected by those laws.

In the past, little direct effort was made by the government to understand what effect, if any, a given law might have on the family institution. For example, until recently, women with children on welfare received more support if their husbands left them. Social workers had to spy on families to be sure that there was no husband around. In essence, the welfare system worked to break up families.

More recently, various income maintenance experiments that ensure support to all members of a family even if the marriage is terminated have been tried. One rationale for these experiments was that the family surviving economically is less apt to break up than one that is not. Yet, in actuality, another effect was also discovered, the independence effect (Steiner, 1979, pp. 2–6). For some women who are

Government and Family Policy

guaranteed an income for themselves and their dependent children, divorce is the outcome because the guaranteed income allows them to be independent of their husbands. In surveying these experiments, Bianchi and Farley (1979, p. 548) conclude:

> The net outcome of the opposing effects (increased stability vs. increased independence) depends upon the magnitude of the support level and the income of the family in the absence of support. Most discussions of the negative income tax or other income maintenance programs envision modest levels of support which would be focused upon families near the poverty level. The experiments conducted thus far suggest that, in such circumstances, the independence effect will far outweigh the income effect and rates of family dissolution will increase.

Family policy research is aimed at uncovering these kinds of practical relationships between governmental actions and the family. President Carter established the first official Office for Families in the Health, Education, and Welfare department in 1979. One of its jobs is to do family policy research.

The White House Conference on Families is another sign of growing governmental concern for the family. The conference has been fraught with controversy and although originally scheduled for 1978, did not take place until 1980. Most states also had family conferences during 1979 and 1980 as preludes to the national conference. The following excerpt from the report on the White House Conference on Families will give you an idea of the kinds of issues raised at these conferences.

> The number one concern cited at the hearings was the sensitivity, or insensitivity, of federal, state and local government toward families. Policies covering tax, welfare and foster care were among the policies critics claimed ignored or undermined families.
>
> Economic pressure was the number two concern, with the impact of inflation, poverty, and unemployment the most frequently cited problems. Support for specific family structures, such as traditional families, single parent families, and extended families was the third major concern.
>
> Hearings participants mentioned child care — its cost and availability — as their fourth concern, while education followed as number five. Among issues raised that related to education were its quality and availability, home/school relations, moral concerns, and the responsiveness of educational systems to diverse needs.
>
> Concern six covered health care issues, while the seventh focused on work and families, i.e., the conflict between work and family responsibilities, the need for flexible employment practices, discrimination in the workplace, increased participation in the work force, and redefinition of the relationship between business and families.
>
> The eighth most frequently cited issue was family life education, including preparation for parenting and marriage, and sex education. Number nine concern was children and parents, involving the need for responsible parenting and supports for parents and children. The tenth major concern was the roles community institutions, both religious and secular, can play in supporting families.

Issues eleven through twenty-five were, in order of frequency: family violence, family planning, financial assistance to families, housing, media, divorce and separation, law (divorce and custody), alcohol and drug abuse, tax policy, families and aging, families and handicapping conditions, adoption and foster care, social services, marriage and military families.

Americans have mixed feelings about government formally declaring interest in the family.* Many fear it will lead to more governmental interference in their lives. On the other hand, intentionally or not, the government is a part of every family.

Hard and fast data in such an intimate personal field of study as the family are difficult to produce. Most of the data come from surveys and from clinicians who work in the field.

Some Words about Marriage and Family Data

Survey data are often problematic for three reasons. The first problem is that the sample may not be representative of the population in which you are interested. For example, if you are interested in the cohabiting behavior of college students, which college students do you survey? Certainly state university students will give different answers than students from a small denominational college where dormitory residence is required. You must always ask whether the sample surveyed really represents the population about which you want to draw conclusions.

A second problem with survey data is who *actually* responded. The researcher will, in most cases, set up a representative sample. However, responding to surveys is not mandatory but depends on voluntary cooperation. Although 100 percent of the sample may indeed be representative of the population about which you want to generalize, you will be fortunate if 50 to 80 percent of those in the sample cooperate. Thus you need to know if those who cooperated with the survey are the same as those who didn't. For example, Alfred Kinsey and his associates worked hard to draw a representative sample of Americans to interview about their sexual behavior. They took people from all geographic areas and from various social classes. But can we be sure that the people who volunteered to discuss their most intimate sexual behavior with the interviewers behaved the same sexually as those who did not volunteer? Of course, we can't, and thus there will always be a question about how truly representative of Americans the two monumental Kinsey studies really are.

The third problem with surveys is the difficulty of validating the respondents' answers. Are they telling the truth? The more intimate the questions, such as those about marriage or sex habits, the more likely the respondents are to hedge their answers or perhaps not even answer at all. Researchers try to overcome this problem by making surveys anonymous but, again, we can never really be sure that an

*For those interested in a detailed look at the problems of family policy, see the special issue of the *Journal of Marriage and Family*, August, 1979, which is totally devoted to this topic.

answer is true. Also, while respondents might not actually lie, sometimes memories are inadequate, or what we think we'd do in a hypothetical situation is not at all what we would actually do in a real life situation. Thus, always be careful about uncritically accepting all data that surveys yield.

Clinicians such as marriage counselors, clergy, psychologists, psychiatrists, and others who work with families supply a great deal of data to the research field. These data are usually anecdotal, and unfortunately the clinicians' conclusions may be overgeneralized. Also, because they work with those seeking help, they may only see troubled families. After working eight hours a day over long periods with people who have problems, clinicians may come to hold an overly pessimistic view of the family.

Data on individual cases are usually valid for those cases, but can such data be generalized to the entire population? In most cases, probably not. On the other hand, group data does not accurately predict what an individual will do. For example, data from large group studies indicate that the chances of divorce go up if one's parents are divorced. Yet, we all know persons who are long married and indeed have worked harder to make their marriage succeed because their parents were divorced. Does this mean that the group data are incorrect? No, not at all. The statistics are correct for the group, but cannot predict the behavior of any specific individual within the group. As Sherlock Holmes (in *The Sign of the Four*) once said, "While the individual man is an insoluble puzzle, in the aggregate he becomes a mathematical certainty. You can never foretell what any one man will do, but you can say with precision what an average number will be up to. Individuals vary but percentages remain constant."

In general, then, remember to be cautious about immediately accepting all supposed facts in the field of marriage and family research.

Summary   Marriage and family are of vital interest to most people. Almost all of us have been reared in families of some kind and most of us will also participate in a family of our own throughout much of our life. However, there are many conflicting viewpoints about the American family and its future. Some see the family as we have known it as obsolete, a relic of some bygone era. Others see the family as viable and more important than ever. That the family is changing cannot be debated. What can be debated is whether or not the family is improving. I believe that the family is important and that there are opportunities to improve its health which our society should encourage.

The basic assumptions on which this book is based are: (1) the family is the basic unit of human organization, (2) the American family is in some ways unique, (3) the structural form by which a family system fulfills its functions will vary, (4) a free and creative society will have many structural forms of the family, (5) the family is the basic economic unit, (6) the family is increasingly important if there is technological and social change, (7) the attitudes of family members toward environmental influences are more important than the environmental influences themselves, (8) each person can marry any one of a number of persons and build a satisfying relationship, (9) all family relationships will change with time, and (10) the fully functioning family can act as a buffer against mental and physical illness.

Because there are many opinions about marriage and family, these assumptions will not necessarily be acceptable to everyone. They are, though, the organizational structure around which this book is based. Healthy debate about them will help to clarify your thinking and hopefully lead to new insights.

Remember that research in the field of marriage and family is not easy to do and must be evaluated carefully. Most research will be of two kinds, surveys and clinical. Both types have problems of which you should be aware.

I hope that healthy debate is generated by the Scenes from Marriage, "The Family is Alive and Well" and "The Family Is Sick and Dying." Contrast these two points of view in your own mind. Which position do you take now that you have read the chapter? Is it different from the one you had before reading? If so, why? If not, why? What are your own personal assumptions about marriage? How widely shared do you think they are? What do you think would happen if a married couple had widely differing assumptions about what the marriage should be? How would a more tolerant social attitude toward alternative forms of relationships affect marriage? From what you see around you, what direction do you think marriage will take in America over the next ten years?

How Healthy is the Family?

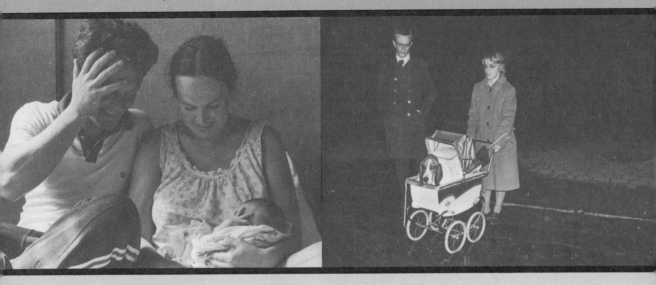

When perusing the vast literature on marriage and family, it is clear that there is great diversity of opinion on how healthy the family is, of what value marriage is, and whether the many changes and alternatives suggested will really solve the problems encountered in marriage. Perhaps a good way of summarizing the continuing diversity of opinion about the future of the American family is to simply present the two extremes — "the family is alive and well" and "the family is sick and dying."

The Family Is Alive and Well:
The Family Is Not "Dying"*

If Prof. Mary Jo Bane of Wellesley College is correct, we Americans for years have been singing a dirge over an institution that is neither dead nor dying but is in fact as healthy as it has ever been.

The institution is the American family, and the requiem goes like this:

There was a time when the extended family — two or three generations living under

*Reprinted with permission of The National Observer, Dow Jones & Company, Inc. 1977. All Rights Reserved.

the same roof — was the norm. This gave nurture to children and care to the aged, who otherwise might have been packed off to an old folks' home. But the extended family is almost extinct nowadays, and the family itself — indeed, even the institution of marriage — is in peril because of a soaring divorce rate, one-parent households, the increasing number of working mothers, and a mobile, rootless population. Result: Children don't get the kind of nurturing they once did, family bonds have weakened, and old folks' homes are filled with people whose children don't want the bother of caring for them.

That's cause for lamentation, all right, except for one thing: Bane says it isn't true. A 34-year-old assistant professor and associate director of Wellesley's Center for Research on Women, Bane refutes what she terms the romanticized, mythical view of the American family in her recent book, Here to Stay: American Families in the Twentieth Century.

Bane's book is a statistical analysis of past and current data on U.S. population characteristics. Using the same data they do, she reaches conclusions diametrically opposite those of such well-known behaviorists as Urie Bronfenbrenner and popular authors such as Vance Packard (*A Nation of Strangers* and *The Naked Society*).

Her thesis, advanced in her book and in interviews with The Observer, is the American family is still strong because:

☐ The extended family never really existed on a wide scale. Data from colonial America show that only 6 per cent of U.S. households contained children, parents, and grandparents. The latest figures, for 1970, show it's still 6 per cent.

☐ More families have two parents now (84.3 per cent) than in colonial days (70 per cent).

☐ What divorce is doing to disrupt families today, death did in earlier times. As the death rate has dropped, the divorce rate has increased — but most divorced people remarry to stay.

☐ It's doubtful that Americans move more often now than they did in the Nineteenth Century. So if mobility is fraying America's family and social fabric, it has been doing so for a long time.

☐ There's no evidence that yesterday's mothers, laboring from dawn to dusk to do housework without labor-saving devices, devoted more time to their children than today's working mothers do.

Bane says her goal was to separate "myth from reality." That's vital, she adds, because public officials create policies regarding the family, abortion, divorce, and welfare on the basis of accepted general assumptions. "Assuming that the family is dead or dying may lead to policies that, in their desperate attempt to keep the patient alive, infringe unnecessarily on other cherished values . . . [or] bring about its untimely death."

"There's a general tendency to romanticize the past; it's persistent through history. In the Seventeenth Century, people were talking about how bad the family was, saying it was falling apart. Even scholars fail to take a long view of statistical data, thus they don't see the longer-term trends nor perceive the longer perspective. You really have to look at the family in a large context."

In doing that, Bane finds yesterday's family was much like today's. "The nuclear family, consisting of parents living with their own children and no other adults, has been the predominant family form in America since the earliest period on which historians have data. . . . Relationships among relatives appear to have been historically what they are now: complex patterns of companionship that only occasionally involve sharing bed and board."

Bane says of extended families: "Three-generational households can exist only where one generation lives long enough to see its grandchildren. . . . People may have wanted three-generational families but lacked the three generations." Death, of course, saw to that.

So whether in frontier forests, on farms, or in cities, yesterday's fathers commonly left homes to work, and mothers stayed behind, tending the brood — mostly without help — until at about the age of 10 the youngsters could contribute their labor at home or elsewhere. Young people usually left home to live with other families for disciplining, apprenticeship, or lodging as they began their working careers.

Working Mothers Compensate Bane refuses to beautify those hard-laboring mothers of yore, saying they frequently ignored their children during a long day's work. They probably gave less attention to their offspring than working mothers do today, she says. "There is no evidence as to how much time mothers a century ago spent with their children. Undoubtedly it was less than contemporary nonworking mothers, since mothers of a century ago had more children and probably also had more time-consuming . . . tasks."

But Bane points out that modern mothers don't spend all that much time solely on caring for the kids either. Recent studies show that the average stay-at-home mom invests 1.4 hours a day specifically on child care.

"There is no evidence that having a working mother *per se* has harmful effects on children," adds Bane. Middle-class working mothers try to compensate by reading more to their youngsters and otherwise spending more time with them than nonworking moms.

Women work now, as in the past, to improve the family's economic position, and time hasn't yielded a way to avoid it. Bane tries to. She suggests a broadly outlined "social insurance" program that in effect would give certain young families the kind of income support during child-rearing years that Social Security now provides retirees. Bane wants children to have "economic decency," and in a way her book boils down to a plea for that.

. . .

Criticism that Americans dump their aged kin in institutions seems overstated, Bane continues. In 1970, for instance, old folks' homes housed just 2 per cent of all Americans aged 65 to 74 and only 7 per cent of the males and 11 per cent of the females 75 and over, census data show.

. . .

The increasing proportion of old people living on their own might [then] reflect better health and better economic conditions. An alternative assumption is that people dislike living alone because they have no children or relatives willing to take them in. . . . The increased proportion of old people living on their own might result from the increasing wickedness of American children or decreasing family sizes.

"It is hard to know whether wickedness is increasing or decreasing. But it is true that people who were over 65 in 1970 were members of the generation . . . that had low marriage rates and high rates of childlessness. Since about 10 per cent never married, and since 15 to 20 per cent of those who did

marry had no children, almost a quarter of the old of the 1970s have no children — wicked or not — to take them in."

Families *have* changed, Bane goes on, but the evidence of caring is too great to allow the conclusion that the American family is in peril. "Children are still raised in families, and families have a lot of strength today." The institution of marriage is healthy, too, she adds.

Mobility's Nothing New Most marital breakups today occur because of divorce. Yet Bane contends that the proportion of youngsters deprived of a parent rose only recently after dropping earlier in this century. The reason: Death rates plummeted and divorce rates have not climbed rapidly enough to offset the drop. Consequently, "The total number of marital disruptions affecting children did not increase," Bane reports.

So why fret over the divorce rate? It's worrisome "in and of itself only if staying together at all costs is considered an indicator of healthy marriages or healthy societies," answers Bane.

Most marriages stay intact, "the vast majority" of divorced persons remarry, and few wed more than twice, Bane points out. "In general, the remarriage rate has kept pace with the divorce rate. . . . We are thus a long way from a society in which marriage is rejected or replaced by a series of short-term liaisons."

But what of Americans' mobility and its supposed deleterious effect on family and community? It's doubtful that "modern America is peculiarly transient," answers Bane. She says Americans were on the move in the Nineteenth Century too. The transients then were mostly young people making short-distance moves away from their parents to set up housekeeping alone or as newlyweds.

And that's also the way it is now, Bane adds. In the 1970s about 20 per cent of the population moved annually with just 4 per cent going out-of-state. The transients tended to be young and to stay within the same metropolitan areas. In fact, half of all Americans live in the same states all their lives. "The historical studies suggested that Twentieth Century Americans are about as mobile as Nineteenth Century Americans. If mobility is destroying community and social life in America it has been doing so for a long time, Bane concludes.   AUGUST GRIBBIN

The Family Is Sick and Dying: The Family—Is It Obsolete?*

The American middle-class family, already stripped of most non-essential duties, now faces an attack on its remaining last bastions. Sex is available premaritally, extra-maritally and non-maritally to more and more Americans. Thus, Morton Hunt reports that to the present generation of young Americans, age 18 to 25, premarital sex runs as high as 81 percent for females and 95 percent for males. Extra-marital sex is reported by about half of the males, and one out of five women. Education has long ago been taken from the family and invested in special institutions, the schools. While in the old days the members of one family often worked one farm, very few families today are also a "work" unit. The rapid rise in women who work (more than 60 percent of all married), or are on welfare, breaks economic dependence as a source of a family bond. Meals can be readily obtained at the mushrooming fast-food franchises, at the supermarket and at "Take-Homes."

Thus, as this short history of the modern family suggests, there is a continued, expanding divesture of missions from the family to other institutions. Now even the upbringing of young children, once considered by social scientists the family duty (indeed, in many societies the marriage is not considered fully consummated until there are offspring), is being down-graded by an increase in the number of persons who decide not to have children at all, and those

*Journal of Current Social Issues, Winter 1977 issue. Reprinted by permission.

who decide that they do not need a family to bring up infants. They either delegate this duty to day care centers, as available to singles as to couples, or do the job on their own. Nine million children under the age of 18 are being raised by one parent only, mostly by women. Thirty percent are under the age of six. There are about 2.4 million one-parent families as compared to 29 million nuclear families. The growth rate of single-parent families has increased by 31.4 percent, almost three times the growth of two-parent families. According to my calculations, if the present rate of increase in divorce and single households continues to accelerate as it did for the last ten years, by mid-1990 not one American family will be left.

The historical trends which propel the decline of the family are now accelerated by an additive, a slew of arguments which justify, legitimate and, indeed, even welcome these developments. They characterize the progressive decline of the nuclear family as "progress" and provide people with additional incentive to take to the exit, to dismantle the often shaky marital bond, instead of providing for a cooling-off mechanism to cope with the occasional centrifugal forces every marriage knows. While we have not reached the stage where breaking up one's family to enjoy "all that life has to offer" has become the thing to do, in many and growing circles the stigma attached to divorce— even when young infants are involved—has paled, the laws' cooling mechanisms have weakened, and reasons which "justify" divorce have grown in acceptance. Indeed "no-fault" divorces, which require no grounds at all, are now available in most states.

Until quite recently these trends were viewed as pathological. In the fifties, for example, the rising divorce rate was defined as a social problem, and marriage counseling was on the rise. The attitude of marriage counselors and that of society-at-large was typified by Dr. Paul Popenoe, marriage counselor and Ladies Home Journal columnist, who asked "Can This Marriage Be Saved?" and month after month related case histories to prove that "yes," it almost invariably could be.

During the sixties, however, an intellectual and to a lesser extent, a public opinion turn around began to take place. The idea that spouses were morally obligated to hold their marriage together and that nine times out of ten they could succeed in doing so if they were willing to work at it moved increasingly to the right of mainstream thinking. Today's popular experts on marriage and the family seldom ask first, "Can this marriage be saved?" but instead, "should it be?" And more and more often the answer given is not only "no" but an optimistic and affirmative "no." This is due to a new popular wisdom which says that people might be better off dissolving an unsatisfactory marriage, and either live single or try again, than to go through great contortions to fix their present marriage. While the many marriage and family experts of the fifties saw their task as shoring up the family's defenses so that it could better withstand attack, a significant contingent among today's experts is ready to view the invading social forces as potential liberators.

Divorce Is Aok Several related lines of argument are currently being used to identify and explain what are seen as positive aspects in the rising divorce rate. The most novel one is the idea that *second marriages are better than first marriages*. Thus, Leslie Aldridge Westoff, a Princeton demographer, writes about "blended" or "reconstituted families" rather than second marriages, in an article entitled "Second-time *Winners*." (The labels are important; blended or reconstituted sounds more approving than "second time around.") Westoff reports that for the couples she interviewed the first marriage was a dry-run. In the second marriage they applied the lessons learned, did not repeat the same mistakes, and chose mates more wisely. "In retrospect many of the couples saw their first marriage as a kind

of training school; . . . divorce was their diploma. All agreed that the second marriage was the real thing at last. With both partners older, more mature, somewhat expert at marriage, everything moves more smoothly, more meaningfully."

. . .

But Westoff herself laments the lack of systematic research on second marriages; her insights are based on a few interviews. She also concedes that second marriages are less stable than first ones. Statistically, 59 percent of second marriages as opposed to 37 percent of first marriages, will end in a divorce, according to Dr. Paul Glick of the U.S. Census Bureau. Nor does she show that such re-marriages, even if they do last, have no detrimental effects on the children.

Disposable Marriages The "if-at-first-you-don't succeed, try, try again" optimism about divorce is at least not down on marriage as an institution. Another increasingly common viewpoint, however, is one which interprets the rising divorce rate as a symptom that something is radically wrong with marriage and/or the family. This school of thought rejects the view that marriage can work once you know yourself well enough and choose the "right" partner; it sees it as *healthy* that individuals in great numbers want to get out of what it views as a decaying social bond. It tends to look upon the rising divorce rate with much the same hopefulness with which a Marxist approaches a new recession: as a condition which cannot be tolerated for long, and hence will force revolutionary changes in social structures. Those who subscribe to this view tend to see new family forms waiting in the wings, from contractual marriages to group-marriages.

Significantly, a common feature of most of these new marital styles is that they seek to take some of the strain off the nuclear family by de-intensifying the husband-wife relationship. One way is by limiting the duration of the relationship a priori to an agreed period of time and defining the terms of the dissolution of the relationship from its very inception. Thus, by this school's terms, divorce has become no more of a crisis than completing a stint in the army or delivering the goods as agreed to a supermarket. Another alternative is to diversify one's emotions by investing them in a large number of intimate relationships, making each one less intense and hence less all-important. Thus, it is often said that sexual fidelity puts too much of a strain on many marriages — acceptance of one or both partners' adultery may well save some relationships, since the couple can stay together while getting the sexual variety, affection or whatever from outside persons. Better yet, it is said, group-marriage secures that you'll always have a mate, even if you divorce one, two, or three. Such deemotionalization and de-emphasis is however a two-edged sword. On the one hand, spouses who do not depend exclusively on each other and who obtain satisfactions from other persons may be able to continue living together for long periods without having to resolve their conflicts, at the risk of bringing them to a destructive head. On the other hand, such relationships may be too shallow to provide the needed emotional anchoring and security many people seek and need.

. . .

After discussing a number of other problems with the family, the author concludes by asking the question:

What Could Be Done? Faced with the progressive dismemberment of the American family, there is surprisingly little public action for two reasons: first, the arguments that the current rate of family break-up may be a blessing in disguise raise doubts concerning the nature and extent of the crisis; and second, public officials feel that there is little the government could or should do in this intimate matter. To my mind, we need a thoroughgoing review of evidence concerning the consequences of family break-up to determine whether or not we have a national social problem on our hands. A Presidential or Congressional Commission could be given the task of investigating the harmful consequences of family dissolution bringing together and examining existing data and, where reliable data are not available, by carrying out studies of its own. Should the Commission find that single-parent families, contractual families and reblended families are doing as well as the declining traditional two-parent families, we can relax and enjoy the marital merry-go-round. Should it establish that the slew of "new" family rationalizations are ill-founded and we have a serious and growing problem on our hands, the very fact that a highly visible study has reached such conclusions, presenting evidence and airing pro and con arguments in public hearings, should help puncture these arguments.

. . .

Second, the "family impact" of various government programs should be assessed and taken into account as old programs are revised and new ones formulated. Thus, day-care centers are a blessing for working women and certainly a better place for a young child than roaming the streets. But they are also costly institutional substitutes for family, and by de-emphasizing the importance of parents in children's lives, they may well further contribute to the erosion of family bonds. More opportunities for *half* time jobs, without loss of privileges (such as benefits and promotion) both for women and men, may provide some parents with an alternative preferable to day-care centers, one which is less costly to the public, less bureaucratic and more compatible with a viable family.

Also, laws which work against the family should be altered, both because the government should not encourage the dissolution of families *and* because laws symbolize public attitudes.

. . .

The regulations governing Social Security benefits for retired persons favor individuals who are single by reducing the total monetary awards to couples. An unmarried woman is eligible to receive 100 percent of her Social Security benefits, whereas this amount is significantly reduced if she is married to a man who is also receiving benefits. This is said to be a significant factor for many retired couples living together rather than marrying. It might be asked — what ill effects result from old people living together unmarried? The answer is that (a) they should be free to choose to live together or marry, but not pushed into living together by government regulations, and (b) older people set models for younger people; "If granny does not marry the guy, why should I?"

. . .

Finally, it might well be advisable that a divorce cooling-off period and opportunities for counseling be reinstituted by those states that went somewhat overboard in making divorce easy and painless. While most divorce reforms are desirable, espe-cially those that remove the necessity of declaring one party "guilty" and the other "innocent" and those which serve to avoid bitter wrangling between spouses which may be communicated to their children, divorce by mail and other reforms which have the effect of divesting divorce of its seriousness over-liberate divorce. The state should not imply that divorce is a trivial matter—something one can do on an impulse. Reinstituting—or beginning again to enforce—a 30-day minimum cooling-off period with opportunities for counseling, if the couple desires, would seem to be a reasonable compromise.

Other steps may well be devised. The main point is that preoccupied as we are with prices, jobs, shortages and energy — all related to the material aspects of our societal existence — we should not neglect what to many sociologists still seems to be the vital cell of our society. The disintegration of the family, one must reiterate these days, may do as much harm to a society as running out of its favorite source of energy.

AMITAI ETZIONI

Chapter 2 〰

Contents

People Liberation: Changing Masculine and Feminine Roles

In the musical "Kiss Me Kate," Kate sings:

I hate men.
I can't abide 'em even now and then,
Than ever marry one of them, I'd rest a virgin rather,
For husbands are a boring lot and only give you bother.
Of course, I'm awf'lly glad that Mother had to marry Father
But, I hate men.
Of all the types I've ever met within our democracy,
I hate the most, the athlete with his manner bold and brassy,
He may have hair upon his chest but, sister, so has Lassie,
Oh, I hate men!
Their worth upon this earth I dinna ken.
Avoid the trav'ling salesman though a tempting Tom he may be,
From China he will bring you jade and perfume from Araby
But don't forget 'tis he who'll have the fun and thee the baby,
Oh, I hate men.
If thou shouldst wed a bus'nessman, be wary, oh be wary.
He'll tell you he's detained in town on bus'ness necessary,
His bus'ness is the bus'ness which he gives his secretary,
Oh, I hate men!

Her negative feelings about men find their counterpart in "My Fair Lady" when the good Dr. Higgins laments:

I'm an ordinary man,
Who desires nothing more than just the ordinary chance
To live exactly as he likes and do precisely what he wants.

An average man am I,
Of no eccentric whim;
Who wants to live his life free of strife
Doing whatever he thinks is best for him.

   Just an ordinary man.

But let a woman in your life
And your serenity is through!
She'll redecorate your home from the cellar to the dome;
Then go on to the enthralling fun of overhauling you.

Oh, let a woman in your life
And you are up against a wall!
Make a plan and you will find she has something else in mind;
And so rather than do either you do something else that neither likes
   at all.

Later, Dr. Higgins asks, "Why can't a woman be more like a man?"

Women are irrational, that's all there is to that!
Their heads are full of cotton, hay and rags!
They're nothing but exasperating, irritating, vacillating,
   calculating, agitating, maddening and infuriating hags!

The lyrics in these songs clearly depict some of the stereotypical attitudes held by our society about the characteristics of men and women. Yet such stereotypes are generally incorrect and, if believed, would certainly limit the interaction between the sexes.

Many theorists are now pointing out the oppression of rigid sex stereotypes, and that what we think of as "natural" sexual behavior is often learned behavior. They see all people benefiting from a balance of what we consider "feminine" and "masculine" behaviors. In the future, we may speak of human qualities instead of "masculine" and "feminine" ones.

Certainly individuals whose choices are not arbitrarily restrained and who are happy and fulfilled by what they have chosen to do in life can function better in marriage than people who feel oppressed and dissatisfied. If the partners can share the decisions and responsibilities of marriage in ways that feel right for them, their satisfaction will be greater than if each is forced into stereotyped behaviors that may not fit. To do away with role rigidity and stereotyping and to move in the direction of "people liberation," so that everyone is free to choose a fulfilling life style, is a proper goal of a free society.

Actually we do not need new roles for the sexes, but an acceptance of the concept of role *equity*. This means that the roles one fulfills are built on individual strengths and weaknesses in contrast to roles built on preordained stereotypic differences between the sexes.

Equity implies the "fair" distribution both of opportunities and constraints (restrictions) without regard to gender. Thus, it may entail inequity in the sense of "not the same" if such an arrangement is freely adopted by the individuals concerned. Equity between the sexes in family life thus embraces variation, i.e., many types of families — not advocacy of a model type of family, be it traditional or liberated. "Constructive liberation" is concerned with variation not just moving from one traditional definition of what is "right and proper" to another, egalitarian one. It is not constructive to move from one prison to another (Rapaport & Rapaport, 1975, p. 422).

Of course, the opening of alternatives makes some people feel threatened and insecure. If roles are tightly prescribed by society and few, if any, deviate from them, people feel safe and secure. However, the American society encompasses a great deal of diversity. People may find that their neighbors have a different life style. Children may point to imperfections in their parents' marital life and question whether people need to get married. They find the mass media criticizing a relationship they may never have seriously questioned. They may read articles praising alternative living arrangements that they were taught were immoral. Under such pressures, confusion, insecurity, anxiety, and resentment result. Unfortunately, these reactions often cause people to cling even more firmly to the status quo; indeed, the extreme attacks on the "traditional American marriage" mounted by radical feminists, gay liberationists, sexual freedom leagues, and others may have seriously undercut a thoughtful and constructive approach to change within the family structure. The thrust of this chapter is recognition of the value of varying forms of marital roles with the knowledge that most people will continue to choose the traditional roles for some time into the future.

Simply stated, whether one is male or female is biologically determined. The behaviors — roles — that go along with being male or female, however, are largely learned from one's society. For example, a French male can cry in public over a sad event; an American male, to be considered masculine, will repress tears in public. Both men are male, but a social behavior (role) assigned their sex differs. We call the behavior assigned biological sex in a given society masculine for the male and feminine for the female.

Male = Masculine and Female = Feminine: Not Necessarily So

Norms and Roles   Before discussing gender development, it is important to understand the meanings of the terms *norm* and *role*. Norms are accepted and expected patterns of behavior and beliefs established either formally or informally by a group. Usually the group rewards those who adhere to the norms and places sanctions against those who do not. For example, a husband who does not support his family is not meeting one of the marital norms of American society. In this case, general social disapproval and, in the extreme, legal sanctions could result because of his failure to fulfill this norm.

Roles overlap with norms inasmuch as they involve people doing the things demanded by the norms. That is, a husband working to support his family is fulfilling his role as husband. Since there are many norms in a society, there are also many roles that a person plays. For example, a married woman may fulfill the roles of sexual partner, chef, mother, homemaker, financial manager, psychologist, and so on. If she works outside of the marriage, she will fulfill roles there too. A married man may fulfill the roles of breadwinner, sexual partner, father, general repairman, and so on. The point is that all people play a number of roles at any given time in their lives. And often conflict between roles occurs because there are so many roles in a complex society. For example, in our society, a woman's mother and wife role may interfere with her career role (see Chapter 8).

The expectation that people will fulfill their roles, and thus meet social norms, is strong. Since roles are so taken for granted, most of us probably are not aware of the pressure to conform. In fact, the expectation that people behave in prescribed ways probably makes much of life simpler for us. But what happens when people behave in unexpected ways? To find out for yourself how unconscious expected role behavior is, try stepping out of an expected role and observe the reactions of those around you!

Norms and roles obviously also play important parts in marriage. That is, each of us brings to marriage, or to any intimate relationship, a great number of expectations about what our roles and those of our spouse should be. Many disappointments in marriage stem from frustration of the role expectations we hold either for ourselves or our spouses (see Chapter 5). The most obvious example is that of a man who assumes that the role of wife is restricted to caring for him, the house, and the children. His wife, however, may believe the role of wife can also include a career, and that the role of husband can include household duties and care of children. These conflicting role expectations will undoubtedly cause conflict for this couple.

Norms and roles, when accepted, tend to smooth family functioning. But problems occur when roles and norms are not accepted or when they are unclear. In many societies, there are very definite goals for marriage, such as increasing the family's land holdings, adding new

A bundle of joy and a little extra work.

workers (children) to the family, or even bringing extra wealth into the family in the form of the wife's dowry. But our society does not set definite goals other than the vague "living happily ever after" we learn about in movies and romantic fiction. And even there "happiness" is not defined.

Furthermore, in societies where roles and norms are stable, people enter into marriage with clear ideas of each partner's rights and obligations. Again, though, in our society almost all norms and roles are being questioned, and none more so than those associated with masculinity, femininity, and sexuality. Because the classification of behavior by gender is so central to human society, and to the concept of marriage as we have known it, this chapter will take a closer look at division according to gender and at the expectations, roles, and norms that arise from such division.

Division of Labor by Gender Division according to gender is society's oldest classification system. All societies recognize differences between the sexes, though not always the same ones. For example, Table 2-1 reveals that all societies do not assign the same work functions to

Table 2-1 Comparative Data on the Division of Labor by Sex

Activity	Number of Societies Where Work Is Done by				
	Men Always	Men Usually	Either	Women Usually	Women Always
Weapon making	78	1	0	0	0
Hunting	166	13	0	0	0
Boat building	91	4	4	0	1
Mining and quarrying	35	1	1	0	1
Trapping or catching of small animals	128	13	4	1	2
Lumbering	104	4	3	1	6
Fishing	98	34	19	3	4
Herding	38	8	4	0	5
House building	86	32	25	3	14
Body mutilations (such as tattooing)	16	14	44	22	20
Burden bearing	12	6	35	20	57
Manufacture of thread and cordage	23	2	11	10	73
Basket making	25	3	10	6	82
Mat making	16	2	6	4	61
Weaving	19	2	2	6	67
Gathering of fruits, berries, and nuts	12	3	15	13	63
Pottery making	13	2	6	8	77
Preservation of meat and fish	8	2	10	14	74
Manufacture and repair of clothing	12	3	8	9	95
Gathering of herbs, roots, and seeds	8	1	11	7	74
Cooking	5	1	9	28	158

Source: W. L. Stephens, *The Family in Cross-Cultural Perspective* (New York: Holt, 1963), pp. 282–283.
Also see Rosaldo, M. Z. "Women, Culture & Society: A Theoretical Overview," in Rosaldo & Lamphere (Eds.), *Women, Culture & Society*, Palo Alto, Ca.: Stanford Univ. Press, 1974.

Table 2-2 Employed Persons by Major Occupational Groups and Sex

Occupational Group	Both	Male	Female
White-collar workers	48.3	40.9	60.6
Professional and technical	14.0	13.7	14.5
Managers and administrators,			
except farm	11.0	14.6	5.0
Sales workers	6.4	5.9	7.2
Clerical workers	17.0	6.7	33.9
Blue-collar workers	34.4	45.9	15.4
Craftsmen and kindred workers	12.9	19.9	1.3
Operatives	16.4	18.3	13.3
Nonfarm laborers	5.1	7.7	0.8
Service workers	13.5	8.2	22.2
Private household	1.9	0.1	4.9
Other service workers	11.6	8.1	17.4
Farm workers	3.8	5.1	1.7
Farmers and farm managers	0.1	3.2	0.3
Farm laborers and foremen	1.7	1.9	1.4
Total employed	100.0	100.0	100.0

Source: U.S. Bureau of Labor Statistics.

the same sex. Although certain work functions may be associated with one sex across many cultures, the table also demonstrates that sex-assigned roles vary from culture to culture to some degree.

Note that most "men always" jobs involve being away from the home and that most "women always" jobs involve being in or near the home. This most likely occurs because women usually care for children and small children are mostly kept in or near the home (Whiting, 1972, 1974). Thus, the woman may work and watch over the children at the same time.

Table 2-2 shows that work differences based on gender persist in modern America. Note, for example, that clerical workers tend to be female while blue-collar workers tend to be males.

However, note also that the tables show that roles overlap, that biology is not necessarily destiny for a given individual. True, individuals are usually biologically either male or female, and this foundation greatly influences some physical characteristics and behavioral tendencies. But the socially taught behaviors assigned each sex — that is, masculine and feminine roles — account for more of the behavioral differences between the sexes than do biological components.

How Sex Identity Develops

Three factors determine one's sex identity. First, sex is genetically determined at conception. Second, hormones secreted by glands directed by the genetic configuration produce physical differences. Third, society defines, prescribes, and reinforces one's sex identity. Problems with any one of these factors can cause faulty sex identity.

Biological Contribution Every normal person has two sex chromosomes, one inherited from each parent, which determines the biological sex. Women have two X chromosomes (XX), men an X and a Y (XY). Thus if the man's X chromosomes combines with the woman's X, the child will be female (XX). If, on the other hand, the man's Y chromosome combines with the woman's X, the child will be male (XY).

At first embryos are all sexually bipotential (Money & Athanasion, 1973). That is, the already existing tissues of the embryo can become male or female. In order for a male to be produced, the primitive undifferentiated gonad must develop into testes rather than ovaries. The male hormone (a chemical substance), testosterone, spurs the development of testes while at the same time another substance (Müllerian-inhibiting substance) causes the regression of those embryonic tissues that would become the female reproductive system. In the absence of these hormones, the female organs develop. The hormones have already started working by the time the embryo is six millimeters long. By the end of the eighth week, the child's sex can be determined by observation of the external genitalia (see Chapter 11, pp. 336 – 337, for a fuller description of embryonic development).

Note that the male appears to develop only by the addition of the male hormones, which are stimulated by the Y chromosome. Without that stimulation, a female develops. This has led some researchers to conclude that the human embryo is innately feminine (Sherfey, 1972).

By puberty, hormonal activity has increased sharply. In girls, estrogen (one of the female hormones) affects such female characteristics as breast size, pubic hair, and the filling out of the hips. Estrogen and progesterone (another hormone) also begin the complicated process that leads to changes in the uterine lining and the first menstruation, followed about a year later by ovulation — the cycle, mediated by these hormones, that causes an egg to mature each month (see Chapter 9, Female Sex Organs, for a fuller discussion of the processes of ovulation and menstruation).

In boys, the active hormone is testosterone. At puberty it brings about the secretory activity of the seminal vesicles and the prostate and the regular production of sperm in the testes (see Chapter 9, Male Sex Organs, for a fuller discussion of this process).

Testosterone also affects such male characteristics as, larger size, more powerful muscles, and the ability of blood to carry more oxygen. Castration (removal of the testicles) generally leads to obesity, softer tissues, and a more placid temperament in the male due to the reduction in the quantity of testosterone.

Because every human starts with the potential of becoming either male or female, each, as a fully differentiated adult, still carries the biological rudiments of the opposite sex. For example, the male has undeveloped nipples on his chest and the female has a penis-like clitoris. In a few rare individuals, even though gene determinants have set the sexual direction, the hormones fail to carry out the process.

Inset 2-1
Transsexualism: A Confusion in Sexual Identity

I was three or perhaps four years old when I realized that I had been born into the wrong body, and should really be a girl. I remember the moment well, and it is the earliest memory of my life.

I was sitting beneath my mother's piano, and her music was falling around me like cataracts, enclosing me as in a cave. . . .

What triggered so bizarre a thought I have long forgotten, but the conviction was un-faltering from the start (Morris, 1974, p. 3).

Morris attended Oxford which led to a glamorous position as correspondent for *The Times* (London). He scored one of the world's historic journalistic coups by climbing 22,000 feet up Mt. Everest with Edmund Hillary and Tenzing Norgay, and flashing first word of their conquest of the peak. The lean, stubble-chinned Morris, whose "manly" stamina made such a feat possible, became a Fleet Street legend. By this time, in spite of his inner contra-dictions, he married, and he and his wife, daughter of a Ceylonese tea planter, had five children. Eventually he resigned from *The Times* to write books, and in this endeavor, too, he distin-guished himself.

However, for all of his out-ward appearance of normalcy, his inner anguish remained. He consulted physicians, and was advised either to wear gayer clothes or to "soldier on"

as a male. His quest for help led him to New York City where he was counseled by Dr. Harry Benjamin, an endocrinologist who has specialized in the study of gender confusion. Dr. Benjamin prescribed female hormone treatments to prepare the way for Morris's sexual changeover. For men, such treatments involve estrogen and progestin to soften the skin and enlarge the breasts. Morris underwent the treatment for eight years and estimates that he swallowed 12,000 pills.

In July, 1972, James Morris took the final, irreversible step. He checked into a Casablanca clinic that specializes in transsexual operations, and submitted to the surgery. The male-to-female procedure is carried out by amputation of the penis and castration, after which an artificial vagina is created, using scrotal or penile tissue or skin grafts from the hip or thigh. Because the penile tissue is still sensitive, male-to-female transsexuals may experience orgasm, though, of course, pregnancy is im-possible.

Today the former James Morris is in virtually every respects a woman, with a new name, the properly an-drogynous Jan since it is used by both males and females; a new relationship with her former wife (divorced, they regard each other as unofficial "sisters-in-law"); and with her children, who now call their father "Aunt Jan."

James Morris was a very

conventional male, who did all of the things that a man was supposed to do. He has turned into a very conventional female, doing the things that a woman is traditionally sup-posed to do. The new Jan Morris enjoys having men open doors for her, flirt with her, and kiss her. She says, "Women who like to feel cherished by a stronger man have every right to their feelings."

Such cases are extremely rare. It is estimated that about 5,000 individuals in the United States have altered their sex by surgery. For them, biology and the environment had failed to work together to produce a stable sex identity.

It is interesting to note that Johns Hopkins Medical Center gave up doing sex change operations in 1979. Their follow-up studies of sex changed persons indicated that the psychological and other gains were minimal and not worth the problems risked with the extensive surgery necessary to accomplish a sex change.

From *Human Sexuality*, a title in the Human Behavior series by John Gagon and Bruce Henderson and the editors of Time-Life Books, 1975.

Such a person has characteristics of both sexes, though neither are fully developed, and is called a *hermaphrodite*.

Hermaphrodites are rare and should not be confused with transsexuals or transvestites. A transsexual is a person who has undergone a sex-change operation as discussed in Inset 2-1. A transvestite is a person who enjoys and gains sexual pleasure from dressing as the opposite sex.

The strength of the sex hormones can be seen when pregnant rhesus monkeys are injected with testosterone for twenty-five to fifty days. The genetically female offspring of the injected mothers have malformed external genital structures, which include a scrotum, a small penis, and an obliterated external vaginal orifice. In addition, the behavior of such pseudohermaphroditic females is altered in the direction of normal male behavior (Perez et al., 1971, p. 7).

The early adaptability of the tissues that grow into mature sexual organs is also quite amazing. Ovaries and vaginas transplanted into castrated male rats within the first twenty-four hours after birth will grow and function exactly like normal female organs. This plasticity of the sex tissues quickly vanishes as the hormones cause further differentiation. Transplants of female organs into male rats more than three days old are unsuccessful.

Environmental Contribution Once a baby is born, the society begins to teach it its proper sex role and reinforces its sexual identity. In the United States, we name our children according to their gender; we give girls pink blankets and boys blue blankets; and at Christmas and birthdays boys receive "masculine" toys and girls "feminine" toys.

In keeping with cultural prescriptions about the way in which males and females are viewed, different attitudes are shown toward children of different sexes and different behaviors are expected and rewarded. For example, boys are encouraged to engage in rough and tumble activities while girls are discouraged from such activities. (This may explain, in part, why men tend to be more interested in contact sports than women are.) Parents provide guidance to help the child assimilate the proper role. Nothing inherent within the child will give rise to the socially sex-appropriate behaviors. Each child must learn —from parents, relatives, teachers, friends—the appropriate behaviors for the culture. (See also p. 378 on accepting the new body image at puberty.)

Occasionally, children fail to learn the role that traditionally accompanies their biological sex. This can lead to the unusual circumstance of a person being one sex biologically but the opposite sex psychologically. Such a case is presented in Inset 2-1.

Biological and Environmental Interaction It seems that the arguments presented in Insets 2-2 and 2-3 are extreme points of view. There are obvious anatomical and chemical differences between the sexes. But the extent to which they dictate behavioral differences is the real point

The first edition of this text [Udry, 1965], based on information available in 1965, presented a thoroughly sociological explanation of the origin of sex differences in behavior. At that time I argued that sex differences were probably completely determined by socialization, and that any innate predisposition to different behavior by the two sexes was trivial. . . . The information available today invalidates my previous explanations. Evidence on the role of sex hormones in differentiating the behavior of other animals has been accumulating for two decades. . . . Now the human data make it possible for us to begin sorting out sex differences into those underwritten by biology, however culturally embellished, and those that are genuine cultural options.

The nervous system is preprogrammed by the fetal androgen [male sex hormone] or its absence, and the programming is evidently permanent. These androgen-programmed differences include at least the following:

1. Males have a predisposition to competition for dominance, while females do not.

2. Males have a greater predisposition than females for high energy expenditure.
3. Females have a greater predisposition to care for infants.

This list is not meant to be exhaustive, nor does it exclude the possibility that other sex differences in behavior are supported by other biological factors which come into play at other times in life.

Sex roles may seem a social accommodation and elaboration on the basic biological differences in behavioral predisposition of males and females. . . .

If differences in the behavior of men and women were solely determined by the social process, then presumably a society with consensus and determination could write its own scenario of the ideal society, specify any particular relationship between the sexes, and differences in the behavior of the sexes it chose, or no sex differences in behavior if that was preferred, and build a social structure to achieve it.

We must now face very strong evidence which undercuts the theoretical support for such a position. It is no longer tenable to believe that

males and females are born into the world with the same behavioral predispositions. Our theory of society and of the relationship between the sexes must accommodate itself to the fact that males and females are born with predispositions to behave differently. In the past, most societies have simply taken that for granted. Sex-role differences in most societies can be viewed as cultural elaborations and specifications which capitalize upon the innate proclivities of males and females to behave differently.

We must now be confident that if it were possible to rear boys and girls alike, they would still come out different. If we are throughgoing in our determination to eliminate sex-role differences, we must recognize that it will be necessary to work at cross-purposes with the natural propensity of the organisms. Specifically, we will have to reward dominance and punish submissiveness in women, while we reward submissiveness and punish dominance in men. No one can be sure what other problems such socialization might create (Udry, 1974, pp. 45–49).

Anthropologists such as Margaret Mead have pointed out that sex-role behavior varies from one society to another (Mead, 1935, 1961). Such variations support the idea that one's sex identity is largely learned. For example, according to Western standards, both Arapesh men and women are feminine. Both tend to be cooperative, have concern for others, and both are passive and unaggressive. The Tchambuli, on the other hand, rear women who are masculine according to Western standards.

Social learning theorists such as Walter Mischel (1971) point out that no other categorization is as important psychologically as the one that sorts people into male and female and their characteristics into masculine and feminine. It is through *sex typing* that an individual acquires and learns to value and practice the proper sex-role behaviors. Biology determines a child's gender. Society then reacts to the child in light of its gender. The child quickly learns that little girls behave this way and little boys behave in another way. The female child models after mother, the male after father. Sex-appropriate behavior is rewarded by the society, inappropriate behavior punished. In America, aggression is part of the masculine stereotype. Studies by R. Sears (1957, 1963, 1965) indicate that sex differences in aggression have been found as early as age three and that they persist throughout life. But are these differences innate? Sears has

shown that boys are given greater freedom in the expression of aggression. They are often rewarded for aggressive behavior, while overt aggression in females is reproved — "that's unladylike." Thus one's sexual identity is largely rooted within the culture. Biology makes the first determination, but the behaviors that characterize one's gender are learned by each person from the society into which they are born.

If sex roles are learned, it is possible for a society to change masculine and feminine behavior. This is a position taken by feminists.

One interesting piece of evidence they point to are those few babies whose ascribed sex differs from their biological sex. Some of these babies have been studied over a twenty-year period, and one researcher (Weitzman, 1975b, p. 108) concludes:

In virtually all cases, the sex of assignment (and thus of rearing) proved dominant. Thus, babies assigned as males at birth and brought up as boys by their parents (who were unaware of the child's female genetic and hormonal makeup) thereafter thought of themselves as boys, played with boys' toys, developed boys' sports, preferred boys' clothing, developed male sex fantasies, and in due course fell in love with girls. And the reverse was true for babies who were biologically male but were reared as girls: they followed the typical feminine pattern of development.

Another two cases further emphasize the relative importance of sex rearing. The child was a genetic male who had been exposed to prenatal androgens and was born with male genitals. However, he had his genitals changed to female and was being reared as a female. In this case, one of two identical twins was reassigned as a female following a surgical mishap. At seven months, the twin boys were to be circumcised by electrocautery. Due to an electrical malfunction, the penis of one of the twins was totally destroyed. Following the recommendations of their doctors, the parents of this little boy elected to have the boy's sex reassigned. At seventeen months, the boy came to the Johns Hopkins clinic for the necessary surgical corrections to give him female external genitals. Money and Ehrhardt reported that since surgery, the parents have made every effort to raise the twins in accord with their assigned sex — one male and one female. According to the reports of the parents, the two children are developing to fit the role expectations of their assigned sex. The mother described her "daughter's" behavior this way (Money & Ehrhardt, 1972, p. 119):

She likes for me to wipe her face. She doesn't like to be dirty, and yet my son is quite different. I can't wash his face for anything. . . . She seems to be daintier. Maybe it's because I encourage it.

of debate. It appears, in general, that the cultural overlay is mainly responsible for behavioral differences.

For example, many women experience premenstrual depression, irritability, and fatigue. This is due to the influence of the various hormones during certain times of the monthly cycle. Generally such feelings occur during the days prior to the onset of menstruation. These symptoms, however, can be exaggerated if one's culture has a negative attitude toward menstruation. (For a fuller discussion of this point, see Bardwick, 1974; Ivey and Bardwick, 1972; and Paige, 1973.) Many cultures, unfortunately, have a "menstrual taboo." Menstruation is seen as something unpleasant and to be avoided. Historically in many cultures the female was avoided and isolated during menstruation, and many myths about the dangers of menstrual blood and potential evils existed. If a woman expects menstruation to be unpleasant and her society emphasizes the unpleasantness, it is obvious that menstruation will be more difficult for her than need be. She may feel worse than necessary, or she may deny that she feels any different at all during menstruation in an effort to minimize the negative cultural stigma. In any case, the negative cultural overlay will only serve to make a normal bodily function more mysterious, more troublesome, and less understood than it should be. In our own society we are coming to realize that a more positive attitude toward menstruation leads to a much more healthy and positive experience for women.

Paula Weideger (1975, p. 189) discusses the many myths and taboos that surround menstruation in America. She concludes that:

> Somewhere between the denial of the menstrual cycle and its bearing on behavior and the overzealous acceptance of only negative aspects of cyclic variation rests a balanced assessment of the ways in which the cycle of menstruation shapes woman's experience. The taboo and its subsequent prejudices form a straitjacket, constricting emotional and intellectual growth. If the flight from taboo leads to the denial of the menstrual cycle, it is as constricting as a docile acceptance (of only the negative).

B. G. Rosenberg and B. Sutton-Smith conclude their 1972 survey of the many theories of sex differences by pointing out that most cultures have preferred to maximize rather than reduce sex differences. It could be, then, that even if some of today's sex differences are reduced, men and women might well invent new differences. Perhaps societies with sex roles are more interesting and productive than those without.

Recent studies of the human brain indicate that there may be gender-related differences in how certain mental processes are controlled and the location of the control area (Goleman, 1978). There are no commonly accepted, observable differences in the physical size, structure, and biochemical components of brains, however, and the degree to which these differences influence behavioral differences is difficult to determine. Table 2-3 looks at some of the stereotypic differences between the sexes and compares them to scientific findings. There seems to be little support for the belief that there are many

Table 2-3 Stereotypic Sex Role Differences Compared to Research Findings[1]

Stereotype	Findings
Perceptual Differences	
Men have: better daylight vision	Mild but in direction of stereotype.
are: less sensitive to extreme heat	"
more sensitive to extreme cold	"
faster reaction times	"
better depth perception	"
better spatial skills	"
Women have: better night vision	"
are: more sensitive to touch in all parts of their body	"
better hearing, especially in higher ranges	"
less tolerant of loud sound	"
better manual dexterity and fine coordination	"
Aggression	
Males are more aggressive. Females are less aggressive.	Strong consistent differences in physical aggression. Inconsistent finding with indirect aggression.
Dependency	
Females are more submissive and dependent. Males are more assertive and independent.	Weak differences that are more consistent for adults than for children.
Emotionality	
Females are more emotional and excitable. Males are more controlled and less expressive.	Moderate differences on some measures. Overall, findings inconclusive.
Verbal Skills	
Females excel in all verbal areas including reading. Males are less verbal and have more problems learning to read.	Moderate differences, especially for children.
Math Skills	
Males are better in mathematical skills. Females are less interested and do less well in mathematics.	Moderate differences on problem-solving tests, especially after adolescence.

[1]This table has been constructed using four main sources:

1. Maccoby, Eleanor E., Jacklin, Carol N. *The Psychology of Sex Differences.* Palo Alto, Calif.: Stanford University Press, 1974.

2. Goleman, Daniel. "Special Abilities of the Sexes: Do They Begin in the Brain?" *Psychology Today.* Nov., 1978.

3. Frieze, Irene H. et al. *Women and Sex Roles.* New York: W. W. Norton, 1978.

4. McGuiness, Diane, Pribram, Karl. "The Origins of Sensory Bias in the Development of Gender Differences in Perception and Cognition." In Morton Bortner (Ed.) *Cognitive Growth and Development.* Essays in honor of Herbert G. Birch. New York: Brunner/Mazel, 1979.

strong and consistent differences between males and females. Yet when we examine all of the studies that have been done on the subject of sex differences, there is support for some mild differences. In every case, however, the differences between persons of the same sex on a given characteristic can be greater than the average differences between the sexes.

However, I believe that the reduction of sex-role stereotypes — or any behavioral stereotypes — is a worthy goal. Furthermore, to argue endlessly over the relative influence of biology as opposed to environment is a waste of energy. Since we know that culture does influence sex roles to a great extent, it is certainly possible to modify sex roles.

Sweden has moved in the direction of reducing sex role differences. Boys and girls are now required to take identical subjects in school. All jobs are open to both sexes. Laws are applied equally. In addition, more radical reformers want to do away with the concept of the male provider, which they interpret as the reason for wage and other discrimination against females (see Linner, 1967). They advocate:

1. Rearing boys and girls in exactly the same way.
2. Practical reorganization of housework.
3. Far-reaching arrangements for collective supervision of children.
4. A children's fund that would enable either the father or mother to remain at home during the first three years of their child's life.
5. Automation and shorter working hours to make it easier for parents to devote equal time to employment and housework.

Perhaps in the future sex roles will become flexible enough so that individuals will be able to choose roles that maximize their own unique capabilities. Only time will tell.

The Androgynous Person   The concept of the androgynous person who exhibits both male (andro) and female (gyno) behavioral characteristics now associated with one or the other sex has become popular among many who are in favor of reducing sex role differences. Abraham Maslow's (1968) self-actualized person (see pp. 163–164 for a fuller discussion of Maslow's ideas) comes close to being such a person, open to both masculine and feminine as well as positive and negative aspects. The self-actualized person has no need to assert dominance or play the coquette. He or she is free to build his or her individualized role.

To create such adults, society would have to train children for competence in many areas without regard to sex. This is the idea that we saw being tried in Sweden.

> In an androgynous society children strive for competence in many areas without regard to sex. They develop motor skills through running and jumping, and hand-eye coordination through needle work, art work, and handling of tools. They learn the skills necessary to take care of themselves, such as cooking, sewing, and household repairs. They play with friends of both sexes, in school as well as out. They engage freely in games of competition as well as games of cooperation

Inset 2-4
A Theory of Sex Role Development

The old argument over whether environment and learning or genetics and biology determine sex role behavior should not be stated in this either/or form. In truth, of course, it is the interaction of these two great molders of behavior that determines one's actual behavior. The following theory tries to take both into consideration. In the early years (stage 1) biological influence is most clearly seen. Children ten through thirteen (stage 2) demonstrate much more socially influenced behavior. Finally, during adolescence (stage 3), there seems to be a more personal psychological orientation directing sex role behaviors.

Stage 1: Biological Orientation
Level I (6 years) Differences between masculine and feminine are expressed primarily in terms of external bodily differences, such as size, strength, length of hair, etc. Social and psychological differences are recognized but are assumed to be the consequence of these external physical differences. Conformity to sex differences is viewed as necessary in order to maintain gender identity and to allow for the expression of innate gender differences.

Level II (8 years): There is a growing awareness that mas-

culine and feminine traits can exist independently from biological and physical features. Emphasis is placed on the ability of the individual to act according to choice, since he or she is no longer limited by physical or biological constraints. Also the role of training, and social conditions are beginning to be recognized. Finally, since children no longer see sex differences as biological necessities, they do not demand the conformity to sex roles characteristic of the younger children.

Stage 2: Societal Orientation
Level III (10 years) Masculine and feminine traits are seen as inherent in the requirements of a system of social roles, and are viewed as fixed and unchangeable. The traits associated with certain adult social roles are assumed to be characteristic of the members of the sex expected to fill those roles. Conformity to masculine and feminine standards is based on the need to satisfy external demands of the social system.

Level IV (12 years) There is a growing awareness that the system of social roles is arbitrary and variable, and may function independently of sex of individual. Stress is put on the individual's freedom to

act according to individual self-interest. Conformity is no longer expected.

Psychological Orientation
Level V (14–16 years) Masculine and feminine traits are based on the adoption of an appropriate psychological identity by males and females. These adolescents admit that sex differences are not biologically based and may not be the result of social necessity but these traits are assessed to a central part of men's and women's identities. Deviation is viewed as "sick" or "abnormal," and conformity to external standards is seen as required for maintenance of marriage and the family.

Level VI (18 years) There is an awareness that masculinity and femininity may exist independent from conformity to traditional standards, roles, and behaviors. Sex-stereotyped traits are not assumed to be crucial aspects of personal identity. Principles of equality and freedom are proposed as standards for behavior, and are used to define an ideal model of personal and interpersonal functioning.

Source: Ullian, 1976.

with friends of the other sex and friends of the same sex. They learn to respect (or to dislike!) each other on the basis of individual differences, not according to sexual category.

Children learn not only self-confidence and a sense of mastery but also attitudes of caring and concern for others. Both sexes are held and touched often as infants and after. They learn to understand and express their own feelings and to recognize the needs and feelings of those around them. Verbal and physical displays of emotion are encouraged as long as they are not harmful to other people (Lindemann, 1974, pp. 185–186).

Whether or not this is an ideal that most Americans want to strive for remains to be seen.

Practical Problems Related to Sex Roles

People locked into stereotypic sex roles that ignore individual differences will, more often than not, feel frustrated and dissatisfied. They may not be able to fulfill their own individual capabilities or to follow their own interests if their society clings too strongly to rigid sex role behaviors. Although the American society is far freer of unquestioned sex role stereotypes than most societies, there still remain some practical obstructions to full freedom to choose roles best suited to individuals, regardless of their gender.

It is interesting to note that we find relative agreement between American men and women when they assess the advantages and disadvantages of their sex roles. Essentially, the perceived advantages of one sex are the disadvantages of the other.

> Masculine disadvantages consist overwhelmingly of obligations with a few prohibitions while the disadvantages of the female role arise primarily from prohibitions, with a few obligations. Thus females complain about what they can't do, males about what they must do. Females complain that they cannot be athletic, aggressive, sexually free, or successful in the worlds of work and education; in short, they complain of their passivity. Males complain that they must be aggressive and must succeed; in short, of their activity. The (sanctioned) requirement that males may be active and females passive in a variety of ways is clearly unpleasant to both (Chafetz, 1974, p. 58).

Women and the Economy The major social restraint to freer role choice is women's disadvantageous economic position in our society. In general, a man can earn more than a woman regardless of their individual skills. This economic differential in earning power locks each sex into many traditional roles. For example, a father who would prefer to spend more time at home caring for the family usually cannot afford to do so. In most cases it would mean giving up a portion of his income and his wife usually cannot earn enough to totally replace the lost income.

Although there are more and better job opportunities for women today, the male-female earnings gap has remained and, in fact, increased in recent years. Table 2-4 shows women's relative earnings as a percentage of men's earnings. Notice the "all workers" figures. In 1956, women averaged 63.3 percent of men's earnings. Since then the figure has dropped to 58.8 percent (in 1975).

Furthermore, the unemployment rate for females is almost double that of males. And the kinds of jobs available to women tend to be those at lower levels — "pink-collar" jobs. Table 2-5 shows the

Table 2-4 Women's Relative Earnings by Occupation, 1956 – 75
(Median Earnings of Full-Time, Year-Round Women Workers as a Percentage
of Men's Median Earnings)

Occupational Group	1956	1960	1965	1970	1975
All workers	63.3	60.7	59.9	59.4	58.8
Professional and technical workers	62.4	61.3	65.2	64.1	65.9
Teachers, primary and secondary	NA	75.6	79.9	79.5	83.0
Managers and administrators	59.1	52.9	53.2	54.6	56.7
Clerical workers	71.7	67.6	67.2	64.0	62.2
Sales workers	41.8	40.9	40.5	42.7	38.9
Operatives	62.1	59.4	56.6	58.4	56.1
Service workers (nondomestic)	55.4	57.2	55.4	55.6	57.1

Source: U.S. Department of Commerce, Bureau of the Census, *Current Population Reports*, series P-60, various issues.

earnings of women in the federal government civil service system. You can see clearly that even in government service, which has led the battle against sex discrimination in jobs, women are overrepresented in the lower grades and underrepresented in the higher grades.

Most women tend to be employed in a relatively narrow range of jobs. You can see from Figure 2-1 that 80 percent of employed women tend to fall into only six basic job categories, with 57 percent of them falling into just two categories, clerical and service workers.

Table 2-5 Earnings of Women and Men in the Federal Government Civil Service System
(Full-Time, White-Collar Employees of Federal Government Agencies as of
November 30, 1977)

General Schedule (GS) Grade	Salary	Number of Women Employed	Women as a Percentage of Total Employed
Total GS Employees	—	615,342	43.1
1	$ 6,561	1,277	65.7
2	7,422	15,818	74.1
3	8,366	73,187	77.5
4	9,391	134,602	77.5
5	10,507	126,060	68.1
6	11,712	60,560	69.6
7	13,014	64,631	49.4
8	14,414	16,374	50.3
9	15,920	54,455	35.1
10	17,532	8,547	32.4
11	19,263	30,621	19.4
12	23,087	16,997	11.1
13	27,453	7,670	6.8
14	32,442	2,878	4.9
15	38,160	1,435	4.5
16	44,756	159	3.4
17	47,500	55	3.2
18	47,500	16	3.7

Source: U.S. Civil Service Commission, *Equal Employment Opportunity Statistics* (Washington, D.C.: U.S. Government Printing Office, 1978), p. 2.

Note: The salary rate shown is basic pay for employees in step 1 of the grade as of October 1978.

Figure 2-1
Occupational profile of the female labor force, 1977.
Source: U.S. Department of Labor, Bureau of Labor Statistics, 1977.

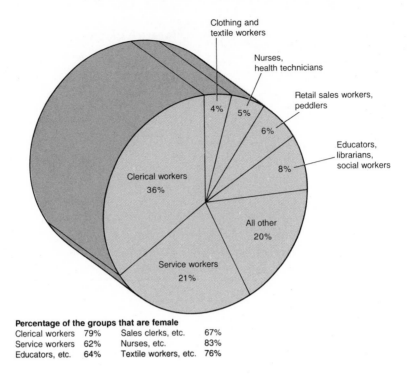

Clothing and textile workers

Nurses, health technicians

Retail sales workers, peddlers

4%   5%

6%

Educators, librarians, social workers

8%

Clerical workers
36%

All other
20%

Service workers
21%

Percentage of the groups that are female

Clerical workers	79%	Sales clerks, etc.	67%
Service workers	62%	Nurses, etc.	83%
Educators, etc.	64%	Textile workers, etc.	76%

Table 2-6 shows the percentage of males in various professions. Note that women have made little, if any, gain in most of them since 1940. However, since 1970, the last year on the table, there have been some dramatic changes. For example, 25 percent of entering medical students are now women, up from 11 percent in 1970. Also, 20 percent of law students are now women, up from 8.5 percent in 1971 (*Time,* 1976, p. 8).

Table 2-7 shows the overall distribution of young women workers in 1977 compared to 1968. You can see that there has been a slight increase in professional, technical, and management participation and a slight decrease in clerical employment. However, the changes have

Table 2-6 Percentage of Males in Various Professions

	1940	1950	1960	1970
Architects	97.7	96.0	97.7	96.5
Lawyers and judges	97.6	96.7	96.2	95.2
Physicians and surgeons	95.4	93.8	93.0	90.8
Photographers	86.3	82.7	88.0	86.2
College presidents and faculty	73.5	76.8	78.1	71.6
Authors	63.9	61.2	74.4	70.7
Social and welfare workers	35.7	30.8	37.2	37.3
Religious workers	25.4	30.4	37.5	44.3
Teachers	24.3	25.4	28.3	29.8
Librarians	10.5	10.9	14.3	18.1
Nurses and student nurses	2.1	2.4	2.5	2.7

Source: U.S. Census Bureau, 1970.

Table 2-7 Occupational Distribution of Young Women Workers (ages 20–34) in 1977 Compared with 1968

Occupation	Distribution (percent)	
	1977	*1968*
Professional, technical, and managerial	24.5	20.0
(of which, teachers[1])	(7.1)	(7.1)
Clerical	38.0	41.7
Services	17.4	16.7
(of which, private household)	(1.4)	(3.0)
Operatives	10.4	14.5
Craftsmen	1.8	0.6
Sales	5.6	4.4
Other	2.3	2.1

Source: Unpublished tabulations provided by the U.S. Department of Labor, Bureau of Labor Statistics.

[1]Excludes college and university teachers.

not been very great considering efforts made on the behalf of women with such legislation as the Equal Pay Act of 1963 and the creation of the Equal Employment Opportunity Commission (EEOC) under Title VII of the Civil Rights Act of 1964. Despite the slowness of the process however, women are gaining economic opportunities. As Barrett (1979, p. 57) concludes:

> The rapid evolution of the law from sanctioning sex discrimination in the guise of protecting the weaker sex, to establishing the principle of equal employment opportunity, and finally to mandating the eradication of discrimination through affirmative action is one of the most significant legislative developments of the post-World War II era.
>
> . . .
>
> Equal employment legislation may open new doors for women, but women themselves must be prepared to walk through them.

Although women's earning power and choice of jobs are more limited than men's, this century has witnessed dramatic changes in women's participation as workers outside of the home. The proportion of women (over 20) in the work force has risen from 20 percent in 1900 to 50 percent in 1978. Even more dramatic and important to marriage is the greatly increased percentage of working married women. It wasn't so long ago that a married woman, especially one with children, was supposed to remain at home, taking care of her house, husband, and children. In 1930, only about 29 percent of married women worked at outside jobs. By 1950, the figure had jumped to 52 percent, by 1960 it was 60 percent, and by 1975, it had risen to 62 percent (U.S. Bureau of Census, 1949, p. 63; 1974, p. 340). In 1978 of approximately 42 million females in the labor force, 23 percent were single; 62 percent were married; and 15 percent were widowed or divorced (Statistical Abstracts, 1977, p. 358; Smith, 1979, p. 4).

What changes can be made in the economic system to make better and fairer use of women in the work force? Equal pay for equal work is certainly the first necessary change. But this can only become a reality when certain attitudes about working women change. Chafetz (1974, p. 124) lists a number of these attitudes, which she calls myths:

Myth 1: Women are only working for "pin money."

Myth 2: Women aren't worth hiring where any training or investment is necessary since they just get married or pregnant or quit.

Myth 3: Women are weak and frequently sick, thus missing too many days of work. For example, California employers are required to have a couch in every ladies' room in larger firms.

Let's take a closer look at these myths. Although there are some women who work because they enjoy it, rather than out of necessity, many women are the sole breadwinners or major contributors to their families. Approximately 5.5 million American families are headed by women, and the recent sharp increase in the divorce rate indicates that this number may well rise. In light of present pay levels for women, it is not surprising to learn that approximately half of these women-headed families, with about 4.5 million children, fall below the poverty line (Amundsen, 1971, pp. 26–27).

Other evidence indicates that the majority of employed wives are married to low-earning men, and the wives' earnings are needed to maintain the family (Suelzle, 1970, pp. 55–56).

Myth 2 rests on a factual foundation: females do quit more often than males. However, many things contribute to this such as low pay, overqualification for available jobs, lack of promotional opportunities, time conflicts between job and marriage responsibilities, and much more. In general, people in low paying jobs have higher "quit rates." Since a higher proportion of women have such jobs, their overall quit rate is exaggerated.

Myth 3 is simply untrue. Females average 5.3 sick days per year and males 5.4 sick days (Suelzle, 1970, p. 55).

A number of societal rearrangements could help the working mother. First, the quality of care provided for children of working mothers is a matter of public as well as private concern. Traditionally children have been cared for by their own mothers. When the mother works outside of the home, other arrangements must be made. Children must be left with other nonemployed women, relatives, or at some kind of child care center. Although professionally run child care centers would seem to offer the most advantageous help to working mothers, most women cannot afford even the modest cost of $8 to $12 per day ($160 to $240 per month) that good private centers currently charge. Consequently, in recent years feminists have argued and worked for government funding of day-care centers. They have had limited success on the state level, but little on the federal level.

Two objections can be made to government funding of day-care centers. The first objection is that government funding will mean too much government control over child-rearing practices. Granting that minimal standards for day-care centers should be established for such things as fire and health precautions, general funding usually provides for much more detailed control. Those who pay the bill usually decide what sort of service will be provided. It is possible that legislation for child care funding would provide for parental control over governing boards of child care facilities. The trend, however, in other segments of public education has been in the opposite direction, toward loosening of local community control and greater regulation from the governmental bureaucracy. Government funding for early childhood care is likely to take the direction for children's care out of the hands of parents.

A second objection to governmental funding, especially from a feminist's point of view, is that it provides a substitute for adequate pay for women workers. In effect, the government is giving a subsidy to employers. Since the government is paying for the child care that their employees cannot afford, employers can keep wages low and still find workers. The government funding does benefit the worker, but at the same time limits her options. If she does not like the kind of care provided in the government-funded centers, she has little recourse. She cannot afford to send her children elsewhere, and it is unlikely that she could influence the center's policies to any great extent.

Consistency and predictability are crucial to the development of very young children. Close parental involvement with those who are providing care is necessary. Paid an adequate wage, working mothers could choose the private child care center that best meets their needs. The resulting demand for quality child care would make it profitable to establish child care centers and a variety would be opened with dif-

Day-care centers become increasingly important as more mothers enter the work force.

Joan and Pamela, each recently divorced, share quite a bit: a job, a paycheck, a house, and their children.

The two friends persuaded a small company to hire both of them to split one secretarial job. One works while the other baby-sits. There are numerous advantages to this arrangement. Each has a job which is necessary if she is to make ends meet since neither receives more than a minimum amount of child support. Each saves money that would go to baby-sitters. Each knows the other well so that the children are left with a friend rather than a stranger. The children also remain in their own home rather than being sent away for the day. In addition, each has time with her own children. Each has reduced her costs by sharing the costs of the house.

They each work three days one week and two days the following week. This schedule gives the company a full-time secretary while each mother works only half time.

The company has also derived some extra advantages from the job sharing. Occasionally one of the women's children becomes sick. The other woman can cover for her at work. If only a single mother were involved, the company would probably have to do without their employee for the day.

Both workers are also fresher and less tired since they are not coping with two full-time jobs every day, mother and employee.

fering educational policies. Even if parents had little direct influence over the programs offered, they would have some indirect control since they would not have to patronize those centers that raised their children in ways inconsistent with their own values.

For the immediate future, government help for early child care would be an improvement over the present situation where children of working mothers often receive only minimal care. In the long run, wage scales for women's jobs must be raised to levels comparable to those for men's jobs (see Chapter 8). That is the best way to help families choose quality child care that will meet their needs (Lindemann, 1980).

Second, in addition to better child care, more part-time jobs at good pay could be created. For example, two women could share one job (see Inset 2-5). They could alternate days, or one could work a morning shift and the other an afternoon shift. In Massachusetts, Honeywell, Inc., offers mothers shortened shifts within school hours. These shifts allow mothers time to be with their children and maintain their home and yet contribute economically to the family. In addition, they would be participating in the world outside the home and maintaining a career, without working themselves into exhaustion as so often happens when a woman works all day and then returns to her homemaking job at night.

Third, maternity leaves should be a normal fringe benefit of all jobs. The man who desires to should also be allowed such a leave to participate with his wife in the birth of their child.

Fourth, business needs to reconsider its age limitations in its hiring practices. The woman whose children have left home is often a reliable and conscientious employee. She may need some training if she has been out of the work world for a long time, but, given that training, she is far freer to devote herself to the job than is her counterpart with children at home, and she is often more stable and experienced in dealing with people than a younger man or woman.

With these suggested changes, women would have more alternatives and would derive more satisfactions. Business would have better workers, because the person who feels worthwhile and productive in all areas of life does a better job and is less prone to quit. Fair pay and a humane system that supports rather than hinders home life certainly are worthwhile social goals.

Credit and the Single Woman Obviously, the lower pay scale for women makes it more difficult for them to obtain credit. For example, for house purchases, loan institutions require that the monthly payment be no more than a certain set percentage of the monthly income. The lower the income, the lower the possible loan.

However, the single, never-married, working woman at least has some credit standing, but the divorced or widowed woman often finds herself stranded without credit. Credit standing until recently has been based almost entirely on the husband. Even a working wife's income has often been discounted in the belief that she is only a temporary worker.

> Susan and Larry Stevens both work and earn well above the national average. Both have and use many credit cards. Unfortunately, one day Larry is killed in an automobile crash. Susan decides to move to another city where her parents are now living. Although she and Larry never had any problems obtaining credit, she now finds herself turned down because she has no credit history. Although she had contributed to their joint income during their entire marriage, her past jobs and savings were not considered assets. In only one way is she lucky. If Larry's credit had been bad, she would have had a negative credit history too.

Recently, through the 1975 Equal Credit Opportunity Act, such unfair practices have been curbed to a degree. The act requires that credit rights be spelled out. Credit may not be refused solely on the grounds of sex or marital status. A woman who qualifies for credit does not need a cosigner. Everyone has the right to know on what grounds credit was refused. Everyone has the right to examine the information used in making the credit decision (but this must be done within sixty days). A woman's income or savings must be counted as equal to a man's. The credit history of "family accounts" must be considered in extending credit to either spouse.

Just how much these regulations will help women remains to be seen, but they are a step in the right direction. Of course, both males and females must be good credit risks if credit is to be obtained. Prompt and consistent payments on loans and accounts is the best way to build a good credit rating.

Women and the Law* Another restraint on freer sex roles has been the legal structure. Our laws are extremely complicated and have often worked to the detriment of both sexes. In the past, laws have considered females to be irresponsible and in need of protection. For example, in California, a married woman had to use her husband's home as her legal address and until a recent change in the law she could not buy or sell stocks or property without her husband's consent and thereby his acceptance of the responsibility for her actions. The current Georgia code (written in 1856) states: "The husband is head of the family and the wife is subject to him; her legal and civil existence is merged in the husband . . . either for her own protection, or for her benefit or for the preservation of public order." This may sound archaic to you, but recent attempts to change this wording were defeated in the Georgia State Legislature.

Although many laws remain in effect that are unfair to one or the other sex, the 1970s and 80s have seen much legal change. The changes have been precipitated mainly by women challenging the laws they felt discriminated against them. Changing laws of living together, divorce, child custody and support, of crimes such as rape and sexual harassment, and of benefits such as social security, have resulted.

A change in a law to make the sexes more equal sounds like a worthy goal. Yet some critics see new inequities resulting. For example, divorce laws that ask equal division of property may leave older women with little work experience much worse off than their ex-husbands. She may rightly have her half of the property but still be unable to support herself. "Rehabilitative alimony" is one legal reaction to this new problem created by changing laws. The idea is that the exhusband should help the exwife financially to retrain herself to become self-supporting.

Many law changes are making work and economic participation fairer to women. One example would be the California statute enacted in 1978 making it an unfair employment practice to discriminate on the basis of pregnancy, childbirth, or medically related conditions. It also requires employers who provide disability insurance programs for their employees to include disability for normal pregnancy as a benefit (AB 1960, Berman, Chapter 1308, Statutes of 1978).

In the criminal courts, women have successfully strengthened rape laws. Punishments for rapists have been made stronger. For example, California now prohibits the granting of probation to any person upon a conviction of rape by force or violence (SB 1479, Deukmejian, Chapter 1308, Statutes of 1978). More important, many states have eliminated the humiliating defense tactic of cross-examining the victim about her previous sexual conduct as if she were on trial. In 1977, Oregon passed a statute that made it a criminal offense for a husband to rape his wife. This is a complete departure from marital law of the past where there was no such thing as "rape" if a couple were married.

*Most of the laws governing marriage and sex roles are state laws and hence do not apply throughout the country.

Inset 2-6
A Steno Who Said "No!"

Adrienne Tomkins says that all she wanted was to get ahead in her career. Tomkins, now 34, was a pool stenographer at the Public Service Electric and Gas Co. in Newark, N.J., when she was offered a tryout position as private secretary to company executive Herbert D. Reppin in August 1973. Her competency, she was told, would be evaluated in three months.

The day of reckoning, as the green-eyed, auburn-haired Tomkins tells her story, occurred nearly three months later. "Since your evaluation is coming up, why don't we discuss it over lunch?" Reppin asked. Not wanting to hurt her chances for promotion, Tomkins reluctantly agreed.

Reppin took her to a restaurant in a hotel, Tomkins says. He suggested a drink at the bar. "This is my new girl," she quotes him as telling his barmates. After two hours at the bar, Tomkins said she was leaving. Reppin, she says, reminded her that he was her boss. By 3 p.m., Tomkins remembers, he was on his sixth drink and gossiping about office love affairs. "All of a sudden," she says, "I heard him say flat out, 'I want to ____ you. It's the only way we can have a working relationship'."

'Trade-offs' Tomkins insists that she tried to leave, but that her boss grabbed her by the wrist and said they were going to a room in the hotel. She talked her way out by saying she had to visit her sick mother. Reppin kissed her, then let her go, Tomkins says.

Reppin's response to this story is as black to white: "I denied the allegations in my deposition and my counsel denied the allegations in court. I did not proposition her, I was not drunk and there were no trade-offs asked for sexual favors in exchange for her promotion."

The total discrepancy in these two stories of the same encounter demonstrates the hazards of pursuing a remedy for sexual harassment. But Tomkins was so certain of her cause that she pursued her complaint for five years.

The day after the ill-fated luncheon date, Tomkins complained to the company's personnel department. The following day, she received a call from a supervisor, who called it "all a big misunderstanding." Furious, Tomkins said she would never return to the job. The supervisor promised to find her a "comparable" position in the company.

The comparable position never materialized. She protested in vain to the company's equal-employment-opportunity staffers. "In those days you had to plead sex discrimination," recalls Tomkins. "There was no such thing as 'sexual harassment'." Un-beknownst to her, her personnel folder was filling up with critical appraisals. In January 1975, Tomkins was fired.

Discrimination By now under treatment from a therapist and still caring for her mother, Tomkins went to Federal court. She and her lawyer, Nadine Taub of Rutgers University Law School, charged that Reppin and the company had violated Title VII of the 1964 Civil Rights Act, which forbids sexual discrimination in employment. U.S. District Judge Herbert Stern held that Tomkins could sue the company, but not Reppin. Tomkins appealed and the U.S. Court of Appeals agreed with her, holding that sexual harassment was a form of discrimination and she could sue Reppin.

Before the facts could be determined at trial, PSE&G, without admitting fault, offered to settle. The company agreed to pay Tomkins $20,000 plus her legal costs, and to restore her personnel file to its state before her luncheon with Reppin. It agreed to set up a panel to hear sexual-harassment complaints. And it agreed to finance a film — produced by Tomkins and Taub — illustrating Title VII discrimination.

Reppin, 52, remains at PSE&G. Tomkins is a computer operator in her hometown of Bayonne, N.J. She received her settlement check last month.

Diane K. Shah with Susan Agrest, *Newsweek*, April 30, 1979.

Sexual harassment is another legal area that is slowly opening to women (see Inset 2-6).

Although the feminine liberation movement supports such changes in the laws, leaders feel that it will take forever to change the thousands of laws now on the books on a one-by-one basis. They place emphasis on the Equal Rights Amendment (ERA) to the Constitution which would make all such changes in one stroke. The amendment simply says:

> Equality of rights under the law shall not be denied or abridged by any state on account of sex. The congress shall have the power to enforce, by appropriate legislation, the provisions of this article.

Thus the ERA would require equal opportunity for job training in public funded programs; equal treatment in military service; correction of inequalities in the criminal justice system; and equal treatment in alimony, child support, child custody, and property rights. The amendment would end the legal support of traditional sex roles. And, like other guarantees of freedom, it entails considerable responsibility as well. For example, marital partners capable of work would share equal financial responsibility for the care of their children and one another.

Although the proponents of the ERA first thought it would quickly be ratified by the 38 states necessary to make it law, only 35 states have thus far ratified the amendment and several of those are considering revocation of their earlier ratification. When it became clear that the amendment would not be ratified by a sufficient number of states at the end of the seven year time limit (March 22, 1979), in an unprecedented vote Congress granted an additional three years to seek enough state ratifications. Even with this time extension, however, there is still a real question as to whether it will ever pass.

The opponents of ERA fear that women will lose some of the advantages that they have had such as the right to support, protective labor legislation, and exemption from the military draft. The debate over draft registration for women brought on by the Russian invasion of Afghanistan in 1980 may well work against the ERA since women would have to serve if it is passed and the draft is reactivated.

Proponents of the ERA argue that far more would be gained than lost for women. They feel that the amendment would put an end to the long tradition of sexual discrimination and give couples more freedom to define the privileges and responsibilities of their relationship, based on personal preferences and capabilities.

Sex Role Stereotypes

The depth of most people's belief in sex role stereotypes is often overlooked and is sometimes hard to believe. Most people simply take the various traditional sex role behaviors for granted. See how you react when reading Scenes from Marriage (pp. 74 – 75), which substitutes male terms for female in an imaginary article for a young man about to wed. Reversing the genders often quickly reveals our sex role stereotypes.

To the degree that our behaviors are dictated by stereotypic thinking about sex roles, we close ourselves to potential growth and broader expression. A husband may have a real need to express his emotions, yet the masculine stereotype forbids him to cry. A wife may be a fine natural leader, yet she may suppress leadership behavior because the stereotype says it is not feminine.

Traditional roles historically reflected the man's greater physical strength and the necessity to defend the family from attack and the woman's child-bearing function. A male's status today is still partially determined by his physical prowess, especially during the school years. The traditional role stresses masculine dominance in most areas of life, in the society as well as within the family. The traditional role also allowed men sexual freedom while severely limiting women's sexuality.

The traditional feminine role was essentially the complement of the masculine role. Man was active, so woman was passive and submissive. Wives helped their husbands, took much of their personal identity from their husbands, ran the home and family, and worked outside the home only if necessary. Woman was the source of stability and strength within the home, from which most of the love and affection flowed.

Table 2-8 points out some of the common American stereotyped sex roles.

Table 2-8 Male and Female Stereotypes

Male Role Tendency	Female Role Tendency
Instrumental leadership; task and power orientation	Expressive leadership; nurturance and support
Analytic reasoning; intellectualizing	Emotional reasoning; intuition
Generalizing	Personalizing
Identity based on achievement; how others see self less important	Identity dependent on feelings of others toward self; status traditionally based on relationships
Attention to issues of large systems; in a group, remarks impersonal and indirect	Attention to small number of others; in a group, remarks addressed personally to another
Anger and blame externalized; vengeance sought	Blame internalized; difficulty expressing anger
Physical distance; hostility-violence in crowded conditions	Greater comfort with being touched; cooperation under conditions of crowding
Fear of failure in the organizational world; get ahead at all costs	Ambivalence about success in the organizational world
Aggression; competition	Cooperation; support
Exhibit strength; hide weakness	Exhibit weakness; hide or repress strength

Source: Rosabeth Kanter, "Women in Organizations: Sex Roles, Group Dynamics, and Change Strategies." In A. Sargent, *Beyond Sex Roles* (St. Paul, Minn.: West, 1977), p. 382.

The Traditional Closed Marriage Marriages that accept traditional sex role assignments have been called "closed marriages" by George and Nena O'Neill. Essentially, they are marriages of possession and reduced freedom. The main tenets of the closed marriage "contract" are (O'Neill & O'Neill, 1972, pp. 52–53):

Clause 1: Possession or ownership of the mate. (Both the husband and the wife are in bondage to the other: "You belong to me.") Belonging to someone is very different from feeling that you belong *with* someone.

Clause 2: Denial of self. (One sacrifices one's own self and individual identity to the contract.)

Clause 3: Maintenance of the couple front. (Like Siamese twins, we must always appear as a couple. The marriage in itself becomes your identity card, as though you wouldn't exist without it.)

Clause 4: Rigid role behavior. (Tasks, behavior, and attitudes are strictly separated along predetermined lines, according to traditional sex-role stereotypes.)

Clause 5: Absolute fidelity. (Physically and even psychologically binding through coercion rather than choice.)

Clause 6: Total exclusivity. (Enforced togetherness will preserve the union.)

You may not agree that this is the kind of psychological contract you agreed to at all. *You* married for love, warmth, companionship. Of course, you did. But, subtly, insidiously, often without knowing it, the clauses of the closed marriage contract begin to foreclose upon your freedom and your individuality, making you a slave of your marriage.

Let's take a closer look at what goes on in a closed marriage.

WHAT DO YOU THINK?

In what ways have stereotyped sex roles affected this conflict?

Why does Mary seem so dissatisfied?

Why doesn't John allow her to take the class?

What role changes can you suggest that might help alleviate their conflict?

A Closed Marriage

John and Mary Doe both come from lower-middle-class families where the wife's role was oriented toward the home and was secondary to the husband's. Their parents say they are satisfied with marriage and their families. John and Mary met while they were attending community college, and they married about a year and a half later. John is now selling insurance, and Mary is busy at home with their three-year-old son. One evening, the following scene transpires:

"John, can't you stop looking at television for a while?"

"Gee, honey, I'm tired and it's a good mystery. What do you want?"

"Just to talk."

"We can talk later."

"You always say that and when later comes, you want to go to sleep."

"Can't you leave me alone and give me peace? All you do is nag. You want me to make more money, so I have to be out more. Yet you want me to be home. I'm not paying enough attention to you. Well, you can't have it both ways."

While at school, Mary had done well and had been an active leader. But now she denies her competitiveness since she fears it is unfeminine. However, she expresses her competitiveness by urging John to earn more, while at the same time belittling his efforts.

Later that same evening, in bed, John tries to be affectionate, but Mary responds by saying, "You wanted to go to sleep, so go to sleep and leave me alone."

"You never seem interested in sex any more."

"Well, you never want to talk to me any more so why should I satisfy your every whim?"

Note how Mary gets back at John by controlling their sexual behavior.

The following conversation is also typical of many:

"John, I'd like to do something besides stay home. There's an interesting art class offered at night that I want to take."

"No, I can't see you being out at night. You should be home with me."

"But it's just one night a week and it doesn't cost much."

"It's not the cost. I just think a wife should be at home with her husband at night."

"Why don't we take it together?"

"No, I haven't got time. You keep me working seven days a week with all your nagging and pushing. I want to do what I want in my little spare time."

"You always do what you want."

"Are you kidding? I'd much rather be at the motorcycle races on Sunday rather than doing gardening work."

"Well, it seems to me that when you aren't working late, you spend your time at home glued to the T.V. That sure isn't doing what I want. Besides, at least you get to meet adults and be out in the world."

John usually responds to these conversations by withdrawing into work and into watching T.V. This withdrawal stimulates Mary to try more frantically to gain his attention, which causes John to withdraw further. Thus a vicious circle develops.

Here we have seen a couple trying to conform to sex role stereotypes that don't quite fit. Mary would like to participate in the world; she would like to exercise some of her competitiveness and dominance, yet the traditional role precludes this. Such behavior does not fit her husband's expectations for a wife. But by not talking directly about her frustration, Mary does not give John a chance to understand her feelings. Since she does not find her role as fulfilling as she expected and since she and John do not talk about it, she may react in negative ways such as nagging, ridicule, and sexual withdrawal. John, of course, may react by withdrawing more, perhaps by coming home later and protesting his "tiredness" and hiding his feelings from Mary, as men have traditionally been taught to do. Once such a vicious circle gets started, it is extremely difficult to break because of the increasing lack of communication.

There are, of course, many relationships in which the partners comfortably conform to traditional sex role expectations. If both have internalized these roles, there will probably be minimal conflict, but marital growth may also be minimal. Unfortunately, genuine sharing and two-way communication will probably be minimal since the traditional masculine role restrains males from sharing their feelings. If there is not genuine sharing of feelings, it becomes very difficult for the partners to make meaningful changes in their relationship, and without such change, stagnation is apt to occur.

If the female has truly internalized the traditional wifely role, she will too often limit herself to a child-centered, home-centered, husband-centered life.* She may feel isolated and restricted. She may have to repress other aspects of herself as Mary did in order to conform to her role as she sees it. Such repression may lead to dissatisfaction and unhappiness. Also, her husband may find himself saddled with someone who is virtually totally dependent on him for the fulfillment of all her needs, for making all decisions, and so on. What starts out to be an ego trip (the helpless idolizing wife and the strong, responsible husband) quickly becomes a heavy burden for many men. Few honest males today would deny that such overwhelming responsibility is extremely difficult and unpleasant, as well as constricting to their own lives (Chafetz, 1974, pp. 169 – 170).

The closed marriage locks the husband into a set of roles that may limit his growth as well as the wife's. He is usually locked into the role of provider, which tends to give him a different set of commitments than his wife. In our competitive society, where success is measured by individual productivity and achievement, the husband must manage two marriages: the first to his career and the second to his wife and family. When there is conflict between his marriage and his work world, the job comes first. This may be difficult for the traditional wife, who is family-centered, to accept. She may feel cheated and rebuffed by her husband because he appears to place a lower value on what for her is the most important part of her life. So long as the economic system is partial to the man, it will be difficult for him to escape the provider role. In the middle classes, the unfortunate antagonism between male economic success and marital life is difficult to resolve. One step that can be taken to limit this conflict is for the wife to participate as much as she can in the husband's life outside the family. He can encourage this by sharing his career experiences and encouraging her interest in his work world. This is especially important if the man's work demands almost total commitment as in medicine or in the ministry. In such cases the wife must participate, perhaps by becoming a volunteer worker, or risk sharing very little with her

*This may cause her problems when the children leave and during widowhood (see Chapter 13).

husband. Here the important factor in the eventual success of the marriage will be the wife's acceptance and respect for her husband's commitment.

Naturally a similar conflict exists for the married career woman. In order to succeed, she will probably have to put even more energy into her career than her husband has put into his, since she must overcome prejudice about career females. Her husband may also become jealous of the attention she gives her career, or resent her encroaching on his domain. Also, unemployed men who are dependent on their wife's earnings are likely to suffer feelings of failure and guilt. Some may respond to these feelings with hostility.

The working wife and mother also faces major problems in coping with the work world and her marriage. First, as noted earlier, the kinds of jobs available to her are more limited than they are for males. Because of the lower pay for most women, she will probably spend as much time on the job as her husband, but bring home much less money.

Second, the full-time working mother is still responsible for the major portion of the household chores. Automation does not get the children off to school on time or make their lunch. If her husband sees himself as locked into the traditional male roles, she will in many cases be carrying two full-time jobs — running the family as well as working. Some husbands of working wives do participate in some of the domestic tasks, but even when they do, their share of the work is usually much less than the wife's (see Chapter 8).

Most of our discussion has focused on the middle-class family. The traditional working-class family in many ways has even more rigidly stereotyped marital roles. The wife is expected to be in the home most of the time unless she is working. The man, on the other hand, fulfills much of his social life in his relations with his male friends. Thus sharing activities and joint participation in family matters seem much less important than in middle-class families. However, while shared conjugal roles may have greater potential for mutual satisfaction, they may also lead to conflict, as we have seen. Segregated roles may leave husband and wife with little to say to one another and yet give each a sense of competence and independence. Rubin (1976) suggests that the lower economic class male may be threatened when his wife works because she will contribute a much higher proportion of the family support than would her middle-class counterpart. By maintaining rigid traditional roles in marriage, he is better able to maintain control and his sense of pride and importance. Working wives in these families express greater satisfaction with their jobs than do their husbands. Her working broadens her world and opens choices for her. He often feels trapped and oppressed by his work. His choices are limited by his low pay and the low prestige of his work. Often his own lack of skills entraps him and he is unable to think about or actually move ahead economically. He feels as though he is in a dead end and often blames the burdens of his family responsibilities for his unfavorable situation.

In general, the closed traditional marriage may give a couple security and reduce conflict on the surface, yet, in the long run, a marriage based on rigid stereotypical roles will probably create resentments on the part of both partners. The rigidity of the marriage also tends to make the marriage fragile and unable to adjust to new strains and pressures.

An Open Companionship Marriage An open marriage is one in which both members are as free as possible to create their marital roles. By becoming aware of the roles society now expects us to fill and by understanding the role expectations that we have learned, we can begin to learn how to choose roles for which we are best suited and that will yield the most satisfactions. Realistically, however, it must be pointed out that such freedom of choice will in itself often cause problems. To make marriage viable, there are tasks that must be accomplished. Who will do the necessary tasks that neither partner wants to do? For example, neither partner may want to be tied to a nine-to-five job, yet in most families someone must earn money. The bills must be paid, the children raised, the car fixed, the house cleaned, the in-laws telephoned, and so forth.

In an open marriage, the main thing is that each mate be committed to the idea of seeking equity in the marriage and communicating openly any feelings of inequity. This also requires that the couple be willing to experiment and change if first solutions fail.

Sally and Jim find, after several years of marriage, that their dissatisfactions with themselves, their marriage, and each other are growing dangerously large. They decide together to take an adult education class called Creative Marriage. The class examines many facets of marriage and family living, first analyzing common marital problem areas and then suggesting creative new ways of trying to approach the problem.

Sally and Jim decide that they will try to rearrange the family responsibilities so that each can have more time to do the things he or she wants to do as an individual. They hope that by being freer as individuals, they will also find more joy in doing things together. Since both Sally and Jim work, each felt put upon by the children and the household chores. Although Sally did most of them, Jim always felt her anger at him for not doing more. Even when he did help, he did not do it happily and then Sally felt guilty for not properly fulfilling her role as housewife. Now they make a list of all the things that have to be done each month to keep the family running smoothly. They each pick out the four things they think they are best at. In one case they picked the same thing. Jim thinks he is good at handling money and Sally thinks she is. They decide that, to be equitable, they will try handling the money on alternate months. The chores neither want, they divide between them. They decide to try the new arrangement for two months and then re-evaluate.

At the end of the two months, they decide to change how they did the chores neither had wanted to do. They had both felt burdened by the chores even though they did not feel unfairly put upon. They decide that rather than dividing the unwanted chores, they will each assume responsibility for all of the chores on alternate weeks. In this way, each will be completely free of the chores for one week and then totally responsible for them the next week. To date, this arrangement is working well for them. Each feels freer and less resentful toward the other and the family is still running efficiently.

This kind of exploring can lead to a great deal more satisfaction than limiting oneself to prescribed roles that may or may not fit. However, seeking equity in marriage means two partners willing to explore and compromise. Each couple will have to sort responsibilities so as to yield the greatest freedom while maintaining love and intimacy. This is no small task, but the rewards can be large. The Couple's Inventory can help you explore your own and your partner's sex role attitudes. Of course, the couple will still be burdened by the stereotypical sex roles held by the general society. For example, Sally and Jim may agree that she is to handle the investments but still find that the banker or stockbroker always asks for him. Be this as it may, however, each couple can work to realize more freedom within their marriage. As one student of changing sex roles suggests (Lindemann, 1976, p. 188):

> A society that has gone beyond narrow ideas of femininity and masculinity to the ideal of the self-actualized person offers the widest possible range of choices to its members. It is a society that has reached a level of material comfort that allows it to put resources into human rather than only material development. The real issue is not the liberation of women so much as the liberation of humanity, the establishment of a society where men and women have equal opportunity to fulfill their hopes and dreams unhampered by oppressive and irrelevant sexual stereotypes.

The idea Lindemann describes seems at last to be more acceptable to many Americans. To start the year 1976, *Time* ran as its cover and feature story "Women of the Year." The first few paragraphs were as follows:

> They have arrived like a new immigrant wave in male America. They may be cops, judges, military officers, telephone linemen, cab drivers, pipefitters, editors, business executives — or mothers and housewives, but not quite the same subordinate creatures they were before. Across the broad range of American life, from suburban tract houses to state legislatures, from church pulpits to Army barracks, women's lives are profoundly changing, and with them, the traditional relationships between the sexes. Few women are unaffected, few are thinking as they did ten years — or even a couple of years — ago. America has

Inset 2-7
Couples Inventory

Personal goal   To look at how sex role behavior influences decision making, autonomy, and intimacy in your relationship with your partner.

Directions   Both partners fill out separate inventories and then compare statements.

1. I am important to our couple because _____

2. What I contribute to your success is _____

3. I feel central to our relationship when _____

4. I feel peripheral to our relationship when _____

5. The ways I show concern for you are _____

6. The ways I encourage your growth are _____

7. The ways I deal with conflict are _____

8. The ways I have fun with you are _____

9. I get angry when you _____

10. I am elated when you _____

11. The way I get space for myself in our relationship is _____

12. The ways I am intimate with you are _____

13. The ways I am jealous of you are _____

14. I have difficulty being assertive when you _____

15. You have difficulty being assertive when I _____

16. The strengths of our relationship are _____

_____

17. The weaknesses of our relationship are _____

_____

18. Our relationship would be more effective if you _____

_____

19. I feel most masculine in our relationship when I _____

_____

20. I feel most feminine in our relationship when I _____

_____

21. I trust you to do/be _____

_____

22. I do not trust you to do/be _____

_____

23. I deal with stress by _____

_____

24. You deal with stress by _____

_____

25. The division of labor in household tasks is decided by _____

_____

26. Our finances are controlled by _____

_____

27. The amount of time we spend with our relatives is determined by _____

_____

28. Our vacation plans are made by _____

_____

29. Our social life is planned by _____

_____

30. Taking stock of our relationship is done by _____

_____

31. I am lonely when _____

_____

32. I need you to _____

_____

Taken from: Alice G. Sargent, *Beyond Sex Roles* (St. Paul, Minn.: West, 1977), p. 87.

not entirely repealed the Code of Hammurabi (woman as male property), but enough U.S. women have so deliberately taken possession of their lives that the event is spiritually equivalent to the discovery of a new continent. Says Critic Elizabeth Janeway: "The sky above us lifts, the light pours in. No maps exist for this enlarged world. We must make them as we explore."

It is difficult to locate the exact moment when the psychological change occurred. A cumulative process, it owes much to the formal feminist movement — the Friedans and Steinems and Abzugs. Yet feminism has transcended the feminist movement. In 1975 the women's drive penetrated every layer of society, matured beyond ideology to a new status of general — and sometimes unconscious — acceptance.

The belief that women are entitled to truly equal social and professional rights has spread far and deep into the country. Once the doctrine of well-educated middle-class women, often young and single, it has taken hold among working-class women, farm wives, blacks, Puerto Ricans, white "ethnics." The Y.W.C.A. embraces it; so do the Girls Clubs of America and the Junior Leagues. A measure of just how far the idea has come can be seen in the many women who denigrate the militant feminists' style ("too shrill, unfeminine") and then proceed to conduct their own newly independent lives. At year's end a Harris poll found that by 63 percent to 25 percent, Americans favor "most of the efforts to strengthen and change women's status in society." Five years ago, it was 42 percent in favor, 41 percent against (*Time*, 1976, p. 8).

Summary   Equity between the sexes, not sameness, is the goal we should be seeking. Yet, gaining such a goal is not easy. First, one is born male or female, though this is not always as clear as it may at first seem. Second, the roles (masculinity and femininity) that go with one's sex are taught by the society. If a society holds hard and fast stereotypes of sex roles, it will be difficult for individuals to achieve equitable roles since variations will be discouraged. Thus for change to occur, individual couples must strive to create equitable roles in their own marriage and at the same time join with others to fight cultural stereotypes. One group working to change stereotypes has been the women's movement. The movement has worked toward the passage of the Equal Rights Amendment (ERA) which will end discrimination by sex if it can be passed by thirty-eight states. Women have also been slowly moving into what have been traditional male fields, and more women than ever, married and unmarried, are now working.

Two important stumbling blocks to people liberation insofar as sex roles are concerned are the economic deprivation of women and laws that discriminate between the sexes. Until women are able to earn the same amount as men for the same work, it will be difficult for couples to change the traditional roles of "man, the provider" and "woman, the homemaker," if they wish to change them. In addition, many kinds of discrimination are built into our system of laws. For example, women in the past have not been able to establish their own credit if married, though this law has recently been changed. Men are discriminated against by our criminal laws and by the armed forces drafting system.

Open marriage means that a couple is free to establish the most meaningful relationship that they can. It means that they are free to establish sex roles that best fit them. It also means freedom of choice within the marriage. Some may choose the older traditional roles. Although the roles may be rigid in a traditional marriage, the tasks necessary to maintain a marriage were clearly spelled out and each partner knew his or her responsibilities. A specific role assignment may be more comfortable for some since it yields efficiency and security. Some may choose to radically alter the traditional roles into new but equally rigid roles. Others may opt to periodically change roles and maintain an always flexible system. The concept of open marriage does not dictate the kind of relationship a couple will have. What it does say is that couples should be free to explore and encouraged to make their own choices. One of the basic suppositions on which this book is based, as you'll remember from Chapter 1, is "A free and creative society is one that offers many structural forms by which family functions may be fulfilled." The best marital roles are those that best fit you.

How to Hold a Wife: A Bridegroom's Guide

Oh, lucky you! You are finally bridegroom to the woman of your dreams!

But don't think for a minute that you can now relax and be assured automatically of marital happiness forever. You will have to *work at it*. While she may have eyes only for you *now*, remember that she is surrounded every day by attractive young men who are all too willing to tempt her away from you. And as the years go by, you will lose some of the handsome muscularity of your youth; you will have to make up in skill and understanding what you will lack in the bloom of youth. It will be up to you to make your physical relationship so exciting, so totally satisfying to her, that she won't be tempted to stray!

Yes, boys, we are talking about SEX. Don't turn away in embarrassment. For if you are to *hold* that wonderful woman, you will have to practice and work hard at making her sex life as marvelous as it can be.

But how?

Here is what you need to know and do to succeed in your marriage, your greatest challenge in life — and the one that will be utterly essential to your wife's future happiness and thus your own.

1. Let's start in with the essentials. You should always be available to your wife whenever she wants you. It is, of course, your husbandly prerogative to say no, but you will be wise to never do so unless you are really ill, for that may tempt her to turn to other men to fulfill her essential needs. She cannot do without sex, so you as a smart husband should always be ready to provide it.

2. That means that you should never let yourself get too tired to perform. The cardinal sin for a husband — and a good way to lose the wife you love — is to fail at your duty to achieve a good erection and to sustain it until your wife is fully satisfied. To never let your work or anything else get in the way of plenty of rest each day, regular but moderate exercise, and plenty of protein in your diet — and stay away from excessive alcohol.

Remember that women's sexual needs vary. Some need it more often than others, and some (lucky you if you are married to a

From Jennifer S. MacLeod, *The Village Voice* (February 11, 1971).

real woman like that!) can achieve multiple orgasms in a single night of love *if* you can do your part!

3. "But how about me?" you may ask. "How about my sexual needs and satisfactions?"

Now man's passion, of course, often does not equal that of woman. But you have a wonderful surprise in store for you, if you concentrate your efforts on your wife's pleasure and don't worry selfishly about your own. For sooner or later you will discover the ecstacy of truly mature male coital orgasm that can be induced only by total surrender to the exquisite sensations of a woman's orgasmic contractions. . . .

4. Remember that your first duty is to your wife. So if you fail to satisfy her (and yourself, too) in the above-described natural way, you should talk to a good psychiatrist who specializes in this kind of problem. She will help you if, for instance, you have not fully accepted the natural masculine role that will bring you the joy of selfless service to others instead of the futile envy of woman's natural leadership role. . . .

5. Now for a subject that may seem trivial: your appearance and dress. Don't overlook it — it is a vital ingredient in marital happiness.

Every woman likes to be proud of how attractive her husband is, so dress to please her. If she likes you to show off your youthful figure, by all means do so! Broad shoulders can be accentuated by turtleneck jerseys (with shoulder pads if needed), as can the well-tapered waist. Small, firm, well-shaped buttocks (very much in fashion this year) can be set off by well-cut clingy stretch pants. . . .

If you do your job well — for husbandhood is the true career for all manly men, worthy of all your talents — you will keep your wife happy and hold her for the rest of her days. Remember that marriage for a man should be *life's Great Adventure*, so *relax — relax — relax — and enjoy.*

Chapter 3 ⁓

Contents

~ The American
Ways
of Love

To most Americans, love and marriage are like hand and glove, apple pie and ice cream, bacon and eggs — they belong together. Where there is one, there should be the other. Of course, we all know of marriages without love, and certainly romantic literature is full of examples of love without marriage. But the traditional ideal, the ultimate in human relationships for most Americans, is the steady, time-honored, and sought-after combination of love and marriage.

Love and Marriage

When Americans are asked "Why do you want to marry?" they often reply "Because I love. . . ." So we Americans marry for love. But, doesn't everyone? What other reasons could there possibly be?

Indeed, there are other reasons. Certainly not everyone has married for love historically. Even today many cultures do not accept love as a reasonable basis for marriage. Love as a basis for marriage may be a unique American contribution to the world. As Ralph Linton pointed out many years ago, "All societies recognize that there are occasional violent emotional attachments between persons of the opposite sex but our present American culture is the only one which has attempted to capitalize on these and make them the basis for marriage" (Linton, 1936, p. 175).

Love in most societies has historically been an amusing pastime, a distraction, or, in some cases, a godsent affliction. For example, courtly love began as a sport among the feudal aristocracy. It exalted both chastity and adultery. Courtly love glorified love from afar and made a fetish of suffering about love affairs. It made a great game of love where men proved their manliness on the jousting field in the name of love and a woman's honor. Adultery was also an integral part of courtly love. The intrigue and excitement of adultery added to the sport and made the love even more sweet. Marriage was not considered the proper place for courtly love. Married love was considered too mundane and unexciting.

The story of the knight Ulrich von Lichtenstein highlights courtly love which seldom found consummation in marriage. At an early age Ulrich pledged his love and admiration to an unnamed lady. He accepted every challenge in an effort to prove himself worthy of serving his love. He was filled with melancholy and painful longings for his lady, a condition which he claimed gave him joy.

The heartless lady, however, rejected his admiration even after his ten years of silent devotion and his many feats of valor. Undaunted, perhaps even inspired by her rebuffs, he undertook a stupendous journey in 1227 from Venice north to Bohemia during which he claimed to have broken the incredible total of three hundred and seven lances fighting his way to Vienna and his lady love.

It comes as something of a shock when by his own statement he stopped off for three days to visit his wife and children. For the fact is that this lovesick Galahad, this kissless wonder, this dauntless knight-errant had long had a wife to lie with when he had the urge, and a family to live with when he felt lonely. He even speaks of his affection for his wife, but, of course, not his love; to love her would have been improper and unthinkable to the ethic of courtly love (Hunt, 1959, pp. 132–139).

On the other hand, ancient Japan felt love to be a grave offense if not properly sanctioned, for it interfered with proper marriage arrangements. Etsu Sugimoto describes this in *A Daughter of the Samurai*:

> When she was employed in our house, she was very young, and because she was the sister of father's faithful Jiya, she was allowed much freedom. A youthful servant, also of our house, fell in love with her. For young people to become lovers without the sanction of the proper formalities was a grave offense in any class, but in a samurai household it was a black disgrace to the house. The penalty was exile through the water gate—a gate of brush built over a stream and never used except by one of the Eta, or outcast class. The departure was public and the culprits were everafter shunned by everyone. The penalty was unspeakably cruel, but in the old days severe measures were used as a preventative of law-breaking (Sugimoto, 1935, pp. 115–116).

As surprising as it may be, such attitudes are still widespread. Marriage in many cultures has been and still is based on considerations other than love. In India, as Inset 3-1 demonstrates, the Hindu place responsibility for finding a suitable mate on the parents or older relatives. The potential mate is judged by his or her economic status, caste, family, and physical appearance. These criteria are not by any means simple snobbery; they reflect the couple's prospects for rapport, financial stability, and social acceptance, all valid concerns in marriage. Even in the United States, such considerations are often found hidden in the ephemeral concept of love, as we shall see in Chapter 4.

Defining Love

Trying to define love is a task that has kept poets, philosophers, and sages busy since the beginning of history. I have said that Americans generally marry for love, or think they do—but what is this phenomenon that causes two people to react to one another so strongly? Is it physical? Spiritual? A mixture of the two? Why does it only occur with some people and not others? Is it the same as infatuation? The questions are endless, yet each person speaks of love, recognizes love, and seeks love whether or not he or she can define just what this vivid and strong emotion is.

The Greek, Sappho, twenty-five centuries ago, described the physical state of love:

> For should I but see thee a little moment,
>   Stright is my voice hushed;
> Yea, my tongue is broken, and through and through me
> 'Neath the flesh impalpable fire runs tingling;
> Nothing see mine eyes, and a noise of roaring
>   Waves in my ear sounds;
> Sweat runs in rivers, a tremor seizes
> All my limbs, and paler than grass in Autumn,
> Caught by pains of menacing death, I falter,
>   Lost in the love-trance.

Sappho, trans. by J. Addington Symonds

The Greeks actually classified love into three elements: *eros* (carnal or physical love), *agape* (spiritual love), and *philos* (brotherly or friendly love).

Eros is basically the physical, sexual side of love. It is needing, desiring, and wanting the other person physically. In the poem above, Sappho is describing the effect of eros. The Romans called eros Cupid, and, as we know, Cupid shoots the arrow of love into our hearts. Eros is that aspect of love that makes our knees shake, upsets our routines, and causes us to be obsessed with thought of our lover.

Agape is the altruistic, giving, nondemanding side of love. It is an active concern for the life and growth of those whom we love. It is most clearly demonstrated by the love of a parent for his or her child. Agape is an unconditional affirmation of another person. It is the desire to do things for the beloved, to care, to help, and to give to the loved one.

Theologian Paul Tillich sees the highest form of love as a merger of eros and agape: "No love is real without a unity of eros and agape. Agape without eros is obedience to moral law, without warmth, without longing, without reunion. Eros without agape is a chaotic desire, denying the validity of the claim of the other one to be acknowledged as an independent self, able to love and to be loved" (Tillich, 1957, pp. 114–115).

Philos is the love found in deep and enduring friendship. It is also the kind of love spoken of in the Bible when it says: "Love thy neighbor as thyself." It can be specific deep friendship for specific people, or it can be a love that generalizes to all people. It is often nonexclusive while eros and agape are often exclusive.

Theories of Love* There are probably as many theories of love as there are persons in love. However, it is worthwhile to examine just a few of them, even if only superficially. To understand how other thoughtful people have theorized about love will help us to understand our own feelings and thoughts about it. And, as we shall see, the better we know our own attitudes and definitions of love, the better we will become in making long-lasting intimate relationships.

In his classic book, *The Art of Loving*, Erich Fromm defines love as an active power in man (people); a power that breaks through the walls that separate man from his fellow man. . . . In love we find the paradox of two beings becoming one yet remaining two (Fromm, 1956). Like the Greeks, Fromm also discusses several kinds of love, including brotherly and maternal love. Brotherly love is characterized by friendship and companionship with affection. Maternal love is characterized by an unselfish interest in your partner and a placing of yourself second to your partner's needs. Mature love for Fromm includes attachment plus sexual response. More importantly it includes the four basic elements necessary to any intimate relationship: care,

*It should be noted that no theories of love enjoy much empirical support.

How do I love thee? Let me count the ways.
I love thee to the depth and breadth and height
My soul can reach, when feeling out of sight
For the ends of Being and ideal Grace.
I love thee to the level of everyday's
Most quiet need, by sun and candle-light.
I love thee freely, as men strive for Right;
I love thee purely, as they turn from Praise.
I love thee with the passion put to use
In my old griefs, and with my childhood's faith.
I love thee with a love I seemed to lose
With my lost saints — I love thee with the breath,
Smiles, tears, of all my life! — and, if God choose,
I shall but love thee better after death.

Elizabeth Barrett Browning

Let me not to the marriage of true minds
Admit impediments. Love is not love
Which alters when it alteration finds,
Or bends with the remover to remove.
O, no! It is an ever-fixed mark
That looks on tempests and is never shaken.
It is the star to every wandering bark,
Whose worth's unknown, although his height be taken.
Love's not Time's fool, though rosy lips and cheeks
Within his bending sickle's compass come.
Love alters not with his brief hours and weeks,
But bears it out even to the edge of doom.
If this be error and upon me proved,
I never writ, nor no man ever loved.

William Shakespeare
Sonnet 116

When God would invent a thing
apart from eating or drink or
game or sport, and yet a world —
restful while in which our
minds can melt and smile. He
made of Adam's rib an Eve
creating thus the game of
love.

Piet Hein

responsibility, respect, and knowledge. People who share all of the elements of mature love are *pair-bonded*. The relationship is reciprocal. Fromm goes on to suggest that a person's need to love and be loved in this full sense arises from the feelings of separateness and aloneness we all experience to some extent. Love is the way to escape these feelings and gain a feeling of unitedness.

Taking off from this idea, Lawrence Casler (1969) considers that love develops in part because of our human needs for acceptance and confirmation. These needs are heightened in a society as competitive and individualized as ours. Thus, it is a relief to meet someone whose choices coincide with our own, who doesn't try to undermine us in some way. We tend to attach ourselves to such a person because he or she offers us validation, and such validation is an important basis for love (see Rubin, 1973, Chapter 7).

Casler points out that American dating may serve to provoke love feelings in the partners more as a by-product than from some innate attraction. For example, a person, for any number of reasons including simple politeness, may pretend to like his date more than he really does. The date, also seeking validation, responds favorably. And this favorable response makes the first person feel good, and feel real fondness now for the person who has made him feel good. As his feelings increase, hers are likely to also. Obviously, it is easier to love someone who loves you than someone who is indifferent.

Of course, falling in love is much more complex than this example because we have many needs besides validation to fulfill. Obviously, sex is one of these needs:

> Society emphasizes the necessity for love to precede sex. Although many disregard this restriction, others remain frightened or disturbed by the idea of a purely sexual relationship. The only way for many sexually aroused individuals to avoid frustration or anxiety is to fall in love — as quickly as possible. More declarations of love have probably been uttered in parked cars than in any other location, some of these are surely nothing more than seduction ploys, but it is likely that self-seduction is involved in most cases (Casler, 1969, p. 33).

Because our society is marriage-oriented, most of us learn early that not only love but marriage as well is a prerequisite to sex. Thus, for most Americans, love, sex, and marriage go together, ideally at least if not always in practice.

In more general terms, the sources of love for Casler are (1) the need for security, (2) sexual satisfaction, and (3) social conformity. If these are the causes of love, what does Casler see as the consequences of love?

First, in this culture, "being in love makes it easier to have guilt-free sex, to marry, and to view oneself as a normal healthy citizen." Love will also create the error of overevaluation (romanticized ideal images; see Chapter 5) of the love object. Love will foster dependency on the love object insofar as the love object is relied upon for much need gratification.

If maturity is, in part, establishing independence, then love, as viewed by Casler, acts as a deterrent to maturity. Although the individual who is unable to love is viewed as pathological in the American culture, Casler's interpretation of love can lead to an opposite interpretation. The individual who is not loving may be in excellent mental health. If, as Casler suggests, the need for love is based largely on insecurity, conformity, and sexual frustration, then the person who is secure, independent, and leading a satisfactory sex life may not need love. Such a person will:

> be a person who does not find his own company boring, a person whose inner resources are such that other persons, although they supply pleasure and stimulation, are not absolutely necessary. We have long been enjoined to love others as we love ourselves, but perhaps we seek love relationships with others only because we do not love ourselves sufficiently.

Ira Reiss (1960) suggests the wheel as a model of love. In the rapport, or first, stage the partners are struck by the feelings that they have known each other before, that they feel comfortable with one another, and that they both want to continue and deepen the relation-

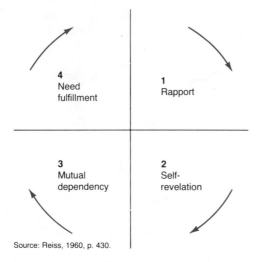

4
Need
fulfillment

1
Rapport

3
Mutual
dependency

2
Self-
revelation

Source: Reiss, 1960, p. 430.

ship. This leads to the stage of self-revelation, during which more and more intimate thoughts and feelings are shared. This sharing deepens the relationship because such sharing is only done with special people, i.e., we are special to one another. As this sharing becomes more and more intimate, a feeling of mutual dependency develops. With it comes a feeling of loss when the partner is not present. More and more personal needs are being met as the couple deepens its relationship. Reiss (1960, p. 143) suggests that it was perhaps the hope of having these deeper needs met that caused the initial rapport.

> These four processes are in a sense really one process for when one feels rapport, he/she reveals him/herself and becomes dependent, thereby fulfilling his/her personality needs. The circularity is most clearly seen in that the needs being fulfilled were the original reason for feeling rapport.

Borland (1975) changes the model slightly, likening it to a clock spring rather than just a simple circle.

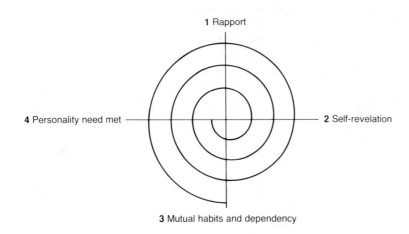

1 Rapport

4 Personality need met

2 Self-revelation

3 Mutual habits and dependency

As these four processes occur and lead one into the other, they wind themselves toward a closer and more intimate relationship with an understanding of the real inner self of the other person. As this occurs, the individuals form an increasingly tighter bond to one another in much the same way as a clock spring tightens as it is wound (Borland, 1975, p. 291).

Romantic Love For many Americans, the idea of romantic love most influences their feelings about attraction and intimacy. This concept of love encompasses such ideas as "love at first sight," "the one and only love mate," "life-long commitment to the one and only," "the continuing excitement of the 'eros' kind of love," "I can't live without him/her," "the perfect mate," etc.

In essence, the concept of romantic love supplies a set of idealized images by which we can judge the object of our love as well as the quality of the relationship. Unfortunately, such romanticized images usually bear little relationship to the real world. Often we project our beliefs onto another person, exaggerating those characteristics that match the qualities we are looking for and masking those that do not. That is, we transform the other person into an unreal hero or heroine to fit our personal concept of the romantic marital partner. In essence, we often fall in love with our own romantic ideas rather than with a real human being when we believe in romantic love.

For example, the traditional romantic ideals dictate a strong, confident, protective, masterful role for a man and a charming, loving, fragile, dependent role for a woman. A woman holding this stereotype will tend to overlook and deny dependent needs of her mate. She will tend to repress independent qualities she discovers in herself. Love for her means each correctly fulfilling the proper role as she perceives it. And, of course, the same holds true for a man with traditional romantic ideals.

Those who "fall in love with love" in this way will suffer disappointment when the real person of their chosen partner begins to emerge. Rather than meet this emerging person with joy and enthusiasm, partners who hold romanticized ideals may reject reality in favor of their stereotypic images. They may again commence to search for the proper object of their love, rejecting the real-life partner as unworthy or changed (see Chapter 5 for a more complete discussion of the problems of idealized expectations). Hopefully, dating and broad premarital experience with the opposite sex will help to correct much of this romantic idealism (see Chapter 4).

In essence, people often fall in love with their romanticized expectations rather than with their spouse. This tends to lead to one of two actions. Either the spouse is rejected or an attempt is made to change the spouse into the romantic ideals. John Robert Clark (1961, p. 18) has a pithy description of the first action:

> In learning how to love a plain human being today, as during the romantic movement, what we usually want unconsciously is a fancy human being with no flaws. When the mental picture we have of

someone we love is colored by wishes of childhood, we may love the picture rather than the real person behind it. Naturally, we are disappointed in the person we love if he does not conform to our picture. Since this kind of disappointment has no doubt happened to us before, one might suppose we would tear up the picture and start all over. On the contrary, we keep the picture and tear up the person. Small wonder that divorce courts are full of couples who never gave themselves a chance to know the real person behind the pictures in their lives.

The second action, attempting to change one's spouse, also leads to trouble. It is difficult to change, and the person being asked to may resent the demand or may not wish to change.

Generally, the rose-colored glasses of romantic love tend to distort the real world, especially the mate, thereby becoming a barrier to happiness. However, this is not to deny that romantic love can add to an intimate relationship. Romance will bring excitement, emotional highs, and color to one's relationship. Hopefully though, a mature love relationship will develop more of the relationship than just the romantic. As intimacy develops in many ways, emotionally, intellectually, socially, and physically, romance takes its place as one of several important aspects of the relationship, not the only one.

Romantic Love and Infatuation Romantic love and infatuation are often confused. Some say that they are the same thing. Others feel that romantic love is "real" while infatuation is not. Others feel that the term infatuation is used to negate one's past feelings of love that have now changed. Love itself is supposed to last forever, so falling out of love means that the feeling for the other person was not really love; it must have been something less — namely infatuation (Udry, 1974). Still others suggest that infatuation may be the first step towards love. The feelings of physical attraction, the chemical arousal, the intense preoccupation with your partner, all characteristics of infatuation, are also the precursors to "real" love. Infatuation can also be used by others to describe your state. "You were infatuated with him before you met me." One's daughter is infatuated with the boy the family doesn't approve of. It is apparent from the many ways in which the term is used that we probably cannot agree completely on the difference between romantic love and infatuation. Ann Landers periodically reprints a suggested list of differences between the two terms:

Love or Infatuation?

Infatuation is instant desire. It is one set of glands calling to another.

Love is friendship that has caught fire. It takes root and grows — one day at a time.

Infatuation is marked by a feeling of insecurity. You are excited and eager, but not genuinely happy. There are nagging doubts, unanswered questions, little bits and pieces about your beloved that you would just as soon not examine too closely. It might spoil the dream.

Love is the quiet understanding and mature acceptance of imperfection. It is real. It gives you strength and grows beyond you — to bolster your beloved. You are warmed by their presence, even when they are far away.

Infatuation says "We must get married right away. I can't risk losing you."

Love says, "Be patient. Don't panic. Plan your future with confidence."

Infatuation has an element of sexual excitement. If you are honest, you will admit it is difficult to be in one another's company unless you are sure it will end in intimacy.

Love is the maturation of friendship. You must be friends before you can be lovers.

Infatuation lacks confidence. When they are away you wonder if they are being true.

Love means trust. You are calm, secure, and unthreatened. Your partner feels that trust and it makes him/her even more trustworthy.

Infatuation might lead you to do things you'll regret later, but love never will.

Love lifts you up. It makes you look up. It makes you think up. It makes you a better person than you were before.

Such a list makes love sound all grownup and infatuation childish. Yet play and childishness are also acceptable and important parts of any intimate relationship.

How can we avoid the pitfalls of romantic love and infatuation? How can we be sure that we are in love with someone just as they are, and not dazzled by our own romantic image of them? Perhaps we can't. However, we will see that love is learned, and part of the process of moving toward a mature, realistic love is simply trial and error.

Furthermore, the most important prerequisite for true love may be knowing and accepting ourselves, complete with faults and virtues. If we cannot deal with our own imperfections, how can we be tolerant of someone else's? As Erich Fromm (1956, p. 59) puts it, "Love of others and love of ourselves are not alternatives. On the contrary, an attitude of love toward themselves will be found in all those who are capable of loving others. *Love, in principle, is indivisible as far as the connection between 'objects' and one's own self is concerned.* Genuine love is an expression of productiveness and implies care, respect, responsibility, and knowledge."

Love Is What You Make It   The more one investigates the idea of love, the harder it becomes to pin down. Everyone is quick to describe it, most have experienced it, and all know the mythology of the romantic ideal even though many disclaim their belief in it. Although there does seem to be some agreement on at least a few of the aspects of love, much of what love is appears to be unique to each person. That is to say, each person seems to define love for themselves. This, of course, may lead to problems for a couple if each member defines love somewhat differently from the other. Thus it is important to examine your concept of love in order to understand it and thereby recognize differences between what you and your partner may mean by it. For

Inset 3-3
Adrenaline Makes the Heart Grow Fonder

A frightened man is a potentially romantic man. So is an angry man, a jealous man, a rejected man, or a euphoric man. Anyone, in fact, who experiences the physical arousal that accompanies strong human emotion is a potentially romantic person in that he has already fulfilled one of the two essential conditions for love and is a step ahead of the person whose emotions are in a quiescent stage. If he should meet an unusually desirable woman while he is in this state, he is likely to be more intensely drawn to her than he would be in normal circumstances.

To love passionately, a person must be physically aroused, a condition manifested by palpitations of the heart, nervous tremor, flushing, and accelerated breathing. Once he is so aroused, all that remains is for him to identify this complex of feelings as passionate love, and he will have experienced authentic love (Walster and Berscheid, 1971, p. 46).

This is a highly simplified account of some fascinating research on emotion and love. Based on the idea that both physiological arousal and the intellectual interpretation or labeling of the arousal are necessary to produce an emotional experience (Schachter, 1964), researchers have found that both positive and negative physiological arousal can lead one to love if the labeling process is strong enough.

For example, in one study, men were led to believe they would soon receive three "pretty stiff" electrical shocks. Later the experimenters told half of them that there had been an error and they would not receive the shocks. A third group used as a control was not told about any electrical shocks. The experimenters introduced each of the men to a young woman and asked later how much each liked her. Those who were still expecting the electrical shock and those who had been told to expect one initially, but later told that they wouldn't be shocked, exhibited more liking for the woman than did the control group. The experimenters concluded that the fear, though irrelevant to the emotion of liking, facilitated the attraction. Likewise, the relief from fear, which is also emotional, seemed to facilitate attraction.

Another example might be the fact that many American women of traditional upbringing label their sexual experiences as love. They have been taught that sex without love is taboo. If they feel highly aroused sexually, then social pressure leads them to label their feelings as "love." This then justifies their sexual feelings and thereby reduces their guilt if they act on their sexual feelings.

example, A. L. Scoresby (1977, p. 168) suggests that: "since love is the word symbol we are accustomed to use in explaining great varieties of marital events, if actual feelings of love are not determinant of happy marriages, then mutual agreement about what love means is. Love is, after all, the most often given reason for getting married, and loss of love is the most often given reason for dissolving a marriage." So, if a couple can agree on what love is, on what loving acts are, and, most of the time, can act on this agreement, then their chances are great of maintaining love in their relationship.

So, let us begin by examining those aspects of love where there seems to be at least some agreement. Most people agree that there is a strong physical attraction between lovers at least during the early stages of their relationship. This attraction is often accompanied by a variety of physiological reactions such as more rapid breathing, in-

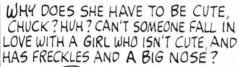

creased pulse rate, and muscular tension. In other words, the person "in love" experiences general emotional arousal when thinking of the loved one or when in his or her presence.

Of course, such a reaction could be just sexual attraction and infatuation rather than love. But, if the physical attraction is accompanied by a strong and growing emotional attachment, and if there is a marked tendency to idealize and be preoccupied with the person, then the reactions are more indicative of love.

Generally, there is a feeling of openness between lovers. Both feel they can confide in the other. Both feel the other likes them as they really are, so they can be more open, more honest, more communicative — in a word, more intimate — than in nonlove relationships. One way of viewing love may be as "intimate self-disclosure" (Schulz & Rodgers, 1975, p. 2).

Such open sharing of your true feelings can, of course, be risky. A person in love is easily hurt, as all lovers, past and present, will attest. Thus, to love is always an adventure because there is danger involved. Indifference is the opposite of love. A lover cares, a lover reveals more of himself or herself, and a lover is therefore vulnerable to being hurt. When hurt occurs, a lover may react to the pain with hostility and anger, and, at times, with hate. Indifference is the reaction of someone who doesn't care, who isn't hurt — who isn't in love.

Another way of thinking of love is to ask whether the experience of loving is leading to personal growth. Most people in love experience an expansion of self. Being loved by another leads to feelings of confidence and security. Many people feel encouraged to venture into new and perhaps unknown areas of themselves. "I feel more emotions than I've ever felt before." "I used to feel awkward meeting new people, but when I'm with Mary, I have no trouble at all meeting strangers." "Bill makes me feel like I can do anything I want."

Probably most Americans will agree on the characteristics of love thus far discussed: physical attraction, emotional attachment, self-disclosure and openness, and feelings of personal growth. Yet how these characteristics are expressed by individuals will vary greatly, and such variance can lead to communication breakdowns. To say and mean "I love you" is one thing. We all recognize the word but it has become so worn by its indiscriminate passage through time that we no longer can identify it with certainty or clearly tell what it represents (Lasswell & Lobsenz, 1980, p. xii).

Two people very much "in love" may have quite different ideas about what this means and how to express it. For example, it is not uncommon for one partner to feel quite loving toward the other while at the same time the other feels unloved. It is as if they are on two different emotional wavelengths. "But you never tell me that you love me," she may say. "I shouldn't have to tell you. I do loving things for you," he replies. Those "loving things" may in his eyes include such actions as bringing home the pay check, fixing broken appliances, avoiding arguments. In her eyes they are merely things any good man should routinely do. She defines evidence of love as words of endearment, gifts, touching, tenderness — the kinds of behavior that he is perhaps uncomfortable with. And yet he knows he loves her. But she is not getting the message. In other words, love is more than emotion. Love is also an intellectual concept. It is what you think it is. It is how you define it and this will probably differ to some extent from how your partner defines it (Lasswell & Lobsenz, 1980, pp. 4–5).

Because we usually assume that our meaning of love is the same as our partner's, we may often feel unloved when, in fact, our partner's expression of love is simply unrecognized. The emotional script in this case is (Lasswell & Lobsenz, 1980, p. 15):

> I, like every man and woman, want to be loved. But I have my own idea, grounded in my personality and attitudes and experience, of what loving and being loved means. Moreover, locked in the prison

of my own ways of thinking and feeling, I assume that my definition of love is the only correct one. As a result, I want and expect to be loved in the same way that I love others, with the same responses that I interpret as the evidence of lovingness.

But I am not loved in that way. Instead (and quite logically, if one could be logical about love), I am loved the way my partner thinks and feels about love, the way he or she understands and expresses it. In my own distress, I do not recognize that my partner is experiencing the same incongruity in reverse. Puzzled, hurt, unable to communicate our confusion to each other, we both unreasonably feel unloved.

Thus, in a truly loving relationship, each partner must try to learn the meaning of love as defined by the other partner and incorporate the differences into one's own concept of love. Ideally, in a successful love relationship, each partner's concept of love grows to include the other's concept. As our personal definitions of love move closer together, our chances of feeling loved increase.

Styles of Loving*

Marcia Lasswell and Norman Lobsenz agree with our thesis that love is defined by each individual in a unique manner based upon a person's life experiences. They feel that these definitions of love and one's attitudes towards love, although unique, can be classified into six general styles. Most people will be a mixture of these styles, with one or two predominating. It is valuable to understand various styles of loving since they are basic to each adult and will characterize their intimate loving relationships.

Best-Friends Love When Jennifer and Gary told their families they were going to be married the news was a pleasant surprise to everyone. "We knew they were close," said Jennifer's mother. "After all, our families have lived on the same block for years and the children went through school together. But we never dreamed they would fall in love." Neither did Jennifer and Gary. "Actually it's not as if we fell in love at all. It's more like we're comfortable with each other. We have a really warm and easy relationship, so why bother to search for anyone else?"

In this case a comfortable intimacy has developed out of close association over a substantial period of time. For persons in whom this style predominates, love grows through companionship, rapport, mutual sharing and dependency, and gradual self-revelation. There is seldom any assumption at the outset of the relationship that it will flower into love or marriage. Friendly lovers find it hard to conceive of becoming emotionally involved with someone they do not know well. They rarely fantacize about other potential lovers. Even if this thought should occur to them, they would probably want to share it with their partners. After all, isn't that what a best friend is for? Such persons

*This material has been taken from *Styles of Loving* by Marcia Lasswell and Norman Lobsenz. Garden City, New York: Doubleday & Co., 1980.

tend to speak of their love as "mature" compared to some of the other styles, which they are likely to see as infatuation.

Typically, a person with this love style is the product of an emotionally secure and close-knit family. He or she has usually been able to count on parents and siblings for companionship, warmth, and support. In many respects, this style of love resembles a good sibling relationship. The divorce rate is low for best-friend couples, but if such a relationship does break up, the lover will most likely want to remain close to his/her former partner. After all, two people who had once loved one another could not become enemies simply because they ceased to be lovers.

Game-Playing Love   To the game-playing lover an emotional relationship is a challenge to be enjoyed, a contest to be won. The more experienced one grows at the game, the more skilled one's moves can be, and often a wide range of strategies are developed to keep the game interesting. Commitment is virtually anathema to this style lover. The object of the game is to play amiably at love, to encourage intimacy, yet to hold it at arm's length. The other person is usually kept emotionally off balance, and the game player's affections are never to be taken for granted.

Game-playing lovers have many artifices. For example, they avoid making long-range plans with partners. Dates are usually arranged on a spur-of-the-moment basis. They are careful not to go out with the same person too often; that might lead him or her to believe there was some prospect of stability. Much of this kind of love style is found prior to marriage when a one-to-one commitment is not required or expected. Obviously, men and women who play at love have both charming and infuriating qualities. They are usually self-sufficient, making few demands on the other person, and preferring not to have demands made on them. They tend to be amusing, quick-witted, self-confident. On the other hand, they tend to be self-centered. The charge often is made that game-playing love is not truly love at all, that it is hedonism at best and promiscuity at worst. But the true game-player believes in playing fair and tries not to hurt the other person.

Logical Love   The logical lover concentrates on the practical values that may be found in a relationship. This style has been called love with a shopping list. "I could never love anyone who didn't meet my requirements for a husband and father (or wife and mother)." Moreover, logical lovers are quite realistic. They usually know exactly what kind of partner they want and are willing to wait for the person who comes closest to meeting their specifications.

It is not uncommon for a lover of this pragmatic bent to avoid any relationship that he or she does not think has a good chance of becoming permanent. "Why should I waste my time?" In one sense, logical love is an updated version of the traditional "arranged" match-making of earlier times. The modern logical lover may believe that romance does have some place in love, but he or she feels more strongly that love should be an outgrowth of a couple's practical compatibility.

Pragmatic lovers consider themselves in love so long as the relationship is perceived as a fair exchange. If matters turn out to be not what they seemed, logical love calls for a two-step response. First, an effort is made to help the partner fulfill his or her original potential. If such efforts fail, then the relationship is ended. Not surprisingly, logical love requires patience: patience to find the proper partner; patience to work out problems; and if the relationship should break up, patience to wait to end it until a reasonable and logical time.

Possessive Love The possessive lover presents perhaps the most unfulfilling and disturbing love style. Alternating between peaks of excitement and depths of despair, capable of shifting in an eyeblink from intense devotion to intense jealousy, he or she is consumed by the need to possess the beloved totally, and simultaneously to be possessed by the other person. The fear of loss or rejection is omnipresent. Despite this bleak picture, the pattern is usually considered one of the most common definitions of being in love.

At the root of possessive love are two seemingly contradictory emotional factors. On the one hand, such lovers are enormously dependent. At the outset of the love affair they may be too excited to sleep, eat, or think clearly. Unable to control their intense reactions, they often feel helplessly at the mercy of the beloved. Yet at the same time such lovers are demanding, often placing great emotional burdens on the other person. Supersensitive, the possessive lover is constantly on the alert for the slightest sign that the partner's affection may be slackening. If such a sign is detected, or even imagined, the anxiety-ridden lover demands immediate reassurance.

When affairs with possessive lovers break up, the ending is usually bitter and angry. The possessive lover finds it almost impossible to see his or her former partner again or to retain any concern or affection for him or her. It is easy to give possessive love a bad name and to concentrate on its unpleasant characteristics. Nevertheless, it has been our experience that many perfectly adequate and emotionally healthy people evidence this style of love to some degree. They prefer intense togetherness. They see jealousy as a natural part of being in love.

Romantic Love Cupid's arrow piercing the heart and instantaneously awakening passionate devotion — no other image so accurately delineates this style. The romantic lover is often as much in love with love itself as with the beloved. Love at first sight is not only possible but almost a necessity. The typical romantic lover seeks a total emotional relationship with the partner. Moreover, he or she expects it to provide a constant series of emotional peaks. The fires of this love style are fueled in large part by a powerful sense of physical attraction.

Once they have found each other, two romantic lovers are likely to be in each other's arms quickly. There is a great urgency to merge physically as well as emotionally. Obviously the intensity of this initial attraction and passion cannot be maintained indefinitely at the same high level. When it begins to taper off, the romantic lover must either substitute fantasies for realities or confront the growing evidence that the other person is not perfect.

One must be willing and able to reveal oneself completely, to commit oneself totally, to risk emotional lows as well as highs, and, finally, to survive without despair if one's love is rejected. A romantic does not demand love, but is confidently ready to grasp it when it appears.

Unselfish Love Unselfish love is unconditionally caring and nurturing, giving and forgiving, and at its highest level, self-sacrificing. It is a characteristic of this love style that one has no sense of martyrdom, no feeling of being put upon. Rather, it rests upon the genuine belief that true love is better expressed in giving than in receiving. This style of love is sometimes called *agape*. In a sense, men and women with this style of love never actually "fall in love." Rather, they seem to have a reservoir of loving kindness that is always available. They are ruled less by their own needs than by the needs of others. Unselfish love occurs less often in real life than imagined. Not many people have the emotional fortitude to be so giving. Even if they have, however, their altruism is not necessarily devoid of all personal rewards. An unselfish lover experiences in return feelings of satisfaction, recognition, even gratitude.

If there really are such styles of loving as set forth by Lasswell and Lobsenz, where do they come from and how do we learn them? Essentially we learn the meaning of love and how to demonstrate it from those around us — our parents, siblings, peers — and from the general culture in which we are raised. For example, such a simple thing as birth order will influence our definition of love. An only child becomes accustomed to a great deal of adult attention. He or she may feel unloved if their spouse (who is the third of four children and received relatively little adult attention) does not attend to them all of the time.

Our personal experiences mold our attitudes and behaviors. Thus, the way we express love and what we define as love are the results of our past experiences.

Actions and Attitudes The attitudes a person brings to love, to dating, and later to marriage have developed over many years. Since no two people experience the same upbringing, it is not surprising to find great attitudinal differences between people, even when they are "in love." Many of the difficulties we experience in our interpersonal relationships stem from conflicting attitudes and unrealistic expectations rather than from specific behavior. For example, a few socks on the floor is not as upsetting to a new wife as is her husband's general

Learning to Love

WHAT DO YOU THINK?
What do you personally mean when you say, "I love you?"

What do your parents mean when they say "I love you" to each other? To you?

Does saying "I love you" carry a commitment to marriage? To sexual intercourse?

How do you recognize if a person is sincere in saying that he or she loves you?

How does love make you feel physically?

attitude toward neatness — does he expect her to wait on him? Often it is necessary to change underlying attitudes if behavior is to change, but this is difficult to do. We take our attitudes for granted without being aware of them. In one of my classes, a young man roundly criticized the double standard. But a day later, when discussing spouses' freedom to be apart occasionally, he stated that he certainly deserved time out with "the boys," but girls probably shouldn't go out with their girl friends after marriage since it might be misunderstood as an attempt to meet other men.

Attitudes generally consist of three components: affective, cognitive, and behavioral. The *affective* aspect is one's emotional response resulting from an attitude, such as "I like blondes." The *cognitive* component consists of a person's beliefs and/or factual knowledge supporting the particular attitude, such as "blondes have more fun." The *behavioral* component involves the person's overt behavior resulting from the attitude, "I date blondes."

Unfortunately, these components are not necessarily consistent. For example, my attitudes may not be founded on fact. I may not act on my attitudes. Or I may voice attitudes that are not really a part of me. The young man above is an example of someone who voices one attitude, support for women, while still favoring another, the double standard.

Where do such attitudes come from? We are not born with them. We learn our most basic attitudes as we grow up, generally from our parents, siblings, and peers. The values of a society are passed on to new members, commencing at birth. This is why we must trace our attitudes toward sex, love, and marriage from early childhood in order to understand adult behavior.

Developmental Stages in Learning to Love As we shall see in Chapter 12, children pass through varying stages of development as they grow to adulthood. Although such stages are actually arbitrary classifications set up by theorists in their effort to understand development, they are very useful to that understanding. Sigmund Freud early delineated four psychosexual stages leading to adult sexual and love expression. Eric Erikson expanded upon these to suggest eight general stages of development across a person's life span (see pp. 374 – 380). A quick overview of Freud's four psychosexual stages is helpful to understanding how we learn to love.

SELF-LOVE STAGE: INFANCY AND EARLY CHILDHOOD During these years young children are so busy coping with their environment that almost all of their energy is focused upon themselves and exploring the environment. Many believe that this early period of self-involvement sets the foundation for subsequent attitudes toward the self. It is important during these early years for the child to receive stimulation, including physical fondling. "By being stroked, and caressed, and carried, and cuddled, and cooed to, by being loved, the child learns to stroke, and caress, and cuddle, and coo to and love others" (Montague, 1972, p. 194). Montague concludes that involvement, concern, tenderness, and awareness of others' needs are communicated to the infant through physical contact in the early months of life. It is here that the child begins to learn the meaning of love and to develop attitudes about intimacy although the infant cannot intellectually understand these concepts. Thus the child deprived of early physical contact may later be unable to make relationships based on love and caring because he or she has not experienced it. Breastfeeding is particularly important because the infant is thereby assured of holding, cuddling, and fondling. Feeding becomes a time of psychological as well as physical nourishment for the child (see p. 375, Chapter 11).

If children are given love and security and are generally successful in learning to master the environment during this first stage, the chances are that their attitude toward themselves will be accepting and positive. These positive self-attitudes are necessary for adults to relate lovingly to others: "The affirmation of one's own life, happiness, growth, and freedom is rooted in one's capacity to love, i.e., in care, respect, responsibility, and knowledge. If an individual is able to love productively, *he loves himself* too; if he can only love others, he cannot love at all" (Fromm, 1956, pp. 59–60).

By loving one's self, Fromm means a coming to terms with oneself, a realistic acceptance of both shortcomings and assets, and a feeling of ease with oneself. People who hate or despise themselves have great difficulty loving others. Thus, even as very small children, we learn about love from the way in which we are loved.

PARENTAL IDENTIFICATION STAGE: EARLY AND MIDDLE CHILDHOOD

During this stage children learn the role, masculine or feminine, that goes with their sex. In many respects children are neuter until they are about five or six years of age. Of course, many parents guide their children toward the appropriate sex role much earlier, but usually the child is five or six before she or he normally makes a deep commitment to the appropriate sex role by identifying with the same-sexed parent (see Chapters 2 and 11).

Although this stage is quite short, usually lasting a few months to a year, it is a crucial period, especially in a culture that has highly defined and differentiated sex roles. For although sex roles are moving closer together in the United States, there is still fairly strong sentiment in favor of the traditional roles: a strong, protective male and a more dependent and passive female.

During this stage it is important for children to have close contact with an adult of their own sex. Under normal circumstances, this would be the father or mother. However, with the increasing number of single-parent families, it might be a grandfather or grandmother or a male or female companion of the remaining parent. One can usually recognize that this transition has been made because the children become more certain of their gender. The boy will probably not want to do the things that he labels for girls and vice versa. Girls and boys will want to take the proper gender roles when playing make-believe house. Children usually talk a lot at this time about what is proper for a girl and for a boy. The importance of this stage to the child's development suggests that parents who can maintain a decent relationship even if apart and who can work together to help the child make the proper identification will make the child's transition go more smoothly. Once children have made this initial identification, such close contact becomes less important. If identification does not occur during this stage, it may occur later, but it will be more difficult for the child to achieve.

Masculine and feminine roles dictate, in part, the way in which an individual demonstrates love. If it is unmasculine for a male to show tenderness, then tenderness may not be a part of his style of love. The sex role that we learn will be an important determinant of our definition of love and an even more important influence on how we display love.

GANG STAGE: LATE CHILDHOOD AND PREADOLESCENCE   This stage coincides fairly well with the usual elementary school years in our society. It is called the gang stage because of the tendency of each sex to avoid the other, preferring to spend time with groups of friends of the same sex. Freud called it the "latency" period because it appeared to him to be a relatively calm time sexually. More recent research has indicated that there is a great deal more sexual experimentation during this period than was first thought. There is some sex play, such as "I'll show you mine if I can see yours."

The main tasks of this stage are consolidation of the socially appropriate sex role and adjustment to cooperative endeavor and formal learning. The gang, or peer group of his or her own sex, helps the child to learn cooperative behavior and the give and take of social organization. In addition, masculine and feminine roles are strengthened by the gang members' approval and disapproval as well as by adult models the gang admires.

During this period the average boy or girl is often openly hostile toward the opposite sex. But the onset of puberty usually signals the end of this stage. The onset of puberty is so varied in our culture that each child will probably enter it at a slightly different time. Thus the primary importance of the gang only gradually diminishes as one by one the members begin to turn their attention toward the opposite sex. The girls' groups dissolve first, since on the average they reach puberty two years ahead of the boys. They have been ahead biologically all the time, but the distance is greatest at the onset of puberty.

ENTERING THE HETEROSEXUAL ADULT STAGE   Children who arrive at puberty earlier or later than the average have additional problems during the transition into the fourth stage, adult heterosexuality. Those who are early often face ridicule and disdain from the gang when they begin showing interest in the opposite sex. The first boy in the gang who suddenly finds himself attracted to one of his sixth-grade female classmates will have to be very careful to keep the gang from finding out, or he will be in for unmerciful teasing and perhaps even ostracism. An early-developing girl faces different problems. She will probably want to date and do the things she sees older girls doing, and her family will most likely set limits on such behavior, paving the way for arguments and conflict. Her peer group, on the other hand, may be titillated by her daring and she may "show off" to keep their approval. This may involve her seeing older, more sophisticated boys who may try to take advantage of her, and who may succeed since she is entering into a game whose rules are not yet known to her.

Children, especially males, who develop late usually suffer through a period of exclusion. They are deserted by friends who are no longer interested in their old activities, and they do not share the new interest in the opposite sex. Often late developers suffer from feelings of rejection and inferiority. They may turn to the company of younger children. This is actually a reasonably satisfactory solution for a boy since his age may bring him a position of leadership in the younger group, thus helping to offset his feelings of inferiority. Some boys may

"I DON'T PLAY WITH GIRLS, MARGARET...."

"... WHERE PEOPLE CAN SEE ME!"

not have to go through a period of exclusion since male gangs usually retain their interest in sports and cars, which the late-developing boy can still share with them. He can also, of course, pretend an interest in girls to go along with his friends and thereby avoid ridicule.

The slow-developing girl finds herself left out more completely, for girls become almost exclusively interested in boys during the transition to early puberty. With her confidence undermined, and lacking compensating support from the group, she faces a difficult time. She may withdraw from social activities, and may suffer from depression that may be masked behind future plans to enter a self-sacrificing vocation. If she remains biologically behind the group for an extended period, say, more than a year or two, she can develop such a strong inferiority complex that she may need additional help and guidance when at last she does catch up biologically.

Children who enter adulthood at the same time as most of their peers avoid these problems. They begin to turn their attention toward the opposite sex and will soon begin dating (see Chapter 4).

Each stage of development becomes the foundation of the next stage. And we must assimilate the lessons of all the stages to become mature, loving individuals.

People who have passed through the first three stages of development successfully reach the heterosexual stage with a positive attitude toward themselves, a fairly clear idea of their roles as a man or woman, and a heightened interest in the opposite sex. They have learned several different kinds of love in their relationships with their parents and their peers. Their definitions of and attitudes about love are fairly well set and so is their own personal style of loving.

Love Over Time

Many of the characteristics of love thus far described are most apparent early in a love relationship and all too often fade over time even though the couple knows they love each other. This implies that love changes over time. That is, being in love at twenty with your new spouse will probably be quite different from the love experienced with your spouse after twenty years of marriage.

David Orlinsky (1972) postulates varying kinds of love relationships over the life cycle starting in infancy and moving through eight stages into parenthood. Let us briefly examine his ideas about love and then consider what further changes in love might occur in the later years of a love relationship.

He suggests that each stage of the life cycle is marked by the emergence of a new form of love experience that is not only exciting but also necessary to the full development of the person. Each love relationship is a medium or vehicle of personal growth.

> One grows as a person through loving, though not only in this way. As one becomes a new and different self through this experience, one also becomes ready to engage in a new and different mode of relatedness to others. Love relationships are not merely pleasant or edifying

Love and intimacy know no age boundaries.

but essential experiences in life, "growthful" in the same generous sense in which travel is "broadening." They are in fact necessary links in the process of personal growth (Orlinsky, 1972, p. 144).

What he is saying, as many others have noted, is that children become loving adults through interacting in loving relationships as they grow up. This preparation is necessary to mature love relationships. We have looked more closely at these early stages and their contributions to mature love in the last section. At this point, we will just take a quick overview of the early stages to help us understand how love might change over time. Orlinsky's first four stages are *infancy*, and *early*, *middle*, and *late childhood*. Each of these stages involves dependency on others. For example, infants must be nursed and children taught. If they are nursed and taught in a loving environment, the chances are good that they will have a positive self-image, a prerequisite for mature adult love. By the fifth stage, *preadolescence*, relations with peers are becoming more important, and the love experience changes to one between equals rather than unequals. In the sixth stage, *youth*, the exciting, passionate, romantic love we have discussed becomes dominant. If a partnership is formed during the seventh stage, *adulthood*, the couple will grow together and find the emotional attachment becoming stronger, and some of the passion may give way to a more enduring, caring, and comfortable relationship with the spouse. The last stage, *parenthood*, is when the couple broaden their love to include children. There will then be a greater proportion of agape or selfless love. This more selfless love is seen by many philosophers and prophets as a more mature, higher order love than just eros alone.

Where might love go from here? Hopefully, it will become more and more a mixture of eros, agape, and philos. Rollo May (1970) calls this mixture "authentic love." Erich Fromm (1956) uses the phrase "mature love" to describe healthy adult love. Mature love preserves the integrity and individuality of both persons. It is an action, not just a passive emotion. Giving takes precedence over taking. Yet this giving is not felt as deprivation, but as a positive experience (Miller & Siegel, 1972, p. 33).

Besides giving, one must be able to receive love if a relationship is to remain loving. Loving is really a reciprocal relationship. By the act of accepting your partner's love, you affirm that person as an accepted and valuable companion (Scoresby, 1977, p. 178).

Hopefully, a couple can maintain an interplay of all three kinds of love throughout most of their relationship. Stated another way, there are social, physical, intellectual, and emotional sides to love expression. Different periods in one's life may find one or another of these aspects dominant and thus the way in which love is shown will vary from time to time. Such changes do not necessarily mean an end of love, but may only signal a changing interplay of all of the factors that comprise it.

So the route love might take in a relationship that lasts a lifetime is basically the pattern of dependency, mutuality, passion, caring and respect, and then perhaps dependency again in old age. Of course, there are other courses that love can take and we will look at them in Chapter 15, where couples find their love has diminished or died.

Love is not a form of matter that can be isolated and analyzed. The very fact that after thousands of years of human existence we are still asking "what is love?" indicates that the question has no definite answer. Love, it seems, is what you make it.

Summary   American youths are given relative freedom to choose a mate. Unlike other societies where mate choice is directed by rigid prescriptions and parental and social guidance, young people here seek their own mates with a minimum of social interference or parental participation. American mate choice is usually based on the nebulous concept of romantic love. "I will marry the person with whom I fall in love."

"Love" is a difficult word to define. One helpful approach was proposed by the ancient Greeks who classified three possible kinds of love: eros, sexual love; agape, spiritual love; and philos, brotherly or friendly love. Mature love includes all three aspects.

Our attitudes about and personal definition of love guide mate selection and lead each of us to form a set of idealized expectations as to the kind of mate we desire. These expectations, if highly unrealistic, often cause disappointment because the partner cannot live up to them. Overromanticized expectations of what a mate and a marriage should be almost ensure disappointment in, and subsequent failure of, a relationship.

Attitudes about love and marriage develop through a number of stages as one grows from infancy to adulthood. Each stage presents problems that the developing person must successfully overcome if, as an adult, mature love relationships are to be sustained. The first stage is the *self-love* stage. During this early period children begin to come to terms with themselves, establishing security, trust, and self-respect. In the *parental identification* stage, children identify with their like-sexed parent and begin to incorporate the masculine or feminine roles of their culture. In the *gang* stage, further consolidation of appropriate roles is accomplished in addition to learning interpersonal relations and communication skills. Finally, the *heterosexual adult* stage is reached, which is the stage of adult sexuality and eventual marital fulfillment.

Such stages, of course, are only theoretical and will vary with cultures and individuals. Yet the idea that we develop our attitudes toward love and marriage as we grow up is important. Child-rearing practices, the immediate family, and the general subcultures in which one is reared will all influence one's attitudes toward intimacy. Conflicting experiences during childhood may lead to confusion as an individual strives for intimacy. And differing childhood experiences may lead to conflicts between lovers as they try to relate to one another. Awareness of these differences and concern for the other individual will make the transition to mature love more likely. And, finally, knowing and accepting ourselves is a necessary first step on the path to a successful love relationship.

The Love Research

Love has always been one thing, maybe the only thing, that seemed safely beyond the research scientist's ever-extending grasp. With an assist from Masters and Johnson, behavioral scientists have, to be sure, dug rather heavily into the topic of human sexual behavior. But whereas sex might now be explored scientifically, love remained sacrosanct.

Or so we thought.

Love was a taboo topic for researchers as recently as 1958, when the president of the American Psychological Association, Dr. Harry F. Harlow, declared in faintly mournful tones, "So far as love or affection is concerned, psychologists have failed in their mission. The little we know about love does not transcend simple observation, and the little we write about it has been written better by poets and novelists." Since the poets and novelists had always been notoriously contradictory about love, defining it as everything from "a spirit all compact of fire" to "a state of perceptual anesthesia," this was a pretty severe indictment.

But the psychologists did not take this charge lying down. Instead, they rallied to the call and started a quiet revolution. Over the past dozen years, and at a positively accelerating pace, behavioral scientists have begun to study love. They have done so on their own terms, with the help of such tools of the trade as laboratory experiments, questionnaires, interviews and systematic behavioral observation. And although the new love research is still in its early stages, it has already made substantial progress. The research has proceeded on several fronts, including explorations of the psychological origins of love, its links to social and cultural factors and the ways in which it deepens — or dies — over time.

Recent studies of falling in love have indicated that there is a sense in which love is like a Brooks Brothers suit or a Bonwit dress. For one person's feelings toward another to be experienced as "love," they must not only feel good and fit well, they must also have the appropriate label. Sometimes a sexual experience contributes to such labeling. One college student told an interviewer that she was surprised to discover that she enjoyed having sex with her boyfriend, because until that time she had not been sure that she loved him. The pleasant surprise helped to convince her that she was actually "in love."

Paradoxically, however, people sometimes label as "love," experiences that seem to be negative rather than positive. Consider the rather interesting case of fear. Ovid noted in *The Art of Love*, written in first-century Rome, that an excellent time for a man to arouse passion in a woman is while watching gladiators disembowel one another in the arena. Presumably the emotions of fear and repulsion stirred up by the grisly scene would somehow be converted into romantic interest.

Ovid himself did not conduct any controlled experiments to check the validity of the fear-breeds-love principle, but two psychologists at the University of British Columbia, Drs. Donald L. Dutton and Arthur P. Aron, recently did so. They conducted their experiment on two footbridges that cross the Capilano river in North Vancouver. One of the bridges is a narrow, rickety structure that sways in the wind 230 feet above the rocky canyon; the other is a solid structure upriver, only 10 feet above a shallow stream. An attractive female experimenter approached men who were crossing one or the other bridge and asked if they would take part in her study of "the effects of exposure to scenic attractions on creative expression." All they had to do was to write down their associations to a picture she showed them. The researchers found that the men accosted on the fear-arousing bridge were more sexually aroused than the men on the solid bridge, as measured by the amount of sexual imagery in the stories they wrote. The men on the high-fear bridge were also much more likely to telephone the young woman afterward, ostensibly to get more information about the study.

The best available explanation for these results comes from a general theory of emotion put forth by Dr. Stanley Schachter of Columbia University. Schachter's experiments suggested that the experience of emotion has two necessary elements. The first is physiological arousal — a racing heart,

heightened breathing, sweating and the like. These symptoms tend to be more or less identical for any intense emotion, whether it be anger, fear or love. The second necessary element, therefore, is the person's subjective labeling of his or her arousal. In order to determine which emotion he or she is experiencing, the person must look around and determine what external stimulus is causing the inner upheaval.

This labeling is a complicated process, and (as Ovid apparently knew some 2,000 years ago) mistakes can happen. In the Capilano Canyon study, subjects apparently relabeled their inner stirrings of fear, at least in part, as sexual arousal and romantic attraction. This sort of relabeling is undoubtedly encouraged by the fact that the popular stereotype of falling in love — a pounding heart, shortness of breath, trembling hands — all bear an uncanny resemblance to the physical symptoms of fear. With such traumatic expectations of what love should feel like, it is no wonder that it is sometimes confused with other emotions. As the Supremes put it in a song of the 1960s, "Love is like an itching in my heart."

In the case of the Capilano Canyon study, of course, one cannot say that the subjects actually "fell in love" with the woman on the bridge. But the same sort of labeling process takes place in more enduring romantic attachments. In the process, social pressures also come crashing into the picture. Young men and women are taught repeatedly that love and marriage inevitably go together, and in the large majority of cases they proceed to act accordingly on this assumption.

. . .

The pressure to label a promising relationship as "love" seems especially strong for women. Sociologist William Kephart of the University of Pennsylvania asked over a thousand Philadelphia college students the following question: "If a boy (girl) had all the other qualities you desired, would you marry this person even if you were not in love with him (her)?" Very few of the respondents (4 percent of the women and 12 percent of the men) were so unromantic as to say yes. But fully 72 percent of the women (compared with only 24 percent of the men) were too practical to answer with a flat no and, instead, pleaded uncertainty.

One of Dr. Kephart's female respondents put her finger on the dilemma, and also on the resolution of it. She wrote in on her questionnaire, "If a boy had all the other qualities I desired, and I was not in love with him — well, I think I could talk myself into falling in love."

Whereas women may be more highly motivated than men to fall in love with a potential spouse, men tend to fall in love more quickly and less deliberately than women. In a study of couples who had been computer-matched for a dance at Iowa State University, men were more satisfied than women with their dates, reported feeling more "romantic attraction" toward them and even were more optimistic about the possibility of a happy marriage with their machine-matched partners. In a study of dating couples at the University of Michigan, I found that among couples who had been dating briefly — up to three months — boyfriends scored significantly higher than their girlfriends did on a self-report "love scale." These men were more likely than their partners to agree with such statements as "It would be hard for me to get along without _____," "One of my primary concerns is _____'s welfare" and "I would do almost anything for _____." Among couples who had been together for longer periods of time the male-female difference disappeared.

. . .

Skeptics may point out, of course, that a paper-and-pencil love scale does not really measure how much people love each other, but simply how much they *say* they love each other. But there is some corroborating behavioral evidence for the scale's validity. For example, scores on the scale checked out with the well-known folk wisdom that lovers spend a great deal of their time gazing into each other's eyes. Surreptitious laboratory observation through a one-way mirror

confirmed that "strong lovers" (couples whose members received above-average scores on the love scale) made significantly more eye contact than "weak lovers" (couples whose scores on the love scale were below average). Or, as the popular song puts it, "I only have eyes for you."

Whereas men seem to fall in love more quickly and easily than women, women seem to fall out of love more quickly and with less difficulty than men, at least in the premarital stages. For the past several years, my coworkers and I have been conducting an extensive study of student dating couples in the Boston area. We found, to our initial surprise, that women were somewhat more likely to be "breaker-uppers" than men were, that they saw more problems in the relationship and that they were better able to disengage themselves emotionally when a breakup was coming. Men, on the other hand, tended to react to breakups with greater grief and despair.

These tendencies run counter to the popular stereotypes of women as star-struck romantics and men as aloof exploiters. In fact, women may learn to be more practical and discriminating about love than men for simple economic reasons. In most marriages, the wife's status, income and life chances are far more dependent on the husband's than vice versa. As a result, the woman must be discriminating. She cannot allow herself to fall in love too quickly, nor can she afford to stay in love too long with "the wrong person." The fact that a woman's years of marriageability tend to be more limited than a man's may also contribute to her need to be selective. Men, on the other hand, can better afford the luxury of being "romantic."

Sociologist Willard Waller put the matter most bluntly when he wrote, some 40 years ago, "There is this difference between the man and the woman in the pattern of bourgeois family life: a man, when he marries, chooses a companion and perhaps a helpmate, but a woman chooses a companion and at the same time a standard of living. It is necessary for a woman to be mercenary."

As more women enter business and professional careers, and as more men make major commitments to homemaking and child-rearing, it is likely that this difference will diminish.

In spite of these culturally based sex differences, the usual course of love is probably pretty much the same for human beings of both sexes. A key task for love researchers is to explore the stages and sequences through which love develops. To this end, Drs. L. Rowell Huesmann of the University of Illinois at Chicago Circle and George Levinger of the University of Massachusetts recently developed a unique computer program, called RELATE, that simulates the development of close relationships. Given information about the personalities of the two partners and following a built-in set of rules and assumptions, RELATE is able to generate a "scenario" of the likely course of their relationship. In its maiden effort along these lines, RELATE simulated the relationship of two hypothetical sweethearts, John (who was described to RELATE in the computer-language equivalent of "attractive, but shy") and Susan (introduced to RELATE as "outgoing and popular").

After a few minutes of whirring and clicking, RELATE came up with its prediction. It hypothesized that after a period of time during which they interacted at a superficial level, "John learns that Susan is willing to disclose intimacies in response to his disclosures, and he confides in her completely. This leads the pair into active striving for a deep romantic involvement." By the end of RELATE's love story, John and Susan were both oriented toward a permanent relationship, although neither had yet proposed marriage.

Since John and Susan are only hypothetical, it is impossible to know how accurate RELATE's scenario really is. Moreover, Drs. Huesmann and Levinger freely acknowledge that at present the simulations are greatly oversimplified, providing at best pale reflections of the events of real-life relationships. But the computer-matchmaker has already proved to be of value to re-searchers in refining their models of the development of love in real life.

Note, for example, that John and Susan's romance did not get very far until John learned that Susan would reciprocate his disclosures. My study of Boston couples, conducted in collaboration with Drs. Letitia Anne Peplau (now at UCLA) and Charles T. Hill (now at the University of Washington) has confirmed RELATE's working assumption along these lines, to wit: love is most likely to flourish when the two partners are *equally involved* in their relationship. In our study of 231 dating couples, 77 percent of the couples in which both partners reported that they were equally involved in 1972 were still going together (or, in some cases married) in 1974, as compared with only 45 percent of unequally involved couples.

The importance of equal degrees of involvement makes it clear that love, like water, seeks its own level. As Columbia University sociologist Peter M. Blau explains, "If one lover is considerably more involved than the other, his greater commitment invites exploitation and provokes feelings of entrapment, both of which obliterate love. . . . Only when two lovers' affection for and commitment to one another expand at roughly the same pace do they mutually tend to reinforce their love."

Because of this mutual reinforcement, love will sometimes beget love — provided that the first person's love is communicated to the second. To help make the point, Dr. Paul Rosenblatt of the University of Minnesota sifted through anthropologists' reports of "love magic" in 23 primitive societies, from the Chaga of East Africa to the Kwoma of New Guinea. He came to the conclusion that although love magic often works, it isn't really magic. Instead, such exotic practices as giving one's "victim" a charmed coconut, flashing a mirror at her or blowing ashes in her face all serve to heighten the woman's love by indirectly communicating the man's love for her. When love magic is practiced without the victim's knowledge, it is not nearly so effective. (Other studies have made it clear, however, that expressions of love must also be well-timed. If too much affection is expressed too soon, equity is undermined and the tactic will backfire.)

Dr. Rosenblatt's study illustrates quite directly what some observers fear most about the new love research — that it will rob love of its magic and mystery. Sen. William Proxmire is one of those who takes this point of view. In a much-publicized statement last year, Sen. Proxmire identified a study of romantic love sponsored by the National Science Foundation as "my choice for the biggest waste of the taxpayer's money for the month of March. I believe that 200 million Americans want to leave some things in life a mystery, and right at the top of the things we don't want to know is why a man falls in love with a woman and vice versa."

. . .

My view of the matter, and that of other love researchers, is rather different. We are quite aware of the difficulties inherent in the attempt to study love, and we have no illusion that we will ever unlock all of love's mysteries. But we also believe that especially at a time when many people are terribly confused about what love is or should be, the scientific study of love can make a positive contribution to the quality of life. To shun this task is no more justified than the taboo until several centuries ago against scientific study of the human body, on the grounds that such research would somehow defile it. In the words of one of the most humane of modern psychologists, the late Dr. Abraham H. Maslow, "We must study love; we must be able to teach it, to understand it, to predict it, or else the world is lost to hostility and to suspicion."

ZICK RUBIN

Chapter 4 ~

Contents

American Dating
and
Mate Selection

Every society has a system, formal or informal, by which mates are selected and new families are started. In the United States, mate selection is carried out by relatively unrestricted dating among the young. That is, the selection process is fairly informal. However, once the couple decides that each is indeed his or her choice for a future mate, the system becomes more structured and engagement and marriage usually follow.

Puberty signals the beginning of adult sexuality. Children are now biologically able to reproduce, and the male-female relationship takes on an overtly sexual nature.

Adolescent years in most Western cultures are a time of sexual stress because although biology has prepared the individual for sexual intercourse and reproduction, society has traditionally denied and tried to restrain these biological impulses by placing restrictive rules and taboos on adolescent sexual behavior. For most, stress lasts until the individual marries, for it is primarily in marriage that our culture allows its members to freely engage in sexual activities. If, in round figures, puberty commences for boys at fourteen years of age and they marry at twenty-four years of age on the average, it means that there is a ten-year period of stress after biology prepares a man for adult sexuality before the society condones sexual intercourse (i.e., in marriage). There is a comparable nine-year period for females, assuming that puberty commences at approximately twelve years of age and she will marry on the average at about twenty-one years of age.

There are instances when the stress period is less evident, such as when the average age of marriage is low. Some societies practice child marriage, which eliminates this period of sexual stress. Some cultures, such as the Polynesian, are also highly permissive in allowing sexual activities among the young. In fact, an anthropological study by George Murdock (1950) found that of 250 societies throughout the world, 70 percent permit nonincestuous sexual relations before marriage.

The stress period can also be reduced by prolonging the gang stage. The middle and upper classes of most European countries keep girls and boys more segregated than in the United States. Many of the schools there are segregated according to sex. Early adult behavior, such as dating, using makeup, and heterosexual school activities such

**Puberty
and
Sexual Stress**

as dances, is discouraged. The middle-class European girl of fifteen or sixteen is, on the average, most similar to the American girl of eleven or twelve. She still spends most of her free time with her gang of girl friends, bike riding, going to movies and cultural events, and youth hosteling in the summer. Contact with boys is limited and usually confined to teasing and flirtation. However, American culture is influencing European youth, and this description may be invalid soon.

Our society encourages early contact between the sexes. Even elementary schools promote coeducational dances and parties. Some parents worry that their children will not become popular and pressure them into developing an early interest in the opposite sex. Makeup, adult fashions, and bras for pre-teens are advertised as ways of increasing popularity. The teen-age market is large, and business has evolved a subeconomy that creates and caters to the tastes of adolescents (see Stone & Church, 1973, pp. 447–448). Much advertising is based on sex appeal, thus heightening the tensions of this period.

The stress of emerging sexuality is compounded by the extended opportunities a young American couple have to be alone together. The automobile has not only revolutionized transportation and contributed to the highly mobile American way of life, it has also revolutionized early sexual experimentation. Recently, vans have literally become mobile bedrooms. A boy and girl can be alone at almost any time in almost any place. The feeling of anonymity and distance from the social system is increased. Group control and influence are lessened, and there is no one who might comment or report on their behavior.

Thus, what we find in America is a society that supposedly prohibits premarital sexual relations, yet through the mass media and the support of early boy-girl relations, actually encourages them. In essence, a young couple is often thrown completely onto their own resources to determine just what their sexual behavior will be. In the end, they will make the decision about the extent of their sexual relationship based on their attitudes, peer influences, and the pressures of the moment.

American Dating   Mate selection through dating is an American invention and is relatively new, having started after World War I, mainly because of the emancipation of women and the new mobility of the car. Some see dating as the most significant mechanism of mate selection in many centuries. In place of the church meeting, the application to the girl's father, the chaperoned evenings, modern youth meet at parties, make dates via telephone, and go off alone in cars to spend evenings together.

Modern youth are so accustomed to having almost free access to one another that it is difficult to appreciate just how hard it was for a young man to meet a young woman not too long ago at the turn of the century. Schools were not coeducational, thus you were not surrounded by students of the opposite sex after elementary school. An introduction of the young man to the young woman's parents had to be arranged and this was not always easy. If the parents approved of the young man, there was little leisure time that the couple could spend together as most young people worked hard in addition to their studies. What little time they had together was usually spent doing things with other family members.

Why Do We Date? We date for many reasons in addition to mate-seeking. Dating serves to fill in time between puberty and marriage. It is often simple recreation, fun, an end in itself. It is a way to gain social status by who one dates and how often one dates (see Winch, 1971, pp. 530–531).

Dating helps to familiarize people with the opposite sex. Because Americans live in small nuclear families, they may have had little opportunity to learn about the opposite sex if they had no opposite-sex siblings near their own age. Dating is an opportunity for the sexes to interact and learn about one another. It is also an avenue to self-knowledge. Interacting with others gives one a chance to learn about one's own personality as well as the personalities of others. Dating allows one to try out a succession of relationships. And one learns something about marital and familial roles by relating with the opposite sex.

In early adolescence, dating is mostly considered fun and recreation and learning about oneself. But the older one becomes, the more serious dating becomes, and the more concerned with mate selection. Thus dating patterns can be placed on a continuum leading from casual dating to marriage (see Figure 4-1).

In general, mate selection in America may be viewed as movement down two paths (see Broderick, 1967). One is the path of commitment and the other is the path of physical intimacy. At first, com-

Today people date for many reasons besides mate selection.

Casual recreational dating
of numerous persons

↓

Multiple dates
with fewer persons

↓

Going steady

↓

Informal commitment
to marriage such as
"pinning" in fraternities
and sororities

↓

Engagement

↓

Final commitment

↓

Marriage

Figure 4-1
A continuum of dating.

mitments are very superficial: "Let's spend an evening together." Finally, at the end of the path, there is the deep-seated commitment: "Let's spend our lives together." The intimacy road runs from casual hand-holding to a full and continuing sexual relationship. Unfortunately, the emphasis in America on sex may lead to neglect of other important aspects of a relationship. Social compatibility, development of shared interests, and increased knowledge of one another are all important, especially if the relationship is to become permanent.

Patterns of Dating Adolescent boy-girl interactions have become increasingly more individualized in the past few years. This great variation makes it difficult to describe a common American dating pattern. In general, formal dating, where a boy approaches a girl beforehand and arranges a meeting time, place, and activity for them, has declined in the larger urban areas such as Los Angeles and New York City. Formal "going steady," where class rings and lettermen's jackets are given by the boy to the girl, has also declined in these areas. However, one still finds more traditional, formalized dating in small cities and towns. The movie *American Graffiti* depicted boy-girl interactions in the 1950s and early 1960s. Actually, the film shows the typical pattern of adolescent interaction today in small-town America. Main Street is cruised on Friday and Saturday nights, dates are prearranged, and afterwards everyone meets at a drive-in restaurant or couples head into the countryside to neck and pet. Many go steady for a good portion of their high school years.

There is another generalization we can make. The first date used to be the first time a couple would become acquainted. It usually involved a function or activity, such as going to the movies. By concentrating on the activity, some of the difficulties and embarrassments of getting to know one another were avoided. After all, you can't talk if you are at a movie theater. Today, young people generally know one another better before actually dating. They have chatted with each other and perhaps done things together in the context of a larger group. Their first date comes more casually; they may decide on the spur of the moment to go to the beach together. Couples still go steady, but again, the relationship seems less formal, more relaxed and casual. Also, once past a period of almost total preoccupation with one another, there seems to be more group activity, going out with other couples or once in a while with girlfriends or boyfriends. It seems, then, that dates of the 1950s were more task-oriented, what will we do on our date, while today dates have become more person-relationship oriented, what will the relationship be on our date.

Since there is a diversity of dating patterns, let's take a look at the two ends of the spectrum. First, we'll follow a young couple through an extended period of dating and observe how the traditional, more formal game is played. Then we'll jump to the other end of the spectrum and look at dating as a "happening" where there are few formal guidelines and little commitment.

TRADITIONAL DATING AND GOING STEADY   Let's start when our hypothetical couple are first allowed to begin dating. Age at first dating varies greatly with each family and with social class, but, in general, people are dating earlier, so that dating at eleven and twelve, especially for a girl, is not unusual. Let us further assume that the boy has just reached the age of legal driving (15 or 16) and is able to talk his father out of the family car for his date.

The boy will probably have known the girl superficially for some time. They attend the same school and have met at various school functions. Although it requires courage, he finally asks her to a movie on the coming Saturday night. A movie is usually a safe first date for a young adolescent since it requires so little interaction with one's date. Neither has to worry about being boring or having nothing to say since the movie will occupy their time. At the appointed time, the boy proudly arrives to pick up the girl. Although she has been ready for some time, she is discreetly "not ready." This serves a twofold purpose; she does not appear overeager (her mother has told her to play hard to get) and it gives her parents a few moments to look him over and discuss the evening's rules with him, mainly at what time to return. Then she makes her entry and they leave.

In the darkened theater, the boy strongly feels the pressure of his friends and the anonymous larger group of peers loosely defined as "the boys" to approach her physically. And he is, of course, under pressure from himself, wanting to prove to himself that the girl likes him, thus boosting his self-esteem. The intimacy road leading to sexual contact enters dating immediately. The boy generally pays for the date, at least at first, and this pressures the girl into paying him back, usually with some kind of physical response. The double standard, where sexual advances are expected of the boy, but are inappropriate for the girl, still operates in traditional dating. To feel masculine and proud among his peers, the boy wants to at least try to have some type of physical contact with the girl. Thus, as he sits watching the movie, the first of many conflicts concerning sexuality arises. He notices that her hands are lying one inch in his direction on her lap. Perhaps this is a clue. Should he attempt to hold her hand? If she vigorously rejects this advance, someone in the row might notice and he'll be embarrassed. If, however, she accepts, how will he be able to withdraw his hand when it becomes sweaty and begins to cramp? Will she take it personally as some kind of rejection if he does withdraw it?

The fascinating characteristic of traditional American dating is what one may call "escalation." In other words, resolution of this first minor intimacy conflict does not end the problem. If the girl accepts his first advance, then the pressure he feels to prove his masculinity will actually increase since the whole procedure is designed to test just how far he can go toward overt sexuality with the girl. Granted, much of this pressure may be unconscious for the boy, yet he feels the need to prove himself. Naturally the further the boy moves, the more pride he will feel when bragging to his friends of his success with girls. Thus, once he has taken her hand, he must now look to the slightly greater problem of attempting to place his arm around her. The reward of increased intimacy is obviously greater, but so are the risks. If she vigorously rejects his attempt, the whole movie house will notice (at least, it will seem this way to him). If she accepts, there is always the cramped shoulder to look forward to as well as the necessity of facing the new escalation level and all of its ensuing conflicts and insecurities.

The girl is having conflicts too because she does not want to lose her reputation and yet at the same time she does not want him to think her a prude and not ask for another date. Of course, she may just have gone out with him to have a date and doesn't really want to date him again. In that case, total rejection of his physical advances will serve to let him know further dates are not desired. If she does like him, she wants to encourage him, but not too much. How much physical contact can she allow the boy without leading him to think she will eventually go all the way?

If the relationship continues, the couple will gradually limit their dating to each other. They enjoy the security of knowing they always have a date. They find being together comfortable, and it's a relief to them not to have to face the insecurity of a new date. Of course, going steady requires a higher degree of commitment than casual dating, but this ability to commit oneself becomes the foundation of later marriage. Going steady helps the couple to understand what kind of commitments are necessary to marriage.

Going steady, though, does create problems. The phenomenon tends to add pressure to the sexual conflicts experienced by the young couple. Their contact is much more frequent, and it may become harder for the girl to retain her virginity and still encourage the boy. Also, an American boy tends to be possessive. He tends to regard any attention or compliments paid to his steady as insulting and he tries to restrict her social interaction to himself. Of course, she may resent this, and fights may result.

On the whole, starting early and remaining in a steady relationship throughout adolescence is probably disadvantageous to later adult relations. The young person who has always gone steady is unlikely to have had enough experience with a broad cross-section of the opposite sex to have developed his or her interpersonal abilities to the fullest. Going steady early also tends to lead to earlier marriage and the data about the stability of early marriages is quite negative. If dating is to work as a method of mate selection, then it is important to date enough to insure a reasonably good mate choice.

On the other hand, dating so many people that no longer-term relationships are formed during the premarital dating period is also dysfunctional. The young person never gets any practice in the give and take of long-term relationships. Thus, ideally, one must date enough people to understand the many individual differences that are to be found and at the same time experience some longer-term relationships in order to gain knowledge of the commitments and compromises necessary to maintain a relationship over time.

"GETTING TOGETHER": DATING AS A "HAPPENING"   At the other end of the spectrum is dating as a "happening." In this case, there is no orderly progression from the first parent-approved date to going steady to eventual marriage. Here meetings and even dates tend to "just happen," are spur of the moment affairs. One of these casual "dates" can end with the couple having sex, or they may never even think of sex. They may decide to "hang out" together, or they may just drift away and not see each other again — it all seems to depend on the "vibes" of the moment.

For example, the boy may notice the girl at a local coffeehouse or other neighborhood hangout. When he comes back with a fresh cup of coffee, he moves his chair nearer to hers. He notices that she laughs at some of his jokes. A day or two later, he bumps into her on the street and asks if she wants to go along to the beach. On the way they find they both like the same rock groups, and that both were hitching in Europe last summer. Sex depends on how they feel at the moment, and is considered no big thing to either of them. The boy does not expect her to be a virgin, and would be surprised if she were.

The problems of this type of dating are, as you might expect, almost the opposite of those of going steady. Rather than too limited experience with the opposite sex, here there tends to be too much experience and too little commitment. Neither the boy nor the girl is likely to feel chosen or special when he or she knows the partner is likely to have sex with anyone who turns up. Since both have learned to avoid conflict or "scenes" by moving on, neither has ever learned to work things through or compromise. Since marriage involves commitment and compromise, both are bad marriage prospects if this is their only experience.

Probably our own personal dating experiences will fall somewhere between traditional dating and "getting together," depending on where we live, our upbringing and values, and what our peers are doing. Regardless of the style of our dating, each person has the problems of finding dating partners, coping with "bad" dates, and avoiding exploitation during the date. The fact that American dating today is so informal and without rules compared to mate selection processes historically and in other countries, means that each young person has to make his or her own decisions about what is best for them personally. Of course, when we say "make their own decisions" we realize that there will be many social and cultural pressures guiding them, but these pressures are not as clear-cut nor is there just one clear set of pressures as we have sometimes found in the past.

Living Together   In Chapter 14, *The Alternatives*, we will examine premarital cohabitation, or living together, in detail. However, we discuss it here as well because a number of factors have combined to make it a part of the American dating game for increasing numbers of American youth. After reviewing the research on nonmarital cohabitation, Macklin (1978) concluded that about 25 percent of undergraduate college students have been involved at some time in such an experience. Thus, for many young Americans, living together is a characteristic of the dating period and may play a role in the mate-selection process.

Without going into detail, there seem to be at least six factors that have contributed to the increase in nonmarital living together: availability of effective contraception, skepticism regarding traditional values leading to changing premarital sex norms, the relaxation of the surrogate parent role played in the past by our educational institutions, the availability of off-campus living, peer support, and economic necessity.

Although there are many reasons for living together, at this point we will examine only the relationship between living together and the two dating systems we have been discussing, traditional dating and "getting together" dating. With traditional dating, living together is a formal mate-selection step. In Figure 4-1, page 114, living together would most likely fall just before or go along with the engagement step. The couple has already been together for some time, they are committed to one another, and thus living together becomes a logical extension of their ongoing relationship. These couples tend to see it as a trial marriage.

On the other extreme, the more casual couple may view living together less formally. The girl may be eager to get away from her parents who seem, to her at least, to be her jailers, always trying to separate her from her friends and from fun. She may bring little more than a sleeping bag and some clothes with her. Meals are apt to be from cans or at a local hamburger joint. Just as there is little or no formal commitment and few promises in the "dating as a happening" relationship, there are no formal rules or responsibilities in the living-together arrangement. When one tires of it, he or she moves on.

As a mate-selection device, living together may play the same roles as any dating can. It can teach one in more detail about individual differences and the responsibilities and commitments necessary to maintain a long-term relationship. It can help to improve and make more intimate a relationship. On the other hand, it may destroy a relationship. As mentioned, we will examine living together in detail in Chapter 14.

Premarital Sexuality

As we have seen, movement down the path of intimacy is a part of American dating. For most, it is a gradual movement characterized by increasing escalation of sexual intimacy. Traditional American dating often evolves into a sexual game of offense versus defense. With each step, the couple moves closer to sexual intercourse. Since, in traditional dating, it is the boy who pressures the girl for greater physical intimacy, it is she who is constantly on the defense. Since her value system will probably be vague or confused because of the swiftly changing and pragmatic character of American society, the continuing pressure on her to become more intimate will often cause her great confusion and insecurity.

Continuing escalation of physical intimacy moves from the first cautious hand-holding at the movies to necking, petting, and, in some cases, intercourse. The rapidity of the escalation depends on the inner security of each member of the couple, the length of time and exclusiveness with which they date each other, and what their friends do. The more insecure the young people are, the more they will seek security in conforming to what they believe the peer group is doing. Time is obviously an important factor. To place vigorous young adults who like one another together for long periods of time without supervision in a culture that promotes sexuality is obviously going to lead to sexual activity.

But it is up to the individual couple to make the decision of how far they will go. I call this strategy "sex — not-sex," and it is usually the female who makes up the rules. Since she must control how far the male goes sexually, she must have a personal definition of what sexual behavior is. She knows that actual intercourse is sex, but she is probably unsure of how to categorize all the other behavior: kissing, necking, and various degrees of petting. If she can categorize kissing as "nonsex," she can kiss as much as she likes and feel no guilt. If, on the other hand, because of upbringing, she categorizes kissing as "sex," she will feel guilty when she engages in such behavior. Premarital sex in America is largely a matter of learning how to handle guilt.

When one asks a cross-section of young American women what they define as sexual behavior, there is no one agreed-upon answer. One girl may become upset at any action beyond kissing. Another may be able to indulge in mutual masturbation with little if any conflict because she has defined all but actual intercourse as nonsex. In reality, in the broadest sense, intimate physical contact of any kind between male and female is sexual behavior.

The boy feels he cannot judge where any one girl will draw the line, and he will be insecure in a new girl's presence until he knows the rules whereby she plays the game. He also may be timid and afraid of overt sexuality although he is obliged to hide any fears by the masculine stereotype that demands he be a sexual initiator.

The young adult can become centered on sex to the exclusion of most other things. And even the final solution to escalation problems, sexual intercourse, does not end the preoccupation with sex. Instead, it often serves to exaggerate it.

Although premarital relations are against our societal standards, they are not uncommon. The classical sexuality studies of the past forty years indicated that some 85 percent of unmarried American males and about 50 percent of unmarried females engaged in sexual intercourse (Kinsey et al, 1948, 1953). Age, social class, education, and strength of religious ties were all important determinants of such behavior.

Is There a Sexual Revolution? The answer to this question is vigorously debated. From such data as Kinsey's, we can see that the taboo against premarital intercourse is violated by many. The incidence of premarital intercourse is probably even higher than the figures indicate, since some individuals may decline to answer questions about their sexual behavior. However, numerous studies about the incidence of premarital sexual intercourse seem to point to the following conclusions.

During the 1960s, being frank about sex became popular, leading to the unsupported belief that premarital sexual intercourse was increasing greatly. There was, in fact, a great deal of smoke, but little fire. Premarital intercourse rates remained substantially the same as they had been since the 1920s (see Bell, 1966). The difference was that sex was discussed more openly.

However, commencing in the 1970s, premarital intercourse rates, especially for women, began to rise. The rates for American females had remained relatively low, around 20 percent, throughout this century until the late 1960s. King et al (1977) compared the percentage of college students having premarital intercourse in 1965, 1970, and 1975 (Table 4-1) and found little increase for the college men but a great deal of increase for the college women, although their rates remained lower than the men's.

In addition, King et al found that the college students' rejection of premarital sexual intercourse as immoral had dropped dramatically. Students strongly agreeing with the statement "I feel that premarital intercourse is immoral" showed continual decline over the years studied (Table 4-2).

Robert Bell and Kathleen Coughey (1980) also compared female premarital intercourse experience during three different time periods, 1958, 1968 and 1978. They broke their figures down according to both the type of relationship in which premarital intercourse occurred (dating, going steady or engaged) and according to the girl's religion (Jewish, Protestant, and Catholic). In each category their figures also showed a progressive increase (see Table 4-3).

Zelnik and Kantner (1977) found that the prevalence of sexual activity among never-married American women (ages 15–19) increased 30 percent between 1971 and 1976. The median age for first intercourse also declined slightly during this time from 16.5 to 16.2 years of age. *Redbook* magazine (September, 1975), in a study of 100,000 readers, found that 80 percent of the women had engaged in premarital sex, and that for almost half of them, the experience had occurred before age eighteen.

It is clear from such figures that the double standard wherein the male participates in premarital sexual activity and the female does

Table 4-1 Percentage of 1965, 1970, and 1975 College Students Having Premarital Intercourse

	Males	Females
1965	65.1	28.7
1970	65.0	37.3
1975	73.9	57.1

Table 4-2 Percentage of Students Strongly Agreeing with the Statement,
"I feel that premarital sexual intercourse is immoral."

	Males	Females
1965	33.0	70.0
1970	14.0	34.0
1975	19.5	20.7

not is declining. Although more American females are engaging in premarital sex, they are still more conservative than their male counterparts with respect to both attitude and practice. The figures in Table 4-3 show that as relationship commitment increases, so does premarital intercourse. It appears that while many more single women are having coitus, they do so with men they love and hope to marry.

Many of these studies may be biased in the direction of showing a high percentage of premarital sexual activity since the respondents are volunteers. Generally, volunteers in studies of sexuality tend to be more liberal. For example, in Hunt's (1973) study only one in five persons contacted agreed to participate in the study. Those who refused may have quite different experiences from those who did participate. But, be that as it may, the figures for premarital sexual experience are so much higher than in previous studies that, at the very least, they show continued movement in the direction of increasing premarital sexual experience for young women. Bascially, young women's premarital sexual experiences are coming more to resemble those of young men.

Although the sexual mores of American youth are becoming more permissive, adults tend to react negatively to these changes. Most adults still support a position against premarital intercourse. The most common reasons they list for this position are:

1. Religious attitudes prohibit such behavior.
2. My own upbringing and personal moral code prohibit that kind of behavior.
3. Sex relations before marriage lead to serious problems — illegitimate children, damaged reputation, psychological problems.
4. Premarital sex contributes to the breakdown of morals in this country.
5. Sex is sacred and belongs only in marriage.

Table 4-3 Females, Percentage Having Intercourse by Dating, Relationship and Religion, 1958, 1968, 1978

	Jew			Protestant			Catholic			Total		
	1958	1968	1978	1958	1968	1978	1958	1968	1978	1958	1968	1978
Dating	11	20	45	10	35	56	8	15	46	10	23	50
Going Steady	14	26	64	20	41	79	14	17	63	15	28	67
Engaged	20	40	69	38	67	88	18	56	69	31	39	76

It is easy, of course, for middle-aged individuals to urge young people to suppress their sex drive, but the fact remains that sexual needs are among the most basic human needs. It is extremely difficult for young adults to accept admonitions against premarital sex. Instead of discussing standards of behavior that have not been adhered to for some time, adults need to discuss openly and honestly the problems youth face. Any ultimate decision about premarital intercourse will be made by the young couples themselves. Surely, rather than lectures about morality, it is better to supply them with as much good information as possible so that their decision will be sound and based on a firm foundation of knowledge rather than ignorance.

Deciding for Yourself   There are four major areas for the couple contemplating premarital sexual intercourse to consider: (1) personal principles, (2) social principles, (3) religious principles, and (4) psychological principles.

Every person has a set of personal principles by which to guide his or her life. The following are some personal questions young adults should ask themselves when contemplating premarital intercourse:

1.   Is my behavior going to harm the other person or myself, either physically or psychologically? Will I still like myself? What problems might arise? Am I protecting my partner and myself against V.D. and pregnancy?
2.   Will my behavior help me become a good future spouse or parent? Do I believe sex belongs only in marriage?
3.   Is my sexual behavior acceptable to my principles and upbringing? If not, what conflicts might arise?

Of course, there are no general answers to questions such as these. Each individual has his or her own personal principles and personal manner of applying the principles in a particular situation, but the fact remains that most young adults should confront such questions if they engage in premarital sexual experimentation.

Again, questions arise when one considers general social principles. Our society has long supported certain rules concerning premarital sex. If enough people break such rules, pressure is placed on the society to change them. Thus each person who decides to act against the established code adds his or her weight to the pressure for change. Before you make such a decision, you should ask yourself:

1.   What kind of behavior do I wish to have prevail in my society? Is premarital sex immoral? Will premarital sex contribute to a breakdown of morals? Is this desirable?
2.   What kind of sexual behavior do I feel would make the best kind of society? Would I want my friends to follow in my footsteps?
3.   Am I willing to support the social rules? What will happen if I don't?

Questions concerning religious principles will also need to be answered. Most of us have had religious training, and we have learned attitudes toward sexual behavior from that training. In a study of several hundred junior college students' attitudes toward premarital sex, I found that 90 percent of those who were against it gave religion as their primary reason. The following are some questions you should ask yourself:

1. What does my religion say about sexual conduct? Do I agree?
2. Am I willing or able to follow the principles of the religious body to which I belong?
3. Do I feel there is a conflict between the sexual attitudes of my church and society? My church and my friends?

Psychological principles may be the hardest to uncover. Since the socialization process begins at birth and continues throughout· one's lifetime, it is difficult, if not impossible, to remain completely unaffected by society and family. Many of our attitudes are so deeply ingrained that we are unaware of them. When our behavior is in conflict with these attitudes, there will usually be stress and guilt. Thus some of the psychological questions that must be grappled with are:

1. Can I handle the guilt feelings that may arise when I engage in premarital sex?
2. How will premarital intercourse influence my attitudes and the quality of sex after marriage?
3. What will I do if I (or my partner) get pregnant? Can I handle an abortion? A child? Marriage?

Possible Problems Associated with Premarital Sexual Relations As American mores have relaxed, the differentiation between premarital and marital sex activities has lessened. However, there are still a number of problems that are clearly related to premarital sex.

Venereal disease is more prevalent among unmarried participants in sexual activities. This is true because the chances of having more than one sexual partner are greater for unmarried people. The chances are also greater of having short duration sexual encounters where the lines of communication are less open. This may lead, especially for women, to later discovery of venereal disease, thus increasing the chances of permanent damage. Venereal disease is discussed fully in Chapter 9, p. 283.

Unwanted pregnancies are a second problem. Despite improved birth control methods, especially birth control pills, premarital pregnancies have continued to increase. The U.S. Census Bureau estimates that the number of illegitimate births per 1000 unmarried women, aged fifteen to forty-four, has increased from 14.1 in 1950 to 24.1 in 1974 (Statistical Abstracts, 1976, p. 58). However, illegitimacy rates do not give the whole picture because many babies conceived out of wedlock are legitimized by subsequent marriage. Perhaps as many as one-third of all first-born babies are conceived out of wedlock. CBS (1980) has reported that over half of all teenage births resulted from out of wedlock pregnancies.

Table 4-4 Illegitimate Live Births by Race and Age of Mother, 1950 to 1974

Race and Age	1950	1960	1965	1970	1974
Total numbers (1000s)	141,600	224,300	291,200	398,700	418,100
Percent of all births	3.9	5.3	7.7	10.7	13.2
Rate per 1000 unmarried women	14.1	21.6	23.5	26.4	24.1
White women	6.1	9.2	11.6	13.8	11.8
Negro and other women	71.2	98.3	97.6	89.9	81.5
Age of Mother (1000s)					
under 15	3,200		6,100		10,600
15 – 19	56,000		123,100		210,800
20 – 24	43,100		90,700		122,700
25 – 29	20,900		36,800		44,900
30 – 34	10,800		19,600		18,600
35 – 39	6,000		11,400		8,200
40 and over	1,700		3,700		2,300

Source: Statistical Abstracts, 1976, p. 58.

An unwed pregnant woman has limited alternatives available to her. She may marry. She may seek an abortion (see Chapter 10). She may give birth to the baby and then give it up for adoption. She may simply desert the infant. She may keep the child and go on welfare, or let her parents care for the child while she works or continues with school. But, regardless of how one handles a premarital pregnancy, the problems are many and stay with one for years.

Dawn and Jim:
But I Want to Keep the Baby Even If We Aren't Married
Dawn is twenty years old and a college junior, majoring in business administration. She has gone with Jim for two years. He is a senior in premed and has been accepted for medical school. She has recently discovered that she is pregnant. In the past both she and Jim have agreed to postpone marriage until they are finished with school and Jim has established himself.

Jim is quite mad at her for becoming pregnant. "How stupid of you to forget to take your pill, especially in the middle of the cycle when you knew your chances of pregnancy were higher. Are you sure you didn't do it on purpose? You could have told me and I could have used something although I don't like to. It isn't natural. It is really up to the girl to protect herself and you were plain dumb to forget after all this time."

Dawn doesn't quite agree. "You're having sex with me, too. I don't see why birth control is always just *my* responsibility. You know as well as I do that I didn't want to get pregnant. It wasn't my fault that I forgot. After all, you didn't have to make love to me. You were the one that was hard up and pushing, not me. But now that

I'm pregnant, I'm going to keep the baby. A lot of my friends are doing it. Having a baby before you are married isn't half as bad as it used to be. I really don't care what you or our folks think, it's the modern thing to do."

Jim objects strongly. "Well, I'm not going to marry you under these conditions. We agreed to wait until I was finished with medical school and you blew it. The only thing you can do is get an abortion. They're easy to get now. There is nothing to them physically and I'm willing to pay for it. Keeping the baby will just foul up our lives and tie us down. We'll have plenty of time to have children after we're finished with school."

"No abortion for me," replies Dawn. "I don't think they're right. Besides, I don't expect you to marry me. I wouldn't want you to feel forced into anything. I've only a year of school left and I'm sure my folks would watch out for the baby until I'm working and independent. Then, with child care, I'll be able to take care of it just fine, without you."

"Well, if you're that stupid, I'm glad to find out now," retorts Jim. "I won't be a part of such a dumb plan. Unless you do the smart thing and get an abortion, I'm through with you, pregnant or not."

WHAT DO YOU THINK?

How will they resolve their conflict? What would you advise?

What would you do if you were Jim? Dawn?

What kind of attitudes show through Jim's statements? Dawn's?

How would your parents react to such a situation?

What are the alternatives open to the couple?

How do you feel toward illegitimacy? How do you think society feels today?

Whose responsibility is birth control? Why?

Early commitment and isolation are frequent partners of premarital sexual involvement. Sex is such a powerful force in young people's lives that it often overrides other aspects of a relationship. Sexual involvement often excludes growth in other areas such as the social or intellectual. Also, sexual relationships often make for exclusivity, thus narrowing a young person's interpersonal experiences. In essence, the sexual part of the relationship tends to override other aspects. It may lead to commitment on a sexual basis alone rather than to a total relationship. An early commitment based on only one aspect of a relationship (sexual) is usually an unstable basis for any long-term relationship.

The *quality of the sex act may be impaired* by premarital sexual experience. Masters and Johnson (1966) point out that fear, hostility, and conflict are the three mental states that most often cripple the sex life of both men and women. They feel that it is through education that these three can be defeated. In their treatment conferences with couples they examine the history of the couple's past sexual experiences and slowly guide them toward overcoming the negative emotional reactions that may be attached to early unhappy sexual experiences. Assuming that the couple's sexual problems are only mental in nature, they help the couple through actual practice and desensitization to become more satisfactory sexual partners to one another. They find that early unsatisfactory sexual experiences have often negatively influenced an individual's whole attitude toward sexuality. Unfortunately, as long as society holds taboos against early sexual experience, indulging in such experiences as premarital intercourse may be (for some) a factor working against later sexual fulfillment. Trainer (1965), in his excellent book on the physiology of the sexual act, reports between 25 and 40 percent of first-year wives are unable to achieve a climax. These women are not, for the most part, frigid, since this term implies deep emotional or physical problems that render the woman unable to achieve satisfaction. By and large, those women who do not find a full and rewarding sex life in this culture are the victims of twisted social mores. They have been taught that sex is unpleasant or that a "nice" girl never desires sex, or they suffer from deep-seated guilt over their behavior. A fair number of sexual problems are also reported among American men.

It is apparent from the statistics reported earlier (p. 121) that premarital sexual intercourse is becoming more prevalent, and thus an increasing number of American youth may be initiated into sexual intercourse under the often adverse circumstances that surround much premarital sexual activity. It is the author's hypothesis that early sexual experiences largely set the attitudes that an individual will hold toward sexual intercourse throughout his or her life. If one's early sexual experiences occur premaritally, the chances are that the quality of such experiences will be under less than optimum conditions. As a result, large numbers of our youth may begin their adult sexual life with negative attitudes toward the sexual act. Premarital sexual experiences in our culture are often of relatively poor quality for two major reasons.

First, the environment in which these early clandestine experiences take place is almost always negative and is seldom, if ever, conducive to relaxed, uninhibited sexual contact. Many of these contacts take place in the automobile; having to duck each time a car passes hardly helps the boy or girl relax and feel secure. Relaxation and security are both important psychological attributes to the successful sex act. The general environment is especially important to the girl's ability to find satisfaction. The boy is much more direct in his sexual response and almost regardless of the environment can achieve satisfaction through ejaculation. The girl has a more diffuse physiological response and this response is much more dependent upon her psychological state of mind than is the boy's response. The girl who is highly afraid of being caught,* who is suffering from intense guilt over her action, and who may be feeling used and manipulated by the boy is seldom going to find great satisfaction in sexual intercourse. Indeed, most girls report that their first experience with intercourse was not very enjoyable. Only 18 percent in a large recent study reported their first experience to be "thrilling," and only 10 percent reported having had an orgasm (Wolfe, 1980, 255). This is not to deny that it is pleasurable and exciting, but in light of what it could be, she may find herself disappointed. Such disappointment may breed many greater problems in her attitude toward sex. Since most of the modern literature as well as the movies and television depict sexual satisfaction for the female as a wild and violent complete climax, her ensuing disappointment is

---

*If the place of first intercourse is the home of the girl, one can imagine the potential guilt for some girls if their parents are highly moralistic.

often interpreted as personal shortcomings. She may begin to feel that something is wrong with her sexually and this, of course, increases her anxiety, which renders her even more incapable of finding satisfaction. Thus, the early sexual experience of an individual, if negative, may start a "vicious circle" pattern of behavior. Actually, in most cases, there is absolutely nothing wrong with the girl. If the environment is one of security and romance, if the boy is sophisticated enough to appeal to the girl on a total basis, that is, psychologically as well as physically, offering her intellectual rapport, warmth, and a feeling of self-respect, and if her conception of the experience is realistic, in all likelihood she will experience a great deal of satisfaction. Although we have discussed the problems of the disappointed girl, it should be noted that when the girl shows disappointment, it is also terribly threatening to the boy who may react with his own inferiority feelings since he appears unable to satisfy her. His ability to satisfy is, of course, one of his chief masculine ego defenses and he is highly vulnerable to insecurity in this area.

The second reason for the generally poor quality of premarital sex is the general ignorance of the young American male. As implied above, it is important that the boy address himself to the psychological state of the girl as well as to her physical state. Candlelight, music, sweet nothings whispered in the ear, in a word, romance, is an important ingredient to successful sexual experience for the girl. Yet the American male is usually lacking in his understanding of these dimensions. If he does understand them, he often becomes too preoccupied with himself or too embarrassed to do anything about them. In addition, he can't admit to others, and *occasionally* even to himself, that he does not know all there is to know about sex. Indeed, it is often found that the boy who is the biggest braggart about sex knows the least.

Thus, because of the generally poor environment in which most premarital intercourse must take place and the lack of knowledge and ineptness of the young couple, many American youth are experiencing a disappointing baptism to adult sexuality. In light of the wonderful place intimate physical contact can and should play in the life of the family, this is extremely sad commentary upon our society.

Again the reader should remember that the problems just described, although prevalent in the society, do not appear in every case. Some couples can premaritally experience the joys of adult sexuality, but they are probably the exception rather than the rule.

Although sexual intercourse is the end result of the physical intimacy path (p. 113), it no longer signifies total commitment. Current research does not support the popular idea that "sexual relations and psychological commitment are related." Peplau et al (1977) found that sexual intercourse was not significantly related to pair continuance. In the past, of course, it usually was. Sexual intercourse was more closely restricted to marriage or at least to a strong commitment to marriage. The shotgun wedding was a common end for the couple caught having premarital sexual relations, especially if a pregnancy resulted. Today, however, sexual relations are not necessarily a precursor to a long-term commitment.

Finding the One and Only: Mate Selection

Chapter 3 pointed out that "love" is the major reason Americans give for marriage. Yet is love really the magic wand that directs our mate selection? We certainly fall in love. There is no doubt about that. However, who we are attracted to and why is a complicated, still to be understood, process. Critics who argue against using love as a basis for marriage feel that Americans are seduced by the romantic ideal into ignoring all the practical considerations that help ensure a successful marriage; i.e., social and economic levels, education, age, religion, and so forth. Yet this is not really true. Our social system does take these factors into consideration and a close inspection of love finds that it does indeed incorporate some of these factors. You don't fall in love with just anybody.

First of all, there is a field of "desirables," or people to whom you are attracted. Within this field is a smaller group of "availables," those that are available and free to return your interest. You can meet them, they are not in love with another, they are unmarried, etc.

Availability is closely related to how we live. Our communities are usually organized into neighborhoods according to social class, and in America this usually means by economic level. So the people who live near-by will be socially and economically like us. Thus, middle-class whites tend to marry middle-class whites, lower-class whites tend to marry lower-class whites. Catholics tend to marry Catholics. This idea that like marries like, or, more specifically, that we tend to marry within our own group, is called *endogamy*.

Of course, there are exceptions to the rule of endogamy, but, generally, society aims us toward loving — and marrying — someone similar to ourselves. If you don't marry the girl or boy next door, you are likely to marry someone you meet at school. The American system of neighborhood schools and selective college attendance makes education one of the strongest endogamic factors directing mate selection. Or you may find your future mate through your family's social circle, your job, or your church. All of the groups you join tend to some degree to limit their membership to people who are similar in socioeconomic status as well as in their more obvious reasons for being part of the group.

Strange are the ways of love, but even so, it seldom happens that a banker's college-educated daughter falls in love with the un-educated son of an unskilled factory hand.

Alan Kerchhoff and Keith David (1962) suggest that we select a mate by passing him or her through a series of successive filters (see Figure 4-2). Proximity and "suitability" of background act as the initial filter. The couple has the likelihood of meeting if they live or work close to one another, and they will be interested in further exploration if each seems, at first appearance, suitable to the other. Suitability is determined by one's values, most of which are learned and internal-ized from one's parents and peers. The second filter is a more thor-ough exploration of attitudes and values. For example, the couple question each other about mutual friends, activities, and interests: "Oh, where do you go to school?" "I know some people who go

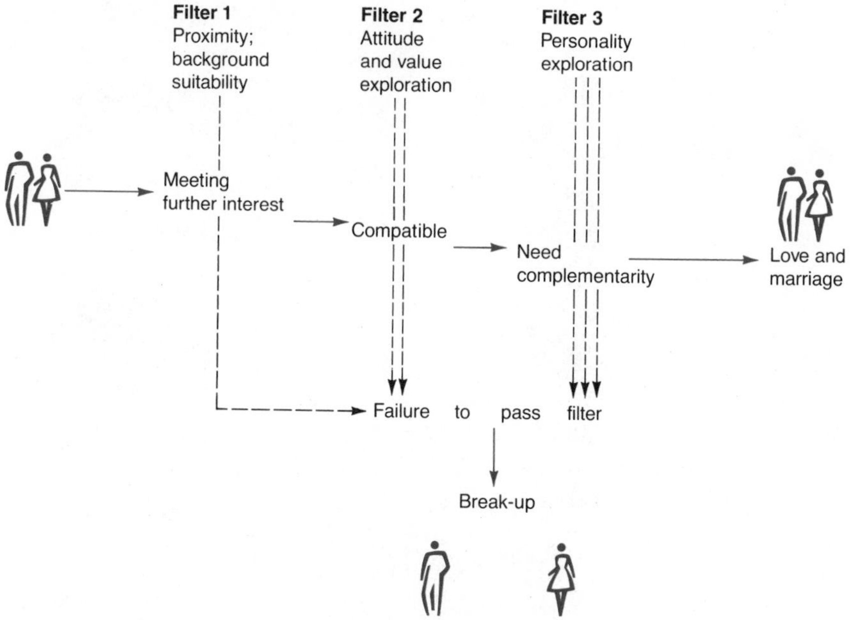

Filter 1
Proximity;
background
suitability

Filter 2
Attitude
and value
exploration

Filter 3
Personality
exploration

Meeting
further interest

Compatible

Need
complementarity

Love and
marriage

Failure   to   pass   filter

Break-up

Figure 4-2
Mate selection as
successive filters.

there, do you know Jim Black and Sally Bowles?" "What classes are you taking?" "Really, I'm taking French next semester." "Do you ski? I'm going next week." If the couple's attitudes and interests prove compatible, they will progress toward more subtle personality exploration, finding out whether their needs for affection, independence, security, and so on, are also compatible.

This kind of model is useful in understanding that mate selection is an ongoing evolving process. However, such an exact fixed set of filters or processes have yet to be proved (Levinger et al, 1970; Kerckhoff, 1977; Rubin & Levinger, 1974).

Theoretically, two principles guide mate selection. Endogamy, as we have seen, is marriage within a certain group, such as a caste, class, or religion. *Exogamy*, on the other hand, is a requirement that people marry outside their group. In our culture, requirements to marry outside your group are limited to incest and sex, that is, you may not marry a near relative or someone of your own sex. All states forbid marriage between parents and children, siblings (brothers and sisters), grandparents and grandchildren, and children and their uncles and aunts. Most states forbid marriage to first cousins and half-siblings, although some states do not. About half the states forbid marriage between stepparents and stepchildren, and about the same number prohibit marriage between a man and his father's former wife, or his son's former wife.

Until recently, most states had other prohibitions about whom one could marry. These prohibitions were generally termed *mis-*

Endogamic factors tend
to work against cross-
racial marriages.

cegenation laws because they prohibited interracial marriages. Most of
these laws were originally aimed at preventing white-Indian marriages,
but they also were used to prevent white-black and white-Asian marriages. As recently as the end of World War II, thirty of the forty-eight
states had such laws. Gradually, though, some states declared them
void; and, finally, in 1967, the U.S. Supreme Court declared all such
laws unconstitutional. By chance, the defendant's surname was Loving,
so the name of the landmark case, *Loving* v. *Virginia*, fits in well with
the American romantic ideal.

The other rule of exogamy, which until quite recently has been
taken for granted, is the requirement that we marry someone of the
opposite sex. This, of course, helps to ensure reproduction and con-

tinuance of the species. In the past few years, attempts by homosexuals to obtain more rights have also led to a ceremony called marriage for homosexuals. So far, though, such marriages have no legal value.

Endogamic and exogamic principles tend to guide our mate selection even though Americans tend to hide such mundane factors under the title of "love."

First Impressions to Engagement* Let us look more specifically at the mate-selection process for you, the individual. First impressions are usually belittled as superficial and unimportant. Yet without them, the process cannot begin. A favorable first impression must be made or there is no further interaction. *Physical attractiveness*, although subjective, tends to create the first appeal. This seems true for people of all ages, from children to the elderly. Fair or not, good-looking individuals are given preferential treatment. They are seen as more responsible for good deeds and less responsible for bad ones (Seligman et al, 1974), their evaluations of others have more potent impact (Sigall & Aronson, 1969), others are more socially responsive to them (Barocas & Karoly, 1972) and more willing to work hard to please them (Sigall et al, 1971). Physical attractiveness is more important to male evaluations of females than vice versa (Miller & Revinbark, 1970).

It is interesting too that there is a "halo effect"** operating in regard to physical attractiveness. Physically attractive persons are imbued with other positive qualities that might not actually be present. Dion, Berscheid, and Walster (1972) found that both males and females rated pictures of attractive individuals of both sexes as more sexually warm and responding, interesting, poised, sociable, kind, strong, and outgoing than less attractive people. They are also seen to be more competent as husbands and wives and to have happier marriages. Thus to be physically attractive is usually a real advantage at the first-impression stage of a relationship. However, this is not always true. Some persons are known to avoid highly attractive persons in order to enhance their chances of acceptance.

Your impressions of *cognitive compatibility* (how the other thinks, what their interests are, etc.) are also an important element of first impressions. In general, similarity seems to go with attraction because (1) another's similarity itself is directly reinforcing, (2) another's similar responses support the perceiver's sense of self-esteem and comfort, and (3) such responses indicate the other's future compatibility (Huston & Levinger, 1978, p. 125).

Generally, in choosing a partner, two factors must be considered after the first impression has aroused interest. First, you must believe that the potential partner's attributes will be found desirable. Second, there must be a degree of anticipation that the potential

---

*Much of the material in this next section is available in the fine research review article "Interpersonal Attraction and Relationships" by Ted L. Huston and George Levinger, found in the 1978 *Annual Review of Psychology*. Annual Reviews Inc.: Palo Alto, Calif.

**The "halo effect" is the fact that first impressions tend to influence succeeding evaluations.

partner will react favorably to your initiation of further interaction. Except for traditional females who won't take the initiative in pursuing a relationship because they feel it is improper to do so, most people will pursue it if the potential partner is in the field of "eligibles" and the two factors mentioned are favorable.

We usually try to further a relationship by various attraction-seeking strategies. In order to draw a potential partner's attraction, we may attempt to buoy the other's esteem by conveying our feelings that we think highly of them. We will probably try to do things for them. We will tend to agree with the other person and we will attempt to ascribe attractive characteristics to ourselves (Jones & Wortman, 1973).

Attraction tends to lead to *self-disclosure*. Intermediate degrees of disclosure may in turn lead to greater attraction, but this depends on the desirability of the information disclosed. Self-disclosure tends to lead to reciprocity. This is usually the early phase in a relationship when a lot of exciting mutual sharing takes place. "Is that the way you feel about it?" "That's great, because I feel the same way." As more is disclosed, the excitement increases because the potential for a meaningful relationship seems to be rapidly increasing. However, the speed with which one discloses personal aspects is also important. Perceived overly quick disclosure seems to arouse suspicions rather than trust (Rubin & Levinger, 1975; 1976).

Stambul and Kelly (1978), using retrospective reports of courtship provided by newlyweds, identified four relationship dimensions that interacted during courtship and finally led to marriage. The four dimensions are (1) love, (2) conflict and negativity, (3) ambivalence (mixed feelings), and (4) maintenance (problem-solving efforts and attempts to change behavior). Love and maintenance activities were reported to increase as a couple moved from casual dating through serious dating to engagement. Conflict and negativity increased from casual to serious dating and then leveled off, presumably as a consequence of the couple working out the terms of their relationship. Particularly interesting was the way the dimensions were interrelated at various stages. Early in the cycle, love was associated with efforts to maintain the relationship. Later on, however, love had little to do with maintenance activities. Instead, such activities were associated with conflict. Ambivalence was tied to conflict early in the relationship. Later it had more to do with concerns about love than conflict (Huston & Levinger, 1978, p. 140).

Although there has been much research done on interpersonal attraction, some of which we have been examining, our efforts to predict the evolution of a given individual relationship based on the personal characteristics of the partners have been primative at best and certainly not very successful (Huston & Levinger, 1978, p. 141). In fact, to date it has been next to impossible to determine in advance who one should marry to ensure a successful relationship.

As an example of the complexity of this matter, let us take a look at two marriages, one built on similar needs and one on complementary needs. In a marriage of similar needs, the partners begin with similar interests, energy levels, religion, socioeconomic background, age, and so on. They share many characteristics and hence seem well selected for each other. Ideally their relationship can lead to mutual satisfaction, but this is not always so. If, for example, the partners are competitive, the result can be disastrous. Consider the case of Henry and Hazel:

Henry and Hazel are alike in most respects, including being computer programmers, but Hazel has advanced more rapidly because her boss happens to like her. Henry, being competitive, feels like a loser and begins to resent his wife. He subtly puts her down and gradually becomes more critical of women in general. The more success Hazel has, the poorer their relationship becomes because Henry cannot accept, let alone find joy in, her success. To him, it only points up his weaknesses.

By contrast, a marriage of complementary needs is one in which each partner supplies something that the other lacks. For example, an extrovert may help an introvert become more social; an organized partner may help bring structure to the life of a disorganized partner; a relaxed partner may create an environment that helps ease the stress of a tense partner. This can be most beneficial but it cannot be counted on to happen reliably because often such differences begin to polarize the partners rather than drawing them together. For example, consider Carol and Otis:

Carol is so organized that Otis counts on her to pay the bills, make social arrangements, find the nail clippers, and so on. The more Otis depends on her for these things, the more organized Carol feels she needs to be, and she begins to try and organize Otis. On his part, Otis resents this pressure and becomes passively resistant (procrastinates and becomes forgetful and careless). Polarization has occurred.

Unfortunately there are no fully satisfying techniques for selecting marriage partners for lasting satisfaction. Even trial marriages have proven relatively ineffective (Hill, Rubin & Peplau, 1976). By way of summary, we can certainly point out some of the reasons for marrying that reduce marital success chances and, in addition, some helpful selection factors that seem to improve chances.

Reasons for Marriage that Tend to Reduce the Chances of Success

1. *Love at first sight*: It is easy to understand falling in love at first sight but hard to justify selecting a marriage partner on this basis alone.

2. *Escape from home*: Rather than dealing with a current relationship, many persons run away, hoping a new person or a new environment will be better. A marriage so conceived is often the first of a series of failures.

3. *Avoiding loneliness*: Loneliness can sometimes drive a person into a hasty marriage. To seek companionship in marriage is certainly a proper goal. However, if overcoming loneliness is one's only motivation for marriage, chances are high that this reason alone will not sustain a long-lasting relationship.

4. *Sexual attraction*: Unfulfilled sexual attraction, or guilt over sexual involvement, is a popular, yet weak, reason for marriage. An unusually fulfilling sexual relationship alone is not reason enough to marry.

Reasons for Marriage that Tend to Increase the Chances of Success

1. *Similar socioeconomic backgrounds*: Social research has clearly demonstrated that a similar socioeconomic status improves the chances of success in marriage.

2. *Similar energy levels*: Similar — or dissimilar — activity levels are fundamental to every other aspect of the relationship. For example, consider a marriage where the energy levels are dissimilar:

> Bill is a quiet person who needs eight to nine hours of sleep to function well the next day. His tempo is slow and deliberate but he finishes everything he starts. His slowness causes him to be habitually late. Joyce, his wife, needs little sleep and appears to be a bundle of energy. She does many things, finishing most of them quickly. She is always ready earlier if they are going out and finds she always seems to be waiting for Bill and nagging him to hurry. She likes companionship in the evening and dislikes going to bed before midnight. Bill usually wants to go to bed around 10 P.M. and is annoyed if she doesn't accompany him. Over several years of marriage the conflicts engendered by their differing energy levels have grown. They wonder if they should look for new partners better suited to their activity levels.

3. *Openness to growth or desire for stability*: A good relationship can occur between two partners who want stability or between two partners who want growth or change, but differences between partners in this respect are extremely difficult to overcome. For example, consider this marriage where the partners differ:

> Mary is comfortable with routine and stability. It makes her feel safe and secure to know exactly what is going to happen today, tomorrow, and next week. On the other hand, her husband, Jack, is very spontaneous and dislikes committing himself too far in advance to any plan of action. He says that this allows him freedom and flexibility, which he feels is necessary if a person is to grow and avoid stagnation. Their differing philosophies about growth and stability cause them to continually disagree.

Although it would be great to find "the one and only," apparently our chances of doing this are slim. In fact, within limits, any number of persons can become satisfactory and long-lasting partners, for the key to a successful relationship is more in the building and maintenance rather than in the selection of the imaginary perfect mate (see Chapters 5 and 6). The marriage ceremony is really a commencement, not a culmination. The key to successful relationships is not the initial mate-selection process so much as it is the couple's learning to communicate and compromise with one another.

The last step in the mate selection process before marriage is generally engagement, though this step is often less formal than it used to be. Engagement is a public announcement of a couple's intention to marry and serves as the preparation period for marriage. Often, the couple spends more time with each other's families. Parents seek to know the intended spouse better. The families sometimes arrange to meet. The couple now spends time discussing fundamentals such as living arrangements, children, and vocational plans, exploring each other's likes and dislikes, and personalities. In fact, E. Burgess and P. Wallin's classic study *Engagement and Marriage* (1953) indicates that the longer the length of friendship before marriage, the better the marital adjustment.

Engagement

Types of Engagements   There is the short, romantic engagement lasting from two to six months. Time is taken up with marriage plans, parties, and intense physical contact. Normally, such a short engagement period fails to lead the couple to more insights into one another's personalities. Indeed, so much time is taken up with marriage preparation that the couple may not have enough time for mutual exploration of their relationship.

The long, separated engagement, such as when one partner is away at college, also presents problems for the couple. There are two distinct philosophies of separation: "Absence makes the heart grow fonder" and "out of sight, out of mind." Unfortunately, in reality, the latter tends to prevail. Prolonged separation tends to defeat the purposes of the engagement. Also, the question of exclusivity of the relationship is raised. Does one date others during the separation? Dating others may cause feelings of insecurity and jealousy, while separation without dating is lonely and may cause hostility and dissatisfaction. In general, this type of engagement is usually unsatisfactory to both members of the couple.

Another engagement possibility is the long but inconclusive engagement. Here the couple puts off marriage because of economic considerations, deferance to parental demands, or just plain indecisiveness. When a couple is engaged for years but the engagement never culminates in marriage, it is probably a good sign that all is not well between them.

About one in four engaged couples break up temporarily. In addition, about half of the women and a third of the men in the Burgess and Wallin study had been previously engaged. The major reasons for the breakups appear to be simple loss of interest, recognition of an incompatible relationship, and the desire to reform the prospective mate. The major areas of disagreement tend to be matters of conventionality, families, and friends. However, broken engagements can be considered successful because the couple had the time during this formal commitment period to look more closely at one another and could realize that their marriage would not succeed.

Functions of Engagement What should a sensible engagement do? How can engagement help the couple achieve a better marriage? Basically, the couple should come to agree on fundamental life arrangements. Where will they live? How will they live? Do they want children? When? Will they both work? How will they handle their income and expenses?

The couple also needs to examine long-range goals in depth. Do they want similar things from life? Are their methods of obtaining these things compatible? Do their likes and dislikes blend? What role will religion play in their lives? How will they relate to one another's family? Friends? Work associates? They may not be able to answer such questions with complete finality, but at least tentative answers should be agreed upon. In fact, the most important premarital agreement may be an agreement as to how answers to such questions will be worked out in the future. A couple with a workable, problem-solving approach to life is certainly in a good position to find marital success.

Of course, it is during engagement that wedding plans are made.

An important part of the engagement is the premarital medical examination. It serves several useful functions. It might be that one of the partners has a general health problem that will require special care by the other partner. For example, marrying a diabetic means that diet will have to be carefully controlled and insulin administered periodically. There may be anatomical problems that would interfere with sex and/or conception. The girl's hymen may be totally blocking her vagina, which would make first intercourse difficult. The boy may have a low sperm count, which would make conception more difficult. Both need to be checked and cured of any possible venereal disease. The Rh factor in each partner's blood needs to be determined as this factor is of major importance in future pregnancy. Information on mutually acceptable methods of birth control can be given at this time. And, finally, each partner will have the opportunity to talk over questions about the coming marriage.

Such premarital counseling is always a good idea because often there is a certain blindness that comes with "being in love." It can be very helpful to discuss your ideas and plans with an objective third person such as a minister, marriage counselor, or mutual friend. A truly successful engagement period leads either to a successful marriage or to a broken engagement. An unsuccessful engagement in all likelihood will lead to marital failure.

The onset of puberty signals the beginning of adult sexuality. The age of sexual maturity, however, does not coincide in America with social acceptance of overt sexual behavior, especially sexual intercourse. Marriage is the socially accepted vehicle for sexual intercourse. Since marriage for most Americans does not occur until they are in their late teens or early twenties, there is a period of several years during which there is conflict between the dictates of biology and society. This is called the "sexual stress period."

Although much of our society does not consider premarital intercourse a legitimate outlet of sexual energies, a great deal of premarital intercourse is taking place. There appears to be increasing acceptance of premarital intercourse among American youth despite societal pressures against it. However, since there are social mores against premarital intercourse, those engaging in it usually face conflict within themselves. Questions about social, personal, religious, and psychological principles should be answered by anyone contemplating premarital intercourse.

Mate selection and sexuality for the young are handled mainly through the American invention of dating. Although dating varies greatly from person to person and place to place, there is some recognizable pattern to traditional dating, especially outside the large metropolitan areas. American dating is controlled by the youth themselves and involves relative freedom for the boy and girl to be alone together. This intensifies the pressure for the pair to move toward premarital intercourse as a means of handling their sexual drives.

Mate selection is an involved process that is not yet fully understood. However, it is fairly clear that similarities of socioeconomic backgrounds, energy levels, and degrees of restraint, help to increase the chances of marital success.

Engagement is the formal mate-selection step that signifies the couple's intention to marry. Engagement serves the important function of helping the couple to better understand one another and the marital relationship they will be entering. In most cases they come to know their potential in-laws more intimately during this time. Public announcement of their intentions places their relationship at a new level.

Summary

Teenage Sexuality

The continuing sexual revolution means that more and more parents will be confronting their children's sexuality long before their children have married. The double standard has more or less allowed parents to overlook their son's sexuality. An occasional "rubber" might slip from his wallet at an embarrassing moment, but this is far less threatening to most parents than finding birth control pills in their sixteen-year-old daughter's bathroom.

As we saw earlier (p. 120), Zelnik and Kantner (1977) found that the prevalence of sexual activity among never-married American women (ages 15-19) increased 30 percent between 1971 and 1976. The median age for first intercourse dropped to 16.2 years of age in 1976. Wolfe (1980, 255) found that 20 percent of her survey sample of women had had their first sexual experience by the age of fifteen.

Premarital pregnancy is usually the parent's greatest fear for their sexually active daughter, and such fear is well founded. As you read on page 123, illegitimacy has been increasing. The percentage of illegitimate births to teenage mothers has gone up even faster than the overall rates. In 1955, 30 percent of all illegitimate children were born to teenage mothers. By 1976, that figure had risen to 41 percent (U.S. Bureau of Census, Statistical Abstracts, 1977, 59).

It seems to many parents that society is conspiring with their daughters to increase sexual activity. The courts have now ruled that contraceptives may be prescribed for underage girls without parent's consent or knowledge (Carey vs. Population Services International, U.S. Supreme Court, 75-443, 1977). Even more controversial and upsetting to parents is another recent court decision (Planned Parenthood of Central Missouri vs. Danforth, U.S. Supreme Court, 428, U.S. 52, 1976) allowing abortions for underage girls without notification of parents nor their consent.* Thus, the trauma of abortion can be borne by a teenage girl without her parent's knowledge unless she comes forth with the information.

Such changes in the nation's laws recognize teenage sexuality by assuming that the teenager can take full responsibility for her

*For discussion of the changes in the law, see George Beiswinger, "The High Court, Privacy and Teenage Sexuality." *The Family Coordinator*. April, 1979, 191–198.

or his sexual activities. Such an assumption is challenged by many parents.

Sexuality among teenagers has created some surprising new problems. For one thing, there is the marked increase in venereal disease which, unattended, is far more serious than children care to know. For another, the new sexual rules place demands for performance on girls or boys who may be shy or slow, or maturing at a different rate from their peers. There may be no reason now to say "no" unless the reason is "I don't want to," and just such a strong assertion is hard for many young people who may find themselves undressed and in bed with a stranger when they really wish they were home having milk and cookies in the kitchen with their brothers and sisters. Peer pressure and social image have always deviled teenagers but now the stakes seem higher than ever and "going all the way" is thought to be a sign of that much-desired adulthood. Many children think they must act cool and easy about their bodies when the truth is they are still awkward, uncomfortable and anxious. Many others separate sexual feelings from emotional attachment of feelings of love and, consequently, have great trouble making any kind of real commitment when they are no longer driven by sexual need (Roiphe, 1975).

Indeed, this last point was echoed by many women polled in the large Cosmopolitan Survey reported by Wolfe in 1980. Thirty-three percent of these women said the sexual revolution had trivialized sex and caused a loss of emotional intensity; while twenty percent reported that they now had trouble refusing a man and sometimes had sexual experiences they didn't actually want. "The sexual revolution has given men an excuse for avoiding any sort of commitment. They never wanted commitment, and now we've let them think we don't want it either." "The sexual revolution has made women talk themselves into sexual behavior they don't really desire, under the pressure of being labeled uncool or possessive." Wolfe reports (265) that so many readers wrote negatively about the sexual revolution, expressing feelings for vanished intimacy, and the now elusive joys of romance and commitment, that perhaps a sexual counterrevolution is beginning in America.

If such sentiments are being expressed by many of the 106,000 women polled by Cosmopolitan (and these are the so-called liberated women volunteering to be surveyed), perhaps increasing teenage sexual expression is not as responsibly handled by the teenagers as the courts have assumed. Perhaps it is time that society supported parents in helping their teenage children to cope with emerging sexuality rather than labeling as old fashioned the concerned parents trying to maintain some control.

Chapter 5 ～

Contents

⁓ Marriage, Intimacy, Expectations, and the Fully Functioning Person

Marriage is the most intimate of all human interactions. At its heart, marriage is an interpersonal relationship between two persons, a man and a woman. Most people try to fulfill their psychological, material, and sexual needs within marriage. To the degree that they are successful, the marriage is successful. We know, however, that success in meeting these needs is difficult to achieve. This is reflected in America's high divorce rate (see Chapter 13).

You may remember that one of the primary functions of the contemporary American family is to provide emotional gratification to members, help them deal with emotional crises, and grow in the most fulfilling manner possible. In other words, marriage and the family *ideally* act as a haven, from which individual members can draw support and security when facing the challenges of our rapidly changing, technological society. A fully functioning family helps its members grow, mature, and become self-actualized individuals. A good marriage acts as a buffer against mental health problems—against alienation, loneliness, unhappiness, and emotional depression. In a word, ideally, marriage can be therapeutic, a curative to the problems of its members.

Modern marriage obviously has a long way to go before it can truly fulfill these positive functions. In this chapter and the next we shall explore marriage as an interaction between two individuals, suggest a philosophy and techniques, and present case histories to help individuals create marriages that are nurturing and supportive of self-fulfillment. Although we will be discussing interpersonal relations in the context of marriage, it is clear that the insights are applicable to any kind of human relationship: boyfriend-girlfriend, employer-employee, parent-child, and so forth.

Marriage

Most Americans expect to find fulfillment within marriage. Today, about 95 percent of the population will be married at some time during their life (Glick & Norton, 1977). They expect marriage to fulfill all of their psychological, sexual, and material needs. Never before have people asked so much of the marriage institution. Such high expectations contribute to great disappointments, as we shall see on p. 156. Failure oftens reflects high hopes, and certainly most Americans enter marriage with high hopes.

This chapter was written in collaboration with C. Norman Jacobs, a licensed psychologist in private practice in Santa Barbara, California.

Fulfilling Needs in Marriage

PSYCHOLOGICAL NEEDS You may remember that our sixth basic assumption (Chapter 1) is: "The family becomes increasingly important to its individual members as social stability decreases and/or people feel more isolated and alienated."

Mobility, increased anonymity, ever larger and more bureaucratic institutions, and lack of social relatedness all contribute to increasing feelings of loneliness and helplessness. Because of these feelings, our psychological need of intimacy has increased greatly, and we hope to find intimacy in marriage (Bach & Deutsch, 1970, pp. 14–15):

> What men and women seek from love today is no longer romantic luxury: it is an essential of emotional survival. More and more they hope to find in intimate love something of personal validity, personal relevance, a confirmation of one's existence. For in today's world, when men and women are made to feel as faceless as numbers on a list, they want intimate love to provide the feelings of worth and identity that preserve meaning and sanity.

Marriage will hopefully supply love and affection, emotional support and loyalty, stability and security, and romantic fulfillment as well as companionship. But this is a big order, which we will investigate more thoroughly in this chapter and in Chapter 6.

SEXUAL NEEDS Marriage is the only legitimate outlet for sexual energies recognized by American society. Indeed, sexual intercourse is a state-mandated part of marriage. If sexual needs are not fulfilled in a marriage, the marriage can be dissolved. Thus American spouses must function as lovers to their mates as well as fulfilling the long list of psychological needs. (See Chapter 9 for a fuller discussion of sexuality.)

MATERIAL NEEDS "Room and board" is a part of every marriage. Breadwinning and homemaking are essential to survival. Material needs also affect how successfully psychological and sexual needs are met. Marital disruption is considerably higher among families in economic trouble than among families satisfactorily meeting material needs. (See Chapter 7 for a detailed discussion of the family as an economic unit.)

Society recognizes that fulfilling these three areas of needs is a valid responsibility of the marriage institution. In fact, so important are the meeting of these needs for individuals, that failure to do so is recognized by all states as legitimate reason for divorce.

You and the State: Legal Aspects of Marriage Every society has some kind of ceremony whereby permanent relationships between the sexes are recognized and given status. The society (or the state) sets minimum standards for marriage in the interest of order and stability. In Western societies, the state is basically interested in supporting a monogamous marriage, assuring the "legitimacy of issue," protecting property and inheritance rights, and preventing marriages considered unacceptable, such as between close relatives.

In the United States, marriage laws are determined by individual states. But while there are differences in requirements, all states recognize marriages contracted in all other states. The language of California Senate Bill No. 252 is typical of many state bills relating to marriage:

> Marriage is a personal relation arising out of a civil contract, to which the consent of the parties capable of making that contract is necessary. Consent alone will not constitute marriage; it must be followed by the issuance of a license and solemnized as authorized (S.B. 252, Chapter 2, Article 1, Sec. 4100).

Marriage in the United States is a contract with obligations set by the state. Like all contracts, the marriage contract must be entered into by mutual consent, the parties must be competent and eligible to enter into the contract, and there is a prescribed form to the contract. However, unlike most contracts, which are between two parties, the marriage contract involves three parties, the man, the woman, and the state. The state prescribes certain duties, privileges, and restrictions. In addition, the contract cannot be dissolved by the mutual consent of the man and woman but must be dissolved by state action.

Table 5-1 is a summary of state marriage eligibility requirements. All states set minimum age requirements, and most require a medical examination and a waiting period between the examination and license issuance.

In a few instances a couple may be exempt from the marriage license law. Section 4213 of the California Civil Code allows couples living together to marry without applying for a license, provided they are eighteen or older. A certificate of such marriage must be made by a clergyman, delivered to the parties, and recorded in the records of the clergyman's church. Thirteen states recognize common law marriage if

Table 5-1 Summary of State Marriage Laws

State	Age With Consent		Age Without Consent		Blood Test Required	Wait for License	Wait after License	Common Law Marriage	Community Property
	Men	Women	Men	Women					
Alabama[b]	17	14	21	18	Yes	None	None	Yes	No
Alaska	18	16	21	18	Yes	3 days	None	No	Yes
Arizona	16[h]	16	18	18	Yes	None	None	No	No
Arkansas	17	16[j]	21	18	Yes	3 days	None	No	No
California	—[h]	—[h]	18	18	Yes	None	None	No	Yes
Colorado	16	16	18	18	Yes	None	None	Yes	No
Connecticut	16	16	18	18	Yes	4 days	None	No	No
Delaware	—[m]	16[j]	18	18	Yes	None	24 hours[c]	No	No
District of Columbia	18	16	21	18	Yes	3 days	None	No	No
Florida	18	16	21	21	Yes	3 days	None	No	No
Georgia	18	16	19	19	Yes	None[b]	None[k]	Yes	No
Hawaii	17[e]	16	20	18	Yes	None	None	No	No
Idaho	16	16	18	18	Yes	None[l]	None	Yes	Yes
Illinois[a]	—[e]	15[e]	21	18	Yes	None	None	No	No
Indiana	17	17	18	18	Yes	3 days	None	No	No
Iowa	18	16	18	18	Yes	3 days	None	Yes	No
Kansas	—[e, h]	—[e, h]	18	18	Yes	3 days	None	Yes	No
Kentucky	18	16	18	18	Yes	3 days	None	No	No
Louisiana[a]	18	16	18	18	Yes	None	72 hours	No	Yes
Maine	16	16	18	18	No	5 days	None	No	No
Maryland	18	16	21	18	None	48 hours	None	No	No
Massachusetts	—[h]	—[h]	18	18	Yes	3 days	None	No	No
Michigan[a]	—	16	18	18	Yes	3 days	None	No	No
Minnesota	—	16[a]	18	18	None	5 days	None	No	No
Mississippi[b]	17	15	21	21	Yes	3 days	None	No	No
Missouri	15	15	21	18	Yes	3 days	None	No	No
Montana	—[h]	—[h]	19	19	Yes	5 days	None	Yes	No

Source: Adapted from a table compiled by William E. Mariano, *The World Almanac and Book of Facts*, 1975 Edition; Copyright © Newspaper Enterprise Association, Inc., New York, 1974, p. 961.
And from Laurel Leff. "You, Living Together and the Law." *Cosmopolitan*, 1978 (Dec.). pp. 194–200.
Many states have additional special requirements; contact individual state.
[a]Special laws applicable to nonresidents. [b]Special laws applicable to those under 21 years. [c]24 hours if one or both parties are residents of state; 96 hours if both parties are nonresidents. [d]None, but male must file affidavit. [e]Parental consent plus court's consent required.

a couple can prove they have lived together as husband and wife for seven or more years.

The state also sets a number of other standards. It limits how closely within family relationships one may marry. It considers a marriage invalid if consent to marry is obtained by fraud or under duress, if there is mental incapacity, if there is physical inability to perform sexually, or if either party is already married.

No particular marriage ceremony is required, but the parties must declare, in the presence of the person solemnizing the marriage, that they take each other as husband and wife, and the marriage must be witnessed, usually by two persons. Although some states are quite specific, there is a general trend away from uniform marriage vows. Traditional vows reflect the permanence expected in marriage by society (although such permanence seems difficult to achieve): ". . . to have and to hold from this day forward, for better or worse, for richer,

State	Age With Consent		Age Without Consent		Blood Test Required	Wait for License	Wait after License	Common Law Marriage	
	Men	Women	Men	Women					
Nebraska	18	16	19	19	Yes	5 days	None	No	
Nevada	—	16	18	18	None	None	None	No	Yes
New Hampshire[a]	14[e]	13[e]	18	18	Yes	5 days	None	No	No
New Jersey[a]	—	16	18	18	Yes	72 hours	None	No	No
New Mexico	16	16	21	21	Yes	None	None	No	No
New York	16	14	18	18	Yes	None	24 hours[g]	No	No
North Carolina[a]	16	16	18	18	Yes	None	None	No	No
North Dakota[a]	—[h]	15	18	18	Yes	None	None	No	No
Ohio[a]	18	16	18	18	Yes	5 days	None	Yes	No
Oklahoma	18	15	21	18	Yes	None[f]	None	Yes	No
Oregon	18[e]	15[e]	18	18	Yes	7 days	None	No	No
Pennsylvania	16	16	18	18	Yes	3 days	None	Yes	No
Rhode Island[a,b]	18	16	18	18	Yes	None	None	Yes	No
South Carolina	16	14	18	18	None	24 hours	None	Yes	No
South Dakota	18	16	18	18	Yes	None	None	No	No
Tennessee[b]	16	16	21	21	Yes	3 days	None	No	No
Texas	16	16	18	18	Yes	None	None	Yes	Yes
Utah[a]	16	14	21	18	Yes	None	None	Yes	Yes
Vermont[a]	18	16	18	18	Yes	None	5 days	No	No
Virginia[a]	18	16	18	18	Yes	None	None	No	No
Washington	17	17	18	18	d	3 days	None	No	Yes
West Virginia	18[h]	16	18	18	Yes	3 days	None	No	No
Wisconsin	18	16	18	18	Yes	5 days	None	No	No
Wyoming	18	16	21	21	Yes	None	None	No	No
Puerto Rico	16	16	21	21	f	None	None	No	No
Virgin Islands	16	14	21	18	None	8 days	None	No	No

[f]None, but a medical certificate is required. [g]Marriage may not be solemnized within 10 days from date of blood test. [h]Statute provides for obtaining license with parental or court consent with no stated minimum age. [i]Under 16, with parental and court consent. [k]All those between 19 and 20 cannot waive 3-day waiting period. [l]If either under 18 — wait full 3 days. [m]If under stated age, court consent required.

for poorer, in sickness and in health, to love and to cherish, 'till death do us part."

About 75 percent of all marriages in the United States take place in a church. The state vests the clergy with the legal right to perform the marriage ceremony. Most faiths in the United States consider marriage a sacrament. God is called on to witness and bless the marriage: "Those whom God hath joined together let no man put asunder."

The marriage ceremony commits the couple to a new status. It sets minimum limits of marital satisfaction. Typical of these directives are those found in Title 8, Husband and Wife, of California's Senate Bill No. 252:

> Husband and wife contract toward each other obligations of mutual respect, fidelity and support.

> The husband is the head of the family. He may choose any reasonable place or mode of living, and the wife must conform thereto.

> Neither husband or wife has any interest in the property of the other,

Community Property

...rights, obligations, and respon-sibilities. Yet, we don't get to read the contract before we sign it. Indeed, if we did, we might not sign it at all.

Many people are beginning to ask why the marriage contract cannot be written to the personal specifications of the couple marrying. Although a personal contract is void where it contradicts a state marital obligation, such contracts can be useful in getting any couple to think out more clearly just what they expect, and what is expected of them, in a marriage. Such a personal contract may be private, known only to the partners. Some may choose to make the contract or parts of it public in their marriage ceremony. Others may attempt to make it legally binding by having an attorney draw it and making it a matter of public record. Contracts may cover any arrangements the couple wants to spell out. In general, they cover such things as whether children are desired, and, if so, when and how many. They cover whatever economic arrangements the couple plans. (This is especially true of remarriages.) They cover household responsibilities. In more open marriages, the contract may spell out what the partners' expectations and limitations are in regard to

others. Some contracts cover a set period of time, after which they can be renegotiated.

Susan Edmiston (1972) has more detailed suggestions in her Utopian Marriage Contract:

1. The wife's right to use her maiden name or any other name she chooses.

2. What surname the children will have: husband's, wife's, a hyphenated combination, a neutral name or the name the children choose when they reach a certain age.

3. Birth control: Whether or not, what kind and who uses it. (One couple — the wife can't use the pill — splits the responsibility 50-50. Half the time she uses a diaphragm, the other half he uses a condom.)

4. Whether or not to have children, or to adopt them, and if so how many.

5. How the children will be raised?

6. Where the couple will live: Will the husband be willing to move if the wife gets a job offer she wants to take? Separate bedrooms? Separate apartments?

7. How child care and housework will be divided: The spouse who earns less should not be penalized for the inequities of the economic world by having to do a larger share.

8. What financial arrangement will the couple embrace? If husband and wife are both wage earners, there are three basic possibilities.

a. Husband and wife pool their income, pay expenses, and divide any surplus. (This was Leonard and Virginia Woolf's arrangement. At the end of the year, after payment of expenses, they divided the surplus between them equally so each had what they called a personal "hoard.")

b. Husband and wife pay shares of expenses pro-portional to their incomes. Each keeps whatever he or she has left.

c. Husband and wife each pay 50 percent of expenses. Each keeps what he or she has left.

If the husband earns sig-nificantly more than the wife, the couple might consider (a) that the disparity is a result of sexist discrimination in employment and there should perhaps be some kind of "home reparations program" to offset this inequity, and (b) whether the couple really has an equal partnership if one has greater economic strength, and therefore possibly greater power psychologically, in the relationship.

9. Sexual rights and freedoms. Although any arrangement other than monogamy would clearly be against public policy, in practice some people make arrangements such as having Tuesdays off from one another.

10. The husband might give his consent to abortion in advance.

but neither can be excluded from the other's dwelling (except under certain circumstances recognized by the court).

The respective interests of the husband and wife in community property during the continuance of marriage relations are present, existing and equal interests under the management and control of the husband.

Note that these directives give authority to the man in a number of areas. The feminist movement is trying to change such laws so that marriage can truly be an arrangement between equals. These laws might also be found invalid if the Equal Rights Amendment is passed (see Chapter 2).

Marriage, then, is much more than "just a piece of paper." It commits the couple to a new set of obligations and responsibilities. In essence, the couple in many ways marries the state and it is the state to whom they must answer if the prescribed responsibilities are not met.

The Transition from Single to Married Life

Married life is indeed different from single life. Suddenly, marriage brings duties and obligations. One is no longer responsible for only oneself but now shares responsibility for two people and perhaps more if and when children arrive.

Furthermore, your identity is changed with marriage. No longer are you simply you, you are now Bill's wife or Marge's husband or Randy's father or mother. You become interdependent with the others in your family, and lose the independence you had when single. You enter a double-person pattern of life: planning together, working together, and playing together become more important than what you do as an individual. Decisions now involve the desires of two people and often become a discussion or debate and end in a compromise rather than you simply doing what you want (Bowman, 1974, pp. 195–198).

The transition from dating to establishing a home and family is often a large step for both partners. The girl may have cooked some lovely dinners for her boyfriend, but cooking 1095 meals a year for two on an often tight budget is a far greater challenge. Planning out a month financially is certainly more difficult than raising money for a weekend of skiing with one's girlfriend or boyfriend. In fact, living within some kind of a family budget is a difficult transition for many newly marrieds. Prior to their marriage they were used to spending their income as they wished. Now another person must be consulted and what they earn must be shared (see Chapter 7).

Leisure time activities, which are often spontaneous and unplanned when one is single, now must be planned with another person, and often compromises must be worked out. As we shall see with Bill and Marge, conflicting leisure time pursuits are difficult to resolve.

New relations must be developed with both sets of parents after marriage. One's primary relationship is now with one's spouse

rather than with one's parents. Also, one must learn to relate with one's in-laws. Prior to marriage, there usually isn't much interaction with the parents of the girlfriend or boyfriend. But, after marriage, interaction will be more frequent and more important. Failure to build a satisfactory in-law relationship makes married life much more difficult since one's spouse's parental relationship is usually very important to them.

The sexual relationship may also involve a big transition. Premarital sexuality may have been restrained, covert, and only partially satisfying. Hopefully, the marital sexual relationship will become fully expressive and satisfactory to both partners. However, this may not occur if one or both of the partners have been taught excessive control and repression of their sexual impulses. The large number of sexual technique manuals, lack of sexual enjoyment, and the increasing interest in sex therapy attest to the problems in this area of the relationship and the greater openness about sex.

There are, of course, many other transitions that must be made if a marriage is to be successful. Basically, all the transitions are from the self-centeredness of childhood to the other-centeredness of adulthood. To consider the likes and dislikes of one's partner, to compromise one's desires at times in favor of the other's, to become a team that pulls together rather than in opposing directions, to become a pair that has more going than the sum total of the two individuals making up the pair, these are a few of the things that indicate a successful marriage. If the majority of transitions cannot be made by one or both partners, the chances of the marriage being successful are slim.

Bill and Marge — Married Singles

Both Bill and Marge were active singles until they met, fell in love, and married in their mid-twenties. Bill's single life pattern had involved a great deal of time for sports, especially trips to the desert to ride his motorcycle with other dirt-bike enthusiasts.

Marge had spent a great deal of time with her office colleagues, going to picnics, bowling on the office team, and window shopping on Saturdays. Sunday was reserved for church. Although she had dated a great deal, her religious background had restricted her sexual activities. She had spent much of her time on dates defending herself. Although she was no prude about her sexuality, she did not feel it necessary to sleep with every date.

As the newness of marriage begins to wear off, both Bill and Marge find themselves somewhat bored and uncomfortable with the other's activities. Marge did go out to the desert twice when Bill went motorcycling, but she found it dirty, boring, and lonely since she didn't know the other women and the fellows were away from camp riding all day.

Bill doesn't like bowling although he tried once or twice. He doesn't like being alone at night either and so pressures Marge to give up the bowling team. "After all, why am I married if I have to be alone in the evening?" he complains.

Marge also has great difficulty relaxing and enjoying sexual relations with Bill. For so long, her impulses, when approached sexually, had been to back away and defend herself that she finds it difficult to change. Bill, feeling this tension in her, takes it as a rejection of himself rather than as a transition stage that Marge has to pass through.

He begins flirting with other women because it makes him feel good when they respond. He even entertains the idea of going out with other women behind Marge's back. "It's Marge's hangup that our sex life isn't very good," Bill often says.

Gradually, each falls back into old single-life patterns and they spend less and less of their time together. Although they are still married, they do almost nothing together. Bill spends more and more of his time on motorcycle trips, and Marge has joined a second bowling team. Their friends wonder if they ever see one another.

Of course, the transition from single to married status does not end the need for change. As time passes, the marriage also will change and require further transitions of both partners. For example, the coming of children places a whole new set of demands on the married couple (see Chapter 12).

In general, the couple contemplating marriage seldom realizes the extent of the changes necessary, both in themselves and in their partner, to make a successful marriage. After all, "love" should take care of all of the transitions from single to married life. "We can get along now, of course we'll get along after we marry."

Marriage: A Myriad of Interactions

Each day we usually interact with numerous people. On the job, we talk with colleagues, receive instructions from superiors, and give orders to those who work for us. At the stores we talk with salespeople. On our way home we interact with the other drivers or with people on the bus. However, all of these human interactions are relatively simple. For example, when buying something at a store, I simply want to make my purchase. I don't need to know how the salespeople are feeling, how their children are doing in school, how their sex life is going, how they feel about their jobs. I need only relate to them as a customer. The interaction begins and ends at a rather superficial level.

This is not so with marriage. The family, perhaps more than any other institution, is an arena of intimate and complex interaction. Not only are there literally hundreds of interactions within a family each day but they vary in infinite ways. We can think of these interactions as ranging from pure intellectual interaction with no emotional involvement to strong emotional involvement. Note in the following conversations how the interactions move from superficial and intellectually distant to ones showing care, commitment, and emotional involvement:

"Good morning. How are you feeling?"
" 'Morning. Fine. How're you?"

"Good morning. How are you feeling? Did you sleep well?"
" 'Morning. I slept fine. Hope you did, too."

"Good morning. I'm really glad to see you looking so well this morning! I'm glad the headache went away."
" 'Morning. It's great not to be in pain. Thanks so much for reminding me to take those aspirin, they really did the trick! Don't know what I'd do without you!"

"Good morning! You know, it's always wonderful to wake up in the morning with you!"
"It makes me feel so good when you say that! I'm so happy with you!"

The first interaction is pretty superficial, a general morning greeting. The next, while still fairly superficial, demonstrates more concern and awareness of the other person. The concern deepens in the next interaction — the first speaker remembers the other's headache of the previous day or night and is happy that the partner is out of pain. The partner expresses gratitude for the concern and for the partner's aid. And the last interaction demonstrates a deep emotional level of sharing between the partners.

Let's also look at some of the role interactions that go on in a marriage:

man	⟷	woman
lover	⟷	lover
friend	⟷	friend
provider	⟷	provided-for
provider	⟷	provider
spendthrift	⟷	budgeter
father*	⟷	child*
child*	⟷	mother*
child*	⟷	child*
taker	⟷	giver
giver	⟷	taker
teacher	⟷	learner
learner	⟷	teacher
learner	⟷	learner
employer	⟷	worker
worker	⟷	worker
colleague	⟷	colleague
leaning tower	⟷	tower of strength
tower of strength	⟷	leaning tower

Obviously, the list of possibilities is endless! And think of the complications that can arise when children enter the picture (children will be discussed in Chapter 12). Remember also that cross interactions can occur, such as between lover and friend or lover and teacher. For example, the friend can interact with the woman, the lover, and so on down the list. Thus, when I wake up in the morning and say to my wife "How do you feel?", it is far more meaningful than saying the same thing to a passing acquaintance. It could mean, "I am concerned about you," as a friend, "I'd like to have sex with you," as a lover, "will you be able to work today?" as an employer, and so forth. And to further complicate matters, the spouses may not agree on what the meaning is. She may take it to mean he'd like to make love before getting up, whereas he really meant to inquire how she was feeling as she was sick the day before. Complicated, isn't it?

To manage successfully the hundreds of interactions that occur in marriage all of the time would be a miracle indeed. But to manage them better each day is a worthy and attainable goal. If people can be successful in marriage, the chances are they will also be successful in most other interpersonal relations because the others will almost certainly be far simpler than the marriage relationship.

WHAT DO YOU THINK?

What kind of marital role expectations do you think you have learned?

Are they similar to the roles your parents fulfilled in their marriage?

What do you think are the two most important roles your spouse should fulfill?

What would you do if your spouse disagreed with you and didn't wish to fulfill one of these two roles you consider important?

*These are not interactions between real children and real parents, but interactions that involve one partner acting like an authority or parent and the other partner reacting as a dependent child. The child-child interaction involves the partners acting like children with each other.

Marital satisfaction, of course, depends on a great many factors. In addition, each couple may value the factors differently, thus making it very difficult to identify any general principles. But, if we are to understand the dynamics of prolonged, mutually fulfilling marriages, we must identify some of the generally important elements on which they depend.

Several basic factors do show up clearly in the literature on marital satisfaction. [Good summaries of this literature can be found in Hicks and Platt (1970) and Laws (1971).] These include:

1. *Length of marriage:* Generally, satisfaction is rated higher at the beginning and in the later years of marriages, with a drop in satisfaction experienced in the middle years (see number 2, below) (for a fuller discussion of this factor and the next, see Rollins and Cannon, 1974).

2. *Children:* Children tend to put a strain on marriages, and some of the drop in satisfaction experienced in the middle years of marriages is probably due to the effect of children. Childless couples on the average report greater marital satisfaction.

3. *Adequacy of performance of marital roles:* A recent study (Chadwick et al, 1976) indicates that "adequacy of role performance of both self and spouse and spouse's conformity to expectations [see also number 5, below] emerged as the strongest predictors of satisfaction." Mary Hicks and Marilyn Platt (1970) found that the husband's performance was crucial since in most cases he was the economic support of the family and his status determined theirs.

4. *Similarity of socioeconomic background:* Having similar religious and social class backgrounds, and similar educational levels reduces conflict in a marriage and increases communication. The partners feel they can understand and are understood by each other.

5. *Shared expectations about appropriate marital behavior:* Again, shared expectations reduce conflict and give each partner a sense of security in knowing the other will behave appropriately. The reverse is also true: Marital satisfaction goes down when spouses do not conform to each other's expectations of appropriate behavior.

In that regard, Judith L. Laws (1971) found that the wife's conformity to her husband's expectations was more crucial to the marriage's success than the reverse. She also found that wives were more tolerant of disappointment when their husbands' behavior did not conform to their expectations than were husbands when their wives did not conform to expectations. James Hawkins and Kathryn Johnson (1969) add that a person who experiences a lack of conformity between his or her expectations and personal behavior will also experience a lowering of marital satisfaction.

Marital Expectations

In a very real sense, humans create their own world. The wonderful complexity of the human brain allows us to plan, organize, and concern ourselves with what we think should be as well as what is; we predict our future and have expectations about ourselves, our world, our marriage, our spouse, and our children. In our earlier discussion of "love" (Chapter 3) we noted that love often acts like the proverbial "rose-colored glasses" in that we don't see the people we love as they really are, but rather as we wish (expect) them to be.

In essence, the world is as we perceive it, and our perceptions are based in part on the input of our senses as well as what we personally do with that input — accept it, reject it, interpret it, change it, color it — essentially, put our own meaning on it. The study of how people experience their world is called *phenomenology*. It is important to realize that most people react to their perceptions of the world rather than to what the world may be in scientific reality. A simple example may clarify this point. Let's say we place a straight metal rod halfway into a pool of clear water. The rod will appear bent or broken because of the refraction of the light waves by the water. Yet, since we have measured and examined the rod scientifically, we know it is straight. But, how would people react if they knew nothing about light refraction and had never before seen a partially submerged object? To them, the rod is bent, and they would act on that perception. On the other hand, most of us have learned that light waves will be refracted by the water and appear bent, so we will assume that the rod is straight even though our eyes tell us it is bent. In other words, because of our training, we have learned that our perceptions do not always reflect the objective world — we have learned that appearances can be deceptive.

How does all this relate to marriage? Unfortunately, when it comes to our interactions with other people, we often forget that our perceptions may be deceived by appearances or that our spouse may have different perceptions or even a different "reality." For example, consider the following situation:

> Jim asks his steady out for Friday night. She says she's sorry, but she has to go out of town to visit her grandparents (she is actually going to do this). Jim becomes jealous and angry and accuses her of having a date with someone else. No matter how she reassures him that she is indeed visiting her grandparents, he remains unconvinced. When she returns from her visit, he is even more angry and upset because of her refusal to tell him the truth as he feels it to be.

Jealousy can be a very difficult emotion with which to cope. We can see that his behavior is being dictated by his own subjective view of the world, not reality. Yet, even though we know and his girl knows that his view is incorrect, the difficulty is just as real as if he were correct. Since he is angry, they may fight and not speak to each other for a week. If Jim finds out from others that she was indeed visiting her grandparents, he will be apologetic and sorry that he acted "that way." Remember, we act on our perceptions and they are not necessarily the same as objective reality.

The Honeymoon Is Over: Too High Expectations

> One morning, after Jim and Sue have been married for about a year, Sue awakens and "realizes" that Jim is no longer the same man she married. She accuses him of changing for the worse: "You used to think of great things to do in the evenings, and enjoyed going out all the time. Now you just seem to want to stay home." Jim insists, of course, that he has not changed, he *is* the same person he has always been, and that, indeed, he always said he looked forward to quiet evenings alone with her.

This interaction may be signaling that the honeymoon is over for Jim and Sue. This is a very important point in most marriages. It usually means that the unrealistic, overly high expectations about marriage and one's mate created by "love" are being reexamined. In a successful relationship, it means that subjective perceptions are becoming more objective, more realistic. It means also that we are at last coming to know our mate as a real human being rather than as a projection of our own expectations.

Unfortunately, however, some people throw away the real person in favor of their own idealizations. In essence, they are in love with their own dreams and ideals and not with the person they married. Originally their mate became the object of their love because the mate met enough of their expectations that they were able to project their total set of expectations onto them. But this state of affairs is possible only so long as they are able to overlook and deny the things in the mate that don't fit their idealized image of what a mate should be. Living together day in and day out makes it only a matter of time until each partner is forced to compare ideals with the real flesh-and-blood spouse and seldom, if ever, will the two coincide exactly.

Romantic ideals lead us to expect so much from our mate and marriage that disappointment is almost inevitable. But how we cope with this disappointment determines, in part, the direction our marriage will take when the "honeymoon is over." If we refuse to reexamine our ideals and expectations and instead blame our mate for the discrepancy, then trouble lies ahead. On the other hand, if we

Some conflict in marriage is to be expected.

realize that the source of disappointment is within, caused by our own unrealistic expectations, we can then look forward to getting to know our mate as a real human being. Further reflection also makes it clear that recognition of our mate as a real human being complete with frailties and problems rather than as some kind of perfect godlike creature greatly eases the strain on the marriage and on ourselves. No one can live up to perfection. That is, realizing the humanness of our partner allows us to relax, to be human as well. If my partner can make mistakes and be less than perfect, so can I, thank goodness. Of course, each person can work to become better. But who will ever be perfect?

But, consider what can happen if we are unwilling to give up our expectations of an ideal mate:

Carol, the Perpetual Seeker

Carol's father died when she was eight years old. Her mother never remarried because she felt no other man could live up to her dead husband. Through the years Carol was told how wonderful and perfect her father had been, both as a man and as a husband.

As a teenager, Carol fell in love often and quickly, but the romances always ended soon, usually, she said, because the boy would disappoint her in some way. The only romance that lasted was when she met a boy while on a summer vacation to California. Even though they knew one another for only a month, they continued their romance via mail during the following year. They met again the next summer. Carol was now nineteen. Three months after parting when school resumed, after many letters declaring their love and loneliness, Carol was asked to come to California and marry her friend. She assured her mother that he was the right man: strong, responsible, and loving, just as her father had been.

They married and everything seemed to go well. However, by the end of the first year Carol's mother was receiving letters telling of how Carol's husband was changing for the worse, how he wasn't nearly the man Carol had thought him to be. She was questioning whether he would ever be a good father, and noted that he didn't have the drive for success that her dad had had at his age.

Two years after marrying, Carol divorced her husband. She had met an exciting, great man who had given a talk to her women's sensitivity group. He was all of the things her husband wasn't, and, incidentally, all of the things her father had been. She married him not long after her divorce was final.

Carol is now thirty years old and married to her third husband, about whom she complains a great deal.

WHAT DO YOU THINK?

Why does Carol seem to find so little satisfaction with her husbands?

Why did Carol's romance persist so long with her first husband before marriage while all of her earlier relationships dissolved quickly?

What are the qualities of your dream spouse?

How does your relationship with your parents influence your marriage ideals?

How can Carol find satisfaction with her husbands?

Love or Marriage? That disappointment with marriage is almost inevitable makes sense if we consider that our prevailing cultural view of marriage as expressed in the mass media is one of overly high romantic expectation. We are also led to expect that the powerful emotional sensations of romantic love will remain indefinitely throughout our marriage.

One of the greatest disappointments newly married couples face is the fading of romantic love with time. Romantic love depends on an incomplete sexual and emotional consummation of the relationship. Physical longing is a tension between desire and fulfillment. In a marriage where sexual desire is fulfilled, romantic love changes to a more stable feeling of affection which, while less intense and frenzied than romantic love, is more durable. However, since we have been flooded with romantic literature and movies about love and marriage, we are often quite unprepared for this natural change in the emotional quality of the relationship. For example, let's take a look at a not untypical couple:

> Allison fell in love with Mike when she was sixteen and he was seventeen. Neither of them had ever been in love before. After two years they are still deeply in love and Mike persuades Allison to marry him because he is tired of dealing with their guilt about pre-marital sex, worrying about pregnancies, and hiding their intimacy from parents. But, after two years of marriage, Allison finds herself not nearly as excited by Mike as she had been earlier. The couple is struggling to make a living and she feels that "the bloom is going from the rose." One day, as she listens to a lecture from her art history teacher, she feels a lump in her throat, a thumping in her heart, and a weakness in her knees. This was the way she felt about Mike two years ago, and she suddenly realizes that she doesn't have these feelings for Mike any more. She can't tell Mike and she is afraid of her feelings for the teacher, so she drops the class and tells Mike it's time for them to have a baby.

It's clear that Allison believes feelings of sexual attraction are "love." Since American folklore says you can't love more than one person (at least at the same time), she must either hide from these feelings of tension and longing, as she does, or believe that she is no longer in love with Mike and perhaps consider a divorce. Narrowly defining love as only "the great turn on" means that all marriages will eventually fail since that intense feeling fades with time.

Mixed Expectations   But, even if expectations about marriage are realistic, spouses may have different expectations about marital roles. This is especially true in regard to roles that each expects the other to play in marriage. Roles that have historically been fulfilled by one sex or the other are no longer clear-cut. For example, the husband is no longer only the breadwinner and the wife is no longer only the homemaker. However, as we have learned, many of our expectations about role behavior have come from our experience with our parents' marriage. And often we are unaware of these expectations. For example, consider the possibilities for conflict in the following marriage:

Randy and Susan: Who Handles the Money?

In Randy's traditional Midwestern family, his father played the dominant role. His mother was given an allowance with which to run the house. His father made all of the major monetary decisions.

In Susan's sophisticated New York family, both her mother and her father worked hard at their own individual careers. Because they both worked, they decided to each control their own money. While both contributed to a joint checking account used to run the household, individual desires were fulfilled from their own personal funds. There was seldom any discussion about monetary decisions since each was free to spend his or her own money.

Randy and Susan get married after Susan has been teaching school for a year and Randy gets a good position with a New York bank. Randy feels that since he has a good job, it is no longer necessary for Susan to work. He can support them both, which he feels is the proper man's marriage role. He sees no reason for Susan to have her own bank account. After all, if she wants something, all she has to do is ask him for it.

WHAT DO YOU THINK?

Who do you think should control the money in marriage? Why?

What feelings will Susan have when she asks Randy for money to buy a new dress?

What do you think will happen if she quits her job as he wants?

Who controls the money in your family?

Did your parents have any areas of conflicting expectations? If so, what were they?

Chapter 14 examines some of the many alternatives open to people contemplating close intimate relationships today. This increasing diversity of relationships also means that children in the future may be raised quite differently from the way we were. Thus, their expectations of marital roles will also probably be quite different from ours. And their marriages may quite well involve a flexible interchange of roles.

80 Percent I Love You — 20 Percent I Hate You*   Many people hold the expectation that their partner will meet all of their needs, indeed that it is their duty to do this if they love you. To the extent that they fail to live up to this expectation, they are "bad" spouses. However, human beings are complex. It is probably impossible for any two people to completely fulfill one another's needs. If a pair could mutually satisfy even 80 percent of one another's needs, it would be a minor miracle.

The expectation of total need fulfillment within a marriage ruins many marital relationships. Even if the minor miracle of one's spouse meeting 80 percent of your needs occurs, the following destructive interaction will often also occur. As time passes, the spouse with the unmet needs longs to have them satisfied. He will accuse his spouse of failure and indifference. "What's wrong with you that you can't or won't meet my needs?" he keeps asking. Conflict will grow since the accused spouse feels unfairly accused, defensive, and inferior. Life will revolve more and more around the negative 20 percent rather than the positive 80 percent. This is especially true if the partners are possessive and block each other from any outside need grat-

*Adapted from Frank Cox, *Youth, Marriage and the Seductive Society*, 2nd ed. (Dubuque, Iowa: Wm. C. Brown Company, 1974), pp. 147–148.

ification. Unless such interaction is broken, it is quite possible for a spouse to suddenly "fall in love" and leave his mate for someone else. These sudden departures are catastrophic to all the parties. And the ensuing relationship also often fails because of the same dynamics. For example, the newly "in love" spouse has met a person who meets some of his unfulfilled needs and because these needs have become so exaggerated, he concludes that at last he has met the "right" person. "Right" means someone who will meet *all* of his needs. In his excitement, he often overlooks the fact that the new love does not fulfill certain other needs that have long been met by the discarded spouse. Since those needs have always been met, they are taken for granted. But careful inventory of the new love's need-meeting potentials might disclose the fact that she is incapable of meeting a large portion of the 80 percent which the former spouse met. Hence, in a few years, the same conflicts will reappear, granted over different unmet needs, and the whole process of disenchantment will reoccur.

Let's take a closer look at this process. We'll call our spouses Carl and Jane. They are very much in love. Their friends are amazed at how compatible and well-suited they are to one another. Each expects total fulfillment within the marriage. Jane enjoys staying up late and insists that Carl, who likes to go to bed early to be fresh for work, stay up with her as she hates to be alone. At first, Carl obliges but he gradually returns to his habitual bedtime. But, of course, he can't sleep well since he feels guilty leaving Jane alone, which, she reminds him, demonstrates his lack of love and uncaring attitude. She tries going to bed earlier, but also can't sleep well since she isn't sleepy, and so she simply lies there resenting Carl. She begins to tell him how he has failed her, and he responds by listing all the good things he does in the marriage. Jane acknowledges these good things but dismisses them as the wrong things. He doesn't really do the important things that show real love, such as trying to stay up later. Naturally, sex and resentment are incompatible bed partners, and their sex life slowly disintegrates. They begin to hate the other for not fulfilling their needs, for making them lose their identity in part, and because their sex life has become so unsatisfactory. Then Carl, working overtime one Saturday, spontaneously has intercourse with a willing secretary and is soon "in love." Sex is good, reaffirming his manhood, and the woman loves to go to bed early. He divorces Jane and marries his new "right" woman. Unfortunately, they also divorce three years later because Carl can't stand her indifference to housekeeping and her abominable cooking. He reminds her periodically during their marriage that Jane had kept a neat house and prepared excellent meals.

Such dynamics are prevalent in "love" marriages. This is true because "love" blinds, thus reducing the chances of realistic appraisal and alternative seeking. To the person who believes in love as the only basis of marriage, the need to realistically seek alternatives is a signal that love has gone. But:

> The happy, workable, productive marriage does not require love or even the practice of the Golden Rule. To maintain continuously a

union based on love is not feasible for most people. Nor is it possible to live in a permanent state of romance. Normal people should not be frustrated or disappointed if they are not in a constant state of love. If they experience the joy of love for ten percent of the time they are married, attempt to treat each other with as much courtesy as they do distinguished strangers, and attempt to make the marriage a workable affair — one where there are some practical advantages and satisfaction for each — the chances are the marriage will endure longer and with more strength than so-called love matches (Lederer & Jackson, 1968, p. 59).

The Self-Fulfilling Prophecy   There is evidence suggesting that the expectations you hold about another person tend to influence that person in the direction of the expectations (see, for a more extensive discussion, Rosenthal and Jacobson, 1968). Thus, to hold *slightly* high expectations about another person is not totally unproductive as long as the expectations are close enough to reality that the other person can fulfill them. But remember that to expect something different of a person implies that you don't approve of the person at the present time. Also, expectations that are clearly out of another's reach tell that person that he or she is doomed to failure since the expectations can't be met. This often happens to children. They never seem to be able to meet their parents' expectations. Sometimes children feel so frustrated by this that they deliberately do the opposite of what their parents seem to desire in an effort to free themselves from impossible expectations. "All right, if you are never satisfied with my schoolwork, no matter how hard I try, I'll stop trying." Such dynamics are also often found in marriage. If your mate constantly expects something of you that you can't fulfill, you may begin to feel incompetent, unloved, and unwanted.

On the other hand, positive and realistic expectations about our spouse, or anyone else for that matter, may very well be fulfilled since the other person will then feel good about him or herself and will often act on this positive feeling.

It is clear that the closer we can come in our expectations and perceptions to objective reality, the more efficient our behavior will generally be. If we expect impossible or difficult behavior from our mate, we doom both our mate and ourselves to perpetual failure and frustration. If, on the other hand, we accept ourselves and our mate as we are, then we have the makings for an open, communicative, and growing relationship.

How can we be realistic in our expectations of others and of marriage? Perhaps we can never be totally realistic, but if we can accept ourselves basically for what we are, can feel respect and genuine liking of ourselves, can admit error and failure and start again, can accept criticism, and can be self-supportive rather than self-destructive, then we will be on the right road. But, of course, if these were easy steps, we would all be living happily ever after. Although a great deal is known about

The Self-Actualized Person in the Fully Functioning Family

helping people to live more satisfying lives, a great deal remains to be learned. Individuals are complex and vary greatly and no single answer will suffice for everyone. Thus we need many paths by which people can travel to self-actualization. In this chapter and the next we will try to map some of these directions by examining common marital conflicts and possible solutions to these conflicts. Our first step will be to set up ideal yet realistic goals toward which we may move in our quest for maturity and mental health.

Characteristics of Mental Health*   The National Association for Mental Health has described mentally healthy people as (1) feeling comfortable about themselves, (2) feeling good about other people, and (3) being able to meet the demands of life. Each of these three short statements is then amplified by a series of descriptive phrases.

MENTALLY HEALTHY PEOPLE FEEL COMFORTABLE ABOUT THEMSELVES
Mature people are not bowled over by their own emotions — by fears, anger, love, jealousy, guilt, or worries. They take life's disappointments in their stride. They have a tolerant, easy-going attitude toward themselves as well as others; and they can laugh at themselves. They neither underestimate nor overestimate their abilities. They can accept their own shortcomings. They respect themselves and feel able to deal with most situations that come their way. They get satisfaction from simple everyday pleasures.

Notice that this description recognizes that people's lives have negative aspects — fear, anger, guilt, worries, and disappointments. Mentally healthy people can cope with such negative aspects of life. They can accept failures without becoming uptight or considering themselves failures because of temporary setbacks. And, what is more, they can laugh at themselves, which is something maladjusted people can seldom do.

MENTALLY HEALTHY PEOPLE FEEL GOOD ABOUT OTHER PEOPLE   Mature people are able to give love and consider the interests of others. They have personal relationships that are satisfying and lasting. They expect to like and trust others, and take it for granted that others will like and trust them. They respect the many differences they find in people. They do not push people around, nor do they allow themselves to be pushed around. They can feel part of a group. They feel a sense of responsibility to their neighbors and country.

As you have probably noticed, this description includes a great deal of common sense. Certainly we would expect people who are considerate of other people's interests to have lasting relationships. Furthermore, as we noted before in our discussion of self-fulfilling expectations, if we approach people in an open, friendly manner, expecting to like them, they will feel warmed by our friendliness and will most likely feel friendly toward us. If, on the other hand, we

*This section is adapted from Frank Cox, *Psychology* (Dubuque, Iowa: Wm. C. Brown Company, 1973), pp. 500–505.

approach people as if we expect them to cheat us, the chances are that they would be suspicious of us, and keep their distance.

Another aspect of this description is that it recognizes that people are gregarious, or, as the popular song says, "People need people." Mature people recognize this need, and are also aware of the responsibilities that people have toward one another.

MENTALLY HEALTHY PEOPLE ARE ABLE TO MEET THE DEMANDS OF LIFE
Mature people do something about problems as they arise. They accept responsibilities. They plan ahead and do not fear the future. They welcome new experiences and new ideas and can adjust to changed circumstances. They use their natural capacities. They set realistic goals for themselves. They are able to think for themselves and make their own decisions. They put their best effort into what they do, and get satisfaction out of doing it.

Abraham Maslow and Actualization   Abraham H. Maslow spent a lifetime studying people, especially those he called self-actualized people. These were people he felt had reached the highest levels of growth, people who seemed to be realizing their full potentials. They are people at the top of the mental health ladder. Let's take a look at some of the characteristics they share:

1. A more adequate perception of reality and more comfortable relations with reality than occur in average people. Self-actualized people prefer to cope with even unpleasant reality rather than retreat to pleasant fantasies.
2. A high degree of acceptance of themselves, of others, and of the realities of human nature. Self-actualized people are not ashamed of being what they are, and they are not shocked or dismayed to find foibles and shortcomings in themselves or in others.
3. A high degree of spontaneity. Self-actualizing people are able to act freely without undue personal restrictions and unnecessary inhibitions.
4. A focus on problem-centeredness. Self-actualizing people seem to focus on problems *outside* themselves. They are not overly self-conscious; they are not problems to themselves. Hence they devote their attention to a task, duty, or mission that seems peculiarly cut out for them.
5. A need for privacy. Self-actualizing people feel comfortable alone with their thoughts and feelings. Aloneness does not frighten them.
6. A high degree of autonomy. Self-actualizing people, as the name implies, for the most part, are independent people capable of making their own decisions. They motivate themselves.
7. A continued freshness of appreciation. Self-actualized people show the capacity to appreciate life with the freshness and delight of a child. They can see the unique in many apparently commonplace experiences.

In addition, Sidney Jourard (1963, p. 7) lists such traits as a democratic character structure; a strong ethical sense; an unhostile sense of humor; creativeness; a feeling of belonging to all humanity, including occasional mystical experiences about this sense of connection; and a resistance to *enculturation* (being overly influenced by one's culture).

Let's take a deeper look at this last trait. Self-actualized people, like other individuals, learn from and accept many of their culture's teachings. But they are aware of these cultural beliefs and can be critical of some of them. They are simply not a rubber stamp of the culture. The relationship between mentally healthy people and their culture is one of delicate balance. If there is too much emphasis on culture, then individuality is lost, as it has been in many totalitarian cultures. Yet overemphasis on the individual may lead to anarchy and the ultimate destruction of the culture. Also, extreme nonconformity to one's culture, which may appear to be individuality, is often uncritical control by the culture since the person, to nonconform, must act as the opposite of the culture — the culture is still controlling the behavior.

Jourard (1963, p. 7) sums up the qualities of the fully healthy person:

> Healthy personality is manifested by the individual who has been able to gratify his basic needs through acceptable behavior such that his own personality is no longer a problem to him. He can take himself more or less for granted and devote his energies and thoughts to socially meaningful interests and problems beyond security, or lovability, or status.

Living in the Now Marriages are constantly troubled because one or both spouses cannot live in the present. Aren't the following remarks familiar? "I'm upset because Christmas now reminds me of how terrible you were last Christmas." "This is a nice dinner but it doesn't compare with the one I want to fix next week."

All phases of time — past, present, and future — are essential for fully functioning people. To retain what has been learned in the past and use it to better cope with the present is an important attribute of maturity. To project into the future and thereby modify the present is another important and perhaps unique characteristic of people. Past and future are used by the healthy person to live a fuller, more creative life in the present.

But, just as retention and projection of time can help us behave in a more efficient manner in the present, it can also hamper present behavior. In the conversations above, the present Christmas is being ruined because of the past Christmas. Probably the spouse is now being perfectly pleasant, yet the other is unhappy because he or she is dwelling on the past rather than enjoying the present. Of course, people who do not learn from the past are doomed to repeat mistakes, yet people must develop the capacity to learn from the past without becoming entrapped by it.

Much the same can be said of the future. To plan for the future is an important function. Yet people may also hamper their behavior by projecting consequences into the future that keep them from acting in the present. For example, look how a husband's performance fears can create a lonely night for himself and his wife:

> James knows his wife is in a loving mood but he is tired and afraid that if they make love he will fail to satisfy her. When she approaches him, he says he doesn't feel good and goes off to sleep in the guest room.

James may have been correct, but, on the other hand, he may not have been, and by avoiding the situation he has assured his wife's dissatisfaction.

As we saw, some persons live a frustrated life because their expectations of the future are unrealistic. Remember Carol and her three husbands? Carol projects idealized expectations onto her husbands. Rather than letting them be the persons they are, she expects them to act in a certain manner (like her father). She is so busy expecting her husband to behave as she thinks he should that she derives no satisfaction from his actual behavior.

People who can learn to let go of past animosities and hurts and who can plan intelligently for the future without belittling the present find a great deal of happiness in the present.

The Goals of Intimacy

It seems clear from the foregoing discussions in this chapter and in Chapters 3 and 4 that to build a satisfying and successful intimate relationship is a difficult and complex task. Many factors will influence the success of such relationships. Certainly if we prepare in advance to meet the problems so often found in intimate relationships of all kinds, if we know the skills of open communication and problem solving *before* they are needed, before hostilities and inability to communicate make problem solving more difficult, then we stand a better chance of maintaining and fulfilling intimate relationships.

What is being proposed is that marriage be treated as a complex vehicle to personal happiness and that, like any vehicle, preventive maintenance and regular care will minimize faulty operation.

Marriage counselors see many couples whose marriages are so far gone that little if anything can be done to help them. But most American couples commence their marriages "in love." They do not deliberately set out to destroy their love, their partner, or their marriage. And yet it is hard to believe that the couples in the marriage counselor's office or the divorce court ever felt love and affection toward each other. Too often they are bitter, resentful, and spiteful. Their wonderful "love" marriage has become a despised trap, a hated responsibility, an intolerable life situation.

Why? I believe it often happens because we are not generally taught the arts of "getting along" intimately with others, solving problems and conflicts as they arise, nor are we taught the skills necessary to create a growing and meaningful existence in the face of the pressures and problems of a complex world. According to Paul Popenoe (1974, p. 3): "Far more could be done to handle marital difficulties more intelligently and successfully, and failure to teach how this can be done, both before and after marriage, is a notorious deficiency of contemporary treatment of the subject of marriage."

To get along intimately with another person, to create a fully functioning family, we need to be clear on what the basic goals of intimacy are. In the most general terms, I see them as identical to some of the functions of the family that we discussed in Chapter 1 (p. 10). In particular, I see the basic intimacy goals of the family as (1) providing emotional gratification to members, (2) helping the members deal with crises and problems, and (3) helping the members grow in the most fulfilling manner possible. We can see how a marriage can fulfill these functions in the following examples:

Emotional Gratification

Pete loves to tinker with things and it makes him feel important if he can fix something in the house for Gail. Gail loves to knit and Pete loves sweaters, so she feels worthwhile and appreciated when she knits him a sweater. Pete finds he enjoys sex with Gail because of the giving and receiving of affection that goes on between them. Gail knows she can sound off when she gets angry, since Pete understands and doesn't put her down. Both partners are having emotional needs met as well as meeting many of the needs of the other.

Dealing with Crises

When Pete has a crisis in the office, he tells Gail about it, and she listens, offers support, asks questions, and, very occasionally, offers advice. When he is through telling her about it, Pete often feels he understands the situation better and is more ready to either accept or change it.

Growing in a Fulfilling Manner

Gail wants to be less shy, and Pete encourages her to be more assertive with him and to role-play assertiveness with others. Gradually, she finds she can overcome her shyness, in large part because Pete encourages and supports her.

Certainly it does not seem to be asking too much of a marriage to supply emotional gratification to the partners, to help them better deal with crises that arise, and to encourage each to grow in a personally fulfilling manner. Yet, marriage often fails this assignment, or to put it more accurately, marriage partners often fail to create a marriage in which these positive elements thrive.

Hopefully some insight into how to go about creating a fulfilling intimate relationship can be gained from reading the Scenes from Marriage at the end of this chapter, "Warm Fuzzies and Cold Pricklies."

Summary

Marriage is the socially accepted relationship through which sexual drives are fulfilled. It is, of course, much more than this — it is the generally accepted mode of life for most Americans. Marriage is really a three-way relationship that involves the man, the woman, and the state. The state sets certain eligibility requirements that must be met in order for a couple to marry. In addition, the state prescribes certain obligations that each partner must fulfill in marriage. The marriage ceremony actually commits a couple to a new status with certain privileges, obligations, and restrictions. In addition to state-mandated marital obligations, some couples are writing their own marriage contracts, stating goals, obligations, and responsibilities that they wish to be a part of their marriage. Such contracts, if properly written, are considered legal so long as the couple has not disregarded state-mandated duties and obligations.

Marriage is many things but, more than anything else, it is the constant interaction between the family members and the many roles that each fulfills within the family relationship. How does one interact with another person at the intimate level of marriage? Basically, how we interact will be determined by our attitudes and expectations about marriage and our partner. These attitudes and expectations of the larger culture are assimilated by us from our parents. However, when our expectations and attitudes differ from our spouse's, there will usually be conflict in the marriage.

The basic goals of intimacy in a marriage are emotional gratification of each partner, helping each deal with crises, and helping each grow in a fulfilling manner. The ideal goal of family is to provide an environment in which each family member is encouraged and free to become the most actualized person that he or she is capable of becoming. Each family member will have to try to maintain his or her own balance and growth while at the same time contributing to the well-being of all others within the family unit. This is a large order and means that all will have to try to understand themselves and "keep their own heads on straight" if they are to help and support the other family members.

Self-actualizing people are many things but essentially they are people who feel comfortable about themselves and others. They are able to meet most of the demands of life in a realistic fashion. They tend to use their past experiences and ideas about their future in such a way so as to enhance the present rather than to escape from the present. They are not prisoners of their past, but rather are free to use it to improve the present. Intimacy includes the commitment to help each other realize to the fullest possible degree all of the human potentials inherent in each individual family member. Granted that this is a difficult and at times impossible task, it is certainly a worthy goal toward which to strive.

Warm Fuzzies and Cold Pricklies

Once upon a time, a long time ago, there lived two very happy people called Tim and Maggie with two children called John and Lucy. To understand how happy they were, you have to understand how things were in those days. You see, in those happy days everyone was given at birth a small, soft, Fuzzy Bag. Anytime people reached into this bag they were able to pull out a Warm Fuzzy. Warm Fuzzies were very much in demand because whenever people were given a Warm Fuzzy, it made them feel warm and fuzzy all over. People who didn't get Warm Fuzzies regularly were in danger of developing a sickness which caused them to shrivel up and die.

In those days it was very easy to get Warm Fuzzies. Anytime that somebody felt like it, she might walk up to you and say, "I'd like to have a Warm Fuzzy." You would then reach into your bag and pull out a Fuzzy the size of a little girl's hand. As soon as the Fuzzy saw the light of day, it would smile and blossom into a large, shaggy, Warm Fuzzy. You then would lay it on the person's shoulder or head or lap and it would snuggle up and melt right against her skin and make her feel good all over. People were always asking each other for Warm Fuzzies, and

since they were always given freely, getting enough of them was never a problem. There were always plenty to go around and, as a consequence, everyone was happy and felt warm and fuzzy most of the time.

One day a bad witch became angry because everyone was so happy and no one was buying her potions and salves. This witch was very clever and she devised a very wicked plan. One beautiful morning she crept up to Tim while Maggie was playing with their daughter and whispered in his ear, "See here, Tim, look at all the Fuzzies that Maggie is giving to Lucy. You know, if she keeps it up, eventually she is going to run out and then there won't be any left for you."

Tim was astonished. He turned to the witch and said, "Do you mean to tell me that there isn't a Warm Fuzzy in our bag every time we reach into it?"

And the witch said, "No, absolutely not, and once you run out, that's it. You don't have any more." With this she flew away on her broom, laughing and cackling hysterically.

Tim took this to heart and began to notice every time Maggie gave up a Warm Fuzzy to somebody else. Eventually he got very worried and upset because he liked Maggie's Warm Fuzzies very much and did not want to give them up. He certainly did not think it was right for Maggie to be spending all her Warm Fuzzies on the children and on other people. He began to complain every time he saw Maggie giving a Warm Fuzzy to somebody else, and because Maggie liked him very much, she stopped giving Warm Fuzzies to other people as often, and reserved them for him.

The children watched this and soon began to get the idea that it was wrong to give up Warm Fuzzies any time you were asked or felt like it. They, too, became very careful. They would watch their parents closely and whenever they felt that one of their parents was giving too many Fuzzies to others, they also began to object. They began to feel worried whenever they gave away too many Warm Fuzzies. Even though they found a Warm Fuzzy every time they reached into their bag, they reached in less and less and became more and more stingy. Soon people began to notice the lack of Warm Fuzzies, and they began to feel less and less fuzzy. They began to shrivel up and, occasionally, people would die from lack of Warm Fuzzies. More and more people went to the witch to buy her potions and salves even though they didn't seem to work.

Well, the situation was getting very serious indeed. The bad witch who had been watching all of this didn't really want the people to die, so she devised a plan. She gave everyone a bag that was very similar to the Fuzzy Bag except that this one was cold while the Fuzzy Bag was warm. Inside of the witch's bag were Cold Pricklies. These Cold Pricklies did not make people feel warm and fuzzy, they made them feel cold and prickly instead. But, they did prevent people from shriveling up. So from then on, every time somebody said, "I want a Warm Fuzzy," people who were worried about depleting their supply would say, "I can't give you a Warm Fuzzy, but would you like a Cold Prickly?" Sometimes, two people would walk up to each other, thinking they could get a Warm Fuzzy, but then they would

change their minds and would wind up giving each other Cold Pricklies. So, the end result was that while very few people were dying, a lot of people were still unhappy and feeling very cold and prickly.

The situation got very complicated because, since the coming of the witch, there were less and less Warm Fuzzies around, so Warm Fuzzies, which used to be thought of as free as air, became extremely valuable. This caused people to do all sorts of things in order to obtain them. Before the witch had appeared, people used to gather in groups of three or four or five, never caring too much who was giving Warm Fuzzies to whom. After the coming of the witch, people began to pair off and to reserve all their Warm Fuzzies for each other exclusively. If ever one of the two persons forgot and gave a Warm Fuzzy to someone else, he or she would immediately feel guilty about it because he or she knew that the partner would probably resent the loss of a Warm Fuzzy. People who could not find a generous partner had to buy their Warm Fuzzies and had to work long hours to earn the money. Another thing which happened was that some people would take Cold Pricklies — which were limitless and freely available — coat them white and fluffy and pass them on as Warm Fuzzies. These counterfeit Warm Fuzzies were really Plastic Fuzzies, and they caused additional difficulties. For instance, two people would get together and freely exchange Plastic Fuzzies, which presumably should make them feel good, but they came away feeling bad instead. Since they thought they had been exchanging Warm Fuzzies, people grew very confused about this, never realizing that their cold prickly feelings were really the result of the Plastic Fuzzies.

So the situation was very, very dismal and it all started because of the witch who made people believe that some day, when least expected, they might reach into their Warm Fuzzy Bag and find no more.

But, not long ago, a young woman with big hips born under the sign of Aquarius came to this unhappy land. She had not heard about the bad witch and was not worried about running out of Warm Fuzzies. She gave them out freely, even when not asked. They called her the Hip Woman and disapproved of her because she was giving the children the idea that they should not worry about running out of Warm Fuzzies. The children liked her very much because they felt good around her and they, too, began to give out Warm Fuzzies whenever they felt like it. The grown-ups became concerned and decided to pass a law to protect the children from depleting their supplies of Warm Fuzzies. The law made it a criminal offense to give out Warm Fuzzies in a reckless manner. The children, however, seemed not to care, and in spite of the law they continued to give each other Warm Fuzzies whenever they felt like it and always when asked. Because there were many, many children, almost as many as grown-ups, it began to look as if maybe they would have their way.

As of now it is hard to say what will happen. Will the grown-up forces of law and order stop the recklessness of the children? Are the grown-ups going to join with the Hip Woman and the children in taking a chance that there will always be as many Warm Fuzzies as needed? Will they remember the days their children are trying to bring back, days when Warm Fuzzies were abundant because people gave them away freely?

CLAUDE M. STEINER

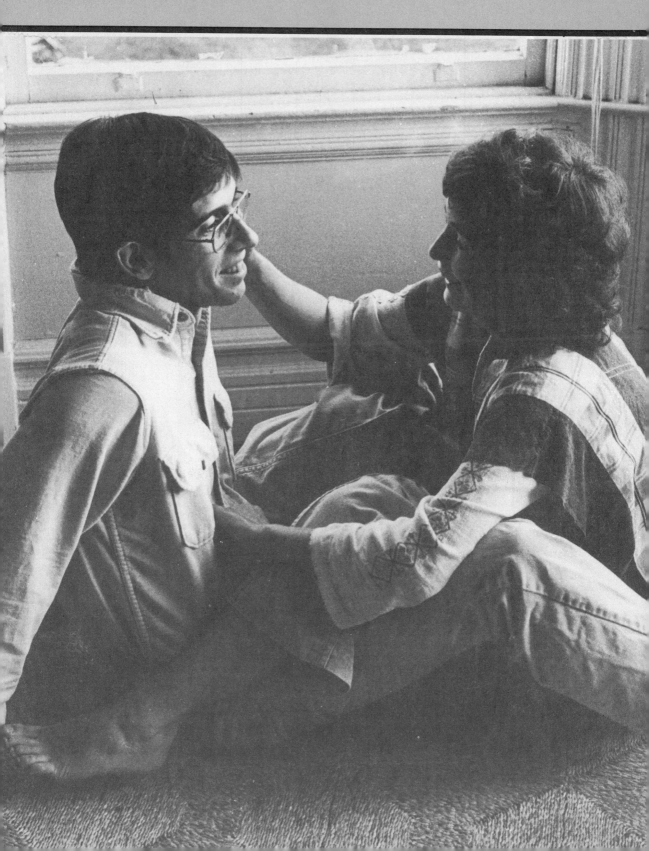

Chapter 6 ~

Contents

Communication
in
Marriage

Building and maintaining a marriage that fulfills the goals defined in Chapter 5 (that is, a marriage that supplies emotional gratification to each partner and helps each to deal with crises and to grow in a fulfilling manner) can only be achieved by the active processes of talking, listening, negotiating, and problem solving. We generally call this process *communication*, which is simply conversation with a purpose, a purpose that can always be seen as seeking emotional gratification, or, more specifically, as avoiding pain and seeking pleasure. Try it yourself. Can you think of any verbal statement that does not have as its ultimate purpose the avoidance of pain or the seeking of pleasure? It may seem like semantic manipulation, but any conversation can be reduced to this fundamental purpose.

I know you believe you understand what you think I said, but I am not sure you realize that what you heard is not what I meant.

In marriage, true communication is a mutual understanding, a *knowing* of one another, so that pleasure is maximized and pain minimized for both partners. A possible complication, of course, is that the achievement of pleasure for one may cause pain for the other, or that the avoidance of pain for one may add to the pain of another. Thus our definition of successful marital communication must be refined. Successful marital communication is a conversation that leads to pain reduction or pleasure enhancement for one partner, with due regard to the impact on the other partner.

Successful communication is the cornerstone of any relationship. Such communication must be open, realistic, tactful, caring, and valued. But it is not always easy to maintain this kind of communication unless all family members are committed to the belief that good communication is important to life satisfaction. This sounds simple, yet couples in marital trouble almost always list failure to communicate as one of their major problems.

Good communication is especially important and especially difficult in marriage because of the intensity of the emotions in a love relationship. High emotional levels tend to interfere with rationality and logic, and thus with clear communication. If you have ever had trouble communicating when calm and collected, imagine the potential problems when you are excited and emotionally aroused. Yet, it is only through clear communication that each partner can know the needs of the other. When conflicts arise, the only chance to resolve

This chapter was written in collaboration with C. Norman Jacobs, a licensed psychologist in private practice in Santa Barbara, California.

them is if each partner is able to communicate fairly about the problem, define it clearly, and be open to alternative means of solution. Good communication also helps minimize hostilities. For example, unexpressed dissatisfactions tend to create hostility, but fairly expressed dissatisfaction allows the other partner to understand the problem and to act to reduce the partner's dissatisfactions and thus deflate the hostility.

Conflict management is essential to all intimate relationships. This is true because there is bound to be conflict in any long-lasting relationship. When one considers that two people marry only after many years of growing up and learning multiple attitudes, it is really surprising that the two can get along at all on an intimate day-to-day basis since what each individual has learned about handling interpersonal relationships will be to a large extent peculiar to that individual. For example, one partner may learn that you do not talk about problems until everyone is calm and collected. This has meant that sometimes a problem is not brought up for several days. The other partner has learned that you always speak your mind immediately. To wait, she or he has been taught, only makes things worse. You can see immediately that these differing beliefs about when to communicate will cause difficulty.

Communication is, of course, also affected by the general society. For example, American men are taught to be less communicative, less self-disclosing about their feelings than American women. The traditional American masculine role is one of strength and silence. To be expressive, sensitive, and tender is considered feminine. But obviously the latter three traits are important in good communication even if the traditional masculine role denies them to males. Thus

Clear communication can minimize hostile moments in a relationship.

marital communication is certainly affected by general societal values about masculinity and femininity as well as by the individual communicative skills of the partners.

It is important to emphasize this influence of the general society and its institutions. Most people encountering problems in their marriage tend to believe that the problems are personal. That is, they believe that the problems are unique to their partner, their family, themselves, or the immediate circumstances. Locating the source of problems within the couple and their marriage reinforces the myth that marriage to the "right" person will solve all problems and result in a happy family life (Feldberg & Kohen, 1976, p. 158). Certainly many problems are unique to a given family, but it is equally true that many family problems arise because of pressures placed on the family by the general society. For example, as we saw in Chapter 2, stereotypical sex roles may lock a family into rigid patterns of behavior that cause problems for the individual family members and therefore stress for the family.

What Causes Communication Failure?

Failure to communicate is not usually an accident. The failure is usually intentional, though not overtly or consciously so. *People choose not to communicate!*

Often when a marriage is disintegrating, the partners say "We just can't communicate" or "We just don't talk to each other any more." They identify a deficiency of communication as the cause, when actually it is usually not a deficiency but a surplus of negative or aversive communication that causes the disintegration. Of course, a deficiency of talk may eventually replace the unproductive aversive talk, but the deficiency is not the cause of the problem.

Failure to communicate with others usually begins with a breakdown of internal communication. Anger, emotional maladjustment, stress and strain, and faulty perceptions can all lead to blind spots and overly strong defenses. If we become rigid and inflexible, we may be threatened by new experiences and change. Our self-image may become unrealistic, causing us to filter all communications to fit this faulty self-picture. When this happens, it is very hard to have good communication. In general, those of us who don't have our heads on straight (see Chapter 5) have a great deal of trouble communicating.

Aversive Communication

Let's return to our basic principle of human behavior: people seek pleasure and avoid pain. And let's refine the principle a bit more: people first avoid pain and then seek pleasure, since in the hierarchy of human needs, pain avoidance is a basic guide for survival. This is a crucial point in our understanding of communication failure because motivation to communicate will be most urgent when avoiding pain. Unfortunately, the quickest means of changing the spouse who is giving us pain is by threatening him or her. That is, by creating pain ourselves with an aversive communication, we hopefully get the

Inset 6-1
Can We Really Be Totally Open All the Time?

It is a popular notion now that the more open, the more honest the self-disclosure, the better the communication, and thus the better the relationship. Yet research does not support this idea. Certainly there is a correlation between openness and satisfaction, but it turns out that both too much and too little self-disclosure can reduce satisfaction with a relationship (Cozby, 1973).

A. L. Rutledge (1966) has noted that after marriage, restraints tend to be released, so that manners are forgotten, frankness overrides tact, and hostility results. If the hostility and frankness become too overwhelming, the couple tends to limit their self-expression and to withdraw from communication altogether.

B. R. Cutler and W. G. Dyer (1965) have found that nearly half of the "nonadjustive responses" for both husbands and wives come as a result of open sharing of feelings about violated expectations. Contrary to popular belief about the benefits of such sharing, this open communication did not lead to improved relations.

Shirley J. Gilbert, who has studied communication in families, says, "What is being suggested is that there exist pros and cons of openness and that previous research does not suggest the existence of an unequivocal relationship between self-disclosure and satisfaction in human relationships (1976, p. 224).

Actually the real question is *how* to disclose rather than whether to disclose or not. What is said (the content), how positive or negative it is, and the levels on which it is said (superficial to deeply meaningful, intellectual to emotional) — all have to be taken into account. For example, M. J. Bienvenu (1970) has found a number of elements that differentiate between good and poor communication for couples. These elements include the handling of anger and of differences, tone of voice, understanding, good listening habits, and self-disclosure. The elements that contribute to poor communication are nagging, conversational discourtesies, and uncommunicativeness.

Certainly both partners must share a willingness to communicate. But equally important is that they learn how to communicate successfully, and that they remain aware of each other's weak and sensitive points. For example, people who are insecure, and feel inferior and worthless, tend to be self-deprecating. They also tend to be fearful of open communication and usually react with hostility to what they perceive to be unfair criticisms. On the other hand, people with a high level of self-esteem tend to be comfortable with open communication and are willing to disclose their own feelings and to accept their partner's feelings.

So, how one discloses thoughts and feelings, especially negative ones, strongly influences how the communication will be accepted. Those who believe it is important to keep everything out in the open, to express themselves always to the fullest, must also concern themselves with *how* this is done or they may find such openness backfiring and actually destroying communication rather than enhancing it.

spouse "off our back." This is counterproductive in the long run, since our partner will most likely respond on the same level, creating a "vicious circle" and we both become losers. That is, we respond negatively to our partner's negative response, and the communications continue, each more hostile and aversive, until one of us retreats and stops communicating altogether. This kind of communication is a power struggle in which the winner is the one who generates the most aversion. The loser feels resentful and probably engages in typical loser's behavior such as deceit, procrastination, deliberate inadequacy, sarcasm, sullenness, and so forth. Any verbal input by the loser is now likely to be an emotional discharge of the resulting resentment and hostility. Often the loser will begin to meet needs outside the marriage, at which point communication failure will become an intentional goal. The loser stops talking or becomes deliberately misleading because he or she knows that his or her behavior is unacceptable to the winner. Also, the loser stops talking because communication has become so painful.

An example of aversive communication is one that starts out to deal with one conflict only to lead to a confusing kaleidoscope of other marginally related disagreements, one following on the heels of the other and connected only by the pain each partner causes the other:

"Where did you put my socks?"

"You mean the socks I have to crawl under the bed to find every time I do the laundry?"

"Yes, every time you do the laundry — the second Tuesday of every week."

"With the machine that's always broken, that nobody fixes."

"Because I'm so busy working to pay for tennis lessons and ladies' luncheons."

"And losses at Tuesday night poker bashes."

"I'm sick of this argument."

"Well, you started it."

"How?"

"Well, I can't remember, but you did."

More examples of positive and negative communications may be seen in Table 6-1.

There is a sense of order in successful communication where communications flow smoothly back and forth between sender and receiver. First, there are three general conditions that must be met for successful communication to occur:

Developing a Flow Chart of Communication

1. *Commitment*: the partners must be motivated to work on their relationship.
2. *Growth orientation*: the partners must accept the fact that their relationship is dynamic and changing rather than static.
3. *Noncoercive atmosphere*: the partners have to feel free to be themselves, to be open, to be honest.

These conditions are difficult to attain, and we shall look at each in more detail later. First, the message must be "encoded" and sent to the partner via some communication channel, e.g., verbal or written. The partner (receiver) must "decode" the message and, to ensure that it has been correctly received, must feed back what has been decoded to the sender (source). The source either verifies the message or through correction, negotiation, and problem solving resends the message and the process is repeated. This circular pattern may have to be

Table 6-1 Negative and Positive Responses in Communication

Negative		Positive[1]	
1. Ordering, directing, commanding	"Stop ordering me around." "You can't buy that." "Don't talk to me like that."	1. Providing self-direction and choice	"You appear very disappointed." "Let's discuss whether that would be a good purchase." "When you talk like that, I feel frightened."
2. Warning, admonishing, threatening	"Listen to me or else." "If you won't, then I'll find someone who will."	2. Seeking causes for differences	"What did I say that turned you off?" "Help me to understand why you don't want to . . ."
3. Exhorting, moralizing, preaching	"You should tell your boss you want that raise."	3. Choosing one of several alternatives	"Which do you think would be best for you, . . . for us, . . . for all involved?"
4. Advising, giving solutions or suggestions	"Why don't you try . . ." "You ought to stay home more."	4. Exploring possibilities	"What could you try?" "Would it help you if . . ."
5. Lecturing, teaching, giving logical arguments	"It makes more sense to do it this way." "The Browns are happy and they don't have a new car."	5. Considering consequences	"Which way seems to get better results for you?" "Let's think about what would result from each decision."
6. Judging, criticizing, blaming	"You are wrong." "It's all your fault." "What a stupid idea!"	6. Sharing responsibility	"Those two statements seem to conflict." "Let's do what we can to solve it." "Let's see if that idea will work."
7. Praising, agreeing, evaluating[2]	"I think you are absolutely correct." "You do so many good things."	7. Expanding openness	"This seems like a difficult decision for you to make." "You sound discouraged. I'll listen."
8. Name calling, ridiculing, shaming, categorizing	"You're no good." "You're just like all the other men/women." "You're a liar."	8. Enhancing self-esteem and uniqueness	"I love you." "I appreciate your understanding." "Your interpretation is different from mine."
9. Interpreting, analyzing, diagnosing	"If you weren't so tired you could see my point." "You don't care what I think."	9. Increasing sensitivity	"If you prefer, we can discuss this at another time." "Right now, I'm feeling so alone and left out."
10. Reassuring, sympathizing, consoling[2]	"Don't worry about that." "All men/women go through that at some time."	10. Expressing care and concern	"What worries you about that?" "This is an especially difficult time for you."
11. Probing, questioning, interrogating	"Where have you been?" "Now, tell me the real reason you feel that way."	11. Giving freedom and privacy	"I've missed you a lot." "You don't need to explain if you would rather not."
12. Withdrawing, distracting, humoring, diverting	"You're funny when you are mad." "Why don't you tell me something new!"	12. Accepting, giving attention to the other person	"I understand that you are feeling mad because . . ." "That point is something you haven't mentioned before."

Source: From Richard Hunt and Edward Rydman, *Creative Marriage* (Boston: Holbrook, 1976), pp. 50–51.

[1]Most of the positive responses are ways of saying to the partner, "Yes, I'm listening." More explicit listening invitations are "I see," "Tell me about it," "This seems important to you," and "Okay, let's work on it together." As you become aware of negative responses in your interaction with your partner, substitute more positive responses that show your care and concern for him or her.

[2]Praising and reassuring may be negative responses when the other person has a problem because such responses tend to prevent that person from sharing feelings that are more threatening or painful. Don't be too quick to reassure. Later, when the partner has sufficiently explored all of the feelings that are associated with the problem, expressing appreciation and confidence in the partner will be positive.

repeated several times before successful communication is achieved (see Figure 6-1).

In addition to the basic conditions, communication requires that five skills be mastered (see Gordon, 1970, for a more thorough discussion of these skills, which we will discuss briefly):

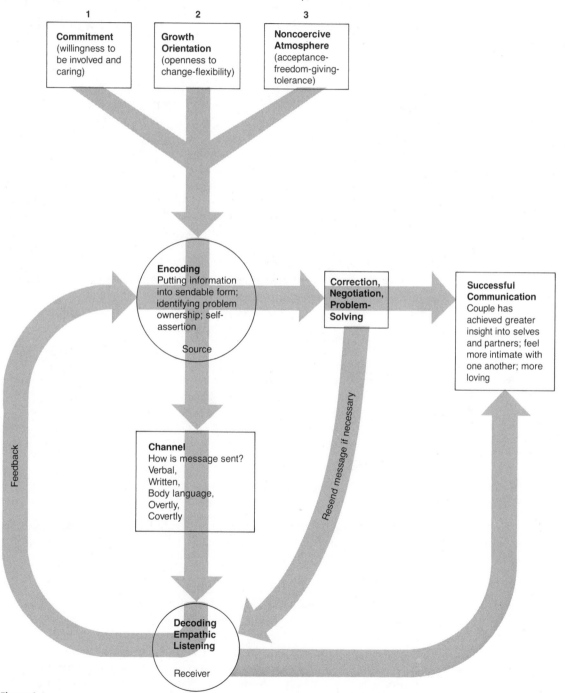

Figure 6-1

Communications flow chart. The three conditions necessary to successful communication are shown at the top.

1. Identifying ownership of the problem.
2. Self-assertion by the owner of the problem.
3. Empathic listening by the other partner.
4. Negotiating.
5. Problem solving.

Commitment Simply stated, commitment means active involvement in working to build and maintain the relationship as well as commitment to the partner as a person. Marriage counselors are often seen when there has been so much pain and suffering that the commitment of one or both marital partners has ceased. There is then little hope of resolution. Often one member of the marriage is still committed enough to want counseling, while the other, who has covertly given up hope and commitment, is very resistant to counseling and fears being drawn back into a painful trap. Sometimes the noncommitted partner will enter treatment only in the hope that a dependent spouse will become strong enough to survive without the marriage. This leads to an added complexity if the dependent partner, sensing abandonment, avoids getting stronger in the hope that the noncommitted partner will stay in the marriage. Overt commitment of both partners is essential to building and maintaining a marriage.

Many uncommitted partners allow the other to plan activities, anticipate problems, make necessary adjustments, and so on. Sometimes this kind of relationship works. But, more often than not, there is resentment on the part of the partner with the greater commitment. Paradoxically, in a relationship, the one who cares the least, controls.

> Alice is more committed to their marriage than is Roger. For their summer vacation she wants to go to San Francisco while he wants to go backpacking. Since he is not as committed to the relationship, it is easy for him to say "Go to San Francisco if you want, but I'm going backpacking and you can come along if you like." Alice can plead with Roger to consider her desire but, more likely, she will resign herself to going backpacking.

Although commitment is a precondition to effective communication, the five communication skills discussed later also help increase each partner's commitment to the relationship.

Growth Orientation Individuals change over time. The needs of a forty-year-old person are somewhat different from the needs of a twenty-year-old. Marriage must also change if individual needs are to be continually met within the marriage framework. Yet change is often threatening. It upsets comfortable routine and is therefore often resisted. But, of course, such resistance will be futile since time does not stand still. So, it is far better to accept and plan for change. An individual oriented to growth is someone who incorporates the inevitability of change into his or her life style. This implies not only an acceptance of some change but intentional and orderly change in a chosen direction.

> Going to a large social gathering was something Helen anticipated with pleasure but which her husband Art dreaded. However, they were both oriented to growth and Art wanted to be more comfortable in social situations. So they decided to actively work on helping Art to change his dread to an enjoyment of social interaction. Helen, at Art's suggestion, began to invite just one or two couples over to their house, since Art always felt more comfortable at home. He soon began to enjoy these small get-togethers. Helen gradually expanded the get-togethers. Although Art is still not perfectly at ease away from his home in large groups, he is much more comfortable than before and accompanies Helen most of the time.

Had Helen and Art not been growth-oriented, they might have grown apart or become resentful of one another. Helen might have chastised Art for his social inabilities and gone out without him, leaving him home to brood and resent her. On the other hand, Art might have been dictatorial and not allowed Helen to go to large social gatherings, with the likely outcome that she'd have felt entrapped and hostile. Yet, because neither was afraid of change and because each felt that change in Art would be beneficial, they set out deliberately to encourage this process. Notice that they were both committed to the change. If only one partner desires change, particularly in the other partner, and the other disagrees, then there will be conflict and often diminished communication. Successful communication requires a positive regard for each other and noncoercion.

Noncoercive Atmosphere   The goals of marriage will usually be lost if either partner is subjugated in all ways by the other. Free and open communication cannot exist in a one-sided totalitarian relationship. When any two persons share a common goal, the issues of responsibility and authority arise. The situation in marriage is not unlike that in government. A marriage can be laissez faire, where both partners are free to do their own things. It can be democratic, where responsibility is shared and authority is delegated by equitable agreement. A marriage can also be an autocracy, where authority is assigned to a single leader.

Ideally, most Americans state they desire to establish a democratic marriage. In reality, this is the most difficult pattern to maintain, although I believe it is ultimately the most satisfying arrangement.

When power is invested in an authority, a coercive relationship usually results. At least one partner feels a loss of freedom and often both feel this loss since there are ways the subjugated person can manipulate the authority as well as vice versa. Free and open communication cannot usually coexist with coercion.

Mike and Daphne have been married six months. She pleads with him to give up his weekly poker game because she is afraid to be alone. He feels unfairly restricted and calls her a child. She in turn calls him an immature "jock" who can't give up the boys. One thing leads to another and he finally walks out of the room and slams the door. She tearfully runs to the bedroom and locks herself in, leaving him to nurse his guilt. Although he apologizes profusely, she won't come out. So Mike stays home, having had his physical coercion overpowered by her emotional coercion. He is resentful and she is frightened and resentful. The intimacy that they felt in their court-ship is being dissolved by the acid of resentment created by coercive acts committed by both of them.

It is clear that successful communication will not survive long in such an environment. Sharing responsibilities, giving control voluntarily, and feeling relatively free in a relationship greatly facilitate communication.

Instead of the above sequence, Mike and Daphne might have worked out a compromise that would have satisfied both of them. For example, Daphne, knowing how much Mike enjoys his weekly poker session, might have supported him in this desire, hopefully leading him to respond to her fear of being alone. He could suggest that he reduce the number of times he play poker. Or perhaps she could plan to visit her parents that evening or do something with a girlfriend. If each felt the other was noncoercive and supportive of their desires, it would then be far easier to work out compromise solutions.

Communication Skills When all is going well with a couple, they usually don't think about communication. Yet this is the best time to build communication skills since disruptive forces are minimal. The skills will be there if and when things go wrong and problems arise. It is apparently irreconcilable conflicts that destroy relationships. And such conflicts become irreconcilable in most cases because the partners have failed to develop their communication skills.

IDENTIFYING PROBLEM OWNERSHIP Clarifying responsibility or problem ownership is an important first step in communication. Of course, this is not always easy. A problem can belong to either partner or it can be jointly shared. The key question is "Who feels tangibly affected?" That is, to own or share ownership of a problem, we must know and openly admit that we are personally disturbed by it. For example, let's take a look at the following situation:

Jane feels that her husband Ray is losing friends because he drinks heavily and becomes belligerent. But he isn't concerned about his behavior. He feels people exaggerate his behavior, thus refusing ownership of the problem. Since he doesn't have a problem, no change on his part is necessary.

In addition to accepting ownership of a problem, one must be tangibly affected by it. In the above situation if Ray's behavior does not interfere with Jane's friendships, it does not affect her, and she does not own or share ownership of the problem. The fact that she might be concerned for him does not make it her problem. She can, of course, share her observations with him. However, if Jane is tangibly affected by his behavior, she does, at least, share the problem. For example, if their friends stop calling them, then her needs are being tangibly interfered with. If she communicates this to Ray and he refuses to admit to it, then, as paradoxical as it may seem, Jane owns the problem. If, however, Ray acknowledges that his behavior is affecting Jane, then the problem is jointly owned.

Assuming ownership of a problem is extremely important, yet we often shun responsibility. Some people feel that if they don't pay attention to problems, the problems will disappear. However, the reverse is generally true. In the long run, unattended problems usually become worse. Denial effectively cuts off communication and prevents change.

Modern American society has, unfortunately, too often encouraged individuals to "cop out" of problems by supplying many scapegoats on which responsibility can be placed:

"My parents made me this way because they rejected me as a child."

"My father beat my mother when he drank, so I can't relate to men because of my deep hostility at his behavior."

"The establishment controls everything, so why bother to change?"

"American society is racist, I am black, and therefore all my problems are caused by society."

Of course, the list could go on and on, but these examples should give an idea of what must be avoided if we are to solve personal problems. For instance, it may be true that you have problems because your parents rejected you, but they are still *your* problems. Rejecting parents are not going to suddenly become loving parents in order to solve your problems. Obviously, your parents have problems of their own, but you can't make them solve their problems, you can only work to solve your own. The first step toward solution is assuming responsibility for a problem if it is yours.

An important caution must be added to the discussion of problem ownership. Forcing problem ownership onto your partner can also be "blaming," which is highly destructive. Some people use this aspect of good communication in a negative manner; i.e., to *show* the other person that they are wrong and that they blame them for causing all the trouble because "it is *their* problem." The same kind of comment can be made about the next skill we will discuss, self-assertion. One partner can really attack the other under the guise of being assertive, thus perverting a positive communication skill into a disguise for harmful communication.

If the problem is mine, then I will use skill 2, *self-assertion*. If my partner owns the problem, then I will try to use skill 3, *empathic listening*. If we both own the problem, we will alternate these two communicational skills.

SELF-ASSERTION   Self-assertion is the process of recognizing and expressing one's feelings, opinions, and attitudes while at the same time being aware of the feelings and needs of others.

Some people are nonassertive. They fail to make their feelings and thoughts known to others. This makes communication almost impossible.

Mary feels Jim is becoming less affectionate. He doesn't seem to hug her and touch her as much as he used to. Mary always liked the close physical contact and misses it. But it has always been hard for her to talk about her physical desires with anyone, much less a man, and so she says nothing. Her anxiety and discomfort grow. She feels that if Jim really loved her, he should recognize how miserable she feels and give her more physical contact. She becomes increasingly hostile to him until one day he asks, "What's the matter?" She replies, "You ought to know, it's your fault."

Jim is completely in the dark. Mary's nonassertive behavior has precluded successful communication and thus foreclosed solving the problem.

Some of the personal reasons for nonassertive behavior are fear, feelings of inferiority, lack of confidence, shyness, and embarrassment. Besides personal reasons, society and its traditional role expectations may influence nonassertive behavior. For example, in Mary's case, she may have incorporated the traditional American feminine role of being passive and nonassertive, of expecting the male to solve her problems. But, whatever the reasons, if we can't express our needs, we cannot expect others to magically recognize and fill them for us.

In contrast to nonassertive individuals, aggressive individuals completely bypass tact and recognition of other's needs in expressing their feelings. They demand attention, support, and whatever they want at the moment, often overriding the rights and feelings of others. In fact, they often seem unaware that other people have rights and feelings, and they can hurt other people without being aware of what they are doing. However, not all aggression is destructive. Used in a constructive manner, aggression offers emotional release, can let a partner know how intensively the other partner is feeling, and can help both partners learn how to cope with all kinds of aggressive and emotional behavior (for a fuller discussion of how to use aggression constructively, see Bach and Wyden, 1968).

Self-assertive people, on the other hand, are free to express themselves and are aware of the feelings and needs of others. Self-

As we saw in Chapter 2, the traditional sex roles of a strong, silent male and submissive, emotional female lead to stereotyped behavior and to communication difficulties. Carol Pierce and Janice Sanfaco (1977) have studied and outlined some of this traditional conditioning, and point to the following results:

Women are encouraged from childhood to feel it is better to have a man's approval than a woman's approval.

Women are set in competition with other women for male approval.

Women experience lines of power as going from women to men.

Women are taught to be reactive rather than proactive.

Women learn to live for and through others and to define themselves in terms of others.

Women are expected to be selfless helpers and not to have needs for a lot of space, both territorial and psychological.

On the other hand, men are taught: to be self-sufficient, intact, a closed system; they are not expected to acknowledge their dependence needs.... Eventually men begin to deny to themselves that they even

have such needs. They lose touch with their feelings, become task-oriented, compartmentalized, mechanical, totally rational and therefore totally dependent on women to fill their needs for nurturing and caring of their own personal relationships and interaction with others (women playing the role of facilitator between father and child, adult son and father, man and friends). Men are now ripe for women's "psyching-out."

For women this necessitates the development of mental processes and styles characterized by continual forethought as to how to "use" another person. Hence, women learn to be schemers. Women often learn to gear their thoughts to what will make a man feel comfortable; the best way to make a man appear pleasing and smart to others; what problems a man needs to talk about; and how to make a man feel fascinating and powerful.

The cost to women in this process is that they learn to deny their own wants and needs and, hence, do not gain a sense of self-esteem, integrity as an individual, and autonomy. They have little feeling of being powerful enough to shape their

environment. Women frequently "psych-out" to get male approval, to compete with other women, to manipulate, because these are the modes familiar to them. Whereas, in those interactions characterized by the sharing of straight, factual knowledge, giving orders or advice, and the initiating of sexual encounters, one sees the preponderant type of communication behavior of men in a male-dominated world. Many men are now experiencing a revolution to learn those behaviors and expressions necessary to grow emotionally and to relate in a more personal way.

"Psyching-out" then is a mode of behavior where a person constantly takes on the responsibility of figuring out what is most helpful and pleasing to another person, hoping the result will be that in return he/she will be liked, appreciated, and will receive attention. The problem is that because of role-stereotyping, the same kind of attention is seldom initiated or returned to women, and the giver is frequently neither noticed nor appreciated (Pierce & Sanfaco, 1977, pp. 97–98).

assertive people's communications are also about themselves rather than critical of other persons. For example, contrast the statement, "This kind of behavior is hard for me to handle and makes me angry even though I don't want to be" with "You make me mad." The second statement is almost useless to successful communication. It judges and places blame on the other person. It will usually only provoke a defensive comment on the part of the person to whom it is said.

It may seem surprising that special help with self-assertion should be required in building a relationship. In fact, many people believe that selfishness and self-seeking assertions are the basis of marital difficulty, and that what is needed is less self-assertion. However, our definition of self-assertion includes awareness of the other's feelings and needs. We certainly need to be less destructively aggressive in our relations but we must not confuse that with being non-assertive.

It is important to be aware that recognition and expression of needs do not necessarily lead to their fulfillment. For example, I may recognize and express my desire to smoke, which is self-assertive. If, however, other people in the room find cigarette smoke unpleasant and tell me so, they are also being assertive. This conflict can be resolved in several ways. I may be able to go outside and smoke, thus satisfying my needs and not interfering with the needs of other people. Or I can recognize that smoking would be more unpleasant to them than pleasant to me, and forgo smoking in their presence. In any case, I have still been assertive — I have recognized and expressed my need, though I have not fulfilled my desire. Self-assertion does not mean "getting one's way" all the time.

Note though that the definition of self-assertion does include recognizing needs and inner feelings. This is not always easy, as the following example shows:

Alice has to conduct a P.T.A. meeting tomorrow morning and she is both anxious and resentful about it. She has put off planning the meeting until there is almost no time left. Harry comes home and says, "How about going to the movies tonight?" Alice blows up and says, irritatedly, "I still have dinner to cook and dishes to do, as the old saying goes — 'man works from sunup to sundown, but woman's work is never done.' " Harry responds, "If women have it so tough, why do men get all the ulcers and heart attacks?"

And so the argument rages on without chance of solution because Alice has not recognized the real source of her irritation, namely, her anxiety about the P.T.A. meeting. But, why doesn't she?

Perhaps she doesn't want to admit to herself that she is afraid of conducting the meeting. She avoids thinking about the meeting and thereby avoids the fear that arises when she does. Or maybe she knows she is afraid but doesn't want Harry to see this weakness, so she covers it from him by starting an irrelevant argument.

Self-assertion requires self-knowledge. That is, successful communication depends in large part on knowing oneself. In any relationship there will be known and unknown dimensions. One way of diagramming and discovering these dimensions is called the Johari window (see Figure 6-2).

Let's see how to use the Johari window. As you begin a new relationship with another person, one where you both are committed to helping each other grow, you can both draw Johari windows. The

Things about myself that I . . .

		do know	don't know
Things about myself that the other . . .	does know	**common knowledge**	**my blind spots** (such as an irritating mannerism I'm unaware of)
	does not know	**my secrets** (things I've never shared about myself)	**my unknown self** (things neither you nor I know about myself)

Figure 6-2
The Johari window.

easiest window to fill in is that of common knowledge. At the beginning of the relationship, common knowledge will probably only include such things as height, hair color, weight, food preferences. As the relationship continues, you will be able to fill in some of the other's blind spots, perhaps such things as insensitiveness, always wanting one's own way, nervous laughter, bad breath, snoring. Then, as you continue to develop trust in each other, you can begin to fill in your secrets, perhaps feelings of inferiority, fears of homosexuality, being afraid to be alone at night. By now you may be discovering aspects of each other's unknown self; these may be hidden potentials, talents, or weaknesses that are uncovered by the relationship itself, the interaction between the two of you and your friends. And, as you get to know each other better, the blind spot and secret areas will become smaller as more information is moved into the common knowledge window.

Of course, you don't have to have a new relationship to use the Johari window — it can illuminate behavior and knowledge in on-going relationships. In fact, the process of exploring new dimensions of the self and the other person is exciting and never-ending. Yet, unfortunately, many couples share little common knowledge because there is little self-knowledge on the part of each partner. People who are afraid to learn about themselves will usually block communication that might lead to self-insight. Aversive reactions, as we saw earlier, are excellent ways to stifle communication. For example, consider the following interaction:

> Jim feels his wife Jane looks unusually good one evening and says, "I really feel proud when men look at you admiringly."
> Jane replies, "When you say that I feel like a showpiece in the marketplace."
> "Why don't you get off that feminist trip," he retorts.

Her aversive reply to his statement will probably make him more reluctant to express his feelings the next time. In essence, her aversive response punished him for expressing his feelings. But why did she respond aversively? It's hard to know. She may simply have been in a bad mood. Or, perhaps she has always felt negative about her appearance, and thus needs to deny Jim's feeling since it is inconsistent with her self-image. Her appearance might be a blind spot in her Johari window. Regardless of how objectively attractive Jane may be, if her view of herself is negative, that is what she will believe. In this case Jim has failed to listen empathically (see skill 3, below) to understand Jane's feelings. His own response in the interaction above shows that he is also avoiding communication.

So, we can define the communication skill of self-assertion as learning to assert oneself without making the other person defensive.

EMPATHIC LISTENING   Of all the skills we have been discussing, none is probably more underrated and overlooked than that of being a good listener. We are all very ready to give our opinions and often not really ready to listen to the other's opinion. To be a good listener is an art in itself and much appreciated by most people. To be a good listener may be one of the most therapeutic things we can do for our intimate relationships.

Real listening keeps the focus on the person who is talking. By focusing on the speaker, the listener actively tries to reduce any personal filters that distort the speaker's messages. Usually, however, the listener is actively adding to, subtracting from, and in other ways changing the speaker's message. For example, someone says, "I wrapped my car around a tree coming home from a party last night." I might be thinking, "Well, you probably were drinking (inference) and one should not drive when drinking (value judgment)." Although I have no evidence of any drinking, I have immediately put my own meaning on the statement. Also, if the speaker recognizes my negative implications, he or she might react with anger or cease talking to me.

Empathic listening, on the other hand, is nonjudgmental and accepting. To the degree that we are secure, we can listen to others without filtering their message. To really listen and to understand another means that we allow our own self to be open to new self-knowledge and change. However, for the insecure, this can be frightening. For example:

George is very unsure of Gloria's love for him and fears she may one day leave him. At dinner she comments, "I really like tall men with beards." George feels his clean-shaven chin and begins to feel insecure. He doesn't hear much of the ensuing conversation because he is busy trying to decide whether she would like him to grow a beard or if she has a crush on another man. He has completely filtered out the part about tall men since he is tall and therefore not threatened by that.

George has put his own inferences onto Gloria's comment and becomes increasingly upset as he ponders, not what she actually said, but what he thinks she means by what she said.

It is interesting to note that it is easier to listen empathically to a stranger than to someone close. Married persons often state that some friend or acquaintance understands them better than their spouse. This may well be true. Our emotions often get in the way of our hearing. For example, when George's secretary says she likes tall men with beards, George doesn't even think about it, he simply says "that's nice."

When one listens empathically, what happens to the speaker? The speaker really feels that the listener hears and cares. In essence, the speaker feels nonthreatened, noncoerced, and, of course, free to speak — one of our preconditions for successful communication.

There are several components of empathic listening. Obviously the listener must feel capable of paying close attention to the speaker. If we are consumed by our own thoughts and problems, we obviously cannot listen to another. But when we know that we cannot listen well, we should point that out (self-assertion) and perhaps arrange to have the discussion at another time. For instance, all too often family members bring up problems at the end of the day when everyone is tired and hungry or at other inopportune times and then become even more upset because no one is willing to listen. We all need time, a quiet environment, and a peaceful mind to be good empathic listeners.

Part of our attention should also be directed to the body language of the speaker. Emotions are reflected throughout the body although they are less specific than verbal communication. When we pick up bodily communications, we should check them out with the speaker because of their less specific meaning.

Feedback is another key component of empathic listening. The listener must periodically check perceptions with the speaker. This is best done by rephrasing the speaker's words. This allows the speaker to have reassurance that she or he is being listened to and accurately heard, to have the opportunity to correct the listener's perceptions, and to have the opportunity to hear her or his ideas from the listener's perspective.

Some examples of feedback are:

Speaker: I'm not getting out of bed today.
Listener: Is there a problem?
Speaker: You're always working.
Listener: I know. Is it interrupting something we need to do?
Speaker: Why don't we get out of this town?
Listener: I don't understand why. I guess you don't like it here.
Speaker: Nobody does any work around here but me.
Listener: It sounds like you feel tired of all the work you have to do.

Note that empathic listening involves an effort on the listener's part to pick up feelings as well as content. If the listener is incorrect, the speaker can correct when the listener feeds back what she or he thinks was said.

Remember though that we are discussing enhancing good problem-solving communication. Much communication is for play and fun, to establish contact, or to impart information. To use the skills helpful to problem solving inappropriately can also *cause* problems.

Exercises for Sending and Receiving Feeling Messages

People often intermix sending and receiving messages. For example, the speaker may be overconcerned with the effect the message might have on the listener, and may thus modify and change the message so that it is not quite what was originally meant. In other words, the sender fails to send a true message because of fear about how it will be received. And, as we have seen, the listener may indeed put a personal interpretation on the message, or may be thinking about how to reply, and thus not really concentrating on getting the entire message.

When feelings are involved, as in conflicts between family members, messages are even more likely to get changed. So practice in sending — self-assertion — and receiving — empathic listening — will help keep the two separate and enhance clear, good communication.

The following exercise should give you and your family and/or friends the opportunity to improve both your ability to assert yourself clearly and your ability to listen effectively. Begin by choosing a speaker and a listener. The speaker should send a brief, personally relevant communication in which she or he recognizes and owns some feeling. The listener then repeats, to the best of his or her ability, the speaker's statement. The others listen attentively and, after the listener has responded, share with the speaker any other feelings they think were involved in the communication but which the speaker did not express. When the message is clearly understood by both speaker and listener, they should change places. All members of the group should have a chance to practice as senders and receivers.

The exercise serves two purposes:

1. The speaker does not receive a critical reaction and therefore does not have to defend the statement. This hopefully frees the speaker to deal more honestly with feelings and also to hear the message she or he has communicated.

2. The listener gets practice in effective listening without having to react, interpret, or evaluate. This hopefully frees the listener from feeling he or she has to resolve or somehow deal responsibly with the feelings the speaker has expressed, so the listener can concentrate on what is actually being said.

In the practice situation the burden of reaction is lifted from the listener. Thereby he or she may concentrate on receiving the message accurately and clearly. They feel a strong connection with the speaker. On page 191 there are examples of poor sending and receiving as well as examples of clear communication where listening and speaking are well separated. (For a thorough discussion of training in communication skills, see Schauble and Hill, 1976.)

For example, if someone asks you to "Please pass the butter," it would *not* be appropriate to reply, "Oh, you feel like having some butter on your bread." About the best this remark will do is invoke muttering from the requesting person about "there you go using that dumb psychology again" while he reaches for the butter. To know when and how to listen is an invaluable skill, but it too can be misused.

NEGOTIATING   If the problem is jointly owned, then the situation calls for negotiation. In this case the partners alternate between self-assertion and empathic listening. Usually the most distressed partner starts with self-assertion. But since the problem is jointly owned, the listener's feelings are also involved, so it is imperative to switch roles relatively often to be sure that each person's communications are understood by the other. Set a time period, say, five to ten minutes for

Inset 6-4
Fighting Fairly in Love and Marriage

Many couples state that their basic problem is that they fight all the time. Yet, rather than a problem, fighting is a normal part of any intimate relationship. The problem is not whether one fights or not, but how one fights. Fighting is simply a form of communication and all of our principles apply. George Bach is a therapist who gives fight training to help increase intimacy rather than destroy it (see Bach and Wyden, 1968). The following dialogue is an example of pointless fighting. It is followed by the same fight done in a constructive manner. Within the parentheses are Bach and Wyden's analysis of the interactions.

Ralph: I don't like the way the kids handle money.
Betsy: What's the matter with it? They're good kids.
Ralph: Yes, but they haven't learned the value of money.
Betsy: They're just kids. Why not let them have their fun? They'll learn soon enough.
Ralph: No, I think you're spoiling them.
Betsy: How in the world am I doing that?
Ralph: By giving them the idea that money grows on trees.
Betsy: Well, why don't *you* set a better example? You might start by spending less on your pipe collection.
Ralph: What's that got to do with it?
Betsy: Plenty. When the kids see you waste money on nonessentials, they feel they have the same rights.

Ralph: I shop for my pipes. They're very carefully selected.
Betsy: Maybe, but whenever I send you to the market, you always spend more than I would. You're always dragging in stuff we don't really need.
Ralph: OK, OK. I know you're a better shopper at the market, but that's your job, you know, not mine.
Betsy: Well, then, don't blame me for the kids.

After several training sessions, we asked the Snyders to refight the same fight before one of our training groups. Here is how it went the second time around:

Ralph (*starting with a specific objective, not a general observation*): I want you to stop slipping the kids extra money beyond the allowances I give them.
Betsy (*showing Ralph why his idea may be difficult to accomplish*): But you're not around. You don't know their needs.
Ralph (*spelling out his objective further*): I want to know their needs. I want them to come to me with their money needs.
Betsy (*justifying her past practices*): Well, you know what goes on. I tell you everything. You know where the money goes.
Ralph (*specifying the real issue that this fight is all about*): That's fine, but it's not the point. I believe the children should learn more about responsibility — having to justify getting the money from me and spending it wisely.

Betsy (*making sure he's serious*): You really want to supervise all this piffle?
Ralph (*reconfirming the stakes as he sees them*): Don't you see the importance of teaching them early responsibility for money matters?
Betsy (*specifying the reasons for her opposition*): Frankly, no. They are good kids and they're having a good time. I like to give them a little extra now and then. I enjoy it when they have fun. They'll learn responsibility soon enough.
Ralph (*sizing up the results of the fight thus far and re-checking his wife for more feedback*): I can see we really differ on this issue. Do you understand my position?
Betsy (*reconfirming her understanding of Ralph's real objective*): Yes, you want us to teach the kids responsibility.
Ralph (*seeking a meeting ground, at least in principle*): Yes, don't you?
Betsy (*agreeing to his principle but dissenting from his method*): Yes, but your method would deprive me of something I enjoy doing, and I don't believe I am overdoing it. You know I'm careful with my money.
Ralph (*hardening his stand*): Yes, you're a careful shopper and all that — I have no complaints about that — but I must ask you to stop slipping the kids extra money. That's the only way to control careless spending.
Betsy (*realizing that she'll probably have to give some ground*): I see you really are concerned with this specific issue.

Ralph (*elaborating on the reasons for his firm stand*): I love the children as much as you do and I don't want to see them develop into careless adults.

Betsy (*offering a proposal for a compromise*): I don't think they will, but since this seems to mean so much to you, let me suggest something. Why don't you tell me how much you think would be reasonable to give them "extra" and for what occasions, and I'll stick to it.

Ralph (*checking out that Betsy isn't likely to compromise further*): You still want to keep giving them extra money?

Betsy (*reconfirming her stand*): Yes, I do. I enjoy it, as I told you.

Ralph (*accepting Betsy's compromise, proposing details on how to make it work, and offering another compromise as a conciliatory gesture*): Well, let's sit down and budget how much money they should get from us altogether, for everything every week, how much for extras, and so on. It's not so terribly important to me who gives them the money, as how much and what for.

Betsy (*confirming Ralph's acceptance and offering a further implementing proposal showing that she too is now trying to accomplish his objective*): OK. Let's figure it out; then, every weekend, you can sit down with the kids and me and see that we didn't go over the limit.

Ralph (*confirming that he understands and approves her latest idea*): Yes, I could vary the regular pocket money, depending on how much you've slipped them.

Betsy (*offering another suggestion to make sure their new plan will work and maybe show Ralph that she was right about the kids' sense of responsibility after all*): Certainly, you can also ask them how much they've spent and what for. Then you would find out all about their needs and learn how responsible they can be.

Ralph (*nails down the deal and specifies the date it goes into effect*): OK. Let's try it this Saturday (Bach and Wyden, 1968, pp. 65–68).

each partner to speak and then listen. Remember that listening will take extra effort to avoid the temptation of thinking about your side of the problem while the other is speaking, which, of course, interferes with empathic listening.

When roles are exchanged, the partner who was listening should first restate the assertive partner's position (feedback) so that any necessary corrections can be made before going on to his or her own assertions. The very fact of knowing that the speaker's position must be restated to her or his satisfaction before your own position can be presented works wonders to improve listening ability.

This simple procedure of reversing roles and restating the other's position before presenting your own is also amazingly effective in defusing potential emotional outbursts. Much frustration usually builds up because partners do not listen to one another and therefore often feel misunderstood. But with this process, even if your partner strongly disagrees with your position, at least you both have the satisfaction of knowing your position will be heard and understood by the other. This is a large step toward better communication and certainly helps avoid "the dialogue of the deaf" which all too often occurs in marriage.

PROBLEM SOLVING Now that ownership of the problem has been established, clarification of the problem started, and some of the emotion surrounding the problem discharged, we are ready to solve the problem. Of course, by now the problem will have been greatly diminished, or the partners may even discover, once they have truly expressed themselves and listened to the other, that the problem has disappeared. However, if the couple still feels they have a problem, they can now apply the scientific method to solving it.

There are seven steps to scientific problem solving:

1. Recognizing and defining the problem.
2. Setting up conditions supportive to problem solving.
3. Brainstorming for possible alternatives (establishing hypotheses).
4. Selecting the best solution.
5. Implementing the solution.
6. Evaluating the solution.
7. Modifying the solution if necessary.

The first two steps have already been accomplished if the couple has used the skills discussed. Step 3, brainstorming, helps to broaden the range of possible solutions. Brainstorming is producing as many ideas as possible in a given time period. That is, if you select a half hour to brainstorm the problem, you both call out any ideas you have as fast as

possible — without pausing to evaluate. That is, all ideas are put out regardless of whether or not they are ridiculous or possible. All too often negative judgments stifle creative thinking, so it is important to suspend any evaluating until you have both run out of ideas or reached the end of the time period. You can, however, jot down ideas as they occur so you won't forget any — but just jot them down, don't think about them.

Once you have both run out of ideas, or of time, you can begin to select the best solution. Be sure to read both lists of ideas so that all will be considered. Then use the skills of self-assertion and of empathic listening to evaluate the likely ideas. It is a good idea to decide on an amount of time to use to defend and judge each idea.

Once the best idea has been agreed on, of course, it must be acted upon, or implemented. If the problem has been a serious one, it is a good idea to schedule periods when you can both discuss how the solution is working out. If the solution has solved the problem, then you will not need to use step 7. If, however, you are still experiencing difficulties, you may have to modify the solution in light of your evaluation sessions. Or you may have to go back to the possible alternatives generated during the brainstorming session and reselect another possible solution to test.

Summary

Nowhere are communication skills more important than in the marital relationship. Couples having marital trouble almost always report communication failure as a major problem. Basically, communication failures occur because one or perhaps both partners choose not to communicate or lack the skills of communication.

Although communication problems are often the result of personal problems and inadequacies of the partners, the general society can also facilitate or hinder good communication. Society's support of stereotypical sex roles, especially that of the strong, silent male, certainly restricts good communication.

When most people talk about failure in communication, what they really mean is that communication has become too aversive, that it causes too much discomfort. In other words, there is too much negative and hurtful communication rather than there simply being no communication. But if the aversive communication continues too long, the couple may indeed stop communicating.

There are three basic conditions that must be met before good communication can be assured. First, there must be a commitment to communicate. Both parties must want to communicate with one another. Second, there must be an orientation on the part of the partners to growth and improvement of the relationship. Each must be willing to accept the possibility of change. Third, neither partner must try to coerce the other with communications. The communication should not be so aversive and attacking as to cause the other partner to be defensive or to withdraw from communicating.

When these basic conditions are met, problem-solving skills can be called into play. Basically, five skills are involved in successful communication. The ownership of the problem must be identified, each partner must be willing to speak up and state his or her position and feelings (self-assertion), each must be a good listener (empathic listening), and each must be willing to negotiate and work with the other to solve the problem.

Fighting fairly and using problem-solving skills will enhance any relationship and keep it alive and growing. But failure to communicate clearly and fight fairly will usually cause disruption and the ultimate failure of intimate relationships.

Games, Strategies, and Schemes

A couple's communications can easily fall into set patterns that reduce and destroy the chances for successful communication. These patterns are often called games, strategies, and schemes since their actual purpose is covert or not clearly communicated. Games, strategies, and schemes interfere with good communication, and though they sometimes seem to reduce conflict in the short run, in the long run they deepen communication problems. So it is important that any such patterns be quickly recognized and dealt with by couples. Scenes from Marriage thus includes examples of several of these destructive patterns.

The Mind-Reading Act

Sue Bernard is sweet, bright, and attractive. At 105 pounds, five feet one inch tall, she seems incapable of driving Sam, her 220-pound ex-tackle husband, into frantic confusion. Yet she can, and she is very, very good at it.

Every day, Sam Bernard returns home on the five-thirty commuter train. All the way up from the station he thinks of getting

home, of a Scotch and soda, some soft music, and his sweet Sue who can be fragile, cuddly, a small but strong bulwark against the nasty competitive world of stocks and bonds.

It is now 6:05 P.M. at the Bernard residence. Sue has seen Sam come up the walk. She opens the front door just as Sam reaches for it with his key. The welcoming is thus a bit unnerving, especially as she gasps, "Oh, darling, you look so tired!"

Thus doubly taken aback, Sam feels a bit vulnerable. He responds without protest to her mothering invitation to sit in his favorite chair while she gets him a drink.

Her wide brown eyes peer steadily over the rim of her gin and tonic (Sam also has one, since she didn't ask—and he didn't say —that he preferred a Scotch and soda).

"Darling, you're angry about something. Yes," continues Sue before Sam has a chance to reply, "you are. You forget how well I know you. Why don't you tell me what it's about?"

"Sue, I don't know what you're getting at. I am a little *tired*. I am not angry." His voice starts to get strident.

"All right, if you won't say. I don't see why you can't share anything with me any more. I just wanted to help."

"Damn it, I don't need help. I'd like to listen to Miles Davis and relax a bit before dinner. Is that asking too much?"

"Well, I like that! I told you you were angry. Now you're taking it out on me. You're mean and nasty and I'm getting sick and tired of it," says Sue petulantly, flouncing off to the kitchen.

Sam can hear the clanging of pots and the mild banging of dishes, a sure sign that sweet Sue is sour. Sitting and sipping the bitter gin and tonic, Sam feels his stomach ache as if a big tackle had put an elbow into his gut. He is puzzled and despairing.

Sam has unwittingly encouraged Sue's destructive "mind reading" by not dealing with it specifically. He has permitted Sue to control and anger him almost any time she wishes.

Husbands play the mind-reading game, too. This vicious process could have worked the other way around. For example, Sue might have been looking ahead to Sam's return, and he might have entered the front door saying, "Oh, I see you've had a bad day?"

"No, as a matter of fact . . ."

"The house always looks a mess when you've been feeling bad. Are you beginning to be pre-menstrual?" And then it would have started.

Sometimes both spouses practice this arcane art. While it makes for interesting listening for a marital therapist, it is hell for both participants, who join the world's most misunderstood people.

What can be done to help the mind reader refrain from practicing this destructive technique?

The spouse who wishes to correct this behavior in his or her mate can do so *if* he or she skillfully and consistently follows the proper method, even for a short period. He or she must *always agree* with the mind reader. In fact, it is desirable to *overagree*, as in the following dialogue.

Sue: Oh darling, I know you're just beat. You must sit down here.

Sam: Thanks, darling. You're right. I've *never* been so tired. Could you get me a drink while I lie down?

Sue: Certainly, sweetheart. You've had a bad day, I can see that.

Sam: You don't know the half of it. Everything went wrong. To begin with, I may have to fire my secretary. Did I tell you some of the things that girl did?

Sue: Oh, excuse me, darling, I must see to supper. I'm sure you'll feel better after a hot meal.

Sam: Well, I don't know if I'll be able to eat anything, but I can try.

Sue: (*Retreating in confusion*): Oh, that's fine, hon. I'll call you.

This technique depends on the principle of the *reductio ad absurdum*, in which by carrying something to its logical conclusion one shows it to be ridiculous. What the mind reader says is usually irrefutable, so argument does no good. But he doesn't expect agreement, and when he gets it he becomes confused, for he depends on omnipotence and surprise in order to retain the advantage. Now he is suddenly afraid to continue; he doesn't know where his remarks may lead.

This is not an easy technique to use, but some practice before a mirror will help (Lederer and Jackson, 1968, pp. 225–226).

The Private Freedom Cult

It is hard to argue with a woman like Terry when she says "No relationship is good if the partners aren't free. If they can't be individuals, they go stale and have nothing to give each other. That's what's wrong with most couples today."

Mark agreed. It followed that there was to be no exclusivity in their relationship in bed or out. She wanted no commitment. She wanted to stay loose. Dates should be broken even on short notice if either partner felt he did not really want them. In a museum, Terry might say, "You keep looking at Flemish painting; I'm going to the Egyptian Room." And she was irritable if Mark said he'd go along.

She told Mark she loved him. Sometimes she acted this out sexually, with wild abandon; twice she made love with him all night. But at other times she was repelled by his physical affection, and became angry when he touched her. Her capacity for excitement turned Mark on. But he felt rejected when she asserted her independence.

She began mentioning other dates that she had on these independent days. Then one night in bed, she mentioned something amusing that a male friend of hers had said at breakfast that morning. When Mark protested, she reminded him of her previously announced credo, and of the fact that he, too, was free.

"The only way I can live with or love someone," she said, "is with no questions asked, no questions answered."

On the other hand, she assured Mark that he was really central in her life, that he was her real love. Lately, she had been saying this more and more often. Also, Terry called on his time with less and less warning. She would phone on an impulse to suggest seeing a movie in an hour, or to make love right away. Mark was afraid to reject these overtures. Even if he had plans, he would break them. For Terry responded to any hint of refusal with something like, "Of course, you *should* do what you most want to do right now." But her voice was cold.

The situation was maddening for Mark. He was involved in a totally undisciplined pairing. The partners made no attempts to calibrate their real wishes. It seemed to Mark that he was being used, that Terry wanted him at her beck and call, while claiming freedom for herself and giving only lip service to *his* freedom. He allowed this to continue against his own better judgment but ultimately asked for professional advice.

A few weeks later Mark was able to tell Terry that he wanted to test his newly stiffened backbone. Terry seemed merely amused. When Mark flatly refused some of her last-minute summonings, she verbally shrugged the refusal off. As usual, she treated Mark coldly on these occasions and he would relent for fear of losing her.

Finally, he made a testing demand. If he was really central in her life, if she really loved him, Mark said, he felt entitled to reserve some prime time for himself. He wanted her to spend weekends with him. She argued. Mark merely said he would accept whatever decision she made and that this would indicate to him the reality of their relationship. She became very irritable but assented. They made a date for Friday night a week in advance, quite unusual for Terry, who said she hated commitments and thought that life was much richer when lived by impulse and surprise.

Friday at seven, Mark was at her door. She did not answer the bell. He used his key and found a note. "Had to go out. Sorry. Terry."

Mark waited three hours before he left, never to see her again. He had the answer.

Terry is an "autonomy worshipper." This is another, sometimes intractable, form of being nonintimate. Autonomists — who are more often male — like intense semblances of intimacy, such as sexual passion. This is often bait for them, as it was for Mark, who was passive with women. He did not have to reach out for sex, and he deluded himself that he had conquered Terry.

The realistic pairer cannot be exploited for long by the autonomist, who, while seeming to grant freedom, always asserts control. Any passionate assertion of self tends to make the autonomist flee, as Terry did when Mark made a realistic demand for change.

Chapter 7 ~

Contents

The Family
as an
Economic System

Americans have more money per person than most people on earth. The gross national product (GNP) divided by the total population of men, women, and children gives each individual more than $9646 per year (all GNP figures are based on the year 1978). Table 7-1 indicates how this compares to other nations.

Americans also spend more than any other people. In 1978, Americans consumed an estimated $1340 billion in goods, or about $14,000 per household. Most of this money is spent by family units to support family members. The family in modern America is actually the basic economic unit of the society in that it is the major *consumption* unit. In the early years of our country the family was also the major production unit. Ninety percent of the population once worked in agriculture on family-owned farms. However, over the years, large corporations took over the farms, combining them into ever-larger units, and most farm workers became factory workers. Thus, today's average family is not directly involved in economic production. Most families support themselves by having one or more of their members work for outside employers.

As a consuming unit, however, the family exerts great economic influence. A couple anticipating marriage and children are also anticipating separate housing from their parents. This means a refrigerator, stove, furniture, dishes, television, and so on. And how will the new American family acquire all of these? Probably by the use of credit, perhaps not an American invention, but certainly an American way of life. And how much do Americans owe? Approximately $300 billion, or about $1333 per person for outstanding personal credit

Table 7-1 Per Capita Income for the Top Ten and Lowest Ten Countries

Top Ten	Dollars Per Person	Lowest Ten	
Switzerland	$13,853	Afghanistan	Less than $200 per person
Kuwait	13,000	Burma	"
Denmark	10,948	Pakistan	"
Sweden	10,440	Vietnam	"
W. Germany	10,415	Tanzania	"
Belgium	9,938	Ethiopia	"
Norway	9,849	Zaire	"
United States	9,646	Nepal	"
Netherlands	9,367	India	"
Saudi Arabia	9,330	Laos	"

(*Santa Barbara News Press*, Nov. 7, 1979, F-14). About 36 percent of this is accounted for by indebtedness for automobiles.

"Buy now, pay later!" "Why wait? Only $5 per week." These and many more are the economic slogans of modern American society. The extension of credit to the general population has produced a material standard of living the likes of which the world has never seen. We may, on the promise of future payment, acquire and use almost anything that we desire. Not only may we acquire material goods, we may also travel, educate ourselves, and use many services such as medical and dental care, all without immediate monetary payment. If the credit system were suddenly ended, the degree to which it supports the economy would become glaringly clear. Traffic congestion would end as the majority of autos would disappear from the road. Many buildings, both business and residential, would become empty lots or smaller, shabbier versions. Thousands of televisions would disappear from living rooms. A vast amount of furniture would also vanish from our homes. If debtor prisons were reestablished at the same time, practically the entire population would be incarcerated!

Any discussion of marriage must include an analysis of the part that finances will play in the relationship. In the past it was widely believed that money mattered little to the general success of a marriage. Many of the classic studies indicated little if any relationship between amount of money and marital success. Unfortunately these results led many later writers to exclude financial adjustment as a significant influence on the general marital relationship. This was an error. Although the actual amount of money earned by a family may not relate to marital success, each partner's attitude toward money and finance is often crucial.

Money is involved in everything we do, yet few people consider the study of personal finance, money management, investment, and budget of interest. Most Americans appear more willing to discuss their sex lives than their monetary situation. Asking a person what he or she earns or what something has cost is often considered an affront, or, at the least, an invasion of privacy. But the recent unusual economic climate, a frightening mixture of inflation and recession, has brought economics more strongly into the spotlight than at any time since the Great Depression of the 1930s. However, even in good economic times, married couples often quarrel over money. General economic stress is often a major contributing factor to marital failure.

Essentially, quarrels over money revolve around allocation of resources and control of the allocation. What should we buy? When should we buy? Who should buy? Who should make the spending decisions? Such questions become particularly troublesome if the partners have divergent attitudes about money. For example, consider a person who comes from a background of thrift and practicality and who takes pleasure in making a good buy. Such a person will be excited about buying a used car at wholesale rather than at retail blue book price and will probably brag about the purchase. Any minor problems with the car will not be upsetting because of the value of the

Answer the following questions[1] without discussing them with your partner. Then have your partner answer them. If you answer the questions differently, it may indicate points of attitudinal differences and possible conflict. You should each discuss the reasoning behind your answer and how your two positions can be reconciled.

1. Are you comfortable living without a steady income?
2. Did your parents have a steady income?
3. Do you consider yourself to come from an economically poor, average, or wealthy background?
4. Do you think that saving is of value in America's inflationary economy?

[1]Some of these questions are from Landis, 1970, p. 509.

5. Do you have a savings account? Do you contribute to it regularly?
6. In the past, have you postponed buying things until you had saved the money for them, or did you buy immediately, if possible, when you desired something?
7. In the past, have you often bought on installment?
8. Do you have credit cards? How many? Do you use them regularly?
9. Do you have money left over at the end of your regular pay period?
10. Do you brag about making a really good buy or finding a real bargain?
11. If it were possible to save $100 a month, what would you do with the money?
12. Possible answers to question 11 are listed below. Rank them in order of importance using 1 for what you

would most likely do with the $100 and 10 for what you are least likely to do:
  a. Save it for a rainy day.
  b. Save it so you can buy something for cash rather than on credit.
  c. Invest it.
  d. Use it for recreation.
  e. Use it for payments for a new car.
  f. Use it for travel and adventure.
  g. Use it to buy a home or property.
  h. Use it to improve your present living place.
  i. Divide it in half and let each spouse spend it as he or she chooses.
  j. Use it for an attractive wardrobe, eating out, and entertaining.

"good buy." However, the partner comes from a luxurious environment that places value on achieving just what you want and measures success by an economic standard. This partner feels that a new car of the appropriate model is the proper vehicle to buy. A used car, especially a "steal," will be considered a mark of poor taste and economic failure. Obviously, the married life of such a pair will be filled with conflict over money matters.

Credit buying has allowed the average American a higher standard of living than was ever dreamed possible. It has given Americans the means for a healthier, more fulfilling life about which, in centuries past, one could only dream. However, despite these positive results, the system can boomerang and place people in a slavery system that traps them subtly but with psychological cost. This entrapment and loss of freedom usually comes from ignorance of the system and blind acceptance of the persuasive and seductive output coming through advertising. A clear understanding of economics and the relationship

Why a "Slavery" System?

of debt to personal freedom enables people to make the system work for instead of against them.

"Slavery" appears to be a strange term to use to describe the economic system of one of the freest countries on earth. Yet credit and debt are directly opposed to personal freedom. To contract to pay for a new automobile over a period of thirty-six months, for example, involves gaining the use of the automobile but losing a degree of personal freedom. Regardless of circumstances or what you do with the car, you have promised and legally made yourself responsible to pay a certain amount each month for the next three years. If at the end of one year, you wish to take a lower paying but more satisfying job, or to return to school to improve skills, you would be unable to do so unless you can make adequate arrangements to continue payments on the car. Even if you decide to return the car it does not cancel the debt. If the credit company is gracious enough to allow you credit for the money received by them when the car is sold, the chances are that there will still be some debt because the car depreciates in value faster than the debt is reduced during the first year or two. Although the remaining debt will be smaller, it still exists, and so does your obligation.

Thus any debt curtails a certain amount of personal freedom. If you cannot at least partially resist the temptations of credit buying, you can become so obligated as to lose almost all freedom. This modern economic slavery is far more seductive than historical slavery systems based on power. In real slavery, a person knows who the enemy is and where to direct the hostility engendered by the loss of freedom. But in the American system it is the individual who has placed himself or herself in the slavery of debt. There is no one but oneself to blame then for the predicament. No one is forced to keep buying "goodies" on "easy" installments. Unfortunately, too many small, easy payments can add to heavy sums — often too heavy for the marriage to bear.

Joe and Mary — Slow Drowning in a Sea of Debt

Let's now take a closer look at a hypothetical, newly married young couple and follow them through their first few years of confrontation with the American economic system. This will make clear the slow and often insidious nature of the loss of freedom and eventual entrapment suffered by so many families. For many young couples, marriage actually means a drastic reduction in their standard of living. Accustomed to living at home, to sharing their parents' standard of living (usually created by twenty years of their parents' earnings), the newlyweds are cast economically onto their own. Beginning jobs are scarce and pay is low compared to the parents' earnings. If the newlyweds don't understand this and attempt to maintain the parental standard in their new marriage, they are likely to be entrapped in the economic slavery system.

When Did Joe's Entrapment Begin? Joe's actual entrapment began before his marriage. Joe is shorter than most of the other boys in high school, and finds he is not as popular with girls as some of his taller friends. Like most of his friends, he has always been interested in automobiles. He now figures that if he had a good car, he would probably be more popular. He also notes that his parents often judge their friends, in part, by the cars they drive. Thus he feels that his car should be one of the better ones. He has a job as a stockboy at a local supermarket, and since he lives at home and doesn't have any living expenses, he feels he can use the money he's earning to pay for the car. It seems so simple. His parents don't object to his buying a car, but make it clear that they are in no financial position to help him. So he goes ahead and contracts to pay $110 a month for the next three years. Of course, the $110 is not his only expense now — he has all the general expenses of an automobile: tax, license, insurance, gas, upkeep, and, quite likely, modifications (lowering it, raking it, adding magnesium wheels, four carburetors, a tape deck, and whatever else is popular).

The automobile is one of the few products in the American inflationary economy that usually loses money.* But the practical reason for the auto, transportation, is rarely considered by young men. For many, the car is much more than this. It is an extension of one's ego. (In general, the relationship between the strength of ego and the cost of the car is inverse. That is, the weaker the boy's ego, the more important the car.) It is one's means to prestige and status. It gives one a feeling of power since one can make the car do whatever one wants. Many adolescent boys drive hundreds of aimless miles per week. The figures on car theft demonstrate dramatically the importance of the auto to the young American male. The FBI national figures show a heavy preponderance of male youth involved in car theft. (See p. 214 for car costs.)

Joe soon attracts a wonderful girl with his new symbol. Although she first noticed him because of his new car, Mary finds him to be a nice person and is soon going steady with him. The pressures of the American dating game build up, and they consider themselves deeply in love. Joe is near the end of his senior year in high school and will soon be able to work full time. If he stays at the supermarket and becomes a checker, he will be earning $900 to $1400 a month. This seems like a fortune compared to the $140 he now receives as part-time help. Both Joe and Mary have also always heard that two can live as cheaply as one — another of the great modern hoaxes.

Looking at the rapid rise in yearly minimum salary needed for a family of four, it is obvious that his new salary is really only at survival level in today's inflationary economy (see Inset 7-2).

Setting Up Their New Apartment   Finally, Joe and Mary marry and set up housekeeping. At first, they are the envy of their friends. They are now independent, out from under parental domination, and can participate in so many things that were previously taboo. Soon Joe finds that his salary isn't going as far as he anticipated. Somehow rent, food,

*A few cars become classics and, if well maintained, may actually appreciate in value.

and basic necessities are eating huge chunks of his new, large salary. Before his marriage, he thought he would have enough to update his car a bit, go on some nice trips now that he and Mary are legally married, and model their apartment after those seen in *Playboy*. But now Mary says they have to have a new washing machine, that it's something all young married couples have to have. When they go to look at washing machines, the salesperson convinces them that they should buy the deluxe model with five washing speeds and three water temperatures. Of course, it's $70 more than the ordinary machine, but then again, according to the salesperson, it's far superior, and the payments are the same, just stretched a little longer for the deluxe model. Of course, the salesperson doesn't tell them that the motor and all basic parts are the same in both models. But the salesperson does add that there's a special this week on the matching dryer, which they can get for $30 less with free installation. It's a great opportunity, and would only add $2 more per week. Joe is beginning to feel a little nervous about adding these payments to the $110 he is still paying on the car, but Mary does seem very happy, and he supposes the machines will make life easier for both of them. He still wishes he had his car fixed up, however.

Gradually Joe is going to find that his salary is claimed before he receives it — the couple will reach the point where they no longer have the freedom of decision over their income. One obvious problem is that they are starting off with large purchases, some of which they don't really need. A washer and dryer are really unnecessary items for a young couple without children.

Credit to Cover Credit A year after their marriage, their first child is born — with concomitant hospital, doctor, and general care bills. A surprising number of salespersons come knocking at their door to help them get their youngster started off right. First there are disposable diapers, a must for the modern mother. Then there is a photographer who will take regular pictures of the child so they will have a permanent record of the child's growth. There are toys that will help increase their child's intellectual growth. And, of course, they now need a set of encyclopedias.

One month Joe discovers that his paycheck doesn't quite cover their monthly costs. At first, they panic, but then Mary remembers an ad she saw that says all their debts can be wiped out by combining them into one large package loan. In fact, the ad said, "Borrow enough money to get completely out of debt." At the time it didn't seem to make sense but now it does. With a sigh of relief they go down to the finance company and soon have things financially under control again. The discount interest rate is 10 percent but they don't really care as long as they can meet the payments.

Rather than continue Joe's story, suffice it to say that five years after his marriage, Joe is in bankruptcy court. No, he hadn't gambled on a big investment speculation, he had simply slowly drowned in a rising sea of debt.

Credit, Borrowing, and Installment Buying

Money is borrowed for two basic reasons: to buy consumer goods and to invest in tangible assets.

Consumer debt is high-priced money because it is used for consumable goods such as cars, furniture, and clothing whose value diminishes with time. Discount, or hard, interest is usually charged for consumer debt. This kind of interest is charged on the total amount of the loan for the entire time period.

Investment debt, or real-property debt, is lower-priced money because it is used for tangible assets such as real estate or businesses whose value is permanent. If, for some reason, the debt is not paid, the creditor may assume ownership of the asset and sell it to regain the loaned money. Simple interest is charged for investment debt. This kind of interest is charged only on the unpaid balance of the loan.

Examples of Actual Interest Costs

Hard or Discount Interest If you borrow $1000 for three years at 10 percent hard interest per year, you must pay $100 per year interest for the use of the money ($0.10 \times \$1000 = \$100$). Each month you will pay $8.33 interest ($\$100 \div 12$ months $= \$8.33$). In addition, you will pay back the principal of $1000 in thirty-six equal monthly installments so that it is all paid off at the end of the three years. The monthly principal

Table 7-2   Comparative Costs of Consumer Credit

Lenders	Type of Loan	Annual Percentage Rate[1]	Remarks
Banks	Personal loans (consumer goods) Real-property loans General loans	10–18[2]	60% of all car loans, 30% of other consumer-good loans; real-property loans have lower interest rates since property retains value, which may cover defaulted loans.
Credit Cards	Personal loans Cash loans	18[2]	Used as convenience instead of cash; credit is approved for the card rather than individual purchase; no interest charged if bills are paid in full each month; cash in varying amounts, depending on individual's credit rating, may also be borrowed against.[3]
Credit Unions	Personal loans Real-property loans	9–15[2]	Voluntary organizations in which members invest their own money and from which they may borrow.
Finance Companies	Personal loans Real-property loans	12–40	Direct loans to consumers; also buy installments credit from retailers and collect rest of debt so that retailers can get cash when they need it.
Savings & Loan Companies	Real-property loans	11–16[2]	Low interest rates since real property has value that may cover defaulted loans.

[1]Interest rates vary due to pressures of inflation and recession.
[2]If the institution charges interest on the *face amount* of the loan over the entire period of the loan, then double the listed interest rate to get the true interest rate. See example 1, following.
[3]See example 2, following.

payment will be $27.77 ($1000 ÷ 36 = $27.77). Thus your total monthly payment is $36.10, or your interest plus your principal payment ($8.33 + $27.77 = $36.10).

Although you will pay $100 interest each year on your $1000 loan, the fact is that you do not actually have use of the full $1000 for the entire three years. Each month you pay back $27.77 of the loan. As the table shows, at the end of a month (after one payment), you only owe $972.23 ($1000 minus your principal payment of $27.77 = $972.23) of your $1000 loan. Each month what you actually owe (or retain) on the loan is reduced by your principal payment until at the end of the three years (thirty-six payments) your loan is paid off.

		Payments			
	Original Loan	Interest Payment	Principal Payment	Total per Month	Balance
First month	$1000	$8.33	$27.77	$36.10	$972.23
Second month		8.33	27.77	36.10	944.56
Third month		8.33	27.77	36.10	916.79

With hard interest, the stated interest (10 percent in this case) is paid each year of the loan even though with each payment a portion of the loan has been paid back. The true interest rate in such a case is figured by doubling the stated interest rate (in this case it would be 20 percent). This is done because, on the average, you don't really have the full amount of the loan ($1000) to use. You actually have the full $1000 to use only before you make your first payment. After your first payment, you have only $972.23, as the table shows. After the second payment, you have only $944.56 left, and by the thirty-sixth or last payment you have only $27.77 left. By adding up the amount of loan you actually still have after each payment and dividing by the length of the loan (in this case, thirty-six months) you will find that you only have an average of $500 to use. Yet you pay $100 per year interest. This means your real interest on this loan is 20 percent ($100 interest ÷ $500 average cash available from loan = 20 percent).

Actually, all you have to remember is that on a discount or hard interest loan, you pay interest on the full amount of the loan each year even though you have paid back part of the loan. Such interest is usually figured for the full term of the loan and is added to the face amount of the loan immediately when you receive the loan. Thus, in our example, you would sign for a $1300 debt ($1000 principal + $300 interest = $1300) but only receive $1000 in hand. The rule of thumb to figure the actual interest rate on this type of loan is simply to double the stated interest rate.

Credit Card Use If you run a balance on your credit card rather than paying promptly at the end of each month, you are charged interest at 1½ percent per month or 18 percent per year. In addition, there is a one-time transaction charge of 4 percent of each cash advance and 1 percent of each loan advance.

If you are short of money and use your credit card to borrow $100 in cash during your vacation and take three months to pay it back, the loan will cost you $4.00 for the transaction and $1.50 per month interest, or a total of $8.50 for the use of $100 for three months.

Home Loans If you decide to buy a $50,000 home, you may receive a loan of $45,000 for thirty years at 10 percent simple interest (interest rates for home loans have varied dramatically in the past few years, from lows of 9 percent to highs of 16 percent). Simple interest is charged only on the principal balance. For example, to pay off your $45,000 loan and interest in thirty years, your payments will be $394.91 per month. Actually $375 of your first payment will be for interest and $19.91 will be credited against the principal. Thus, for your second payment, you will owe interest on a principal of $44,980.09. Now $374.83 of your second payment will be for interest and $20.08 will apply to the principal. Each month you will pay less interest and more against the principal. However, at the end of thirty years, while you have paid off the $45,000 loan, you will also have paid about $75,000 in interest! (At present, you can deduct interest charges from your income tax, which somewhat reduces the actual amount of money that interest charges cost you.)

Table 7-3 more clearly shows the costs of a mortgage. The figures represent a 30-year loan for $30,000 at a 9 percent interest rate. Table 7-4 shows what monthly payments would be at different rates of interest on a $100,000 house when $30,000 is put down ($70,000 owed) or $50,000 is put down ($50,000 owed).

Table 7-3   A Standard Thirty-Year Mortgage at 9 Percent Interest

Year	Monthly Payment	Outstanding Balance	Total Paid
1	$241	$29,795	$ 2,892
2	"	29,570	5,784
3	"	29,326	8,676
4	"	29,057	11,568
5	"	28,764	14,460
10	"	26,828	28,920
30	"	0	86,760

Total Interest Paid = $56,760

Table 7-4   Twenty-Five-Year Mortgage on a $100,000 House

	Example A	Example B
Down Payment	$30,000	$50,000
Amount Borrowed	70,000	50,000

Interest Rate	Monthly Payments	
8%	$540	$386
9	586	420
10	636	454
11	686	490
12	737	527
13	789	564
14	842	602

Because it was often very difficult to determine actual amounts of interest charged in credit transactions, the Truth in Lending Law was passed in July 1969. Under the terms of this law, lenders must clearly explain what the credit costs of the transaction will be.

Financial Problems and Marital Strain

Joe's story is not unusual. Those in financial trouble today tend to be blue-collar workers earning a steady salary of $6000 to $10,000, in their forties, married twelve years with two children, and carrying an average debt of $5000, owed to 12 creditors.

One way out of debt problems is to declare bankruptcy. The basic law that allows one to do this is Chapter XIII of the National Bankruptcy Act, the Wage Earner Plan. This is not actual bankruptcy, however. First, one goes to court and with the aid of a lawyer draws up a budget and plan for repayment of debts, usually spread over a thirty-six-month period. The plan is filed with the local bankruptcy court and, once accepted, a trustee is appointed who receives the payments and distributes them to the creditors. The trustee is paid 5 percent of the amount distributed. Unfortunately, according to R. L. Miller (1975, p. 147), this plan only works for half of the people who use it.

If the debtor cannot meet the court-supervised payments, the only legal way to cancel the debts is to declare bankruptcy in a U.S. District Court. Declaring bankruptcy means giving up all that one owns. The court only allows one to keep such essential things as the tools of one's trade, clothing, basic furniture, and, in some cases, one's home (what one can keep varies from state to state). The rest of one's assets will be sold and the money distributed to the creditors. Even if the assets do not cover the debts, declaring bankruptcy does mean that all debts are legally canceled except for taxes, alimony and child support payments, and any debts that others may have cosigned (which become their debts). While one may get rid of debts, one suffers the loss of most of one's property, has a black mark against future credit ratings, has lawyer and court fees to pay, and cannot declare bankruptcy again for six years.

The Bankruptcy Reform Act of 1978 generally makes it easier to plead bankruptcy. State standards used to vary widely but now an individual may choose either the state standard or a federal exemption. (The law does allow a state to prohibit debtors from choosing the federal exemption and several states have already enacted such a ban.) The federal exemption allows the debtor to keep an interest of up to $7500 in real property used as a residence and up to $1200 in a car. Debtors may also keep an interest up to $200 in each of a number of individual categories like clothing, jewelry, and so forth.

Going through bankruptcy procedures does not seem to help people be more prudent with their purchases. It seems that 80 percent of those who file for bankruptcy use credit and are in debt trouble again within five years (Miller, 1979, pp. 119–120).

Even if bankruptcy is declared, both spouses may have to work just to keep the family financially afloat. Unfortunately, the second salary will often be more token than real if the family has small children. (See Chapter 8, pp. 242–243.) Once the children are in school or are old enough to care for themselves, however, the second salary will be a real help.

Although bankruptcy is unpleasant in any case, at least those who invested were attempting to move ahead and were trying to make the system work for them instead of vice versa. Today's bankrupt young family often has had no chance to even try a different approach financially. The 1975 total of 254,485 bankruptcy filings represents a 20 percent increase from 1973. In 1950, 22 out of 100,000 people nationally filed bankruptcy. In 1971, the figure was 90 per 100,000. Fiscal 1978 showed a drop from the 1975 all time high, however, to 210,000. In fiscal 1980 there were about 240,000 bankruptcies.

But What about Joe and Mary?   Under the court-supervised payment plan, Joe is slowly paying off their debts, including those incurred by the birth of their second child. Both he and Mary resent not being able to buy new things, including a new car now that theirs is so out-of-date, but it seems as if every cent of his and her new salary is earmarked for the old debts. Mary nags him a lot since she comes home from work tired and feels she should be spending more time with the children as they grow up. She keeps asking him why he doesn't get a better job. At one time he did investigate going back to school to qualify for a market manager position. But he would need to spend two years in school, and Mary cannot earn enough to support the family during those two years. Instead, he has taken a second job as a night watchman. He is so tired when he comes home that the least little noise is painful and he finds himself constantly yelling at the children to be quiet or Mary to make them be quiet. He also finds he is usually too tired to make love at night. At work he finds himself envying the younger, unmarried men who are driving new, fast cars. Why, he wonders, did he get married in the first place? Mary sometimes wonders the same thing.

It is obvious that financial pressures have put a great strain on this marriage. In fact, in view of this pressure and the fact that they married in their teens, it is quite likely that Joe and Mary's marriage will end in the divorce courts.

Are Joe and Mary alone to blame for their predicament? Why didn't they make the system work for them? Why didn't they wait awhile before making major purchases? Why didn't they postpone children for a year or so in order to get on their feet economically? What are the answers to such questions as these? In the midst of the wealthiest nation in the world, how could this couple have been economically strangled to death? (See the continuation of Joe and Mary's story in Chapter 8.)

The Seductive Society: Credit and Advertising

As so often occurs, the actual behavior found in our society bears little resemblance to the basic traditional truisms being taught in the family or school. Buying and spending have quietly taken the place of thrift and saving. The traditional values, though often still preached, are really no longer practiced. Actually, in a productive, inflationary economy such as ours, they are no longer even virtues. For example, after an income tax reduction in 1965, President Johnson urged the public to spend the additional money they now had. Even thirty years ago, such a statement would have been heresy. At the time the president made the statement it went almost unnoticed. Spending is important in a credit, inflationary society. Goods must be kept moving. The failure of the consumer to buy can immediately produce dire consequences for the economy. A slowdown in any one of the basic industries affects the whole economy, not just the one industry. The auto industry is a good example of this. A slowdown in the sale of cars affects literally hundreds of subsidiary industries as well as most of the other major industries such as steel, rubber, and aluminum. If the consumer fails to buy, then production must be cut back, which means laying off workers, thus compounding the problem by loss of these workers' buying power as consumers. In order to keep goods flowing, a whole new field of endeavor has opened, namely, stimulation and creation of wants and desires in the consuming mass population.

John Kenneth Galbraith in his classic work, *The Affluent Society* (1958), mentions that the theory of consumer demand in America is based on two broad propositions:

1. The urgency of wants does not diminish appreciably as more of them are satisfied.
2. Wants originate in the personality of the consumer and are capable of indefinite expansion.

These two propositions go a long way toward explaining why actual income bears little resemblance to a family's feeling of economic satisfaction. Many Americans are dissatisfied with the amount of money they make, yet Americans command a better standard of living than has ever before been known. The most dissatisfied group is that of professionals, where income is generally high, but, of course, so are the aspirations. Thus economic contentment appears to relate more to one's attitudes and values than to actual economic level.

Advertising and need stimulation have become essential parts of the American economic picture. A family or individual has to be made to want new material goods for more than rational, practical reasons. For example, though a well-made automobile can last ten years with care, such a longevity for the average car would greatly upset automobile production. The auto industry has met this problem with the yearly model change or the concept of built-in obsolescence, often under the guise of improvement. In all fairness to the auto industry, it should be noted that many yearly model changes are improvements but, on the other hand, there has often been change for its own sake so that the older models would appear less desirable.

Today's youth grow up in a completely different economic atmosphere than their parents. Until quite recently, they have known nothing but an affluent society. Even the recent period of relative job scarcity, inflation, and recession has had little effect on spending habits. For example, with gas prices and car prices at all time highs, 1976 saw near record car sales.* Buying, spending, credit, and debt are

*However, 1980 was a poor year for American auto sales, although imports still did well.

In its 1979 annual car costs survey, Hertz Corporation concluded that the national average was 38¢/mile for mid-sized automobiles and 32¢/mile for compacts. In 1977, a mid-sized car cost 30.1¢/mile. Thus, in just two years, the average per mile cost of driving a mid-sized car rose over 26 percent. A good deal of this increase came from the rapid gasoline price increases in the latter half of 1979. A mid-sized car now costs about $3800/year or $316/month if driven 10,000 miles.

The company said its estimates include costs for gasoline, oil and other service station items, maintenance, parts and repairs, licenses, fees, insurance, loan interest, and depreciation. These costs are calculated for a car purchased new, kept three years, and driven 10,000 miles a year.

Hertz broke down the costs for a mid-sized car on a city-by-city basis. You will note that there are large differences ranging from 44.2¢/mile in Los Angeles to 27.2¢/mile in Cincinnati.

Los Angeles	44.2¢
New York	43.9¢
Denver	38.8¢
San Francisco	36.9¢
Minneapolis	34.4¢
Seattle	33.9¢
Houston	33.7¢
Miami	33.3¢
Chicago	33.0¢
Milwaukee	32.9¢
Washington, D.C.	32.6¢
Pittsburgh	32.0¢
Boston	31.9¢
Dallas	31.3¢
Atlanta	31.2¢
St. Louis	30.9¢
San Diego	30.8¢
Cleveland	29.4¢
Detroit	29.2¢
Cincinnati	27.2¢

Car costs will continue to climb · with inflation and increasing gasoline prices. For many young people, an automobile is their first large purchase and first indebtedness. If costs continue to escalate, however, the car may become a luxury that few can afford.

now familiar accompaniments of marital life. The advantages of such a system cannot be denied. Yet youth must also be aware of the dangers of such a system in order to utilize it to their fullest advantage. Joe and Mary became trapped and lost their economic freedom because they never had a chance to stand apart from the system and analyze the negative aspects against which they needed to be on guard.

The power of advertising appeals and the ability to immediately satisfy one's needs or desires are a very formidable and seductive pair for mature adults to cope with, much less youth. How well can a young couple resist the invitation to use a store's credit again when they have almost paid off their bill? An official looking check arrives in the mail and indicates that they may now obtain $500 more merchandise for nothing down and no increase in the monthly payments that were otherwise about to end. If they understand thoroughly the meaning of what exercising their desires in this manner means, they can make use of some or all of the offer with no danger. On the other hand, it could turn out to be the straw that breaks the camel's back if, when added to the rest of their financial debt, it pushes them into economic disaster. The young couple must remember that personal freedom and indebtedness vary inversely. The more debt they take on, the less personal freedom they have.

In *The Affluent Society* (1958, p. 155), Galbraith pointed out that a "direct link between production and wants is provided by the institutions of modern advertising and salesmanship. These cannot be

Table 7-5 Fifty Leading National Advertisers (Total ad dollars in millions: 1978)[1]

#	Company	$	#	Company	$
1	Procter & Gamble	$554.0	26	Gulf + Western	126.8
2	Sears, Roebuck & Co.	417.9	27	J. C. Penney Co.	125.0
3	General Foods	340.0	28	International Telephone & Telegraph Corp.	122.7
4	General Motors Corp.	266.3	29	Colgate-Palmolive Co.	122.5
5	Kmart	250.0	30	CBS Inc.	122.3
6	Philip Morris Inc.	236.8	31	General Electric	121.3
7	Warner-Lambert Co.	211.0	32	Seagram Co.	120.0
8	Ford Motor Co.	210.0	33	Heublein Inc.	118.0
9	Bristol-Myers Co.	192.8	34	Anheuser-Busch	116.6
10	Chrysler Corp.	188.9	35	American Cyanamid	115.0
11	American Home Products Corp.	183.0	36	Kraft Inc.	114.2
12	R. J. Reynolds Industries	182.6	37	Richardson-Merrell	105.0
13	American Telephone & Telegraph Co.	172.8	38	Pillsbury Co.	104.0
14	General Mills	170.0	39	Gillette Co.	99.0
15	Mobil Corp.	163.0	40	Revlon Inc.	92.0
16	PepsiCo Inc.	156.0	41	Consolidated Foods Corp.	91.5
17	Beatrice Foods Co.	150.4	42	SmithKline Corp.	91.2
18	Unilever	145.0	43	Ralston Purina Co.	91.0
19	Norton Simon Inc.	144.6	44	Nabisco Inc.	90.9
20	Esmark Inc.	141.4	45	Eastman Kodak Co.	86.1
21	RCA Corp.	140.0	46	Chesebrough-Pond's	84.7
22	Coca-Cola Co.	138.8	47	B.A.T. Industries	82.4
23	McDonald's Corp.	136.8	48	Kellogg Co.	79.6
24	Johnson & Johnson	134.0	49	Loews Corp.	78.9
25	U.S. Government	128.5	50	Sterling Drug	78.0

Source: *Advertising Age*, Sept. 6, 1979.
[1]Based on measured media expenditures only; does not include local advertising.

reconciled with the notion of independently determined desires, for their central function is to create desires — to bring into being wants that previously did not exist." Vance Packard, in *The Hidden Persuaders* (1958), early exposed the extent to which advertising influences the public's attitudes, values, and behavior. He questioned the morality of some advertising techniques that manipulated the consumer into buying regardless of the consequences. In concluding his book, he asked a series of provocative questions that young married couples might well consider:

1. What is the morality of the practice of encouraging housewives to be non-rational and impulsive in buying family food?
2. What is the morality of manipulating small children even before they reach the age where they are legally responsible for their actions?
3. What is the morality of playing upon hidden weaknesses and frailties — such as our anxieties, aggressive feelings, dread of non-conformity, and infantile hangovers — to sell products?
4. What is the morality of developing in the public an attitude of wastefulness toward national resources by encouraging the "psychological obsolescence" of products already in use? (Packard, 1958, p. 143)

In 1978 approximately $23 billion was spent on advertising (see Table 7-5 for the top 50 advertisers), the majority of it to create new wants and desires which will, in turn, add new frustrations to the already monetarily unhappy American family who already live at one of the highest material levels in the world. The average child, for example, now sees some 25,000 commercials on television each year, or 225 minutes of commercials each week! There are over 6,000 advertising agencies and 500 companies that do various kinds of research on advertising effectiveness (CBS, 1973).

An Alternative: Investment

There is a popular belief that one's chances of earning $1 million are currently much less than they were for one's grandfather. But the number of millionaires today actually far exceeds the number in grandfather's time. Granted, $1 million may be worth considerably less in buying power today, but it is still a healthy mark of affluence, to say the least. A gradual inflationary economy is also an economy in which money can be easily made by a person who is intelligent and willing to work. Needless to say, another important qualification is the ability to stay clear of early economic entrapment as has been described. For most young people, the necessity of gathering the first small amount of capital is crucial. Everything in the system works against them. In the early years, they must stay alert to keep the system from entrapping them and thereby canceling their attempt to accumulate initial investment capital. If they can win this battle and start on the road to financial success, they will be using the system to their advantage rather than being used by it. When one compares costs of living in America with those in other countries as in Table 7-6, it is clear that America still offers a great deal economically to its citizens.

Thinking about investments even on a very modest scale is important if a person or a newly married couple are to make the economic system work for instead of against them. Figure 7-1 shows the broad range of investment opportunities from which one can choose. They range from the very conservative, low-yield bank savings account to the highly speculative gambles for high return on such things as mining and oil exploration. You might ask "How can the average newly married couple even consider investments? It's all they can do to set up housekeeping in this day of inflation." This is a legitimate question. However, the couple who plan investing into their life, even if only at a later date, have the greatest chance of economic prosperity and freedom. A positive attitude toward investment is actually even more important than investment itself. Such an attitude recognizes that "money makes money," that there is value in budgeting and staying free of consumer debt, that controlling desires in early years may lead to greater rewards later, and that the American economic system, if used properly, can free one from economic worries. Even if a couple can put aside only a few dollars a month toward future investments, they stand a good chance of improving their economic position compared to their friends who have no interest nor knowledge of investing. (See "Gaining Freedom Through Investment, p. 253.)

Table 7-6 What's the Difference: Washington, D.C., London, Moscow[1]

Amount of Work Time Necessary to Buy Certain Goods

Commodity	Washington, D.C.	London	Moscow
Milk (1 liter)	7 minutes	9 minutes	18 minutes
Hamburger meat, beef (1 kg)	43	57	128
Sausage, pork (1 kg)	31	43	145
Potatoes (1 kg)	2	4	7
Apples, eating (1 kg)	11	15	40
Sugar (1 kg)	5	11	59
White bread (1 kg)	8	12	18
Eggs (10)	10	20	18
Vodka (0.5 liter)	52	161	380
Cigarettes (20)	9	22	23
Weekly food basket for four people	12.5 hours	21.4 hours	42.3 hours
Soap, toilet (150 grams)	5 minutes	6 minutes	23 minutes
Lipstick	26	50	72[2]
Panty hose	22	11	427[2]
Men's leather shoes	8 hours	11 hours	33 hours
Men's business suit	20	25	68
Refrigerator, small (120 liters)	43	35	208
Color TV set, large (59 cm screen)	86	177	713
Automobile (Ford Fairlane/ Granada/Volga GAZ-24)	4.1 months	8.5 months	35 months

Source: Radio Liberty Research Supplement, March 1979. Worktime is based on average take-home pay of male and female manufacturing workers. Income taxes, Social Security taxes (U.S. & U.K.), health insurance premiums (U.S. & U.K.), and unemployment insurance (U.K. only) have been deducted from wages: family allowances (U.K. & U.S.S.R.) have been added for a family of four. In dollars, hourly take-home pay in January, 1979 was $4.61 for American workers, $3.25 for British workers, and $1.38 for Russian workers.

[1]Table is used by courtesy of the National Federation of Independent Business, 150 W. 20th Ave., San Mateo, California 94403. A complete table showing many other items such as production and education statistics in poster form may be obtained free from the above address. Ask for "What's the Difference, Washington, D.C., London, Moscow."

[2]Some items, such as lipstick and panty hose, could not be found by any surveyor in Moscow in any state retail store at the time of the survey. The price given is that seen in the past.

Figure 7-1

The investment continuum. Note that the percentage return increases in successful investments as the risk increases. The chances of striking gold are slim, but if you do, the return is great. Percentages also change with economic conditions. They do, however, give a rough idea of the return you might expect on a successful conservative investment of a given type.

Low return Low risk	4–9%	5–12%	9–13%	10–15%	6–15%	10–20%	12–22%	20%–inf.	50%–inf.	100%–inf.*	High return High risk
	Bank savings	Savings and loan	First mortgage	Second mortgage	Syndications	Apartment rental	Commercial rental	Franchises	Land speculations / Commodities	Oil and mining / Invention backing	

Bonds — Preferred — Common blue chip — Mutual funds — Common big board — Over-the-counter

Low return / Low risk — Stocks and bonds — High return / High risk

*"100%–inf." means 100% upwards without limit (infinite).

Effective Money Management

The most important step in reducing marital conflict over money is to determine ahead of time how most money decisions will be made. There are at least five possible ways to handle monetary decisions: (1) the husband can make all the decisions, (2) the wife can make all the decisions, (3) one spouse can control the income but give the other a household allowance, (4) each spouse can have separate funds and share agreed-upon financial obligations, and (5) the spouses can have a joint bank account upon which each can draw as necessary (Landis, 1970, p. 516).

Once an agreement is reached, most day-to-day monetary decisions can be handled automatically. Then the next step in reducing monetary conflict is to agree on a budget. (See Scenes from Marriage, pp. 231–233.) A budget is actually a plan of spending to assure attaining what is needed and wanted. For example, a family's income must cover such basic necessities as housing, food, clothing, transportation, and hopefully, leave some money for discretionary expenditures such as vacations and recreation. How Americans actually spend their money is shown in Table 7-7 and Figure 7-2.

Naturally, the first step is to allot money for necessities. Assuming there is some money left over, it can then be divided among other wants the family may have. The rapid inflation we have been experiencing has made planned spending more important than ever. For example, it is estimated that the spontaneous food shopper spends approximately 10–15 percent more for food than the shopper who has a planned food budget and a shopping list of needed items.

Table 7-7 Summary of Annual Budgets for a Four-Person Family at Three Levels of Living, Urban United States, Autumn 1977 and Estimated for 1980[1]

| Component | Lower | | Intermediate | | Higher | | Item as Percentage of Total Budget | | |
| | | | | | | | Lower | Inter-mediate | Higher |
	1977	1980	1977	1980	1977	1980			
Total budget	$10,481	$13,640	$17,106	$22,236	$25,202	$32,500			
Total family consumption	8,657	11,277	13,039	16,900	17,948	23,400			
Food	3,190	4,090	4,098	5,300	5,159	6,600	30%	24%	20%
Housing	2,083	2,700	4,016	5,200	6,085	6,900	20	23	24
Transportation	804	900	1,472	1,900	1,913	2,450	8	9	8
Clothing	828	900	1,182	1,500	1,730	2,250	8	7	7
Personal care	282	310	377	400	535	700	3	2	2
Medical care	980	1,100	985	1,250	1,027	1,300	9	6	4
Other family consumption[2]	489	540	909	1,150	1,499	1,950	5	5	6
Other items[3]	472	530	763	1,000	1,288	1,700	5	4	5
Taxes & deductions	1,352	1,750	3,303	4,300	5,965	7,600	13	19	24
Social Security & disability	632	700	961	1,250	985	1,300	6	6	4
Personal income taxes	720	800	2,342	3,000	4,980	7,400	7	14	20

Source: U.S. Department of Labor, Bureau of Labor Statistics News, Wahington, D.C.
[1]The estimates for 1980 were made by adding approximately 30 percent to each of the 1977 figures and rounding off. This accounts for a 9 percent inflation rate each year.
[2]Other family consumption includes average costs for reading materials, recreation, tobacco products, alcoholic beverages, education, and miscellaneous expenditures.
[3]Other items include allowances for gifts and contributions, life insurance, and occupational expenses.
NOTE: Because of rounding, sums of individual items may not equal totals.

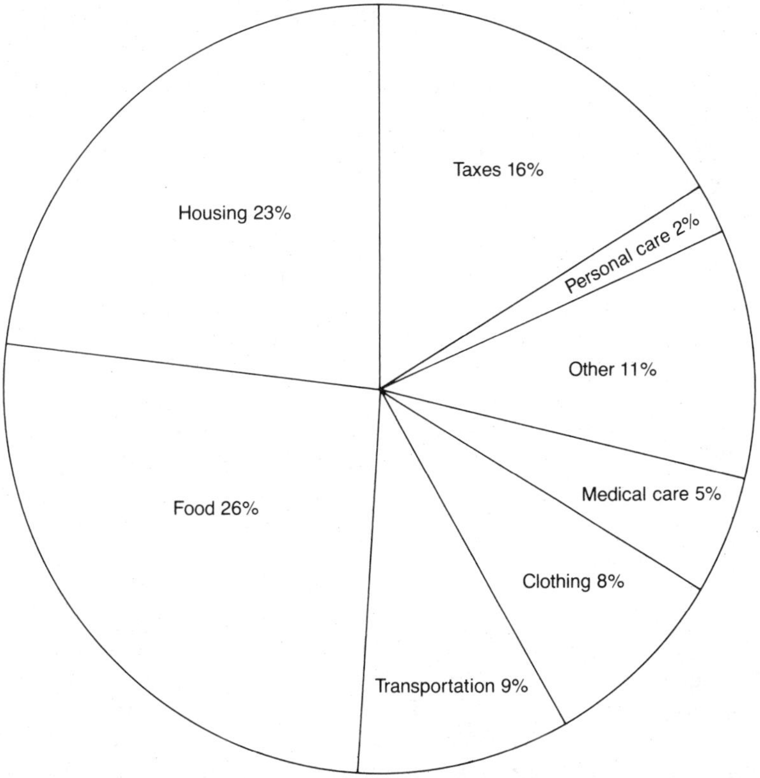

Taxes 16%

Housing 23%

Personal care 2%

Other 11%

Medical care 5%

Food 26%

Clothing 8%

Transportation 9%

By living within a budget (see Table 7-8), a family can avoid many of the problems that defeated Joe and Mary. In addition, by budgeting even a small amount to savings, they can make investment possible. Saving is really only deferred spending. But by deferring immediate spending, it becomes possible to use the money to earn additional income.

A budget should only be used for a specified time. It must be changed and updated to reflect changing family circumstances. For example, the newly married couple may feel well off if both work. They have two incomes and minimal expenses. But danger is ahead if they become accustomed to using up both incomes. For example, if they decide to have children, it usually means the wife will give up her

Table 7-8   Suggested Budget for Necessities for a Family of Four

Item	Low Income Percentage Range	Median Income Percentage Range
Food	25–35	20–30
Housing	25–35	20–30
Transportation	16–20	12–18
Taxes	12–15	20–23
Clothing	10–15	10–15
Health and Insurance	8–12	8–14
Recreation and Savings	4–10	8–12

income, at least for a while. Expenses also go up because of the children. Thus income often drops and expenses rise with children, which can throw the family into an economic crisis unless they have economically planned for both eventualities.

Another stage that the family must plan for is if and when the children go to college. This usually means a drastic rise in expenditures. The cost of putting a child through college averages more than $20,000 if room and board are considered.

After children have become independent, the spouses can usually enjoy a comfortable period of relative affluence. They must, however, plan carefully for their coming retirement. Without such planning the couple may end their lives in a state of poverty, especially if inflationary pressures exist.

As dull and uninteresting as budget planning may sound, the family that does not put time into planning their finances may find themselves facing increasing monetary strain, which may even lead to the destruction of the marriage. This is especially true when there is a high rate of inflation.

Inflation

There have been many, and often revolutionary, social and economic changes since World War II. Certainly one of the most noticeable changes, especially in the 1970s and continuing in the 1980s, has been the increasing rate of inflation with which families have had to cope. Each day we are surprised, dismayed, and angry at increased nominal or absolute costs of almost everything we buy.* Bread is more than $1 a loaf, yet it seems only yesterday that it was 50¢ a loaf. The last new car you bought ten years ago cost $2800, tax and license included. Today, the same model is priced closer to $8000. "Buy now before the price increases," is an often repeated advertisement that feeds our fears about inflation. Those on fixed incomes, slowly, month by month, drop farther into poverty. The demands for increased wages, just to stay even with inflation, become more insistent. Public opinion polls find that inflation constantly rates as one of the major concerns of the populace. Books on personal finance now start with a discussion of inflation in the first chapter (Miller, 1979).

Constantly rising prices and recent stagnation of real income combine to bring more and more wives into the labor force. A thorough understanding of inflation can help today's family make better use of their resources.

Americans born after 1940 have only known an inflationary economy, one with constantly rising prices. Beginning with World War II, the rate of inflation has averaged 5–6 percent a year. The rate dropped at the beginning of the 1960s but then began to rise again until it reached a dramatic double digit high of 12 percent in 1974. Thereafter it declined until 1978 when it went to 9 percent and 1979 when it reached a new post World War II high of over 13 percent, the highest rate in 33 years (see Figure 7-3).

*Nominal price is the absolute price in dollars you pay for an item, $1 for a loaf of bread, $8000 for an automobile.

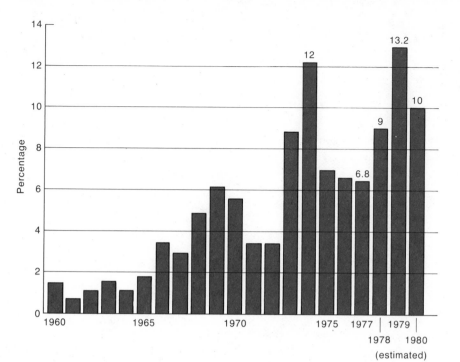

Figure 7-3 **Inflation Rates**
The figures cover each full year. The highest gain was in 1979 when the Consumer Price Index soared to 13.3 percent (U.S. Department of Labor).

Prices do not always rise, although young Americans might not believe it. Figure 7-4 shows what the Consumer Price Index (CPI) has done since 1860. Where the index has dropped, it indicates a recession or depression in the economy. Overall, however, the CPI has risen over 600 percent in the past 100 years. In just the past 12 years, the CPI has risen 129 percent. Goods costing $100 in 1967 cost $229.90 in December, 1979.

Figure 7-4
Consumer Price Index has its ups and downs (mostly ups).

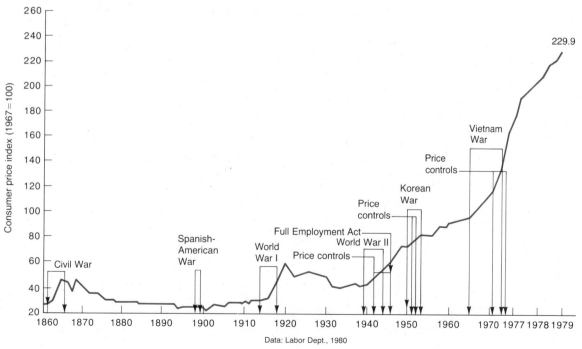

Data: Labor Dept., 1980

Figure 7-5

Rise in nominal and real per capita income in the United States. Per capita personal disposable income is expressed in current dollars. That is, it is not corrected for changes in the price level. We know it has been going up steadily from 1919 until the present, except for the Great Depression when it started going downhill. Figures have been corrected for inflation. (All figures expressed in terms of 1972 dollars.) Source: Business Conditions Digest.

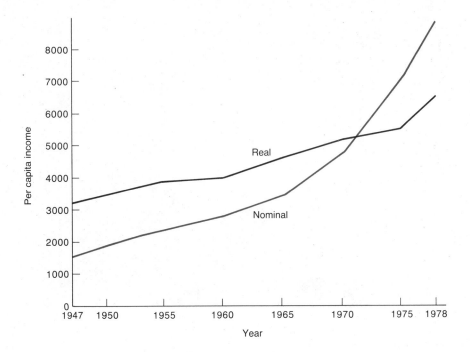

Inflation rates by themselves only tell half of the real story of the American economy, however. Inflation simply says that the nominal prices have risen. However, income has also risen during this time. If income rises at the same rate as prices, one's buying power remains the same. Thus, a more important measure of the economy than just the inflation rate is the *real per capita income*. This is computed by taking the per capita income increase and subtracting out the inflation rate. If my income increases 10 percent in a year during which inflation is only 5 percent, my real income (buying power) has increased just 5 percent. Figure 7-5 shows that most people have actually increased their real income (buying power) since World War II. However, in the seventies and thus far in the eighties, there have been years where the real per capita income has declined.

The CPI* is the most common indicator used in popular media to measure price fluctuations. It is an average of prices of several thousand common goods and services purchased by all urban workers. Because it is an average, it tends to mask actual price fluctuations for a specific item. Thus it is important that the consumer look at the relative price of a product rather than just at the nominal or absolute price. Although most goods have greatly increased in nominal price, some relative prices have actually decreased. For example, compared to 1967, the base year, when the CPI was set at 100, the index rose to 198.4

---

*There is controversy over how accurately the CPI measures inflation. Some economists feel that it overstates housing and interest costs. Others feel that the monthly publication of the CPI itself fuels inflation.

in 1978, indicating that the CPI-measured average prices had almost doubled in the preceding eleven years. But television sets rose to only 102 on the index, and thus compared to the average CPI gain during those years, their relative price dropped to 51.4 on the index. In other words, television sets have not gone up much in absolute cost between 1967 and 1978 and, relative to other goods on the CPI, are much cheaper in 1978 than they were in 1967. Automobiles, however, have increased in price at the same rate as the CPI. So, although overall prices as measured by the CPI are going up, some goods go up more slowly than others and therefore become relatively better buys.

Some individual goods have actually decreased in absolute price during this time. This may be seen in some areas of electronics such as the popular hand-held digital display calculators. Decrease in price has occurred because of technological breakthroughs that lower the production costs in the electronics industry.

Another way to see the relationship between inflation of prices and income is to compare the actual amount of income needed to remain at the same purchasing power level from 1950 to 1979. A family that earned $10,000 in 1950 needed $12,219 in 1960, $16,130 in 1970, and $27,738 in 1979 to retain their initial 1950 purchasing power of $10,000. Table 7-9 shows both the absolute and real weekly earnings for nonagricultural workers in 1976 and 1977, and Table 7-10 shows gains and losses for a wider variety of workers.

Although there is a great deal of lip service paid to the cause of reducing inflation, little has actually been done about it by the government. Factually, compared to many other countries, the United States has had a relatively low rate of inflation since World War II. Many countries have experienced 40, 50, and even 100 percent inflation rates per year. The government also benefits from mild inflation as Table 7-11 shows. In recent years California has been a good example of the increased government income that accrues from inflation. As prices go higher, sales tax revenues increase, and, as Table 7-11 demonstrates, so do income taxes. Despite the big property tax cut embodied in California's Proposition 13 that was passed by the people in 1978, the state surplus of funds remained almost as high (between five and six billion dollars) after the property tax reduction.

Increased revenue to the government and the politician's fear of recession combine to keep government from doing much about mild inflation, except talking. Increasing energy costs are one of the

Table 7-9 Gross Weekly Earnings for Private Nonagricultural Workers in March, 1977

	Current Dollars	1967 Dollars
March 1977	$183.45	$102.95
March 1976[1]	$176.29	$103.40

Source: Department of Labor Statistics, May, 1977.
[1]Note that the buying power was actually 45 cents lower in 1977 than it was in 1976.

Table 7-10 Who's Ahead in Real Pay, 1977–78. (Here is how buying power of workers' weekly paychecks — real pay — has changed during the last year. Changes are affected by average hours worked as well as by wage rates, taxes and inflation.)

	Average Weekly Pay Before Taxes	Gain in Pay 1977-78	Change in Real Pay — Allowing for Higher Prices, Taxes[1]
Those Ahead . . .			
Farm operators	$230.38	$49.23	+$21.45
Tire-factory workers	372.22	58.68	+ 19.17
Metal-can makers	368.94	57.06	+ 18.02
Steelworkers	412.16	60.01	+ 16.61
Metal miners	364.04	54.94	+ 16.52
Petroleum-refinery workers	411.65	44.00	+ 3.55
Bank clerks	155.73	9.73	+ 2.92
Aluminum workers	399.81	41.72	+ 2.48
Oil, gas-field workers	388.07	40.07	+ 1.99
Aircraft workers	355.91	33.31	+ .38
Laundry workers	132.86	11.41	+ .18
. . . And Behind			
Social Security pensioners	$ 58.62	$ 3.47	−$ 1.49
Construction workers	328.99	29.72	− 1.97
Wholesale trade workers	239.68	20.89	− 2.10
Clothing workers	146.52	10.78	− 2.12
Auto workers	395.60	35.74	− 2.13
Retired federal workers	163.62	12.70	− 2.36
Retail clerks	133.42	8.84	− 2.50
Local bus drivers	286.86	23.12	− 3.52
Paper mill workers	296.24	24.18	− 3.68
Veterans on full disability	211.48	13.58	− 4.23
Sporting-goods workers	176.33	11.75	− 4.76
Furniture workers	194.57	11.91	− 6.05
Meatpackers	309.33	22.71	− 6.06
Electric, gas-company workers	329.80	24.56	− 6.09
Food processors	241.80	16.12	− 6.16
Printing and publishing workers	255.46	15.95	− 7.20
Schoolteachers	282.10	14.77	− 10.08
Federal government workers	348.65	18.17	− 11.58
Cigarette factory workers	288.79	9.69	− 14.82
Telephone workers	311.24	9.40	− 16.77

Source: U.S. Department of Labor, Agriculture, and HEW, Civil Service, Veterans Administration, National Education Association.
[1]After federal income and Social Security taxes and adjustment for the rise in consumer prices. Assumes a family of four for tax purposes, except for retired federal workers who are assumed to be married couples.
Note: Latest available weekly pay usually December, 1978. Farm operators often include family members instead of individual workers.

major causes of recent inflation along with an inflationary mentality that has been created in the last few years.

Living with Inflation It appears that some degree of inflation will influence the economy for the foreseeable future. Americans must take it into consideration if they are to be successful economically. There are a number of things that can be done to combat mild inflation.

1. *Minimize your cash holdings.* Cash obviously loses value at the rate of inflation. If I bury $1000 cash to protect it from theft for a

Table 7-11   A 9.4 Percentage Increase in All Prices and Salaries over a One-Year Period[1]

	Gross income	Federal income tax	Effective rate	After-tax income in year 1 dollars
Year 1	$14,000	$1,600	11.4%	$12,400
Year 2	15,316	1,890	12.3	12,164
Year 1	20,000	3,010	15.1	16,990
Year 2	21,880	3,506	16.0	16,646
Year 1	30,000	6,020	20.1	23,980
Year 2	32,820	7,035	21.4	23,361

[1]Because of graduated income tax rates, even families lucky enough to get raises matching the big increase in living costs wound up losing purchasing power. Here we show how a 9.4 percent inflation outruns a 9.4 percent pay raise.

year during which the inflation rate is 10 percent, inflation robs me of $100. At the end of the year I only have $900 in purchasing power. Thus, I want to minimize my cash holdings. For example, the balance in your checking account should be no larger than necessary to cover the checks you write since checking accounts traditionally do not earn interest, or interest is minimal. Excess funds should be placed in interest-earning savings accounts.

2. *Select high yield savings accounts whenever possible.*   There are now many savings plans paying interest rates from 5 to 16 percent. Generally, the higher the interest, the longer the funds must remain invested and/or the higher the minimum amount required in the savings account. In the longer term accounts, there are substantial penalties if you withdraw your funds before the end of the term. Hence, one must thoughtfully spread one's savings over a number of different kinds of accounts. For instance, you will want to keep a small balance to cover unexpected expenses in a regular passbook account where you can withdraw at any time without penalty. You will probably only earn between 5 and 6½ percent interest on this money. You may want some money in a six-month to one-year term account on which you may earn from 6½ to 12 percent, although the higher yields usually require large minimum deposits such as the $10,000 required on T-bill accounts in savings and loan institutions. If you have enough funds, you can place more monies into longer-term, higher-paying savings certificates.

3. *Try to have a cost-of-living clause tied to your employment contract.*   Many unions have been successful in gaining this for their members. Thus, if inflation increases the CPI by 10 percent, cost-of-living clauses take effect and the worker's income is automatically increased to match. This, of course, also acts to maintain the inflation.

4. *Try not to let inflation panic you into buying before you are ready.*   We are constantly told to buy now before prices increase. Yet, as we pointed out, some prices may actually decline relative to the CPI even though they go up in absolute terms. Even with large cost

One thing about Americans. They turn every adversity into an asset.

Take the energy crisis. Please.

When we were told to cut back on the use of big appliances for small baking and heating jobs, there were no less than 500 small appliances that flooded the market.

There's a deep fat fryer for two shrimp, a grill for one hamburger and Teflon top for one egg. There's a mini-oven for baking two biscuits at a time and an excuse-the-expression twoholer to bake two doughnuts.

There are crocks to accommodate an entire meal, a skillet for cooking one-dish meals, and woks if you're feeling Oriental.

There are popcorn poppers, waffle grills and miniature percolators for one cup of coffee. There are hot beverage makers, bean pots, chili pots and electric units to keep your pots hot after you've unplugged them.

There are electric socks, blankets, handwarmers, and here's a must — a unit that will heat your golf balls to insure you a more satisfying "hit" in cold weather. Where you plug in the unit is your challenge.

There are electric clocks that will not only awaken you by radio, but will project the time on the ceiling of any darkened room in large digital numerals.

There's an electric gun that looks like a six-shooter that fires out hors d'oeuvres, cookies and canapes. There are electric salad spinners to rid your greens of moisture, an electric knife and an electric sharpener to sharpen your electric knife.

When you cut down on your energy by bringing in a pizza, there's an electric heating element to heat up your pizza if it has turned cold.

Do you have to spend time away from your appliances? No. There's a new unit for you that plugs into the cigarette lighter of your car, camper, van or boat. You can make stews in it, bake cookies, toast sandwiches or heat soups.

And don't forget the electric plant turner to assure your favorite blossoms that they will always be turned toward the light.

Americans have rallied so well to the challenge of having to cut back that I am reluctant to tell them about my new discovery of an appliance that cooks several meals at a time, heats up the kitchen, keeps food warm, cooks it, bakes it, has a see-through glass, cleans itself, heats golf balls and tells time.

I call it an oven.

Erma Bombeck

items such as automobiles that have risen in cost as fast as the CPI, you might want to postpone buying. If your present auto has two more years of trouble-free life, then drive it those two additional years and you will probably save more money even though the new car will cost you more absolutely two years in the future.

Example: The new car cost this year is $8000. If you bought it outright (no payments), you'd lose 10 percent interest per year that the money could be earning in a savings account. Thus you'd lose $1600 of potential interest in the two years. If the inflation rate was also 10 percent per year, the car would cost you $1680 more two years from now (10 percent × $8000 = $800 the first year. 10 percent × $8800 = $880 the second year. Adding the two yields $1680 as the price increase of the car over two years). Considering that your income stays at least even with inflation, the car will actually cost you relatively less if you buy it two years from now at the higher price, because the money you would have spent on the car earns interest for the two years. Of course, if you don't have the money and must buy the car on credit, the figures will not apply.

5. *Learn about investments.* Money earns money. The wise investor can stay ahead of inflation. For example, real estate has stayed ahead of inflation in many parts of the country. By this, we mean that it has gone up in price faster than the CPI has risen. Unfortunately, inflation brings with it a certain amount of irrationality. Thus we see speculation causing unusual and unpredictable surges in prices. Gold and silver are two good examples of what irrational speculation can do to prices. The small, prudent investor would do well to avoid the irrational investments in favor of more predictable ones. (See p. 253)

6. *An inflationary period tends to favor the borrower.* Money borrowed today is paid back in cheaper dollars in the future.

   Example: I borrow $10,000 at 10 percent interest per year for a five-year period. During that period inflation is 10 percent per year. In essence, I am paying nothing for the use of the money. I will have paid $1000/year or $5000 in simple interest at the end of five years. However, at the end of five years, the $10,000 I pay back is worth *only $5000 in buying power because of the accumulated 50 percent inflation which has halved the value of my dollars.*

7. *Try to buy wisely.* Watch for bargains such as year-end sales and seasonal price reductions.

8. *More members of the family can work.* This suggestion is discussed in more detail in Chapter 8. Higher inflation rates are partially responsible for the increasing number of married women seeking employment.

9. *Conserve and save.*

Proper use of insurance can protect a family from catastrophic financial setback. Every family must have at least three kinds of insurance: medical, automobile, and if they own their own home, fire insurance.

A Word About Insurance

Medical coverage is an absolute necessity. Medical costs have become so high that no average family can sustain the costs of a prolonged illness. For a young, healthy couple, coverage can be limited to catastrophic illness with a large deductible, perhaps as high as $500. This is the least expensive type of medical coverage. However, when children arrive, a policy that covers more everyday kinds of medical problems with a lower deductible should be sought. A family of four may have to pay $50 to $150 per month for medical coverage depending on how comprehensive it is. In addition to insurance plans such as Mutual of Omaha and Blue Cross, there are also prepaid foundation type plans such as the Kaiser plan where one may have full medical coverage at a certain facility, hospital, or clinic for a specified yearly fee.

Many employers now offer group medical plans as part of their fringe benefits, which helps to reduce health coverage costs for their employees. In such cases, the family will not need to supply their own medical coverage.

The government is also entering the health field more strongly with Medicare plans of various kinds (Social Security disability and

Workmen's Compensation insurance). Many suggest that health services will one day become a branch of government but unless you are very poor, you must cover for health emergencies or face potential financial ruin at this time. One example of rising medical costs should suffice to convince you of the importance of medical coverage. A knee cartilage removal cost about $200 in 1950. In 1980 the cost was $2500.

Automobile coverage is also essential. It is so important that many states make it illegal not to be covered. Property damage and liability are the crucial elements. Covering one's own car for damage is less important unless, of course, it has been bought on time. In this case, the lender requires collision damage on the car.

If you own your own home or other real property, it is necessary to have fire coverage. This is a mandatory condition of borrowing mortgage money. Because of inflation, such coverage should be raised periodically to keep up with rising construction costs. Homeowner's package policies give much more protection than just fire coverage alone. They usually include coverage for such things as theft, personal liability, wind and water damage, and personal belongings.

Even if you do not own your own home, it might be a good idea to have a personal belongings insurance policy. Such things as stereo equipment, cameras, furniture, and clothing are surprisingly expensive to replace if they are stolen or lost in a fire. Insurance, on the other hand, is usually quite inexpensive.

Life insurance is also important, but not an absolute necessity. There are many kinds of life insurance and newly married couples are often pushed by insurance agents to overinsure or choose an unnecessarily expensive policy. Remember that the purpose of life insurance is to protect one's estate and provide for the family until the children are independent. The best protection for the least money is term insurance. In term insurance, a given amount of insurance is bought for a set period of years, usually five. As one becomes older, the premium becomes higher since the chance of death increases.

Savings life insurance policies are very expensive and should usually be avoided by young couples. For example, a young couple can buy about $16,000 worth of five-year term life insurance for $100 a year but that amount will only pay for $6000 worth of coverage in an insurance plus savings policy.

Insurance agents tend to push savings life insurance since both they and the company earn a great deal more on this type of policy. However, the savings aspect of the policy yields only 2 to 3 percent return. By investing the substantial difference in cost between term and savings life insurance, a couple can have a great deal more insurance protection and at the same time accumulate savings at a much faster rate.

Basically, the amount of life insurance needed by a couple will depend on the number and ages of their children, their standard of living, and their other investments. What life insurance must do is to protect the family if the major monetary contributor should die. It should cover death costs, outstanding debts, and supply enough for taxes and to allow the family to continue functioning. Just how much this will be depends on each individual family. In some families the wife and children may also be insured.

Home ownership is a way of life for most Americans. A higher percentage of families own their own home in the United States than in any other nation in the world. As you will see in Chapter 15, one's home is a major source of savings for many retired Americans. Yet within the last four years, skyrocketing real estate prices and the highest ever interest rates have shattered the home ownership dream for many families.

Housing prices have risen dramatically. By September, 1979, the average new house price reached $74,300, up from $61,900 just one year earlier. A previously occupied house was up to $63,700 from $53,700 in September, 1978.

Mortgage interest rates have risen over the past ten years from a low of 6 percent to 16 percent at the beginning of 1981. Although there will be future variations, the rates will remain higher than they have been historically. The would-be home buyer is caught between the high prices and high interest. The family will have to put down a much larger sum of money to keep monthly payments realistic. They will also have to earn a large income to qualify for the higher loans. For example, to qualify for a $65,000 mortgage carrying 12 percent interest rate, a family would have to earn over $40,000 a year.

Smaller homes, condominiums, and cooperatives may help to keep prices within reach. There may also be some lower interest mortgages available through government funding if a family can qualify. However, today's long-range picture for home ownership by the young family is increasingly bleak.

Summary

The family is the major unit of consumption in the United States. In order for a family to survive it must have the economic ability to provide food, shelter, and transportation for its members. Hopefully, there will also be money to supply some pleasurable and recreational activities as well. The family that is economically successful stands a much better chance of surviving than the family that fails economically. For example, the poorest segment of the American society has the highest rate of divorce.

Credit use in the United States has allowed Americans to maintain the world's highest standard of living. Yet this easy availability of credit can also curtail individual and family freedom when it is abused and/or misunderstood. Future payments for present goods or services can lock the person making the agreement into an inflexible life pattern. Money must be earned steadily to meet the payment schedule. For many families the debt burden is so large that almost all funds are allocated automatically to pay the many payments due each month. The family has little or no monetary flexibility to meet unforeseen emergencies or to act quickly if a good investment opportunity arises.

On the other hand, a thorough understanding of credit, installment buying, interest costs, and budgeting can work to a family's benefit, allowing them to invest in the American economy and perhaps achieve not only economic security but freedom as well. Investments are a means of supplementing income and making money work to produce more money. The family able to save and invest even a small portion of their income is freer of possible economic entrapment and stands a better chance of survival than families who cannot control wants and desires and spend their total income.

Investments can be plotted along a continuum from low risk, low return to high risk, high return. Examples of low-risk, low-return investments are bank savings and savings and loan accounts. Risk and return increase with such investments as first and second mortgages, syndications, apartment houses, commercial property, and franchises. While the rate of return can be very high for such speculations as land, commodities, oil and mining, and invention backing, the risk is too high for young couples with limited funds to consider. The stock market is another investment outlet. Here again there is a continuum from low risk, low return to high risk, high return.

The day-to-day handling of money can be a problem in a family if the partners have different values about money. However, conflict can be minimized if the couple decides ahead of time how most monetary decisions will be made. Their choices are to let the husband make all decisions, to let the wife make all decisions, to let both have separate funds and share agreed-upon obligations, or to share a joint account upon which each can draw as necessary. Budgeting will also allow them to plan for necessities and to see how their income is spent. Deciding together how to use income left over after meeting necessities is another way to reduce monetary conflict.

Inflation is the number one economic enemy of the newly married couple. Inflation rates have risen in recent years as have wages. However, in the past two years wages have not risen as rapidly, so that many people find that their real income has actually gone down. It is important for families to understand inflation so that they can take steps to guard against it. Proper budgeting and good investments are two steps that a family can take to reduce the unwanted effects of inflation.

Insurance should be considered a necessity. A couple needs medical coverage, automobile coverage, and life insurance. If they own a home, they need fire insurance also. Couples should start with a medical policy that protects them against catastrophic illness and then, as children arrive, change to broader coverage. This pattern should also be followed with life insurance. The couple should buy term insurance, increasing the amount of the coverage as needed to protect family members.

The American dream of a large home for every family shows strong signs of fading in the face of drastically increased housing prices. Smaller homes, condominiums, and cooperatives will probably be the housing of the future.

How to Budget Your Income*

Once you decide to do some positive money management, you must figure out a budget and try to stick to it. The budget is a planning tool to help you reduce undirected spending.

Steps in Budget Making

Very briefly, after the income and goals of the relevant spending unit are determined, these basic steps should be followed to create a spending plan.

1. Analyze past spending by keeping records for a month or two.
2. Determine *fixed expenses*, such as rent, and any other contractual payments that must be made—even if they come infrequently, such as insurance and taxes.
3. Determine *flexible expenses*, such as for food and clothing.
4. Balance your fixed plus flexible expenditures with your available income. If a surplus exists, you can apply it toward achieving your goals. If there is a deficit, then you

*This section is adapted from Roger Miller, *Personal Finance Today*. St. Paul, Minn.: West Publishing Co., 1979, pp. 53–56.

must re-examine your flexible expenditures. You can also re-examine fixed expenses in view of reducing them in the future.

Note that so-called fixed expenses are only philosophically fixed in the short run. In the longer run, everything is essentially flexible, or variable. One can adjust one's fixed expenses by changing one's standard of living, if necessary.

The Importance of Keeping Records

Budget making, whether you are a college student, a single person living alone, or the head of a family, will be useless if you don't keep records. The only way to make sure that you are carrying out the plans implicit in your budget is by having records to show what you are actually spending. The ultimate way to maintain records is to write everything down, but that becomes time-consuming and, therefore, costly. Another way to keep records is to write checks for everything. Records are also important in case of problems with faulty products, services, or the Internal Revenue Service. Thus, you serve at least two purposes by keeping good records.

Which Records to Keep at Home Here are eleven types of records that you should keep at home. Not all of these records are directly related to budget making; some are for such purposes as insurable losses, lost credit cards, and the like.

1. *Income*: paycheck stubs, record of self-employment income, W-2 Forms (given to you at the end of the year by your employer(s), 1099 Forms (indicates interest, dividends, etc., earned during the year).
2. *Most canceled checks*: keep at least one year and, in some cases, a minimum of seven years.
3. *Insurance policies*: automobile, home owners, fire, health, life, and so on.
4. *Large purchases*: all receipts and canceled checks for the following: autos, furniture, equipment, appliances, stereos, and so on. These should be kept as long as you own the item.
5. *Home improvements*: all receipts and canceled checks must be kept until you are no longer a home owner. You can reduce taxes this way.
6. *Investment transactions*: a register of all stock transactions, confirmations of purchases and sales sent to you by brokers, and receipts.
7. *Tax-deductible items*: canceled checks and receipts for interest, taxes, contributions, business expenses, medical and dental expenses, and drugs (should be kept at least three years after tax-filing deadline).
8. *Tax returns*: copies of all returns, worksheets, and schedules to be kept three years after date of tax-filing deadline.
9. *Information on valuables*: canceled checks and receipts on art, antiques, and jewelry and appraisals of same. These records should be kept as long as you own the item, plus three years after any sale, for income-tax purposes.

10. *Credit cards*: all credit card numbers, telephone numbers and/or addresses, and/or prepaid envelopes to notify of loss or theft; update constantly.
11. *Other current documents*: warranties, loan contracts, service contracts.

Things to Keep in a Safe Deposit Box There are a number of items that you want to keep in a safe deposit box. Although they don't specifically relate to budget making, they are part of sensible and complete record keeping.

1. *Personal documents*: birth certificates, marriage certificate, military records, naturalization papers.
2. *Securities and properties*: deed to a house, car titles, stock certificates, insurance policies, bonds.
3. *Wills*: all current wills; originals should be kept by those who will carry out the will.
4. *Inventory of personal and household items*: make complete and update in case of loss or damage. Take photographs, and perhaps make a tape-recorded inventory.

General Budgeting

Figure 7-6 is a monthly general-budget form that encompasses both estimated and actual cash available and fixed and variable payments.

You will note that the savings category is located under the *Fixed Payments* heading. This is because the money in your savings account may be used to pay such fixed annual expenses as auto, fire, and life insurance, and it is necessary to plan to save in advance for these expenses.

The key to making a budget work for you is to review your figures every month to see how your monthly estimates compare to your spending.

Figure 7-6

A general way to budget.

Cash Forecast, Month of _____	Estimated	Actual
Cash on hand and in checking account, end of previous period	_____	_____
Savings needed for planned expenses	_____	_____
Receipts		
Net pay	_____	_____
Borrowed	_____	_____
Interest/dividends	_____	_____
Other	_____	_____
Total cash available during period	_____	_____
Fixed Payments		
Mortgage or rent	_____	_____
Life insurance	_____	_____
Fire insurance	_____	_____
Auto insurance	_____	_____
Other insurance	_____	_____
Savings	_____	_____
Local taxes	_____	_____
Loan or other debt	_____	_____
Children's allowances	_____	_____
Other	_____	_____
Total fixed payments	_____	_____
Flexible Payments		
Water	_____	_____
Electricity	_____	_____
Fuel	_____	_____
Telephone	_____	_____
Medical	_____	_____
Household supplies	_____	_____
Car	_____	_____
Food	_____	_____
Clothing	_____	_____
Nonrecurring large payments	_____	_____
Contributions, recreation, etc.	_____	_____
Other	_____	_____
Total flexible payments	_____	_____
TOTAL ALL PAYMENTS	_____	_____
Recapitulation		
Total cash available	_____	_____
Total payments	_____	_____
Cash balance, end of period	_____	_____

MARILYN BERGER

Chapter 8 ～

Contents

The Subtle Revolution: The Working Woman

The increasing number of working wives relates, in part, directly to the inflationary economy. For years, the popular opinion was that when a married woman worked it was for the extras, the luxuries, yet today this is not true. Statistics indicate that 68 percent of the female labor force work of necessity (Smith, 1979, p. 69). As inflation has accelerated, the second income in a family has become increasingly necessary to maintain a given standard of living. And, there are many other important reasons besides inflation for the married woman to enter the labor force. This chapter will examine these phenomena in detail.

The Working Wife

Joe and Mary Revisited

In the last chapter (p. 212), you'll remember we left Joe trying to pay off his debts under a court supervised bankruptcy payment plan. Mary was busy at home with their second baby. Another different, more common scenario for this story is that Mary goes to work to help make ends meet. In this way, Joe is able to avoid the drastic step of declaring bankruptcy, at least for a while, and probably indefinitely.

In years past, the working woman generally, and the working wife in particular, was an unusual phenomenon. The labor force included few women prior to 1900. Married women were full-time wives and mothers and considered derelict in their duty if they worked outside of the home. In 1890, only 3.7 million women were in the labor force. They accounted for 17 percent of all workers and represented 18 percent of the female population over fourteen years of age. Only 4.5 percent of married women were in the labor force (Smith, 1979, p. 3).

By 1978, 42 million women, 50 percent of the female population over age sixteen, were in the labor force (Smith, 1979, p. 3). In 1975, 62 percent of married women were in the labor force (Statistical Abstracts, 1976, p. 358). One-third of them were mothers with young children (Smith, 1979, p. 1). Over the past thirty years, six out of ten additions to the work force have been female and most of them have been married (Smith, 1979, p. 1). Thus, the traditional marriage in which the husband works to support the family while the wife remains home caring for the family has become a minority pattern. Labor department projections indicate that this traditional type of family, with the mother in the home constantly, will describe only 25 percent of married women's families by 1990 (Smith, 1979, p. 18). Today's American family is a dual career family in which both husband and wife work outside of the home.

Smith (1979, pp. 4–7) discusses a number of factors other than the constant inflationary pressures of the American economy that have led to the increased numbers of married women working outside the home.

1. Real wages (adjusted for inflation, see p. 222 have increased dramatically. As this happens, the relative cost of staying home with the family all day becomes too large, and more women are drawn into the labor force. The opposing effect of increased real income for a family is less economic pressure to work and greater financial means to enjoy leisure pursuits. However, this effect has not been dominant. Rather, increased real income has drawn women into the work force. One reason might be that desires for increasingly higher standards of living have outpaced the real income increase. Secondly, in the recent years of high inflation, real income has not really increased very rapidly. Indeed, in some years it has actually declined (p. 223). Thus, despite increasing real income, women have not remained home to enjoy it, but have entered the labor market to participate in the higher wages. Increased income also permits the reduction of unpaid labor in the home by the woman, since labor-saving devices and domestic help can be purchased.

2. There has been a tremendous increase in the kinds of jobs available to women. The importance of physical strength in many industrial jobs has diminished. Service jobs, such as clerical and sales, have expanded greatly. The opportunity for part-time work has also increased. Equal opportunity legislation (Chapter 2, p. 55) has created demands for women in jobs previously unavailable. Because of the greatly increased demand for women workers, their wages have increased, although they remain well below men's wages (Chapter 2, p. 53).

3. Declining birth rates have certainly contributed to women working more. Women with small children are the least likely to work outside of the home (Glick, 1979). As the years diminish during which small children are at home, the woman is freer to seek work and fulfillment outside of the home.

4. Increasing education has contributed to women working outside the home. College attendance has gradually increased from only a small percentage of women fifty years ago to equal or even higher percentages than we find among men (Glick, 1979). Many public institutions of higher learning now have more women than men enrolled. Better education certainly creates job opportunities. More importantly, the educated person's awareness tends to increase, and as a result, he or she will seek fulfillment as well as

the chance to make a broader contribution to society. The role of wife and mother becomes only one of many roles that the educated woman may see herself in as she becomes more aware of her potential.

5. Attitudes about the role of the woman in the family have changed greatly during this century. In 1930, only 18 percent of surveyed women believed married women should have a full-time job outside of the home (Smith, 1979, pp. 4–7). Oppenheimer et al (1976) report that in 1964 54 percent of the women surveyed agreed that a working mother could still establish a close relationship with her children. By 1970, that percentage had risen to 73 percent. Today most women believe that working outside the home is important for personal satisfaction, rather than just for earning additional money.

Work Availability: A Double-Edged Sword for Married Women

Increasing work availability for women has also meant increasing independence. Not only does this mean increased freedom within marriage, but it can also mean increased freedom from marriage. There is little doubt that the working woman's ability to support herself has freed her to seek changing roles. As Smith (1979, pp. 23–24) says:

> To the extent that employment provides a woman with a reason and the means to postpone marriage, with meaningful roles other than motherhood, and with the ability to support herself after divorce, women's employment has contributed to these changes in marriage formation and dissolution.

In the past, a woman's inability to support herself trapped her into marriage. She had to have a husband to survive. But with economic opportunities opening up, this has become increasingly untrue. She is now able to make it on her own, even when she has children. Thus, she does not need to remain trapped in an unhappy, unfulfilling marriage. One result of work availability for women, then, is the fact that it frees them from marriage if they so desire.

The other edge of the sword is that through working outside of the home, a woman's family life can be improved and enhanced. Her earnings can increase the family's standard of living. She can help alleviate her family's monetary restraints. For example, when Mary goes to work, she reduces the pressure on Joe. Hopefully this will help him feel happier and more satisfied with his family life. The family can take longer vacations together. They can afford better housing in a nicer neighborhood. They can help their children increase their education. Thus, by working the wife can contribute greatly towards the family's well-being.

In addition to the direct economic advantages of having an additional wage earner in the family, there are numerous other advantages. As mentioned, the husband may be under less economic pressure. The working wife may derive great personal satisfaction from her work just as many men do. By having contact with other adults outside of her family, she may feel more stimulated and fulfilled. This is especially true if she has small children at home. Her self-esteem may increase, knowing she is more of an equal partner in her marriage.

Of course, the results of increased independence experienced by the woman who enters the work world are hard to predict. Each individual will react differently. The point is that increased independence for the woman, made possible by her participation in the work world, is now a fact of life. For some women, it may effectively end their marriage and harm their family. For others, it will greatly enhance their marriage and family. Regardless of what it may do in a particular case, there is no doubt that women's participation in the world of work has been revolutionary to the individual woman, to women, and to the family and society in general.

What Are the Effects of Female Employment on the Time of Marriage?

As pointed out in the previous section, employment of a married woman can have either positive or negative effects on her marriage. A working woman is more likely to postpone marriage (Moore & Hofferth, 1979, p. 28; Smith, 1979, p. 104) because she is able to support herself without marriage. Although this seems to support the idea of employment as an alternative to marriage, overall marriage rates have not declined. About 95 percent of contemporary American women are expected to marry at some time in their lives (Glick, 1977, pp. 3–15). The young woman who works tends to postpone marriage rather than reject it altogether. On the other hand, employment seems to act as a "dowry" for older women, particularly those with children contemplating remarriage (Oppenheimer, 1977; Moore & Hofferth, 1979, p. 19). Apparently men are more willing to marry a woman with children if she is able to help support the children and herself. This, of course, reduces the economic burden on a new husband.

The age at first marriage has risen slightly in the past few years. This might be due to both the increasing education of women and their greater participation in the work force. Moore and Hofferth (1979, p. 29) summarize the effect of women working on time of marriage as follows:

> To the extent that increased employment of women raises occupational aspirations and educational attainment, age at marriage will continue to rise. Employment does not seem to lead many people to develop tastes or life-styles that preclude eventual marriage, however. Nevertheless, there may be a slight increase in the proportion never married among those who turned 20 during the 1970s to about 7%. Rather than indicating a rejection of marriage, this will probably reflect the inability among some of those who postpone marriage to find a suitable partner when ready for marriage and some increase in the frequency of cohabitation.

Sickness and death may seem like far-fetched consequences of female employment, but when one considers that women have, within the traditional role, made nurturing and home production their principal concern, the loss or diminution of these services might be feared to lead to poorer health among family members. Women, of course, as they opt for the working world, are exposing themselves to job tensions, commuting accidents, and occupational hazards; consequently, their mortality may rise (Waldron, 1976). Especially given the picture of over-work and strain in households with two full-time earners plus children, it seems possible that less attention can be given to proper diet and rest. Parents cannot afford to take the time to relax or to be ill, so their physical health may deteriorate. Two-job couples may consequently have shorter life spans.

On the other hand, the higher incomes of families with employed wives may provide the wherewithal for an adequate diet and preventive medical care. Husbands who are freed from the omnipresent concern of supporting their families might enjoy lower blood pressure and fewer heart attacks. Husbands may be able to turn down overtime or leave a job that is harmful to their long-term health. These benefits from women's rising labor force participation might lengthen the average life span, particularly among men.

At this time, no studies are known that have addressed this issue. If it is the case that increases in female employment affect longevity and the incidence of disease, however, the ramifications are enormous. The frequency and length of widowhood would be lessened. Fewer retired people might be unmarried. Pension systems and health care services would be affected. If the strains experienced by two-earner families are reflected even in the incidence of sickness and death, the importance of flexible and part-time employment becomes self-evident. Clearly, this is a topic that merits research attention.

Our speculation at this point is that the long-run effect of women's working will be to equalize the life span, lengthening men's lives but shortening women's. A shorter life span would be less likely, however, to the extent that both sexes reject the aggressive, competitive model of employment.

Moore and Hofferth

Marriage & Family Review, Vol. 2, No. 2, Summer 1979

As with time of marriage, female employment seems to have differing effects on the possibility of marital disruption. A woman can support herself outside of marriage if necessary. On the other hand, by contributing to the marriage economically, she can improve the quality of her family's life and consequently the stability of her marriage.

Studies on this question yield mixed results. Nye and Hoffman (1974) reviewed the literature and concluded that families in which the wife is employed are no more likely to separate or divorce than those in which she is not employed. However, if the wife earns more than the husband or if he is periodically unemployed, the probability of divorce or separation increases (Moore & Hofferth, 1979).

An interesting and controversial side question concerns the effect of welfare aid on marital disruption. Two different research

How Does Employment of the Wife Affect Divorce and Separation?

teams have reported that receipt of welfare or income maintenance decreases marital stability (Hoffman & Holmes, 1976 and Hannan & Tuma, 1977). In addition, welfare recipiency severely depresses re-marriage rates in the first two years after divorce. However, this negative effect seems to disappear after two years has passed.

The Working Wife's Economic Contribution to the Family

Mary Decides to Go to Work

Joe manages to keep the family afloat financially until their second child is two and one-half years old. Mary and Joe realize, especially with the high inflation rate, that they simply aren't going to make it comfortably on his earnings alone. Mary has heard that a local company is expanding and needs new employees. She applies for a job, receives it, and suddenly finds herself to be a full-time working mother. Although her income is relatively small compared to Joe's, she feels her $800/month will not only get them out of debt, but allow them a few luxuries they have had to forego. Hopefully, it will also allow them to save a little money toward a house down payment.

Unfortunately, Joe and Mary quickly learn that her $800 does not raise the family income by that amount. Before Mary can go to work, arrangements must be made for *child care*. They have several choices. Mrs. Smith, an older mother down the street, also needs some extra money and is willing to keep both children at her house during Mary's working hours for $30/week. Joe's mother is also willing to keep them one day a week for free. There is a day-care center near Mary's work that will care for the children for $25/week. What the center charges is related to a family's income, so that the weekly cost will vary from family to family. Mary decides to leave the children with Mrs. Smith for four days a week ($24/week) and Joe's mother for the remaining day (free). This way the children will be with people they know as well as staying in their own neighborhood. If this doesn't work out, she can put them into the day-care center. Thus, her monthly child care costs are $96. This leaves $704 of her paycheck.

Transportation must be considered. There is a bus that goes past her place of work. The route is circuitous and requires her to leave the house about one-half hour earlier than if she drove. Thus, the bus both ways will cost an additional hour of time plus about $22/month ($1/day). Taking the bus also means that Joe will have to drop the children off each morning at the sitter's. They decide that buying an old economy car is probably the best solution. This way, Mary can deliver and pick up the children, stop at the market on her way home, if necessary, and generally be more efficient. Joe borrows $1200 for 24 months at 15 percent interest and buys an old VW from a friend. The car is in good shape and other than a new set of tires, needs no work. There are additional insurance costs, however. He covers only liability, feeling that since the car is so old, it isn't really worth the cost of collision coverage. The total monthly cost for the car is $100. The breakdown is as follows:

Payment	$ 65	Hard interest adds up to $360 for two years. This makes a total debt of $1560. Divide by 24 months to get monthly payment of $65.
Insurance	$ 10	
Gas and maintenance	$ 25	
Total	$100/month	

Subtracting $100 more from Mary's monthly paycheck leaves $604.

Taxes and social security are also deducted from Mary's paycheck. She takes no deductions for the children and finds that another large bite has been taken from her paycheck. In addition, her income added to Joe's puts the family in a much higher overall tax bracket. They will receive a refund at the end of the year when they file because of child care costs and other higher deductions, but when all is said and done, the taxes and social security costs average about $150/month. Thus, Mary's monthly check shrinks to $454.

There are also miscellaneous costs associated with Mary going to work. She simply doesn't have time for as much food preparation and household work. She uses more partially prepared foods such as frozen dinners that tend to be more expensive. She also sends more clothing out to the laundry. In addition, she has had to buy some new clothes to wear to work. These costs add up to about $100/month. The bottom line is that her $800/month pay will actually add only about $354 to the family income. This amounts to about 43 percent of her gross pay. In fact, studies indicate that the working mother will spend between 25 and 50 percent of her income in order to work depending on the age of her children, type of work, and other factors unique to her situation (Vickery, 1979, pp. 159–299).

Because women tend to hold lower paying jobs, as we saw in Chapter 2, the actual amount of money they contribute to the family tends to be small. Yet for many families this contribution is increasingly important. In the past, when the working wife was the exception, her work was viewed as a family insurance policy, a buffer against hard times. Today, for many families, her income has become necessary for survival. What this means is that many families no longer have an economic buffer between themselves and hard times. They become accustomed to living on two incomes; thus, if either is lost, family finances become precarious, if not impossible.

It seems strange to hear a mother of two small children reply to the question "What do you do?" with "Oh, nothing, I'm just a housewife." Obviously, a mother with two small children does a great deal of work

Household Activities

for her family inside the home. She certainly doesn't "do nothing." Thus, when she takes a job outside of her home, something has to change inside her home. Mothers with children at home average about thirty-six hours per week working in the home (Walker & Woods, 1976). Generally, their time is divided into three major household activities: (1) meal preparation and cleanup, about 30 percent of their time; (2) care of family members, 15–25 percent of their time; and (3) clothing and regular house care, which accounts for another 15 percent of their time.

What happens to all of this work when mother takes an outside job? Essentially nothing. It still must be done and mother still does it. She simply cuts down the amount of time she gives to each task and donates much of her leisure time (weekends) to household tasks. Many people suggest that the husband and children will increase their share of the housework. Factually, their increase in household work, especially the husband's, is small. Studies yield varying results about increased household work by husbands of working wives. Some show an increase as low as only six minutes a week, while others show as much as a two hour weekly increase (Moore & Hofferth, 1979, 113–115).

Although husbands don't appreciably increase their share of the household work when their wives go to work, they are generally sharing more household work than they have in the past, whether or not their wives work. This stems from changing attitudes about sex roles and the increased emphasis on egalitarian marriage in the United States. Despite this, certainly one result of going to work for most wives is "overload" and strain. They are simply forced to do two jobs, one inside the home and one outside. Their leisure time is greatly reduced. The quality of their household work diminishes. Time becomes their most precious commodity.

Mary Seeks Part-Time Work

Mary works for seven months at her new full-time job. This helps Joe to get all of their debts paid off. However, she finds that she is increasingly fatigued. She and Joe never seem to have fun together any more. All she wants to do if she does find some free time is sleep. The house is looking bad. She hasn't had fun cooking a meal in months. She feels guilty about the little time she is able to spend with the children. She finds herself grumpy and unhappy a lot of the time. Mary decides, now that they are out of debt, to see if she can find a part-time job. She finally does, and with a sigh of relief, quits her full-time job.

Part-Time Work   As suggested in Chapter 2 (p. 58), the creation of more and better part-time jobs for mothers with young children would help alleviate the overburden experienced by the full-time working mother. Between 1965 and 1977, the number of workers on voluntary part-time schedules increased nearly three times as rapidly as the number of full-time workers. Most of this increase was among women (see Figure 8-1), so that by 1977, women held nearly 70 percent of the part-time jobs (Barrett, 1979, p. 81).

Approximately one-half of all women who work part time state "taking care of the home" as their reason for preferring part-time work. The part-time schedule effectively reduces the overload on the working mother. Unfortunately, it also drastically reduces her economic contribution to the family. This is due not only to working fewer hours, but also to the lower pay standards for part-time work (see Table 8-1).

On an hourly basis, part-time work generally pays 75 percent of full-time work. Part-time work seldom gives fringe benefits, job protection, or advancement opportunities. Those who seek part-time employment are usually assumed to be intermittent workers without long-term commitment to a career. Failure to gain fringe benefits, especially health insurance, combined with low pay in part-time jobs may keep some people on welfare. Welfare recipients are eligible for free medical care under the Medicaid program, and welfare payments in some cases can be as much as can be earned in a part-time job.

However, as more and more mothers enter the work force and prove to be good workers, part-time jobs may take on more and more of the advantages that come with full-time work. As we saw in Chapter

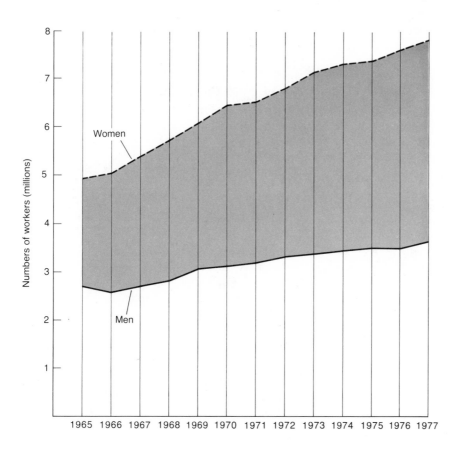

Figure 8-1
The growth in part-time employment for men and women, 1965–1977.
Source: U.S. Department of Labor, Employment and raining Adminis-tration, *1978 Employment and Training Report of the President*, p. 226.
Note: Excludes agricultural workers and part-time workers who want full-time jobs but cannot find them.

Table 8-1 Earnings of Part-Time versus Full-Time Workers by Occupation and Sex, 1977

Occupation[1]	Percentage of the Work Force on Part-Time Schedules	Median Hourly Earnings		Part-Time Earnings as a Percentage of Full-Time Earnings
		Full-Time	Part-Time	
Women				
All workers	29	$3.85	$2.87	74
Sales	54	3.05	2.64	86
Clerical	24	3.91	3.06	78
Services (nondomestic)	47	2.95	2.59	88

Source: Unpublished tabulations from the Current Population Survey provided by the U.S. Department of Labor, Bureau of Labor Statistics, 1978.
Note: Data for part-time workers include persons who usually work from 1 hour to 34 hours per week. Data for full-time workers include persons who usually work at least 35 hours per week.
[1]The detailed occupations shown include 70 percent of all female part-time workers.

2, there are some genuine problems for an employer hiring two part-time people to do one full-time job. For example, social security contributions will be higher for the two workers than for the one full-time worker, even if the rates of pay are identical. Hopefully, as the advantages of part-time work are recognized, such inequities can be removed for the employer.

Mary's New Part-Time Job

Mary's new half-time job pays her $350/month. However, with her mother-in-law's help, she is able to do away with child care costs. Transportation costs remain the same, $100/month, leaving her $250. Taxes and social security are reduced to $70/month, leaving $180. Miscellaneous costs are also reduced to $50/month. Thus, in the end, she is able to contribute only $130 extra dollars to the family, compared to the $354 she contributed when working full time. This is just enough to keep them out of debt. There is a great deal less strain on Mary, however, and hence on the family.

Marital Satisfaction When the Wife Works

As with so many areas we have discussed, the question of marital satisfaction is double-edged. The family may gain satisfaction through the wife's economic contribution. The family may lose satisfaction because she is no longer able to supply some of the caring and services to the family that she did as a full-time wife and mother. Economic strain may be reduced when she works. Psychological and physical strain may be increased.

Moore and Hofferth (1979, pp. 118–122) find that the research evidence on marital satisfaction when the wife works is mixed. After reviewing many studies, they conclude that wives who work from choice rather than economic necessity, those whose husbands are favorable toward their employment, and those who work part time are happier with their marriages than full-time housewives.

Although we have spoken mainly of the working wife's economic contribution to the family, Chapter 2 made it clear that her participation in the world of work may also pay her psychological dividends. Work may allow her to use some of her skills that go unused in the homemaker role. She will meet and interact with a wider variety of adults. She will gain more power in relationship to her husband. Her feelings of integrity, self-respect, competency, self-determination, and accomplishment may increase if she has desired employment and has successfully solved the problems of working and caring for her family.

The evidence of husbands' satisfactions with their marriage when their wife works is also mixed, but tends to indicate that they are less satisfied than the wives. As Moore and Hofferth (1979, p. 121) report:

> Evidence from other studies suggests that many husbands accept their wives' work grudgingly; that men may have more trouble than women do adapting to nonstereotypical roles; and therefore that men experience greater difficulties resolving the resulting stress. Other researchers note that in going to work a woman is frequently expanding into a new role, one that is higher in status than that of homemaker, while a husband who assumes homemaking functions is adopting a role of lower status — a role that may strain not only his sense of status and identity but his feeling of competence as well. Furthermore, a busy wife may not be able to provide the same level of physical and emotional support that a full-time homemaker can, so a husband may well come to feel he is losing out on all fronts.

On the other hand, a second income can provide the husband additional freedom. He can cut down on moonlighting and overtime work. He might be able to take a temporary reduction in pay to enter a new career or job he finds more satisfying. Increased free time may allow more family enjoyment and leisure time pursuits.

Traditionally, only a small minority of mothers with children under age six have been employed. In 1970, about 28.5 percent of such mothers were in the labor force. By 1977, this had risen to 37.6 percent, and by 1990 it is projected to be 44.8 percent (Monthly Labor Review, 1977, 1978; U.S. Dept. of Commerce, Bureau of Census, 1977). Two factors have worked to keep the mother of young children out of the labor force. First, the logistics of caring for the children and working outside the home are often unsolvable. Second, there has been a long-standing belief that a mother belongs with her children, especially when they are young. Due to earlier studies of the effects of prolonged separation of children from caring parents (orphanage and foster home placements, war orphans, etc.), many people believe that the mother's absence during the early years will do great harm to the child. Yet effective child care by other than the true biological mother certainly does not necessarily lead to severe problems in children. Actual effects of substitute child care are just as difficult to uncover as are the effects of natural parenting. The effects depend on (1) the quality of the substitute care, (2) the characteristics of the child, (3) the mother's reasons for working and the quality of the time she does spend with the child, and (4) the general social acceptance of substitute child care.

The quality of substitute child care can be excellent. It can provide for the child both physically and psychologically. A loving, caring baby sitter is often an important and happy influence on a child. The kibbutzim of Israel supply successful substitute care to large groups of young children. Substitute child care cannot be wholly praised or condemned but must be examined as to its specific merits. It can be good or bad for a child just as the child's biological mother can be.

Individual children will react differently to the partial loss of their mother and the substitution of another manner of care. Again their reaction can be positive or negative. A hyperactive, disruptive child may experience much negative feedback in a large day-care center. This same child may thrive with an attentive individual baby sitter.

If the mother is an unhappy, frustrated homemaker and prefers the work world, her child will probably be better off with a substitute. It is not really the quantity of time a mother spends with her child, but rather the quality of the time that counts. A working mother may spend less time with her children, but if she strives to make it high quality time, it may actually improve her relationship with her children.

Mary Tries to Improve the Time She Spends with Her Children

When she was a full-time homemaker, Mary found that her two children were always under foot. She never seemed to have a minute's peace. They were calling "Mommy, Mommy, Mommy," at her so much that she almost never paid attention to it. In fact, sometimes when she heard it, she'd deliberately hide from the children to escape their constant pressure. Now that she works, she finds she enjoys spending time with them. She looks forward to the weekends so she can do projects with them and give them her undivided attention. She spends much less time with them now that she works, but she enjoys that time more than she ever has.

It is interesting to note that daughters of working mothers as compared to daughters of nonworking mothers view women as more competent (Broverman et al, 1972) and view female employment as less threatening to marriage. This seems to indicate that their mothers did a decent job of rearing them even though they worked outside of the home. Obviously, a working mother may shortchange her children. On the other hand, she may also be able to provide for them better.

To this point, we have basically been discussing women taking jobs in the labor market. However, a short- or long-term job is not the same as a long-term career. Essentially we can place work onto an attitudinal continuum according to the degree of commitment (Kahn & Wiener, 1973, p. 153).

Basic attitude toward work as	Basic additional value fulfilled by work
1. Interruption	Short-run income
2. Job	Long-term income—some work-oriented values (one works to live)
3. Occupation	Exercise and mastery of gratifying skills—some satisfaction of achievement-oriented values
4. Career	Participating in an important activity or program. Much satisfaction of work-oriented, achievement-oriented, advancement-oriented values
5. Vocation (calling)	Self-identification and self-fulfillment
6. Mission	Near fanatic or single-minded focus on achievement or advancement (one lives to work)

Most women in the labor force occupy one of the first three levels. Although many men also occupy one of these first three levels, there is a far higher percentage of men than women in the latter three categories. This is true, of course, because it is the man who has traditionally been the family breadwinner while the woman has been the

Inset 8-2
The Two-Career Family

Marjorie Smith, a trust officer at Chase Manhattan Bank, is up every morning at 6 o'clock. After making breakfast and laying out clothes for her daughter Suzy, 5, she leaves for work. At that point, her husband, Lee, takes over — getting Suzy dressed and walking her to school. At 5 o'clock, after a long, hard day at the office, Marjorie picks up their daughter at a day-care center. Once home, the Smiths continue their hectic schedule, doing the laundry, dashing through a supper of soup and sandwiches, and dividing up the other household tasks — grocery shopping by Marjorie, vacuuming by Lee. The only trouble is that the routine rarely works. "The norm is frantic phone calls and schedule changes," says Lee with a laugh. "Valium has to rank with the invention of the wheel."

The Smiths are one of a growing number of couples whose daily life is fraught with the hassle of keeping two careers and a family afloat. There are now more than 20 million working married women, and many of them are committing their ambitions and energies to full-time careers. For these working couples, the problems — and pleasures — of coping with their households and two separate careers are creating a whole new life style for which there are few traditional rules. "The two-career families are pioneers, experimenters with little cultural support," observes Suzanne Keller, a professor of sociology at Princeton University. "I'm always impressed with how bravely these couples do manage the struggle."

Tensions The emotional demands in a two-career family are profound. They fill some mothers with waves of guilt for leaving their children to the care of others, they force husbands to redefine traditional roles, and they create new tensions between couples whose time is spent as much on their careers as on each other. Many young couples are postponing having children and some are deciding to forgo having children altogether. A small but significant number of couples are literally moving in separate directions, pursuing their careers in different locations and returning to their marriage on weekends.

Perhaps the most visible example of this new kind of family is Carla and Roderick Hills. She was Secretary of Housing and Urban Development…Roderick was chairman of the Securities and Exchange Commission. The Hillses manage their high-powered life by inviting guests to share meals with their four young children, guarding Sundays jealously, and employing a live-in housekeeper.

For couples with fewer financial resources, things are more complicated. Page Crosland doesn't have full-time help and feels tied to her desk at her public-relations job in Atlanta. Her husband David, who has his own law practice, can tend to their two children more easily and, recently, he was the only father at a PTA meeting. "Right now I think it's a real challenge to communicate with my kids." says David, thirty-eight. "If Page and I both wanted to play tennis or act in the theater, we'd have problems." Page, thirty-five, admits that David handles the children so well she sometimes

homemaker. However, as women have increasingly entered the work force and as attitudes about sex roles have changed, more and more career opportunities are opening to them. The real two-career family will become a more visible reality in the future. A career may be denoted by (1) a long-time commitment including a period of formal training, (2) continuity in that one moves to higher and higher levels if successful, (3) mobility in order to follow career demands.

In most families with career men, his career will dictate much of the couple's life. Where they live, how they live, and for how long feels "he's X'ed me out." Still, she thinks she's found the best solution. "There's strain in our marriage because I work," she says, "but there would be more strain if I didn't work."

In most cases, it is children who compound the difficulties of the two-career equation. In Atlanta, Penny and John Dendy had been married more than five years before they had their son, Hunter. Penny took a six-month maternity leave from her job as a research assistant, and when she returned to work, she enrolled Hunter in a parent-owned day-care center. At first, it was a disaster. "He cried all day long, and I cried all the way to work," confesses Penny, twenty-seven. She almost quit her job. "I felt I was doing everything poorly and the only way to solve it was to stop working." The shock was just as great to husband John, thirty-one, an architect. "We had to figure out how to get through the day not really knowing what our roles were," says John.

. . .

Some couples have decided that they do not want to add the extra burden of caring for children to the already formidable difficulty of coping with separate careers. In Chicago, David Firnhaber, thirty-two, and his wife, Genny, thirty-one, spend their combined income traveling and entertaining instead of worrying about PTA meetings. "We're happy with the life we have," says Genny, who came from a big family, as did her husband. "Having children was not romantic for either one of us. We know it's a lot of hard work." David is equally sure he does not want children. "We like the freedom to unwind at the end of the day," he says, sipping a glass of wine. "Or just to take off when we get home from work." Many psychologists agree that children can tip the scale in dual-career families. "Once children arrive, that's when it becomes sticky," says sociologist Pauline Bart. "One of the things that facilitate it is having money to purchase goods and services. Otherwise the woman usually ends up doing at least a job and a half."

Increasingly, many ambitious couples are pursuing jobs in separate cities and chatting about the day over long-distance instead of over dinner. Charlotte Curtis, associate editor of *The New York Times*, has had a happy weekend marriage for three and a half years with William Hunt, a Columbus, Ohio, neurosurgeon. "It's ideal for people who have serious occupations," says Curtis. "And besides, he's in the operating room from 8 in the morning until 9 at night and often I'm meeting a 1 A.M. deadline, so we wouldn't see each other that much anyway." It's only for "grown-ups" though, she cautions. "After all, you have no idea for five days what the other person is doing," says Curtis. "You can't be neurotic or insecure. Just one independent person hitched up to another."

will depend on his career demands. These demands are relatively easily met if the wife is a homemaker or simply works at one of the first three levels. However, a two-career family can have possible conflict between the partners over career demands as well as all of the kinds of problems that any family will have when both partners work. For example, the president of a local community college is married to a woman who is also a high-level school administrator. When he won the job of president, it meant moving several hundred miles to a new college. After much discussion, the couple decided that each should continue their own career. They are now a "weekend family." Each spends the week at their jobs and they visit each other on the weekends. Since they now have a house in each city, they take turns visiting. This couple does not have children to complicate the situation.

Summary   Many consider the number of women entering the work force to be the major revolution affecting the American family this century. In the past, the woman's, and especially the mother's, place was in the home. This is no longer true. Today, in most families, the woman is an active participant in the economic support of her family. Her movement into the work world has been speeded recently by the higher rates of inflation that have made it harder for all families to make ends meet.

Although now a permanent and large part of the American labor force, women still earn a disproportionately lower income than their male counterparts. In addition, the working mother is often overburdened, doing her job as well as being the major worker in the home.

Increasing job availability has also contributed to making women more independent than they have been in the past. This has brought pressure upon many marriages, because women now have a realistic alternative to a bad marriage, moving out and supporting their families themselves. A woman's increasing independence of course reaps rewards for the family. They are financially better off. Her additional earnings may help them to invest and start the economy working for them. Pressure is taken off of the husband or father to be the only breadwinner. In general, a woman's participation in the work world can lead to a more egalitarian relationship within the marriage.

Unfortunately, the lower incomes generally received by women tend to blunt some of the possible advantages of working. The costs of working including clothes, transportation, increased taxes, and child care often make the woman's real economic contribution small and even "not worth it" at times. However, as the woman improves her skills, as she becomes a more indispensable part of the work force, as she gains political power, as she becomes more career as opposed to just job oriented, the pay differential between the male and female worker declines.

Gaining Freedom Through Investment

Often when the wife works, enough extra money is brought into the family that a modest investment program can be undertaken. I can only superficially discuss a few of the many investment opportunities here. Each person must make her or his own decisions about saving and investing. For example, a young family with small children should lean toward conservative investments that require little personal time since they probably have little free time at this stage in their lives. Each couple must consider their personal interests and their financial goals. For example, the family in which the husband or wife has flexible time (perhaps they own their own business, do free-lance work, teach and have considerable vacation time, and so on) can consider apartment house ownership and management. Where time is rigidly structured, the family can investigate the stock market, real estate or business syndicates, mortgage purchase, house trading, and so on.

Savings accounts are necessary in order to gather the first capital for investment but generally they do not yield enough in light of yearly inflation. Certificates of deposit are available at interest rates up to 16 percent per year but require that the savings be left in the account for stated periods of time up to eight years to earn this maximum interest. Generally, enough money should be kept in savings accounts to meet emergencies but using such accounts for investment is not worthwhile with our present inflation rate.

Let's take a closer look at specific investments. Remember though that the percentages will only be realized if the investment is successful.

First Mortgage Money is loaned with real estate as security for the debt. If the debt is not paid, the land and/or building is taken over by the lender. First mortgages are quite safe so long as no more money is loaned than the property is worth. For example, most savings and loan institutions only lend 80 percent or less of the selling or appraised price of a property, thus assuring themselves that their loan will be covered in case the property must be sold to recover the debt. Buying first mortgages usually cannot be considered by young couples since they require a good deal of money. For example,

80 percent of a $50,000 house is $40,000. Also, the money is usually tied up for a long time, twenty to thirty years in most cases.

Second Mortgage This kind of investment can be considered by a young couple since the amount of money required can be quite low. This is the same kind of loan as a first mortgage but more speculative since it is given after a first mortgage has already been placed against the property. (The first-mortgage holder has first claim on the property in case of default.) A second mortgage is often made when the buyer of a property doesn't have enough cash for the down payment or to make up the difference between the price and the first mortgage. For example, if a house is bought for $45,000, the first mortgage is $35,000, but the buyer might have only $5000 for the down payment. The buyer is therefore $5000 short of the sales price. A short-term second mortgage of $5000 will make up the difference.

Second mortgages are usually for only a few years, seldom more than seven, and more often only for two to three years. They can be in any amount, thus making them real investment possibilities for young couples. They may be purchased from real estate agencies and money brokers. Ads for both first and second mortgages may be found in the classified newspaper sections. In general, one should not invest more in a second mortgage than the buyer has put down on the property. One should also be sure that the property is worth the price paid, so that in the case of default, sale of the property will realize enough money to cover both the first and second mortgages.

Although the standard interest rate for most second mortgages is ten percent, (in many states it can now be higher), one can often earn more by buying the second at a discount. Let's say that the previous owner of the $45,000 house took the second mortgage of $5000 from the new buyer. However, the previous owner finds that he is in need of cash before the mortgage is due. In order to make the second mortgage more attrac-

tive to investors, he offers to sell the mortgage at a 10 percent discount. Perhaps there is still $4000 due on the mortgage. The discount means that the new investor would get the mortgage of $4000 for $3600, thus effectively increasing the profit margin.

Syndicates Money for investment is raised by a group of individuals who form a partnership and usually buy real estate or a business. For the young couple, it is often possible to join such a venture in the position of a limited partner. There will be a few general partners who actually put the deal together and run the investment on a day-to-day basis. They will also assume the risks beyond each of the limited partner's investment. All the limited partner does is to put into the venture some minimum amount of money. For example, the limited partner shares might cost $1000 each. The limited partners have no responsibility in the management and no risk other than their initial investment. If the venture is profitable, they share in the profits. Such syndicates are often advertised in the financial pages, but more often one finds out about them through other investors and professional money management people. State laws control the syndicates so that the investor knows how the money is going to be used and what liabilities will be assumed as well as what profit will be paid if the venture works well.

Apartment and Commercial Rentals This kind of investment requires time as well as money since the rentals must be managed and maintained constantly. However, apartment management for other owners is a good way for a young couple to get started. They not only make money, but learn the fundamentals of property management before actually investing in apartments themselves. Commercial rentals are generally beyond the economic means of young couples, so they won't be discussed here.

If a couple has time and is handy at minor repairs, then buying and living in a duplex or triplex is a good start toward property ownership. The rents help with the payments and maintenance and, in addition, the value of a well-located property will follow the upward inflationary trend. (A more thorough example of property investment will be found on pages 256 to 257.)

Franchises This kind of investment involves buying a business such as MacDonald's, Radio Shack, Sambo's, or Colonel Sander's Kentucky Fried Chicken. The advantage is that one starts a business supported by a large company's reputation, experience, backing, and advertising. The new owner must use the parent company's products and maintain a given standard of service. The price for good franchises is high, but many of the larger companies have loan funds that can help the new owner buy in and get started.

Land Speculation and Commodities These are really speculations rather than investments and should be avoided by the small investor since the risk of loss is high. Both involve gambling on the effect the future will have on the desirability of the land or the price of the commodity (commodities are farm products such as corn, wheat, cattle, or oats, or raw materials such as copper, silver, gold, or timber). Let's look at one commodity speculation. Suppose a cattle raiser needs money or decides to avoid the risk of changing prices by entering into a future's account. The calves are bought at today's prices and then are sold to the future's account at the going rate for year-old steers. (The cattle raiser still has to feed the calves for the year, but has been assured of a moderate profit by this transaction.) The speculator who buys the account hopes, of course, that the price of beef will be higher when the steers are actually ready for market. Obviously risks are high since such unpredictable things as the weather, governmental policies, and the international situation affect commodity prices. For example, remember what happened to the price of beef when wheat reserves were sold

to the Soviets and the price of feed for cattle skyrocketed. On the other hand, often so much of a particular commodity is produced that prices drop (this has happened in recent years with milk and pork).

Oil and Mining and Invention Backing These are even more speculative investments and should not even be considered by a young family entering the investment market.

Another major form of investment is the stock market, or stocks and bonds. We will again consider these investments in some detail, starting at the low-risk, low-return end of the continuum and continuing to those investments that involve more risk and also more return.

In general, stocks, bonds, and notes of various kinds are bought through stock brokerage firms. These firms are members of various stock exchanges through which they buy and sell. The customer pays a small fee to the brokerage house to buy or sell.

Bonds Bonds are a form of IOU or promissory note that companies issue when they need funds. They are usually issued in thousand-dollar multiples. The issuing company promises to pay the bondholders a specified amount of interest for a specified amount of time at the end of which the bond will be redeemed for the face amount. Because of this generally low risk, bonds usually offer low interest rates. There are several different kinds of bonds: U.S. Savings, corporation, and municipal bonds. U.S. Savings Bonds are the safest investment but are also long-term and low interest. Because of inflation, an investor can actually be losing money over the period of the bond. Corporation bonds are relatively safe since the company pledges the properties it owns as collateral. Municipal bonds are similar except that a government unit offers the bonds, usually to complete a building or park project. Although relatively safe, as city finances have become more strained in recent years, there is some doubt that some municipal bonds will be repaid at the expiration date. Municipal bonds have the advantage of having their interest exempt from federal income taxes.

Stocks A stock is a piece of paper (stock certificate) that gives the owner the right to a portion of the assets of the company issuing the stock. Like bonds, they are issued when companies need money, usually for expansion. Unlike bondholders, stockholders are part owners of the company they have invested in, and can vote at stockholders' meetings. The stocks of large companies are usually listed on stock exchanges, either regional ones around the country or the two largest, the New York Stock Exchange and the American Stock Exchange. These organized exchanges set minimum requirements that must be met by a company in order to have its stock listed. For example, the New York Stock Exchange specifies that a company must have at least $10 million in tangible assets, at least $2 million in annual earnings, and at least 1 million shares divided among 2000 or more shareholders. Stocks are also sold over the counter in markets that are less organized than the exchanges. These stocks are usually not traded as often as those listed on the exchanges, and are issued by smaller and less well known companies (over-the-counter stocks offer the highest risk and highest return).

1. *Preferred stocks.* These are called preferred because when earnings are distributed or when a company is liquidated or goes into bankruptcy, holders of preferred stock are paid first.

2. *Common stocks.* Most stocks are common stocks. They are the last to earn and normally fluctuate more than bonds and preferred stock. While common stocks usually pay dividends, most investors hope to buy the stock at a low price and sell it at a higher price after a rise in the stock market. Blue chip stocks are those of strong companies such as General Motors or IBM. The stronger the company, usually the safer the stock.

Mutual Funds Mutual funds are companies that buy and sell large blocks of stocks. The investor can buy shares in such companies rather than shares in "real" companies. However, each mutual fund stock really represents a share of the large and diversified group of shares the fund owns. There are two kinds of mutual funds, closed end and open end. Closed-end funds usually do not issue stock after the initial issue. Many closed-end mutual funds are listed on the New York Stock Exchange, and their shares are readily transferable in the open market and can be bought and sold like other shares. Open-end funds, on the other hand, usually issue more shares as people want them and are not listed on the stock exchange.

The young family should consider diversified investment rather than place all of their capital into one venture. For example, in the stock market, the mutual fund is safer than the single stock since it represents a widely diversified holding of stocks. Before considering any investment, however, the family should be sure they have enough insurance to have basic security (see A Word About Insurance, pp. 227 – 228).

A Three Year Real Estate Investment Let's now trace a simple investment program through a three-year period. Real estate in California has been one of the best investments since World War II, so we shall invest in this field. The program outlined is highly conservative and deals only with the buying, selling, and management of well-located, already occupied apartment houses. The percentage return in real estate is greatly increased by dealing in land, building, and commercial properties, but, of course, so is the risk.

Our couple decides to postpone having children for two years so that the wife can work and add her salary to their savings. They also decide to restrain their buying and travel until their investment begins to pay off. When they have saved $4000, they use the money for a down payment on an old building with two units that costs $40,000.

They take first and second mortgages for the remaining $36,000. The income from the units covers the monthly costs of mortgage payments, property tax, and maintenance.

A year and a half later, with money saved from the wife's salary, they buy another building, an older duplex that costs $30,000. They put down $3000 and take out mortgages on the remaining $27,000. They also invest $500 plus their time to modernize the building. (In general, we are not considering the time they put into minor repairs and improvements such as painting.) Six months later, they sell the building for $38,000. Their costs (realtor's fees and the $500 in improvement) are $2500, so their net capital is $5500, or a 83+ percent rate of return on their $3000 down payment!

Three years after their first building purchase, they use its equity and the $5500 they made from the sale of their second building to buy a seven-unit newer apartment house. The equity and cash come to $15,000 as a down payment on the building, which is worth $90,000, leaving $75,000 to be financed by first and second mortgages. Again, the monthly expenses are covered by the apartment rents. The following table summarizes their three years of real estate investment.*

Our example is not just hypothetical but represents an actual case. Although this couple faced hardship during the early years of their marriage, they were soon in a position that greatly increased their security and freedom. Within six years they were financially well ahead of their friends who had not chosen to save and invest. They had

Table 8-2   Real Estate Investment

Initial investment	$ 4000
Second investment	3000
Total investment of saved capital	7000
Total worth of investment represented by third building	15,000
Net increase in 3 years	8000
Percentage increase in 3 years	114

traveled widely, bought a nice house, and broadened their investments. Although no cash was available at first from any of the buildings, the value of each building increased with inflation. An additional increase was effected by their improving the properties. In the later investments, more money could be put down, thus leaving smaller debts and allowing for some cash to be taken from the building income for other purposes such as travel.

The technique of buying a property, improving it, and trading it on a larger, more costly property is known as "pyramiding." The percentage of total gain is somewhat misleading since no fair payment for the family's time and work has been included. This, of course, is taken in the form of overall profit when the investment is liquidated.

You might ask "But what if the real estate market turned down?" Obviously, families must be alert and work to understand their investment market. Money is not made by luck but by the intelligent consideration of all factors bearing on the investment. This requires hard and diligent study. But even if there were a general depression and this family could not meet their payments, they would actually lose only $7,000 in cash and three years part-time labor. While this would be regrettable, it would not plunge them into debt since it represents saved money. It is also better to have gambled for economic growth than to have spent the money on consumer goods that lose value quickly.

*These figures will vary greatly depending on the area in which you are buying real estate. In very desirable areas, the building will cost a great deal more, thus requiring larger down payments. However, relative figures will remain about the same. They will simply all be higher.

Chapter 9 ⌒

Contents

⌒ The Biological Foundation: Sexuality

What is sex? This may seem like a strange question in this modern, enlightened age. Everyone knows what sex is. Sex is for having babies (reproduction). That's certainly true, yet if sex were only for reproduction, why don't humans mate like other animals, once a year or so? Why don't human females go into heat, attract males, become pregnant, and later give birth? Why are humans always interested in sex regardless of where females are in their reproductive cycles? If sex is only for reproduction, why do humans spend so much time talking about, reading about, thinking about, and having sex?

Perhaps sex is for human pleasure. But if sex were just for fun, why are there all the restrictions on sexual behavior? Why does society so often regulate sexual expression through religion? If sex is just for fun, why does religion restrain sexual behavior and try to focus it toward a higher purpose?

Well, then, perhaps sex is for love. But what is love exactly? Does sex always mean love? If masturbation is sex, does it mean I love myself if I do it? Love is for emotional closeness, intimate communication, and ego-enhancement. So, if sex is for love, it must also be ego-enhancing, a means of intimate communication, and a way to be emotionally close.

Certainly sex can be for all of these things. In addition, sex is sometimes only for biological and/or emotional release as, for example, when a male has a wet dream during which semen and sperm are released. That doesn't sound much like love, does it? Sex can be an expression of love but it can also be used for many other things.

For example, it may be used to possess another person, such as when women are considered to be male property. It may be used to gain status, such as when a king marries the daughter of another king to increase his holdings and thereby his prestige. It may also be used for violence as in the case of rape. It may also be a business as in the case of prostitution. It may be used indirectly as in advertising where appeals based on sex are made to sell many different kinds of products.

It is obvious from this short discussion that sex is many things to human beings. If sex were only for reproduction or only for love or only for fun, there certainly would be little controversy about it and no need to control it. But, of course, sex isn't just for one purpose, but for many. It is this fact that causes people to be so concerned and, at times, so confused about the place of sex in their lives.

Human Sexuality in the United States

For better or worse, the place of sexuality in the American society has changed rapidly in the last twenty years. Generally, sexual expression has become freer, more diverse, and more open to public view. The famed double standard, which promoted sexual expression for men while limiting it for women, has begun to break down in the face of the feminine liberation movement. Better understanding one's own sexuality has become an important goal in many people's lives.

In fact, better understanding and acceptance by women of their sexuality may be one of the real revolutionary changes affecting the family and all intimate relationships during the 1980s (Reiss, 1980). Reiss predicts that the incidence of sexual dysfunction will decrease in the 1980s in part because women will gain increasing control over their own sexuality.

Traditionally, the male has set the stage for sexual expression. He has usually initiated and guided sexual encounters. Hence, he has been able to engage in sexual activity at the times, in the places, and in the manner he desires. The woman has had to react to him. It seems clear that in this circumstance, the chances for him to derive pleasure from the sexual contact are far greater than her chances. He has sex when he feels interested, ready, and capable. She may or may not feel this same confidence when he initiates sexual interaction. Hence, the chances are greater that she will fail to feel satisfied more often than he will. The chances are also greater that she will make excuses to avoid sexual activity since she traditionally has been placed in an automatically defensive, reactive position about sexual relations.

As she becomes freer to initiate sexual activity and to express her own desires, she will be able to set the stage for sexual expression or at least to share in the decision. Thus, she too will be able to pick times for sexual activity when she feels interested, ready, and capable. Obviously if she can pick these times, her chances of sexual satisfaction are increased. There is no need to make excuses to avoid sexual relations if you are the initiator.

If women could gain sexual equality, they could then channel sexuality into their lives in their own way and at their own pace. In general, sexual equality should serve to reduce sexual dysfunction in both men and women. If each person is free to express themselves sexually with their partner and respects that freedom for their partner, then chances of sexual exploitation of one partner by the other are reduced. Without exploitation and manipulation, the chances for sexual fulfillment and enjoyment are greatly increased. Freedom of sexual expression also includes the freedom to say "no."

In a sense, greater sexual diversity and freedom create as well as solve problems. Freedom means responsibility. I must assume personal responsibility for my actions if I am free to choose my actions. In the past when the mores, taboos, and traditions tightly surrounded sexual expression, responsibility was removed from me. I could always blame the rules for my lack of satisfaction, for my failures, for my unhappiness. But the America of the last twenty years has rapidly removed the rules from my sexual expression. The decisions are now up to me and this can be frightening.

Freedom of sexual choice for the young unmarried individual can be much more threatening than for the married person whose sexual expression is a mandated part of the relationship. The sexual mores in many parts of the American society have changed from supporting postponement of sexual intercourse until marriage to pressuring young people to engage in premarital sexual relations. Don't be old-fashioned. Get with it. Everyone does it. Especially for young women, the harder decision now seems to be to say "No, I don't wish to have sexual intercourse with you or at this time." This is quite a change from the old fear of losing one's virginity. A young woman is now all too often made to feel guilty and inadequate if she doesn't participate in sexual relations. Virginity is maligned often because it represents past traditions and morality and, of course, it is supported by all the wrong people, i.e., parents, grandparents, ministers, and those who aren't liberated.

Yet, part of a healthy model of sexual behavior is the freedom to choose to participate or not in sexual relations. "It is my body." Respect for me as an individual will allow me this choice. Being coerced into sexual relations, either physically or psychologically, seldom leads to a healthy experience.

Healthy sexual expression is a primary part of human intimacy. Indeed, the word intimacy often implies sexual activity. As we try to make good decisions for ourselves about sexual intimacy, it is perhaps helpful to think about what is meant by healthy sex. Of course, there is debate over this. For some, no sexual involvement before marriage is healthy. Others will argue that complete sexual freedom is healthy. Despite these two opposing positions, it seems that one can in less extreme terms discover some foundations that will help to promote "healthy sex."

Does My Sexual Expression Enhance My Self-Esteem? If my behavior adds to me, increases my self-respect and my positive feelings about myself, and in general helps me to like myself better, then the behavior is most apt to be healthy. Behavior that creates negative self feelings and causes loss of self-esteem is better avoided. Low self-esteem, as we saw in Chapter 5, creates many problems, especially in our intimate relationships. Thus for any behavior, not just sexual, one judgment each of us can make is: does my behavior increase my self-esteem?

Is My Sexual Expression Voluntary (Freely Chosen)? It is not always easy to answer this question. Obviously, being raped is not voluntary sexual expression and certainly not health-enhancing. However, things are not always so clear-cut. Is my behavior voluntary when I have sexual intercourse out of fear of losing my boyfriend if I don't put out? Perhaps it is, yet the element of fear raises a doubt. Does the fear make me feel I must do it? Does the fear rob me of voluntary choice? Does the fear cause me to overlook the broader question: If I will lose him only because I will not have sex at this time, is he really someone with whom I want to have an intimate relationship? If my decision is really mine, independent of peer and social pressure, then the chances increase that my chosen behavior will be healthy.

Is My Sexual Expression Enjoyable and Gratifying? This may sound like a strange question to ask. Isn't all sex fun and enjoyable? It should be if it is healthy, but we often find that it is not. Many people report disappointment with their early sexual encounters. A few people report that they seldom derive much joy from sexual encounters. For most, however, positive answers to the first two questions will help to answer this question positively. In general, enjoyable and gratifying sexual expression tends to occur most often within intimate all-encompassing human relationships. This is not to deny that at times sex for sex is gratifying. However, close intimate relationships that involve one in many ways, intellectually, emotionally, socially, and physically, tend to promote healthy sexual relations.

Will My Sexual Expression Lead to an Unwanted Pregnancy? Sexual relations leading to wanted children is healthy. Sexual relations using birth control methods and thereby avoiding unwanted children can also be healthy. There are some who for religious reasons will disagree with the latter statement. For them healthy sex might mean abstinence if children are not desired at a given time. For most people, however, sex leading to unwanted pregnancy is to be avoided if sexual expression is to be healthy. We will discuss the problems of unwanted children in Chapters 10 and 11. Taking steps to prevent unwanted pregnancy is an important element in healthy sexual expression.

Will My Sexual Expression Pass Venereal Disease to My Partner? It is obvious in the medical sense that healthy sex does not propagate venereal disease. Thus, knowledge of venereal diseases and taking precautions against them must be a part of healthy sexual expression.

In a sense, healthy sex is knowledgeable sex. Knowing oneself so that self-esteem may be enhanced, knowing how to make voluntary choices and being independent enough to make them, knowing what is enjoyable and gratifying, knowing how to prevent unwanted pregnancies, and knowing how to guard against and what to do about venereal disease—these are the foundation blocks to healthy sexual expression. In a nutshell, "Knowledge breeds responsible behavior, ignorance just breeds" (Canfield, 1979).

Human Sexuality Compared to That of Other Species

No society has ever been found where sexual behavior was unregulated. True, regulations vary greatly—one spouse, multiple spouses, free selection of sexual partners, rigidly controlled selection, and so forth. Actually, the specific regulations include almost any arrangements imaginable if one takes a cross-cultural view of sexuality. Within a given culture, however, the regulations, whatever they may be, are usually strictly enforced through taboos, mores, laws, and/or religious edicts. To transgress from them may bring swift and sometimes severe punishment as in the case of stoning to death the woman involving herself in an adultery, as has been done in some middle eastern cultures.

Why do humans always surround sex with regulations? Certainly among lower animals sex is controlled, but the controls are usually identical throughout the species, dictated by built-in biological mechanisms. Humans have regulated sex precisely because their biology has granted them sexual freedom of choice. Sexual behavior can occur at any time in humans. Among animals, sexual behavior occurs only periodically, depending on the estrous cycle of the female in all mammals below primates. For mammals, sexual behavior is basically for reproduction. Thus, sexual responsiveness is tied directly to the period of maximum fertility in the female. The female gives clues such as odor change and genitalia swelling, to which the male responds.

In lower animals sexual behavior is controlled by lower brain centers and spinal reflexes activated by hormonal changes. In general, the larger the cortex, the higher the species, and the more control the animal has over its own responses. So we come to the humans with their large cortex and what do we find? An animal with few built-in restraints and hence many variations in sexual behavior. Without built-in guidelines, human sexuality is dependent on learning, and since different societies and groups teach different things about sexuality, there are many variations in sexual attitudes and behavior. Sexual compatibility, in part, depends on finding another person who shares your attitudes about sex.

Since sex for human beings is less tied to reproduction, sexual expression can serve other purposes as well. For example, Desmond Morris (1967, pp. 65–66) notes:

> The vast bulk of copulation in our species is obviously concerned, not with producing offspring, but with cementing the pair-bond by producing mutual rewards for sexual partners. The repeated attainment of sexual consummation for a mated pair is clearly, then, not some kind of sophisticated, decadent outgrowth of modern civilization, but a deep-rooted, biologically based, and evolutionarily sound tendency in our species.

Human sexuality differs significantly from that of other animals in several other important ways besides the greater freedom from instinctive direction. It appears that human females are the only females capable of intense orgasmic response. The sexual behavior of the human male, however, still resembles the sexual behavior of male primates; it depends largely on outside perceptual stimuli and is under partial control of the female in that she usually triggers his sexual response (Barclay, 1971, p. 61). Of course, with the human this trigger can be indirect, such as when the man fantasizes.

Another important difference is that human females are most sexually responsive immediately before and after the menstrual flow

WHAT DO YOU THINK?

What do you think is the major purpose of human sexuality? Why?

Do we need any controls on human sexuality? Why or why not?

What controls would you have if you feel they are needed?

If you feel there should be no controls, how would the institution of marriage be affected?

rather than at ovulation when pregnancy can occur.* According to A. M. Barclay, "This difference, coupled with the development of the orgasm in females, might tentatively be interpreted to mean that humans are the only species to derive pleasure out of sexual behavior without becoming involved in its reproductive aspects" (1971, p. 61).

The major difference, however, remains that much of human sexuality depends on what the individual thinks rather than on biology. Thus, compared to other species, human sexuality is:

1. More pervasive, involving humans psychologically as well as physiologically.
2. Much more under conscious control rather than instinctual biological control.
3. Far more affected by learning and social factors, and thus more variable within the species.
4. Largely directed by an individual's beliefs and attitudes.

*A recent study at Wesleyan University seems to dispute this, finding that women, like other mammals, become more sexually aroused when they are most fertile (see Adams, Gold & Burt, 1978).

5. Less directly attached to reproduction.
6. Able to serve other purposes such as pair-bonding and communication.
7. More of a source of pleasure.

Marriage is society's sanctioned arrangement for sexual relations. Sex is the foundation of most human intimate relationships. Sex is the basis of the family, procreation, and the survival of the species. Sex is communication and closeness. It can be pleasuring in its most exciting and satisfying form. It is certainly right and proper to study marriage by viewing humans as the sexual creatures they are. And though thoughts and attitudes toward sex are the most important part of human sexuality, we must start with the biological foundations if we are to fully understand sexuality and the male-female bond. Thus the remainder of this chapter is mainly concerned with the physiology of sex.

When describing human anatomy, we must always think in terms of two descriptions, male and female. Yet, the development of male and female anatomical structures rests on a common tissue foundation. As described in Chapter 2, hormonal action triggered by chromosomal make-up differentiates the tissues into male and female organs. Figure 9-1 shows this differentiation, and the homologues (similar in origin and structure, but not necessarily in function) of external male and female genitalia.

It is interesting that human sex organs have always been of great interest to people, more so than other organs. Many past societies have glorified the genitals in their arts (see Figure 9-2). But the advent of Christianity brought a more negative attitude toward sexuality in general, limiting it to reproduction and denying its more pleasurable aspects. The interest in sexuality went underground, so to speak, and graphic display of sexual activities became known as pornography.

Although the genitalia have been studied medically in modern American society, it is only recently that they have been studied as organs of sexuality. As one gynecologist puts it (Neubardt, 1971, p. 2) gynecology

> is a subspecialty concerned with the diagnosis and treatment of diseases of the female genital tract . . . Gynecology requires four years of residency. It is a thorough and intensive program that has consistently produced highly skilled and extremely well qualified practitioners. . . . Yet under these ideal circumstances, in a discipline focused entirely on the genital tract, in my four years of training there was absolutely no time devoted to the consideration of sexuality. It was never even mentioned. Our consideration of the vagina involved its tensile strength, its supports, its distensibility, its bacterial flora. . . . The vagina as a source of pleasure was simply never mentioned.

Human Sexual Anatomy

Answers to *Sex Knowledge Inventory*

1. T	6. F	11. F	16. T
2. T	7. F	12. T	17. F
3. F	8. F	13. F	18. F
4. F	9. F	14. T	19. T
5. F	10. T	15. F	20. T

Figure 9-1

External male and female genitalia: development from undifferentiated to differentiated stage.

Undifferentiated

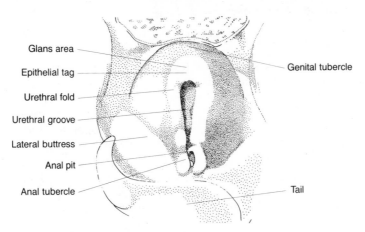

Glans area

Epithelial tag

Urethral fold

Urethral groove

Lateral buttress

Anal pit

Anal tubercle

Genital tubercle

Tail

Male   **Embryo**   **Female**

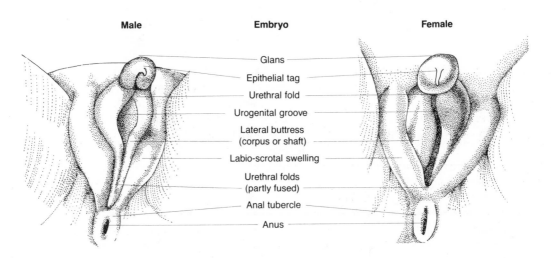

Glans

Epithelial tag

Urethral fold

Urogenital groove

Lateral buttress (corpus or shaft)

Labio-scrotal swelling

Urethral folds (partly fused)

Anal tubercle

Anus

Fully Developed

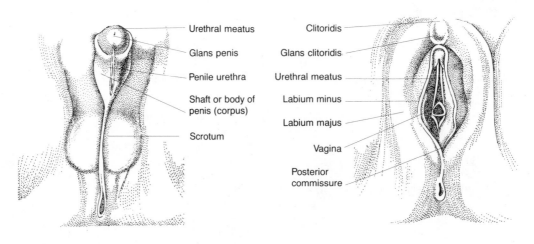

Urethral meatus

Glans penis

Penile urethra

Shaft or body of penis (corpus)

Scrotum

Clitoridis

Glans clitoridis

Urethral meatus

Labium minus

Labium majus

Vagina

Posterior commissure

Figure 9-2

(a) A phallic terra cotta figure from the Near East, probably during the Roman period. (b) A Mexican terra cotta figure from the third or fourth century B.C.

(a)

(b)

Fortunately, the medical schools have begun to correct this oversight and study human sexuality. For example, at a recent regional meeting of the Society for the Scientific Study of Sex the following papers were presented: "Feminine Sexual Hygiene," "Penile Sensitivity, Aging and Degree of Sexual Activity," "Clitoral Adhesions: Myth or Reality," and "The Vaginal Clasp."

Male Sex Organs Although most people's interest focuses on the external organs of both sexes because of their obvious sexual connotations, the internal ones are regarded as the primary organs of procreation (see Figures 9-3 and 9-4).

The testes in the male produce *spermatozoa* (or sperm for short). If the coiled tubules within the testes that produce the sperm and store it were straightened out, they would be several hundred feet

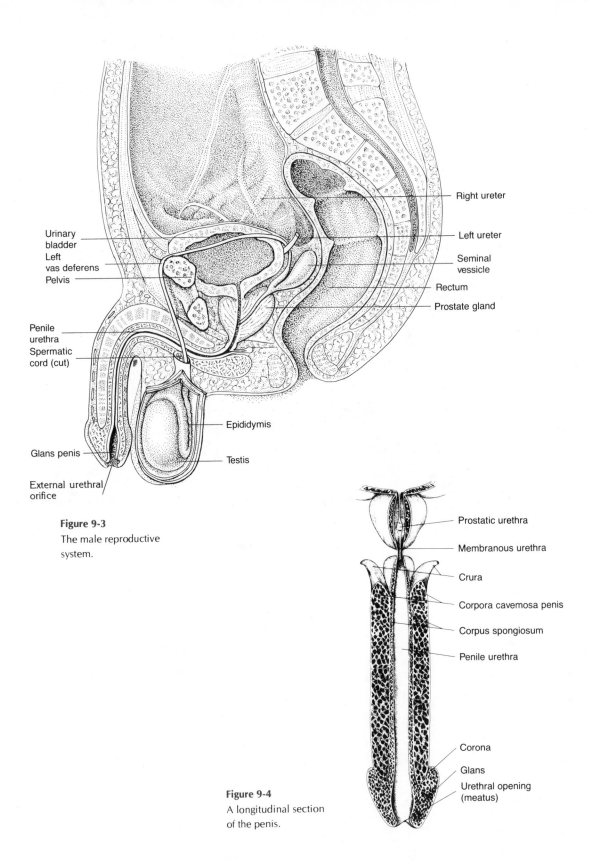

Right ureter

Urinary
bladder

Left
vas deferens

Pelvis

Left ureter

Seminal
vessicle

Rectum

Prostate gland

Penile
urethra

Spermatic
cord (cut)

Glans penis

External urethral
orifice

Epididymis

Testis

Figure 9-3
The male reproductive
system.

Prostatic urethra

Membranous urethra

Crura

Corpora cavemosa penis

Corpus spongiosum

Penile urethra

Corona

Glans

Urethral opening
(meatus)

Figure 9-4
A longitudinal section
of the penis.

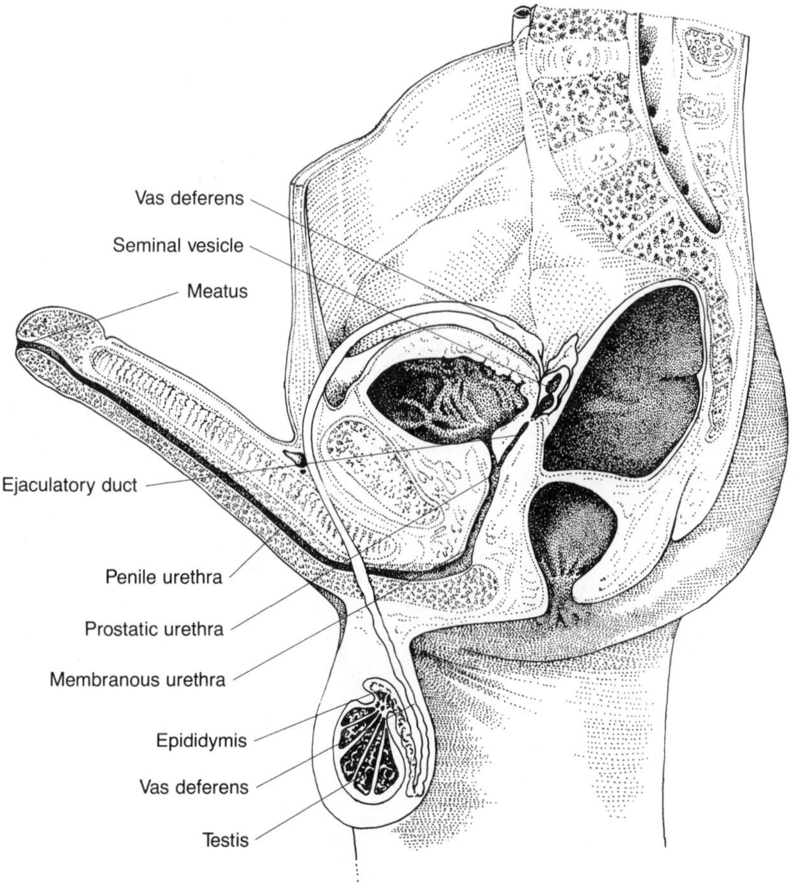

Figure 9-5
The passage of
spermatozoa.

Vas deferens

Seminal vesicle

Meatus

Ejaculatory duct

Penile urethra

Prostatic urethra

Membranous urethra

Epididymis

Vas deferens

Testis

long. Other special cells within the testes produce the important hormone *testosterone*. It is this hormone that directs the developing tissue toward maleness and, at adolescence, causes the maturing of the sexual organs and the appearance of secondary sexual characteristics such as deepening voice and facial and body hair. Figures 9-5 and 9-6 show the course taken by the spermatozoa in ejaculation. Spermatozoa are matured and stored in the *epididymis*. With ejaculation, they travel up the *vas deferens* where it joins the duct of the *seminal vesicle* in the lower abdomen. The two seminal vesicles produce a secretion, *semen*, which increases the volume of the ejaculatory fluid, which empties into the ejaculatory ducts. These ducts then empty into the *urethra*, which is the canal extending through the penis. (The urethra is the canal through which urine is discharged but urine and semen can never pass at the same time. Sexual arousal and ejaculation inhibit the ability to urinate.) The *prostate gland* surrounds the first part of the urethra as it leaves the bladder. This gland secretes a thin fluid that helps alkalize the seminal fluid, and, in addition, the muscle part of the prostate helps eject the ejaculatory fluid out of the penis. The last contribution to the seminal fluid comes from the *Cowper's glands*, two pea-sized structures flanking the urethra. During sexual

Figure 9-6
The route of a sperm from
its origin to its fer-
tilization of an ovum
during ejaculation.

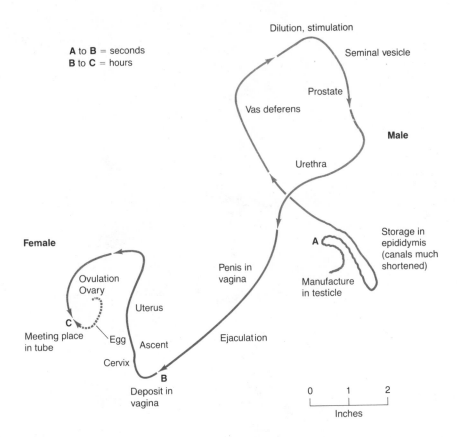

arousal they secrete an alkaline fluid that further neutralizes the acidic environment of the urethra.

The ejaculatory process begins with contractions of the ducts leading from the *seminiferous tubules* in the testes and simply continues on through the system. The actual amount of ejaculate varies according to the male's physical condition, age, and the time elapsed between ejaculations. Usually about a teaspoon of fluid is ejaculated, but this contains several million sperm. The ejaculate must contain 60 to 100 million sperm per cubic centimeter of semen to be considered of normal fertility.

The strength of the ejaculatory response also varies: the semen may simply ooze out of the urethra or it may be discharged as far as several feet beyond the penis. The ejaculatory amount is reestablished in the healthy male within twenty-four hours.

Ejaculation is accompanied by a highly pleasurable sensation known as *orgasm*. (This will be discussed more fully later.) Figure 9-6 diagrams the route taken by the sperm for fertilization to take place. The testes are particularly sensitive to temperature and must remain at a slightly cooler level than the body to produce viable spermatozoa. Hence, when the temperature is very hot, the sac will hang further down. When it is cold, the testicles will be pulled up close to the body. Occasionally, the testicles won't descend into the scrotum properly and sterility results. However, surgery and hormone treatment usually can correct this (McCary, 1967, p. 43). Sometimes only one testicle descends, but one is usually enough to ensure fertility.

In order to have sexual intercourse, it is necessary for the male to have an erection. He does not have voluntary control of this and cannot always be sure that he will be capable of intercourse. This fact sometimes leads to sexual insecurity in males. Failure to achieve and hold an erection long enough for sexual intercourse is called *impotence*. Both erection and ejaculation can occur without physical stimulation, such as with a nocturnal emission which is usually accompanied by an erotic dream.

Figure 9-4 shows the three cylindrical bodies of spongy erectile tissue that run the length of the penis. Sexual arousal causes the dilation of the arterioles, and small valvelike structures (polsters) emit blood into the vascular spaces of the erectile tissue. The rate of blood inflow is greater than the rate of outflow, so the volume of blood in the penis increases. As the erectile tissue becomes engorged with blood, the penis stiffens into an erection. The average penis is 3 to 4 inches long in a flaccid state and approximately 6 inches long when erect. Size variations are less in the erect state than they are in the flaccid state.

Modern technology has succeeded in duplicating the erection's mechanism. Dr. Brantley Scott, a urologist at St. Luke's Episcopal Hospital in Houston, Texas, has successfully implanted a mechanical device to aid men who cannot become erect. The device consists of two silicone rubber cylinders implanted into the penis, two bulbs in the scrotum, and a liquid storage area in the pelvic region. To make the penis erect, one bulb is squeezed and the liquid flows into the cylinder. The penis remains erect until the other bulb is squeezed to evacuate the fluid back to the storage area.

Female Sex Organs As we did with the male sperm, let us trace the course of development and ultimate fertilization of the female egg (ovum). Eggs are produced in the female gonads or *ovaries*. It is estimated that each ovary contains 50,000 to 200,000 tiny sacs or *follicles*, but only 250 to 400 will become active during a woman's lifetime and produce eggs (see Figure 9-7). Each woman is born with all her primordial eggs and does not actually produce them as the male produces sperm. After puberty, normally one egg every twenty-eight days will ripen and burst from a follicle and enter the *Fallopian tube*, where fertilization may occur.

Each month, normally, a ripe egg is produced and released. This cycle is known as *menstruation*, and release of the ripe egg from the follicle is called *ovulation*. The easiest way to describe this process is to label the first day of menstrual flow as day 1 because it is easy to observe. On an average, the cycle lasts twenty-eight days with menstruation lasting five days. Individuals may vary considerably from these averages.

Follicle-stimulating hormones (FSH) are released from the anterior lobe of the pituitary gland, which is a pealike gland suspended

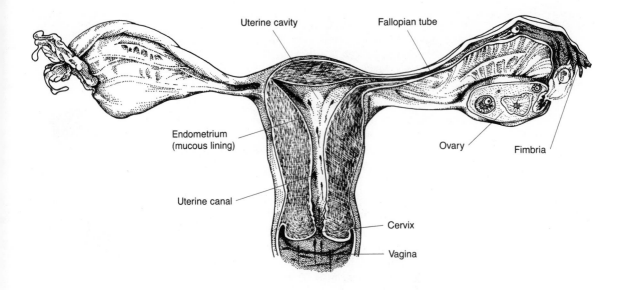

Uterine cavity

Fallopian tube

Endometrium
(mucous lining)

Ovary

Fimbria

Uterine canal

Cervix

Vagina

Figure 9-7
A schematic illustration
of the development
of a fertilized egg. An
ovum is shown leaving the
ovary. Later it is fer-
tilized in the upper
Fallopian tube. The fer-
tilized ovum, or zygote, will
cleave daily as it con-
tinues down the Fallopian
tube to the uterus. It
floats in the uterus for
several days and then
is implanted in the uterus
wall.

from the base of the brain. It produces at least nine different hormones that play important roles in the proper growth of the child. The follicle-stimulating hormone activates the ovarian follicles and two to thirty-two follicles and eggs begin to ripen. The follicles mature at different rates of speed. By the tenth day the most mature follicles look like rounded, fluid-filled sacs. The maturing follicles begin to produce *estrogen*, which prepares the uterus for implantation of the fertilized egg. At this time, one of the follicles speeds its growth. The others, developed to various extents, regress and die. Occasionally a woman may produce more than one ripe egg per cycle and thus be prone to

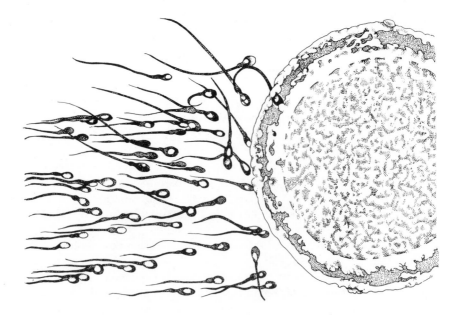

Figure 9-8
Sperm swim toward a
mature ovum and swarm
around it until one
of them penetrates the
outer edge of the egg.

Inset 9-2
Fertility Drugs: A Mixed Blessing

"They just kept coming. We weren't expecting anything like this."

Mark Levy, 27, of Fairfield, Ohio, had good reason to be surprised and excited last month. His wife Pamela, 28 and previously childless, had just given birth to quintuplets — a phenomenon that until recently happened only once in every 41 million births. But quintuple deliveries and other multiple births have become more commonplace lately; Pamela, like thousands of other women, had been taking a fertility drug called Pergonal. Doctors estimate that women who become pregnant after treatment with Pergonal are many times more likely, and women who take another fertility drug called Clomid slightly more likely, than other women to have more than one baby.

The Levy quints are doing well, and their parents seem to be adjusting to the startling increase in the size of their family. But many of the multiple births that result from the use of fertility drugs turn out to be mixed blessings at best. The infants are usually born prematurely, and because of overcrowding within the womb are likely to suffer even more problems than most "preemies." The prospect of multiple births also puts a strain on pregnant women. They are usually dismayed when they first hear the news. In fact, many families feel that they are simply unprepared — physically, financially, and emotionally — to cope with more than one new baby at a time. Most women nonetheless profess to be delighted after they find themselves the mothers of twins, triplets, or even quints.

Multiple births are not the only problems that go with fertility drugs. Though many, perhaps even the majority of women who take fertility drugs experience no ill effects, a number develop potentially serious illnesses. Researchers found that women who took Clomid occasionally developed ovarian cysts, which, without skillful treatment, can rupture and cause internal hemorrhaging and death. The incidence of cysts is higher with Pergonal.

Casual Use. Most fertility experts insist that the drugs are indeed safe — if they are used with care and discretion. Unfortunately, says Manhattan Gynecologist Edward Stim, who rarely prescribes the drugs, they are sometimes given on a casual, "Why not give it a try?" basis. Clomid, a synthetic hormone-like drug, seems to work by stimulating the pituitary gland to release hormones that help to ripen the ovum. Pergonal, a hormonal extract from the urine of postmenopausal women, primes the ovaries so that another hormone — human chorionic gonadotropin or HCG — can ensure the release of the ovum. Neither treatment should be used unless doctors have first determined that a woman's inability to have a baby is caused by a failure to ovulate, which accounts for only 5 to 10 percent of all cases of infertility.* The experts urge that patients be monitored carefully to prevent the development of cysts.

Some doctors feel that women faced with giving birth to litters should consider having abortions. "If there are more than three fetuses, it's a disaster," says one fertility expert. But Dr. Robert Kistner of Harvard Medical School, a pioneer in Clomid treatment, feels that multiple pregnancies can and should be prevented before they start. Kistner treats women who do not respond to Clomid alone by priming them first with small doses of Clomid and Pergonal then checking their estrogen (female hormone) levels to estimate how many eggs they are about to release.

If his test indicates that the patient will yield only one or two, he administers HCG to trigger release. If the test suggests the ripening of more than two eggs, he withholds the drug; the small doses of Clomid and Pergonal alone are insufficient to produce ovulation. Kistner's system appears to be effective. Of 80 patients treated with Clomid and Pergonal in sequence, most of those with simple ovulation problems became pregnant and had babies. Only one woman had more than one baby, and she had only twins.

*More common causes: male sterility and infections that scar the lining of the uterus and Fallopian tubes.

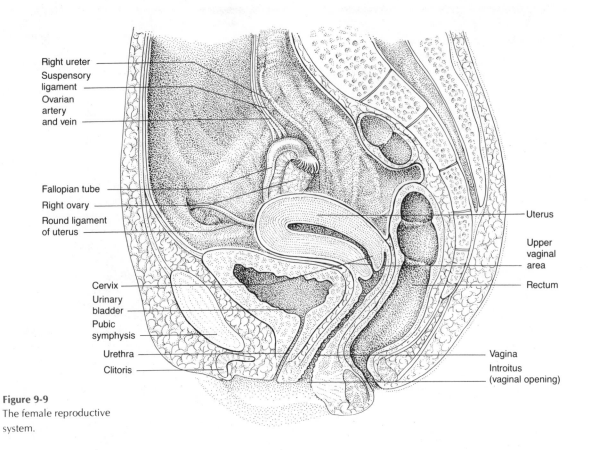

Figure 9-9
The female reproductive system.

Right ureter

Suspensory ligament

Ovarian artery and vein

Fallopian tube

Right ovary

Round ligament of uterus

Cervix

Urinary bladder

Pubic symphysis

Urethra

Clitoris

Uterus

Upper vaginal area

Rectum

Vagina

Introitus (vaginal opening)

Figure 9-10
External female genitalia.

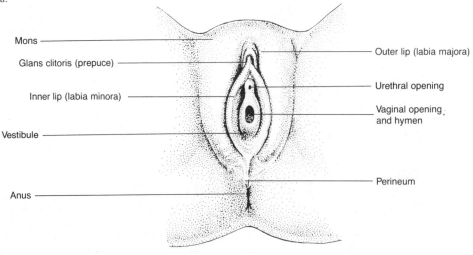

Mons

Glans clitoris (prepuce)

Inner lip (labia minora)

Vestibule

Anus

Outer lip (labia majora)

Urethral opening

Vaginal opening and hymen

Perineum

multiple births. Recently, many women who took certain chemicals designed to increase their fertility have had multiple births, indicating that the chemicals stimulate numerous follicles to continue ripening.

By about day 13, the egg is ready to be released. This is accomplished by the *luteinizing hormone (LH)*, also produced by the pituitary gland. The luteinizing hormone causes the follicle to rupture, which is ovulation.

The egg survives for about twenty-four hours. Sperm can normally survive from one to three days after being deposited in the vagina. If ovulation occurred between the twelfth and sixteenth days of the cycle, intercourse any time between the ninth and the eighteenth day might cause pregnancy (see Figure 9-11).

As the egg has been developing, estrogen has also worked to enrich and thicken the uterine lining (*endometrium*) (see Figure 9-12).

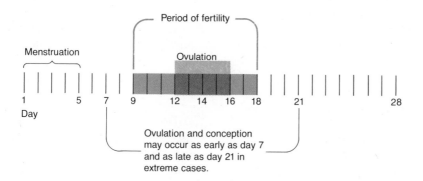

Figure 9-11
Timing of the menstrual cycle.

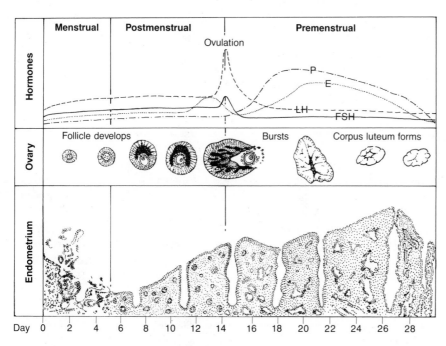

Figure 9-12
Lining build-up.

Blood engorges the tissue to make it a nourishing environment for the fertilized egg. If fertilization does occur, the fertilized egg will be implanted in the thickened uterine wall and the menstrual cycle will be suspended for the duration of the pregnancy (see Chapter 11). Usually, however, fertilization does not take place and the menstrual cycle is completed. Without fertilization, the estrogen level falls and the thickened uterine lining, as well as the remnants of the unfertilized egg, are shed through the cervix and vagina. About two ounces of blood are lost in an average menstrual period. There may be some cramps in the pelvic region as well as general discomfort at this time. In addition, many women report some fatigue, irritability, depression, and psychic distress just before menstruation. This premenstrual tension is probably the result of the shifts in hormonal levels.

The remaining organs of the female reproductive system, the *vagina*, *clitoris*, and other external genitalia (Figure 9-10) are important to sexual behavior. The vagina averages about three and a half inches when it is relaxed and can stretch considerably during intercourse and childbirth (see Chapter 11). The clitoris is extremely important to female sexuality, being highly erogenous. It is located just under the upper part of the labia minora (Figure 9-10).

Sources of Total Sexual Outlet

Sexual behavior is highly varied. Name the behavior, and someone will have tried it. Actually, the Kinsey researchers (1948, 1953) found that practically all orgasms experienced by men and women could be attributed to sexual intercourse or coitus, masturbation, sex dreams, heterosexual petting, or homosexual relations.

Coitus and masturbation account for the vast majority of orgasms for most Americans. Sexual outlet is, of course, very much influenced by such factors as age, marital state, cultural mores and taboos, and so on. For example, more young unmarried Americans reach orgasm by masturbation than married couples. For married couples, coitus is the major sexual outlet.

The Physiology of the Sexual Response

We have only recently begun to understand the physiology of the human sexual response. In a series of controversial studies, William H. Masters and Virginia E. Johnson (1966) pioneered research using human subjects engaged in sexual activities. Before these studies, most of our knowledge was derived from animal research. Among other techniques, Masters and Johnson actually photographed the inside of the vagina during sexual arousal and orgasm. As controversial as this research was, it opened up a whole new field of study, gave us a new understanding of the human sexual response, and paved the way for providing programs to help those having sexual difficulties.*

*Recently, Masters and Johnson's work has been criticized for methodological errors and slipshod reporting. See Zilbergeld and Evans, 1980, for an overview of this criticism.

For both men and women, the sexual response is divided into four phases: *excitement*, *plateau*, *orgasm*, and *resolution*. (A partial description of these phases, first for females and then for males, follows.) The responses in all the stages for both females and males are usually independent of the type of stimulation that produces them. In other words, the basic physiological reactions are the same regardless of whether they are produced through manual manipulation, penile insertion, or some other manner.

The Female Sexual Response Sexual response begins with the excitement phase, which may last anywhere from a few minutes to several hours. The breasts swell with blood. The skin may also be flushed, the nipples may become erect, and there may be general muscle contractions in the thighs, back, abdomen, and throughout the body. The clitoris becomes engorged with blood (tumescent); then vagina walls begin to sweat a lubricating fluid that facilitates the entrance of the penis. The inner portion of the vagina balloons, increasing in size, and the uterus may have irregular contractions. The labia minora increase in size. Blood pressure, heart rate, and breathing rates all increase.

The next phase, the plateau phase, lasts from only a few seconds to about three minutes. Tumescence and the sex flush reach their peak. Muscle tension is high and the woman experiences a complete physical and emotional absorption with the impending climax. The clitoris withdraws beneath its hood and can only be stimulated indirectly. (The idea that direct stimulation of the clitoris is necessary for female orgasm is untrue. Indirect stimulation is effective, and, in fact, the heightened clitoral sensitivity during this phase may make direct stimulation uncomfortable.) Muscle rigidity reaches a peak as shown by the facial grimace, rigid neck, arched back, and tense thighs and buttocks. The labia minora change color dramatically. (In women who have not borne a child, the color will become pink to bright red. In women who have had children, the color will become a pink to a deep wine.) Blood accumulates in the arteries and veins around the vagina, uterus, and other pelvic organs. This pelvic congestion is relieved by the orgasmic phase.

The third phase, orgasm, is usually the most pleasurable. During orgasm, most of the built-up neuromuscular tension is discharged in three to ten seconds. Orgasm is so all-absorbing that most sensory awareness of the external environment is lost. The whole body responds though the sensation of orgasm is centered in the pelvis.

> Of all the widespread muscle responses, the muscle contractions . . . that surround the lower third of the vagina cause the most unique phenomenon. These muscles contract against the engorged veins that surround that part of the vagina and force the blood out of them. This creates the orgasm. These contractions, in turn, cause the lower third of the vagina and the nearby upper labia minora to contract a number of times (Kogan, 1973, p. 86).

The last phase, that of resolution, finds the body returning in ten or fifteen minutes to its normal prestimulated condition. However, if orgasm does not take place, the resolution phase may last as long as twelve hours or more. Women have the capacity of repeating the cycle immediately after resolution and can experience multiple orgasms if stimulation is continued.

The Male Sexual Response   The four stages of the sexual response cycle cause the same changes in the male as they do in the female, with a few additions. For example, during excitement, the penis (as well as the man's breasts and nipples) becomes engorged with blood until it erects. Also, the sperm begin their journey from the epididymis to the penis.

The next and major difference occurs during the orgasmic phase. Orgasm for the male is reached by the ejaculation of the semen and sperm through the penis (there is no counterpart of ejaculation in the female).

Once the male ejaculates, penile detumescence (loss of erection) usually follows quickly in the resolution phase though complete detumescence takes longer. Unlike the female, who can reach repeated orgasms, the male usually experiences a refractory (recovery) period during which he cannot become sexually aroused. This period may last only a few minutes or it may last up to several hours depending on such factors as age, health, and desire. Since in our society the male has usually been taught that it takes time to become sexually aroused again after ejaculation, the refractory period may be partially due to psychological as well as physiological factors.

The male who is sexually aroused for a length of time without ejaculating may experience aching in his testicles and a general tension. This can last for an hour or two. Such tension may be relieved by masturbation if a sexual partner is unavailable.

Some Unmasked Myths   Masters and Johnson's research put to rest a number of myths about human sexuality.

First, it established beyond question that women can have multiple orgasms.

Second, it established the fact that there is no such phenomenon as dual orgasms, one clitoral and the other vaginal, in the woman. Regardless of how she is stimulated, the orgasm is the same.

Third, it established that, within normal ranges, the size of the penis and vagina have little to do with the experience of orgasm. For example, the back two-thirds of the vagina is practically without nerve endings and plays little part in orgasm. Most of the stimulation occurs in the front third of the vagina, the labia minora, and the clitoris.

Fourth, as mentioned earlier, it is not essential to stimulate the clitoris directly for orgasm to occur though such stimulation produces the quickest orgasm for most women.

Last, it is not necessarily true that the female responds more slowly. When she regulates the rhythm and intensity of her own sexual stimuli, the time required for her to reach orgasm is about the same as for the male. The female's much-discussed slowness in arousal is probably due to cultural repression rather than some physiological difference.

In addition to these very specific findings, Masters and Johnson's work changed our ideas about some more general aspects of sexuality. For example, masturbation is now considered by many sexologists to be an important and necessary part of sexual expression rather than a taboo behavior. Some women who have never experienced orgasm are best taught by first teaching them the techniques of masturbation. Once they have learned how to have an orgasm, they can transfer the learning into bed with their partners. The rationale behind this is that so many emotions surround the sex act (for example, shame and guilt about the failure to achieve orgasm, disappointment and perhaps insecurity on the part of the partner) that it becomes almost impossible for her to enjoy it or to change her behavior. The direct stimulation of masturbation encourages orgasm and being alone eases the emotional turmoil associated with the sex act.

In general, Americans' attitudes toward sexual expression have become more open as they have learned more about their sexuality. Rather than ignoring and/or hiding sexuality, it is important to understand it so that you may use it to enhance your life and bring greater joy and intimacy to your marital relationship.

There are a number of basic differences between male and female sexuality that are well documented, yet controversial. These differences stem from both biological and cultural sources (see Chapter 2 for a discussion of the biological and cultural background of male-female differences).

Differences between Male and Female Sexuality

Certainly, in the young teens, male sexuality is far more genitally oriented than female sexuality, which is more socially oriented. When young males are sexually stimulated, there is an increased flow of seminal fluid. This buildup causes a preoccupation with the genital area and the need to ejaculate.

Males are generally easily aroused by visual stimuli or mental imagery caused by pictures of nude women and pornography (see Barclay, 1971). In general, the male is simply more preoccupied with sex than is the female. For example, the Kinsey researchers found that, by age twenty, 92 percent of the males studied had masturbated to the point of orgasm, whereas only 33 percent of the females had (Kinsey et al, 1953, p. 197). Furthermore, the researchers found that about one in four married women had not experienced orgasm at age twenty-five, and they proposed that approximately one in ten would never experience orgasm during their married lives (ibid, p. 513). By contrast, the average male, by his wedding day, had already had 1,523 orgasms (1948, p. 520). As L. Saxton (1977) summarizes, "It is not surprising, then, that the average male often feels betrayed and dejected by the

People have long sought the ideal *aphrodisiac*, a substance that would arouse sexual desire. The search has thus far failed, although there is an extensive folklore about such things as powdered rhinoceros horn and "Spanish fly" or cantharis. Alcohol is the most widely used sexual stimulant in America, but in reality it is a depressant and will effectively inhibit the sexual response in the male if ingested in large amounts. Its apparent action as an aphrodisiac stems from its psychological effects. It loosens controls and inhibitions and thereby indirectly stimulates sexual behavior.

Marijuana has mixed effects on sexuality. There is no evidence of heightened physical reactions but there is some sense distortion that probably heightens sexual sensitivity with a compatible partner (see Kogan, 1973, p. 342). It also acts as alcohol does, reducing control and inhibition.

LSD, by distorting time, may seem to prolong the sexual experience. However, a bad trip will have disastrous effects on one's sexuality.

The amphetamines (speed) do stimulate the male to maintain a prolonged erection, but long-term use destroys general health as well as sex drive and ultimately leads to impotence. Cocaine has similar effects. Since these drugs have a drying effect on vaginal secretions, prolonged intercourse may be uncomfortable unless extra lubrication is supplied.

The Roman philosopher Seneca knew the best aphrodisiac: "I show you a philtre, without medicaments, without herbs, without witch's incantations. It is this: If you want to be loved, love" (quoted by Wedeck, 1962, p. 302).

WHAT DO YOU THINK?

What differences between male and female sexuality have you found troublesome?

There has always been a double standard of sexual conduct for the sexes in America. How does this affect sexual differences between the sexes?

Must sex and love always go together? Why or why not?

indifferent sexuality or antisexuality of his wife." It is equally no wonder that some women come to think of their husbands as preoccupied with sex. To the degree that this general difference is cultural, and probably most of it is, women will probably become more overtly interested in sex as the women's liberation movement gains strength and as they learn more about their own sexuality.

Another important difference is that the degree of sexual response variation is far wider in women than in men. Some women never achieve orgasm, and some only when they are thirty to forty years of age. At the other extreme, some women have frequent multiple orgasms. Neither of these extremes is true for males (Masters and Johnson, 1966). There is also an interesting difference in the reported subjective feelings of pleasure with repeated orgasm. Women who experience multiple orgasms usually find their second and third orgasmic episodes the most pleasurable. But most men report greater pleasure from the first ejaculation after a period of continence rather than from a repeated orgasmic experience immediately after a refractory period (ibid, p. 216). This might be explained in part by the relatively greater volume of seminal fluid in the first ejaculation, especially the first after a period of continence.

The sexes also reach their peaks of sexual activity at different ages. The average male reaches his peak of sexual activity in his late teens and early twenties. The female tends to reach this peak in her early thirties.

Another difference is that females tend to have a cyclic increase in sexual desire related to the menstrual cycle. Most women report increased sexual desire just before menstruation and a few report increased desire right afterward. Recent evidence (Adams, Gold & Burt, 1978) also indicates increased female sexual arousal close to ovulation. There is no counterpart of this cyclical heightened desire in the male. It is also interesting to note that sterilized women report an increase in sexual enjoyment since they are free of fear of pregnancy. Such differences should be understood so that they do not cause misunderstanding and conflict.

Venereal Disease

Unfortunately, no discussion of human sexuality is complete without mention of the most social of human diseases, an oft-found bedmate, venereal disease (see Table 9-1).

The incidence of venereal disease in the United States has been drastically reduced by the use of antibiotics such as penicillin. Recently, however, there has been an epidemic of venereal disease. In

Table 9-1 Venereal Diseases

Disease	Cause	Incubation Period[1]	Characteristics	Treatment[2]
Syphilis, Primary	Bacteria	7-90 days (usually 3 weeks)	Small, painless sore or chancre, usually on genitals but also on other parts of the body	Penicillin and broad spectrum antibiotics
Secondary	Untreated primary		Skin rashes or completely latent; enlarged lymph glands	Same
Tertiary	Untreated primary		Central nervous system can be invaded causing various paralyses; heart trouble; insanity	Same
Gonorrhea	Bacteria	3-5 days	Discharge, burning, pain, swelling of genitalia and glands; if males put off treatment, the penis is affected and may lose ability to erect, permanent sterility may result; 80 percent of infected females do not experience symptoms	Same
Chancroid	Bacteria	2-6 days	Shallow, painful ulcers, swollen lymph glands in groin	Sulfa drugs, broad spectrum antibiotics
Lymphogranuloma venereum	Virus	5-30 days	First, small blisters, then swollen lymph glands; may affect renal area	Broad spectrum antibiotics
Genital herpes	Virus	Unknown	Blisters in genital area; very persistent	Pain-relieving ointments

Note: As soon as you suspect any venereal disease, or notice any symptoms, consult your doctor, local health clinic, or local or state health department. Both syphilis and gonorrhea, in particular, can be easily treated if detected early; if not, both can become recurrent, with dire results.
[1] If venereal disease is diagnosed, all sexual partners during the incubation period and up to when the disease is discovered should be examined medically.
[2] Local health clinics or local and state health departments will have more detailed information on current treatment and follow-up.

fact, after the common cold, gonorrhea and syphilis are the most common infectious diseases in the United States. In 1973, approximately 2 million people were treated for gonorrhea in the United States (U.S. National Center for Health Statistics, 1975). (About 300,000 new cases of syphilis were treated in that same year.) Over 75 percent of reported VD occurs in young adults, ages 15 to 30. In 1980 it was estimated that one out of two high school students will have contracted gonorrhea by the time they graduate (U.S. Public Health Services Center for Disease Control, 1975). Since these statistics are based on reported cases, in all likelihood they underestimate the actual level of venereal disease.

At least three factors play a role in the resurgence of VD. First, the pill has become the major method of birth control, replacing the condom that affords some protection against VD infection. Second, the antibiotics themselves have lulled people into apathy. "Who cares about VD, it's easy to cure," appears to be a common attitude. (Unfortunately, while this is partly true, cure depends on prompt treatment, and also, new forms of more resistant strains of the infecting organisms are appearing.) Third, the increased sexual activity among the young, especially the increased number of sexual partners, has contributed to the widespread outbreak of VD.

If you, your spouse, or a sexual partner suspect one of the venereal diseases, have a physical checkup as soon as possible. In most cases, the disease does not "go away," though some of the symptoms change or even disappear. Begun early, treatment is effective; delayed, the disease may recur or become more dangerous. Also, anyone seeking treatment will be treated with confidentiality. If a venereal disease is diagnosed, all people who have had sexual contact with the carrier should be notified and should also have physical checkups. Hopefully, with increased public awareness of venereal disease, the incidence can be cut back to earlier low levels.

Summary   Sexuality pervades the life of humans. This is mainly because human sex is to a great extent free from instinctual control. Although sexuality is a biological necessity, much of the way in which sex is manifested is learned. For this reason, there is far greater variation in sexual behavior among humans than among other animals. All human societies try to control sexual expression, but the controls vary from one society to another. Because of the variability of sexual expression and the often conflicting teachings about sexuality, there is confusion both within societies and within individuals about sexuality. However, in all societies, human sexuality serves other purposes than procreation such as communication, strengthening the male-female bond, increasing intimacy, pleasuring, having fun, and generally reducing tension.

Understanding of sexual physiology has increased greatly as science and medicine have learned more about the functioning of the body. It is clear that males and females are physiologically very similar, having developed their sexual organs from common structures. The main difference in function is the ejaculatory response of the male. Another major difference is the cyclical preparation for pregnancy that the female goes through each month.

Basically, both males and females share the same physical responses during sexual activity. These are called the excitement, plateau, orgasmic, and resolution stages. It is during the orgasmic stage that the major difference between the sexes takes place: the ejaculation of the male. Also, the male must go through a refractory period after the resolution stage before he can have another erection.

Unfortunately, venereal disease all too often accompanies sexual activity. The two major venereal diseases are syphilis and gonorrhea, both of which are on the increase. This increase is attributed to use of the pill rather than condoms, people believing that modern drugs have eliminated the diseases, and, most of all, to youth's increased sexual activity and variety of sexual partners.

The Mechanization of Sex

Since sex is such an important part of most people's lives, there is a growing industry that attempts to educate people about their sexuality: Manuals of sexual techniques, classes in the art of increasing sensual awareness, encounter groups to get rid of sexual inhibitions, and weekend retreats for anonymous sex have all become part of America's mechanization of sex. In fact, many people have come to consider sex a kind of tool which one must be trained to use. There is no doubt that sex can be used as a tool and that some people are less adept than others with it. However, if sexuality is limited to simple mechanics, much of the joy and beauty that can be part of the experience is lost. How we feel about sexuality is far more important than actual technique.

A knowledge of sexual technique is, of course, helpful, but emphasis should be placed on the totality of the experience of human sexuality. Sexual pleasure for humans occurs as much in the head as in the body. The following letter spoofs America's preoccupation with "how to" sex manuals.

Dear Alex Comfort,

I'm just a housewife, but I sure want to thank you for your lonely struggle for sexual freedom. Your book, The Joy of Sex, enriched my life, particularly that terrific section on "sauces and pickles" (I've been getting into them with relish, if you know what I mean).

Now comes your new book, More Joy. It just knocks me out—that's all I can say. It is really heartwarming to read that "there is nothing to be afraid of, and never was." You took the words out of my mouth when you wrote that all our sexual complications are produced by "garbage" people who oppose "sexual turned-on-ness." (I really admire your way with words!)

Imagine how the garbage people will scream when they learn that you say "All people are both straight and gay if they'd let themselves be," or "The energy American men have spent trying not to express bisexuality . . . would solve the power shortage." My husband George doesn't know this yet, and I bet he won't take to your interesting suggestion that one of the advantages of anal intercourse between a man and a woman is that the male partner can close his eyes and pretend that he's in bed with another man.

He's also far behind us free spirits on the aggression frontier, Dr. Comfort. Even after your first book, he refused to tie me up, spank me, or push me around in the loving way you recommend.

That's why I adored the idea in your new book about batacas—the plastic-foam bats that sexual partners can smack each other with. I rushed out and bought a pair, and while George was taking off his shoes, I crept up behind him (nude, of course) and gave him a loving bataca shot behind the right ear. As he got up off the floor, he shrieked, "Don't tell me that dingbat has written another book!" and ran right downstairs to our coffee table. He found it there, of course, and kept howling and slapping his thigh as he read your keen advice. Not even another bataca thump could make him stop laughing. He's just repressed. All the money I've invested in ropes, pulleys, electric gadgets and batacas, and George still doesn't think they have much to do with expressing affection. It burns me up.

I guess the only thing to do is to consider group sex—the big new message in More Joy. I like your idea that we shouldn't call them "orgies" any more but merely "sharing." After all, who's against sharing? I can believe it when you say that everyone comes back from an orgy—oops, I mean from a sharing—feeling "breathless, guiltless and ready to return to propriety." Maybe that's because "the main experience in sharing is quietude, and the intention is sensual rather than sexual." I must say I don't really get this, probably because I am just a housewife, but it sounds uplifting and I guess that's the point.

Your section on jealousy is a dilly. You know, the part where you say that if you find out somebody's been messing with your mate, you can react with pride at the compliment to your taste and luck instead of carrying on "like a backward five-year-old

who sees another child with his tricycle."

What gets me is the dumb argument that you've solved all sexual problems by leaving the emotions out, probably because you recommend "cool sex" instead of old "hot sex," with its "tragic intensities." These people haven't even noticed that you included 13 lines on the subject of love in your new book, and actually defined love (very movingly, I might add) as "the mutually satisfying sharing of each other's experience and the experience of each other." Now I guess they'll stop thinking of you as some sort of cold, potty Englishman dishing out new versions of Mechanix Illustrated for the U.S. suburbs. After all, The Joy of Sex has sold 3 million copies, and More Joy sold 150,000 copies even before its official publication date. Can so many people be wrong?

It's getting late, and George is still over there giggling and slapping himself over your book. I told him you are a serious man—a Ph.D., an expert on aging, and author of six books on sex, plus poetry and novels. I even told him about the field research you did at the Sandstone sexual freedom ranch in Malibu, selflessly watching people make love (and participating) so your book would be accurate. He knows your Joy books got raves from big sex experts all over California, and that some people in the Midwest are actually showing up at bookstores with prescriptions for the books. Still he giggles, the insensitive brute....

The only problem I have with the book (and I hate to be a compulsive naysayer, as you might put it) is with those drawings. Since I look forward to another book (More, More Joy?), I am enclosing a photo of a penis so your artists will know what one looks like. I hope I am not being too bold.

Millions will bless you for pointing out that sharing in group sex can be a religious experience. I certainly hope, if you're ever in the neighborhood, you come and worship with me.

Yours in joyful free expression,
Betty Jo

Chapter 10 ～

Contents

∼Family Planning

The place and function of children within the family varies from culture to culture and over time. In countries with high infant mortality, women have to bear many children to ensure that at least some will reach adulthood. Thus pregnancy may be nearly a perpetual state. In some cultures, a male heir is the major aim of reproduction. When the United States was still an agricultural nation, it was important to have many children to help work the land. Children were major economic contributors to the family. In modern urban America, however, the costs of rearing children far outweigh the income they will bring into the family. Thus, from a strictly economic point of view, children have become a liability. The Department of Agriculture estimates that an average family spends $50,000 to $80,000 rearing a child to age eighteen.

From the point of view of society as a whole, it is perhaps even more important that we consider carefully the possible consequences of having children. Because of concern about worldwide overpopulation, a couple may now decide to have only two children (reproduce themselves only), to have no children, or to adopt children.

Family Planning in America Today

I consider the ideal family to be one that allows all children to grow up in the most healthful manner possible. Aside from environmental considerations, this definition implies that: (1) children are wanted by both partners, (2) the partners are healthy enough physically and psychologically to supply love and security to children, (3) family economics are such that children can be properly nourished and kept physically healthy, and (4) the family can supply their children with sufficient educational opportunity to learn the skills necessary to survive and enjoy success within the culture.

A Child Should Be Wanted The most important idea above is that children should be wanted by their parents. Unwanted children are often social problems. Unwanted children are more likely than others to grow up in psychologically unhealthy homes, are more likely than others to become delinquents, and, when they become parents, are more likely to be poor parents themselves and breed another generation of unwanted children. "This is a vicious circle if ever there was one.... It is ruinous to the social system" (Hardin, 1964).

There are many reasons why parents may not want children. We have already mentioned the problems of finances and overpopulation. Then, many children are unwanted because they are illegitimate. And couples may prefer not to have children because of the limitation they place on their freedom, especially the mother's. Many feminists argue that not only is motherhood not necessary to a woman's feelings of fulfillment, it may even prevent her from being fulfilled in other ways.

> When motherhood is no longer culturally compulsory, there will certainly be less of it. Women are now beginning to think and do more about development of self, of their individual resources. Far from being selfish, such development is probably our only hope. That means more alternatives for women. And more alternatives mean more selective, better, happier, motherhood—and childhood and husbandhood (or manhood) and peoplehood. It is not a question of whether or not children are sweet and marvelous to have and rear; the question is, even if that's so, whether or not one wants to pay the price for it. It doesn't make sense any more to pretend women need babies, when what they really need is themselves (Rollin, 1970, p. 27).

Whatever the reason, parents who do not want a child should not have one.

It is difficult to say just what the effects of being unwanted are on a child, but they are certainly negative. At one possible extreme, there are many children in pitifully battered condition lying in the wards of local hospitals, having been beaten by fathers and mothers who could not cope with them (see Scenes from Marriage, Chapter 12 for more on child abuse). While not so devastating, a Czechoslovakian study (Matějcék, Dytrych & Schüller, 1979) of 110 boys and 110 girls born in 1961–1963 to women denied legal abortion on initial request and again on subsequent appeal showed some interesting negative characteristics when compared to a matched group of children whose mothers had not requested an abortion. In general, those children born of mothers denied an abortion: (1) had a higher incidence of illness and hospitalization, (2) had slightly poorer school marks, (3) showed somewhat poorer social integration into their peer group, (4) had come to the attention of school counseling centers more often, (5) had a less stable family life, and (6) showed generally poorer adaptation, more frustration, and increased irritability (especially the boys).

In reviewing all of the data from the continuing longitudinal study of the Prague children, it is also clear that a woman's original rejecting attitude toward her pregnancy does not inevitably lead to behavioral difficulties in the child. The belief that every child unwanted during pregnancy remains unwanted is not necessarily true. It is equally untrue that the birth of an originally unwanted child causes a complete change in maternal attitude. Not every woman who becomes a mother will love her child. In sum, the study confirms the risk of potentially unfavorable developmental consequences of compulsory pregnancy for the unwanted child and thus the desirability of preventing unwanted pregnancies (David & Baldwin, 1979, pp. 867–868).

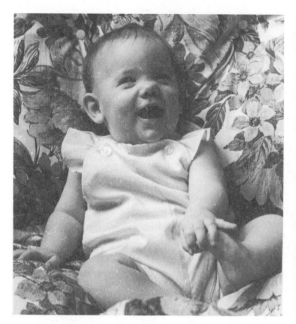

Are We Ready for Children? Thus, the first question a couple should answer when thinking about raising a family is "Do we really want children?" The answer rests on answering questions like the following: "How much time do we want for just each other and establishing a home? How much more education do we want or need for the jobs and income we want? Are we ready to give a baby the attention and love it needs? Can we afford to provide it with the food, clothing, and education we want for it? Can a child successfully fit into the style of life we feel is best for ourselves?"

Most experts in the field of family planning advise young couples to wait awhile before having their first child. This gives them time to make the important early adjustments to each other, to enjoy one another's individual attention, and to build some economic stability before coping with the additional responsibility of a child.

The decision to have children is one of the most important marital decisions, and yet it is often made haphazardly. Having children generally means assuming long-term responsibilities, usually for eighteen to twenty years or more. When children are young, great amounts of time and energy and money must be devoted to their well-being. Adolescence usually brings a period of unrest, strain, and conflict. If higher education is decided on, financial strains on the family will be greatly increased. There is almost no time when children do not make heavy demands on their parents, sometimes even long after they have become adults.

On the other hand, there are also many rewards. There is joy in watching a child grow and become competent and assume a responsible role in society. There is joy in learning to know another person intimately. There is just plain fun in doing things together as a family.

Wanted and cared for or unwanted and neglected?

Birth Control   Modern techniques of birth control, though far from perfect, have made better family planning possible. However, the idea of birth control has long been a part of human life. The oldest written records mentioning birth control date back to the reign of Amenemhet III in Egypt around 1850 B.C. The woman is advised to put a pastelike substance in the vagina where it will block the male sperm from reaching the egg.

Pliny's *Natural History*, written in the first century A.D., lists many methods of birth control: potions to be taken orally, magical objects, suppositories and tampons of primitive sorts, and physical action such as jumping to expel the semen. Most of the time, of course, such early birth control methods were unsuccessful.

However, two ancient birth control methods gradually evolved into the first really effective contraceptive techniques. First, the ancient attempts to block the cervix so that sperm could not penetrate to the egg evolved into the vaginal diaphragm, or cervical cap, when vulcanized rubber was invented. The most sophisticated historical prototype of the modern cervical cap was the use of a half lemon, squeezed of its contents and inserted over the cervix; the residual citric acid, which is mildly spermicidal (causing the death of sperm), provided additional protection (Peel and Potts, 1970, p. 62). Second, the early attempts to cover the penis evolved into the modern condom. Starting in the sixteenth century, the penis was covered to protect it from venereal infection. In the 1840s, manufacturers began to make condoms of inexpensive rubber and later of latex.

However, despite the long history of birth control, modern birth control and family planning has had a difficult and eventful history. An Englishman named Francis Place, the father of fifteen children, was the founder of the birth control movement. In the 1820s he posted handbills advising contraception to counteract the effects of the growing industrialization and urbanization that he felt were creating poverty. His handbills recommended that women should place a piece of sponge tied with a string into the vagina before intercourse, and remove it easily afterward by pulling the string.

In the United States, there was a long hard battle waged by people like Margaret Sanger that lasted well into this century. The Puritan morality in the United States opposed birth control. Although contraceptives were advised for the highest ethical reasons as a means of avoiding poverty, misery, and marital discord, the promoters were accused of immorality and often were brought to trial and fined. In 1873, Congress passed the Comstock Law prohibiting the distribution of contraceptive information through the mail. Numerous states also passed repressive laws. For example, the right of physicians to prescribe contraceptives was a legal issue in Connecticut until 1965 when the state law banning prescription of contraceptive devices was overthrown by the U.S. Supreme Court in *Griswold and Duxton v. State of Connecticut.*

Of course, family planning is possible without the aid of mechanical contraceptive devices. Infanticide (killing infants) has been practiced historically in many cultures, though it is no longer acceptable by modern ethical standards. Simple marriage postponement acts as an effective birth deterrent, providing illegitimacy is controlled. In China today, marriage is discouraged until the woman is twenty-four and the man is twenty-seven. Rigid peer group control has reduced illegitimacy to a low level. Discouraging early marriage and controlling illegitimacy have reduced the Chinese fertility rate considerably (see Sidel, 1974).

Withdrawal and abstinence also reduce fertility rates. France, for example, has long had a relatively stable population of near 50 million. Since contraception is frowned on by the Church, population stability has mainly been achieved by withdrawal (coitus interruptus), even though it is only fifty percent effective. Other methods of sexual outlet, such as masturbation, oral sex, and homosexuality, serve a contraceptive purpose as well as a sexual purpose.

Contraceptive Methods Although family planning in itself is generally healthful, methods of implementing it may have mixed results insofar as health is concerned. Table 10-1 examines the various contraceptive devices, describes them, and indicates their effectiveness as well as possible side effects. Effectiveness is stated as the number of sexually active women out of 100 who get pregnant in the course of one year when using each method. Without some method of birth control, between 80 and 90 out of 100 sexually active women would get pregnant in the course of one year.

Planning a family requires deciding how many children are desired, and how far apart they should be. Questions regarding birth control must also be answered: "Who will be responsible for using a birth control method? What method will be used? How will the method chosen affect our sex lives? What will be the cost of the method?" These questions need to be discussed and a mutually acceptable birth control method decided upon by each couple desiring to plan their family.

The general requirements for an *ideal* contraceptive, which obviously does not exist yet though research continues, are that it should be harmless, reliable, free of objectionable side effects, inexpensive, simple, reversible in effect, removed from the sexual act, and give protection against venereal disease (Guttmacher, 1969). While the following contraceptives do not fulfill all of these requirements, they do meet many of them.

THE CONDOM   The condom is a sheath of very thin latex or animal gut that fits over the penis and stops sperm from entering the vagina when ejaculation occurs. The user must put the condom on as soon as his penis is erect. He places the rolled-up condom over the head of the erect penis and unrolls the condom to the base of the penis, leaving a small space at the tip to collect the semen. Both he and his partner must be careful not to puncture the condom anywhere with their nails or rings. After ejaculation, the male must hold the condom around the

Table 10-1   Contraceptives

Popular Name	Description	Effectiveness (Pregnancies per 100 women using method for 1 year)

The pill
  oral contraceptive
  (consultation with
  physician required)
	Contains synthetic hormones (estrogens and progestin) to inhibit ovulation. The body reacts as if pregnancy had occurred, and does not release an egg. No egg — no conception. The pills are usually taken for 20 or 21 consecutive days. Menstruation commences shortly after cessation of pill ingestion.	Combined pills, 0.3–1.5[1]
		Sequential pills, 1–3[1]

IUD
  intrauterine device
  (consultation with
  physician required)
	Metal or plastic object that comes in various shapes and is placed in the uterus and left there. It is not known exactly how it works. Hypotheses are that endocrine changes occur, that the fertilized egg cannot implant in the uterine wall due to irritation, that spontaneous abortion is caused. Doctor's fee varies.	3–5

Diaphragm and jelly
  (consultation with
  physician required)
	Flexible hemispherical rubber dome the woman inserts into the vagina to block entrance to the cervix thus providing a barrier to sperm. Usually used with spermicidal cream or jelly.	6–10

Chemical methods	Numerous products to be inserted into the vagina to block sperm from the uterus and/or as a spermicide. Vaginal foams are creams packed under pressure (like foam shaving cream) and inserted with applicator. Vaginal suppositories are small cone-shaped objects that melt in the vagina. Vaginal tablets also melt in the vagina.	8–12 More effective when used in conjunction with another method, such as the diaphragm.
Condom	Thin, strong sheath or cover, usually of latex, worn over the penis to prevent sperm from entering the vagina.	12–15
Withdrawal (coitus interruptus)	Man withdraws penis from vagina before ejaculation of semen.	16–18
Rhythm	Abstinence from intercourse during fertile period each month.	24–38

NOTE: Individuals vary in their reaction to contraceptive devices. Advantages and disadvantages listed are general ones.
[1] If taken regularly, pregnancy will not occur. If one or more pills are missed, there is a chance of pregnancy. Combination pills contain both estrogen and progesterone. Sequential pills contain estrogen only for the first 15 or 16 pills and then contain progesterone only. This pill has now been removed from the market.

Advantages	Disadvantages	Cost
Simple to take, removed from sexual act, highly reliable, reversible. Useful side effects: relief of premenstrual tension and some unpleasant feeling associated with menstruation, reduction in menstrual flow and regularization of menstruation, relief of acne, general family	Weight gain (5–50% of users), breast enlargement and sensitivity; some users have increased headaches, nausea, and spotting. Increased possibility of vein thrombosis (blood clotting) and slight increase in blood pressure. Must be taken regularly. A causal relationship to cancer can neither be established nor refuted.	$7–$9/month
Once inserted, user need do nothing more about birth control. Reliability good, reversible, relatively inexpensive. Must be checked periodically to see if still in place.	Insertion procedure requires specialist and is uncomfortable and often painful. Uterine cramping. Increased menstrual bleeding. Between 4–30% are expelled in first year after insertion. Occasional perforation of the uterine wall. Occasional pregnancy that is complicated by the presence of the IUD.	$25–$75 for insertion
Can be left in place up to 24 hours. Reliable, harmless, and reversible. Can be inserted up to 2 hours before intercourse. Control of pregnancy is entirely up to woman.	Many women do not like to use it since it requires self-manipulation of genitals to fit and is messy due to cream. If improperly fitted, it will fail. Must be refitted periodically, especially after pregnancy. Psychological aversion may make its use inconsistent.	$25–$40 for fitting
Foams appear to be most effective, followed by creams, jellies, suppositories, and tablets. Harmless, simple, reversible, and easily available.	May be minor irritations and temporary burning sensation. Messy. Must be used just prior to intercourse and reapplied for each act of intercourse.	$5–$7 for month's supply
Simple to obtain and use; free of objectionable side effects. Quality control has improved with government regulation. Protection against various venereal infections.	Must be applied just prior to intercourse. Can slip off, especially after ejaculation when penis returns to flaccid state. Occasional rupture. Interferes with sensation and spontaneity.	25¢–50¢ each
Simple, costless, nothing required.	Requires great control by the male. May be some semen leakage before ejaculation. Possible psychological reaction against necessary control and ejaculation outside the vagina. May severely limit sexual gratification of both partners.	
Approved by the Roman Catholic Church. Costless, nothing required.	Woman's menstrual period must be regular. Demands accurate date keeping and strong self-control. Difficult to exactly determine fertile period.	

base of the penis as he withdraws his penis from the vagina or some semen may spill from the now loose condom and the sperm may still find their way to the uterus.

The condom has always been a popular method of contraception in the United States and though briefly eclipsed by the pill and the IUD, it is now coming back into widespread use because of the possible dangerous side effects of those other methods of birth control. Condoms may now be openly displayed and sold in forty-six states and are thus easily acquired. They have an additional advantage in that they afford protection against venereal disease. Their disadvantages are that they diminish sensation and interfere with spontaneity.

As noted in Table 10-1, the risk of pregnancy with condom use is quite low. At least some of the pregnancies occur because of careless removal of the condom. Some may occur because of a puncture in the condom. Both risks can be reduced if, in addition to the male's using a condom, the female uses a vaginal spermicide.

THE DIAPHRAGM   The diaphragm is a dome-shaped cup of thin latex stretched over a collapsible metal ring. It is only available on prescription from a doctor. Because of differences in the size of the vaginal opening, the diaphragm has to be carefully fitted to ensure that it adequately covers the mouth of the cervix and is comfortable. The fitting should be checked every two years, and after childbirth, abortion, or a weight loss of more than ten pounds.

Once she has been fitted properly, the woman can insert the diaphragm herself. She can insert it either dome up or down, whichever feels more comfortable. Before insertion, she should spread a spermicidal jelly or cream over the surface of the dome that will lie against the cervix. Then she squeezes the diaphragm flat with one hand, holds the labia apart with the other, and pushes the diaphragm up along the back of the vagina as far as it will go. Then she tucks the front rim behind the pubic bone. It helps if she squats, lies down, or stands with one foot raised while inserting the diaphragm. After it is inserted, she should feel the cervix through the dome to make sure that it is completely covered.

The diaphragm can be inserted just before intercourse or it can be inserted several hours beforehand. If it is inserted more than two hours before intercourse, some spermicide should be inserted into the vagina, or the diaphragm should be taken out and spermicide applied to it again. Additional spermicide should be inserted into the vagina before any additional acts of intercourse. The diaphragm must be left in place for six hours after the last act of intercourse to give the spermicide enough time to kill all sperm.

The diaphragm is removed by hooking the front rim from behind the pubic bone with a finger and pulling it out. It should be washed with mild soap and water, rinsed, and gently patted dry. It should also be examined for holes or cracks in front of a bright light. It is usually dusted with cornstarch before being put away.

As noted in Table 10-1, the diaphragm when used with a spermicide is highly effective. In addition, it has no physical side effects.

However, like the condom, it dampens spontaneity. It also loses effectiveness when fresh spermicide is not used for additional acts of intercourse, and many women do not like to break the "mood" of sexuality by taking time to use additional spermicide. Some women also do not like to touch their genitals.

The main causes of pregnancy when using a diaphragm are inaccurate fitting and incorrect insertion. Sometimes, too, the vaginal walls expand during sexual stimulation and dislodge the diaphragm.

THE INTRAUTERINE DEVICE (IUD) The IUD is a stainless steel or plastic loop, ring, or spiral that is inserted into the uterus by a doctor. A sterile device is used to insert the IUD into the cervical canal and a plunger is used to push it into the uterus. The protruding threads are trimmed so that only an inch or an inch and a half remain in the upper vagina. They can't be felt during intercourse. The best time for insertion (and removal) is during menstruation since the cervical canal is most open then and there is no possibility of an unsuspected pregnancy.

Just how or why the IUD works is still unknown. As Table 10-1 notes, theories range from its producing biochemical changes, interfering with the implantation of eggs, interfering with the movement of eggs or sperm, to its causing spontaneous abortions. As also noted in the table, it is quite effective, being second only to the pill in overall effectiveness. Its other advantages are that, once inserted, it can be used indefinitely and requires nothing further for its use, it doesn't interrupt sexual activity, it is fully reversible, and it has a low long-term cost.

However, it has quite a few disadvantages. The most common is abnormal menstrual bleeding. Bleeding starts sooner, lasts longer, and becomes heavier after IUD insertion. Bleeding and spotting between periods are also fairly common. Women who have never been pregnant often experience pain, mostly uterine cramps and backache. The uterine cramps usually disappear in a few days, though they may be severe enough to require removal of the IUD.

Intrauterine devices are spontaneously expelled in about 10 percent of the women who try them, and if the women do not notice the expulsion, an unwanted pregnancy may result. Most expulsions occur during menstruation, so it is a good idea to check sanitary pads or tampons for the device. The threads can also be felt periodically to make sure the device is still in place.

A more serious complication that may occur is pelvic inflammatory disease. About 2 to 3 percent of women using the device may develop the disease, usually in the first two weeks after insertion. Most of these inflammations are mild, however, and can be treated with antibiotics. In very rare cases, the IUD may puncture the wall of the uterus and migrate into the abdominal cavity, requiring surgery. Pelvic infection, usually caused by bacteria, also seems to be more common among IUD users (Time, May, 1980, p. 60).

Most of the risk of pregnancy when using an IUD occurs during the first few months of use, so an additional method of contraception should be used for that period. The failure rate tends to decline rapidly after the first year of use. Pregnancy may occur with the device in place, but the rate of spontaneous abortion for such pregnancies is 40 percent (compared to 15 percent for all pregnancies). There is little additional risk of birth defects for babies born of such pregnancies. The device usually remains in place during the pregnancy and is expelled during the delivery. One particular make, the Dalkon Shield, has been taken off the market because there was an unusually high pregnancy rate among its users, and when pregnancy did occur, its users developed uterine infections at a much higher rate than nonusers (*Time*, 1974, p. 81).

THE PILL (ORAL CONTRACEPTION) The pill is a combination of the hormones estrogen and progesterone, and must be prescribed by a doctor. The daily ingestion of these hormones bluffs the body into thinking it is pregnant so it stops further ovulation. Since no mature eggs are released, pregnancy cannot take place.

Until recently, there were two kinds of pills, the combination pill and the sequential pill. However, the Federal Drug Administration requested withdrawal of the sequential pill since it appears to pose an increased risk of cancer of the uterine lining compared to combination pills (*Santa Barbara News-Press*, March, 1976). The combination pill consists of a monthly supply of twenty or twenty-one identical tablets. The woman takes pill 1 on day 5 of her menstrual cycle, counting the first day of the cycle as day 1. She takes another pill each day until all the pills have been taken. Menstruation will usually begin two to four days after the last pill.

The pill should be taken at about the same time each day. If a pill is forgotten, it should be taken as soon as possible, and the next pill should be taken at the scheduled time. If two pills have been forgotten, an additional form of contraception should be used for the rest of the cycle.

If menstruation does not occur when expected, a new series of pills should be started a week after the end of the last series. If a period doesn't start after this series, a doctor should be consulted.

During the first two weeks of the first pill cycle, women should use an additional method of contraception for complete protection.

As Table 10-1 notes, the pill, taken properly, is the most effective method of contraception today. It is relatively simple to use, does not affect spontaneity, is inexpensive, and is reversible. However, irregular use does not afford protection. It is also the most widely used method. As many as 8 million American women used the pill in 1975. However, in 1977, this had dropped to 6 million, mainly due to increased surgical sterilization (Johns Hopkins, 1979).

More serious, though, are the side effects, ranging from relatively minor disturbances to serious ones. Among the former are symptoms of early pregnancy (morning sickness, weight gain, and swollen breasts, for example) which may occur during the first few months of pill use. The symptoms usually disappear by the fourth month. Other problems include depression, nervousness, alteration

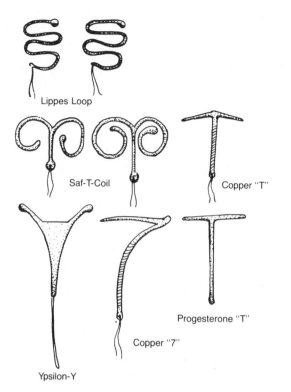

Lippes Loop

Saf-T-Coil

Copper "T"

Progesterone "T"

Copper "7"

Ypsilon-Y

(a) Some commonly used IUD's

Cream or jelly

Spring (coil-spring type)

Dome of soft rubber

(b) A diaphragm; spermicidal cream is
squeezed into cup and around the rim
before insertion.

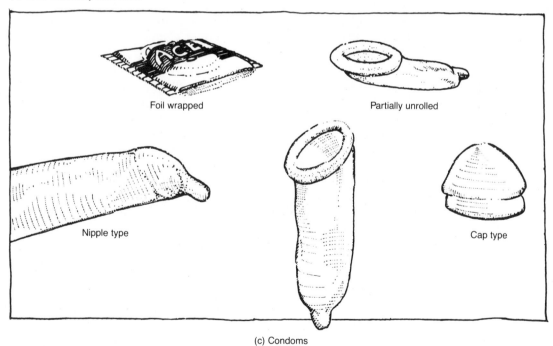

Foil wrapped

Partially unrolled

Nipple type

Cap type

(c) Condoms

Figure 10-1
Types of contraception.

in sex drive, dizziness, headaches, bleeding between periods, and discharge from the vagina. Yeast fungus infections are also more common in women taking the pill. The more serious side effects include blood clot problems and the possibility of a link between pill use and uterine cancer. Although the incidence of fatal blood clots is low (about 13 deaths among 1 million pill users in one year), women with any history of unusual blood clotting, or who have had strokes, heart disease or defects, or any form of cancer should not use the pill (see, for a more complete discussion of oral contraceptives, *Population Reports*, 1975). The arguments over the relationship of pill use and cancer continue to rage and may only be resolved at some time in the future when large numbers of women have been using the pills over many years. If there is a relationship, it appears to be minimal at this time with the chances of death from cancer caused by pill use being far less than the chances of maternal death in childbirth.

If a woman becomes pregnant, she should immediately cease taking the pill. Continued ingestion of female hormones may disturb the cardiovascular development of the fetus according to research done at the Drug Epidemiology Unit at Boston University (*Santa Barbara News-Press*, March, 1977).

RHYTHM   Rhythm is based on the fact that usually only one egg per month is produced. Since the egg only lives for twenty-four to forty-eight hours if it is not fertilized, and since the longest period that sperm released into the uterus are capable of living is forty-eight to seventy-two hours, conception can theoretically only occur during four days of any cycle. Predicting this four-day period is what is so difficult. If each woman had an absolutely regular monthly cycle, then rhythm would be much more reliable than it is. Unfortunately, all women are not regular. In fact, about 15 percent have such irregular periods that the method cannot be used at all.

To use the method, a woman keeps track of her menstrual periods for a full year. Counting the day menstruation begins as day 1, she notes the length of the shortest time before menstruation starts again and also the longest time. If her cycle is always the same length, she subtracts 18 from the number of days in the cycle, which gives the first unsafe day. Subtracting 11 gives the last unsafe day. For example, a woman with a regular twenty-eight-day cycle would find that the first unsafe day is the tenth day of her cycle and the last is the seventeenth day. Thus, she should not engage in sexual intercourse from the tenth to the eighteenth. Figure 10-2 shows the twenty-eight-day cycle.

If a woman's cycle is slightly irregular, she can still determine unsafe days by using the formula. In this case she subtracts 18 from her shortest cycle to determine the first unsafe day, and 11 from her longest cycle to find the last unsafe day. Table 10-2 gives the unsafe days for periods of varying duration.

VAGINAL SPERMICIDES (CHEMICAL METHODS)   These come as foams, creams, jellies, foaming tablets, and suppositories. Foams are the most effective since they form the most dense and evenly distributed barrier

1 Menstruation begins	2	3	4	5	6	7
8	9	10 11 Intercourse on these days leaves live sperm to fertilize egg.		12 13 14 Ripe egg may also be released on these days.		
15 16 Ripe egg may be released on any of these days.		17 Egg may still be present.	18	19	20	21
22	23	24	25	26	27	28
1 Menstruation begins again.						

Figure 10-2
The 28-day cycle.

to the cervical opening. Tablets and suppositories, which melt in the vagina, are the least effective.

Foams are packed under pressure (like shaving cream) and have an applicator attached to the nozzle. Creams and jellies come in tubes with an applicator. A short time before intercourse, the woman places the applicator into the vagina (like a sanitary tampon) and pushes the plunger. The effectiveness of vaginal spermicides only lasts for about half an hour, so another application is necessary before each act of intercourse.

Table 10-2 How to Figure the "Safe" and "Unsafe" Days

Length of Shortest Period	First Unsafe Day after Start of Any Period	Length of Longest Period	Last Unsafe Day after Start of Any Period
21 days	3rd day	21 days	10th day
22 days	4th day	22 days	11th day
23 days	5th day	23 days	12th day
24 days	6th day	24 days	13th day
25 days	7th day	25 days	14th day
26 days	8th day	26 days	15th day
27 days	9th day	27 days	16th day
28 days	10th day	28 days	17th day
29 days	11th day	29 days	18th day
30 days	12th day	30 days	19th day
31 days	13th day	31 days	20th day
32 days	14th day	32 days	21st day
33 days	15th day	33 days	22nd day
34 days	16th day	34 days	23rd day
35 days	17th day	35 days	24th day
36 days	18th day	36 days	25th day
37 days	19th day	37 days	26th day
38 days	20th day	38 days	27th day

Vaginal spermicides are generally harmless, relatively easy to use, readily available in most drugstores, and do not require a prescription. However, as Table 10-1 shows, they are not very effective, though their effectiveness can be increased by using them with a diaphragm. Other disadvantages are that they are messy, may interrupt the sexual mood, must be reapplied for each act of intercourse, and sometimes cause a burning sensation or irritation. If the latter persists, a doctor should be consulted.

WITHDRAWAL (COITUS INTERRUPTUS) Withdrawal is simply what the name implies in that, just before ejaculation, the male withdraws his penis from the vagina. It is probably the oldest known form of contraception. It is free, requires no preparation, and is always available. However, as Table 10-1 points out, it has a very high failure rate. Other disadvantages include the necessity of tremendous control by the male, who must deny himself the natural outcome of the sexual act, plus the fear that withdrawal may not be in time, which can destroy sexual pleasure for both partners. The woman also may be denied satisfaction if the male must withdraw before she reaches orgasm. Also, there may be some semen leakage before withdrawal, which can cause pregnancy.

DOUCHE A douche is applying a stream of water to a body part to cleanse or treat it. As a contraceptive method, it is probably useless and may in fact serve to wash the sperm on into the uterus, thus increasing the chances of pregnancy. There are a number of commercial douches now being advertised, but their use should be limited. Using a substance other than water can cause a bacterial imbalance in the vagina, leading to yeast and other infections.

Sterilization Sterilization is the most effective and permanent means of birth control. Despite the fact that in many cases it is irreversible, more and more Americans are choosing sterilization as a means of contraception. The Association for Voluntary Sterilization estimates 10 to 12 million people in the United States have been voluntarily sterilized and about 1 million more are being sterilized each year. They further estimate that about 90 million people in the world are now sterilized.

VASECTOMY This is the surgical sterilization of the male. It is done in a doctor's office and takes about thirty minutes. A local anesthetic is used. Small incisions are made in the scrotum and the vas deferens tubes, which carry the sperm from the testes, are cut and tied. The male may feel a dull ache in the surgical area and in the lower abdomen. Aspirin and an ice bag help relieve these feelings. Usually he can return to work in two days.

He can have sex again as soon as he doesn't feel any discomfort, usually in about a week. However, another method of contraception must be used for several weeks after the operation since live sperm are still in other parts of the reproductive system.

Although the male's testicles will continue to produce sperm after the operation, the sperm will now be absorbed into his body. His seminal fluid will be only slightly reduced. Hormone output will be normal and he will not experience any physical changes in his sex drive. However, some males do experience negative psychological side effects. For example, some equate the vasectomy with castration and feel less sexual (Kogan, 1973, p. 121). Such feelings probably do interfere with their ability to perform sexually. Postvasectomy psychological problems occur in perhaps 3 to 15 percent of those who have the operation (Lear, 1969, p. 1,207; Wolfers, 1970, p. 297). On the other hand, many men report they feel freer and more satisfied with sexual intercourse after a vasectomy (Kogan, 1973, p. 120).

In about 1 percent of vasectomies, a severed vas deferens rejoins itself so that sperm can again travel through the duct and be ejaculated (Insel & Roth, 1976, p. 193). Because of this a yearly visit to a doctor so that semen can be examined is a good safety precaution.

One of the major drawbacks of a vasectomy or other sterilization is that in many cases it is irreversible. Thus the husband and wife should be sure to discuss the matter thoroughly before deciding on this method of contraception.

If reversal is desired, the tubes can be reconnected in about 40 percent of vasectomies (Guttmacher, 1973a). Also, doctors at the University of California Medical Center in San Francisco have recently reported much higher success with reversal operations using improved techniques (San Francisco Chronicle, 1975). In selected cases, up to 90 percent of men undergoing microsurgical vasovasotomy (reconnecting the vasa, or tubes) subsequently ejaculate sperm and three-quarters are able to impregnate their wives (Brody, 1979).

TUBAL LIGATION   This is the surgical sterilization of the female. It has been, until quite recently, a much more difficult operation than vasectomy since the Fallopian tubes lie more deeply within the body than the vas deferens. The operation is done in a hospital rather than a doctor's office since it requires a general anesthetic and a hospital stay of about three to four days. One or two small incisions are made in the abdominal wall, the Fallopian tubes are located and each is severed, a small section of each is removed, and then the two ends of each tube are tied. The incisions can also be made through the vaginal wall, which will not leave a scar and requires shorter hospitalization (however, recent pregnancy or obesity make this approach more difficult or impossible). Both ligations take about thirty minutes.

Besides being more difficult than vasectomies, the procedure is also riskier. About 7 percent of the women experience problems after the operation, mainly from infections (Insel & Roth, 1976, p. 193). Some women also experience abdominal discomfort and menstrual irregularity. Most women, however, have no aftereffects and continue to have a regular menstrual cycle.

The more recent procedure is called laparoscopy. Again, it is a hospital procedure that requires a general anesthetic. However, the operation only takes fifteen minutes and does not require overnight hospitalization. A tiny incision is made in the abdomen and a small light-containing tube (laparoscope) is inserted so the surgeon can see the Fallopian tubes. The surgeon then inserts another small tube carrying high-intensity radio waves that burn out sections of the Fallopian tubes. The incision is so small that only a stitch or two is needed and it can be covered by a Band-Aid. Most women leave the hospital two or four hours after surgery.

Both forms of tubal ligation have a failure rate of about 3 in every 1000 cases (Insel & Roth, 1976, p. 194). Attempts to reverse the sterilization have failed in more than half the cases.

Women who have been sterilized tend to report an increase in sexual enjoyment since they are now free of the fear of pregnancy. A few women report reduced sexual enjoyment because of the loss of fertility that they may equate with femininity (Easley, 1972, p. 58).

While a *hysterectomy*, which is the surgical removal of the uterus, does end fertility, it is an extreme procedure and should only be used when a woman has uterine cancer or other problems of the uterus and not just for birth control reasons.

Tomorrow's Contraceptives

As probably became obvious in the discussion of the different contraceptive methods, the ideal method is still to be discovered. Researchers hope to find a safe, simple, and reversible contraceptive. They also want to find one that does not need to be taken every day and that doesn't require a doctor's prescription. The following lists should give you a better idea of some of the recent research in the field of contraception.

Possible Future Female Methods of Contraception

1. *One-time implant* An elongated plastic capsule filled with synthetic progestin will be inserted into an arm or leg where it will remain in the fatty layer just under the skin. The progestin will be leaked at a regulated rate, fooling the woman's body into thinking she is already pregnant so no new eggs will be released. If she wishes to become pregnant, the capsule will be easy to remove. However, there are presently serious disadvantages to the use of progestin. These include uterine bleeding and delays of a year or longer in the return of ovulatory cycles (Insel & Roth, 1976, p. 199).

2. *Continuous low-dosage progestin* Again, the constant presence of progestin will fool the body into thinking it is already pregnant so no new eggs will be produced. Possible sources of the progestin will be implanted capsules as above, or through a removable vaginal insert, pill, long-term injection, or IUD, or perhaps through skin contact with a progestin-impregnated ring or cosmetic. However, the same problems as noted above are still likely to occur.

3. *Immunization against eggs or sperm* Theoretically a woman could be sensitized against her own egg cells (or against sperm) so that she would produce antibodies that would inactivate them as if they were a foreign disease. So far, though, human testing has not been undertaken since researchers do not know how long the immunity would last or how to control it, and they are worried that the allergic reaction could upset other disease-fighting systems (Insel & Roth, 1976, p. 201).

4. *Once-a-month pill* A combination pill of estrogen and progestin that has to be taken only once a month would eliminate the accidents that now occur among pill takers who forget to take a pill or two during the monthly cycle.

5. *Postcoital estrogen pill (morning-after pill)* A form of morning-after pill is already in use. This contains large doses of artificial estrogen and is taken for five days after otherwise unprotected intercourse. However, the large doses have caused nausea, vomiting, and other undesirable changes in metabolism. Also, there is some evidence that the synthetic estrogen used in the pill may cause cancer. Continued research may discover a less dangerous form of estrogen.

6. *Long-term injection* Long-term (every ninety days) injections of progestin have been found to be almost completely effective in preventing pregnancy. However, progestin has the side effects noted in number 1 above. Present research is trying to discover a safe combination of estrogen and progestin that will also be effective, perhaps for periods of as long as six months.

7. *Once-a-month injection* A lower dosage of estrogen and progestin might be safe and only have to be injected every month. It might be possible to package the hypodermics already loaded, much as insulin is now packed for diabetics.

8. *Reversible tubal occlusion* Instead of cutting and tying the Fallopian tubes, attempts have been made to plug them by injecting liquid silicone into the tubes. In animal experiments, however, such plugs have been easily dislodged (Insel & Roth, 1976, p. 201). However, other substances may not dislodge so easily, and since the plug could be removed, the woman could later decide to become pregnant.

9. *Improved ovulation-detecting devices* If ovulation can be pinpointed accurately, then rhythm can become a reliable method of birth control. Recently a small, battery-run device called an Ovulometer has come on the market. The device registers changes in body temperature and voltage that occur during ovulation. By touching her body with electrodes, a woman can tell if ovulation has taken place (*San Francisco Chronicle*, 1976).

10. *Contraceptive nasal spray* Hormones contained in the spray go directly to the area of the brain that regulates ovulation and act to stop ovulation. So far, five inhalations a month have kept rhesus monkeys from becoming pregnant.

Possible Future Male Methods of Contraception

1. *One-time implant* This would be an as yet undiscovered chemical that would prevent sperm from being produced. The chemical would be placed into a plastic capsule that would be implanted in an arm or leg and slowly leak the chemical into the body. If the male decided to have children, the capsule could be easily removed. Unfortunately, while some chemicals have been found in animal experiments to suppress sperm production, side effects in humans have been severe.

2. *Immunization against sperm* The male would be sensitized to his own sperm so that he would produce antibodies that would attack them as if they were a foreign disease. As noted for female immunization, however, human testing has not been undertaken since researchers do not know how long immunity would last, how to control it, or what effect it would have on other immune reactions.

3. *Once-a-month or daily pill* Some combinations of hormones or chemicals will prevent maturation of sperm when taken orally. So far, as noted above, a safe combination has not yet been discovered.

4. *Long-term injection* A sperm suppressor will be injected every three to six months. Again, no safe suppressor has been discovered to date.

5. *Reversible vasectomy* Instead of cutting and tying the vasa deferens, they would be plugged with some substance. Experimenters have tried blocking the flow of sperm with removable clips and plugs, but so far these have damaged the vasa (tubes), and have interfered with full restoration of fertility. In some cases, the sperm have made a new path around the plug, so that birth control was not achieved. Another technique has involved implanting small mechanical valves. In the closed position, the valves prevent sperm from reaching the penis. If fertility is desired, another operation is performed to change the valves to open. However, a possible problem with all vasectomy reversals is that some vasectomized men develop antibodies to their sperm, which might persist after the reversal and eliminate the possibility of successful fertility (Insel & Roth, 1976, p. 201).

Abortion　In the United States, the 1960s witnessed mounting interest in abortion as a method of birth control. Although each state had restrictive legislation against abortion, there were many illegal abortions, which sometimes killed and often harmed the expectant mother because of nonsterile or otherwise inadequate procedures.

Other countries use abortion successfully to control population and to help women avoid unwanted pregnancies. Japan, for example, was for years plagued by overpopulation, and then, in 1948, enacted the Eugenic Protection Act which, in essence, allowed anyone to obtain a legal abortion. Consequently, abortion became a major method of birth control. It has been estimated that for every birth prevented by contraceptive devices in Japan, two births are prevented by abortion (Hart, 1967). In the first eight years after the act was passed, the birth rate fell from 34.3 to 17 per 1000, and it has remained at this lower level (ibid). In addition to the liberalized abortion policy, Japan has also mounted a massive educational campaign to make the populace aware of the need to reduce family size.

After a number of states liberalized their abortion laws, the U.S. Supreme Court on January 22, 1973, in *Roe v. Wade* and *Doe v. Bolton*, made abortion on request a real possibility for the entire country. Essentially, the Court ruled that the fetus is not a person as defined by the Constitution and therefore does not possess constitutional rights. More specifically, the Court said that in the first trimester (twelve weeks) of pregnancy no state may interfere in any way with a woman's decision to have an abortion as long as it is performed by a physician. In the second trimester (thirteen to twenty-five weeks) a state may lay down medical guidelines to protect the woman's health. Most states that do permit abortion permit it by choice only through the twentieth week. After that there must be clear medical evidence that the mother's health is endangered or that the baby will be irreparably defective. Only in the last trimester may states ban abortion, and even then an abortion may be performed if continued pregnancy endangers the life or health of the mother. About 20 percent of all pregnancies now end with an induced abortion.

The proponents of abortion on request believed they had won a final victory, yet this conclusion has proved premature. A 1974 Gallup poll indicated that the American public was closely divided on the abortion issue. Somewhat surprisingly, men tended to favor the Court ruling while women tended to oppose it. Gallup asked the following question: "The U.S. Supreme Court has ruled that a woman may go to a doctor to end pregnancy at any time during the first three months of pregnancy. Do you favor or oppose this ruling?" A 1977 national poll by Yankelovich yielded almost identical figures. Forty-eight percent approved of abortion while 44 percent did not (*Time*, November 21, 1977, p. 115). See Table 10-3.

Public attitudes about abortion are strongly divided.

Table 10-3   Results of 1974 Gallup Abortion Poll

| Respondents | Percentage | | |
	Favor	Oppose	No Opinion
National	47%	44%	9%
Men	51	38	11
Women	43	49	8
College graduates	67	27	6
Grade school graduates	25	57	18
Under 30 years	55	38	7
30–49 years	44	50	6
50 and older	43	43	14
Protestants	48	41	11
Catholics	32	61	7
Married	46	45	9
Single	56	36	8

WHAT DO YOU THINK?

Why do you suppose that more women than men opposed abortion on request?

Why do you think there is an educational difference?

Why do you think there is an age difference?

The proabortionists believe a woman's body belongs to her so she should have the right to determine whether to pursue pregnancy to completion. They also believe that laws governing abortion are an unconstitutional invasion of privacy.

They also argue that overpopulation is the major threat to civilization and humanity. Thus to fail to use every acceptable method to reduce population growth is immoral and shortsighted and will ultimately lead to world disaster.

Third, they argue that it is more immoral to have unwanted children than it is to seek abortion. The unwanted child suffers and becomes the source of many of society's problems. Problems are created both for and by unwanted children.

Garret Hardin, professor of biology at the University of California at Santa Barbara and an outspoken proponent of free abortion, has pointed out that:

Critics of abortion generally see it as an exclusively negative thing, a means of nonfulfillment only. What they fail to realize is that abortion, like other means of birth control, can lead to fulfillment in the life of a woman. A woman who aborts this year because she is in poor health, neurotic, economically harassed, unmarried, on the verge of divorce, or immature may well decide to have some other child five years from now – a wanted child. If her need for abortion is frustrated, she may never know the joy of a wanted child (Hardin, 1964).

The American Friends Service Committee makes the following statement:

We believe that every child should be wanted by and born into a family that is able to feed, clothe, educate and, above all, love him; that the family is the basic unit of our society and that the married life of the parents should encompass sexual activity whether or not for purposes of procreation; that an appropriate contraception, which spaces children and eliminates the fear of unwanted pregnancies, strengthens family ties and establishes a sense of responsible parenthood; that in view of the problem of overpopulation, every couple has a responsibility to society as well as to their own family, not to overburden the world with more lives than it can sustain.

We believe that responsible parenthood demands consideration not only of the number of children individual parents want but also of the effect of that number on society as a whole (American Friends Service Committee, 1970, pp. 62–65).

Abortion is not as dangerous to the mother as is childbirth. The maternal death rate in New York is 29 per 100,000 births, while the death rate from legal abortions is only 3.5 per 100,000 abortions. Deaths from pregnancy and birth in England are about 20 per 100,000 deliveries. In Japan, the death rate is about 8 per 100,000 from abortions.

Women have always sought abortions and always will. By making it illegal, society fosters a black market in abortions and increases the woman's chances of injury and death.

Right-to-lifers, a strongly antiabortion group, received a boost for their position from lower courts. Dr. Kenneth Edelin, chief resident of obstetrics and gynecology at Boston City Hospital, was convicted of manslaughter for performing an abortion on a woman who was twenty to twenty-two weeks pregnant (*Time*, 1975). The aborted fetus weighed 600 grams or about 1½ pounds. The jury ruled that the fetus had, in fact, been alive when it left its mother's body and was therefore a living baby. However, in December, 1976, the Massachusetts Supreme Court overturned the ruling. The court declared that "the defendant had no evil frame of mind, was actuated by no criminal purpose, and committed no wanton or reckless act in carrying out the medical proce-

Antiabortion groups believe that abortion is murder. Since murder is not condoned in our society, we should not condone abortion.

An important factor is just when the fetus comes alive. Quickening, the first feeling of movement on the part of the fetus by the mother, has been used in the past to decide when abortion should no longer be undertaken. If one accepts this, then before quickening occurs, abortion would be acceptable since the fetus is not yet considered alive. However, the embryo is actually alive from the minute that conception occurs. Most medical authorities indicate that abortions are relatively safe physically up until the twelfth week of pregnancy and the Supreme Court's decision used the twelfth week as a point of demarcation. By the twelfth week, the embryo is three inches long, weighs one ounce, has nails beginning to appear on stubby toes and fingers, has a beating heart, has eyes, and its gender can be determined. It is clearly recognizable as a living human being. (see Chapter 11).

Social utility is not a viable criterion in matters that involve life and death and essential liberties. While a huge proportion of unhappy lives and a whole network of social ills can be traced to the unwanted child, no one can predict with certainty how a child will turn out. No one can say that an unwanted child won't later be wanted and loved. How many people, even unhappy ones or ones in trouble from time to time, seriously wish they had never been born? The social utility argument reduces human life to the value of a machine — how well does it work (Lessard, 1972)?

Antiabortion groups believe that easy availability of abortions will lead to prom-iscuity. The Christian heritage in the United States not only bans abortion but has a great deal to say about sexual mores. By making abortion freely available, promiscuous behavior is encouraged since the consequences of the act are removed. The possibility of pregnancy means that one needs to contemplate sexual intercourse in a responsible manner since it is possible that the act will involve a child for whom responsibility must be taken. Free abortion leads to irresponsible sexual activity since one need not be responsible for a child even if pregnancy does occur.

Abortion can lead to severe psychological trauma. The feelings of guilt, the frustrated desire to have had the child, and feeling responsible for the death of the child, all these and many more psychological reactions can and do occur and are every bit as much a threat to the mother's health as the continued pregnancy.

Evidence is also beginning to demonstrate physical problems associated with abortion. In Athens, Greece, during 1966–1968, 29 percent of 8312 previously pregnant women admitted for delivery acknowledged one or more previous induced abortions. In the group admitting previous induced abortion, the average number of abortions per woman was two. Of this group, the percentage of stillbirths (born dead) and premature births was double that of the control group (the remaining 71 percent). Studies from other countries agree with these findings (World Health Organization, 1970; Philippe et al, 1968). Another study from Greece indicates that about one-third of all women subjected to induced abortion were permanently infertile (Pantelakis et al, 1973). Thus far, however, such findings have not been reported in the United States. Approximately 1 million abortions were performed in the United States in 1974 and very few negative aftereffects have been reported to date. But this is an area in which more research should be undertaken.

dures'' for the abortion. However, both that decision and the 1973 Supreme Court decision did not clarify the question of when life begins. According to the Supreme Court, ''We need not resolve the difficult question of when life begins. When those trained in the respective disciplines of medicine, philosophy, and theology are unable to arrive at any consensus, the judiciary ... is not in a position to speculate as to the answer" (U.S. Supreme Court, January 22, 1973).

The legal debate over abortions still continues. In fact, in June 1977, the U.S. Supreme Court decided that the states and localities are free, if they wish, to deny Medicaid money for abortions. Both houses of Congress jumped on the bandwagon by passing provisions that forbid Medicaid payments for abortions. In essence, this means that abortions will only be available to those who can afford them. However, in 1980, the Supreme Court refused to block a federal judge's order forcing the federal government to pay for poor women's medically necessary abortions.

Where the continuing debate will go from here is anybody's guess but one thing is sure, the question of abortion will remain a controversial one for some time.

The debate over induced abortion tends to cloud the physical act of abortion itself. First of all, spontaneous abortion occurs in 10 percent or more of all diagnosed first pregnancies by the end of the tenth week after conception. If undiagnosed first pregnancies are taken into account, the figure is probably closer to 25 percent. Interestingly, a high percentage of spontaneously aborted embryos are abnormal. There is also evidence that emotional shock plays a role in spontaneous abortions as well as abnormalities of the reproductive tract. There is also some evidence that excessive manipulation of the cervix during induced abortion is related to later spontaneous abortions.

Abortion is a fairly simple procedure, though usually more unpleasant than abortion advocates claim. The major method of legal abortion used to be *dilation and curettage (D and C)*. In this method, the cervix is held by a clamp and dilated by having increasingly larger metal dilators inserted until the opening into the cervix is about as big around as a fountain pen. At this point a curette (a surgical instrument) is used to scrape out the products of conception. An ovum forceps (a long, grasping surgical instrument) may also be used. The woman is instructed not to have sexual intercourse for several weeks. It may take her ten days to two weeks to fully recover from the procedure. The doctor will usually want to see her again to make sure everything is healing properly.

Vacuum aspiration is now the preferred method of abortion since it takes less time, involves less loss of blood, and has a shorter period of recovery than a D and C. In this method the cervix is dilated by a speculum (an expanding instrument) and a specially designed vacuum-suction tube is inserted into the uterus. A curette and electric pump is attached to the tubing and suction is applied to the uterine cavity. The uterus is emptied in about twenty to thirty seconds. The doctor will sometimes also scrape the uterine lining with a metal curette. The entire procedure takes only five to ten minutes. The woman may return home after a rest of a few hours in a recovery area. She is usually told not to have sexual intercourse and not to use tampons for a week or two after the abortion (see Figure 10-3).

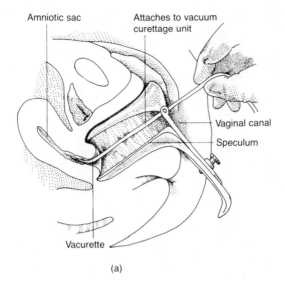

Amniotic sac

Attaches to vacuum
curettage unit

Vaginal canal

Speculum

Vacurette

(a)

Figure 10-3
Vacuum aspiration, an
abortion method, takes
only five to ten minutes;
it can be performed
up to the twelfth week
of pregnancy. (a) The
vacuum aspiration
process. (b) An operating
unit for vacuum
curettage.

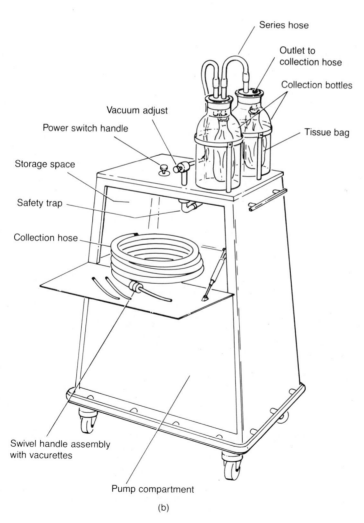

Series hose

Outlet to
collection hose

Collection bottles

Tissue bag

Vacuum adjust

Power switch handle

Storage space

Safety trap

Collection hose

Swivel handle assembly
with vacurettes

Pump compartment

(b)

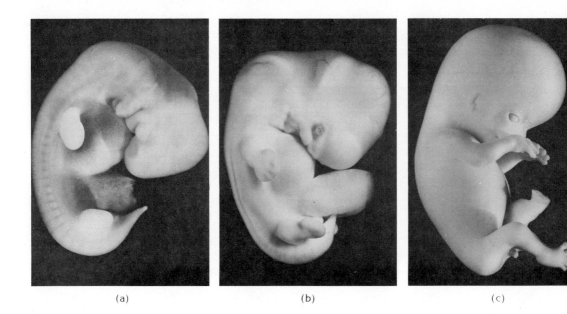

(a)   (b)   (c)

Figure 10-4
Examples of fetal
development. Ages are:
(a) 33 days; (b) about
6 weeks; (c) about
9½ weeks.

After the fourteenth week, a different method, called the *saline procedure*, must be used since the fetus is now too large to be removed by suction and a D and C may now cause complications. By this time, the safest abortion is to stimulate the uterus to push the fetus out, or to cause a miscarriage. (When a fetus dies, the uterus naturally begins to contract and eject the dead fetus.) In order to kill the fetus, a local anesthetic is given and a long needle is inserted through the abdominal wall into the uterine cavity. The amniotic sac (see Chapter 9) is punctured and some of the fluid is removed. An equal amount of 20 percent salt solution is then injected into the sac. The injection must be done slowly and carefully to avoid introducing the salt solution into the woman's circulatory system. She must be awake so that she can report any pain or other symptoms. Once the fetus is dead, which occurs immediately, the uterus begins to contract in about six to forty-eight hours. Eventually the amniotic sac breaks and the fetus is expelled. In up to 50 percent of the cases, the placenta does not come out automatically and a gentle pull on the umbilical cord is necessary to remove it. In about 10 percent of the cases, a D and C must be performed to remove any remaining pieces of the placenta. The saline procedure should be carried out in a hospital and the woman should remain there until the abortion is complete. The recovery period is longer than for the other forms of abortion and complications are more frequent. Thus, although it should be a considered decision, the decision to have an abortion should be reached as quickly as possible.

Recently Dr. K. Sune D. Bergstrom, head of the Karolinska Institute in Stockholm, Sweden disclosed details of a new chemical abortion procedure that may make the above described methods obsolete in the future. A synthetic prostaglandin is the chemical used in a suppository that is placed into the vagina. The chemical causes muscle contractions within one to five hours after a "missed period."

The uterine contractions lead to abortion. The new suppositories have been classed as an investigative new drug by the U.S. Food and Drug Administration and experimentation with them is beginning in the United States. If all goes well, they may be available to the public in the 1980s.

The decision to have an abortion is difficult, of course, and certainly should not be made lightly. Whenever possible, it is wise for the woman considering an abortion to discuss the decision with the prospective father, parents, physicians, counselors, and/or knowledgeable and concerned friends.

Professional abortion counseling can be obtained at local Planned Parenthood chapters and in thirty-four states with the Clergy Consultation Service on Abortion. Both agencies are listed in local telephone directories. Abortion is certainly not a recommended means of birth control and should only be used as a last resort. A woman who is well informed about sex and contraceptive devices should never be faced with having to make an abortion decision.

Infertility

Although many people think only of contraception when hearing the phrase "family planning," problems of infertility are also important aspects of family planning. Alan Guttmacher, past-president of Planned Parenthood–World Population, estimates that 15 to 20 percent of married couples cannot have any children or as many as they want because they are infertile or subfertile (Guttmacher, 1969). Infertile for a male means that he is not producing viable sperm and for a female it means she is either not producing viable eggs or has some other condition that makes it impossible for her to successfully maintain a pregnancy. Guttmacher estimates that in general about one-third of all married couples do conceive the first month they try, and that about 60 percent conceive within the first three months.

Essentially, there are three phases in the treatment of infertility: education, detection, and therapy. Young couples should persist in trying to conceive for at least one year. If they are not successful they should seek help from a physician. Often if the couple learns more about how conception occurs and the possible reasons for failure to conceive, they will feel less tense and anxious and thus increase the chances of conception.

Prerequisites of Fertility   There are at least nine biological prerequisites for achieving parenthood (Guttmacher, 1969, pp. 205–206). Four pertain to the male:

1. Healthy live sperm must be produced in sufficient numbers. Ordinarily a single normal testicle is all that is required, though usually both assume an equal role in producing sperm. In order to function properly, a testicle must be in the scrotal sac. In the male embryo each testicle is formed in the abdomen and descends into

the scrotum during the seventh month of intrauterine life. Very infrequently, one or both testicles fail to descend. If they have not descended by five or six years of age, the boy is usually treated with a hormone to stimulate testicular growth. This makes the testicle heavier, which in some instances brings about descent. If hormone treatment fails, surgery is performed, usually about the eighth year of life.

2. Seminal fluid (the whitish, sticky material ejaculated at orgasm) must be secreted in the proper amount and composition to transport the sperm.

3. An unobstructed seminal "thruway" must exist from the testicle to the end of the penis.

4. The ability to achieve and sustain an erection and to ejaculate within the vagina must be present.

The other five biological requirements for reproduction pertain to the female.

1. At least one ovary must function normally enough to produce a mature egg.

2. A normal-sized uterus must be properly prepared by chemicals (hormones) fed into the bloodstream by the ovary to become the "home" of the developing fetus.

3. An unobstructed genital tract, from the vagina up through the Fallopian tubes to the ovary, must exist to enable the egg to pass down and the sperm cells to pass up.

4. A uterine environment must adequately nourish and protect the unborn child until it is able to live in the outside world.

5. Miscarriage must be avoided and the infant must be delivered safely.

It is not uncommon for couples seeking fertility help to conceive before treatment begins, and for adoptive parents to conceive shortly after they decide on adoption. Clearly, emotional and psychological factors are tremendously important to the process of conception. Psychological factors actually account for approximately one-quarter of subfertility cases (Guttmacher, 1969).

Causes of Infertility Males account for about 33 percent of sterility problems (Kogan, 1973, p. 216). For example, *impotence*, the inability to gain or maintain an erection, precludes sexual intercourse and thus conception. Often impotence is psychological in nature though it can be caused by alcohol, general fatigue, or a debilitating disease. Low sperm count is another possible reason for infertility. An ejaculation that contains fewer than 100 to 150 million sperm limits the possibility of conception. Infectious diseases such as mumps can damage sperm production. Sterility can also occur if the testes have not descended into the scrotum since the higher temperature of the body reduces production of healthy sperm. Also, undescended testes are often abnormal in some way, which is why they didn't descend, and which also affects production of healthy sperm. A prolonged and untreated venereal disease can cause permanent sterility.

If a couple contacts a physician as they should about their apparent infertility, it is easier to test the man first because the tests are quite simple compared to fertility tests for the female. Basically the tests involve collecting a sample of ejaculate and analyzing it for the number and activity level of the sperm and also for abnormal sperm.

Unfortunately, some men tie fertility and manhood closely together. They consider an examination for possible fertility problems an attack on their manhood and may refuse to cooperate. It is obvious, however, that both partners must share in the search for a solution to infertility.

In a woman, both ovarian abnormalities and vaginal infections can cause infertility. A woman must ovulate if she is to conceive. Almost all mature women menstruate but in about 15 percent of a normal woman's cycles an egg is not actually released (Young, 1961). In a few women, even though they menstruate, ovulation very seldom occurs thus making them almost infertile.

A woman may have a problem in conceiving if the tract from the vagina through the uterus and Fallopian tubes to the ovary is blocked. If the egg and sperm cannot meet, obviously conception cannot occur. It is possible to determine if the Fallopian tubes are open by filling them with an opaque fluid and X-raying them.

Another possible problem can arise from the chemical environment of the woman's internal reproductive organs. Too acid an environment quickly kills the sperm. Also, the chemical environment may make implantation of the fertilized egg into the uterine wall difficult or impossible. In the latter case, the woman may conceive and then spontaneously abort (miscarry) the embryo.

Methods of Treatment When the cause of infertility rests with the husband, *artificial insemination* is sometimes used to induce conception. This consists of taking sperm from the husband if possible or from an anonymous donor if not and injecting the sperm into the wife's vagina during her fertile period. Even if the husband's sperm count is low, his ejaculate can be collected and the concentration of sperm increased to bring it within the normal range necessary for fertilization. Sperm banks have been established where sperm is frozen and stored for later use. It seems to remain viable for long periods. Sperm that has been frozen for up to three years has been used for successful fertilization. Mary Ann Oakley (1974, p. 37) estimates that more than 100,000 human births have resulted from artificial insemination. However, there are numerous controversies surrounding this practice, especially when the sperm has come from someone other than the husband. Questions of legitimacy and parental responsibility have arisen. But, biologically, it is a perfectly acceptable manner of overcoming a man's infertility.

When the cause of infertility rests with the woman, *fertility drugs* have been used to stimulate the ovary to ovulate. However, the drugs often overstimulate ovulation and cause multiple births. Overstimulation may be reduced by the recent discovery of the chemical structure and the subsequent synthesis of the luteinizing-hormone-

Inset 10-3
A Sperm Bank for Nobel Prize Winners

Robert K. Graham, 74, a wealthy California businessman, calls it a "moderately expensive hobby." Fairly interesting too. Graham collects sperm from Nobel-prizewinning scientists —five so far— and offers it to young women who have high IQs. According to the Los Angeles *Times*, which broke the story last week, Graham has shipped frozen sperm to several unidentified women, and three of them — all on the East Coast — are pregnant. Says he: "This is just the beginning."

Graham several years ago began writing to Nobel laureates, asking for sperm donations. Five said yes, and Graham made collections in the San Francisco and San Diego areas for his subterranean sperm bank — the Hermann J. Muller Repository for Germinal Choice — built on his ten-acre estate in Escondido, Calif.

A member of Mensa, a group of 33,000 people who have IQ scores in the top 2%, Graham first revealed his project last summer in an interview published in the Mensa *Bulletin*. He was seeking to place his Nobel sperm with bright women who were healthy, under 35 and preferably married to a sterile man. Two dozen women applied,

and those who were chosen received physical descriptions of the anonymous Nobel donors — plus Graham's own assessments. "A very famous scientist," he wrote on the description of one of the five available mail-order fathers (to whom he has assigned numbers 10 through 14), "a mover and a shaker, almost a superman." Replied one of the women: "I'm very excited about this...I'm tentatively going to select No. 13 because he's the youngest of the donors and has the highest IQ." As a condition for receiving Nobel sperm, the applicants agreed to send Graham regular reports on the pregnancy and, after birth, on the child's health and IQ.

So far only one of the sperm donors has revealed himself to the press: Laureate William Shockley (Physics, 1956), whose genetics opinions are regularly attacked as racist. Says he: "I don't regard myself as a perfect human being or the ideal candidate, but I am endorsing Graham's concept of increasing the people at the top of the population." Steve Broder, who directs a Southern California sperm bank called Cryobank and is a former adviser to Graham, says he saw "three or maybe four" Nobelists donating to the

depository. "I see nothing extraordinary in all this," he adds. "It's quite normal for potential mothers to come in and ask for sperm with a high IQ."

Many Nobel winners are taking a dim view of Graham's project. Stanford's Burton Richter (Physics, 1976) reports that his students are beginning to ask whether he supplements his salary with stud fees. "It's somewhat weird," he says. "What they are trying to do is create an intellectual superman, and selecting winning Nobel Prize scientists is not the way to do it." Charles H. Townes (Physics, 1964) of the University of California at Berkeley dismissed the project as "snobbish," and the Salk Institute's Dr. Renato Dulbecco (Medicine, 1975) disqualified himself. Said he: "I was vasectomized long ago."

Graham's project may not even make good sense on its own terms. Nobel sperm may be bright, but the donors are usually far along in years. Shockley, for example, is 70, and recent studies suggest that the chance of having a mongoloid child increases not only with the mother's age, but with the father's too, especially if he is 55 or older.

Time Magazine, March 10, 1980, p. 49.

releasing factor of the hypothalamus, which controls the release of the egg from the ovary (see Kogan, 1973, p. 216).

Recently, *sex therapy* is being used to help couples with non-physical problems that affect their sex life and their ability to conceive. Obviously, intercourse is necessary for conception to occur. But if a couple is having problems with premature ejaculation, impotence, or the spouse's lack of sexual enjoyment, they may avoid having intercourse.

Sex therapists usually use techniques devised by Masters and Johnson (see Masters and Johnson, 1966, for a fuller discussion of these techniques) to guide the couple to a more satisfactory sexual relationship. In general, the couple is seen together. To reduce their performance expectations and fear of sexual failure, they are prohibited from having intercourse for a period of time. The therapists give them a series of exercises, which they perform at home and then discuss with the therapists. The discussions also deal with sexuality in general and with the couple's specific problems. In the exercises they are told to explore each other in sensual, rather than specifically sexual, ways. They learn to give and receive pleasure, and also learn what gives the partner pleasure. As they become more knowledgeable and relaxed about sexuality, they are led, through further structured exercises, to have increased comfort with intercourse.

Sex therapy has recently suffered from a sudden popularity that is leading to ethical problems. For example, some therapists are having sexual intercourse with their clients in the name of therapy. Others are using sexual surrogates, substitute partners, to help their clients overcome sexual problems (see Kaplan, 1974). Although such practices might be justified on theoretical grounds, there are ethical and moral questions involved. Masters and Johnson recently commented that they feel only half a dozen of the many sex therapy clinics are legitimate, using well-trained staff and proven procedures. Recently several state legislatures have considered licensure regulations for sex counselors. In California, sex counselors are required to have master's degrees and supervised training.

Despite these ethical and moral problems, sex therapy is a major breakthrough in the treatment of not only infertility problems due to impotence and frigidity, but all sexual problems.

In the past, for example, an impotent male had little chance to overcome his problem because he failed every time he attempted intercourse. Getting and maintaining an erection is a complex interaction between a man's chemistry and his psychological state of being. No matter how physically healthy a man is, if he is psychologically in the wrong place, he will not become erect. Failure leads him to worry and fear that he will fail again. Such worry and fear works against achieving an erection. A vicious circle is thus created wherein the more he tries to become erect, the less chance he has of being successful. Sex therapy can break this pattern of fear, failure, and more fear by setting up situations in which the impotent man can be successful, thus lessening his fears and increasing his future chances of success.

Much the same is true for the nonorgasmic woman. However, in her case failure to achieve orgasm does not necessarily hinder her ability to become pregnant. But it may lead to disinterest and/or fear of sexual relations and thus lower her frequency of sexual intercourse, which will reduce her chances of becoming pregnant.

For the woman who cannot become pregnant, it is now possible for a human egg to be fertilized outside her body and then implanted within her uterus. This controversial technique is discussed in further detail in Scenes from Marriage at the end of this chapter.

Summary   Family planning is an important part of marriage. The decision to have children should be just that, a decision made rationally by the couple. Yet many pregnancies are unplanned, the resultant children unwanted, and the consequences to the marriage often devastating. Basically the couple should ask themselves if they can help all their children grow into adulthood in the most healthful possible manner. They should not only want the children they have, they should also be healthy and economically equipped to feed, clothe, and educate their children.

Birth control has a long but relatively unsuccessful history. Recent technological advances have led to much more reliable contraceptive methods, though the perfect contraceptive has yet to be invented. The pill, IUD, condom, and diaphragm are all popular and effective methods of birth control. Less effective methods, ranging from the more to the least effective, are vaginal spermicides, rhythm, withdrawal, and douches.

Recently, abortion laws have been revised, making abortion on demand a reality. The revisions have generated a great amount of controversy and it is quite possible that more restrictive laws may again be introduced. Be that as it may, abortion is a presently available method of birth control, though it is one that requires a great deal of thought before undertaking.

Sterilization as a form of birth control has also become increasingly popular during the 1970s. Although usually irreversible, recent advances are opening up the possibility of reversible sterilization procedures.

Family planning also helps couples to have children when there are fertility problems. The increased understanding of reproduction has helped to solve some of the problems that cause infertility. Probably 15 to 20 percent of American couples have some infertility problem. During the 1970s, in addition to correction of physical problems such as low sperm count, failure to ovulate, blocked Fallopian tubes, and so on, efforts have been made to help couples who have sexual problems that stem from their upbringing or from some psychological problem. The couple who cannot successfully have sexual relations obviously will not be able to have their own children, unless by artificial insemination. Sex therapy, although controversial, is proving helpful to such couples.

In general, the couple who plan their family realistically and control reproduction increase their chances of having a happy sex life and a fulfilling marriage. To leave reproduction to chance too often leads to problems and unhappiness.

The First Test Tube Baby*

She was born at 11:47 P.M. with a lusty yell, and it was a cry heard round the brave new world. Louise Brown, blond, blue-eyed and just under 6 pounds, was the first child in history to be conceived outside her mother's body. Her birth last week in a dowdy British mill town was in its way a first coming — variously hailed as a medical miracle, an ethical mistake and the beginning of a new age of genetic manipulation. But perhaps more important, as Dr. Patrick Steptoe proudly reported, "The anxieties are over. We've got a nice, healthy, normal baby."

Steptoe and his medical collaborator, physiologist Robert Edwards, had achieved their breakthrough with just a minor variation on the technique they had been developing for twelve years, and the crucial element was apparently timing: the fertilized egg, reimplanted in Louise's mother's womb slightly ahead of earlier schedules, survived for almost the normal nine months to a Caesarean birth. But that was enough to promise fresh hope for millions of childless women, hundreds of whom immediately besieged Steptoe with requests to help them conceive children.

There were widespread misgivings over the next possible steps: surrogate mothers who might rent out their wombs, or tailor-made babies whose genes might be altered in the test tube. "I fear that we may be slipping away from doctoring the patient to doctoring the race," said Father William Smith of New York's Catholic archdiocese.

Few doubted, however, that Louise's birth represented a major advance in medical research, with the promise of additional breakthroughs in embryo research, the understanding of birth defects and their prevention, treatment of infertility and — paradoxically — the development of new contraceptives.

From Rabbits to People

Steptoe and Edwards had few precedents to guide them in their development of the test-tube-baby technique. The first report of an in-vitro fertilization came in 1936 from Dr. Gregory Pincus of Harvard University; he united a rabbit egg and sperm. Eight years later Dr. John Rock, also of Harvard and, like Pincus, a major figure in the development of the contraceptive pill, claimed to have fer-

*Source: Newsweek, "All About That Baby," August 7, 1978, pp. 66 – 72.

tilized a human egg outside the body and watched it divide into three cells. In 1961, Dr. Daniele Petrucci of the University of Bologna shocked the world with his claim — backed up by movie films — that he had fertilized twenty separate human eggs in vitro. There were even rumors that Petrucci had reimplanted some of them. But so bizarre did the idea of test-tube babies appear to most scientists and laymen that the research was either ignored or greeted with outraged disbelief.

The scientific community was hardly more receptive when Steptoe and Edwards started their historic collaboration, and in the early years the pair proceeded cautiously. Edwards took the lead in perfecting means of fertilizing human eggs and improving the chemical solutions necessary to keep them alive and healthy outside the body. Steptoe, in the meantime, worked on the mechanical technique of removing ova from would-be mothers and returning the dividing, fertilized eggs to the womb. His major contribution — and perhaps the most important event in the chain that led to last week's birth — was to pioneer use of the laparoscope. A foot-long tube equipped with its own eyepiece and internal lighting, it can be inserted through a small slit in a woman's abdomen and used to select a ripening egg that a suction needle can then remove from her ovaries.

Success came slowly. In 1970, the pair reported in the journal *Nature* that fertilized human ova had grown to the eight- and

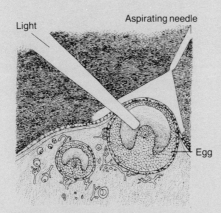

(a) Extraction of egg. In the first step of the process, the doctor uses a laparoscope, a surgical tool with lens and light, to look for a mature egg, and removes the egg, using suction from a needle.

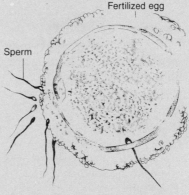

(b) Fertilization in lab. The egg is transferred to a culture dish containing nutrients and sperm. A single sperm penetrates the egg, fertilizing it; the remaining sperm cells are deflected.

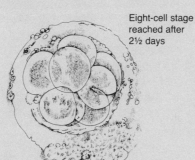

(c) Cell division in lab. The fertilized egg is placed in another solution and begins to divide after resting for about a day. At the eight-cell stage, it is already to be returned to the uterus.

(d) Implantation in womb. The ball of cells is placed in the uterus through the cervix, using a plastic tube called a *cannula*. Days later, the growing sphere attaches itself to the uterine wall.

sixteen-cell stage, and a few years later they started serious efforts to reimplant such test-tube ova, which are no larger than the period at the end of this sentence.

Conceived in a Cottage

In 1975, Steptoe and Edwards produced their first definite pregnancy, but the embryo reimplanted itself in the patient's diseased Fallopian tube rather than in the uterus, and it miscarried after ten weeks. The researchers nonetheless remained confident they were on the right track, and continued to make small alterations in the procedure.

Lesley Brown was an excellent subject. "She was in an age group that was highly suitable," explained Steptoe in a news conference last week, "not too old and highly fertile." Shortly after her visits started two years ago, Steptoe removed Mrs. Brown's diseased Fallopian tubes. That operation destroyed any faint chance that she might be able to conceive normally, but it gave the obstetrician an unobstructed internal view of his patient's ovaries when he took the first step in creating Louise. At that point, Mrs.Brown was given hormone treatment to stimulate egg production before she made the crucial visit to Oldham, for the actual conception of her child. It took place in Dr. Kershaw's Cottage Hospital, a little-used brick building originally donated to the town by an Edwardian eccentric.

Operating in the institution's tiny, white-tiled surgical theater, Steptoe extracted an egg from his patient. Edwards placed the egg in a small jar, where it was mixed with John Brown's sperm and sustained by special fluids. Once fertilized, the egg was transferred to another nutrient solution. The researchers monitored the egg as it divided into two, four and, finally — after more than 50 hours — eight cells.

Now came the crucial point of difference. In previous experiments, Steptoe and Edwards had tried to simulate the natural development of the egg, which is normally fertilized within the Fallopian tube and has multiplied into 64 or more cells by the time it reaches the womb. But new research with rhesus monkeys — though it involved only implantation of conventionally fertilized eggs — suggested that an embryo as small as two cells might survive in the uterus. So the researchers decided to reimplant Lesley Brown's ovum at the eight-cell stage, reducing the complexities of sustaining its development outside her body. She had already received a second batch of hormones to prepare her womb chemically to receive the embryo.

The Brown fetus survived and thrived. Lesley Brown checked into the Oldham Hospital's maternity ward, where she assumed the name Rita Ferguson, to allow doctors to monitor her around the clock. Other mothers told reporters that she was quiet and subdued, spending her time knitting, watching television and doing crossword puzzles. She chewed gum, developed a craving for mints, and couldn't resist disobeying Steptoe's orders by taking an occasional puff from a cigarette — and blowing the smoke out a window to conceal it.

Premature but Beautiful

Steptoe had expected the birth to occur sometime this week, but when Lesley developed a mild case of high blood pressure, threatening complications in the delivery, he decided to deliver the baby immediately by Caesarean section. In a ten-minute conventional operation, he left the mother with a horizontal "bikini cut" and brought forth Louise, several days premature and weighing just 5 pounds 12 ounces. The baby's looks benefited from the operation: because they don't have to struggle through the birth canal, babies delivered by Caesarean section tend to look prettier than children who undergo normal births. "She has a marvelous complexion, not red and wrinkly at all," boasted her father to the Daily Mail. Edwards, a godfather of sorts, added a unique view: "The last time I saw the baby it was just eight cells in a test tube. It was beautiful then, and it's still beautiful now."

Chapter 11 ~

Contents

Scenes from Marriage:
BIRTH WITHOUT VIOLENCE: THE LEBOYER METHOD

⌒ Human
Reproduction

D espite all the talk about effective birth control methods, zero population growth, and sex as a means of communication rather than reproduction, most Americans do have children, and most of the children are desired, cared for, loved, and a source of happiness (along with some heartache) to their parents.

For a mother listening to her six-foot son discuss the finer points of football, for a father escorting his lovely twenty-year-old daughter down the aisle, it may be difficult to remember the beginnings: the love-making; the missed menstrual period that led mother to think "Maybe I'm pregnant"; to remember the thrill of feeling a tiny yet unseen foot kick and dad placing his hand on mom's tummy to feel it too; the scary feelings when labor started and the movielike rush to the hospital; dad and mom holding the little red, wrinkled seven-pound newborn son or daughter and counting all of the fingers and toes to make sure they are all there; the long debate over the name; the wet spot on dad's suit after hugging the baby goodbye before going to work; the first tooth, the first sickness, the first bicycle, the first day in school, the first date, high school graduation, marriage, and then the new cycle when suddenly a little one hugs them and says "Hi grandad, hi grandma."

Conception

All of us, with our billions and billions of cells and complex organs, have grown from the union of two microscopic cells — the ovum or egg cell (about 0.004 inch in diameter) and the sperm (about 0.00125 inch in diameter) — and we weighed only 0.005 of a milligram or one-twenty-millionth of an ounce at conception!

The possibility of conception begins with ovulation, which will release one mature egg (containing twenty-three chromosomes, fat droplets, protein substances, and nutrient fluid all surrounded by a tough gelatinous substance or membrane) to find its way to a Fallopian tube and begin a three-day journey to the uterus. Fertilization must occur within twenty-four hours of the release of the egg or it will die and be eliminated (see Figure 11-1).

The other necessary ingredient for conception is a sperm cell. Like the egg, the sperm contains twenty-three chromosomes within its nucleus (the head), but it also contains a tail which gives it mobility. There are about 400 million sperm in an average ejaculation. They are

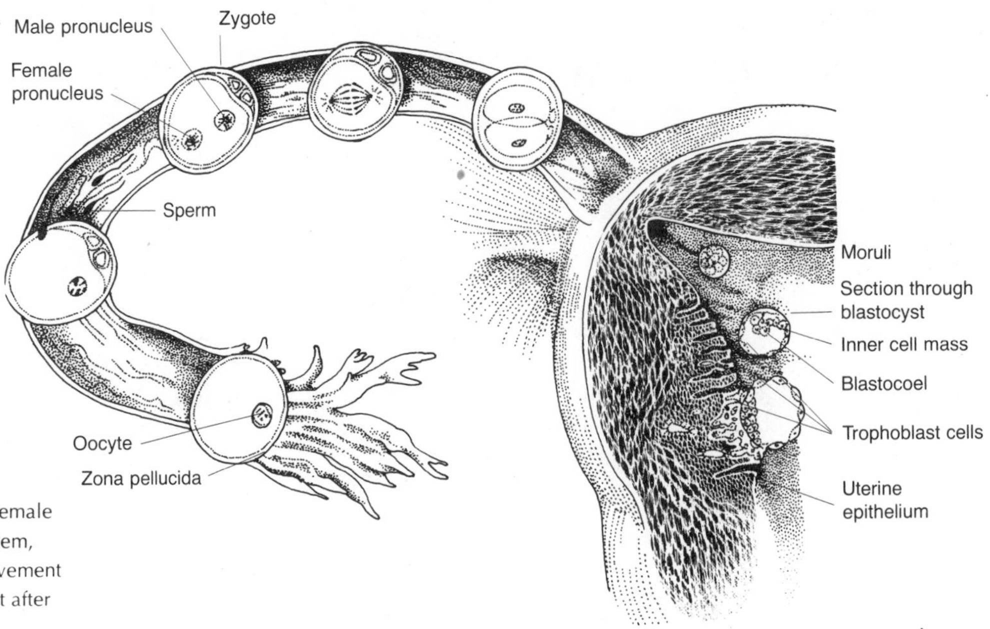
Male pronucleus
Zygote
Female pronucleus
Sperm
Oocyte
Zona pellucida
Moruli
Section through blastocyst
Inner cell mass
Blastocoel
Trophoblast cells
Uterine epithelium

Figure 11-1
One side of the female reproductive system, showing egg movement and development after fertilization.

so minute that enough of them to repopulate the earth could be stored in a space the size of an aspirin tablet.

When sperm are deposited in the vagina after an ejaculation, they are affected by the presence of an egg. If an egg isn't present, sperm will swim erratically in all directions. But when an egg is present, they will swim directly toward it (see Figure 11-2). By using their tails, they can swim at a rate of three to four centimeters an hour (Katchadourian and Lunde, 1972, p. 101). Actually, their great numbers are necessary since the job of reaching the egg is so arduous that only a few thousand will actually reach the tube that contains the egg. Many will die in the acidic environment of the vagina. Many will also go up the wrong tube or get lost along the way. Those that do reach the egg will have to overcome another obstacle — the outer membrane of the egg. Each sperm that reaches the egg will deposit a bit of enzyme on the membrane that will dissolve a minute part. Finally, one sperm will manage to enter the egg and fertilize it. Once this occurs, the egg will become impervious to all the remaining sperm and they will die.

Sperm remain viable within the female genital tract for about forty-eight hours; the egg remains viable for about twenty-four hours.* Thus conception can only occur during approximately three days of each twenty-eight-day cycle. For example, if intercourse occurs more than forty-eight hours before ovulation, the sperm will die, and if it occurs more than twenty-four hours after ovulation, the egg will have died. The rhythm method of birth control is based on this fact (see Chapter 10).

*The average length of life of the sperm and egg are approximate. It may be that their lives will be shorter or longer depending in part on the chemistry of the reproductive system of the woman at the time.

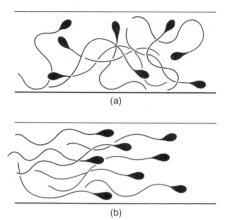

(a)

(b)

Within thirty-six hours after fertilization, the egg divides in half, and then divides again. The dividing continues as the egg floats down the Fallopian tube, with the cells getting smaller with each division (see Figure 11-3). By the time the floating mass of cells reaches the uterus (in about three to four days), it will contain about thirty-six cells. This cluster, called a *blastocyst*, then becomes hollow at the center. The outermost shell of cells, called the *trophoblast*, multiplies

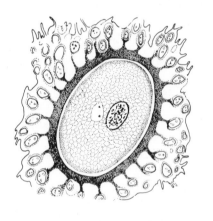

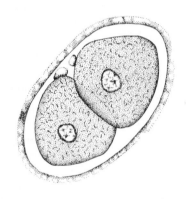

Figure 11-3
Cell division after conception.

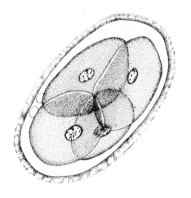

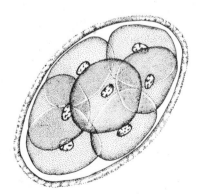

Table 11-1 Male Deaths
per 100 Female Deaths
by Age Group, U.S., 1970

Age	Male Deaths
Under 1	139.6
1–4	122.1
5–14	174.0
15–24	277.5
25–34	204.8
35–44	161.5
45–54	171.6
55–59	193.1
60–64	189.4
65–69	159.2
70–74	133.8
75–79	108.6
80–84	89.5
85 and over	64.5
Total, all ages	128.2

Source: U.S. National Center
for Health Statistics, *Monthly
Vital Statistics Report,
Provisional Statistics, Annual
Summary for the United States,*
1970.
Note: These data do not cover
deaths of U.S. civilians or
members of the armed forces
that occurred outside
of the U.S.

faster, attaches the blastocyst to the uterine walls, and eventually becomes the placenta, umbilical cord, and amniotic sac. The inner cells separate into three layers. The innermost layer (the *endoderm*) will become the inner body parts; the middle layer (the *mesoderm*) will become muscle, bone, blood, kidneys, and sex glands; and the outer layer (the *ectoderm*) will eventually become skin, hair, and nervous tissue (see The Course of Prenatal Development, pp. 336–337).

On the sixth or seventh day after fertilization, the blastocyst will be implanted in the uterine wall and the cells will begin to draw nourishment from the uterine lining.

Boy or Girl?   Sex determination takes place at conception. The female egg always carries an X chromosome. The sperm, however, may be either of two types, one carrying an X chromosome and the other a Y chromosome. If the egg has been fertilized by an X sperm, then the child will be female (XX). If, on the other hand, the egg has been fertilized by a Y sperm, then the child will be male (XY) (see Chapter 2 for a complete discussion).

Many more males are conceived than females. In fact, approximately 140 males are conceived for every 100 females. However, only 106 males are born for every 100 females. We have no conclusive evidence why this is so. Some suggest that the Y sperm move more quickly than the X sperm, thus more reach the egg earlier. Actually, the male is the weaker sex insofar as survival is concerned. In all age groups up to age eighty, males perish at a greater rate than females (see Table 11-1).

Multiple Births   The human female normally conceives only one child at a time, so multiple births have always been unusual. Twins occur about once in every 90 births, triplets once in 9000 births, and quadruplets once in 500,000 births (Katchadourian and Lunde, 1972, p. 124). Mortality rates are significantly higher for multiple births. The infants are often born somewhat prematurely and are usually smaller in size than normal. The famous Dionne quintuplets, five girls, weighed a total of thirteen pounds, six ounces at birth (generally, a baby weighs about seven and a half pounds).

Most twins are *fraternal*, which means they developed from two separate eggs that were fertilized simultaneously. Such twins are no more similar in physical characteristics than are any other siblings (brothers or sisters). About a third of twins are *identical*, which means they developed from the subdivision of a single fertilized egg, and usually shared a common placenta. Unlike fraternal twins, their genetic makeup is identical, so they have very similar physical characteristics, and are always the same sex.

Recently, the so-called fertility drugs have contributed to the multiple birth phenomenon (see Scenes from Marriage, p. 275). Some women who fail to ovulate properly have been given a gonadotropin to stimulate proper ovulation. In numerous cases the use of these hormones has caused multiple births. In one case, an Australian woman

Landrum B. Shettles (1972) aroused much interest and considerable debate with his article "Predetermining Children's Sex." After numerous correlational studies, he offers the following suggestions to help to determine the sex of one's offspring.

A male offspring is more apt to be conceived if:

1. An alkaline douche is used immediately before intercourse. (Add two tablespoons of baking soda to one quart of water.)
2. Intercourse takes place as soon after ovulation as possible.
3. Penile penetration is as deep as possible.

4. The woman achieves orgasm.

A female is more apt to be conceived if these recommendations are reversed.

Shettles' reasoning is as follows: To favor the birth of a boy, it is logical to create an environment in which the smaller, more numerous Y sperms can outdistance the larger X sperms. The age (viability) of the sperm and egg are also important factors in determining whether conception occurs. The availability of a fresh sperm and fresh egg favors a male birth. A fresh egg and an older sperm favors a female birth; this combination is more likely if sexual intercourse occurs two or three days before ovulation. Deep penile penetration during emission results in the deposition of the sperm near the favorable alkaline secretions within the cervix. This, combined with the alkaline orgasmal secretions and an alkaline douche, makes it possible for the Y sperm to outdistance the X sperm in the competitive race to the awaiting egg. By using such concepts, it has been reported that couples can select the genetic sex of their children with an 80 to 85 percent chance of success.

gave birth to nine infants, none of whom survived. With increased understanding of the reproductive functions, the risk of multiple births may be reduced.

How does a woman know if she is pregnant? Since the union of the egg and the sperm does not produce any overt feelings or sensations, the question "Am I pregnant?" isn't easy to answer in the early stages of pregnancy. Although pregnancy is the most common reason for menstruation to stop suddenly in a healthy female, it is certainly not the only reason. For example a woman may miss a period due to stress, illness, or emotional upset, so a missed menstruation is not a sure sign of pregnancy. In addition, about 20 percent of pregnant women have a slight flow or spotting usually during implantation of the fertilized egg into the uterine wall (Katchadourian and Lunde, 1972, p. 76; Schulz, 1979, pp. 129–130). In about two to three weeks after the missed period, some other symptoms of pregnancy will probably occur. The most common is feeling nauseous in the morning ("morning sickness"), though vomiting usually doesn't occur. The nausea usually disappears by the twelfth week of pregnancy. The breasts and nipples will probably also begin to undergo changes in shape and coloration. The breasts will probably become fuller and the areolae (the pig-

Pregnancy

mented areas around the nipples) will begin to darken, and veins will become more prominent. Sometimes the breasts will tingle, throb, or hurt because of the swelling. There may be an increased need to urinate, partly because the growing uterus is pressing against the bladder and partly because of the hormonal changes that are taking place. Again, somewhere around the twelfth week of pregnancy, the uterus will be higher in the abdomen and will no longer press against the bladder, so urination will return to normal. The hormonal changes may also cause feelings of fatigue and sleepiness. Some women find that they need to sleep more often and for longer periods and are always tired during the first few months of pregnancy. Sometimes there are increased vaginal secretions. However, some women do not experience any of these symptoms, some experience only a few, and none experience them severely.

Pregnancy may also have some cosmetic effects. Skin blemishes will often abate and the complexion will look healthy and glowing. In the latter stages of pregnancy pink stretch marks may appear on the abdomen, although most of them will disappear after birth.

Pregnancy Tests Usually, a physician can tell if a woman is pregnant by a simple pelvic examination. It is possible to actually feel the uterine enlargement and softening of the cervix by manual examination after six to eight weeks of pregnancy. However, since most women want to know as soon as possible if they are pregnant, chemical tests are used to discover pregnancy earlier. The well-known frog and rabbit tests for pregnancy are based on the fact that a special gonadotropic hormone is produced following implantation of the fertilized egg in the uterine wall. The hormone is found in the woman's urine about ten days to two weeks after her menstrual period would normally have started. The test involves injecting a small amount of the subject's urine into an animal that has not had its first ovulation. If gonadotropic hormones are present, they will cause the animal's ovaries to mature and form eggs within two days. Although these tests have been used for years, they are awkward and slow because the animals have to be cared for and it takes several days for the animal to react to the injection.

More recently, a test of agglutination, the clumping together of human chorionic gonadotropin (HCG), is being used. This process avoids the use of animals and takes only a few minutes. A reaction will occur from one to fourteen days after menstruation should have started. The test involves taking a urine specimen in the morning and placing a drop on a slide. The proper chemicals are then added. In a negative reaction, agglutination will be visible in two minutes. If the woman is pregnant, no agglutination will occur at two minutes (see Figure 11-4).

Several tests examine the woman's blood serum, also seeking changed levels of HCG. One is called a radioimmunoassay (RIA). In this test it takes about seventy-two hours of incubation to get a reading. Even newer is the Biocept-G technique that has reduced the necessary incubation period to a mere thirty minutes and gives accu-

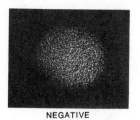

NEGATIVE   POSITIVE

Figure 11-4
Negative and positive pregnancy test reactions. In a negative test, agglutination (clumping) will be visible within two minutes. In a positive test, no agglutination will occur at two minutes.

rate results within a few days after a missed menstrual period. In this case, a blood sample is mixed with radioactive iodine with which the HCG will react if present.

The tests are considered 95 to 98 percent accurate, but can give inaccurate results if they are performed too early (before enough hormone shows up in the urine), if there are errors in handling or storing or labeling the urine, or if the test animal (if an animal test is used) doesn't respond as it should (Boston Women's Health Book Collective, 1976). Sometimes it may take several tests to determine if a woman is pregnant because she may produce very low levels of hormone and there may not be enough in her urine to give a positive result even though she is pregnant. It is very rare for a pregnancy test to give a positive result when the woman is not pregnant.

It is also quite possible to have a *false pregnancy* (pseudocyesis) in which the early physical signs may be present though the woman is not really pregnant. Pregnancy tests, which are inexpensive, will clarify the situation and usually end the symptoms (unless there is a physical problem causing the symptoms).

Because the menstrual cycle is easily affected by one's emotions, uneasiness and emotional upset about engaging in sexual activity may disrupt a woman's monthly cycle enough to delay her period or even cause her to skip a period altogether. Unfortunately, emotional reaction and physical reaction interact to increase her problems in this case. For example, if a woman has sexual intercourse and worries that she might be pregnant, the worry may actually postpone her period, causing her further worry, which further upsets her menstrual timing, which causes further worry, and so on. Again a pregnancy test is 98 percent accurate if done by a professional, inexpensive, and a way to resolve the worry.

Since 1976, a number of home pregnancy-test kits have come onto the market, selling for around $10 (see *Newsweek*, Sept. 3, 1979, p. 69). They work on the same system as the HCG tests we have already discussed and may be used from seven to ten days after a menstrual period is missed. Although the accuracy of these tests is high if they are used correctly, misuse can lead to false conclusions. Doctors fear that diagnostic errors with such home tests may lead to serious health hazards. For example, the early stages of uterine cancer may produce a false positive reading and thereby delay treatment of the cancer. A false negative would lead a woman to conclude that she is not pregnant and she may well continue to take drugs or smoke and threaten the well-being of her unborn child. A doctor's visit costs money but it is well worth the precaution if you think you are pregnant. There are clinics such as those run by Planned Parenthood that give pregnancy tests for a minimal charge, or for nothing.

The following comments capture some of the feelings that a woman may have as the early signs of pregnancy begin to appear.

> Your period is late.
>
> Well, there's nothing unusual in that, you tell yourself. You just need a good night's sleep, or maybe you're catching a cold.
>
> After a few days, you say, "It's late because I'm anxious." You try to think about something else. You try so hard you can hardly bring yourself to wake up in the morning — as long as you stay asleep, you don't have to think about anything at all. "I'm exhausted," you say, "that's why it's late."
>
> After a week has gone by, it begins to look as if your period is not just late, it is altogether absent.
>
> Even that is not so unusual. You have heard of many women who have skipped periods completely during times of stress or illness. You begin to search your memory for other things you have heard — about hot baths that bring on delayed menstruation, about running up five flights of stairs, jumping off porches, taking laxatives. But mixed in with the hearsay and old wives' tales, you cannot quite force out of your mind one hard fact:
>
> You had intercourse last month, so the odds are more than even that you are pregnant.
>
> This is somehow unthinkable if you have not planned to be pregnant, and especially if you have never been pregnant before. It is *your* body, known, familiar; you realize in an abstract way that it is equipped for pregnancy, but the idea that it should suddenly begin to function in this strange and unfamiliar way without your willing or intending it seems utterly unreasonable. How can it happen to you? (Guttmacher, 1973, pp. 1–2).

The Course of Prenatal Development   The average duration of pregnancy is 266 days, or 38 weeks, from the time of conception. For the first two months, the developing baby is called an embryo; after that, it is called a fetus. (The change in name denotes that all of the parts are now present.) The sequence of its development is shown in Table 11-2.

Environmental Causes of Congenital Problems   Although the developing fetus is in a well-protected environment, it is still possible for negative influences from outside to affect it. Sometimes these cause birth defects, which are called *congenital* problems. (These should not be confused with *genetic* problems, which are inherited through the genes.) Alan Guttmacher estimates that some 15 million persons in the United States suffer from some sort of congenital defect (Guttmacher, 1973b). The National Center for Health Statistics also estimates that about 1300 children aged one through four die each year because of congenital problems.

The developing fetus gets its nourishment from the mother's blood through the umbilical cord and placenta. There is no direct

DES (diethylstilbestrol) is a synthetic estrogen. During the 1940s, doctors in Boston prescribed DES for pregnant women who had histories of miscarriage, bleeding, or diabetes because they felt that low estrogen levels accounted for the problems. In 1948, they reviewed 632 pregnancies treated with DES in fifteen states and generally found that the treatment had reduced the pregnancy problems.

Based in part on these generally positive findings, other physicians began to prescribe DES to pregnant women. In 1966, a form of vaginal cancer, clear cell adenocarcinoma, began to appear in young women between the ages of fourteen and twenty-two. This had been extremely rare in such young women heretofore. After much investigation, Drs. David Poskanzer and Howard Ulfelder revealed a significant link between the cancer and exposure to DES before birth. In 1971, a registry was established to gather more information on this rare condition. By 1978, a total of 350 cases had been reported. In about two-thirds of these cases, the mother of the women exhibiting the cancer had been given DES during her pregnancy.

After a great deal of research, there seems to be a clear link between exposure to DES before birth and increased risk of vaginal or cervical cancer. However, the risk is not high, being estimated at no more than 1.4 per thousand exposed daughters up to age twenty-four, and the risk may be even lower. The point of the DES story is: when one is pregnant, the safest course is to avoid ingestion of all drugs as much as possible. Unlike thalidomide, the effect of DES on a few fetuses was very limited and appeared only years later.

Adapted from Annabel Hecht. "DES: The Drug with Unexpected Legacies." *FDA Consumer.* May, 1979, pp. 14–17.

intermingling of the blood, though some substances the mother takes can be transmitted to the fetus. When you consider the extremely small size of the fetus during its early months, you can see how a small amount of a substance can do a lot of harm. We'll take a look at some of the more common causes of congenital problems below, but remember that this is an area where much has still to be learned, so, if you are pregnant, it is wise to avoid taking any drugs, especially during the first three months, and also to restrain the use of alcohol and/or cigarettes throughout the pregnancy.

DRUGS If the mother is addicted to a narcotic, especially heroin (and also methadone), the child will be born addicted, and will suffer withdrawal symptoms if it is not given heroin and then gradually withdrawn from it.

Furthermore, most common prescription drugs affect the fetus. According to The Boston Women's Health Book Collective (1976, p. 256), "Some antihistamines may produce malformations. General anesthetics at high concentrations may produce malformations. Cortisone reaches the fetus and placenta and may cause alterations. Antithyroid may cause goiter in infants. And tetracycline may cause deformities in babies' bones and stain their teeth." *The New York Times* (December 12, 1974) adds:

Table 11-2   Prenatal Development

Time Elapsed	Embryonic or Fetal Characteristics	Illustrations
28 days 4 weeks 1 month	¼ – ½ inch long head is one-third of embryo brain has lobes and rudimentary nervous system appears as hollow tube heart begins to beat blood vessels form and blood flows through them simple kidneys, liver, and digestive tract appear rudiments of eyes, ears, and nose appear small tail	
56 days 8 weeks 2 months	2 inches long 1/30th of an ounce in weight human face with eyes, ears, nose, lips, tongue arms have pawlike hands almost all internal organs begin to develop brain coordinates functioning of other organs heart beats steadily and blood circulates complete cartilage skeleton, beginning to be replaced by bone tail beginning to be absorbed now called a fetus sex organs begin to differentiate	
84 days 12 weeks 3 months	3 inches long 1 ounce in weight begins to be active number of nerve-muscle connections almost triples sucking reflex begins to appear can swallow and may even breathe eyelids fused shut (will stay shut until the 6th month) but eyes are sensitive to light internal organs begin to function	
112 days 16 weeks 4 months	6–7 inches long 4 ounces in weight body now growing faster than head skin on hands and feet forms individual patterns eyebrows and head hair begin to show fine, downylike hair (lanugo) covers body movements may now be felt	

Time Elapsed	Embryonic or Fetal Characteristics	Illustrations
140 days 20 weeks 5 months	10–12 inches long 8–16 ounces in weight skeleton hardens nails form on fingers and toes skin covered with cheesy wax heartbeat now loud enough to be heard with a stethoscope muscles are stronger definite strong kicking and turning can be startled by noises	
168 days 24 weeks 6 months	12–14 inches long 1½ pounds in weight can open and close eyelids grows eyelashes much more active, exercising muscles may suck thumb may be able to breathe if born prematurely	
196 days 28 weeks 7 months	15 inches long 2½ pounds in weight beginning to develop fatty tissue internal organs (especially respiratory and digestive) still developing baby born now has fair chance of survival	
224 days 32 weeks 8 months	16½ inches long 4 pounds in weight fatty layer complete	
266 days 38 weeks 9 months	Birth 19–20 inches long 7–7½ pounds in weight (average) 95 percent of full-term babies born alive in the U.S. will survive	

Among the drugs known to damage the human fetus are the antibiotics streptomycin, tetracycline, and sulfonamides taken near the end of pregnancy; excessive amounts of vitamins A, D, B₆, and K; certain barbiturates, opiates, and other central nervous system depressants when taken near the time of delivery; and the synthetic hormone progestin, which can masculinize the female fetus.

In addition, animal studies have implicated such common drugs as aspirin, antinausea compounds, phenobarbital, and the tranquilizer chlorpromazine as possible causes of fetal abnormalities.

The article also mentions that two commonly prescribed tranquilizers, Librium and Equanil/Miltown, may cause defects when taken early in pregnancy (for a more complete discussion of the effects of drugs on the fetus, see Bowes et al, 1970).

The saddest and most widely publicized instance of drug-related birth defects came from the widespread use of thalidomide. Thalidomide was a very effective sleeping pill and tranquilizer, believed to be safer than most other sedatives. It was widely used in Europe during the 1960s and was sampled by many women in the United States before cases of seriously deformed babies began to get attention. Many of these children had only small, flipperlike appendages attached to their shoulders rather than arms and hands. Others had stunted arms and legs. Needless to say, the drug was taken off the market, and legislation requiring more stringent testing of drugs in this country was passed.

INFECTIOUS DISEASES   Certain infectious diseases, if contracted by the mother, especially during the first three months of pregnancy, may harm the developing fetus. The best-known of these is German measles (rubella), which can cause blindness, deafness, or heart defects in the child. Some women who contract German measles elect to have an abortion rather than risk having a deformed child.

Venereal diseases also affect the fetus. Herpes (see p. 283), for example, can cause a spontaneous abortion, or inflammation of the brain or other brain damage. Syphilis and gonorrhea can be contracted by the newborn baby. If the mother has syphilis, the baby will have the symptoms of the second and last syphilitic stages (see pp. 283–284). Gonorrhea can affect the newborn's eyesight, and as a precaution, silver nitrate or another prophylactic agent is applied to the eyes of all newborns. This has almost totally eradicated the problem.

RADIATION   According to B. A. Kogan (1973, p. 167):

Radiation reaching the testes or ovaries, and thereby the reproductive cells, can cause changes in the structure of DNA (genes). Mutation rates are increased by radiation. Since over 99 percent of mutations are harmful and since they do accumulate in man, the threat to future generations is apparent. Depending on the amount, moreover, radiation may cause chromosomal breaks and translocations. So another danger of radiation is related to chromosomal aberrations. Thus radiation may be one of the causes of a wide variety of genetic disorders, ranging from the mental retardation of phenylketonuria to the mental retardation of Mongolism (1973, p. 167).

Radiation, of course, penetrates the mother's body, so it will also reach and affect the fetus. The worst abnormalities occur if the mother is X-rayed during the first three months of pregnancy, when the embryo's major organs are developing. Even one pelvic X-ray can cause gross fetal defects during this period. Thus, if pregnancy is suspected, the woman should avoid all X-rays, even dental X-rays.

Rh BLOOD DISEASE The Rh factor (named for the rhesus monkey, in whose blood it was first isolated) is a chemical that lies on the surface of the red blood cells in most people. People with the chemical are considered Rh positive; those without are Rh negative. Only about 15 percent of white and 7 percent of black Americans are Rh negative. If a child inherits Rh-positive blood from the father, but the mother is Rh-negative, the fetus' Rh-positive factor is perceived as a foreign substance by the mother's body. Like a disease, it thus causes the mother's body to produce antibodies in her blood. If these enter the fetus through a capillary rupture in the placental membrane, they destroy red blood cells, which can lead to anemia, jaundice, and eventual death unless corrective steps are taken. Only small amounts, if any, of the child's antibody-stimulating Rh factor reach the mother through the placenta during pregnancy, so the first child is usually safe. However, during delivery, the afterbirth (placenta and remaining cord) loosens and bleeds, thus releasing the Rh-positive substance into the mother that then causes her system to produce antibodies. Once these are produced, she is much more easily stimulated to produce them during future pregnancies involving Rh-positive children. Thus, each succeeding child will be more affected than the previous child. With complete replacement of the child's blood at birth, many can be saved. An even better treatment is now available that can essentially eradicate Rh problems. An Rh immunoglobulin that blocks the mother's immunity system can be injected into the mother, thereby preventing production of the antibodies that attack the red blood cells of the fetus. Before this treatment became available, about 10,000 infants died and another 20,000 had major birth defects due to Rh complications (Apgar & Beck, 1973).

SMOKING Heavy smoking adversely affects pregnancy. It increases the risk of spontaneous abortion, of premature birth, and of low birth weight in babies brought to term. Premature birth and low birth weight increase the chances of infant sickness and death. Babies of smoking mothers also remain smaller than babies of nonsmoking mothers for some time. Obviously it would be best if pregnant women cut down on their smoking or stopped altogether (*Human Nature*, 1978, p. 13).

Controlling Birth Defects Once a woman learns that she is pregnant, she should arrange for regular visits to a physician. Regular prenatal care will help to avoid birth defects and will help dispel any fears she may have.

DIET The expectant mother should eat a good, well-balanced diet with plenty of fluids. If there is any doubt about the adequacy of the diet, the doctor should be consulted since the mother's diet has a direct effect on the fetus. Protein and vitamin deficiency can cause physical weakness, stunted growth, rickets, scurvy, and even mental retardation in the fetus (Montagu, 1962). Poor diets can also cause spontaneous abortions and miscarriages or lead to stillborn children.

An inadequate diet leaves the mother more prone to illness and complications during pregnancy, both of which may cause premature birth and/or low birth weight. As we have seen, premature and low-birth-weight babies are more prone to illness and possible death than normal-term babies.

Good nutrition helps prevent stillbirth, low birth weight, and prematurity. It also helps prevent infections, anemia in mothers, and brain damage and retardation in children. Good nutrition lessens complications during pregnancy, and helps mothers feel better, and have strong, lively babies.

AMNIOCENTESIS Recently a test has been developed for detecting genetically caused birth defects, such as Down's syndrome (Mongolism), amino acid disorders, hemophilia, and muscular dystrophy, to name some of the more common disorders. The procedure is called *amniocentesis* and involves taking a sample of the amniotic fluid and studying sloughed off fetal cells found in it. Amniocentesis should be done between the fourteenth and sixteenth week of pregnancy. The test can be performed in a doctor's office, though the laboratory work will take another fourteen to eighteen days to complete. In addition, the fetus' sex can be recognized by this test.

In general, it is a good idea to have the test if you have already had a child with a hereditary biochemical disease; if you are a carrier of hemophilia or muscular dystrophy; if you have already had a child with a genetic abnormality; and if you are over forty, since the risk of having a child with a genetic abnormality increases with age.

If the test indicates the presence of a birth defect, the woman, her husband, and the doctor can discuss their options, including possible abortion.

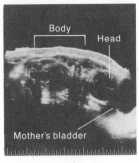

Sonograph of fetus.

ULTRASOUND IN OBSTETRICS   Ultrasound sonography, because it is safe and noninvasive, has become a major means of obtaining data about the placenta, fetus, and fetal organs during pregnancy. It can replace the X-ray as a method of viewing the developing child in the uterus, thus avoiding radiation exposure for both mother and child (Hobbins, 1979).

Basically, ultrasound works on the principle that different tissues give off different speed echoes to high frequency sound waves directed at them. Thus, by moving a transducer (sound emitter) across the maternal abdomen, an echogram outline of the various organs/fetus can be obtained. Using a "real time" transducer that gives off several simultaneous signals from slightly differing sources, one can obtain a picture showing movement of the different organs, such as the heart. The echogram allows the physician to learn about the position, size, and state of development of the fetus at any time after about the first ten weeks of pregnancy. This procedure can, for example, tell a physician ahead of birth if the fetus is going to be born in the normal head-first position or in some problem position (Wells & Devey, 1978).

Ultrasound is a very simple procedure compared to X-rays because the picture is immediately available. The patient's abdomen is greased for good contact and then a small transducer (about the size and shape of a small tape recorder microphone) is moved across her abdomen, painting a black and white picture on the screen as it moves.

Intercourse During Pregnancy   Although some people regard intercourse during pregnancy with suspicion, research indicates that there is nothing wrong with it (Masters & Johnson, 1966). Indeed, the couple should not lose the close contact as well as physical relief afforded through intercourse.

> There is some evidence that erotic feelings increase for the woman during the second trimester of pregnancy. By the third trimester, most women lose sexual interest to a degree. Couples should exercise some care to avoid excessive pressure on the abdomen, deep penile penetration, and infection. Since the uterine contractions of orgasm are similar to labor contractions, intercourse during the last three weeks of term should probably be avoided. Also spotting or bleeding or pain contraindicates intercourse. In the later stages of pregnancy, the rear entry position with the wife lying on her side is usually most comfortable (McCary, 1967, p. 314).

If a woman has miscarried or has been warned that she is apt to miscarry, intercourse should be avoided during the first three months of pregnancy, especially around the time the period would be due. But such prolonged avoidance of intercourse is quite unusual. In most normal pregnancies, intercourse poses no real threat to the pregnancy. Indeed, some doctors suggest that the contractions of orgasm are helpful to pregnancy since they strengthen the uterine muscles. Intercourse also provides exercise for the muscles of the pelvic floor. And, in addition, focusing on the feelings of complete relaxation after orgasm can help one to learn to relax during labor contractions.

Many women report that sexual relations are very important to them during pregnancy. They feel that continued sexual contact maintains their close emotional ties with their husbands. They feel that their husbands' interest shows acceptance of the pregnancy and of their changing body shape. In other words, sexual contact means tenderness, caring, sharing, and love. Many women also feel freer in their sexual behavior since they obviously no longer need to fear pregnancy.

However, in later pregnancy there is need for caution and gentleness. The woman will often feel bloated and uncomfortable. Positions will become more limited as the pregnancy progresses. Toward the very end, a strong orgasm might induce labor, although the chances are small unless labor is imminent anyway. It is probably best to avoid intercourse during the last few weeks before birth. This does not mean, however, to avoid lovemaking. To hold one another, to caress, to be intimate is certainly important as birth draws near. It will help to allay anxieties and let the expectant mother know that she is not alone but has loving support.

Birth
By the time nine months have passed, the mother-to-be is usually anxious to have her child. She has probably gained somewhat more than twenty pounds. On the average, the extra weight is distributed as follows:

Amniotic fluid	2 lbs.
Baby	7 – 8 lbs.
Breast enlargement	2 lbs.
Placenta	1 lb.
Retained fluids and fat	6 + lbs.
Uterine enlargement	2 lbs.

There are two important objections to gaining too much extra weight: excessive weight can strain the circulatory system and heart and many women find it difficult to lose the extra weight after the baby is born. On the other hand, dieting during pregnancy to remain within an arbitrary twenty pound weight gain limit is also risky since, as we pointed out earlier, good nutrition is important during pregnancy.

Although 266 days is the average length of time a child is carried, the normal range varies from 240 days to 300 days. It is therefore difficult for the physician to be exact when estimating the time of delivery. Actually, there is only about a 50 percent chance that a child will be born within a week of the date the doctor determines. In

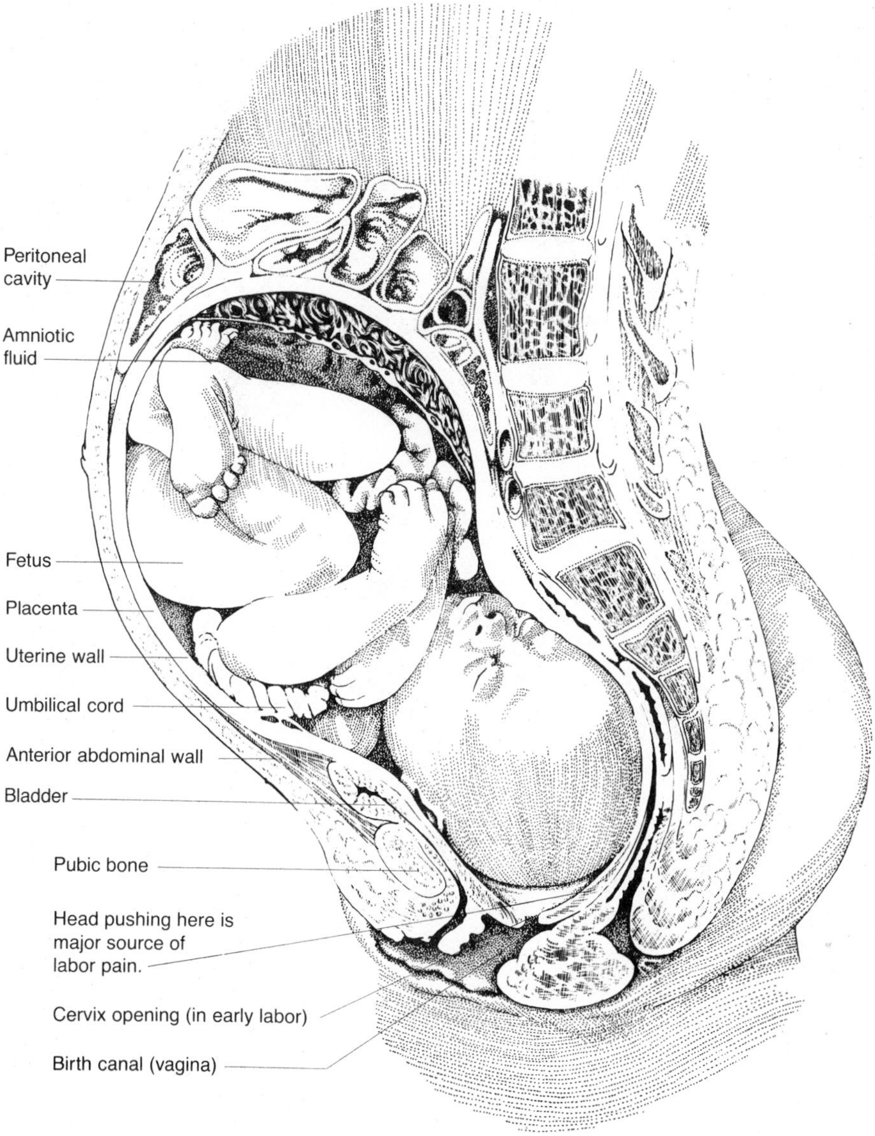

Figure 11-5
The position of the
fetus prior to birth.

Peritoneal
cavity

Amniotic
fluid

Fetus

Placenta

Uterine wall

Umbilical cord

Anterior abdominal wall

Bladder

Pubic bone

Head pushing here is
major source of
labor pain.

Cervix opening (in early labor)

Birth canal (vagina)

general, the expected birth date will probably come and go without
any sign of imminent birth. Although this can be wearisome for the
expectant mother, it is perfectly normal.

Labor Three to four weeks before birth, the fetus "drops" slightly
lower in the uterus (called *lightening*) and is normally in a head-first
position (see Figure 11-5). The cervix (the opening to the uterus)
begins to soften and dilate (open). There may be occasional contractions of the uterus which the first-time pregnant woman may mistake
for labor (false labor). These early contractions are irregular and are
usually not painful.

Essentially, there are three stages to labor. The first two are
illustrated in Figure 11-6. The *first stage* is the longest, lasting eight to

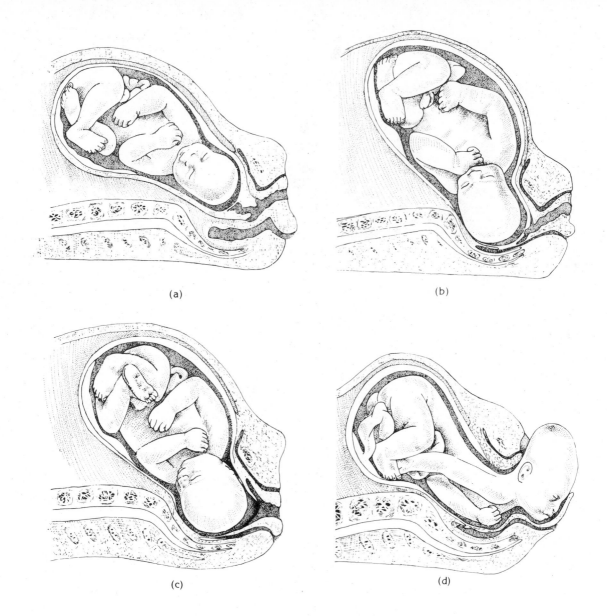

(a)

(b)

(c)

(d)

Figure 11-6

Events in the birth process.
(a) Before labor begins;
(b) early stages of labor,
dilation of cervix begins;
(c) cervix completely
dilated; baby's head starts
to turn; (d) late stage
of labor; baby's head
begins to emerge.

twenty hours on the average for the first child and three to eight hours for subsequent children (Kogan, 1973, p. 201). During this time the cervix must dilate enough for the baby to pass through. (The contracted and closed cervix has held the baby in the uterus until now.) The bag of amniotic fluid, a salt solution which suspends, cushions, and maintains the embryo at an even temperature, will break some time during the labor process, except in about 10 percent of pregnant women who will experience breaking shortly before labor commences. The uterine contractions become more frequent and longer lasting until the baby finally descends into the birth canal (vagina). During this first stage, there is little the mother can do except rest, try to relax, and try to remain as comfortable as possible.

Guide to First-Stage Labor Progress

Signs of Labor

1. Bloody show/mucous plug
2. Gush of water
3. Contractions

Real labor will include #3 and may or may not include #1 & #2. You may have "false labor" for days or weeks before the onset of real labor. Your due date is not always the best guide as to when labor will start.

Ways to Check for Real Labor

1. Change of activity does not change contractions.
2. Contractions increase in length.
3. Contractions become closer together.
4. Contractions increase in intensity.

Call the Doctor When

1. Contractions are 10 minutes apart or less, lasting 45-60 seconds or more for 1 hour.
2. Bag of waters breaks.
3. Anything more than a bloody show appears from vagina.
4. Anything unusual happens.

Early Labor

1. The cervix is thinning and opening or dilating slightly.
2. Labor is generally easy at this point and spirits high.
3. Continue your activities and pay attention — it's fun.

It's the Real Thing

1. Contractions are regular now and the cervix is opening.
2. Spirits are high but the realization that labor is work is starting to dawn.
3. Relax and use slow easy abdominal breathing. Going to bed is not necessary unless desired.

Late Labor

1. This is really hard work. Contractions are intense and close.
2. It takes real concentration on relaxation and abdominal breathing.
3. Birth is getting near.

Transition

1. Confusion is perhaps the best definition. Changing gears going from first-stage contractions to second-stage contractions.
2. Contractions may get closer together or farther apart.
3. Ride with each contraction; it may be your last in first stage.
4. The urge to push signals second stage.

At first the contractions may be thirty minutes apart but gradually they will come more often until they will be occurring every few minutes. The expectant mother should head for the hospital as soon as she ascertains that she is having regular labor pains.

In the *second stage*, the uterine contractions push the child down through the vagina into the outside world with about a hundred pounds of force. During this stage, the mother can actively help the process by pushing or bearing down, thereby adding another fifteen pounds or so to the pressure created by the uterine contractions. This stage may be as short as fifteen to twenty minutes or can last an hour or two.

The *third stage* is delivering the afterbirth or detached placenta, which occurs five to twenty minutes after the birth of the child. During this time the uterus contracts and begins to return to its normal size, and there is minor bleeding.

Although there is a certain amount of pain connected with a normal birth, knowledge of the birth process, the source of labor pain, and a relaxed and confident mental attitude will reduce such pain to a minimum. It is wise for both expectant parents to take classes that teach about the impending birth. Local Red Cross units, county health facilities, and adult education programs usually offer such courses. As mentioned earlier, prenatal care from a doctor should be sought as soon as one becomes pregnant. Although most births are normal and as described, a certain number will be abnormal such as when the child presents feet first rather than head first. In many cases the doctor can recognize the potential problem and be prepared ahead of time.

Fetal Monitoring   During the past few years, fetal monitoring during birth has become more popular. During labor, electronic sensors are placed on the mother's abdomen. During the second stage of birth, an electrode is attached to the baby's scalp. These electrodes record the baby's heartbeat as well as the uterine contractions. Ultrasound techniques (p. 341) also display a picture of the baby and offer another measure of heart beat. These monitoring techniques allow the physician to keep close watch on the baby. Fetal distress can be recognized quickly.

Considerable criticism has been aimed at this kind of technical monitoring, mainly because it is associated with increased caesarean section births (p. 347). However, many claim that such monitoring has reduced infant mortality rates. It seems obvious that monitoring of both mother and baby during birth can be important to successful birth. Whether or not monitoring leads to unnecessary caesarean births, as the critics claim, really is a separate question that should be investigated rather than put forward as an argument to cease monitoring.

Birth Pain   The uterine contractions, which are simple muscle contractions, usually don't cause pain, though prolonged or overly strong contractions can, of course, cause cramping. The majority of pain arises from the pressure of the baby's head (the largest and hardest part of the baby at the time of birth) against the cervix, the opening into the birth canal. In the early stages of labor, the contractions of the uterus push the child's head against the still contracted cervix and this point becomes the major source of labor pain. By trying to relax at the onset of a uterine contraction, by breathing more shallowly so as to raise the diaphragm from the uterus, and by lying on the side with the knees somewhat drawn up, a woman can reduce labor pain to a minimum.

Once the child's head passes through the cervix, there is little or no pain as it passes on through the vagina. Hormonal action has softened the vagina to such an extent by this point that it can stretch up to seven times its normal size. An additional difficulty may occur at birth as the child passes out of the mother into the outside world. There is often a slight tearing of the perineum or skin between the vaginal and anal openings since the skin may have to stretch beyond its limits to allow the infant to exit. In most cases the doctor will make a small clean incision called an *episiotomy* so that the skin does not tear. The incision is sewn after the delivery.

As early as 1882, under certain circumstances such as when a baby is too large to pass through the mother's pelvis, or a very long, hard labor, the baby is removed via a *Caesarean section*. In this operation, an incision is made through the abdominal and uterine walls and the baby is removed. The recovery period is longer than for a normal birth. Although many people believe to the contrary, it is quite possible for a woman to have several babies in this manner or to have one by Caesarean section and the next normally. This operation is almost always done as a last resort to save the baby's or mother's life (McCary, 1967, p. iii).

Recently the percentage of 'C'-section births has increased, rising to around fifteen percent of all births and even higher in specific hospitals. This has led to controversy because the C-section is more traumatic to the mother's body than is natural birth. Interestingly, it is far less traumatic to the child since there is no prolonged pressure on the child as there is in the normal birth process.

The hospitals contend that better monitoring of the child just prior to birth and throughout the process leads to early recognition of possible problems and many of these can be headed off by a C-section. They admit that monitoring has led to a higher proportion of C-sections but it has also served to reduce infant mortality.

The popular but erroneous legend that Julius Caesar was delivered surgically gives the operation its name. Probably the term *Caesarean* originated from an ancient Roman law, which was later incorporated into a legal code called the Lex Caesarea. This statute, aimed at trying to save the child's life, made it mandatory that an operation be performed on a woman who died in the advanced stages of pregnancy (McCary, 1967, p. iii).

Natural Childbirth   In recent years, many women, especially young women having their first child, have sought an alternative to the automatic use of anesthesia and the rather mechanical way many American hospitals used to handle childbirth. Many years ago (1932), Grantly Dick-Read coined the phrase "natural childbirth" and suggested in his book *Childbirth Without Fear* that understanding of birth procedures by the mother could break the pattern of fear, tension, and pain too often associated with childbirth. Thus natural childbirth means knowledgeable childbirth, and not simply childbirth without anesthesia or at home.

General anesthesia for childbirth recently has become much less popular, even in hospitals, since it slows labor and depresses the child's activity, thus making the birth more difficult even though less painful. The caudal or spinal block is now administered in about 10 to 20 percent of births. The spinal block produces a temporary loss of feeling below the waist. It is normally given in stage two of labor, when the baby has passed into the birth canal or vagina. Advocates of natural childbirth question the value of this procedure since most of the mother's pain is over once the child is in the birth canal.

Much more common today is paracervical anesthesia, which involves injection of novocaine or a similar pain-killing substance into the area around the cervix. This quickly deadens the area, thus block-

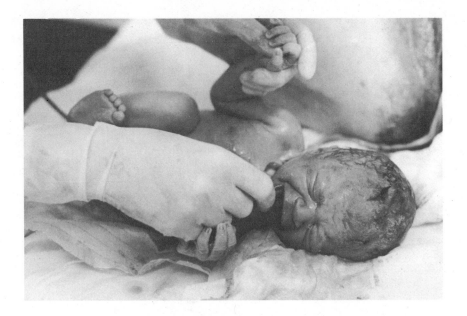

ing out the pain. It is similar to being injected in the gums around a tooth that a dentist will fill. The anesthetic action is very localized and has little if any effect on the baby. Mother is, of course, completely conscious and able to participate in the birth.

Hypnosis is also being used more frequently during labor and delivery to help relax the mother and reduce her sensations of pain. It is particularly useful for women who cannot tolerate the drugs used in anesthesia. It cannot be used with everyone and, of course, the doctor must be knowledgeable about it. It is worth investigating as those who use it report relaxed and relatively uncomplicated deliveries.

Today, more and more physicians are letting the woman decide whether she wants an anesthetic, and if so, what type. Obviously it is important that the expectant mother is informed of the benefits and disadvantages of the available forms of anesthesia so that she can make her choice intelligently.

A couple interested in natural childbirth will find that there are now numerous sources of training and information available.* As mentioned earlier, Red Cross facilities, county medical units, and evening adult schools often provide childbirth preparation classes. The classes provide information on the birth processes, what to expect, and how to facilitate the natural processes. The woman is also taught physical exercises that will help prepare her body for the coming birth. She learns techniques of breathing to help the natural processes along and to reduce the amount of pain she would otherwise experience.

*There are a number of free sources of information on natural childbirth: You can write to the: American Society for Psychoprophylaxis in Obstetrics, 36 West 96th Street, New York, N.Y. 10025; the Association of Mothers for Educated Childbirth (concerned with home delivery), Box 9030, Far Rockaway, N.Y. 11691; and the International Childbirth Education Association/Education Committee, Box 22, Hillside, N.J. 07205.

We have already noted that one of the basic principles underlying natural childbirth is that knowledge reduces fear and reduced fear means less tension and pain. The other basic principle of natural childbirth is to make the mother and father (see below) active participants in the birth of their child rather than passive spectators. For instance, controlled breathing (with the father helping to pace the breathing) supplies the right amount of oxygen to the working muscles, giving them the energy they need to function efficiently. Voluntarily relaxing the other muscles helps to focus all energy on the laboring muscles. Another aspect of the breathing exercises is to focus attention on responding to the contractions, which keeps attention from focusing on the pain. The Boston Women's Health Book Collective notes that selective attention doesn't

> give our minds time or room to register that we might be feeling pain. As a result, some women say they never really felt any pain during labor; others say that feelings of pain kept surfacing but that they were almost always able to control those feelings with increased concentration on the breathing techniques. One woman wrote that there was a kind of beauty in her acceptance of the pain she felt: "I don't think pain is necessarily bad. I had a short, hard labor, and it was clear to me that the incredible euphoria that I experienced afterward was in part a function of the fact that it was very painful. It really was almost positive pain, really worth it in retrospect" (1976, p. 275).

Since the couple has decided to have the child together, it is also important that they learn together about the processes involved, and that the husband is not kept a spectator during the actual labor and delivery. It will be important for the couple to check if the hospital they plan to use will allow the father into the labor and delivery rooms so that he can be there to give psychological support and comfort to the mother. During the early stages of labor, he will be able to remind her of what to do as the contractions increase, he can keep track of the time intervals between contractions, can monitor her breathing, can remind her to relax, massage her (if she finds that a help), and can keep her informed of her progress. In other words, he can help by *sharing* the experience with her. The Bradley and Lamaze methods urge the husband to learn about the birth process and actively participate in it.

Of course, once the baby has passed through the cervix into the birth canal (vagina), things will happen so fast and the woman will be so involved with the imminent birth that the husband's presence and help will be less important.

Rooming-In More and more hospitals are allowing *rooming-in*, which means that the mother is allowed to keep her baby with her, rather than having the child remain in a nursery. Rooming-in is especially helpful to the breast-feeding mother. But both mother and newborn benefit from the physical closeness. The child will cry less since it will get attention and be fed when it's hungry. Many hospitals are planning for rooming-in by connecting the nursery to the mother's room, thus allowing her free access to her infant. In these hospitals, the baby is placed in a drawerlike crib that the mother may pull into her room whenever she wants. If she is tired, she simply places the child into the drawer and pushes the infant back into the nursery where it is cared for.

Alternative Birth Centers Some hospitals have created home-like settings for childbirth. Relatives and friends are allowed to visit during much of the childbirth process. Barring complications, childbirth takes place in the same room that the mother is in during her entire stay at the center. Couples interested in the birth center must apply in advance. The mother-to-be must be examined to be as certain as possible that she will have a normal delivery. In addition, the birth center usually requires that the couple attend childbirth classes. The birth center serves as a compromise between normal hospital birth and home birth. It is part of the continuing trend by hospitals to make childbirth less mechanical and more an experience in which the couple participates as fully as possible.

Home Births Recently some women have elected to have their children at home rather than in a hospital. At home the woman is in familiar surroundings, can choose her own attendants, and can follow whatever procedures soothe and encourage her (have music playing, for example). At home, birth is also a family affair.

But, of course, the immediate question that comes to mind is how safe is home birth? In Europe, where home birth is common, statistics indicate that home birth is just as safe as hospital birth (Boston Women's Health Book Collective, 1976, pp. 269–270). American doctors do not agree and cite many instances of tragedy with home birth that could have been avoided in a hospital. The amount of risk could be reduced by careful prenatal screening of the mother and backup emergency care. If the prenatal screening indicates conditions that might involve a complicated delivery, then the woman should have her baby in a hospital that has the facilities to deal with possible problems.

The emergency backup for a home delivery should include a person who is medically qualified (either a doctor, paraprofessional, nurse, or midwife) to deal with any unforeseen problems. It may be possible in the future to set up some kind of mobile birth unit staffed by trained personnel. The unit, perhaps housed in a converted motor home, could either be parked outside the home or brought to the house by calling an emergency number. In case of emergency, the mother could be quickly shifted to the unit, which would contain any necessary equipment. But, remember, birth is a normal process, and 85 to 95 percent of births do not involve any difficulties (Boston Women's Health Book Collective, 1976, p. 249).

Above, the midwife was mentioned as a medically qualified person, but this is not accepted by many. Although midwives are used in delivery in many modern countries such as Sweden and the Netherlands and were used in our country until the turn of the century, the organized medical profession as well as many others feel that delivery in the hospital by doctors is much safer. In addition, they feel that it would be difficult to enforce standards of competence if delivery by midwives became widespread. On the other hand, England has set high standards and trained midwives since 1902. At the present time there are about 80,000 women registered as midwives in England, of which about 21,000 are actively practicing. In 1970, about 75 percent of all births were midwife-assisted (British Birth Survey 1970, 1975). In England the obstetrician is the leader of the birth team and the midwife does the practical work.

As interest in home births increases and as hospital costs soar (it now costs over $2000 to have a baby with standard hospitalization and delivery), the idea of midwifery is returning in the United States. For example, at the Booth Maternity Center in Philadelphia, the actual number of midwife-assisted births has risen steadily from 254 in 1971 to 1212 in 1976 (Dillon et al, 1978). Some states have now licensed training programs for midwives. In 1977 Congress considered a bill to authorize Medicaid payments to nurse midwives (see *Time*, Aug. 29, 1977, p. 66 for further reading).

Breast Feeding Attached to the natural childbirth philosophy is a strong emphasis on breast feeding. There are many reasons for this emphasis, such as breast feeding being more natural; however, the major reason that psychologists advocate breast feeding is that it brings the mother and child into close, warm physical contact. Since feeding is the infant's first social contact, many experts such as Erik Erikson (1962) and Ashley Montagu (1972) believe that this loving contact is necessary to the development of security and basic trust in the infant. Another advantage to breast feeding derives from the secretion of *colostrum*. This substance is present in the breast immediately after birth and is secreted until the milk flows, usually three to four days after birth. It has a high protein content, but, most important, it is high in antibodies and helps make the child immune to many infectious diseases during infancy. One should also count the warm, loving feelings that arise in the nursing mother as another advantage to breast feeding. Breast feeding also causes hormones to be released that speed the uterus' return to normal.

The new mother needs to prepare for breast feeding as well as understand the natural process if she is to be successful. Her breasts will be engorged, congested, and painful for the first few days after birth. However, mothers who have rooming-in, and who begin to nurse the baby from birth onward (the sucking reflex of a baby born to an unanesthetized mother is very strong), on the baby's demand, usually do not experience engorgement. And the act of breast feeding itself will soon relieve the congestion.

In addition, it helps if the mother massages her nipples before birth to prepare them for the child's suckling. Otherwise, the nipples sometimes become chafed and sore. If the nipples do become sore, exposing them to the air will help. Milk normally begins to flow be-

tween the third and fourth day. The baby is biologically prepared to maintain itself during these days, since it normally has a little surplus fat that tides it over until milk flow begins. Thus the mother does not need to worry or feel a failure if she cannot satisfy the infant's apparent hunger during the first few days.* She should remember, in the words of Ashley Montagu, that "Over the five or more million years of human evolution, and as a consequence of seventy-five million years of mammalian evolution, breast-feeding has constituted the most successful means of administering to the needs of the dependent, precariously born human neonate" (1972, p. 80).

Many new parents may very well decide to bottle feed. There is certainly nothing wrong with bottle feeding so long as the baby receives the holding and close bodily contact that breast feeding supplies. With bottle feeding, the father can also participate and supply

*For those wishing more information on breast feeding, contact La Leche League International, 9616 Minneapolis Avenue, Franklin Park, Ill. 60131.

some holding and physical contact to the baby. Unfortunately the father is too often the forgotten person immediately after birth. He can supply warmth and affection to the baby as well as the mother. Not only does the mother sometimes suffer mild depression after birth, but the father may also suffer from feelings of neglect, jealousy, and simply "being left out" after childbirth. The more of a partnership, the more sharing a couple can have in the whole process of conception, pregnancy, and childbirth, the more satisfaction both the father and mother will receive.

Postpartum Emotional Problems   The first few weeks and months of motherhood are known as the *postpartum period*. Over half of all women who bear children report a marked degree of emotional upset following the birth (Kane et al, 1968).

> Some of us are high, some are mellow, some of us are lethargic and depressed, or we are irritable and cry easily. Mood swings are common. We are confused and a little scared, because our moods do not resemble the way we are accustomed to feel, let alone the way we are expected to feel. If this is our first baby we may feel lonely and isolated from adult society. The special attention and consideration many of us receive as expectant mothers shift to the baby and we too are expected to put the baby's needs before our own (Boston Women's Health Book Collective, 1973, p. 207).

Most women experience a mild depression between the second and fourth days after delivery. This may be due in part to the changing chemical balance within the woman's body as it readjusts to

the nonpregnant state. Some suggest that it results because of the separation of the woman and her newborn immediately after birth (if there is no rooming-in) (Klaus et al, 1972). For most this depression passes quickly. The general emotional reactions to parenthood, however, especially with the first child, continue for a much longer period.

Summary   Pregnancy and childbirth are an integral part of most marriages. Despite the drop in the birth rate and the increasing number of couples expressing the desire to remain childless, childbearing and rearing will be a part of the majority of people's lives. Knowledge of pregnancy and the birth process is important to the act of birth itself. Those who are knowledgeable stand a better chance of having a simple, uncomplicated childbirth.

   Both the egg and sperm cells are among the smallest in the body, yet they contain all of the genetic information necessary to create the adult human being. Both contribute the same number of chromosomes, twenty-three, but the sperm is also responsible for the sex of the child. There are two kinds of sperm, an X sperm, which creates a female, and a Y sperm, which creates a male. Many more males are conceived than females, but, by the end of the first year of life, there are almost equal numbers of males and females. This is because the death rate for males at all stages of life after conception is much higher than the rate for females.

Pregnancy takes several weeks before it becomes recognizable, though some pregnancy tests can determine pregnancy by the end of the third week. A missed menstrual period is usually the first sign. Others might be breast tenderness and coloration change, slight morning sickness, and the necessity of more frequent urination.

The average pregnancy is 266 days or 38 weeks. During this time the mother should try to eat a good diet and be under the care of a physician. She should avoid medicines and being X-rayed as well as stressful life events, if possible. The developing fetus can be affected by the environment. For example, if the mother is addicted to narcotics, or has an infectious disease such as German measles or a venereal disease, or is a heavy smoker, the child may be damaged. Any resulting defects in the child are called congenital defects. Genetic defects are caused by the chromosomes and genes. By removing a small amount of amniotic fluid, a process termed amniocentesis, doctors can analyze it for certain genetic defects such as Down's syndrome (Mongolism), and thus discover defects, if any, before birth.

The birth process is generally divided into three stages. The first is the labor stage, during which the cervix relaxes and opens and the uterus contracts periodically in an effort to push the infant into the birth canal (vagina). In the second stage, these contractions with help from the mother push the child through the birth canal into the outside world. The third stage comes shortly after the baby has been delivered when the placenta or afterbirth is expelled.

In recent years more and more emphasis has been placed on the mother and the father participating as much as they can in the birth of the child. Natural childbirth means knowledgeable childbirth, with the use of drugs reduced to a minimum. Breast feeding is being encouraged as is rooming-in, or keeping the baby with the mother immediately after birth, rather than removing the infant to a nursery in the hospital.

Philosophically, those encouraging natural childbirth believe that for a couple to share together the miracle of creating life can be an emotional high point for the couple. They suggest that care and planning be made a part of pregnancy so that the birth process will function smoothly and the parents will be able to derive the most pleasure and satisfaction from the entire process of bringing a child into the world.

Birth without Violence: The Leboyer Method

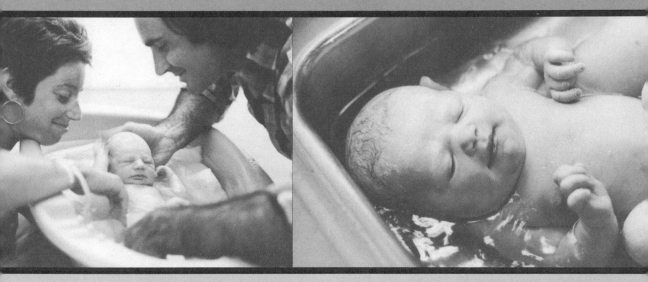

What makes being born so frightful is the intensity, the boundless scope and variety of the experience, its suffocating richness.

People say — and believe — that a newborn baby feels nothing. He feels everything.

Everything — utterly, without choice or filter or discrimination.

Birth is a tidal wave of sensation, surpassing anything we can imagine. A sensory experience so vast we can barely conceive of it.

The baby's senses are at work. Totally.

They are sharp and open — new.

What are our senses compared to theirs?

And the sensations of birth are rendered still more intense by contrast with what life was before.

Admittedly, these sensations are not yet organized into integrated, coherent perceptions. Which makes them all the stronger, all the more violent, unbearable — literally maddening (Leboyer, 1975, pp. 15 – 16).

Many theorists have hypothesized that the trauma of birth leaves an indelible mark on human personality. One of Freud's early followers, Otto Rank, suggested that the birth trauma is the major source of later problems that center around insecurity, because it is this trauma that marks humans with a basic anxiety about life. Little if any of

this kind of thinking has entered the birth routines of American hospitals. In most birth procedures, the mother's comfort is primary, the doctor's efficiency next, and few even consider reducing the impact of birth on the child.

The child emerges out of the quiet, warm, dark, secure environment of the womb into a bright, loud, cooler world, and its source of oxygen and nutrition, the umbilical cord, is immediately severed. The child is hung upside down, slapped, cleaned, and made to function immediately on its own. Little wonder that the child screams, clenches its fist, and has an agonized look on its face. The sensation of the air rushing into its lungs for the first time must be a searing experience. Add to this all of the other new experiences, and life must seem a cacophony of terrifying intensity.

Frederick Leboyer simply tells us to listen to the child. Let the child guide us through the first few minutes after birth. Leboyer's four basic steps are simple. First, once delivery is imminent, reduce the light and be quiet. The infant's vision and hearing will then not be immediately assaulted. Second, as soon as the infant is out, place it comfortably on the mother's warm abdomen which will serve as a nest for the child. Let the child retain the prebirth curved position of the spine until ready of its own accord to straighten and stretch. Third, do not cut the umbilical cord until the child's own systems are functioning smoothly, six to ten minutes after birth. This way the child is doubly supplied with oxygen and there will be no period of possible deficit and related alarm reaction and ensuing terror. During this time, the mother and doctor gently massage the child, simulating the environmental contact the child has so long enjoyed within the mother. Fourth, once the cord stops pulsating, it is cut and the baby is bathed in water similar in temperature to the familiar environment from which it recently emerged. During this time also the baby is held and massaged gently. The hands make love to the child, not briskly rubbing nor timidly caressing, but deeply and slowly massaging just as the child felt within the womb. The child makes contact with the world at a pace that is comfortable for it. And how long might this be? Perhaps ten to twenty minutes is all. Is this too much to ask for a child at this most eventful time in its life?

And what of the Leboyer-born children's later personalities? It might be too early to tell, but they seem noticeably different, especially in their unusually avid interest in the world around them (Leboyer, 1975). Does fear and terror at birth cause many of the problems felt by adult humans? Will reducing the impact of birth on the child help that child become an adult with fewer problems? Only time will tell. But shouldn't we try to reduce birth trauma and see what happens?

On the other hand, there are many doctors who feel that the Leboyer method either does nothing or, in fact, may cause harm, although exactly what the harmful effects might be is unclear. A recent study conducted at McMaster University Medical Centre in Hamilton, Ontario, compared 28 infants delivered by the Leboyer method with 26 who had routine deliveries. The study reported no differences between the infants (*Santa Barbara News-Press* (AP), April, 1980).

Chapter 12 ～

Contents

The Challenge of Parenthood

Marriage and parenthood have often seemed synonymous in the past. Having children was the major goal of marriage. Many popular sayings supported this goal.

Marriage means children.

Having children is the essence of woman's self-realization.

Reproduction is woman's biological destiny.

It is the duty of all families to produce children for the State.

Children prove the manliness and machismo of the father.

Children prove the fecundity, competence, and womanliness of the mother.

Be fruitful and multiply.

Having children is humanity's way to immortality. Children extend oneself into the future.

Children are an economic asset, needed hands for necessary labor.

The beliefs of the past often remain to encumber the present long after the original reasons for the belief have disappeared. So it is today with reproduction and parenthood. For thousands of years humans had to reproduce, had to be parents, if the species was to survive. Besides, they had little choice in the matter since the pleasure of sexual relations usually meant pregnancy.

Marriage has historically always implied the having and rearing of children. Indeed, the primary function of the family was and is to provide a continuing replacement of individuals so that the human species and the particular society continue to exist.

Yet, the dogma of the past has quietly become the liability of the present, for uncontrolled reproduction today means the ultimate demise of the species, not survival. In the past, high infant mortality, uncontrolled disease, and war meant that society had to press all families to reproduce at a high level in order to maintain the population. Women were pregnant during most of their fertile years. Even today in many underdeveloped countries, infant mortality runs as high as 200 per 1000 live births, and because of malnutrition and disease, many women see fewer than half of their children reach maturity.

But, in developed countries, the infant mortality rate has been cut to less than 25 per 1000 live births, and some countries, such as those in Scandinavia, have an infant mortality rate as low as 13 to 15 per

1000 live births. The infant mortality rate in the United States is 16.5 per 1000 live births, the lowest ever recorded in the United States (U.S. National Center for Health Studies, 1975).

Children by Choice

Reduced infant mortality through greater control of disease and pestilence has removed the necessity for most families to have large numbers of children. Since the chances are greater that children will reach adulthood, a family may safely limit the number of children to the number they actually desire.

Because a much larger percentage of children now reach adulthood, the historical pressure on the family to reproduce continuously will have to be modified. The problems of overpopulation pose one of the greatest threats to the survival of the human species. Let's take a look at how population has increased. It took the human population until 1830 to reach one billion. But by 1930 (just 100 years later), another billion had been added. By 1960, just 30 years later, a third billion people were added. The fourth billion arrived in 1975, and by the end of the century it is predicted that we will be adding a billion persons to the world population every five years.

Knowledge of overpopulation dangers, improved and readily available birth control methods, and legal abortions have combined to give newly married American couples greater freedom from unwanted pregnancy. Although the social expectation to have children remains, couples are less likely to be thought of as selfish hedonists or infertile if they remain childless. America's birth rate today is near its lowest point, approximately two children per marriage or 67.8 (66.7 in 1975) births per 1000 women in the childbearing ages of fifteen to forty-four in 1977 (National Center for Health Statistics, 1979). This is approximately 15 births per 1000 population. Many underdeveloped countries, on the other hand, have birth rates of 40 to 50 per 1000 population. If America's birth rate continues at the zero population growth level, the population will reach a high in the year 2015 and start downward around 2020, depending on the amount of immigration from abroad.

The overwhelming number of children preferred by Americans today is two (Glick, 1979; David & Baldwin, 1979, p. 868), whereas in 1945 only 23 percent of the public stated one or two as the ideal number of children. Larger numbers of young educated women are stating a "no children" preference today than at any time in the past. However, stating such a preference and then living by it are two different things. According to Ira Reiss (1980), childlessness among married couples is actually not increasing much, although there is some increase among college-educated partners.

Why Are Children Wanted?

The reasons, conscious or unconscious, why a couple decides to have children very much affect the way in which the child is treated and reared. Since species survival, political, and economic reasons are no longer relevant to having children in modern society (see Chapter 10), it is the personal reasons a couple wants children that need to be investigated. In essence, unfortunately, many of the personal reasons have a selfish element. It is this selfish element that, when frustrated by the child, so often leads to feelings of disappointment and failure on the part of parents. Bernard Berelson (1972) lists six basic personal reasons for having children, each with a large selfish component.

1. *Personal power* Children give parents *personal power*. First, there is the power over children, and it is really a very absolute power during the early years of childhood. Second, having children sometimes gives one parent power over the other. The woman may use the children to bind the man to her or the man may do the same. Children can also represent increased political and/or economic power as in societies where marriage alliances are arranged to control power. In America, the Kennedy or Rockefeller families come to mind when thinking of children as potential power.
2. *Personal competence* Children also offer proof of *personal competence* in an essential human role. "Look what I can do, see how virile I am, see how fertile I am."
3. *Personal status* Tied closely to personal competence is the *personal status* conferred by parenthood. "I have contributed to the society, I can produce and achieve."
4. *Personal extension* Children are also a form of *personal extension*, immortality, life after death. "After all, my children are a part of me, both physically and psychologically."
5. *Personal experience* The plain and simple *personal experience* of having children is rewarding. A parent can feel: "... the deep curiosity as to how the child will turn out; the renewal of self in the second chance; the reliving of one's own childhood; the redemptive opportunity; the challenge to shape another human being; the sheer creativity and self-realization involved."
6. *Personal pleasure* The experience of having children can produce *personal pleasure*, the love involved in having wanted children, caring for them, and enjoying them.

Of course, there are many other personal reasons for having children. For example: "Children will make me an adult." "I'll have something of my own." "People will pay attention to me." "I'll have someone to help and to love," and on and on.

To know and understand our reasons for having children is a small step in the right direction. And to understand that the resultant child is an individual in his or her own right and that this new individual has no responsibility to fulfill our needs and reasons for producing him or her is a *big* step in the direction of enlightened child rearing.

And a woman who held a babe against her bosom said, Speak to us of
   Children.
And he said:
Your children are not your children.
They are the sons and daughters of Life's longing for itself.

**Parental
Effectiveness**

They come through you but not from you,
And though they are with you yet they belong not to you.

You may give them your love but not your thoughts,
For they have their own thoughts.
You may house their bodies but not their souls,
For their souls dwell in the house of tomorrow, which you cannot visit,
not even in your dreams.
You may strive to be like them, but seek not to make them like you.
For life goes not backward nor tarries with yesterday.
You are the bows from which your children as living arrows are sent
forth.
The archer sees the mark upon the path of the infinite, and He bends
you with His might that His arrows may go swift and far.
Let your bending in the archer's hand be for gladness;
For even as He loves the arrow that flies, so He loves also the bow
that is stable.

Khalil Gibran, *The Prophet*

WHAT DO YOU THINK?

Do you want children at some time in the future? Why or why not?

How many do you want (if you want to have children)? Why?

In what ways do you think that your parents were successful in their parenting? In what ways were they unsuccessful?

How would you change the ways in which your parents raised you? Why?

Most people take on the job of parenthood assuming that they will be successful. "Of course, we can be good parents," think most expectant parents. Yet raising children is an extremely demanding job. It is certainly time-consuming since it lasts for twenty years or more. What qualifications do expectant parents consider themselves to have? Well, they all have parents and all have been children. But, as we all know from our own experience as children, all parents fail in their job to some degree. Some failure, especially in the eyes of one's children, does seem to be an integral part of parenting.

> There is no question but that your parents failed you as parents. All parents fail their children, and yours are no exception. No parent is ever adequate for the job of being a parent, and there is no way not to fail at it. No parent ever has enough love, or wisdom, or maturity, or whatever. No parent ever totally succeeds (Close, 1968).

Because of this, great amounts of advice flow forth from almost everywhere — grandparents, doctors, clergy, popular magazines, child experts — all describing how best to rear children. And, of course, a great deal of advice comes from the children themselves who are as yet unblessed with their own children. What fifteen-year-old doesn't know exactly how bad his or her parents are and how to be the perfect parent?

The problem with all this advice is that there is no agreement about the best method to successfully bring up children. In a sense, children come to live with their parents, their parents do not go to live with them. Parents need not think that they must relinquish their lives completely in favor of the child's development. Parental growth and development go hand in hand with child growth and development.

There is no single correct way to rear children. Basically, if children are wanted, respected, and appreciated, they will be secure. If children are secure, they will usually also be extremely flexible and resilient. What is important is for the parents to be honest and true to themselves. Small children are very empathetic; that is, they have the ability to feel as another is feeling. They respond to their parents' feelings as well as to their actions. Parents who are naturally authoritarian will fail in coping with their children if they attempt to act permissively because they have read that this is a beneficial mode of interaction with children. Their children will feel the tension in their parents and respond to that rather than to the parents' overt actions. Thus parents who attempt to be something other than what they are, no matter how theoretically beneficial the results are supposed to be, will generally fail with their children. Parental sincerity is one of the necessary ingredients of successful child rearing. "By and large, the pervasive emotional tone used by the parents in raising children . . . affects subsequent development more than either the particular techniques of child rearing (e.g., permissiveness, restrictiveness, punishment, reward) or the cohesiveness of the marital unit (whether it is stable or broken by divorce or death)" (Berelson & Steiner, 1964, p. 52).

Overconcern and overprotection of children can also cause problems for children. Children need increasing degrees of freedom if they are to grow into independent adults. This means that they must have freedom to fail as well as freedom to succeed. They ought to experience the consequences of their actions, unless, of course, the consequences are dangerous to their well-being. Consequences teach children how to judge behavior. Parents who always shield children from failure are doing them a disfavor. Their children will not be able to modify their behavior to make it more successful since they will be ignorant of the results. Overprotection can sometimes even be dangerous. For example, children taken to beach resorts need to know about and have water skills as soon as possible. Knowledge and skill are the best protection against accidents. The parents who take their children to the beach and then scream hysterically at them the moment they start toward the water are doing only one thing, teaching them to fear the water. Any lifeguard knows that fear of the water may lead to panic if there is trouble, and that panic is the swimmer's worst enemy. Of course, parents need to be aware of small children's activities on the beach. But concern should be shown by helping them learn about the ocean, and by showing them how to have fun in the water and gain confidence in their abilities rather than making them fearful. The best protection for children at a beach is the earliest possible swimming lessons and then watching them quietly to make sure they are not too far out.

It is also important to remember that the family and the child are not isolated from the broader society. Parents are the first to be blamed for their children's faults. Yet the influences on the child from sources outside the family become increasingly powerful as the child grows older. School, peers, friends, and the mass media all exert influence on both parents and children. For example, it is difficult for parents to express their opposition to marijuana use when their teenager's friends are using it and the media present numerous experts giving their opinion that it is not as detrimental to health as either alcohol or tobacco. But, if their child is caught using it, most often it is the parents who are first blamed, not the peers or media.

Parenting, then, is not something done only by parents. How parenting is accomplished and the results of the parenting are both influenced by the family and the larger society surrounding the family. Parents must pay attention to the society as well as to their children. To expect children to become adults reflecting only the values and behaviors of their immediate family is unrealistic. Thus the effective parent must also be the concerned citizen and actively work to better the society at large.

Stimulation and Development

Stimulation is necessary for the development of basic behavioral capacities. Early deprivation of stimulation generally produces slower learning later in life. On the other hand, numerous studies indicate that early stimulation enhances development and later learning. J. Scott, for example, concludes from various research evidence that, "given the present state of our knowledge, the best physical environment in which to rear a child is one that gives him experience with a variety of physical objects which he can manipulate and control freely with minimal restriction. Experiences will give him an opportunity to develop basic motor skills which he can later apply to more specific learning situations" (Scott, 1968, p. 114).

The emphasis on early childhood education and intervention, commencing with the Head Start program in the early 1960s, reflects the recognition of the importance of early environmental stimulation for children. Although there is controversy over the effects of Head Start experiences and the contribution to lasting change in the child made by such experiences, there is little doubt that the preschool years are important to the cognitive development of the child (Weinberg, 1979, p. 912).

Some stress in childhood may also be related to achievement. In a study of over 400 famous twentieth century men and women (Goertzel & Goertzel, 1962), two conclusions seemed to indicate that a child need not be protected from all stress and strain, that, indeed, some manageable stress and strain stimulate achievement:

1. Three-fourths of the children were troubled — by poverty; by a broken home; by rejecting, overpossessive, estranged, or dominating parents; by financial ups and downs; by physical handicaps; or by parental dissatisfaction over the children's school failures or vocational choices.

2. Handicaps such as blindness, deafness; being crippled, sickly, homely, undersized or overweight; or having a speech defect occur in the childhoods of over one-fourth of the sample. In many of these individuals, the need to compensate for such handicaps is seen by them as a determining factor in their drive for achievement.

This study included individuals from all fields and countries, such as Konrad Adenauer, Louis Armstrong, Jane Austen, Lionel Barrymore, Hugo Black, Alexander Graham Bell, Pearl Buck, and Gertrude Stein.

This doesn't mean that parents should deliberately set about introducing stress into their children's lives. Rather, it means that parents may relax and be less concerned if their children are placed in a stressful situation. Children who are secure in the love and warmth of their parents will be able to survive and, in fact, grow in the face of stress. For example, moving away from a neighborhood, from places of familiarity and friends, can be upsetting. Yet studies of the effect of long-distance moves on children show little negative effect. The children seem to make friends easily, the school change is not difficult, and any disturbance in their behavior dissipates quickly (Barrett and Noble, 1973).

Good parents love their children but are also honest enough to know that there will be days when they are angry with them, unfair with them, and in other ways terrible with them. But secure children will survive such episodes.

Enlightened Control of Children

For most parents, control of their children is accomplished in a haphazard manner. If parents liked their own parents, they tend to copy their child-rearing methods. If parents disliked their own parents' methods, they tend to do the opposite. In either case, parents' own experiences as children tend to influence how they themselves parent. The General Mills American Family Report indicates that most parents overwhelmingly use negative techniques to control their children. Table 12-1 shows the percentage of parents reporting use of various disciplinary methods.

Unfortunately, such negative control methods tend to have negative side effects because they serve as model behaviors. A child who is screamed at continually tends to become a child who screams to get his or her way. A child who is treated negatively tends to become a negative child. A child who is punished violently tends to learn that violence is how you change one's behavior. Hostility, low self-esteem, feeling of inferiority and insecurity are frequent reactions of children who are reared by basically negative methods.

Table 12-1 Percentage of Parents Using Various Disciplinary Methods

Method	Percentage
Yelling at or scolding children	52
Spanking children	50
Making children stay in their rooms	38
Not allowing children to play	32
Not letting children watch T.V.	25
Making the child go to bed	23
Threatening the child	15
Giving the child extra chores	12
Taking away an allowance	9

Source: Adapted from General Mills, 1977, p. 104.

Rather than having only a few automatic control techniques, parents must work toward having a wide variety of well-understood child rearing methods. Each child and each situation will be somewhat unique. Therefore, enlightened parents try to react in accordance with each situation. First one tries to understand the child and the problem, then one tries to clearly identify what changes are necessary, and finally one attempts to accomplish the changes in the best possible manner. Thus, enlightened child rearing becomes a rational, thoughtful, directive process as opposed to an irrational, reactive process.

In general, controlling children can be accomplished by using many different methods that vary in intensity from mild to strong. Many parents immediately use strong methods such as punishment when, in fact, a mild method such as distraction might have worked equally well. By first trying milder methods, many of the negative side effects we earlier discussed can be eliminated or at least reduced. Table 12-2 outlines a continuum of mild to strong control methods.

Obviously one must consider the age of the child when using Table 12-2. A two-year-old will not understand 3c, an appeal to his sense of fair play, because this ethical concept has not yet been grasped.

Getting set ahead of time when possible and directing a child's behavior is preferable and much easier than being unprepared and

Table 12-2   Mild to Strong Child Control Methods

1. Supporting the child's self-control
    a.   Signal interference (Catch the child's eye, frown, say something.)
    b.   Proximity control (Get physically close to the child.)
    c.   Planful ignoring (Children often do "bad" things to get attention and if they don't, they will cease the behavior since they are not getting what they want.)
    d.   Painless removal (Remove the child from the problem source.)

2. Situational assistance
    a.   Give help
    b.   Distraction or restructuring a situation
    c.   Support of firm routines
    d.   Restraint
    e.   Getting set in advance

3. Reality and ethical appraisals
    a.   Showing consequences to behaviors
    b.   Marginal use of interpretation
    c.   Appealing to sense of reason and fair play (not useful until child is intellectually able to understand such concepts)

4. Reward and contracting
    a.   Rewards (payoffs) should be immediate
    b.   Initial contracts should call for and reward small pieces of behavior (A reward for picking up toys, rather than a reward for keeping room clean for a week)
    c.   Reward performance after it occurs
    d.   Contract must be fair to all parties
    e.   Terms of contract must be clear and understood
    f.   Contract must be honest
    g.   Contract should be positive
    h.   Contract must be used consistently
    i.   Contract must have a method of change to cope with failures
5. Punishment: See Inset 12-1

Using Discipline and Punishment Effectively

Whether one agrees or not with the use of punishment as a means of teaching children, studies of parental control indicate that it is still the major method used by most parents. Unfortunately, punishment does not always work and, in addition, it has such negative side effects as anger and hostility.

If punishment is used, the parent needs to understand a few simple principles that help to minimize the negative side effects and to maximize its usefulness. If mild punishment is to be effective, there needs to be alternative behavior open to the child. For example, if a child is punished for turning on the television rather than dressing for school, the punishment will work better if the child knows when he or she can watch TV. In this case the child knows that there is another way to do what he or she wants and not be punished. In addition, punishment works best if the child is not highly motivated. For example, a child eats just before dinner. If the child missed lunch, chances are she or he is very hungry (highly motivated), and punishment will probably not be very effective in keeping her or him from eating. If there are alternatives and if the child is not highly motivated, then following the guidelines based on psychological learning theory set forth here will help the parent achieve desired goals while keeping punishment to a minimum.

1. Consider the individual child and the potential negative side effects. *Example*: The author's son reacts strongly to punishment and the reaction lasts for a considerable length of time. He is better controlled by reward or distraction. If punishment is used, it is very mild. The author's daughter is not at all sensitive to punishment. She can be punished, her behavior will change, and there are no lasting side effects.

2. Punish as soon after the act as possible. *Example*: Children are bright, but it is hard for them to associate an act with punishment that comes many hours after the act. The mother who tells the child at 10 A.M. to "Just wait until your father comes home, will you get it," does little more than turn father into an ogre. By the time the father arrives home, little change of behavior will be derived from punishment.

3. If possible, let the punishment flow from the act. *Example*: A child is constantly warned when he reaches toward a hot stove, but it will take time. The child who touches the hot stove is immediately punished by his own action, understands what the word *hot* means, and has learned in one trial. Obviously, one cannot always set up a situation where punishment flows from the act, but when possible it is more efficient.

4. Make the punishment educational and be sure that children understand what their alternatives are. *Example*: Many young children really do not understand exactly what they have done and what new behavior is desired. Mary was punished when her mother found her at the cookie jar before dinner. Later Mary found some cookies on the counter and was again punished. Mary did not understand that she was being punished for eating cookies the first time. She thought her mother did not want her around the cookie jar for fear she might break it. Also, she did not understand that she could have cookies after dinner.

5. Keep the punishment as mild as possible and keep it devoid of emotion. *Example*: Jimmy's mother became so exasperated that she lost her temper and gave him a good spanking. By losing her own temper she simply increased the emotional atmosphere causing Jimmy to become even more upset and also modeled overt anger.

6. Try to punish the act, not the child. *Example*: "You are a bad boy. We don't love you when you are bad." This is a threatening and upsetting statement to a child and really unnecessary. Generally, it is the particular act that is bad rather than the child. When the child changes his behavior, there is no longer a need for punishment, hence the child's relationships should immediately return to normal. By directing punishment at only the act, the child will not continue to be punished by thinking he as an individual is bad and unworthy of love ("I don't like your behavior so please change it. I like you, however.") (Cox, 1973, pp. 234–235).

What were the major methods of control used by your parents when you were a child?

How did you react to these methods as a child?

What do you think of them as an adult? Did they work? Why or why not?

Which methods would you use with your children? Why?

What will you do if you and your spouse disagree on control methods?

surprised by a child's behavior and then trying to react properly. For example, if you give a child a difficult task, stay close (1b, proximity control) so that you can offer help if it is needed (2a).

Firm routines (2c) reduce conflict and the number of overt decisions necessary. For example, an orderly routine at bedtime accomplishes tooth-brushing, elimination, getting into pajamas, story reading, and lights off with little problem. In a sense the child is on automatic pilot and little conflict arises once the routine is established. Such routines are only helpful in certain areas of life and probably work best with the preschool and early school child. Distraction (2b) is very helpful with small children. They usually have short interest spans and their attention is easily shifted from one focus to another. Saying "no" to a child immediately creates a confrontation. ("Don't touch the expensive art book.") However, presenting an alternative and saying "do this" does not necessarily create such a confrontation. ("Why don't you look at this coloring book?" — while handing it to him.)

What Effects Do Children Have on a Marriage?

This is a complicated question for which the research data are mixed. One thing is sure, however: children make the marital relationship more complicated. A couple must contend with communication in only two directions. Add one child and this becomes six-way communication; add two children, and there is now twelve-way communication with which to cope (see Figure 12-1).

It is obvious that whatever effects children will have on their parents are partially determined by the parents' relationship before parenthood. Generally, the arrival of a child is less disruptive if the

Figure 12-1

Adding children complicates communication.

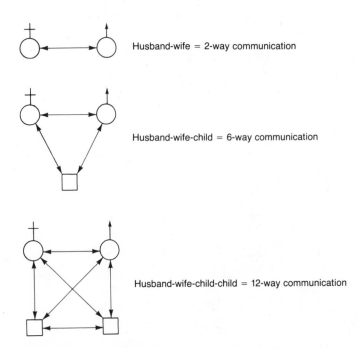

Husband-wife = 2-way communication

Husband-wife-child = 6-way communication

Husband-wife-child-child = 12-way communication

parents have already achieved an effective pattern of communication, mutually acceptable family planning, high marital adjustment, and a strong commitment to the parenthood role. In addition, good maternal health and a calm, nonproblematic baby greatly reduce disruption (Russell, 1974).

But, if a couple's relationship is poor to begin with, children will only intensify their problems. The idea that children will save a marriage in trouble is erroneous. The increased complications will usually hasten the end of the relationship, if not the marriage.

Many couples do report that their happiest time in marriage was before the arrival of the first child and after the departure of the last (Bell, 1975). Also, a general study of the research done during the 1960s on family stability and happiness indicates that children more often detract from, rather than contribute to, marital happiness (Hicks & Platt, 1970). Of course, all research involves averages and group data. The effect children will have on your marriage will depend on your understanding and tolerance of the natural demands and strains that the presence of children creates.

On the whole, the first year of parenthood is viewed by most parents as only moderately stressful. Few first-year parents see their marriage as deteriorating because of parenthood. The problems first-year mothers find themselves now concerned with are: worry about personal appearance, physical tiredness and fatigue, baby interruptions of sleep and rest, worry about loss of figure, and feeling edgy or emotionally upset. First-year fathers are concerned with: baby interrupting sleep and rest, in-law interference about the baby, increased monetary strain, changing plans because of the baby, and additional work required by the baby (Russell, 1974).

In more practical terms, bringing the first new baby home can be quite an experience for the new parents. No matter how much learning they have done, they can never be sure that what they are doing is correct. If the baby cries, they worry. If it doesn't cry, they worry. They will have to adjust to the feeding routine in the first months. It means that the mother cannot venture very far from the baby, especially if she is breast-feeding. The father has to adjust to being in second place as far as his wife's attentions are concerned. An infant is demanding of attention if nothing else. The mother should make an effort to bring the father into the pattern of infant care so that he doesn't feel left out. With the first child, many husbands experience jealousy since they have been used to all their wife's attention and love and suddenly must share it with another. On the other hand, fathers who take an active role with the new infant often don't experience this. Rather, when father and mother share child rearing, the couple may feel drawn even closer together. Perhaps what the couples miss most is time of their own that does not have to be shared with the infant. Especially during the first few years, it seems as if the child dominates everything that they do.

Prospective parents seldom think that children will be with them for probably twenty or more years, and that their effect on the

Historically as well as presently, the American father has played a much smaller parenting role than has the mother. Basically this is because his role usually takes him out of the home, away from the children, to meet his work and support obligations. His absence shifts the burden of parenting disproportionately to the mother. Many fathers indicate that their work in supporting the family is the most important part of their parenting role and so feel that they need to do little else with the children, especially if their wife is not working.

Jean and Jim have two children, a boy aged ten and a girl aged eight. Jim feels that since he is on the job all day, it is Jean's duty to keep the children "out of his hair" when he gets home so that he can relax and recuperate from the day's work. Jean resents this, feeling that she, too, has worked all day. She has also had full responsibility for the children since school was out. She has asked

Jim to watch the children occasionally on Saturday or Sunday so that she may have a day off, but he feels that the weekend should be a family time.

Even if this is the father's attitude, the new father is faced with a number of developmental tasks (Barnhill et al, 1979, p. 232):

1. *Decision-making.* The father must make the decision to accept the reality of having a child.
2. *Mourning.* While the new father gains the role of father, he also undergoes a substantial loss. He loses personal and economic freedom, some of his wife's attention, and much of their relationship's flexibility.
3. *Empathic responding.* The husband who participates in the pregnancy and birth (Chapter 11) will feel more closely involved with his wife and hence with the new child. This developmental task may be missed by the noninvolved father. Such fathers often feel

unknowing about and later somewhat alienated from their children.
4. *Integrating.* The child must be integrated into the spatial, temporal, and social life space of the family. The question "How much time does the husband spend with his wife, and how much time does he spend with the mother of his child?" is answered by the way in which the father integrates these "fathering" and "husbanding" responsibilities.
5. *Establishing new family boundaries.* The new father must now also alter his role as an individual in his extended family. He has moved between generations, becoming primarily a parent rather than a son. In addition, he becomes connected in a whole new series of family relationships transforming his siblings into aunts and uncles, his parents into grandparents, etc.
6. *Synergizing.* The father's last task is developing a sense of trust in the adequacy of the child, the marriage, the family,

marriage will be profound. A spouse who becomes unpleasant or a marital relationship that sours can be escaped by divorce. But you cannot divorce a child who is unpleasant and frustrating. Parents are morally and legally responsible to provide care and shelter for their children until they are of age.

It should be noted that we have been talking about middle-class American families. The general affluence of American middle-class families, their small nuclear family structure, and the trend toward women's liberation all combine to decrease satisfactions deriving from the narrowed and exaggerated maternal role. In the past, women were also productive members of farm and craft teams along with their husbands. Children either shared in the work of the household or were left to amuse themselves. These mothers were usually not lonely and himself. This includes integration of the previous five tasks into a coherent life style, along with the acceptance of his own imperfections and those of his family. Synergizing refers to a state of enhancement that occurs if the father is able to achieve this new husband-father level and function successfully in it.

Even though the American father has not shared equally in the parenting role, recent social changes indicate that he may be participating more in the future. The historical characterization of the harsh, austere, disciplinarian father is being replaced by a more humanistic, affectionate, caring kind of father. Liberation of the woman's role also works to liberate the father's traditional role, hopefully freeing him to be more loving than he has been in the past. Father participation in childbirth, long closed to him, is now more and more encouraged (Chapter 11). As more women move into

careers, more men will have to share a larger portion of the parenting role. A few men are experimenting with fulfilling the home and parent role that used to be limited to their wives while their wives move out into the work world. Although these examples are limited, they are still indicative of a trend to bring more parenting into the father's role. Most experts agree that this would be rewarding to all concerned.

Fathering is much more drastically reduced when families break up. In most cases, children go with their mother, and their father's contact with them is greatly reduced. Many exhusbands are just as happy to escape their parental duties. However, many others desire to maintain their father role. But, even for those who do, the logistics of being with the children enough to remain effective defeat many absent fathers. Contact with the children usually means contact with the exwife, which may be painful. The father's

living situation is often unconducive to having the children stay with him. New commitments limit his time. In most cases, even when the father desires to retain his role with the children, studies indicate that his contract with the children declines rapidly (Hetherington et al, 1976).

But for a few fathers, the breakup of the marriage means coming to know their children better. When they have the children, they are prepared in advance and so devote time to them, whereas they might not have before when the family was intact. More fathers (although very few percentagewise) are obtaining custody of their children and for them, parenting becomes a central responsibility.

For further reading on the father's role in child development, see Lynn, 1974; and the October 1976 issue of *The Family Coordinator*.

or isolated because the world came into their homes in the form of farmhands, relatives, customers, and so on. Such women had no reason to complain of the boredom and solitude of spending ten-hour days alone with their children (Rossi, 1964). In addition to being mothers, they contributed to their family and their society in other important and productive ways.

Today, the idea that a mother must continually remain in the home with her children is losing credence as more and more mothers join the work force. The supposedly negative effects that absent mothers, babysitters, and child care centers have on children have not been found. The majority of studies find no significant differences in the emotional adjustment of the children of working mothers (Nye and Hoffman, 1963; Peterson, 1961; Smith, 1979).

The Growing Child in the Family

The essence of children is growing, changing, maturing, and becoming, rather than sameness. Parents must themselves constantly change in their relationship to the growing child. Just about the time they have adapted and learned to cope with a totally dependent child, they will need to change their behaviors in order to cope successfully with a suddenly mobile, yet still irresponsible two-year-old. Then there are the school years, when the increasing influence of peers signals declining parental influence, and then there are the trials and tribulations of puberty and adolescence, which become the launching stage for the once small, dependent child to go into the world on his or her own to establish a new family and repeat the cycle. As the child grows and changes, the family also changes. In infancy, for example, the mother usually remains close to the child. During elementary school, she often becomes a chauffeur, taking the child to a friend's home, music lessons, after school sports, and so on. Change and growth in the child means parental and family change.

One way of viewing these changes is to see them as a series of social and developmental situations involving problematic encounters with the environment. These situations involve normal "problems" children must "solve" if they are to function fully. This section will focus on *psychosocial* stages rather than biological developmental stages, though the two are, of course, interrelated.

Erik Erikson (1963) identifies eight psychosocial developmental stages, each with important tasks, which describe the human life cycle from infancy through old age.* In each of these stages children must establish new orientations to themselves and their environment, especially their social environment. Each stage requires a new level of social interaction and can shape the personality in either negative or positive ways. For example, if children cope successfully with the problems and resultant stress that come into focus in a given stage, they gain additional strengths to become fully functioning. On the other hand, if children cannot cope with the problems of a particular stage, they will, in effect, invest continuing energy into this stage, becoming, to some extent, *fixated*, or arrested in development. For example, an adult who handles frustration by always throwing a temper tantrum has failed to move out of the early childhood stage when temper tantrums were the only manner of handling frustration. Obviously such an individual is not coping successfully with the stress and problems of adult life.

Notice in Figure 12-2 that each stage can be carried down the chart into adulthood. For example, trust versus mistrust influences all succeeding stages. A person who successfully gains basic trust is then better prepared to cope with the ensuing developmental stages. Naturally, the reverse is also true. A mistrusting individual will have more trouble coping with ensuing stages than a trusting person will.

Let's now take a closer look at the first six stages.

---

*Erikson's stages are theoretical, of course, and though there is controversy over the exact nature of developmental stages, the idea of stages is useful in helping parents understand the changing nature of the growing child and themselves.

Stages								
1 Infancy Oral-sensory 1st year	Trust versus Mistrust (mothering, feeding)							
2 Toddler Muscular-anal 2 to 3 years		Autonomy versus Shame, Doubt (toilet training, self-control)						
3 Early Childhood Locomotor-genital 4 to 5 years			Initiative versus Guilt (increased freedom and sexual identity)					
4 School age Latency 6 to 11 years				Industry versus Inferiority (working together, school)				
5 Puberty and Adolescence 12 to 18 years					Identity versus Role-Diffusion (adult role)			
6 Young adulthood						Intimacy versus Isolation (love and marriage)		
7 Adulthood, middle age							Generativity versus Self-Absorption (broadening concerns beyond self)	
8 Maturity, old age								Integrity versus Despair

Infancy: The Oral-Sensory Stage: Trust versus Mistrust (First Year)
Human beings undergo a longer period of dependence than any other species. Indeed, in the first years, children are completely dependent on parents or other adults for survival. Thus, children's development of trust depends on the quality of care they receive from their parents or the adults who care for them. The prolonged period of dependence makes the child more amenable to socialization (learning the ways of the society). It can, of course, sometimes occur that a child is too strongly or wrongly socialized in the early stages and thereby suffers from needless inhibitions as an adult. Such inhibitions are easily recognized by modern day youth as "hang-ups." During this stage the child demands total care from the parents and is unable to contribute to the family since his responses to his environment are quite limited.

Figure 12-2
Erikson's eight developmental stages.

During the first year the infant must have total care to survive. A parent or some responsible person must be almost continually in attendance. This is a difficult adjustment for many new parents to make because they have enjoyed relatively great personal freedom as well as time to devote to one another. Overnight a newcomer usurps that freedom and has first call on their time. Not only does the infant demand personal time and attention, but many other considerations arise. To go out to a movie now means the additional time and cost involved in finding and paying a babysitter. To take a Sunday drive means hauling special food, diapers, diaper pail, car seat, and so forth. But, for the couple who really want children, the challenge and fun of watching a new human grow and learn can offset many of the problems entailed in the new parental roles.

During this first year the husband must make the adjustment to sharing the wife's love and attention. This can be difficult for an immature husband who is accustomed to being the center of "his" wife's life. Now, suddenly, the baby takes priority. As mentioned earlier, it is not uncommon for a new father to feel some resentment and jealousy over this change in his position. Although most couples are financially strained at this time in their marriage, it is important that they arrange times to be by themselves and remember to pay attention to their own relationship. In the past this was less of a problem because there were usually relatives around who could watch the infant occasionally. Now getting time together usually means paying someone to take care of the child. Such money is, however, well spent if it gives the couple an opportunity to improve their own relationship. After all, it is this relationship that is primary and if it is good, the chances are greater that the parents-children relationship will be good also.

Children learn trust through living in a trusting environment. This means that their needs are satisfied on a regular basis and that interactions with the environment are positive, stable, and satisfying. Parents whose relationship is good are often better able to supply this kind of environment. Also, children have a great deal of empathy, the ability to feel what others are feeling, and this makes them aware of stresses and strains between their parents though they may not intellectually be able to explain what they are feeling.

The term *oral-sensory* derives from the fact that eating and the infant's mouth and senses are its major means of knowing the world.

Toddler: The Muscular-Anal Stage: Autonomy versus Shame and Doubt (Two to Three Years of Age) As children develop motor and mental capacities, opportunities to explore and manipulate the environment increase. From successful exploration and manipulation emerges a sense of autonomy and self-control. This is a time of great learning. Children learn to walk, to talk, to feed and dress themselves, to say "no," and so forth. If parents thought the infant demanding, they learn what "demanding" really can be with their two- and three-year-olds. It seems there is not a minute's peace. Relations between the parents will often suffer during this time because of the constant demands and ensuing fatigue and frustrations engendered in the parents by the child's insatiable demands.

On the other hand, it is exciting to see the child's skills rapidly developing. First steps, first words, and curiosity all make this stage one of quick change for child and parent alike.

During this stage, the parents should try to create a stimulating environment for the child. As we mentioned earlier, stimulation appears to enhance learning skills. Alphabet books, creative toys that are strong enough to withstand the rough treatment given by most two- and three-year-olds, picture books, and an endless answering of questions all help to stimulate the child. This is also the period of toilet training, which needs to be approached in a positive way with humor if it is to be easily accomplished. Once the child is toilet trained, it will be of great relief to parents since the messy job of diaper changing and cleaning is over.

The name of this stage denotes the increasing activity of the child and the toilet-training tasks.

Early Childhood: The Locomotor-Genital Stage: Initiative versus Guilt (Four to Five Years of Age) Children become increasingly capable of self-initiated activities. This becomes a source of pride for parents. It is exciting to see children's capabilities increase. With each passing month they seem more mature, to have more personality, and to become more fun to interact with. As their capabilities and interests expand, so must the parents'. Where children's energy comes from is a constant source of amazement and bewilderment to often tired parents. However, school is just around the corner and with it comes a little breath of free time.

Children who do not increase their capabilities, perhaps because of accident or illness, may feel guilty and inadequate about their chances of success in school.

Locomotor indicates that the child is now very active in the environment, while *genital* refers to sex organ interest and exploration.

School Age: The Latency Stage: Industry versus Inferiority (Six to Eleven Years of Age) At last the children are in school and for a few hours a day the house is peaceful. Now the children's peers begin to play a more active part in the family's life. Relations broaden considerably as parents also become PTA members, den mothers, or little league coaches. This is often a period of relative family tranquility insofar as the child is concerned.

The children's increasing independence also affects the parents. They find that what other parents allow their children to do becomes an important influence on their own children. "Mom, everyone else can do this, why can't I?" becomes a major means for children to try to get their own way.

The children have new ideas, a new vocabulary, and broader desires, all of which can conflict with parental values. Complaints about the children's behavior may also come from other parents, teachers, and authorities. How the children are doing at school becomes a major source of concern.

Also, the children become increasingly expensive as they grow. They eat more, their clothes cost more, and money is needed for school and leisure activities.

Yet, for most families, the elementary school years go smoothly. Children become more interesting, more individual, and increasingly independent. More important for the parents, however, is their own increased freedom from the children since the children are now away from home for part of the day.

It is especially important during this time that parents work together with the children, especially when there is trouble. By this time children are very aware and insightful and can work their parents against one another to achieve their ends unless the parents coordinate and agree. Children can cause conflict between their parents, especially if the parents differ widely in their philosophy of child rearing.

Latency refers to the general sexual quietness of this stage although there is more sexual activity than Freud or Erikson thought.

The Puberty-Adolescence Stage: Identity versus Role Diffusion (Twelve to Eighteen Years of Age)   The tranquility of the elementary school years is often shattered by the arrival of puberty. The internal physiological revolution causes children to reintegrate and requestion many earlier adjustments. *Puberty* means the biological changes every child, regardless of culture, must pass through in order to reproduce the species. *Adolescence* is a broader term that encompasses puberty as well as all of the social and cultural conditions that must be met in order to become an adult. The adolescent period in Western societies tends to be exaggerated and prolonged. There is a great deal of ambiguity and marked inconsistencies of role. Thus children are often confused about proper behavior and what is expected of them. They are not yet adults, but at the same time not allowed to remain children. For example, an eighteen-year-old boy may enter the armed services and participate in battle, yet in many states he may not legally drink beer. The fact that prolonged adolescence is a cultural artifact in no way lessens the very real problems of the period.

The parents are also entering the mid years of their lives and for many this creates problems of requestioning and reordering their lives also (see Chapter 13). Parents must begin to think about coping with the "empty-nest" period of their lives as their adolescent children grow into young adulthood and leave home to establish their own families.

The problems of puberty and adolescence fall into four main categories:

1.   Accepting a new body image and appropriate sexual expression.
2.   Establishing independence and a sense of personal identity.
3.   Forming good peer group relations.
4.   Developing goals and a philosophy of life.

It is during this stage that peer influence becomes stronger than parental influence. What friends say is more important than what parents say. The major problem facing parents now is how to give up the control they have so long had, how to have enough faith in the child to continue the "letting-go" process.

The Young Adulthood Stage: Intimacy versus Isolation   Although some children leave the family in their late teens, many remain longer, especially if they choose to go on to higher education. Seeking a

From *Hold Me!* by Jules Feiffer. © Copyright 1960, 61, 62 by Jules Feiffer. Reprinted by permission of Random House, Inc.

vocation and a mate are the major goals of this period. In the past, success in these two tasks ended children's dependence on the family. Today, however, parents are often called on to continue support of their children for several more years of schooling. They may also have to support a beginning family if a child marries during school. This can be a financially strained period for the family. In addition, studies indicate that unmarried sons and daughters over eighteen can be a strain on their parents' relationship. Both husbands and wives often report that this period when older children are living at home is a dissatisfying time in their marriage (Bernard, 1972).

John is twenty, living at home with his parents, William and Jan. John works and contributes a little toward the food budget. However, his parents find that his living at home is a real strain on their relationship. John has a new car and insists that since it is new, he should have a place in the garage. His father often transports clients in his car and though it is older feels that it must be parked inside so it remains clean. Jan often intercedes in her son's behalf, "Oh, William, it's his first car, let him use the garage." This angers William and he sometimes feels as though it's two against one. He also has wanted a den for years and would like to convert John's bedroom into one. When he encourages John to look for his own place, Jan feels that he is "just throwing him out." "We should be happy that he wants to be with us." However, Jan does find it difficult when John has his friends over. They take the living room and television, leaving her and William with little to do but retreat to their bedroom.

Hopefully, though, by the time their children are grown, parents like and love them, and take pride in a job well done. Now, after twenty or more years, the marital relationship again concerns just two people, husband and wife. Sometimes they discover that their relationship has been forfeited because of the urgency of parenthood. In this case, they face a period of discovery and rediscovery, of building a new relationship between the husband and wife or, of emptiness. Parents must work to maintain their relationship all through the period of child rearing. If they fail to do this, their relationship may become simply "for the children." In this case, when the children leave there is no relationship between the man and wife (see Chapter 13).

Broader Parenting
Perhaps the dissatisfaction and decreased marital happiness felt by some parents result from the American nuclear family where one father and one mother are expected to give a child total parenting: all the care, love, and attention that is necessary for healthy growth. But most societies, including America historically, do not expect one father and one mother to supply 100 percent of a child's needs. Grandmothers and grandfathers, aunts and uncles (real blood relatives or not), older siblings, and many others also supply parenting to children.

In many American suburban families, children and their parents (especially children and their mothers) are basically alone together. The parents cannot get away from the small child for a needed rest and participation in adult activities, nor can the child get away from the parents if necessary. The nuclear family is too often isolated from friends and relatives who might occasionally serve as substitute parents. For example, consider the problem of Susan and her mother:

Susan and her mother have always disagreed but recently, with puberty, the conflict has intensified to such a point that the entire family is in constant turmoil. Susan and her mother simply cannot communicate at this time. Susan feels that her mother doesn't understand her and her mother feels that Susan is too defensive to talk to and won't listen. Susan says her mother is old-fashioned and behind the times. Her mother feels that Susan lacks respect for her elders and is insensitive to others in general. Susan relies on her girlfriends for advice.

Yet Susan needs a female adult with whom she can communicate her fear and anxieties about becoming an adult and from whom she can learn.

In the past, Susan could have turned to a grandmother or an aunt who lived in the family or nearby.

What if parents find they can't really be good parents for a particular child? The child will be trapped in the setting for years. Again, in the past, this child could possibly go and live with relatives who, by temperament, might be better suited to act as his or her parents. Children were sometimes traded between families for short periods, spent summers on a farm, were helped to grow by numerous adults and older children. This extended family meant that no one person or couple were responsible for total parenting. Some critics of the nuclear family suggest that the nuclear family pattern of parents and children always alone together contributes to creating problems in children rather than preventing them. Since the reality of the nuclear family is the only reality small children may know, they cannot correct misperceptions. It is difficult for children to recognize problems, and reorient themselves since they have no other basis by which to compare how adults act.

Broader parenting might be supplied by trading care of children with other families, volunteer community nursery schools, business-supplied day-care centers for workers, and expanding the nuclear family to again include relatives. Volunteering to work in a community nursery is also a way for prospective parents to gain experience with children.

We usually think of adoption being the resort of a couple who cannot physically conceive children. However, there are many other reasons for adoption. A couple may not be able to care for their children, for

Parents without Pregnancy: Adoption

example, so friends or relatives may adopt the children in order to give them a home. Or a couple may feel strongly about the problems of overpopulation and decide to adopt rather than add to the population. Or a husband or wife may wish to adopt their spouse's other children by a prior marriage in order to become their legal parent as well as their stepparent.

The choice to adopt a child is just that, a reasoned decision, a real choice decided on by a couple after a great deal of deliberation and thought. As such, the decision-making process leading to adoption is really an ideal model that all couples desiring children should follow. Adoption takes time and certain requirements such as family stability, finances, and housing must be met by the prospective parents.

Adoptive parents have some advantages as well as disadvantages compared to natural parents. For example, adoptive parents may choose their child. To some degree they may pick genetic, physical, and mental characteristics of the child. They may bypass some of the earlier years of childhood if they desire. On the other hand, they do not experience pregnancy and birth which help to focus the couple on impending parenthood. Of course, some may consider this another advantage of adoption.

A unique parenting problem faced by adoptive parents is that of deciding whether to share the knowledge of the adoption with the child and if so, when? Experts believe the best course is to inform the child from the beginning, but this is often difficult for parents to do. They may fear that such information will affect the child's love for them. They may want to tell them but simply keep avoiding it until it seems too late. Most adoption agencies such as The Children's Home Society supply counseling to prospective adoptive parents on how to handle telling the child. The problems created for both parents and children if the children find out about their adoptive status from others are usually greater and often do harm to the parent-child relationship. The basic trust of the children in their parents may be weakened or perhaps even destroyed if the parents aren't the ones to tell them.

At some time in their lives many adoptive children feel the need to know something about their natural parents. In most legal adoptions, however, records identifying the true parents are unavailable. Some adults who were adopted as children are pressuring states to make information about their real parents available. A few states are moving toward opening adoption records to adopted persons when they reach legal age.

For many years legal adoption was a long drawn-out process wherein prospective parents were put through a strenuous screening process to establish their parental suitability. Recently such screening has been minimized and the long wait for an adoptive child reduced. Also, in a few cases, especially with older children, single people are being allowed to adopt.

Adoption works to give parentless children a home and family as well as to give childless couples children if they so desire. Unfortunately, not all parentless children are easily adoptable. Many minority children are never adopted. Children with defects and health problems seldom are sought by prospective adoptive parents. For the most part such children are reared in various kinds of institutions or by a series of short-term foster home placements.

Adolescent Parenthood and the Single-Parent Family

Today many more adolescent unmarried women who become pregnant are choosing to keep their children than did so in the past. The unwed adolescent mother used to be a major source of adoptive children. But now so many choose to keep their child that adoption agencies are having trouble finding enough children to meet the demand. Although most of these women ultimately marry, until that time they and their children constitute a single-parent family. Add to them those that are divorced, separated, and early widowed, and we find that the single-parent family is becoming a major family form in the United States. In 1978, approximately 19 percent of children under eighteen years of age lived in single-parent families (Glick, 1979).

The rising divorce rate has also been a major contributing factor to the increase in single-parent families. Commencing in 1975, the divorce rate began to level out (Chapter 15) and so we can expect the rate of increase of single-parent families to also show a decline. Remember that single-parent families tend to be a passing phenomenon since marriage rates for single parents are high (Reiss, 1980).

Although family form (nuclear, single-parent, three-generation, foster, etc.) will affect children, the old idea that *only* the traditional two-parent, father-mother family does a good job in rearing children is passing (Marotz-Baden et al, 1979, p. 12). However, there is little doubt that single parenting has more inherent problems than does two-parent child rearing. In many ways the problems of the single-parent family are exaggerated duplicates of the working mother's problems.

The vast majority of single-parent families are women and their children. Thus for them, all of the problems encountered by the working mother are present (see Chapter 8). Low pay, child care problems, overburden caused by working and continuing to shoulder all of the household and child rearing duties face the single mother. The single father may face all of the same problems (except his pay is usually better). However for most fathers the home and child care burdens are new and, at first, often frightening.

Social isolation is one of the problems faced by any single parent. Juggling work, home maintenance, and child care duties usually leaves one little time for either social interaction or self-improvement activities.

Emotional isolation is a second major problem. Having no other adult in the home with whom to share often leads to feelings of loneliness and a sense of powerlessness. If one is a separated or divorced unmarried parent, emotional isolation may be increased by the social stigma that is often attached to these statuses. The early widowed parent, on the other hand, will experience sympathy and support from the society.

Many single parents attempt to alleviate the isolation as well as reduce living expenses by making greater use of shared living arrangements. One study indicates that 23 percent of the single-parent sample had a second adult (usually a relative) living in the household. Only 9 percent of the two-parent families in the study shared their household with another adult (Smith, 1980, p. 77).

Single-parent families headed by women with small earning power suffer numerous logistic problems. Caring for small children during working hours without exorbitant cost is a major concern. Finding adequate housing in a decent neighborhood is often impossible. Even in small cities, female-headed families are concentrated in less desirable blocks of the city (Roncek et al, 1980, p. 167). Larger amounts of welfare aid go to these families than to any others, which is indicative of the financial difficulties they face.

The single adolescent parent faces all of these problems while they themselves are still fighting the problems of self-identity, maturity, and attaining worthwhile vocational skills.* Pay for the adolescent is generally at the lowest levels because of their lack of training and skills.

A study using 1000 thirty-year-olds selected from the 1960 Project Talent participants found that 10 percent of the men and 31 percent of the women had a child during adolescence. Higher incidences of adolescent parenting occurred among blacks and low socioeconomic and low ability groups. Adolescent parenting appeared to negatively affect a number of aspects of the individual's life.

The most immediate consequence of adolescent parenting was termination of school attendance. This directly affected employability so that the adolescent parents were still employed in lower paying jobs at age thirty when compared with nonadolescent parents in the sample.

Having children at a young age also appears to be related to marital dissolution. In a recent study 21 percent of the adolescent parents were or had been separated or divorced as compared to 11 percent of the entire sample (Russ-Eft et al, 1979, pp. 173 – 179).

Perhaps the greatest objection to adolescent parenthood is the fact that the parents assume responsibilities and obligations before they themselves are complete individuals. Their chances for self-growth through extended education, travel, and broadened experiences are reduced because of their parenting responsibilities. One purpose of the usual prolonged adolescence in America has been to allow young persons some freedom from adult responsibilities so that they can concentrate on their own personal development. "To go as far as you can," "to make the most of yourself," are American ideals sought for the young. Very early parenthood almost always works against such ideals.

Summary

Parenthood remains one of the major functions of marriage. Despite decreasing emphasis on it and more tolerance of childlessness for married couples, the vast majority of married couples will become parents.

Planning for parenthood, improving parenting skills, working as a parent team, and understanding the course of development a child passes through in becoming an adult are all important to successful parenting. In addition, understanding how children will affect the parental relationship is very important. No one method has yet been discovered whereby parents can assure the successful upbringing of their children. The fact is that parenthood is a difficult and ever-changing job that demands intelligence, flexibility, emotional warmth, and stability as well as a goodly portion of courage. Parenthood is no easy task and certainly not to be taken lightly.

Children will affect their parents in many ways. Bringing the first baby home immediately changes the life style of the parents.

*About 60% of all unwed mothers are teenagers (Honig, 1978, p. 113).

Suddenly they have another dependent and demanding person to take care of who can, at first, contribute little to the family. Not only is room taken up in the family's living place, but additional funds are needed to care for the new family member. Dad and Mom will both come second to the infant's demands. Although one can divorce a troublesome spouse, there is little that parents can do to escape a troublesome child. Legally and morally, the children are the parents' responsibility until they reach legal adulthood. Even then, parents in many cases will still shoulder responsibility for their children, for example when they go to graduate school.

Erik Erikson (1963) identifies eight psychosocial developmental stages that describe the human life cycle from infancy through old age. The first six are important to parents. They are the oral-sensory stage (first year), the muscular-anal stage (two to three years), the locomotor-genital stage (four to five years), the latency stage (six to eleven years), the puberty-adolescence stage (twelve to eighteen years), and the young adulthood stage (eighteen to thirty, approximately). Each stage has certain tasks that the child must accomplish to become a successful adult. By knowing at what stage a child is and the kinds of tasks that characterize the stage, parents can better understand the child and plan activities that are optimally helpful to the child.

Broader parenting would help parents to do a better job. Having alternative sources of parenting available serves a number of helpful purposes. First, parents would have "time out" periods from their children. This would allow them to concentrate for a short period on themselves and their relationship. It would give them a respite from the burdens and responsibilities of the children. Second, the children would have a broader set of influences and greater stimulation. They would also learn to cope with new and different kinds of people. In general, their experience base would be broader.

Adoption is another avenue to parenthood. It has the advantages of contributing to population control as well as allowing parents greater choice in selection of the children they want. It does, however, have the major problem of having to tell the children that they are adopted.

The single-parent family, although usually transitory, is more common today than ever before. Such a family faces many problems, but with support is capable of doing a good child rearing job. Adolescent parents also face special problems, the main one being that the parents themselves are still in the act of becoming fully functioning adults and parenthood tends to make this job harder.

Parenthood is an important part of most marriages. Good planning will hopefully make parenthood a positive factor in marriages.

Family Violence

In earlier chapters, the importance of the family as a source of love, caring, and emotional support has been emphasized. Yet it is also true that the possibility of violence and abuse of family members exists within the poorly functioning family. Family violence is difficult to measure and document because most of it occurs in the privacy of the home, away from public view. In the past few years great efforts have been made to increase public awareness of family violence; there have been many newspaper and magazine articles as well as T.V. presentations on the battered wife and the abused child. Such publicity has served to bring family violence more into the open.

Violence between Spouses

The most life-threatening situation into which a police officer can enter is a family dispute. Emotions run high and the family members usually feel that their problems are a private matter and that the police officer is an unwanted intruder. Homicide rates are high within families, with about equal numbers of wives killing husbands as

husbands killing wives. Physical damage done by one spouse to another usually involves the husband hurting his wife although the reverse does happen.

In general this kind of violence flares between spouses who do not have good communication skills. Because of this, frustration and hostility build and finally something triggers an emotional outburst resulting in violent behavior.

Some researchers such as Bach and Wyden (1968) maintain that arguing and fighting verbally are integral to all intimate relationships (Chapter 6). They encourage couples to learn how to do it fairly and effectively. Many feel that verbal fighting and aggression will reduce the incidence of physical violence. The idea is that the verbal expression of hostility is cathartic and that "letting it out" will reduce its intensity. In his study of 385 families, however, Straus (1974) found that the greater the amount of verbal aggression, the greater the amount of physical aggression. Physical aggression was less common when people tried to discuss their problems calmly. The use of force for resolving family conflict also acts as a training ground for abuse (Steinmetz, 1977a, p. 21).

Child Abuse

Mistreatment of children by parents hardly seems compatible with mom, apple pie, and Sunday family outings. Yet, there are many parents who physically and emotionally abuse their children. Although statistics are difficult to obtain, it is estimated that at least 1 out of every 500 children die each year from mistreatment and that another 1 million children are victims of physical abuse or neglect (APA, 1976).

In 1973-74, the California Central Registry of Child Abuse reported 17,000 documented cases in just this one state. The problem is so troublesome to California authorities that, as of January 1, 1975, the penal code was amended to increase penalties for child abuse and, perhaps more important, to make it legally mandatory that suspected abuse be reported within thirty-six hours of discovery.

Child Abuse and the Law The following are paraphrased excerpts from Section I, Section 1161.5, of the California Penal Code, effective January 1, 1975:

Any person who willfully causes or permits a child to suffer, or inflicts thereon unjustifiable physical pain or mental suffering, or willfully permits a child to be placed in a situation dangerous to its person or health, is punishable by imprisonment in the county jail for a period not exceeding one year, or in the state prison for not less than one year nor more than ten years.

Any person who under circumstances other than those likely to produce great bodily harm or death, who willfully causes or permits any child to unjustifiably suffer or permits the child to be injured, or places the child in a dangerous situation is guilty of a misdemeanor.

In any case in which a minor is brought to a physician, dentist (there follows a long list of persons, including teachers, social workers, etc.), and they determine from observation of the minor that the minor has physical injury or injuries which appear to have been inflicted by other than accidental means by any person, that the minor has been sexually molested, or that any injury prohibited by the terms of Section 273a has been inflicted upon the minor, shall report such fact by telephone and in writing, within thirty-six hours, to both the local police authority having jurisdiction and to the juvenile probation department; or, in the alternative, either to the county welfare department, or to the county health department. The report shall state, if known, the name of the minor, the minor's whereabouts, and the character and extent of the injuries or molestation.

Reports and other pertinent information received shall be made available to any licensed physician and surgeon, dentist, resident, intern, podiatrist, chiropractor, or religious practitioner with regard to the patient or client; any director of a county welfare department, school superintendent, supervisor of child welfare and attendance, certified pupil personnel employee, or school principal having a direct interest in the welfare of the minor, and to any probation department, juvenile probation department, or agency offering child protective services.

The most important thing about the law is that it becomes mandatory for those in contact with children to report cases of suspected abuse. This helps greatly in uncovering cases that otherwise might be easily hidden.

In general, three elements must usually be present in a family for child abuse to occur. First, the parent must be a person to whom physical punishment is acceptable. It is often found that the abusive parent was abused as a child. The abusive parent has also often been found to be self-righteous and moralistic and to have unrealistic expectations for the child. The parent often expects things of the child that are impossible for the child's level of development. Second, the child is usually difficult and trying. Third, there is usually a crisis event of some kind. The parent has lost a job, is having marital conflict, or something else that has reduced the parent's tolerance level is occurring (Helfer and Kempe, 1974; Starr, 1979, 872–878).

Some cities have recently created telephone hot lines that a parent may use to receive immediate help if he or she feels unable to cope with the child or children. One program to help abusive parents was started in 1970 in Santa Barbara, California. Claire W. Miles became so concerned about child abuse that she installed an extra phone in her home and advertised in the personal column of the local newspaper asking anyone who knew of an abused child to call the number. Within the next month she received twenty-eight calls, many from parents who abused their children. From this simple beginning the Child Abuse Listening Mediation (CALM) program grew. In the first year, CALM was involved in 213 cases. Since that time the program has grown to include educational presentations throughout the country and volunteers who visit the parents as well as the immediate help offered by telephone to the troubled parents.

Help for the Abusive Parent from CALM (Child Abuse Listening Mediation) A good example of the effectiveness and dedication of CALM volunteers is demonstrated in the case of a young mother who called recently for help.

The mother has a son three years old. About two years ago, she had a nervous breakdown and was confined for some time in the psychiatric ward of a hospital. Her baby was cared for by grandparents during her confinement. When she was able to take her baby back, she remarked how fat and healthy he was. The improvement in his physical condition seemed to accentuate her feelings of inadequacy as a mother, and gave her a feeling of even greater insecurity in her relationship with her son. Her child is hyperactive, and her energy is not often a match for his. She has been trying to toilet train him without much success. When she tries to feed him, he throws food all over and refuses to eat. Then later he cries and is cross because he is hungry. Generally she feels that he does nothing right and everything wrong. She is fearful that he is abnormal in some way.

She would like to take him to a nursery school one or two days a week, so she could just be alone and rest, but she can't afford the private nurseries, which are the only ones who will take a child under three or one in diapers. She said, "I don't know what to do — I can't stand it much longer. Can you help me?"

She was told about the volunteer program, and she agreed to have someone come over the next day. A volunteer was selected who lives near her, and who has seven children of her own, ranging in age from ten to one, including a set of twins three years old.

The volunteer found that the girl has no friends here, since she has recently come from the east. Her relatives are all back there. She is lonely and overanxious and tense from being a twenty-four-hour-a-day mother every day. On the initial visit, she didn't want the volunteer to leave, so the volunteer stayed as long as possible, then took the client and child home with her. For two or three weeks, the volunteer invited her over three mornings a week. She encouraged the girl to use her sewing machine to make kitchen curtains. The client gained assurance that there was nothing abnormal about her child, and through association with the volunteer's twins of the same age, the boy began to eat normally without throwing his food around. The mother observed many traits in the volunteer's children similar to those she had worried about in her son, and in a relatively short time has already expressed a relieved sense of relaxation in her relationship with her son. She is being more realistic in her expectations of him, and is gaining self-confidence in her feelings of being able to care for him more adequately.

Sibling Abuse

Probably the most physical abuse occurs between siblings. Young children have fewer ways to express themselves than do adults. They also have less self-control, and thus their frustrations are often expressed aggressively via physical means. Almost 5 percent of surveyed families reported a sibling having used a knife or gun at some time. If this is correct, it is estimated that 2.3 million children have been attacked by a sibling or at least threatened with such a weapon (Steinmetz, 1977b, 1978).

Parental Abuse by Children

Although this type of abuse sounds improbable, there are cases where children physically attack and even kill their parents. This tends to occur most often with troubled teenagers. Although physical abuse of parents by their children is limited, verbal and psychological abuse is common. Children place heavy demands on their parents and seldom fail to react at least verbally when they are frustrated. Verbal abuse heaped on parents by teenage children seems to be the norm during that stage of development.

Although we have focused on physical abuse, both verbal and psychological abuse also takes its toll on family members. Hopefully, families can improve their communication and sharing skills so that abusive and violent incidences do not have to occur.

Chapter 13 〜

Contents

Scenes from Marriage:

Family Life Stages: Mid-Life Crisis to Surviving Spouse

The flush of love and the excitement of exploring a new relationship effectively keep most newly married couples from thinking about later stages of their relationship. After all, who can think about children leaving home when no children have yet arrived? What possible relevance can retirement have for a twenty-three-year-old man receiving his first job promotion? And what newly married woman can be thinking about the very real likelihood that she will spend the last ten to fifteen years of her life as a widow, alone and without this man she now loves and needs so much?

Yet, these are important questions with which almost all married couples must come to grips at some time in their lives. Perhaps one way that the reader can make such questions relevant and meaningful is to consider them in the context of their parent's and grandparent's lives. We cannot expect to live our lives identically to our relative's because we are different individuals and the times in which we live change. Yet, their lives may serve as a preview for some of the changes that will come into our own lives.

If we have children, then the day will come when our children leave home. This is a change that we will have to face just as did our parents and their parents before them. The couple who thinks about and prepares for the inevitable family life changes before they occur stands a better chance of adapting to them in a creative and growth-oriented manner. You will remember that the last basic assumption on which this book is based (p. 10) states:

> Any family relationship can change, just as individuals within the relationship can and do change. Change does not mean the end to the relationship. Indeed, lack of change over time is probably unhealthy and may ultimately lead to the demise of the relationship.

Marriage changes just as people change. Change occurs regardless of one's attitudes towards it. Change can be for the better or the worse. If a marriage changes too much for the worse, then it may end. On the other hand, individuals and families can grow in positive directions to become stronger, more intimate, more communicative, more need-fulfilling, more supportive, and more loving. Since change cannot be avoided, the real question to answer is "Will I cope with the changes in my life and family in a positive growth-oriented manner?" In order to answer this question, we must first consider the changes that can be expected.

An Overview of Family Life Stages

Family life stages are nothing more than classifications through which we hope to gain better understanding of the changes that people go through as they move from birth to death. A developmental stage approach has long been taken in studying children, as we saw in Chapter 12. The prenatal stage, infancy, preschool, school, pre-puberty, puberty, adolescence, and young adult are all well-known developmental stages in the life of the maturing human.

What about stages in the life of a maturing marriage? If we examine the general kinds of problems faced at various marital stages, it seems that for the average American couple, there are six important periods in a long-term marriage: (1) newly married, (2) early parenthood, (3) later parenthood, (4) empty nest (middle age), (5) retirement, and (6) widowhood.

The problems of the *newly married* stage revolve around adjusting to each other, establishing a home, setting directions to the relationship, learning to confront the world as a pair rather than as an individual, and learning to work together to achieve mutually agreed upon goals. These problems have already been discussed in various parts of the preceding chapters.

The advent of children places a couple in the parental role. This change will compound the problems of a newly married couple, especially if children arrive shortly after the marriage, before they have had much time to work out the problems of the first stage.

Early parenthood covers pregnancy, birth, infants, toddlers, preschoolers, and elementary school children. However, when puberty arrives and the children move into junior and senior high school, college, and the young adult world, the problems parents face change drastically. So drastic are the changes that it becomes worthwhile to examine this period in a marriage separately, hence the third stage becomes *later parenthood*. As we saw in Chapter 12, adolescence is actually a combination of puberty, the biological maturing of the child, and the social expectations placed on the child to behave in an adult manner. America, like many western cultures, does not sharply define entrance into adulthood. In fact, the adolescent period in America is nebulous, conflicting and confused because it extends well beyond the achievement of biological maturity. Because of this, many parents find later parenthood to be a trying time. Children become increasingly independent and demanding of freedom, yet parents legally and ethically are still held responsible for their children's actions. It can be a period of strained finances, especially if the children go on to higher education. It is, of course, a period of adjustment by parents to their children's adult sexuality and mate selection attempts. This culminates for most parents in the acceptance of a new family as the children marry and reproduce. Chapter 12 discussed the two stages of parenthood.

Finally, the last child leaves home and the *empty nest* or *middle age* stage begins. For many couples, the parental role continues in that they may still give monetary and psychological support to the newly married children. The grandparent role often continues many of the parental behaviors because children are still part of the couple's lives at times. For others, especially mothers who were child-centered, the empty nest stage can be one of loneliness and loss if the children move far away or reject continued parenting. New interests and goals must be developed to replace the lost parenting functions. The husband will have to assist his wife to reorient her life away from the children and this in turn will usually influence his own. Fathers or career-oriented mothers survive this stage more easily than traditional mothers since many of their goals and fulfillments lie outside the family in the work world. Thus, their feelings of loss when the children leave are normally less severe.

This may be a period during which the husband and wife draw closer. During the earlier marital years many wives devoted their energies to the children and husbands to their work, and therefore they may well have grown emotionally apart. Now, when the children are gone and the husband is established may be the time for a couple to renew their life together, to reinvest in one another, to lay the foundation to the next marital stage, *retirement*.

Increasing life expectancy, automation, and America's emphasis on youth have combined to almost double the length of retirement in the average worker's life during this century. The retiring worker faces the problem of adjusting to leisure after years of basing much of his or her self-worth on working and income production. In addition, the work ethic says that stature is gained by a work orientation, not leisure (Hochschild, 1973). Retirement equals obsolescence in the view of American society. For the productive worker, forced retirement presents a simple option to the retiree: adjust or be miserable (Darnley, 1975, p. 217).*

In a sense, retirement for the man is similar to the empty nest stage for the traditional child-centered wife. It is now he who must cope with lack of purpose and feelings of uselessness. For those who cannot find substitute goals, retirement can be an unhappy period. Indeed, for some it is literally a short-lived period in that death often arrives shortly after retirement for those who cannot seem to adjust (Staley & Miller, 1972). On the other hand, especially for those that have been financially successful, retirement may mean rebirth rather than death. It may signal a new beginning, expanding interests, and rediscovery of the marital partner. Poverty and poor health are the two greatest enemies of the retired. Indeed some 30 percent of men continue to work after age sixty-five, many out of economic necessity.

Inevitably death takes one of the marital partners and so the final marital stage is usually a return to singleness, *widowhood*. In 1976 there were about 7.2 million widows, or approximately 5.3 times the 1.37 million widowers 65 and over (Glick, 1979, p. 304). These statistics point clearly to the fact that widowhood is a far greater possibility than is becoming a widower. Although the percentage of widowed persons in the general population has dropped this century, just as with retirement, the number of years that widowhood may be expected to last has risen dramatically. For example, half of those women widowed at

*Mandatory retirement age was raised from 65 to 70 years effective January 1, 1979.

age sixty-five can expect fifteen more years of life. Thus, especially for women, this final marital stage can be lengthy.

Widowhood is predominantly an older person's problem. For younger widowed persons, remarriage is the solution of choice. However, remarriage becomes increasingly remote with advancing age. In 1975, only 1 percent of the brides and 2 percent of the grooms were sixty-five years old and over (Glick, 1979, p. 303). Naturally, for the widowed person who does remarry, widowhood may not be the last stage of marriage. Remarriage will reinstate an earlier marital stage.

Since the first three stages, newly married and early and later parenthood, have already been discussed in earlier chapters, the remainder of this chapter will be devoted to the last three stages, the empty nest, retirement, and widowhood.

The Empty Nest: Middlescence

For most couples, middle age starts when the children become independent and ends when retirement draws near. Although arbitrary, most people are in this stage between the ages of forty and sixty years.* Better than an arbitrary age range, however, is to delimit this stage by the kinds of changes and problems that occur. For example, a very young mother might face "empty nest" changes by the time she is thirty-five years old.

Historically, middle age is a relatively new stage in marriage.** The much shorter life spans prior to 1900 made it such that most wives buried their husbands before the last child left home. As Glick (1955, pp. 3–9 and 1977, pp. 5–9) points out:

> In 1890 women bore their last child at thirty-two, buried their husband at age fifty-three and attended their last child's wedding at age fifty-five.

> In 1975, women bore their last child at age thirty, attended their last child's wedding at fifty-two, and buried their husband at age sixty-five.

Thus, for most marriages prior to 1900, there was no period of return to simply being a couple alone together. Yet today such a period is not only very likely, but the chances are great that it will last for nearly fifteen years if one considers the father to be fifty-four when the last child leaves home and his death to occur at age sixty-nine.

The changes faced during middle age are somewhat different for men and women. Essentially the woman's problems center on no longer being needed by her children, whereas the man's problems center around his vocation and feelings of achievement and success.

However, for both partners, middle age reactivates many of the questions that each thought had been answered much earlier in their

---

*The census bureau uses the age of forty-five to denote the onset of middle age.
**Life expectancy for persons born in 1900 was about forty-seven years. Today, life expectancy for women is seventy-six and about sixty-eight for men.

lives. Indeed, many of the questions that arise resemble those that were struggled with when the partners were adolescents: "Who am I?" "Where am I going?" "How will I get there?" "What is life all about?" "How do I handle my changing sexuality?" Hence, the term "middlescence" has been coined to describe this stage.

Writers who compare middle age with adolescence and who discover an identity crisis in both periods disagree over what it means (Kerckhoff, 1976). Some see middle age characterized by trying to avoid the recurring bizarre, irrational, sexually confused questions that first occurred at adolescence (McMorrow, 1974). Others, such as Brayshaw (1962), suggest that although middle age may be frustrating and upsetting, such problems can also be growth-producing:

> There are significant parallels between adolescence and middle age. The task of the adolescent is to integrate into life not only his sexuality but the powerful resurgence of idealism . . . Now in middle life there is a sudden breaking through of this suppressed and neglected . . . element in life. . . . We come then to the central question. *What is the second half of life for?* Man has always asked himself "What are we here for?" "What is the purpose of life?" "What is our prime duty?" But in practice, ordinary people find that the cares of bringing up a family obliterate these philosophical questions. We are too busy earning our livings and running our homes and caring for our children. We have no doubt that this is our duty and purpose in life. It is when the children go that the ancient (existential) questions become acutely personal for the second half of life.

Those suggesting that the crisis of middle age is useful say: "Middlescence is the opportunity for going on with the identity crisis of the first adolescence. It is our second chance to find out what it really means to 'do your own thing,' to sing your own song, to be deeply true to yourself. It is a time for finding one's own truths at last, and thereby to become free to discover one's real identity" (LeShan, 1973). In describing the pain and danger that middle-aged people will experience in reexamining their identities, LeShan goes on to compare the process with a lobster's periodic shedding of its shell: it makes the lobster vulnerable, but allows it to grow.

For some, then, it is no wonder that they choose to use their marriage as an escape from facing the existential challenges of middle age. They do not ask the important questions because it is safe to assume that marriage is answer enough. "Who am I?" "I am Mr. or Mrs. Jones." "What is my life all about?" "I am a faithful wife or husband." "I do my duty to the family and help keep it running smoothly." "Where am I going?" "We hope to take a trip to Cape Cod next summer." "My marriage is the answer to all existential questions." "My marriage is my existence."

But to the couples who dare, the crisis of middle age can offer a chance to grow, and the problems can become a vehicle for growth. Marriage enrichment for the middle-aged couple is not to be focused on the improvement of marriage so much as on the improvement of the humans in it. According to LeShan (1973):

One of the most valuable attributes of marriage is that one's partner can truly be one's best friend, and friendship was never more important. If one defines a friend as someone who loves you in spite of knowing your faults and weaknesses, and has even better dreams for your fulfillment than you have for yourself, it can surely be the foundation for what each of us needs most in middle age — permission to continue to quest for one's own identity.

It is not so much what actually happens to us in middle age as it is our attitude about it that really counts. We all experience some kind of crisis in this as in other stages, but how do we use the crisis? If we use it for further growth and expansion of our lives, then our marriage, our relationships, and we ourselves may all benefit and make the second half of our lives even more fulfilling than was the first half.

Middle age can be at least as satisfying as any other life stage.

The Authenticity Crisis of Mid Life Speaking of the mid-life crisis, Gail Sheehy (1977, p. 350) states:

> Deep down a change begins to register in those gut-level perceptions of safety and danger, time and no time, aliveness and stagnation. I start with a vague feeling . . .
>
> > I have reached some sort of meridian in my life. I had better take a survey, reexamine where I have been, and reevaluate how I am going to spend my resources from here on. Why am I doing all this? What do I really believe in?
>
> Underneath this vague feeling is the fact, as yet unacknowledged, that there is a down side to life, a back of the mountain, and that I have only so much time before the dark to find my own truth. As such thoughts grow, the continuity of the life cycle is disrupted. Somewhere between thirty-five and forty-five if we let ourselves, most of us will have a full-out authenticity crisis.

There is infinite variety in the way individuals face the questions that arise when they realize that life is finite. Some people simply look the other way and avoid the questions. Others try to change their external world by relocating, finding a new spouse or a new job. Others seek internal changes such as a new set of values or a new philosophy of life.

Obviously, a person's life circumstances influence the questions and their answers. A child-centered mother out of the occupational world for twenty years may feel real panic as she realizes that she will soon be unneeded by her children. Another mother who has always worked in addition to raising her children may be happy that her children will no longer need her, thus freeing some time to pursue long-neglected interests. Because of these individual differences, our discussion of the mid-life changes must remain general. Some individuals will experience the things we discuss, others may not, and yet others may experience things that are not discussed. Despite these limitations it is worthwhile to examine the middle years of life, because we will all pass through them.

For the traditional wife and mother, the mid-life crisis will revolve around the growing independence of her children and finally their move from home. She has to face her partial failure as a parent (p. 364). She faces feelings of loss and uselessness because she is no longer needed. Her feelings are somewhat akin to the man's feelings when he retires. She often faces reentry to the work world where she may not have used her skills for twenty years. She faces a renewal of her earlier "pair" relationship. It will now be just she and her husband. She faces the biological boundary of the end of her childbearing years. "No more children even if I wanted one." This and the accent on youth in America will cause her to reevaluate her sexuality, asking: "Am I still attractive to men?" "Is there more to sex than I have experienced?" She, as well as her husband, will probably face death in a very personal way when one of their parents and then the other passes away. This event causes many people to direct their thoughts meaningfully towards death and the fact that there truly is an end to life for the first

Five years ago, Jane and Bill Smith and their two older children left their home in Santa Barbara where they were a mathematician and a teacher, respectively. Now they're back as a physician and lawyer-to-be. Bill, an internist with a local medical group, used to be a systems analyst with a large research and development firm. Jane is scheduled to take her bar exam early this year after having taught elementary school for years.

"I read about a program at the University of Miami where they retrain people with Ph.D.'s in the biological sciences to become M.D.'s," said Bill. "There was at the time a plethora of Ph.D.'s and a lack of M.D.'s. Then they let a few people in with degrees in the physical sciences." — He has a doctorate in math — "and discovered that they did just as well."

He spent two years in the accelerated medical school program, which he calls the time of "learning the language," then three years in a Veteran's Administration hospital for his internship and residency, "where I really learned to be a doctor."

Bill said he'd never been exposed much to the hospital environment until he began singing in a barbershop quartet, which was often invited to entertain in rest homes and hospitals. He said he'd had the field of medicine "in the back of my mind" for a long time before he applied. He felt that medicine would be a more self-sufficient career than computers.

"I enjoy the work itself. I never took math home. Nobody cares about the answers except people in the field. However, I never get tired of medicine. When I get home, I get out the medical journals and the texts."

"I knew there'd be 700 applicants and only 28 selected so I didn't get my hopes up. They called for an interview, and three weeks later called again to say that I was 29th, the 'first alternate.' I figured that they told this to many people, so we bought a ping-pong table and settled back into our old routine."

Classes began in Miami on July 1. On July 5, after an afternoon of tennis, the couple arrived home to a telephone call from Miami asking "Can you come tomorrow?" A student had dropped out making room for the first alternate.

Making a quick decision, he packed up and left the next day, leaving Jane to sell the house and furniture plus complete a summer job that she had undertaken.

Bill said the only courses he had in undergraduate school that applied to medical school were a year of chemistry and a course in physiology. But based on his medical school test scores, the lack of preliminary courses wasn't too difficult a problem. "Math training involves more rational thought and medicine is simply more memorization at first."

During his residency his wife took the opportunity to go to law school. When they returned to Santa Barbara she did some volunteer work in the consumer fraud division of the district attorney's office. "Now I'm spending all my time studying for the bar," she said.

As a teacher, Jane said she "was always interested in the political side of teaching. I'm interested in educational law — children's rights, parent's and teacher's rights. I don't think anyone is working in that area here." She said that she was considering this career change even before Bill made his big change.

For both spouses to make such dramatic mid-life changes is certainly unusual. Yet this true story points out that families can make major and dramatic changes and survive and be rejuvenated.

time. In addition to all these changes, the American woman must now face the questions of changing identity and roles aroused by the feminist movement (p. 38).

Thus we see that the mid-life changes faced by women are broad and profound. Of course, both she and her husband face the turmoil within each other created by this stage. If her husband is unhappy and dissatisfied with his work, this adds to her own crisis. If she decides to actively embrace the feminine liberation movement, this may add to the stress and strain felt by her husband.

The typical husband's mid-life crisis revolves around his work world rather than around his family. This is particularly true for the highly successful man. In a competitive economic society such as ours, a person must devote a great deal of energy to his or her work to achieve success. The male is often forced to handle two marriages, the first to his work and the second (in importance also) to his family.

Thus, his mid-life crisis centers around letting go of the impossible dream of youth. He begins to recognize that not all of his dreams will be achieved. For those few men who really have fulfilled their dreams, the mid-life question becomes "What do I do now?" Most men, however, must cope with disillusionment. The feeling that the dream was counterfeit, the vague feeling of having been cheated, "the dream isn't really what I thought it would be," and the growing awareness that perhaps "I won't ever achieve my dreams" are the questions that cause turmoil.

America's emphasis on youth will also cause him problems. "If I haven't achieved it by now, I won't get any more chances." Younger competitive men become a real threat to job security. The subtle comments about retirement now take on a personal significance.

Unfortunately, his dream disillusionment usually carries over into the family. He doubts himself, he doubts his family. He may even blame them for his failure to achieve the dreams of his youth. "If it hadn't been for the family burdens, I'd have made it."

Along with general self-doubts come doubts about sexuality. Unlike his wife, though, these doubts usually do not revolve around physical attractiveness. They occur at a time when his wife's sexuality is at its highest peak (p. 282), and revolve around performance. This, combined with feminine liberation influencing his wife to be more aware and assertive of her own sexuality, can make his self-doubts extremely strong. Self-doubt unfortunately is the male's greatest enemy to satisfactory sexual relations.

In some cases, a rather interesting partial exchange of roles takes place at this time of life. The woman becomes more interested in the world outside of her family. She becomes more responsive to her own aggressiveness and competitive feelings. She returns to the work world, to school, to an interest in public affairs and causes. He becomes more receptive to his long-repressed affiliative and loving promptings. He renews his interest in the family and in social issues outside of his work. He becomes more caring in the way that mother has been caring within the family. Unfortunately, the children are no longer receptive to his new-found parental caring since they are busy seeking their own independence.

Overall, then, for both a man and a woman, mid life usually means rethinking and reevaluating one's life. It is a time of restructuring. The resulting turmoil may destroy the marriage and family or it may result in a revitalized marriage. By recognizing and squarely confronting the issues of mid life, the chances increase that the results will be positive and growth-producing rather than negative and destructive.

Retirement　Retirement usually signals the beginning of disengagement. In many nonindustrialized societies, this is a gradual process. The hardest physical labor is performed by young men and women at the peak of their physical condition. As they age and their own offspring grow to maturity, they assume more administrative and supervisory duties while their children take on the harder physical labor. Ideally, the following generation is ready to take over by the time the parental generation begins to slow down. To some extent this gradual tapering off of duties

Inset 13-2
How Do Couples Judge Their Marriages at Each of the Family Life Cycle Stages?

The following eight-stage family life cycle was developed by Spanier et al (1975, p. 270).

I Beginning families
Couples married less than 5 years with no children

II Childbearing families
Oldest child, birth to 2 years, 11 months

III Families with preschool children
Oldest child, 3 years to 5 years, 11 months

IV Families with schoolage children
Oldest child, 6 years to 12 years, 11 months

V Families with teenagers
Oldest child, 13 years to 20 years, 11 months

VI Families as launching centers
First child gone to last child's leaving home

VII Families in the middle years
Empty nest to retirement

VIII Aging families
Retirement to death of first spouse

Childless families
Families with no children after five years of marriage

Evidence (see Figure 13-1) suggests a general drop in marital satisfaction for both partners, commencing shortly after marriage, bottoming out in the 4th stage (families with schoolage children) and rising thereafter but never regaining the level of satisfaction first found in marriage. Note how the satisfaction levels rise considerably during the last two stages.

There is considerable controversy over this research (Spanier et al, 1975) but it seems clear that feelings of marital satisfaction will change in relation to the various marital developmental stages as well as the general life stages through which each individual passes.

Figure 13-1

Spouses' mean scores on the Locke-Wallace Marital Adjustment Scale by stage in the family life cycle. Newark, Ohio (Spanier, 1975)

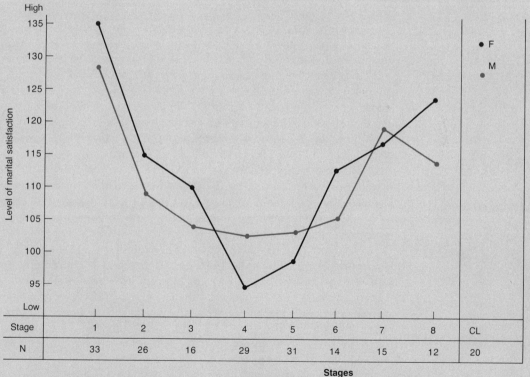

Stage	1	2	3	4	5	6	7	8	CL
N	33	26	16	29	31	14	15	12	20

Stages

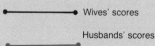 Wives' scores

Husbands' scores

Stage 1 Beginning family
Stage 2 Infant family
Stage 3 Preschool family
Stage 4 Schoolage family

Stage 5 Adolescent family
Stage 6 Launching family
Stage 7 Postparental family
Stage 8 Aging family
CL Childless couple

and the smooth transition of tasks from one generation to the next was done on the farm in rural America.

By contrast, retirement is usually abrupt in the American urban setting, based on reaching a certain arbitrary age or having worked for some specified number of years. In a sense, age categories of employability are created (Winch, 1971, p. 88). For example, child labor laws hold the child out of the labor force whereas mandatory retirement plans force older workers out of the labor market at an arbitrary age.

The abruptness of retirement can cause severe adjustment problems for the newly unneeded worker. The woman in the traditional mothering role faces her retirement at the earlier empty nest stage. But for her, retirement comes gradually as one by one her children gain independence. For the working spouse, on the other hand, he or she is suddenly placed into a totally new role. After forty to fifty years of going to work, they receive a gold watch and pats on the back and are told to go fishing and enjoy their new leisure time (and feelings of uselessness). They are thrust into a new life style that for most retirees is characterized by less income, declining health, and increasing loneliness. They miss their colleagues and the status that was derived from their job. The common question asked by a new acquaintance, "What do you do?", now must be answered by, "Nothing, I'm retired." Since so much of the career person's self-image is defined by their work identity, retirement often means some kind of identity crisis (Darnley, 1975).

A few seem able to find happiness in the "doing nothing" role. "It's great not to have to get up every morning and go to work." Yet most cannot "do nothing" easily and happily after years of working. Many retirees continue to do odd jobs or continue as part-time employees if their occupation permits. For example, a retired school teacher may occasionally substitute teach. Some retirees change activities entirely and start a new vocation or avocation. They may decide to open their own business or actively pursue some long-suppressed interest such as trying to write or paint. Perhaps they busy themselves with volunteer work. There are numerous examples of people being retired and then returning to the work world. Konrad Adenauer assumed the leadership of postwar Germany at the age of seventy-three and actively returned Germany to a powerful world position for fourteen years until the age of eighty-seven.

Generally, those who had broad interests or are able to develop new interests quickly make the best adjustment to retirement. Older (retired) persons who age optimally are those who stay active and manage to resist the shrinkage of their social world. They maintain the activities of middle age as long as possible and then find substitutes for the activities they are forced to relinquish: substitutes for work when forced to retire, substitutes for friends and loved ones lost to death (Havighurst et al, 1968, p. 161).

Money and health seem to be the two most important factors influencing the success of not only retirement but the general adjustment to old age. It takes a great deal of money to live free of economic

Table 13-1 Summary of annual budgets for a retired couple at three levels of living, urban United States, autumn 1978*

Component	Lower Budget	Intermediate Budget	Higher Budget
Total budget[1]	$5514	$7846	$11,596
Total family consumption	5276	7374	10,721
Food	1725	2299	2884
Housing	1831	2641	4139
Transportation	360	701	1299
Clothing	220	369	568
Personal care	156	229	335
Medical care[2]	765	769	774
Other family consumption	220	366	722
Other items	237	472	875

[1]Beginning with the autumn 1978 updating of the budgets for a retired couple, the total budget is defined as the sum of "total family consumption" and "other items." Income taxes are not included in the total budgets.
[2]The autumn 1978 cost estimates for medical care contain a preliminary estimate for "out-of-pocket" costs for Medicare.
NOTE: Because of rounding, sums of individual items may not equal totals.
*From *Bureau of Labor Statistics News*, United States Department of Labor, Washington, D.C., August 20, 1979.

worries (see Table 13-1). Generally, the retiree's income is more than halved upon retirement. The average income for elderly married couples in the mid-1970s was only about $5500 (Porter, 1975, p. 763). Over all, one of every three elderly persons is in a state of severe economic deprivation (Butler, 1973). Finding free time for leisure activities is one of the full-time employee's loudest complaints. It is ironic that when they finally retire and get enough free time, many have little money available to pursue many desires other than those of subsistence. Financial status directly creates the quality of life for the retired couple. Can they travel, indulge their hobbies, and eat well as the television ads depict? They can only if they are financially well off.

The retiree not only must have planned well economically for retirement, but must also have planned for a potentially long-term period with increased life expectancy. Inflation (Chapter 7) is the older person's greatest enemy. Those retired on an essentially fixed income fall further and further behind with each passing day of inflation. A retiree may be financially well off upon retirement, but may have dropped into poverty ten years later because of continued inflation and the shrinking value of the dollar.

Health is the other major influence on people's adjustment to retirement and old age. About 40 percent of those over sixty-five have long-term chronic conditions such as high blood pressure that interfere to some degree with their daily activities (U.S. Office of Human Development, 1976). Although government programs such as Medicare help the elderly to cope financially with health problems, such benefits need to be supplemented monetarily. Thus, money may compound health problems to further reduce the quality of life for the retired. With the high costs of medical care, there are few people who can be completely safe from financial disaster brought on by prolonged or severe health problems.

Assuming that monetary and health problems are not overwhelming, many couples report that the retired period of their lives is one of enjoyment and marital happiness. They are able, often for the first time, to be together without jobs and children placing demands upon them. They can travel and pursue hobbies and long-neglected interests. They can attend to one another with a concentration not available since they first dated. In some ways, a successful retirement is like courting. After years of facing the demands of work and family, after growing apart in some ways, retirement provides the time needed to renew the relationship, make discoveries about each other, and revive the long past courtship that brought the couple together in the first place.

Loss of a Spouse: A Return to Singleness

It is true that one can be faced with the death of a spouse at any stage of marriage. A spouse can die of disease or accident at any time. However, problems of the young widower or widow are much different than the problems spouses face when they lose their partner at the end of their lives and find themselves alone again after the many years of marital partnership. For the young person who loses their spouse, remarriage is most often the solution. Yet, as we saw earlier, remarriage of those over sixty-five is rare, occurring with only about 2 percent of men and 1 percent of women.

Regardless of age, loss of a spouse involves all of the processes that occur whenever death of a loved one is faced. Grieving, feelings of guilt, despair, anger, remorse, depression, turning away from and yet to others at the same time are all normal reactions.

Given time, most of us can overcome our emotional distress when a spouse is lost and go on with our lives. For a few long-married couples, death of one precipitates the death of the remaining partner. This usually occurs when a woman has taken most of her self-identity from her husband. (Inset 13-4)

Widowhood as the Last Stage of Marriage   As we saw in the overview of family life stages (p. 394), the last stage of marriage is overwhelmingly one of widowhood. There are approximately 5.3 times more widows over the age of sixty-five than there are widowers (Glick, 1979, p. 304). Because of this, most of the remainder of this chapter will be concerned with widows. Of course, the older widower faces many of the same kinds of changes and problems,* but the overall magnitude of aging and its associated problems for a society center on the far larger number of widows.

*As a group widowers tend to exhibit more severe problems of disorganization than do widows. They have higher rates of suicide, physical illness, mental illness, alcoholism, and accidents (*U.S. News and World Report*, 1974, pp. 59–60).

Jim was only twenty-eight when Jane was killed in an auto accident while returning from her job. He was left with his son, Mike, who was four years old.

"At first, everyone rushed over and wanted to keep Mike for me. Some of our friends' wives almost couldn't accept 'no' for an answer. Yet I felt that Mike needed to be with me and certainly I needed him."

"It is also amazing to remember who came over the first few days. People that we had hardly known brought food. At first when they asked what they could do, I replied, 'nothing.' Yet they were so obviously disappointed that I finally tried to think of something for them to do. This seemed to make them feel better although I'm not sure it helped me. In a way, I needed things to do, things to distract me from my grief at least for a short time."

"Although I certainly mourned at first, I found that I was often too angry to mourn.

I wanted revenge on the other driver and I was particularly mad at the City for allowing such a dangerous intersection to exist without stop signs. At times I was even angry at my wife for driving so poorly but this always made me feel guilty. Actually I think I was angry at the whole world. Why did events conspire to take her away from me?"

"I had a lot of remorse for things I had put off doing with and for Jane. We really should have spent the money and gone home to see her parents last Christmas. Why hadn't I told her I loved her more often? In many ways at first I felt I had failed her."

"However as time passed I realized that perhaps she had failed me just a little also. At first I could only think of the good things. To think of bad things between us when she wasn't there to defend herself just seemed terrible. Gradually though I have been able to see her, our relationship, as it really was with both good and

bad. I want to preserve her memory for myself and our son but I want it to be a realistic memory, not a case of heroine worship. I do fantasize about her, especially when I'm alone and it really helps me to relive some of the memories but I know that they can't substitute for the present. I must keep living and carrying forward for myself and our son.

"Although I'm not dating yet, I will in the future. She'd not want me to remain alone the rest of my life. Right now, though, I prefer to be alone with our son, with my thoughts and memories. I need time to understand what has happened, time to be sad. I need time for grief, time to adjust to my new single parent role, time to ease the pain. I'll be ready for a new relationship only after I have laid the old one gently and lovingly to rest. When the time comes, I will look forward to marrying again."

As of 1975, there were 75,345,000 women aged eighteen and over, of whom 14% or about 10,104,000 were widows. Seven million plus of these widows were over sixty-five, with a median age of sixty-eight. Of the 67,869,000 men over eighteen, only 2.5% or 1,817,000 were widowers and 1,350,000 of these were over sixty-five with a median age of seventy-one (U.S. Bureau of Census, 1976). Only about half of the population aged sixty-five and older still lives with a spouse.

Thus, the problems of widowhood are for the most part the problems generally faced in old age, but instead faced alone without the spouse. As we have pointed out (p. 404), deteriorating health and declining monetary support are the two major problems faced by the elderly.

In rural America, many parents received monetary and housing support from their grown children when they retired. Thus, a century

My grandmother died only a few months after my grandfather passed away even though she was in good health and had seldom been sick in her life. My grandfather was a strong independent man who worshiped my grandmother and took especially good care of her. He never allowed her to work or to want for anything and remained very much in love with her, often publicly displaying his affection, until he died.

He was an old-fashioned family doctor who made house calls and thought of his patients as his family. My grandmother's entire identity revolved around being "doctor's wife" (that is how she often referred to herself). Her life was his life, and in hindsight I now realize she never developed any of her own interests. In fact, she seemed to have no interests outside of his interests. As "doctor's wife" she took care of him, the family and the house. When the children became independent, she became even more attentive to him and failed to develop any other interests to replace the missing children.

With the arrival of grandchildren, she became the happy mother all over again, taking the grandchildren as often as she could. When grandfather died, we all tried to visit her often and invited her to visit our families. She told us to give her a little time to adjust and that for the present she preferred to stay home. About three months later I found her lying in grandfather's bed having passed away from an apparent heart attack. In retrospect, I think that she had died in spirit when grandfather passed away. The official death certificate indicates "heart attack" as the cause of death. I had no grandmother when I think about it. My grandmother was "doctor's wife" and when he died, her identity died and soon thereafter her body died. I prefer to substitute "broken heart" for "heart attack" on the death certificate.

ago, one tended to grow old on the farm within the family setting. Grandparents gradually turned the farm over to their children, remaining on the farm, giving advice, fulfilling the grandparent role, and being active family members until they died. However, as America urbanized, children tended to move away from their parents and establish independent households within the cities. Often both partners worked at jobs that took them out of the home. Living space diminished so that no room was available for other than the immediate nuclear family. As the children who had moved to the cities grew older, there was no farm to which they could return and thus urbanization slowly moved the care of the elderly out of the children's reach. Fortunately, most Americans own their homes and this often gives them refuge and a major asset in their later years.* More than two-thirds of the elderly remain in their home until death (Streib, 1972). Another 25 percent over sixty-five live with a child. Despite the large amount of generally negative publicity about institutional care for the elderly, only about 2 percent of those in their late sixties live in institutions such as nursing homes (Glick, 1979). The remaining elderly live in a variety of circumstances: with relatives other than children, with roommates, and in rented quarters. Perhaps half a million are well enough off monetarily to buy or lease living quarters in a fancy retirement community such as Arizona's Sun City or California's Leisure World.

*This is fast becoming impossible for today's youth because of skyrocketing housing costs that place a private one-family home out of reach.

The fact that children no longer automatically care for their aging parents means that governmental agencies have had to be created to help the elderly. Government regulated retirement programs and social security have been established to help economically. Medicare and nutrition programs such as Meals on Wheels have been established to help in the area of health. The National Council on Aging in Washington, D.C. publishes a directory of special housing for the elderly. Licensing and supervision of institutional facilities for the aged is being tightened. The elderly themselves are organizing as a power block (the Grey Panthers, for example) to work towards improvement of care and broadening opportunities for people in their later years. Recently, mandatory retirement rules have been successfully challenged in court. Now, those who wish to work longer, and are able to do so, may. Thus, some of the problems the elderly face, especially economic worries, are postponed. Programs such as the Retired Senior Volunteer program, which pays out-of-pocket expenses to those involved in community activities and projects, and the Senior Corps of Retired Executives, which pays them to counsel small businesses, are springing up to keep the elderly active and useful. All of these things bode well for us as we move into the later years of our lives (*Time*, 1975). Yet, the question remains, "If possible, isn't the bosom of the family, the center of intimate relationships, the place to age gracefully and to die with dignity and care surrounding us?" The majority of elderly report that they are satisfied with their family relations (Seelbach & Hansen, 1980, pp. 91–97).

We pointed out earlier that most people finally do make an adjustment to the passing of a loved one. In her study of elderly Chicago widows, Lopata (1979, pp. 110–115) reports the figures for adjustment periods shown in Table 13-2. A few widows reported that they would never be able to establish a new life but only time will tell if their feeling is correct. Lopata makes several interesting points about her sample of widows that probably hold true for many widows. Many of them had never been alone in a home, having gone from the home of the parents directly into one established with marriage. In addition, many of the widows had no occupational skills, never having worked other than perhaps in a few odd jobs prior to marriage. Their traditional socialization was to be passive about the world outside of their home environment. They had always depended on a family support system. Thus, their socialization and consequent life experiences did not adequately prepare them to start a life alone when their spouse passed away.

These factors should diminish as more and more women enter the work force and establish an independent life prior to marriage. The feminist movement's emphasis on individual identity for all women, even when married, should also work to negate the above factors. The upsurge of interest in death and bereavement has also helped the widow to cope with her new role. There is more understanding and empathy for her. For example, programs using widows to counsel one another have been helpful in reducing the adjustment period (Silver-

Table 13.2 Time necessary for elderly widows to adjust and commence development of a new life after the death of a spouse

Time Needed	Percentage
2–11 months	25
One year	20
1–2 years	23
Over 2 years	16
Other	16

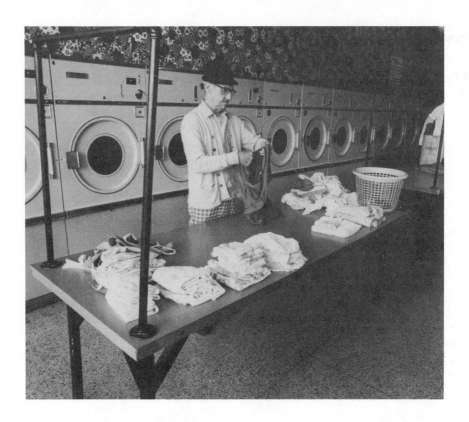

man, 1970).* The Widows Consultation Center in New Jersey carries on an experimental program of group discussion that has been very successful (Hiltz, 1975).

Remarriage is perhaps the best solution for the widow or widower. Yet, as we saw earlier (p. 406), few over sixty-five actually remarry. For widows, the lack of available older men is the major obstacle. Some researchers (Lasswell, 1973, p. 519); Duberman, 1977, p. 13) suggest that polygyny might be an appropriate solution. If the few available older men were allowed more than one wife, remarriage opportunities would be much more available for older widows. Another way to alleviate the problem in the distant future is for women to marry men who are eight to ten years younger than themselves (Glick, 1979, p. 302). This would necessitate a real change in the old American tradition of men marrying women one to two years younger than themselves.

In actuality, many elderly, out of necessity, do live with other older people of both sexes. Living together without marriage is probably more common among the elderly than it is among the young, although current census data do not differentiate by age such "live together" households.

*See Scenes from Marriage at the end of the chapter for more details.

For many retired, widowed, and elderly persons, fulfilling the role of grandparent can bring back many of the joys and satisfactions of family life. Grandchildren can mean companionship, renewal of intimate contact, the joy of physical contact, and the fulfillment of again being needed and useful.

As with the retirement and widowhood stages of marriage, so grandparenting has been greatly extended by increased life expectancy. Most children have contact with one or more grandparents throughout their youth. It is quite possible today for a person's period of grandparenting to be longer than the period in which their own children were at home. Of course, younger grandparents, still married, employed, and living in their own homes do not have the same needs to grandparent that the older, retired, and perhaps widowed grandparents do.

For the older grandparents, the role might be described as "pleasure without responsibility." They can enjoy the grandchildren without the obligation and responsibilities they had to shoulder for their own children. For some, the grandparent role gives a second chance to be an even better parent, especially for males. "I can be, and I can do for my grandchildren things I could never do for my own kids. I was too busy to enjoy my own, but my grandchildren are different" (Neugarten & Weinstein, 1973, p. 507).

Contact with grandchildren can yield a great deal of physical contact for the widow or widower. This is one of the things most often reported missed after one's spouse passes away. In the past, the stereotype of the elderly person has excluded sexual activity. Yet we know today that this is erroneous. Physical contact is an important source of intimacy and emotional gratification, regardless of age (Lasswell, 1973, p. 523).

> The new knowledge that we have about both male and female changes in sexual functioning is going to cause a new kind of sexual revolution — that of the "over fifties!" We now know that menopause has no effect on sexual drive unless the woman thinks it will have such an effect, and then she is only responding to her own negative expectations. And with men, the decrease in testosterone production plays a very small role in decreasing sexual interest, if any. It does increase the time between periods of sexual tension buildup and does decrease the amount of seminal fluid, but it does not affect the erection — only the need and the capacity to ejaculate.

Pfeiffer (1974, pp. 243–251) reports the following data on the frequency of sexual intercourse for men aged 66 to 71:

Sexual Intercourse	Percentage
None	12
Once a month	48
Once a week	26
2 to 3 times per week	2

Although sexual intercourse may be unavailable to the average older widow, much physical contact can be had with grandchildren. Hug-

Grandparenting can be an
especially fulfilling role.

ging, kissing, and affection gained from grandchildren can go a long
ways towards replacing the physical contact earlier had with the missing spouse.

Many grandparents report feelings of biological and psychological renewal from contact with their grandchildren: "I feel young
again." "I see a future." As fulfilling as the grandparental role might
be, many grandparents miss out on it because of the great distance
from them that their children live. Retired grandparents who can afford
to often move closer to their children in order to increase their family
contacts. Although grandparenting is no panacea to the problems of
aging, it can yield a great deal of comfort and satisfaction.

Summary

Families, just as people within them, span a long period of time. Just as individuals change over time, so, too, do families. In this chapter we have tried to trace what some of the common changes might be. Since most of the book is concerned with the early family stages, we have examined only the middle and later stages in this chapter.

When the last child leaves home, the empty nest stage begins. This is usually a time of reassessment for both husband and wife. The reassessment has to do with how their lives will change now that the children are gone. What will they do with the time that used to be devoted to mothering and fathering? How have they lived their lives to date, how do they want to live them in the future? What new directions should be undertaken? What will be their relationship with their adult children, between themselves? How will the grandparent role be fulfilled? What role will sexuality play in their middle years and so forth?

Retirement enters one's thoughts during the middle years, and when it finally comes, the family will have adjustments to make. Time demands will change abruptly; monetary circumstances may shift downward, and, perhaps, feelings of uselessness will have to be coped with by one or both of the spouses leaving the world of work that has for so long been a part of their identity.

At last, death must be faced as one spouse, usually the husband, passes away. Thus for many there is a return to singleness in the later years. Widowhood, in fact, may be an increasingly long period as life expectancy continues to increase.

Despite the passing of one spouse, the family often remains active. Grandparenting can bring small children back into one's life and yield new satisfactions to those aging within the family. For some, however, old age may mean being without family for the first time.

The family institution, then, reflects changes over time, just as do individuals. Our ninth basic assumption on page 10 reflects this fact.

Living as a Widow: Only the Name's the Same

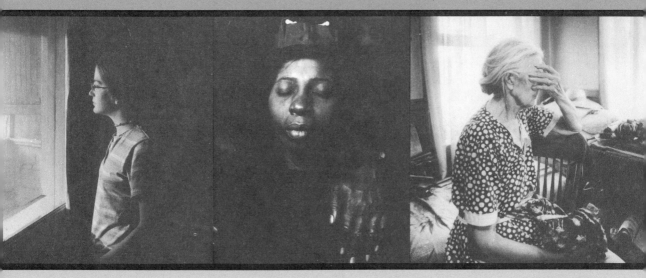

"The funeral was over and suddenly I was all alone," said the grieving widow whose whole life had been wrapped up in being wife and mother. Her children were all grown up and gone. Now her husband. "No one to shop for, no one to talk to. The loneliness was so awful I thought I would go out of my mind." . . .

In the case of Mrs. J., she sat at home, depressed, listening to church music that she and her husband once enjoyed together. One moment, she was determined to find a new home, the next morose and immobilized. Move or stay? She couldn't make up her mind.

Other widows can be encountered after adjustment and re-entry into the world around them. Such as Judge Lucille Buell who was sworn in last year (1974) as a Family Court judge in Westchester County (N.Y.) and who promptly cited her "broad experience in living" — "I was a wife, now I'm a widow. I am a mother [of two college students], a teacher, and a lawyer." Or Vivienne Thaul Wechter, a New York artist and teacher who remembers with warmth "a good marriage that developed over the

years" and who adds: "I always try to have a full life. My advice is not to wallow in your widowhood."

From loneliness to fulfillment, from isolation to involvement, these women are members of a neglected minority — somewhere off in the wings of American society. They tend to be shunted aside, casualties of the worship of youth and of American discomfort with death, caught between the mythology of the swinging single and the frozen patterns of social life built on couples.

More than 10 million women belong to this society of female bereavement, ultimately to be joined by a large majority of married women (given the longer life expectancy of women). Of all the widowed in America, 85 percent are women. They are neither single nor married, divorced nor separated. They are free — but for what?

Mostly, they are Americans looking for roles. Their search goes on without guidelines, with limited sympathy, and with little attention to their problems. As one expert has noted, widows are social pioneers looking for their place in American society.

As the life span increases, American

women are becoming widows later in life and also spending more years as widows.

"The problem in American society — to the extent that a woman's identity is based on being a wife — is that the widow has no place to go," says Dr. Helena Zananiecki Lopata, a foremost expert on widowhood. "She can't be a widow, really, and she can't go back to being single. If she can't be a wife, can't be a widow, can't be single, her identity has to come from something else."

That search for identity, built on the ashes of a husband's death, strikes women unprepared, even when a long illness is involved. Widowhood is something that is not discussed, that is faced suddenly in the full force of grief, surrounded by well-meaning sons and daughters, relatives and friends. They are well-meaning but impatient. Concerned, but filled with misunderstanding and easy, often bad advice.

Widows have been largely left out of the vast American industry of professionalized advice-giving. Toddlers and teenagers get special attention, the just-married and the newly-divorced are recognized as special categories, and so are addicts, alcoholics, the unemployed, and the disabled. But not widows. They are expected to wipe their tears and get going. But how and where?

The fewer resources a woman had as a wife the less she is able to cope as a widow. The less money she has, the greater the effort it will take. The more empty the circle of her relatives and friends, the greater her isolation. The less education and the fewer the skills she has, the fewer her options are. The less flexible she has been as a wife, the more difficult her adjustment as a widow will be. . . .

Psychologically, widows are haunted by loneliness. It comes upon them after they reel under the impact of grief and as they struggle to find their place in the world — alone.

On the practical side, widows confront the legal, financial, and everyday problems commonly handled by husbands in a male-dominated society. They are called upon to perform actions and make decisions they have never faced before.

Finally, in finding their new place in society, they need a new sort of marriage — of attitude and frame of mind with information, know-how, and opportunity. . . .

In general, widows help widows better than anyone else does. This has been evident in the various programs that do exist, particularly the Widow-to-Widow Program developed under the auspices of the Laboratory of Community Psychiatry at Harvard University. Its director, Dr. Phyllis Rolfe Silverman, describes the many advantages a widow possesses as a caregiver: "As a teacher, as a role model, as a bridge person, she helps make order out of the chaos of grief and provides the widow direction in the role transition." . . .

From sympathy and empathy, from a chance to talk to someone who shared the same experience, the widows then could move on to practical questions like legal assistance, social activities, or job-hunting. The idea was so successful that it is being picked up in more places than Dr. Silverman can keep track of. . . .

The death of her spouse often places the widow in a "crisis situation." At the Center in New York, the only professional service of its kind devoted exclusively to widows, the aim is clearly set forth: "Three out of every four wives in the United States eventually face widowhood. Despite this stark fact, no organized effort to help them meet their problems and build new lives for themselves existed until the Widows Consultation Center was established in 1970 as a non-profit, non-sectarian agency."

The Center, whose constant backlog involves a month-long wait, receives a stream of inquiries from all over the country about a many-sided approach that is required in all programs for the widowed. Crisis intervention, in the form of counseling sessions and therapy, helps through the periods of depression that come immediately and often much later. Assistance in solving practical problems is provided by legal and financial experts. (In one example, a widow with $300,000 in the bank felt that she couldn't even afford a taxi.) The Center offers social opportunities along with various group activities. In a variant on the Widow-to-Widow Program, clients who have worked out their own difficulties get involved in helping others. One volunteer-client comes to the center every week and phones widows who are alone and suffering from isolation. . . .

The widows expressed this feeling in various ways: "I don't think anyone who hasn't experienced it can understand the void that is left after losing a companion of so many years—all the happy little things that come up and you think, 'Oh, I must share that'—and there isn't anyone there to share it with."

"You find even though there are people around, there is that great big void that's there. I don't think that the old saying, 'Time heals all wounds' is really true; because we were so close. I find that even being around friends and relatives you can be so lonesome in a crowd." . . .

As expected, Dr. Lopata's research showed that the "more deeply the couple were involved" the more difficult the adjustment. But she adds a counsel that might not occur to a well-meaning relative or friend: the widow "must be allowed to grieve." Specialists use the term, "grief work," and it is the first step on the widow's way back.

Instead of encouraging the widow to forget her loss (impossible, anyhow), relatives and friends must allow her to work through her grief. She faces an emotional trial involving sorrow, guilt, loneliness, and fear. The experts recommend that a widow be encouraged to cry if she wishes, to talk of her late husband, and to describe how bad she feels.

Based on her own first-hand work, Dr. Silverman warns that it is a mistake to judge a widow's state of mind from the fact that her behavior may seem composed at the time of the funeral. For initially the widow is numb, and in handling duties connected with the funeral she is still acting as

her husband's wife. "It is safe to say the real anguish and distress have not yet begun," Dr. Silverman says.

As the widow becomes aware of the finality of the loss, the fact that her husband is gone hits home. It can take her up to two years to accept this fact, and the process of grieving is necessary to her adjustment. If the process is avoided, Dr. Silverman says, it can create its own problems. But when faced it is a "prologue to the future."

Besides "grief work," Dr. Lopata cites four needs that all widows have: namely, companionship, solution of immediate problems, building of competence and self-confidence, and help in re-engagement in the world around them. It is in meeting these needs that relatives, friends, and agencies can aid widows in helping themselves.

Widows appreciate someone "just being there" as they learn to live alone. One widow spoke of "loneliness—nobody to talk to." Another spoke of coming home to an empty house: "It's a very lonely life—you have friends, you feel happy when you're with them, but you have to come home to an empty house." This need for companionship is complicated by the *ups* and *downs* of a widow's state of mind. Those close to her should have a special understanding and patience; they should stand by her, not avoid her.

Faced with her immediate problems, the widow is surrounded by advice—"too much of the wrong kind of advice," according to Dr. Lopata. Generally speaking, a widow should avoid making any important decisions during the first year of widowhood because the chance of making mistakes is great. Her outlook will change after she works through her grief and adjusts to being on her own.

Dr. Lopata is emphatic about a widow's doing her own decision-making: "No one should make decisions for her, unless absolutely necessary to avoid a serious disaster." Instead of advice that increases dependency, independence should be encouraged.

Rather than off-the-cuff advice from the family on technical matters, widows need referral to experts: doctors, lawyers, bankers, and accountants, and counselors. Here is where programs for widows perform valuable service.

Finally, widows need assistance in getting re-connected with society. "Keeping busy" is one frequent piece of advice that makes sense. In the beginning, activity is escape from loneliness, then it takes on meaning for its own sake. It plugs the widow into the life around her. . . .

The goal is to stop being *widows* and to start being individuals — women who have lost a husband and learned to begin again on their own. Such as the widow who recalled how the Widow-to-Widow Program helped her get going:

"I looked around and I saw people worse off than me; they had no money or no family. One woman I know really died after her husband went. The way I was going that could happen to me; I wasn't sure that I wanted that to happen. Then I began to take stock. I was doing things I had never done before, going to meetings [of a widow group], driving people there. People were counting on me. I was needed. I was the one who was always so helpless and here I was helping someone else. I never thought I could change like that."

Then she expressed the life force that fills widows finding new roles in a society that has ignored them: "And I knew then that I had to go on living."

Edward Wakin

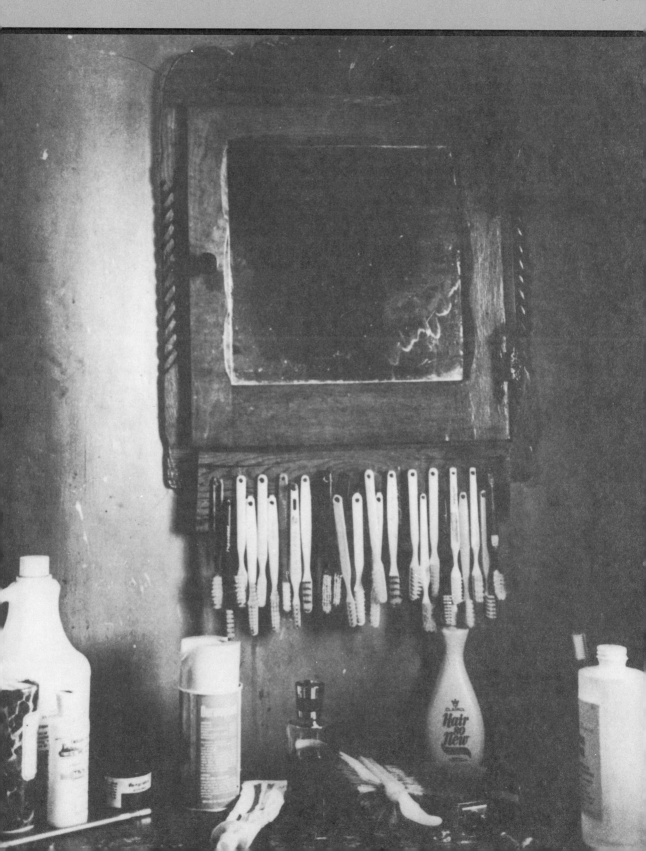

Chapter 14 ～

Contents

Scenes from Marriage

The Alternatives

Traditional marriage is a popular subject of criticism for the mass media. If one attends to the popular press it often seems that the nuclear American family is the source of most of the unhappiness in our society. Numerous "experts" suggest that the traditional family is all but dead. It is soon to be replaced by new and exciting relationships between men and women, parents and children, family and society, which will solve past problems and allow Americans to live fulfilled and happy lives.

It seems that such criticisms reached their height in the late 1960s and early 1970s. Bras were burned to protest the traditional female role in the family. College women insisted they were no longer interested in parenthood. Free sex and drug-oriented communes sprung up by the hundreds. Cohabitation became an American way of life and the marriage certificate was reduced to an unnecessary piece of paper. Handicraft cottage industries returned to the home with the making of leather goods such as sandals and belts, wooden toys, handwoven clothes, etc. Wife-swapping clubs sprung up as couples sought to reenergize their sex lives. The divorce rate soared as people sought the utopian intimate relationship.

However, as we move into the 1980s, much of this turmoil about marriage and the family has died down. Couples are indeed still getting married and having children. Communes and wife-swapping clubs have both lost popularity. The divorce rate has leveled off. Ira Reiss (1980) suggests that the 1980s seem to be a time of consolidation and moderation in so far as the family is concerned. This does not mean that the family is without change. Rather it means that the belief that the family as we have known it can be replaced by some more perfect union has been challenged and found wanting. For example, most people who tried commune life found that it was much more difficult than they had expected. To live intimately with twenty people simply multiplies the problems encountered when trying to live intimately with only one spouse.

Much of the new, when examined historically, didn't prove to be new at all. For example, the popular press gave a lot of attention to cohabitation, especially among college students. But men and women living together without legal sanction is certainly not new in America. Some states (thirteen today, p. 146) have recognized common-law marriage for years (that is, if the partners live together as man and wife long enough, the state accords them marital status without the formalities). Even the criticism of the traditional family was not new.

Throughout the twentieth century there have been constant criticisms of marriage and the family. Suggestions for "new" family forms have always been made by critics of the status quo. For example, in 1936, Bertrand Russell saw marriage collapsing as a social institution unless drastic changes were made:

> In the meantime, if marriage and paternity are to survive as social institutions, some compromise is necessary between complete promiscuity and lifelong monogamy. Although it is difficult to decide the best compromise at a given time certain points seem clear:
>
> Young unmarried people should have considerable freedom as long as children are avoided so that they may better distinguish between mere physical attraction and the sort of congeniality that is necessary to make marriage a success.
>
> Divorce should be possible without blame to either party and should not be regarded as in any way disgraceful.
>
> Everything possible should be done to free sexual relations from economic taint. At present, wives, just as much as prostitutes, live by the sale of their sexual charms: and even in temporary free relations the man is usually expected to bear all the joint expenses. The result is that there is a sordid entanglement of money with sex, and that a woman's motives not infrequently have a mercenary element. A woman, like a man, should have to work for a living, and an idle wife is no more intrinsically worthy of respect than a gigolo (reprinted in 1957, pp. 171–172).

Perhaps the major thing that the great turmoil of the 1960s and 1970s did to and for the family was to broaden the available alternatives for intimacy. If a couple decides not to have children, that is all right. Divorce doesn't mean the end of the world. A cohabitation experience does not make one unmarriable.

Increasing Diversity of Life Styles

Modern America has become remarkably permissive toward and accepting of multiple forms of intimate relationships. Other cultures have had different marital systems, but they have usually disallowed deviance from the system chosen at a given historical time. However, a free and creative society will offer many structural forms of the family by which its functions, such as child-rearing and meeting sexual needs, may be fulfilled. The reasons for America's permissiveness are partly philosophic but mainly economic. For example, as Russell pointed out, "Wives, just as much as prostitutes, live by the sale of their sexual charms." Marriage forms have been historically limited because women have been economically tied to men to support them and the family.

With industrialization and affluence, it becomes more possible to consider alternate life styles and marital forms. For example, affluence allows more people to further their education and thus be exposed to new ideas and knowledge. Affluence also brings mobility and mobility brings contact with new people and new life styles, often without the constraint of immediate supervision by parents. If a person discovers greater personal satisfaction in some alternate life style, affluence makes it possible to seek out others with the same interests. Affluence often makes it possible for people to postpone assuming adult responsibility (earning one's own living), thus allowing wider experimentation and lessening the consequences of failure. Affluence has also given rise to the mass media—magazines, radio, television, and movies—which have spread the news about various life styles and experimental relationships into all parts of the country. In addition, the media have also taken part in creating new life styles by portraying them as desirable and exciting and "in."

In part then because of America's affluence, it seems that the young have a broader choice of acceptable relationships than their grandparents did. Perhaps couples, by choosing wisely the roles that best fit them as individuals, will be able to create growing intimate relationships that are more fulfilling than past family forms. Only time will tell.

In discussing some of the various life styles, we need to remember that some of the problems that seem inherent to the alternative life actually lie within the individual rather than the life style itself. That is, each of us has been reared within a family that holds attitudes and values about its own functioning and worth, and these values and attitudes have become part of us, even if we reject some or all of them. Often when we explore some other life style, feelings of discomfort, awkwardness, and guilt arise because we judge it by old attitudes, some of which we may not even consciously know we hold. Despite intellectual acceptance of a new life style, the old conditioning causes emotional conflict. This often works against the new life style being successful. In addition, choosing a life style that is unacceptable to the general society as well as one's own family and perhaps one's old friends creates further conflict and makes success more difficult. As the society at large becomes more supportive of differing life styles, success will become more likely.

Many alternate relationships (not necessarily accepted by the American society at large) are briefly presented along with statements of possible advantages and disadvantages. Since there is little empirical evidence on the outcomes of such alternative unions, the evaluations of them are often based on opinion rather than fact. It is hoped that these opinions will stimulate the readers to make their own evaluations.

Being Single in the Midst of Marriage Americans marry in greater numbers than do most other people. Being married is the standard role that most of us will play throughout much of our adult life. In fact, to be a "never married" adult past the age of thirty is certainly suspect. "What is wrong with you that you failed to find a mate?" is a question that lurks in the back of many people's minds. For people to be middle-aged and divorced seems more normal to most Americans than for them to have never been married. At least with the divorced or widowed one knows that they were once marriageable. Thus choosing the single life in the midst of marriage is definitely choosing a minority alternative and is to some extent an act of courage since the American society revolves around the married couple.

For most Americans "single" is used to denote a young not-yet-married person rather than a chosen life style. Yet, in actuality, the world includes a much greater variety of people — the divorced, the widowed, as many elderly as young, and an increasing number of people who choose the single life style for a longer, more permanent period.

Despite pressures to marry in America, remaining single is regaining a modicum of respectability. The word regaining is used because marriage has not always been expected of everyone. In fact, just a few years ago, those choosing teaching and nursing careers were actually discouraged from marriage, the feeling being that marriage would divert their energies from their jobs. Historically in Europe certainly, marriage was thought to be a privilege granted those who had gained economic security rather than a required state of being.

Encouragement to marry will undoubtedly remain strong in America, yet several factors are acting to make prolonged single life again more acceptable. The increasing emphasis on self-fulfillment as a major life goal and society's greater tolerance of differing life styles both reduce the pressure to marry. Growth and change are becoming popular goals and they conflict directly with the traditional goals of long-range commitment to stability that marriage requires. The women's movement has also contributed to singleness in that it says to all women "There are other roles you can fulfill that do not necessarily include being a wife and mother." Greater educational opportunity also acts, in some cases, to postpone marriage since going to school usually postpones economic independence.

Statistics bear out the fact that more young Americans are currently choosing to remain single longer than twenty years ago. Single women aged twenty to twenty-four increased from 28.4 percent of the total population of women in 1960 to 40.3 percent in 1975 (*Statistical Abstract of the United States*, 1976, p. 38). Also, for the first time since shortly after World War II, the marriage total for a twelve-month period (ending August 1974) was smaller (by 68,000) than it had been for the preceding twelve months (Glick, 1975). This slight decline continued in 1975 but reversed in 1977. However, if we examine the marriage rate per 1000 population over the years, we can see that there have been many fluctuations in the rate, with the lowest occurring during the 1960s (see Table 14-1).

The median age of first marriage for women increased from 20.3 in 1960 to 21.6 in 1977. The corresponding increase for men was 22.8 to 24 years of age. In 1975, the average age at marriage was about one year older than it had been in the mid-1950s. Also, approximately 35.2 percent of people over the age of eighteen are presently single (*Statistical Abstract*, 1976, pp. 37, 68 and U.S. Bureau of The Census, 1978).

Some take such figures to mean that there is now a definite trend away from marriage toward remaining single (see, for example,

Table 14-1 Marriage Rate per 1000 Population, U.S.

Year	Rate
1910	10.3
1920	12.0
1930	9.2
1940	12.1
1950	11.1
1960	8.5
1965	9.3
1970	10.6
1971	10.6
1972	11.0
1973	10.4
1974	10.5
1975	10.0
1976	9.9

Source: *Statistical Abstract of the United States* (Washington, D.C.: Government Printing Office, 1976), p. 51. and Glick & Norton, 1977, p. 4.

Stein, 1975; and Libby, 1977). However, considering recent economic problems such as inflation-recession and unemployment, it seems premature to conclude anything definite from such statistics. Traditionally, marriage is postponed during economically troubled times. Thus the slight drop in the marriage rate and the larger number of singles over twenty are to be expected.

What effect will remaining single longer have on marriage? Obviously, both partners will be older. Older people used to a long period of singleness may well become more set in their ways and thus find the compromises of the marriage relationship more difficult. Also, parents will be older when they have children, thus increasing the age difference between themselves and their children. Risks during pregnancy and childbirth become greater for older women. Older people will probably have fewer children, with a resultant effect on schools, baby food, the clothing industry, and so on.

On the other hand, later marriage should mean better economic circumstances for the couple. And also people who know they are choosing marriage and are mature enough will be willing to work to make it a positive experience.

But what of the single life itself? What are its advantages? Freedom is probably the major advantage. You need only worry about yourself. Obligations are made by voluntary decision rather than dictated by tradition, role, or law. You have the time to do what you want when you want. Expenses are lower than for a family, and you can change jobs or even cities easily. Independence can be maintained, and the conflicts about activities and life style that can arise in a marriage don't occur.

We have been discussing singleness as if it were one type of life style when in reality there are many types of single life styles. The college student's life style is far different from the working single person's life style, which is again quite different from the singles who have been previously married. Then, of course, there are the many persons who are widowed and spend the later years of their lives as single persons. Indeed, there is a certain amount of segregation among these different types of single persons. In Chapter 15 we will look at those returning to a single life, the newly divorced. Here, however, the focus is on those who choose the single life at least for a few years. These tend to be people in their twenties and early thirties. The media romanticizes this group, presenting descriptions of singles' bars, singles' apartment complexes, and a life style that implies a great deal of sexual freedom (see Inset 14-1). Of course, the popular description does not fit all members of this group. Many singles do not participate in the "singles' life," even though they do choose to remain single.

Possible loneliness, failure to relate intimately, and a sense of meaninglessness are potential disadvantages of singleness. It is interesting and contrary to popular belief, but research notes that old people are less prone to loneliness than young people. Loneliness is particularly prevalent and intense during adolescence (Rubin, 1979). In addition, single people have a higher incidence of mental illness (see

Figure 14-1). It is difficult to say just why the incidence of mental illness is higher for single persons than for married. Perhaps those with a proclivity toward mental illness are bypassed by those seeking mates and are thus forced to remain single. Living closely with another person does serve a corrective function since the other person validates or invalidates many of one's thoughts and actions, thus serving to keep one closer to reality than might otherwise be the case without this interaction. In addition, the social onus placed on the single person may act to increase mental stress. General health is also better for married persons (Verbrugge, 1979, p. 207).

Changing Thoughts on Parenthood Children have long been considered an important element of the family. Historically, in most cultures, many children were produced through the childbearing years since infant mortality was high and had to be offset. For example, a woman might give birth to ten children but see only three grow into adulthood. With modern medicine, the infant mortality rate has declined drastically, especially in Western countries. This and the recognition of the problems of overpopulation have brought about a reduction in the

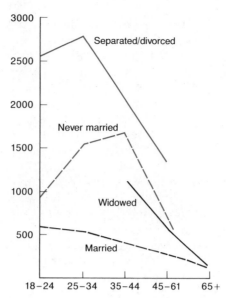

Figure 14-1
Admission rates to out-patient psychiatric services per 100,000 population 18 years of age and over by marital status (National Institute of Mental Health, 1973).

birth rate in the United States. Only ten years ago, the newly wed couple was pressured to have children. Family and friends began to ask what was wrong if the couple didn't have a child within a year or two of the marriage. The couple was chastised as being selfish if they hinted that they did not want children.

Even though such pressure is less direct today, research indicates that husbands are perceived as more psychologically healthy when they have children than when they don't. Wives are liked less and viewed more negatively when they espouse voluntary childlessness than if they are involuntarily childless (Calhoun & Selby, 1980, p. 181). It has also been found that men are significantly more likely to regard childlessness as disadvantageous than are women (Blake, 1979, p. 245).

Today, however, increasing numbers of young people are choosing to remain childless. Of all women who marry in this country, about one in twenty does not become a mother and half of these are childless by choice (Pahlman, 1970; Veevers, 1973). This ratio is currently shifting with more favoring childlessness than in the past.

Recently, couples who choose a childless life are finding some support. Various books, for example *The Case against Having Children* (Silverman & Silverman, 1971) and *A Baby ... Maybe?* (Whelan, 1976), and articles such as "Those Missing Babies" (*Time*, 1974) are supportive of childlessness. Also, in 1971, the National Organization for Non-Parents (NON) was founded to offer support to those couples opting to remain childless in the face of traditional pressures to reproduce when married (Veevers, 1975).

Childlessness offers numerous advantages to the couple. The major advantage is increased freedom. The couple does not have to contend with the responsibilities of children. They are monetarily unencumbered. Current estimates of the cost of raising a child to eighteen years of age range from $50,000 to $80,000. Without children, the couple's time and money are their own to devote to careers, each other, hobbies, travels, and adult life in general. Often the childless couple is a two-career family where both partners are free to invest their energies in their work and meet during leisure times (see Chapter 8). Although the differences are not great, research does lend support to the idea that childlessness is related to enhanced marital adjustment and satisfaction (Houseknecht, 1979, pp. 263–264).

The increased interest in child care agencies, early schooling, and communal child rearing may reflect the desire of couples with children to gain some of the freedom childless couples have. As in the kibbutz settlements of Israel, outside care (other parenting) frees parents of many of the negative aspects of child rearing while allowing them to enjoy the positive aspects. The wealthy have long used nurses and servants to relieve themselves of the day-to-day burdens of parenthood. "Why can't state agencies be used in the same way?" ask some other parents.

Inclusiveness versus Exclusiveness

Traditional marriage in the United States has usually meant exclusiveness. The spouses devote themselves, both physically and emotionally, to one another only. Emotional or physical involvement with others is avoided except at very superficial levels. "Togetherness" perhaps best describes the traditional exclusive American marriage. Extreme emphasis on togetherness, however, can be stifling to both marital partners.

In practice, the exclusive nature of marriage is often transgressed by both wives and husbands. Sexual transgressions have usually been kept secret in the past. Today, however, among a small minority, transgressions have become a part of the marriage. Indeed, multirelationships by spouses are being institutionalized in *group* and *swinging* marriages.

Valid data are difficult to gather on these behaviors because of the general social taboos surrounding them. Most of the following evaluations are thus essentially the personal opinion of those interested in multirelationship marriages.

Group or Multilateral Marriage Group marriage, as the name implies, is "marriage" among three or more persons.* The advantages of such an arrangement are said to be: (1) a broader base of companionship, (2) increased opportunities for personal growth, (3) a more fulfilled life in general, (4) a more enriched sexual life, (5) a stabler economic foundation, and (6) the benefits of multiple parenting for the children.

Unfortunately, despite these claimed benefits, most group marriages have been quite unstable. Part of the reason for their failure has been negative social pressures. But the major reason for collapse is

*Such a "marriage" has no legal validity.

probably the drastic increase in complexity. Instead of the usual marital two-way interaction, there are now multiple interactions. Remember all the roles we found in marriage, and now consider that instead of two there are several people interacting in each role, and it becomes obvious that complexity of relationships can be overwhelming.

Swinging Swinging, or opening the marital relation to include other people sexually while still maintaining emotional exclusiveness, is more common than group marriage. Research here, as on other alternative life styles, is skimpy and therefore suspect. Some say that sexual openness keeps interest and freshness alive in the marital relationship and also gives each partner a more confident self-image. Secretiveness, lies, and ensuing tensions are removed from adultery. Swingers claim that "Sex is fun, so why not enjoy it?"

Usually the husband initiates the interest and makes the first contact, and usually the wife is the first to seek an end to the swinging arrangement (Denfield, 1974). Swingers allow individuals freedom of choice and do not coerce people into doing things against their wishes (although there is obviously the pressure of group expectations). There is a great deal of female homosexual behavior but male homosexual behavior appears to be rare. Swingers actually seem quite similar to nonswingers, with the exception of their sexual behavior. Most swingers feel that swinging has helped their marriage but stress swinging would probably harm a marriage already in trouble. Most swingers believe that they are honest and open about sex and that this is a desirable quality (Bartell, 1971).

It is interesting, however, to note that most swingers return to the traditional marital format after two or three years, apparently because the life style is so strenuous. Research suggests that: (1) many people cannot make the transition to swinging because of inhibitions and guilt, (2) swinging is disruptive of marriage when it is tried but can't be accepted, (3) divorce rates among swingers are higher than average (though this doesn't necessarily mean that swinging was the major cause of the divorce; see, for example, Gilmartin, 1977, p. 183), and (4) venereal disease becomes a real possibility.

A study (Denfield, 1974) of 1175 couples who dropped out of swinging indicates the following kinds of problems. About 10 percent cited jealousy as their reason for dropping out of swinging. Husbands reported more jealousy than wives did. Some husbands became quite concerned about their wives' popularity or endurance capabilities. Wives were more apt to become jealous if the marriage was threatened. Other reasons cited for dropping out were guilt, development of outside attachment (that is, falling in love with another), boredom, separation or divorce, or fear of discovery by relatives or neighbors.

Not all couples who dropped out of swinging reported negative results. About one-third reported at least a temporary improvement in their relationship. They felt that swinging had given them excitement, sexual freedom, new sexual techniques, sexual variety, greater appreciation of mate, and better communication and openness between partners.

Intimate friendships differ from swinging in that the other relationship, which can involve one or both members of a marriage, includes emotional as well as sexual intimacy. However, the married relationship is considered the primary relationship (see Ramey, 1975). Such behavior tries to combine the positive aspects of friendship with open consensual sexual involvement (Ramey, 1975). Extramarital relationships are very difficult to manage because they demand time and energy which in most cases must be taken away from the primary relationship.

Communes Communes, or group living arrangements, represent a viable alternate marital pattern that some find attractive. Communes themselves are markedly diverse: some are agrarian, some urban; some limit sexual contact, drugs, and alcohol, some have no limits; some are based on religious ideals, some on utopian ideals; some have no rules, some have rigid rules, and so on. Carl Rogers (1972, pp. 128–131) listed the following groups in his study of communes (needless to say, these are not the only communes in this country):

1. A rural commune of eleven adults and six children functioning pretty much as an extended family but with sex relationships outside of paired bonds.
2. An urban commune of a dozen professional men and women (and one child) who are paired off, engage in sexual experimentation, and employ encounter group procedures to achieve harmony.
3. A semirural commune, open to anyone, but eventually closed as a public health menace.

4. A coed house near a college, inhabited mostly by students, with great turnover but an eight-year record of stability; work is shared, relationships are nonsexual, and sexual companionship is found outside the house.

5. An urban house containing three men and three women practicing group marriage, with a chart designating who is to sleep with whom on a given night.

6. A group of agricultural communes, unified by religion, going back over 400 years.

7. A highly organized commune of thirty men and women (only two children) stressing work, cleanliness, and sexual freedom.

8. A relationship of urban communes bound together by charismatic leadership, highly structured and emotional group sessions, and a history of drug addiction among members.

9. A rural commune, bound together by Eastern mystical beliefs, and limited to twenty-five members.

Reports suggest that there were approximately 3000 intentional communes scattered throughout America in 1970, although the movement has declined since then (see, for example, Zablocki, 1972). In general, people join communes in order to escape from an increasing sense of alienation and isolation. Alienation often leads people to join rural communes where they can see—and eat—the results of their labor. Communes often sanction ideas or behavior that differ from those of the on-going society at large.

Actually, most communes last less than a year. Only those that are authoritarian or have strong ideals seem to last, though, as one contributor to the *Whole Earth Catalog* ironically noted, "If the intentional community hopes to survive, it must be authoritarian, and if it is authoritarian, it offers no more freedom than the conventional society" (quoted in *Time*, "The American Family: Future Uncertain," 1970).

Living in a Commune

Jerry and Ann have been married for a year. He works downtown in a large city and she works part time at the local university. During their vacation last summer, they visited friends who lived in a rural commune in northern California. Jerry and Ann only stayed overnight but life in the commune seemed pastoral and simple compared to theirs and they began to think about living in a commune. Finally, they decided to quit their jobs and move to the commune.

The commune operates on a laissez-faire basis since most of the members believe that leadership is synonymous with oppression. Most of the members live in couples, though sexual experimentation is tolerated. Drugs, however, are not.

Most of the members live in cabins they have built themselves, so Jerry immediately begins to build a cabin. He and Ann spend time working in the communal garden. Ann, who is a good organizer, also begins working on methods to make handling the chores and

WHAT DO YOU THINK?

What are some of the major ways in which this commune failed?

How would you have solved the problems of this commune?

Why do some urban youth want to return to farming as a way of life?

What are some advantages of living communally? What are some disadvantages?

daily work more efficient. However, after they have been living on the commune for three months, they become aware that the more work they do, the less others seem to do. They also become aware that free loaders seem to wander in and out constantly. And, although the membership seems to stay around twenty-four, only about half of them were there when they arrived three months earlier. The new people seem to share the food but do not remain long enough to share the work.

At about this time, the older members decide that the commune does need rules after all. At a group meeting, job hierarchies, time tables, and work responsibilities are decided on. The group decides that penalties for not working will be denial of communal goods (fruits and vegetables as well as tools and materials) at first, and then, if the person still shirks duties, he or she will be asked to leave. They also decide to discourage visitors for a while.

Ann has begun to notice that though the men talk a lot about female equality and about being nonsexist, actually the women are doing the housework, washing, and cooking. When she mentions this at a meeting, she is told that this division is more efficient, and doesn't she believe in efficiency, and anyway none of the women are strong enough to do the heavy work of building cabins or felling trees. Since the men do the heavy labor, it isn't fair for them to have to do cooking and cleaning too. She finds herself stunned at the hostility in some of the men's voices and notes that the other women seem embarrassed by her bringing the point up.

Several weeks later, while Jerry is away visiting his folks, Ann spends the night with one of the members she has thought warm and loving. But in the morning, he announces to the group at breakfast, "You know, Ann has the potential of becoming a good sexual technician." She feels humiliated and degraded. When Jerry returns, he is told about her infidelity, and he threatens to leave her.

About this time, the health department sends an inspector to the commune, and the commune is cited for unsatisfactory bathroom and kitchen facilities. A county building inspector also cites them for not building to code and for not having building permits. All the structures built without permits will have to come down.

Jerry and Ann decide to return to the city. They still believe in the ideal of communal living, but feel that this group just wasn't suited for them. They think they might try the experience again, but perhaps with a commune that has been in existence for several years.

The major reasons for the failure of most communes appear to be: (1) inability to handle interpersonal conflicts, (2) lack of an economic base, (3) jealousy, (4) lack of a secure one-to-one relationship compounded by the insecurity of relating to an amorphous group, (5) the difficulty of maintaining multiple relationships, (6) lack of privacy, and (7) difficulty of living anarchistically with individuals who are not mature and responsible (Rogers, 1972).

Studies, especially of rural communes, show that the actual living styles may not be as radically different as mass media lead us to believe. Despite women's liberation, the traditional male and female roles, for example, remain essentially old-fashioned in many communes. The women do the daily cooking, cleaning, and child-rearing jobs while the men work at income-producing jobs. Ira L. Reiss (1972, p. 246) concludes that the commune picture that emerges from the research is not one of any radical change in marital relations.

> The radical change seems to be the attempt to achieve close relations in one household, among a relatively large number of people. This is a departure from the suburban nuclear family ranch house, but in many other ways, it is not a departure from the conventional marriage. Perhaps, in time, with a second generation on the commune scene, more radical role changes will appear. But even so it looks as though some form of marital relationship is well established in the commune setting.

Children within the commune setting also present some unique problems. Basically, unless special arrangements are made for children, they face multiple rule makers and rule enforcers. Inconsistency, ambiguity, and contradictions often arise because each adult communal member has a different set of expectations for children. Infractions of the rules are likely to bring several reprimands in addition to those from the parents (for a fuller discussion on children in a communal setting, see Kanter et al, 1975). Parents experience a dilution of control and influence over their children. In some cases, multiple control and responsibility for children practically turns out to be no control and responsibility. In fact, rather badly neglected children come from some of the communes (especially those with heavy drug usage). Because everyone is supposed to be responsible for the chil-

dren, each thinks other adults will be doing the job when, in reality, no one is. But, as we learned in Chapter 12 (Broader Parenting), being able to turn to more adults can also be an advantage for children, as they can find solace and approval elsewhere when in trouble with their parents, and they are exposed to many role models.

Cluster Families   Cluster or extended families are another attempt to regain some of the lost sense of community felt by many Americans. According to a sermon by John A. Crane, Unitarian minister:

> We are so constructed as creatures that we need to have in ourselves a sense of community with others of our kind for our well-being. A sense of community is something we come to feel over a period of time, as we move among people we know well, are close to, people we trust, feel safe with, feel warm toward.
>
> This sense of community used to arise in us naturally, without any conscious effort, in years past, when most of us lived out our lives in the area in which we were born. We met the same people day after day, week after week, some of whom we were quite close to, confided in, and were given confidences in return. We knew all of the storekeepers and tradesmen, often had known them from the time they were children.
>
> In this stable kind of community, with a low level of mobility, we gained both a sense of community and a sense of identity. It didn't require any effort or attention, it was just something we breathed in from our social environment. We came to know ourselves by moving among people who knew us and had known us for some time. We saw ourselves in their eyes each day, in the expression on their faces, in the tones of their voices as they responded to us (Crane, 1974).

A cluster family is an artificially contrived family group that meets for companionship, recreation, and other meaningful experiences but the members do not actually live together. They may choose to eat, play, work, or simply be together. The cluster family provides a large circle of supportive friends for its members. The Unitarian Church of Santa Barbara, California, started the first artificially constructed extended family in 1971, and the concept has spread across the United States and to some foreign countries.

Those interested in joining a family are grouped according to age, sex, and marital status. Thus each family includes married couples, singles, children, old, and young. Usually the family has fifteen to twenty members. Each family has a nonprofessional leader though usually the facilitator is needed only the first three months. Steady, sensitive leadership is necessary though for the extended family group to prosper.

People who join a family must commit themselves to it for at least three months. Each family then develops in whatever ways it wants or members need. Members are expected to make an effort to know and understand other members as well as allowing themselves to be known. Joining a family means "playing, laughing, loving, opening yourself, giving, and receiving. It means growing close to people who, over time, with shared experience, come to matter to you" (Crane, 1974).

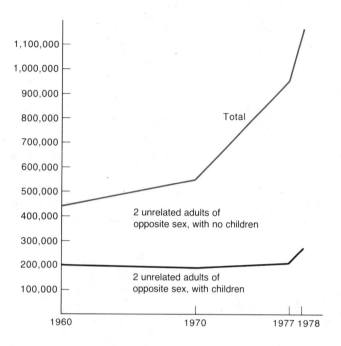

Figure 14-2
Unmarried couples living together in the United States: 1960-1978.
Source: Paul C. Glick and Arthur J. Norton, "Marrying, Divorcing, and Living Together in the U.S. Today." Population Bulletin, No. 5, Vol. 32, Population Reference Bureau, Inc., Washington, D.C., 1977; and U.S. Bureau of the Census, unpublished Current Population Survey data for June, 1975.

Participation in a cluster family also has some potential disadvantages. The activities take time. There are increased complications and strains in interacting with large numbers of people. Also, closeness can sometimes mean getting hurt. And once ties are formed, future separations can be painful (Pringle, 1974).

Cohabitation

Unlike group marriage, swinging, and living in communes, cohabitation has been growing rapidly, especially since 1970. By cohabitation we mean couples who live together in households that contain only themselves and possibly the children of one or both of them, usually by previous partners. The number of such couples has increased from 523,000 in 1970 to 1,137,000 in March of 1978. This accounts for about 2.3 percent of all couples living together. About 76 percent of these couples were living in a household with no other persons present, and the remaining 24 percent had one or more children (see Figure 14-2).

Glick and Spanier (1980) characterize this data by stating: "Rarely does social change occur with such rapidity. Indeed there have been few developments relating to marriage and family life which have been as dramatic as the rapid increase in unmarried cohabitation."

It is possible that some of the increase is accounted for by a greater willingness to divulge the fact of living together outside of marriage. On the other hand, there are an unknown number of couples living together who pass themselves off as married or, at least, do not divulge their living arrangement. They, of course, would not be included in the total figures. It is also true that some of these cohabiting couples have landlady or landlord-tenant, or employer-employee relationships without being intimately involved. However, enough couples are openly living together in intimate relationships that some theorists now consider living together to be an ongoing part of the mate selection process for a growing minority of couples (see Chapter 4, p. 117).

Despite the growing visibility of such couples, they still represent a very small proportion of the population. However, among college students, Macklin (1978) estimates that about 25 percent of the undergraduate population has cohabited and 50 percent state they would if they were to find themselves in an appropriate relationship.

The popular notion that cohabitation is a unique characteristic of the young, especially college students, is not exactly correct. Approximately 40 percent of cohabiting persons are thirty-five years and older. There is also a significant minority of elderly, retired cohabiting couples.

The Nature of Cohabiting Relationships People choose to live together for many reasons, some of which may not be true for every cohabiting couple. First, it is clear that many consider these experiences to be no more than *short-lived sexual flings*. For example, among male cohabiting students in a large research study (Peterman et al, 1974), 82 percent of those twenty years of age or younger reported that their longest cohabitation was three months or less. Sixty-three percent of the males aged twenty-one and twenty-two reported the same average. Among females in the twenty and under age group, 67 percent reported three months or briefer cohabitations, and 48 percent of those aged twenty-one and twenty-two reported the same (Peterman et al, 1974). These couples had no firm future plans. The authors conclude that:

1. The opportunity to cohabit has increased in recent years, especially as college housing arrangements have become less restrictive and the fear of pregnancy has been reduced by improved contraception.
2. There is limited commitment although commitment increases with age and class standing.
3. Most cohabitation experience is probably not in the nature of a "trial marriage" because of its short duration and the living situation in which there are often other persons.
4. A minority of parents are told of the cohabiting experience.
5. Marriage is still the popular choice for cohabitors although cohabitation on a more permanent basis ranks higher than for non-cohabitors.

Generally, living together does not seem to portend some great new experiment leading to a happier life. To date, living together seldom survives long as a permanent form of relationship. Most couples either break up or eventually marry in time (Kapecky, 1972; Bower & Christopherson, 1977).

Second, there are those couples who live together for practical reasons. They are essentially no more than *opposite-sex roommates*.

In this case, the couple live together without necessarily having a deep or intimate relationship. Living with a member of the opposite sex as a roommate affords certain advantages. A woman may feel safer living with a man if she lives in a high crime rate area. They can learn to share skills; for example, she might teach him to cook while he teaches her automobile maintenance. Generally, the couple simply lives together as would two same-sex roommates. They each date others, generally keep their love lives out of their living quarters, and react to one another as friends, each gaining something from living together in partnership rather than separately. The most often given reason for such an arrangement is "to save money." This is especially true of elderly cohabitants.

Third, there are couples who see cohabiting as a *true trial marriage*. As one young woman explained, "We are thinking of marriage in the future, and we want to find out if we really are what each other wants. If everything works out, we will get married" (Danziger and Greenwald, 1973). Some of these couples go so far as to set a specific time period.

Fourth, there are couples who view cohabiting as a *permanent alternative to marriage*. They often express a philosophical rejection of the marital institution as being unfavorable to healthy and growing relationships. They are especially critical of the constraints imposed by

©1977 Universal Press Syndicate

"If you keep bugging me about getting married, I'm gonna break off our engagement."

the laws on partners' rights in marriage. Many of the couples who see consensual union as a permanent alternative to legal marriage write their own contracts in an effort to form a more egalitarian union even though such contracts cannot invalidate state marriage laws.

Many who live together state their desire to avoid what they perceive to be the constraining, love-draining formalities associated with legal marriage. They say "If I stay with my mate out of my own free desire rather than because I legally must remain, our relationship will be more honest and caring. The stability of our relationship is its very instability."

Is the Woman Exploited in Cohabitation Relationships? Obviously the answer to this question will depend on the individual relationship. However, there are some interesting statistics that bear on this question in a general way. There are a number of studies that indicate that males seem less committed to their live-together relationships than their female partners (Budd, 1976; Johnson, 1973; Kieffer, 1972, pp. 79–83; Lewis, 1975; Lyness et al, 1972).

In the Lyness study, couples living together were compared to couples going together. No significant differences were found between the groups in level of trust and reported happiness, both of which were high. A difference was found, however, in the reported degree of commitment to marriage. The couples who were going together, both males and females, were committed to future marriage. But males in the living-together couples were the least committed, far less so than the women with whom they were living. The researchers' tentative conclusions were, in part:

> To a striking degree, living-together couples did *not* reciprocate the kinds of feelings (of need, respect, involvement, or commitment to marriage) that one would expect to be the basis of a good hetero-sexual relationship. The question of whether such a lack of reciprocity is typical of such relationships and thus reflects the difficulties of bringing off a successful nonnormative relationship or whether it is merely typical of those who volunteered for our research cannot be answered (Lyness et al, 1972, p. 309).

We have already seen that many of the cohabitation relationships are short-lived and seem to revolve around the sexual part of the relationship. If the man tends to be less committed than the woman, it appears to be a reasonable assumption that he is often the one to end the relationship, if not directly, then indirectly by refusing equal commitment.

Glick and Spanier (1980, p. 25) also point out that cohabiting men are much *less* likely to be employed than married men, but co-habiting women were much *more* likely to be employed than married women. This might suggest that the men are using the women economically to help themselves get through school or pursue their own interests which at the time do not produce much, if any, monetary return.

It is also of interest to note that although cohabitation appears to be very avant garde, which suggests that those people who are involved in it are liberated, the division of labor in the household tends to be traditional (Macklin, 1978, p. 293; Whitehurst, 1974). That is, the woman does the cooking, cleaning, and household work. Remembering that she is much more apt to be in the workforce than her married counterpart, it is clear that she is often overburdened in the cohabitation relationship.

Perhaps, in general, the woman considering cohabitation should examine carefully the nature of the intended relationship before entering it. One way that she can do this is to answer the questions posed in Inset 14-2.

The Relationship Between Cohabitation and Marriage Many young people argue persuasively that living together provides a good test of future marriage. In a sense, it is like a test marriage without the legal requirements necessary to end the relationship if it doesn't work. Cohabitors espouse a variety of other arguments in support of premarital cohabitation:

1. It provides an opportunity to try to establish a meaningful relationship.
2. It can be a source of financial, social and emotional security.
3. It provides a steady sexual partner and companionship, thus providing some of the central pleasures of marriage without commitment.
4. It provides a chance for personal growth, a chance to increase self-understanding vis-à-vis relating to another person on an intimate basis.
5. Cohabitors would have a more realistic notion of their partner and should generally have less romanticized ideas about the relationship.
6. Cohabitors have a chance to get beyond typical courtship game-playing.
7. Long periods of intimate contact provide an opportunity for self-disclosure and concomitant modification and/or realization of personal goals (Jacques & Chason, 1979, p. 37).

Although these arguments are logical and reasonable, what research we have to date on the quality of marriage after cohabitation experiences finds little if any relationship between cohabitation and the degree of satisfaction, conflict, emotional closeness, or egalitarianism in later marriage (Macklin, 1978). Clatworthy and Scheid (1977) report that while all couples in their sample who had premaritally cohabited considered the experience to be beneficial to their marriage, there was no evidence that they actually had better marriages or that they had selected more compatible mates than noncohabiting couples.

Perhaps the dissimilarities between cohabitation and marriage negate the apparent advantages of cohabitation in so far as future marriage success is concerned. Leslie (1979, p. 159) lists the following dissimilarities between cohabitation and marriage:

Inset 14-2
Sample Counselor Questions for Couples Contemplating Living Together*

Counselor Questions	"Good" Signs and "Concern" Signs
1. Could you talk a little bit about how each of you came to the decision to live together?	**Good signs:** Each partner has given considerable thought to the decision, including the advantages and disadvantages of living together. **Concern signs:** One or both partners have given little thought to the advantages and disadvantages of living together.
2. Perhaps each of you could discuss for a minute what you think you will get out of living together?	**Good signs:** Each individual is concerned about learning more about self and partner through intimate daily living. Both wish to obtain further information about each other's commitment to the relationship. **Concern signs:** One or both partners desire to live together for convenience only. They want to live together to show independence from parents or peers.
3. Could each of you discuss what you see as your role and your partner's role in the relationship (e.g., responsibilities, expectations)?	**Good signs:** Each individual's expectations of self and partner are compatible with those of partner. **Concern signs:** One or both individuals have given little thought to the roles or expectations of self and/or partner. Individuals disagree in terms of their expectations.
4. Could each of you identify your partner's primary physical and emotional needs and the degree to which you believe that you are able to fulfill them?	**Good signs:** Each individual has a clear understanding of partner's needs and is motivated and able to meet most of them. **Concern signs:** One or both individuals are not fully aware of partner's needs. Individuals are not motivated or able to meet needs of partner.
5. Would each of you identify your primary physical and emotional needs in your relationship with your partner? To what degree have these needs been met in the past? To what extent are these needs likely to be met if the two of you were to live together?	**Good signs:** Each partner clearly understands his or her needs. Most of these needs are presently being met and are likely to continue to be met in a cohabiting relationship. **Concern signs:** One or both partners are not fully aware of their needs. Needs are not being met in the present relationship and/or are not likely to be met if the individuals live together.
6. Could each of you discuss what makes this relationship important to you? What are your feelings toward your partner?	**Good signs:** Partners care deeply for each other and view the relationship as a highly significant one. **Concern signs:** One or both individuals do not care deeply for their partner or do not view the relationship as a highly significant one. Partners have an emotional imbalance with one partner more involved in the relationship than the other.

*Adapted from C. Ridley, D. Peterman, and A. Avery. "Cohabitation: Does It Make For a Better Marriage?" *Family Coordinator.* April, 1978, 135–136.

1. In marriage, one partner doesn't keep an address elsewhere to which he or she can retreat when the going gets rough.
2. Couples who live together know that they are not legally bound to one another. They can get out of the relationship with few sanctions.
3. Most living together couples retain a degree of financial independence uncommon in most marriages.
4. Unwed couples have to worry about possible contraceptive failure, but they don't have to plan for children.
5. Cohabiting couples don't necessarily have to make plans for the future.

Counselor Questions	"Good" Signs and "Concern" Signs
7. Could each of you explore briefly your previous dating experiences and what you have learned from them?	**Good signs:** Both individuals have had a rich dating history. Individuals have positive perceptions of self and opposite sex and are aware of what they learned from previous relationships. **Concern signs:** One or both partners have had minimal dating experience. Individuals have negative perceptions of self and/or of the opposite sex and do not seem aware of having learned from their prior relationships.
8. Perhaps each of you could talk for a minute about how your family and friends might react to the two of you living together?	**Good signs:** Each individual is aware of the potential repercussions of family and friends should they learn of the cohabiting relationship. Family and friends are supportive of the cohabiting relationship, or couple has considered how they will deal with opposition. **Concern signs:** One or both individuals are not fully aware of possible family and friends' reaction to their living together. Family and friends are not supportive of the cohabiting relationship.
9. Could each of you discuss your ability to openly and honestly share your feelings with your partner?	**Good signs:** Each individual is usually able to express feelings to partner without difficulty. **Concern signs:** One or both individuals have difficulty expressing feelings to partner or do not believe expressing feelings is important.
10. Could each of you discuss your partner's strengths and weaknesses? To what extent would you like to change your partner, relative to their strengths or weaknesses?	**Good signs:** Each individual is usually able to accept feelings of partner. Individuals are able to accept partner's strengths and weaknesses. **Concern signs:** One or both individuals are not able to understand and accept partner. Individuals have difficulty in accepting partner's strengths and weaknesses.
11. How do each of you handle relationship problems when they occur? Can you give some examples of difficult problems you have had and how you have dealt with them?	**Good signs:** Both individuals express feelings openly and are able to understand and accept partner's point of view. Individuals are able to mutually solve problems. **Concern signs:** One or both partners have difficulty expressing feelings openly or in accepting partner's point of view. Couple frequently avoids problems or fails to solve them mutually.

In discussing the high break-up rate of cohabiting couples, Leslie finds that cohabitors may unknowingly be creating a self-fulfilling prophecy. They enter a relationship partly to see if it will last and, by keeping the possibility of discontinuing the relationship in mind, they actually help to cause the break-up. It is possible that some of the very same relationships might turn out quite differently if the partners entered them with an unshakable determination to succeed. Leslie suggests that living together can be a way for young people to avoid responsibility. It is easier to play house than to be married. If this is true, perhaps this attitude is carried along into subsequent marriages, thus contributing to the marriage's instability.

This piece will use names of two people, Pietro and Tess.

For three years Pietro and Tess lived together without marrying. Such an arrangement had ceased to be scandalous when they took it up, had even become fashionable. It expressed the partners' re-evaluation of the culture, or their liberation from tired old values, or something. It doesn't matter what. Pietro and Tess did it.

They were married a few weeks ago.

The canker in the love nest was the English language. Though English is the world's most commodious tongue, it provided no word to define their relationship satisfactorily to strangers. When Tess took Pietro to meet her parents the problem became troublesome. Presenting Pietro, she said, "Mommy and daddy, this is my lover, Pietro."

Pietro was not amused. "It made me sound like a sex object," he said.

A few weeks later they were invited to meet the president. Entering the reception line, Pietro was asked by the protocol officer for their names. "Pietro," he said. "And this is my mate."

As they came abreast of the president, the officer turned to Mr. Reagan and said, "Pietro and his mate."

"I felt like the supporting actress in a Tarzan movie," said Tess. It took Pietro three nights of sleeping at the YMCA to repair the relationship.

Back to the drawing board, on which they kept the dictionary.

For a while they tried "my friend." One night at a glamorous party Pietro intro-duced Tess to a marrying millionaire with the words, "This is my friend, Tess." To which the marrying millionaire replied, "Let's jet down to the Caribbean, Tess, and tie the knot."

"You don't understand," said Pietro. "Tess is my *friend*."

"So don't you like seeing your friends headed for big alimony?" asked the marrying millionaire.

"She's not that kind of friend," said Pietro.

"I'm his *friend*," said Tess.

"Ah," said the matrimonialist, upon whom the dawn was slowly breaking, "Ah — your — *friend*."

As Tess explained at the wedding, they couldn't spend the rest of their lives rolling their eyeballs suggestively every time they said "friend." There was only one way out. "The simple thing," Pietro suggested, "would be for me to introduce you as 'my wife.'"

"And for me," said Tess, "to say, 'This is my husband, Pietro.'"

And so they were wed, victims of a failure in language.

RUSSELL BAKER
New York Times

Despite such criticisms, cohabitation, especially among college students, seems to be finding more acceptance in our society. However, deciding to cohabit is not a decision to be taken lightly. One needs to consider carefully the ramifications of such a decision. Although we have yet to discuss the legal ramifications, they must also be considered, now more than ever (see Scenes from Marriage, p. 445).

Breaking Up The break-up of cohabiting couples has been largely ignored. In part this may be because one of the philosophical foundations of cohabitation is, it is easy break-up if the relationship fails. Yet for those partners who are highly committed to the relationship, a breakup can be as emotionally uncomfortable as a divorce. At least with divorce, the society does have some support systems (see Chapter 15) to help the person. However, there are no such support systems for the person leaving a cohabitation relationship. As the earlier statistics showed, the break-up rate is high, and thus the number of people who must cope with the trauma of break-up alone or perhaps with only a friend's shoulder to cry upon will be increasing. This problem requires study (Hill, Rubin & Paplau, 1976).

Conclusion

Perhaps, in conclusion, I should note some of the risks involved in the new life-styles. The major risk in opening up choice is error in choice. When choices open up, one must carefully consider priorities. The older restricted system exacted a price; it placed a person in a mold which did not enable him to choose a life-style that would allow maximum self-growth and social contribution. In a more open system people run the risk of acting impulsively. Such precipitate action might destroy long-range life prospects and opportunities. For example, one may impulsively get involved in a sexual encounter, and thereby cause a break in a meaningful relationship; or one may hastily get involved in divorce proceedings, and thereby avoid facing up to faults in oneself. Thus, the price of a more open system is the greater need for a rational examination of the alternatives.

The old system had many people trapped in a rut; the new one may have many people constantly running from one style of life to another, unable to choose wisely (Reiss, 1972, p. 246).

It may be that freedom will encourage people to run from one life style to another as Reiss suggests. On the other hand, it is also possible that freedom will encourage experimentation, which will lead to better decisions. Free inquiry leading to reasoned decisions with opportunities to test one's decisions is the way of science. There is no reason why this method should not help to improve the intimate life of people just as it has helped to improve their material life. In addition, the feeling of having made a free choice as to life style certainly counteracts the feelings of entrapment so often expressed by long-married couples.

Summary

Recently we have witnessed an increasing acceptance of multiple forms of intimate relationships between men and women, probably related to America's affluence, the mass media, and the mobility of the population. But although the popular media make a great deal of alternate relationships to traditional marriage, relatively few people actually participate in many of the alternatives. The social acceptance of alternative relationships seems to be increasing faster than the numbers of people actually participating in them.

Remaining single for a longer period than in the past seems to be one of the emerging life styles. In addition, with the increasing divorce rate, there are increasing numbers of formerly married singles. The single life style is characterized by independence and freedom when compared to the marital life style. Permanence is not a goal of many singles, who instead elevate change and experiencing to the top of their value list, with self-fulfillment a major goal.

Tied closely to singleness is also childlessness. Those who opt to remain single longer also postpone or reject altogether having children. In addition, more and more married couples are also deciding against children. Again, a major goal achieved by such a decision is the gaining of personal freedom. Childless families are often characterized by both the husband and wife working on their own careers.

Traditional marriage has usually meant emotional and sexual exclusiveness. Recently, some married couples have experimented with both emotional and/or sexual relations with nonspouses. In group marriages, the multiple partners relate to all the members of the marriage as they would to an individual husband or wife. In swinging, sexual relations outside of the marriage are allowed but generally emotional involvement is limited to the marriage partners.

Communal living has also increased in popularity. There are many types of communes; rural, urban, monogamous, polygamous, and so on. They all involve members sharing some parts of their lives with the other members. They may all live together in the same structure or they may farm together or they may relate sexually and intimately with the members of the commune. Generally, such shared lives do not hold together long. The average life of a commune is less than a year, though many have lasted much longer, especially those with a religious orientation. Living intimately with so many simply compounds the problems found when just two persons live intimately together.

Living together either as a trial marriage, on a permanent basis, or simply as a short-term arrangement is yet another alternative that more Americans are trying. It is most prevalent among college students and the elderly. With the young, it is seldom a permanent arrangement since most couples who live together either break up or marry. However, enough people are living together for long terms without marrying that the law is beginning to take such relationships into account by allowing each some economic share of things derived from the relationship.

In general, American society is allowing people a broader spectrum of possible intimate relationships. Although only a small minority of people choose alternate intimate life styles, their availability influences all marriages. •

Living Together and the Law

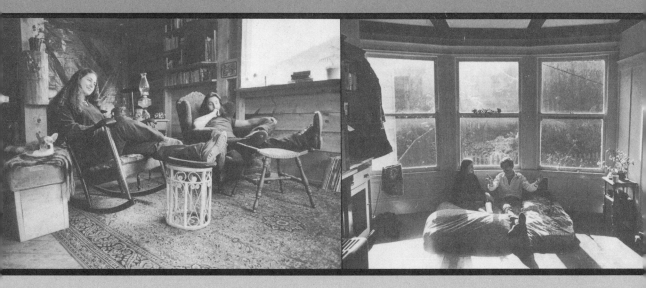

It will come as a surprise to many readers, but as of July, 1976, cohabitation was a crime in 20 states (Lavori, 1976). Indeed, sexual intercourse between unmarried persons is still a crime in 16 states and in Washington, D.C. It is true that such laws are seldom enforced, but if they are, the penalties are stringent. Many states set a maximum fine of $500 and six months in jail. Macklin (1978, p. 300) suggests that such laws may be unconstitutional and may violate one's right to privacy, but at this time they are still the law.

In the states where such laws are in effect, there are numerous ramifications for the cohabiting couple. For example, living together can be grounds for eviction if they are renters. It could also be grounds for losing one's job. Because membership in professional associations and licensing may be conditional on demonstration of moral fitness, such privileges could be denied to someone cohabiting out of wedlock (Macklin, 1978, p. 301).

Palimony

Such laws, however, are so seldom enforced that they are not nearly so meaningful to the cohabiting couple as are several recent court decisions concerning property distribution and the obligation of support.* Perhaps the best known case involved actor Lee Marvin and his "live-in" friend, Michelle Triola. It was in this case that someone coined the term "palimony" to describe settlements made to a nonmarried live-in partner. The term has no legal significance but is descriptive of what Michelle was finally awarded.

Michelle and Lee Marvin lived together for seven years. During this period she acted as a companion and homemaker. There was no pooling of earnings, no property purchased in joint names, and no joint income tax returns filed. They often spoke proudly of their freedom as unmarried cohabitors, and went to some length to keep property separated. Eventually, Lee Marvin asked Michelle to leave the household. He continued to support her for two years after the separation and then refused further support. Michelle then brought suit and asked the court to determine her contract and property rights and to award her half of the prop-

*This section has been adapted from Noel Myricks, " 'Palimony': The Impact of Marvin v. Marvin." *The Family Coordinator.* April, 1980. pp. 210–215.

erty acquired during the period of their relationship.

The trial court dismissed the action as inappropriate, but it was then appealed to the California Supreme Court. That court ruled:

> The fact that a man and woman live together without marriage and engage in a sexual relationship, does not in itself invalidate agreements between them relating to their earnings, property, or expenses. . . . Agreements between nonmarital partners fail only to the extent that they rest upon a consideration of meretricious sexual services (Marvin v. Marvin, 1976).

A meretricious relationship is essentially that of a prostitute to her customer; i.e., sexual services are being paid for. This ruling enabled Michelle to pursue her claim for support payments and established a precedent for unwed couples in that it granted such persons the right to sue for property settlements. Michelle Marvin-Triola became the first unmarried person to win any compensation from a former lover in a U.S. court (Marvin v. Marvin, 1979). She was awarded $104,000 for "rehabilitation purposes so that she may have economic means to re-educate herself and to learn new, employable skills or to refurbish those utilized . . . during her most recent employment, and so that she may return from her status as companion of a motion picture star to a separate, independent but perhaps more prosaic existence" (Marvin v. Marvin, 1979). The award was primarily for retraining, yet some of the funds could be used for living expenses. Such equitable relief is similar to rehabilitative alimony, hence the coined term "palimony." In effect, the judge gave her disguised alimony.

Numerous other cases have been litigated both before and after the Marvin case. In those cases where the courts see the union as meretricious, any implied contracts are illegal. However to 1979, seventeen states had followed the Marvin rationale.

The bottom line is that a given court will have the final word as to a cohabiting couple's obligations to one another if they break up. After a review of many palimony cases, Myricks (1980, p. 214) draws the following conclusions:

1. Distribution of property acquired during cohabitation remains subject solely to judicial decision.
2. Courts should enforce express contracts between cohabitors except where the contract is explicitly founded on payment for sexual services.
3. Without an express contract, courts should inquire into the nature of the relationship to determine if theirs is an implied contract.
4. Courts may compensate a person for the reasonable value of their services regardless of any agreement as to the value of such services.
5. Generally sexual services must be separated from other domestic services to make a valid argument. However, the state of Oregon has ruled more liberally and is willing to disregard the lifestyle of the parties (Latham v. Latham, 1976).
6. An implied contract may be inferred entitling a cohabitant to one-half of the accumulated property where parties have held themselves out as husband and wife (Carlson v. Olson, 1977).
7. Palimony may be provided to a cohabitant for rehabilitation purposes.
8. Lawsuits may be kept to a minimum if cohabitants have written agreements concerning the nature of their relationship although the court may change or invalidate such agreements.

Chapter 15 ～

Contents

Scenes from Marriage:
SINGLE AGAIN

The Dissolution of Marriage

"In sickness and in health, till death do us part." This traditional part of the marriage ceremony might well be changed to the following in modern America: "In happiness and in good health, till divorce do us part."

A hundred years ago in this country, 30 out of every 1000 marriages were ended each year by the death of one of the spouses. Only 3 marriages in every 1000 were ended by divorce. Today those figures are nearly reversed. Divorce, separation, and desertion finish most marriages rather than death.

**Introduction:
Let No Man
Put Asunder**

It seems obvious that the "love match" marriage based on romance and self-gratification, or, in other words, on the fulfillment of all one's needs, must suffer from a high rate of failure. Americans ask a great deal of marriage, and the higher the stakes, the higher the chances of failure.

Basically, the rate of divorce has been rising in this country throughout the century. In 1900, there was about one divorce for every twelve marriages. By 1922, there was one divorce for every eight marriages, and in the late 1940s, there was approximately one divorce for every three and a half marriages. This peak probably occurred as a result of dislocations arising from World War II. From 1950 to 1970 the ratio of divorce to marriage leveled off at approximately one divorce for every four marriages. But then, beginning in 1970, the divorce rate again started to rise until, by 1976, it reached an all time high and then leveled out in 1977 (Glick & Norton, 1977, p. 4). The number of divorced women heading families nearly tripled from 1960 to 1975, going from 750,000 to 2.1 million (Grossman, 1977, p. 48). See Table 15-1.

However, divorce statistics do not yield a complete picture of the incidence of broken marriage. Legal separation claims another 3 percent of all marriages. Desertion, another manner of breaking a marriage, is especially prevalent among the poor, although it is difficult to obtain statistics on desertion since it may not appear in any records. It is usually the husband who leaves, although more wives are now deserting than in the past (Todres, 1978).

It appears, in any case, that dissolution of American marriages is relatively commonplace and becoming more so in the 1970s. Some family experts have begun to call American marriages "throwaway marriages." But a better name is "serial marriages"; that is, Americans

Table 15-1 Number of Divorces and Divorce Rates with Percent Changes from Preceding Years: 1940 to 1978

Year	Number of Divorces	Percent Change in Number	Rate per 1000 Total Population	Percent Change in Rate	Rate per 1000 Married Women 15 Years and Over	Percent Change in Rate
1977[1]	1,090,000	+ 0.6	5.0	–	21.3	+ 0.9
1976[1]	1,083,000	+ 4.5	5.0	+ 2.0	27.7	+ 3.9
1975	1,036,000	+ 6.0	4.9	+ 6.5	20.3	+ 5.2
1974	977,000	+ 6.8	4.6	+ 4.5	19.3	+ 6.0
1973	915,000	+ 8.3	4.4	+ 7.3	13.2	+ 7.1
1972	845,000	+ 9.3	4.1	+10.8	17.0	+ 7.6
1971	773,000	+ 9.2	3.7	+ 5.7	15.8	+ 6.0
1970	708,000	+10.8	3.5	+ 9.4	14.9	+11.2
1969	639,000	+ 9.4	3.2	+10.3	13.4	+ 7.2
1968	584,000	+11.7	2.9	+11.5	12.5	+11.6
1967	523,000	+ 4.8	2.6	+ 4.0	11.2	+ 2.8
1966	499,000	+ 4.2	2.5	–	10.9	+ 2.8
1965	479,000	+ 6.4	2.5	+ 4.2	10.6	+ 6.0
1964	450,000	+ 5.1	2.4	+ 4.3	10.0	+ 4.2
1963	428,000	+ 3.6	2.3	+ 4.5	9.6	+ 2.1
1962	413,000	− 0.2	2.2	− 4.3	9.4	− 2.1
1961	414,000	+ 5.3	2.3	+ 4.5	9.6	+ 4.3
1960	393,000	− 0.5	2.2	–	9.2	− 1.1
1959	395,000	+ 7.3	2.2	+ 4.8	9.3	+ 4.5
1958	368,000	− 3.4	2.1	− 4.5	8.9	− 3.3
1957	381,000	− 0.3	2.2	− 4.3	9.2	− 2.1
1956	382,000	+ 1.3	2.3	–	9.4	+ 1.1
1955	377,000	− 0.5	2.3	− 4.2	9.3	− 2.1
1954	379,000	− 2.8	2.4	− 4.0	9.5	− 4.0
1953	390,000	− 0.5	2.5	–	9.9	− 2.0
1952	392,000	+ 2.9	2.5	–	10.1	+ 2.0
1951	381,000	− 1.1	2.5	− 3.8	9.9	− 3.9
1950	385,144	− 3.0	2.6	− 3.7	10.3	− 2.8
1949	397,000	− 2.7	2.7	− 3.6	10.6	− 5.4
1948	408,000	−15.5	2.8	−17.6	11.2	−17.6
1947	483,000	−20.8	3.4	−20.9	13.6	−24.0
1946	610,000	+25.8	4.3	+22.9	17.9	+24.3
1945	485,000	+21.3	3.5	+20.7	14.4	+20.0
1944	400,000	+11.4	2.9	+11.5	12.0	+ 9.1
1943	359,000	+11.8	2.6	+ 8.3	11.0	+ 8.9
1942	321,000	+ 9.6	2.4	+ 9.1	10.1	+ 7.4
1941	293,000	+11.0	2.2	+10.0	9.4	+ 6.8
1940	264,000	(NA)	2.0	(NA)	8.8	(NA)

Source: U.S. National Center for Health Statistics, *Vital and Health Statistics*, Series 21, No. 29, "Divorces and Divorce Rates: United States," table 1; and *Monthly Vital Statistics Report*, Vol. 27, No. 5 Supplement, "Advance Report: Final Divorce Statistics, 1976," table 1, and Vol. 27, "Provisional Statistics: Births, Marriages, Divorces, and Deaths for 1978," page 1; and unpublished base for rate per 1000 married women 15 years and over.

[1]Provisional data.

tend to marry, divorce, and marry again. Today, 21 percent of all American married couples have divorce somewhere in the background of one or both (*U.S. News & World Report*, Jan. 13, 1975). A high divorce rate apparently does not mean that Americans are disenchanted with marriage, however, since the divorced remarry in great numbers and relatively quickly (see Chapter 16).

Before leaving the statistics of divorce and separation, it is important that the reader realize that such statistics must be interpreted cautiously. For example, the crude divorce rate, the ratio of divorces to each 1000 persons within the population, is greatly influenced by birthrate. A decrease in birthrate will produce a higher percentage of divorce, presuming the total number of divorces remains stable. Because the birthrate has been at an all time low in America, some of the increase in crude divorce rate is accounted for by this fact. Also, as Crosby (1980, p. 57) points out, "Divorce statistics tell us very little about the institution of marriage except that some people choose to dissolve their marriage and others have this choice made for them by their spouses." To conclude that the institution of marriage and the family are in a state of decay and breakdown based on divorce statistics is not valid.

Historically, the American attitude toward divorce has been negative, stemming mainly from the majority Christian heritage. The stigma has a long history. Nearly two millennia ago, only sinful pagans divorced freely; virtuous, spiritual Christians did not. After some centuries, in fact, divorce was formally forbidden by the Church and made legally impossible (there was no civil marriage or civil divorce until recent centuries). To this day, civil divorces of Catholics, even in non-Catholic countries, are not recognized by the Church, and those Catholics who obtain such a divorce and remarry are considered to be in a state of sin and therefore ineligible for Communion, although they are no longer excommunicated.

Divorce: The Legalities

According to Morton Hunt (1969, p. 5):

> As for Protestants, though they have been able to divorce since the Reformation, Christ's injunctions against it have lived on in custom and conscience — in the form of legal difficulties and moral disapproval. Even today, divorce seems to many people an immoral or at least a shameful act. Typically, Dr. Norman Vincent Peale recently wrote in *The Readers' Digest* that to go through with divorce is to demonstrate that one lacks the courage, the intelligence and the unselfishness to make marriage work. The great majority of the divorced are, at least initially, apologetic, embarrassed, and defensive; they feel that in the eyes of the world — and even their own eyes — they have done something "wrong."

Italy allowed divorce for the first time in December 1970. Italy's new divorce law is hardly liberal, yet it took years of effort to gain any kind of divorce law. Couples seeking divorce must be legally separated for at least five years (when separation is mutual) and for six or more years when one partner is opposed. Other grounds cited in the new law are: foreign divorce or remarriage by one spouse, long prison sentences, incest, attempted murder of family members, criminal insanity, and nonconsummation of the marriage sexually. Adultery is not included as a ground for divorce.

For many, attitudes have changed to make divorce a legitimate option and to create an acceptance of divorce as a right and proper way to end an unsuccessful marriage.

The Conservative versus Liberal Battle Over Divorce Divorce laws vary from extreme restriction such as in Argentina and Spain, where no divorce at all is allowed, to extreme permissiveness such as in Japan, where divorce is granted simply on mutual consent. Even within the United States there is great variety since divorce, as well as marriage, is regulated by individual states. For example, until 1949 divorce was not allowed in South Carolina. From 1787 until 1966, adultery was the only grounds for divorce in New York. This led to businesses that planned and documented apparently adulterous situations for couples seeking divorce but uninvolved in real adultery. Since 1969, California has allowed divorce essentially by mutual consent, having dropped the old idea of adversary proceedings in which one member of the marriage had to be proven guilty of behavior that would give the other partner some state-defined ground for divorce.

The reason for such variety in divorce laws is the old philosophic battle between those who believe stringent divorce laws will curtail marriage failure and those who believe that marriages fail regardless of the strictness of divorce legislation. The latter also feel that unrealistic laws do more harm than good.

Until the advent of Christianity, governments in the Western world did not regulate marriage or divorce. In republican Rome, for example, it was customary to marry simply by living together with the stated intention of becoming man and wife. No ceremony was required. The Roman state recognized a marriage as dissolved when the parties separated.

The Christians, partially in reaction to the hedonistic Roman society, advocated strict control of sexuality and hence strict regulation of marriage and divorce. In the Christian ethic, marriage became indissoluble except by death. Sexual intercourse was permitted only within marriage, therefore intercourse was to be limited to only one partner. Marriage was not only an assumption of responsibility for spouse and offspring but a sacrament as well by which the marriage partners acknowledged their belief in and responsibilities to God and their faith in Christ. The Protestant Reformation reestablished the idea of divorce when Martin Luther claimed that marriage was not a sacrament but a "worldly thing." He considered it justifiable for a husband to leave his wife if she committed adultery. This brought back the idea of permissible divorce, but along with it came the idea that one spouse had to be proven a transgressor, thus introducing the adversary approach to divorce that has remained in the Western world to this day. Since religion and government were closely related, laws concerning marriage and divorce came into effect.

Thus the state laid down certain grounds for divorce, rules that if broken by one spouse allowed the other to institute divorce proceedings. In addition, since one spouse had to be proven a wrongdoer to allow divorce, punishments were often established. For example, in the American colonies it was common to deny the guilty spouse the right of remarriage if a divorce was granted. Today payment by one spouse to the other (alimony) is sometimes used to punish the guilty spouse rather than simply to help a spouse become reestablished after marital failure. The adversary-punishment approach to divorce remained the only approach in America until the latter half of the twentieth century.

Slowly, however, the idea that a marriage might be terminated simply because it had broken down, without placing blame on one party or the other, began to find its way into the law of action (how laws are actually applied), and very recently into the law of the books (how the laws are written).

The Legal Sham of Divorce All states set grounds on which a divorce can be granted. Some of these grounds have been adultery, mental and/or physical cruelty, desertion, alcoholism, impotency, nonsupport, insanity, felony conviction or imprisonment, drug addiction, and pregnancy at marriage. In order to obtain a divorce, one of the partners had to prove the other guilty of having transgressed in at least one of the areas accepted by the particular state in which they lived. In addition, all states banned *collusion* (the two agreeing and working together to obtain their divorce) or moving to another state if the only purpose was to take advantage of more lenient divorce laws. Thus, if the letter of the law was followed, divorce would have to be an action taken by one spouse against the other who would have to be proven guilty of some conduct the state of residence found unacceptable and therefore a ground for divorce.

Depending on the particular state, we find such absurdities as drunkenness being twenty-two times more common as grounds for divorce in Florida than in Maryland. This is, of course, because of the difference in the state divorce laws and not because Florida residents necessarily drink more. The most extreme example is New York where, until 1966, when the law was changed to allow other grounds for divorce, adultery was the only acceptable reason. In New York, the partner proven guilty of adultery was not allowed to remarry for three years and then only if the court removed the restriction because of the "guilty" partner's good conduct. There was no room in the laws on the books for a couple to agree to a rational divorce where the goal would be to minimize the problems faced by each.

Yet, the law in practice was often quite different. Only some 10 to 15 percent of divorces are *contested* (that is, in most divorces, both partners agree to the divorce). And, as long as both partners agree to the divorce, and do not fight it in court, divorces have been granted fairly freely and without much substantiation of charges, regardless of the laws on the books. The American divorce system has, in essence, been restrictive on the books and permissive in practice. The courts simply usually do not inquire into questions of collusion, residence, or grounds. They accept the word of the party in court and do not pursue such questions unless asked to do so by the parties and their lawyers. In a sense, America's varying divorce laws are a true democratic compromise. The conservatives have strict laws on the books, and the liberals have permissive courts.

A word needs to be mentioned about the residency requirements that all states tie to divorce. Each state now recognizes divorce in every other state if the other state's residency requirements have been met. And this "if" is not checked in the usual uncontested divorce. The states theoretically do not recognize foreign divorces unless one party actually lives or has lived in the other country. But the formal law again differs from the informal action and the state will do nothing about a foreign divorce even if neither party really lives abroad unless a complaint is received. However, if a complaint is received and the divorce is contested, states may invalidate a divorce where residency requirements have not been met. In cases of remarriage, spouses have sometimes been prosecuted for bigamy when their divorce has been invalidated.

Because the states vary so in their divorce laws, efforts have been made to develop uniform laws for marriage and divorce that all states could adopt. Representative panels of experts have drafted a basic law and submitted it to the states for acceptance by their legislatures. This has been attempted several times in the United States, beginning in 1892 when the National Conference of Commissioners on Uniform State Laws deliberated the divorce law. There was another attempt in 1970. To date, however, none of these efforts to unify state laws have met with much success (see Monahan, 1973, p. 353).

The Move Toward No-Fault Divorce For many years the Interprofessional Commission on Marriage and Divorce Laws has advocated elimination of the "proof of guilt" (adversary) procedure and substitution of "what are the best interests of the family."

California led the way in doing this when it passed a "dissolution of marriage" law (Senate Bill 252) in 1969 which became the model for other states to follow. The law removed fault — the question of who was to blame. Grounds were reduced to (1) irreconcilable differences that have caused irremedial breakdown of marriage or (2) incurable insanity. Section 4507 of the bill defined irreconcilable differences as those grounds that are determined by the court to be substantial reasons for not continuing the marriage and that make it appear that the marriage should be dissolved.

Property allocation was also simplified by dividing it equally under most circumstances. Child support remained the responsibility of both husband and wife. By 1978, most other states had enacted some type of no-fault or modified-fault divorce proceedings. Only three states retained fault as the *only* basis for divorce in 1978.*

Although from a legal view the two grounds are quite vague and open to varied interpretation, in practice it has meant that the

*Illinois, Pennsylvania, and South Dakota.

California courts simply ask the petitioner if his or her marriage has broken down because of irreconcilable differences. The court does not inquire into the nature of the differences, though the court can order a delay or continuance of not more than thirty days if in the court's opinion there is a reasonable possibility of reconciliation.

There is a unique section of the California law that bars evidence of misconduct on the part of either spouse:

> In any pleadings or proceedings for legal separation of dissolution of marriage under this part, including disposition and discovery proceedings, evidence of specific acts of misconduct shall be improper and inadmissible, except where child custody is in issue and such evidence is relevant to establish that parental custody would be detrimental to the child, or at the hearing where it is determined by the court to be necessary to establish the existence of irreconcilable differences (Code of Civil Procedure, Section 4509).

To date, the last point has been ignored by the courts.

In order to preclude people coming into the state only to take advantage of the liberalized divorce laws, California requires a minimum of six months' residency in the state and three months in the county in which proceedings are filed.

Since misconduct of one partner or the other is no longer considered, property settlements, support, and alimony awards are no longer used as punishment. California is one of seven states in which all property acquired during marriage is considered community property belonging equally to each spouse.* As long as the parties to the divorce agree and have divided their community property approximately evenly, the courts do not involve themselves in property settlements. The courts do, of course, set up support requirements for minor children, deeming such minors the responsibility of both parents until they are of age. In practice, this generally still means that the children live with the mother and the father pays.

Alimony can still be granted but not as punishment for wrongdoing:

> In any judgment decreeing the dissolution of a marriage or a legal separation of the parties, the court may order a party to pay for the support of the other party any amount, and for such a period of time, as the court may deem just and reasonable having regard for the circumstances of the respective parties, including duration of marriage, and the ability of the supported spouse to engage in gainful employment without interfering with the interests of the children (Code of Civil Procedure, Section 4801).

Although fault is no longer determined, the judge still has the right to award alimony, though now not as punishment for wrongdoing. In most cases the wife will receive alimony until she is able to get onto her feet financially. Often the wife has devoted herself exclusively to the family for years and has lost what marketable skills she

---

*The other states are Alaska, Idaho, Louisiana, Nevada, Texas, and Washington.

may once have had. In addition, if she is older, finding a job is even more difficult. The judges are tending to award limited-term alimony on the basis of need. For example, in a recent case, the court awarded a wife funds for a college education on the grounds that she had provided such an education for her husband by working to put him through school when they first married and now it would be fair for him to do the same for her. A number of California counties are using the following rough guidelines in awarding alimony. If the marriage has lasted less than twelve years, support will not exceed half the duration. In marriages of twenty years or more, awards of support may be given until remarriage. Generally, however, under no-fault proceedings, the amount and duration of alimony have been drastically reduced (Williams, 1977).

The simplified California law has encouraged a new trend in divorce, namely, "do-it-yourself" divorce. The retention of an attorney in order to obtain a divorce has in the past been mandatory, if for no other reason than to help interpret complicated divorce laws.

Although many attorneys work hard as marriage counselors and do all they can to minimize the problems of divorce, others seem to intensify problems rather than minimizing them:

> And because these divorce proceedings are handled by two lawyers, each of whom is being paid to demonstrate his/her own abilities, what is fair is often completely overlooked in favor of what can be gotten away with. Too many lawyers representing husbands feel they can justify their fees only by working out arrangements by which the husband pays too little. Too many wives' lawyers feel satisfied only when they can point out how little the husband has left (Sheresky & Mannes, 1972, p. x).

Such sentiments are often expressed by recently divorced people. Of course, it might be that the lawyer has simply become the scapegoat. On the other hand, the legal profession may need clearer guidelines for handling divorce as well as some training in counseling and interpersonal relations. Regardless of whether attorneys are involved or not, the couple that can work out their differences before approaching a lawyer and the court are in a much better position to obtain a fair and equitable divorce.

It is extremely important that attorneys who handle divorce cases realize (a) that there are psychological as well as legal factors to the termination of marital contracts and (b) that they attend to these factors as they process their cases. Failure to recognize the psychological aspects in this area of law can lead to a multiplicity of problems and further complicate an already difficult situation. It is not our intention to suggest that lawyers become marriage counselors, but to point out the non-legal issues that directly affect a divorce action (Sabalis & Ayers, 1977, p. 391).

Many Californians are simply going directly to the courts, following simplified procedures from guidebooks written by sympathetic lawyers or knowledgeable citizens, and obtaining their own divorces for the cost of filing ($40 to $60). However, a do-it-yourself approach to divorce is not recommended unless the partners are

Inset 15-1
Humanizing Divorce Procedures*

Because the courts have for so long considered divorce an adversary procedure, it has been difficult for those in the legal profession to think in "no fault" terms. Most of the legal terminology of divorce is derived from criminal law, thus the language used by attorneys and the courts is derived from that same background.

A lawyer is also traditionally trained to take the side of his/her client and do the best possible for them. Thus it is difficult for many lawyers to let go of that training (in fact, unethical of him/her to do so) and concern themselves with the entire family unit. Perhaps not every lawyer should handle divorces. Family law specialization is already a reality in many states. Such a specialization should lead the lawyer to think in terms of protecting all members of the family as they move down the road toward divorce. The family law attorney must

*These thoughts were shared in a talk given at the California Council on Family Relations Annual Conference held in Santa Barbara, California Sept. 26-28, 1980. The talk was entitled, "Drawing Individual and Family Strengths from the Divorce Process," by Meyer Elkin, long time California conciliation court pioneer.

Term	Criminal Meaning	Divorce Meaning
custody	A criminal in jail	A child given to a parent by the courts
custodian	Prison guard	Parent having legal custody of their child after a divorce
visitation	Friends and relatives visiting the person jailed	The noncustody parent visiting his/her child
Defendent	Person against whom legal action is taken	Person being sued for divorce
Plaintiff	Person or state taking legal action against defendent	Person suing for divorce
suit	Legal action to secure justice	Asking for a divorce

think beyond the divorce, especially if children are involved since "parents are forever." All divorce really does is to rearrange family relationships, not end them.

The family law attorney must also encourage self determination on the part of the divorcing couple. They each have strengths and weaknesses and are often better judges of how to change their relationship than are attorneys and courts. The traditional attorney is trained to do everything for his client rather than encouraging the client to take control of the process as much as possible. The family law attorney must learn to become a facilitator to the couple, complementing the couple's strengths and weaknesses.

Emotions are not permissible facts in a court of law. Yet emotions are facts in most divorce proceedings. They must be considered because the close intimacy of marriage cannot usually be dissolved without them.

The law has in recent years recognized the need for family support during the crises of divorce. No fault divorce, conciliation courts, joint child custody, and family law specialization for attorneys are all steps in the direction of humanizing divorce. The changes in the law are not enough, however, we must also work to bring the ideas of no fault and family well being into the consciousness of those working in the legal system.

relatively friendly, in agreement on all matters, including child support, and do not have large assets.

On January 1, 1979, a new law called "summary dissolution" took effect in California. This permits couples who meet several qualifications to get divorced without making court appearances. To qualify, a couple must have no children, less than $2000 in debts, no interest in real property, and not more than $5000 worth of community property excluding automobiles. Also, neither party may have separate property assets exceeding $5000.

The legal steps in obtaining a divorce will again vary slightly from state to state. Using California as a representative state, you must take the following legal steps to obtain a divorce.

1. The first papers must be filed with the county clerk. They include a statistical form and confidential questionnaire (some counties) giving information that the court will find helpful; a petition stating the basic information about your marriage and telling the court what you want done; and a summons or message from the court to the respondent, telling him or her that a petition has been filed.

2. A copy of the summons and of the petition and, in some counties, of the questionnaire must be served on the spouse.

3. The second papers must be filed after a minimum thirty-day wait after the date of service on the spouse. At this time you file the proof of service, a request for entry of default, and a financial declaration. The request for default indicates that your spouse will not fight the divorce so that you can move toward an uncontested hearing.

4. A date for a hearing is now set.

5. At the hearing the judge will ask you to state your name, that the facts on the petition are true, your residency, and the grounds on which the divorce is being sought. He will then talk with you about children, property, and bills, using the information you have supplied him. At this time, you will receive the interlocutory judgment which clears the way for the marriage to be dissolved after the waiting period.

6. The request for final judgment cannot be filed until at least six months after the papers have been served and two months after entry of the interlocutory judgment. When this is received, the marriage is officially dissolved and you are divorced.

Strict versus Liberal Divorce Laws   Those favoring strict divorce laws claim that such laws act to strengthen marriage by forcing couples to work out their problems and assume their responsibilities to make a go of their marriage. Divorce is considered a sign of individual failure in marriage. Yet, in reality, divorce per se is not really the problem, the problem is really marital breakdown. And laws may preclude divorce but they cannot prevent actual marriage breakdown. Laws may deny the freedom to remarry by denying divorce, but they cannot prevent a man and a woman from living together.

Those favoring more liberal divorce laws accuse strict laws of creating undue animosity and hardship, of leading to perjury and the falsification of evidence, and of simply being unenforceable (see, for example, Rheinstein, 1972).

However, simple studies comparing divorce rates and the restrictiveness of divorce laws find that there is a relationship. The more permissive the state's divorce laws, the higher the divorce rate and vice versa (see, for example, Stetson & Wright, 1975; Rheinstein, 1972). But the divorce rate is not necessarily an accurate reflection of marital

Inset 15-2
Divorce and Dad

Pay But Don't Interfere I left home because it seemed easier for Elaine and the kids. After all, I was but one person, they were three. The children could remain in their schools with their friends and have the security of living in the home they had grown up in. I figured I'd come to visit often. I hoped that our separation and divorce would have minimal impact on the children and felt that the family remaining in our home was the way to achieve this.

It certainly hasn't worked out as I first imagined. Visiting the children often is no simple matter. Elaine has a new husband, the children have their friends and activities. And I seem to be busier than ever.

At first I'd just drop by to see the children when time permitted, but this usually upset everyone concerned. Elaine felt I was hanging around too much and even accused me of spying on her. Actually there might have been a little truth in this accusation, especially when she started dating. The children usually didn't have time for me because they had plans of their own. I felt rejected by them.

Next, Elaine and I tried to work out a permanent visitation schedule. I was to take the children one evening a week and one weekend a month. Then she accused me of rejecting the children because I wouldn't commit more time to them. But my work schedule only had a few times when I was sure I would be free and thus able to take the children.

At first, the set visiting times worked out well. I'd have something great planned for the children. Soon, however, Elaine told me that I was spoiling them. She said that they were always upset and out of their routine when I brought them home. Would I mind not doing this and that with them. Gradually the list of prohibitions lengthened. She had the house, the children, and my money to support the kids, yet I seemed to have fewer and fewer rights and privileges with them.

Be sure child support payments arrive promptly but please leave the children alone became more and more Elaine's message.

Since she remarried, my only parental role seems to be financial. I really have no say on what the children do. I feel like I'm being taken every time I write a child support check.

The Missing Dad When Bill and I divorced, I wanted him to see our two children as often as possible and told the judge that he could have unlimited visitation rights. Bill seemed happy and said he looked forward to seeing the children often, both at my place and taking them to his new home. A year has now gone by and Bill almost never visits the children. Each time I ask him about it, he has another excuse. At first he told me that he was too busy getting moved into his place. Then he was working a lot of overtime and was just too pooped to visit. Later, he said his new girlfriend was not comfortable with his visiting here. When I suggested that he take the children to his place, he told me that they did not allow children, something he hadn't realized when he moved in, he said.

I think that the children really need their dad. It is important to them and they miss him. They ask where he is and why he doesn't come more often. I'm embarrassed when they ask since I don't know what to tell them. I really think he just doesn't care.

Even though the court ordered him to pay $200 a month for child support, he is very irregular about the payment and often I have to remind him that it is due. This makes it very uncomfortable, too. Between asking him to visit the children more often and reminding him to send the child support payment, all I seem to do is nag him. In fact, he accuses me of being a worse nag than when we were married, but what can I do?

Divorced Dad Wins $25,000 from Ex-Wife In a verdict described as precedent-setting, a divorced father has been awarded $25,000 because of the serious emotional problems he claims were caused by his ex-wife's refusal to permit visits with their three daughters.

A Fairfax County Circuit Court jury of three men and four women made the award to Harold H. Memmer, a civilian Army worker at Fort Belvoir in northern Virginia. Legal experts believe the verdict is the first of its kind.

Memmer claimed that his ex-wife, who has since remarried and lives in Evansville, Ind., had encouraged the girls, aged 13 and 20, not to talk to him.*

*Santa Barbara News-Press, August 8, 1980.

WHAT DO YOU THINK?

How hard do you think it is for a father to remain in contact with his children after divorce?

How do you think the father in the first story should handle the situation?

What should the ex-wife do to get Bill to visit more often and make payments on time?

In your experience, which of the two cases seems to occur more often? Why?

breakdown. For example, the incidence of separation and desertion tends to be higher in states with restrictive divorce laws.

Strict divorce laws are one of society's attempts to legislate successful marriage. But a better approach might be to make marriages harder to enter. The waiting period between the issuance of a marriage license and the actual marriage could be longer. Premarital counseling could be required. Trial marriages could be sanctioned. More couples seem to be forsaking formal marriage and simply living together, at least for a while, in what appears to be a trial union. This trend might lead to lower divorce rates.

The real issue is whether the law can make marriage successful. I rather doubt it. This does not mean I think there should be no state involvement in marriage. Certainly assigning responsibility for children, assuring some order in property inheritance, and guarding against fraud and misrepresentation are legitimate state concerns. But, beyond those concerns, it certainly seems obvious that state efforts to legislate successful marriage have not worked. Laws that support good human relations might be more helpful. For example, if a couple finds insurmountable obstacles to success in their marriage, then the laws should support their efforts to dissolve the marriage in the most amicable and beneficial manner.

Some Cautions About No-Fault Divorce There is little question that the implementation of no-fault divorce procedures has eased the trauma of divorce by focusing upon the demise of the marriage rather than on the guilt of one of the spouses. The fear that easier divorce laws would lead to skyrocketing divorce rates has not proven to be absolutely true (Dixon & Weitzman, 1980, 298–299). Divorce rates have increased since the first no-fault law in 1970, but many factors have contributed. California, which pioneered the legal changes, ranked 18th in 1976 among the fifty states in number of divorces per 1000 population. From 1969 to 1977, the California divorce rate increased 54 percent while the national rate increased 56 percent (Maher, 1979).

The enthusiasm for no-fault and do-it-yourself divorces, however, must be tempered. As we shall see (p. 462), divorce for most people is traumatic and involves many negative consequences, even under the best of circumstances.

Although on first appearance a divorce settlement that splits assets and responsibilities equally between the couple seems fair and equitable, it favors the man in the majority of cases. This is because the woman's earning power is usually less than the man's. Due mainly to the increasing divorce rates, female-headed families with children have grown greatly in the past fifteen years until they represented about 10 percent of all families in 1979 (Glick, 1979). As a group, these families have the hardest time financially. Approximately 40 percent live below the official poverty line. About 40 percent spend some time on welfare. Perhaps economic settlements should not be even at the time of divorce, but should take into consideration the lower earning power of the woman, especially if she assumes custody of the children, as occurs in most cases.

Property settlements agreed to by the divorcing couple have been found to be incomplete and, at times, grossly unfair to one of the pair. An amicable agreement reached by a divorcing couple based on present circumstances may be totally inappropriate at some time in the future (Leslie, 1979, p. 160).

It is interesting to note that in the past women have been the major partner to institute divorce proceedings. However, several studies indicate that after no-fault divorce legislation becomes law, men become the major partner filing for divorce (Gunter, 1977; Gunter & Johnson, 1979). Although the studies do not suggest the reasons for this reversal, it might be that equal property division does in fact favor the male as we have suggested.

Such cautions are not meant to negate the real advantages and the basic civility that no-fault divorce laws have brought to the procedure. They are simply meant to warn the reader that divorce under any circumstances is difficult and, if not a legal trial, certainly an emotional one.

Divorce But Not the End of the Relationship Many people who contemplate divorce see it as ending their miseries, ending forever a relationship that has become intolerable. Yet this is not always true and certainly is almost never true if children are involved.

Every state has provisions for modifying judgments made by the court at the time of divorce. Requests for change of custody, of support, or of alimony can be made by either spouse at any time. If you believe marital problems end with divorce, you should attend "father's day" in court. Many of our larger cities set aside specific days when motions are heard relative to an errant father's neglect in paying child support or to a vengeful mother's refusal to permit her former husband to visit their children. Sometimes these hearings are emotionally packed scenes, replete with name calling, charges, and countercharges (see, for example, Robbins, 1974, p. 187).

In August 1975, a federal law (Public Law 93-647) went into effect that permits wives access to federal data — IRS records, social security, and so on — to locate deserting ex-spouses who have failed to pay alimony and/or child support. The law also allows the IRS collection service to freeze bank accounts administratively (without going to court) after all other actions have been taken and the errant parent still refuses to pay. Nonpayment of child support is a felony punishable by a $1000 fine and/or one year in state prison. Since this law, many errant fathers have been forced into making their support and alimony payments.

On the positive side, though, many ex-spouses go on to become good friends after the pain of divorce fades. There are cases where a divorced couple remain business partners. Even after remarriage of one or both, there may be friendly interaction between the couples and the new spouse or spouses. Children usually tie a couple together long after divorce. Divorce may thus not be an end to a relationship at all but may only mean that the relationship has changed. Those who look to divorce as a final solution to their marital problems will probably be in for a surprise, especially if children are involved and the marriage is of relatively long duration.

Emotional Divorce and the Emotions of Divorce

Paul Bohannan (1970, pp. 29–30) has described what he terms the "six stations" of divorce. There is the *emotional divorce*, which centers around the problem of the deteriorating marriage. It begins before the second station, the *legal divorce*, and may go on long after the legal divorce. It brings forth the kind of thinking and questioning described in Inset 15-3 and may go on for several years. It is only when one finally lets go of the former spouse emotionally that one really becomes free. Yet, as we just saw, the third and fourth stations, the *economic and coparental divorce*, may mean restraints on freedom for years. The fifth station is the *community divorce*, the reactions of friends and the community to the divorce. The last station is the *psychic divorce*, where the major problem is regaining individual autonomy.

Divorce is not a spontaneous, spur of the moment act as marriage can be. In most cases dissolution occurs slowly, and divorce is actually the culmination of a prolonged period of gradual alienation. In many cases, some two years elapse between a couple's first real thought of divorce and the decree. Willard Waller (1967) delineates the following aspects in the alienation process:

1. Early in the process there is a disturbance in the sex life and affectional response. Rapport is lost, with an attempt to compensate for its lack in some cases. Emotional divorce begins here.
2. The possibility of divorce is first mentioned. This tends to clarify the relationship somewhat, with the initiator taking the lead and the partner remaining passive through the divorce cycle.
3. The appearance of solidarity is broken before the public. The fiction of solidarity is important as a face-saver. Once it is broken, the marriage cannot be the same again.
4. The decision to divorce is made, usually after long discussion, although at times it is made without forethought.
5. A severe crisis of separation follows. Severing a meaningful relationship is a traumatic experience at best, even though it is felt to be the only alternative.
6. Final severance comes with the actual divorce. This may come after a long period of delay and separation. While it is usually thought of as closing the case, the actual legal procedure is necessary before the next stage of the final adaptation can begin.
7. A period of mental conflict and reconstruction closes the case. The former partners enter new social worlds and full estrangement takes place.

So, long before legal divorce, a couple may find themselves beginning the process of emotional divorce. Often the beginnings of the process are not noticeable. What usually happens involves such things as a subtle withdrawal of one partner from the other, erecting barriers that slowly shield each from hurt by the other, gradually shifting concern from "us" to "me," meeting more and more psycho-

How can I be missing her after all of the fighting and yelling we've been doing the past year or two? It's so nice to be in my own little place and have peace and quiet. Damn, it sure is lonely. It's great to be a bachelor again, but after fifteen years of married life, who wants to chase women and play all those games. Wonder why the kids don't call? Keeping house is sure a drag. I wonder what she's doing? Do you suppose she is nicer to her dates than she was to me?

What really went wrong? Two nice kids, a good job, nice home, and I certainly loved her when we married. But she has been so unaffectionate and cold over the years. She never seemed to have time for me. Or was it that I never had time for her? When we dated she was so flexible. She'd do anything with me but after our first child she seemed to become so conservative. She wouldn't do anything daring. I had so little leisure time what with working so hard to give the family a good life. Why couldn't she do what I wanted when I was free? It's really all her fault. Of course, I could have included her more in my work world. Maybe if I had shared more of my business problems with her, she'd have been more understanding. It's true I am awfully short-tempered when the pressure is on. Certainly I didn't listen to her much any more. It seemed as if she only bitched and complained. I get enough of that at the office. You don't suppose there was another person? Maybe it was all my fault. A failure at marriage, that's me. Never thought it could happen to me. When did it start? Who first thought of divorce? Maybe the idea came because all our friends seemed to be divorcing.

On and on the thoughts of this newly divorced man go. Anger, guilt, frustration, conflict, insecurity, and emotional upheaval are the bedmates of divorce. "Our culture says that marriage is forever and yet I failed to make a go of it. Why?" The whys keep churning up thoughts, and endless questioning tends to follow marital breakdown. There are so many questions, doubts, and fears.

logical needs outside of the marriage, and finally, the erosion of the couple's sexual life together. The actual facts or events that lead up to divorce are as varied as the individuals who marry, but one thing that always happens is that each begins to concentrate on the other's weaknesses, shortcomings, and failures rather than on their strengths. The "20 percent I hate you" becomes the point of attention, rather than the "80 percent I love you" (see Chapter 5, pages 159–161). The inability to accept the partner the way he or she is or the inability to accept unwanted change in the partner are at the root of most emotional divorces.

Although many breakups occur during the first few years of marriage, with the peak occurring about three years after marriage, nearly 40 percent of all broken marriages have lasted ten or more years prior to divorce. The median duration of a marriage at the time of divorce in the United States is approximately seven years (Glick & Norton, 1977, p. 8). A couple usually decide on a legal divorce only after years of worsening relations.

Once legal divorce is initiated, many, many emotions will be experienced but essentially they will be the emotions of loss, the grief felt at the death of a loved one. It is true that for a lucky few, perhaps those divorcing quickly after marriage, grief and mourning will not occur. Indeed, for a very few, happiness and joy over regaining freedom may be the major emotions experienced. (See Table 15-2.) But, for most, there will be a period of denial — it really isn't happening — followed by grief, mourning, and a mixture of the following:

Self-pity   Why did this happen to me?

Vengeance   I'm going to get even!

Despair   I feel like going to sleep and never waking up again.

Wounded pride   I'm not as great as I thought I was.

Anguish   I don't know how I can hurt so much.

Guilt   I'm really to blame for everything.

Loneliness   Why don't our friends ever call me?

Fear   No one else will want to marry me.

Distrust   He (or she) is probably conniving with attorneys to take all the property.

Withdrawal   I don't feel like seeing anyone.

Relief   Well, at least it's over, a decision has finally been made.

Unfortunately, unlike the grief and mourning at the death of a loved one, our society offers no ritual, no prescribed behaviors for the survivor of divorce. The community does not feel it necessary to help as it does in bereavement. Indeed, the fact that the spouse still lives often denies the divorced person the opportunity to come to a final acceptance of the break-up since there is always a chance, no matter how small, of recovering the spouse. And, for some rejected spouses, this little chance is exaggerated and becomes the dominant sustaining theme of their life for a long time after the legal divorce. Children and monetary involvement are often excuses for continued contact. Even in cases where marital breakup is hostile and bitter, the plain old loneliness following the break-up often spurs a mate to wish the spouse were home, even if only to fight with and break the loneliness.

Table 15-2 Characterization of the Divorce Experience and Perceptions of "Best" and "Worst" Periods

	Combined Sample	**Female**	**Male**
Characterization of Divorce Experience			
Traumatic, a nightmare	23%	27%	16%
Stressful, but bearable	40%	40%	40%
Unsettling, but easier than expected	20%	19%	24%
Relatively painless	17%	13%	20%
Most Difficult Period			
Before decision to divorce	55%	58%	50%
After decision, but before final decree	22%	20%	25%
Just after the divorce	21%	19%	23%
Now	3%	3%	3%

Adapted from: Stan Albrecht. "Reactions and Adjustments to Divorce: Differences in the Experiences of Males and Females." *Family Relations*, January 1980, p. 61.

The newly divorced often experience a period of bereavement.

Many divorced people may feel a resurgence of hurt, hostility, and rejection when learning of the ex-spouse's new relationships. To hear that one's ex-mate is remarrying is often upsetting and may arouse past hostilities and regrets.

It is probably important that anger be a part of divorce. For it is anger that will finally break the emotional bonds that remain between the ex-spouses, and it is not until these bonds are finally broken that each will be free.

Fortunately, for most divorcing couples, a turning point does come when their energies can finally turn from destruction to construction once again.

Creative Divorce and Rebirth

Divorce is the death of a relationship, but it can also be the rebirth of an individual. Just as death is difficult, so is rebirth. Once the mourning and grief begin to subside, the newly divorced individual faces important choices about life directions. What does one do newly alone? Seek the immediate security of a new marriage? Prepare to live alone the rest of one's life? Make all new friends or keep old friends? Try and maintain ties to the past relationship? Escape into the work world? Seek counseling? Escape through fleeting sexual involvements?

More and more professionals as well as divorced persons themselves are saying "Use the pain and suffering of divorce to learn about yourself. Seek the rebirth of a new, more insightful, more capable person out of the wreckage of failure."

Divorce Counseling and Mediation Divorce counseling is gaining popularity, especially since no-fault divorce proceedings have replaced adversary methods (Coogler et al, 1979). About a fifth of the men and two-fifths of the women divorcing seek outside help with their emotional problems (Hunt, 1969). Usually the first phase is predivorce counseling, which centers around the imminent decision whether to divorce or not. At this point there is still a possibility of saving the marriage. The counselor acts as an objective third party (mediator) and can, hopefully, help the person contemplating divorce come to a good decision. Divorce counseling per se begins when the decision is made and lawyers and/or legal proceedings enter the picture. Such counseling can help the individuals cope with the many conflicting feelings that arise as well as better understand the legalities and alternatives available.

The third phase of divorce counseling occurs after the decree is obtained and is aimed at helping the person get his or her life started again (see Fisher, 1973). In a few states, some divorce counseling is available through the courts. Occasionally the courts require such counseling. Conciliation courts usually attempt to ameliorate the negative effects of marital failure. Their goal at first is trying to save the marriage, but, failing that, to help insure an equitable divorce, "...to protect the rights of children and to promote the public welfare by preserving, promoting, and protecting family life and the institution of matrimony, and to provide means for the reconciliation of spouses and the amicable settlement of domestic and family controversies" (California Code, Section 1730).

Those seeking counseling should not expect to find support for *their* side nor advice which if followed will resolve their problems. They should also not expect to see and feel immediate improvement in themselves and their relations with the ex-spouse. Rather, they will hopefully find clarification and help in assessing strengths and weaknesses so they can generally move toward better understanding and clearer communication. The better the couple's communication and understanding, the less traumatic the divorce will be, for both themselves and their children if there are any.

Children and Divorce Generally, it has been thought that divorce always has negative effects upon the children involved. Many couples remained together only for the sake of the children. Other couples postponed divorce until the children were grown. Yet the effects of divorce upon children are not at all clear. There is no doubt that the immediate effects are unsettling. Long-term effects are probably very mixed. Some children may suffer long-term damage. Others may be much better off after a divorce than they were when the conflicting parents were together. An unhappy marriage is an unhappy home for children, and if divorce promotes parental happiness, then children should also benefit. Although this folk wisdom sounds reasonable, long-term study of divorced families only partially supports it.

Wallerstein and Kelley (1980) did a long-term study of sixty families with children that had gone through divorce. They interviewed them close to the time of divorce, eighteen months later, and again after five years.

Our overall conclusion is that divorce produces not a single pattern in people's lives, but at least three patterns, with many variations. Among both adults and children five years afterward, we found about a quarter to be resilient (those for whom the divorce was successful), half muddling through, coping when and as they could, and a final quarter to be bruised: failing to recover from the divorce or looking back to the predivorce family with intense longing. Some in each group had been that way before and continued unchanged; for the rest, we found roughly equal numbers for whom the divorce seemed connected to improvement and to decline (Wallerstein and Kelley, 1980, p. 67).

What factors appear associated with the 25 percent who adapted well to the divorce? Not surprisingly, children with strong, well integrated personalities who were well adjusted before the divorce were making the best adjustments. Children did significantly better when both parents continued to be a part of their lives on a regular basis. This was true only when the parents themselves were able to work out a satisfactory and non-destructive post-divorce relationship. Aside from these two factors, it was difficult to predict which children would do well and which would not.

Studies (see Wallerstein and Kelley, 1980, for discussion) comparing adults from divorced (divorce occurring when the person was a child) and intact families find that the adults from divorced families more often characterized their childhood as unhappy. They are more likely to suffer from feelings of worthlessness, guilt and despair. Yet such findings might occur because of the kind of relationship their parents had before divorce rather than because of the divorce itself.

What is really clear at this time is that we simply cannot fully understand the effects of divorce on children. There will be immediate effects, usually negative, these will vary from child to child, and for some children, there will be lasting effects that will influence them as adults (Magrab, 1978). It is also clear that the divorced family is usually less adaptive economically, socially, and psychologically to the raising of children than the two-parent family. The one-parent family lacks the support and buffering effect of another adult (Wallerstein and Kelley, 1980, p. 76).

Fortunately most divorced people remarry thereby reconstituting the two-parent family. Of course, in this case children must establish a new successful relationship with the stepparent, which is a new problem unto itself (p. 486).

Despite the general acceptance of divorce in our society, it remains for most people an unpleasant and traumatic experience and for most children, a trying and difficult problem with which to cope.

Creative Divorce The phrase "creative divorce" was popularized by Mel Krantzler (1973) in his book of that name and has come to stand for a movement that declares:

Divorce is not an end, it is a new beginning.
Divorce does not mean the decay and destruction of marriage and

the family in America, rather it means renewed effort to improve marriage and the family.

Divorce is the beginning of a new enriching and enlivening voyage of self-discovery that makes me a happier and stronger person than I was before.

Through divorce, a painful and emotional crisis, I learned that what I went through was what all divorced people go through — first a recognition that a relationship has died, then a period of mourning, and finally a slow, painful emotional readjustment to the facts of single life. I experienced the pitfalls along the way — the wallowing in self-pity, the refusal to let go of the old relationship, the repetition of old ways in relating to new people, the confusion of past emotions with present reality — and I emerged the better for it (Krantzler, 1973, p. 30).

Such attitudes are a far cry from the feelings most initially experience at the break-up of their marriage. Yet it makes a great deal of sense to use divorce as a learning situation rather than seeing it only as a total failure from which nothing good can be derived.

Many groups have sprung up to help the newly divorced move in a positive direction. "We Care" is an organization of volunteers who do just what their name implies — care and help those in mourning, whether it be over the death of a loved one or the death of a relationship. Parents without Partners (PWP) is a nationwide organization of single parents. The primary goal is that of educating single parents in child rearing. The overall purpose is to help alleviate some of the isolation that makes it difficult for single parents to provide for themselves and their children a reasonable equivalent of normal family life.

Many adult education facilities, churches, and other service-oriented organizations offer workshops and group experiences for the newly divorced.

Problems of the Newly Divorced   The major dangers facing the newly divorced are prolonged retreat from social contact, jumping quickly into a new marriage, leading a life based on hope that the spouse will return, or leading a life based on hostility and getting back at the ex-mate. Certainly the first step after any failure may be one of momentary retreat, a turn inward, a time of contemplation, of avoidance of all situations reminding one of the hurt and disappointment, guilt and shame of failure. Unfortunately though, some divorced people make such a reaction their life style. In essence, such people die psychologically and end their lives in every way but physically.

A larger group of divorced persons seek a new relationship as quickly as possible. Discounting those who had a truly meaningful relationship before their divorce and are now fulfilling it as soon as possible after divorce, there are many who can't stand the thought of failure and/or to be alone and thus rush into the first available relationship. These people usually have not had time to reassess themselves or their motives. The idea of facing themselves and the challenges of becoming an independent person are simply too frightening. These are often people who have never really been alone. They married early

Just how long it takes to make the decision to get on with your life I cannot say, but inevitably it must come. Each person must do it in his or her own way, at his or her own speed, and stumble over the obstacles as best he or she can. It's tough, but you must keep moving forward.

The following are tools that can be used effectively. Remember, determination is the key.

1. Be good to yourself; protect the inner child. Turn on your childlike personality, do things to make your inner self feel good.

2. Stay away from guilt trips — he said this, she said that, my fault, his fault, and so on — stay out of that deadly trap. The relationship is over, the marriage didn't jell, remember the good times, and let go.

3. Avoid bitterness and hostility at all costs, it will only hurt you.

4. Take a realistic appraisal of yourself, focus on your good points; stay out of self-recrimination, keep reminding yourself that you are lovable, worthwhile, unique, special — there has never been nor shall there ever be one exactly like you.

5. Stay in the now. Plan time and activities for your internal child. The childlike portion of you is dependent on approval from yourself and others, so give it permission to cry, to express the hurt, and then to laugh and be free.

6. Reach out to others, don't close yourself off — turn on, be excited, get into other people and find something good about them.

7. Make a list of short-range and long-range goals, and do something to activate them.

8. Recognize fear as a useful tool. Fear gives you caution, and with caution there is discrimination, and with discrimination there are useful decisions.

9. Trust your intuitional hunches, be spontaneous; have faith and trust in yourself. Try not to rule out the possibility that all that has happened has a purpose, that in every negative there is a positive to be learned.

Divorce is not a failure, failure only happens when you give up. It's a new lifetime, a new beginning, a new ball game — get with it, dig it, and finally enjoy it (Jursnich, 1974).

and, in a sense, they may never have grown up psychologically. Even though their first marriage may have been unsatisfying, marriage is far preferable to assuming responsibility for oneself. By rushing into a new marriage, they will very likely make the same mistakes over again.

We have already looked at some of the problems of attempting to hold on to a past relationship. Living by false hope serves only to lock the person's life into a kind of prolonged alternation of hope and disappointment.

However, a life based on continuing anger and harassment of an ex-spouse may be the most destructive reaction of all since the ex-spouse is harmed as well as the mate seeking revenge. The horror stories connected with this reaction to divorce are enough to keep people from every marrying. The stories usually involve one of the spouses who spends their time after divorce taking the divorced spouse back to court time and again in an effort to (consciously or unconsciously) punish them. Fortunately, few divorced persons react for long in this fashion.

WHAT DO YOU THINK?

What do you think is the single most important thing that a newly divorced person can do to start on the road to recovery? Why?

What are some things the newly divorced person should avoid doing if he or she wants to speed recovery?

If you were advising a newly divorced person, what would you tell him or her? Why?

The reasons for America's high divorce rate are many and varied. There are the personal reasons that a divorcing couple gives such as communication breakdown, sexual failures, or overuse of alcohol. But more important are the overriding influences that affect all marriages. The general social problems that have their roots deeply in American society and philosophy affect all relationships.

First, as has been mentioned numerous times, Americans ask a great deal of modern marriage, perhaps too much. High expectations often lead to disappointment and failure. Ask nothing, receive nothing, and nothing is disappointing. Ask a great deal, receive a little, and unhappiness often follows. Divorce in this context may not mean the failure of the institution of marriage. Rather, it may mean an attempt to improve one's marriage, to improve the institution.

Tied closely to Americans' high expectations of marriage is the relative freedom allowed individuals in making marital choices. The fourth basic assumption of this book, that a free and creative society will offer many structural forms of the family by which family functions may be fulfilled, acts actually as a second cause for America's high divorce rate. Many choices breed a certain amount of dissatisfaction. Is the grass greener on the other side of the fence? Might one of the alternatives presented in Chapter 14 be better than what I have? Being surrounded by married friends who see marriage as you do and who are committed to it adds strength and durability to one's own marriage. But being surrounded by those who don't support your concept of marriage, who suggest and/or live alternate forms, who deride and chide the kind of marriage you have, is disruptive of your own marital patterns. Although such disruptions might lead to a better present marriage, they are just as apt to lead to further marital complications.

Changing sex roles are also a part of American interest in the general concept of change and its benefits. Pressure is placed on the institution of marriage by all those who question traditional sex roles. For example, a woman who decides that the role of mother is not really for her, who seeks a career and leaves the caring of her children to her husband, is bound to face some disapproval from her family and friends. Certainly the same holds true for the husband who decides at forty to quit his job as an accountant, cease supporting his family, and begin to write adventure stories. Although the end result of sex role changes may be "people liberation," transitory results will continue to be marital disruption for some. Because the changing roles of women and men are listed as a major cause of divorce does not mean that such change will not, in the long run, be good for the family. Certainly many of those advocating change believe the family will benefit.

A fourth reason for the high divorce rate is America's heterogeneity. There are so many kinds of people, so many beliefs, attitudes, and value systems, that family and marriage mean many and differing things to various Americans. Even though people tend to marry people with similar backgrounds, there will still be differences in belief and attitude. For example, consider the situation of a female college graduate interested in pursuing both a family life and a career; she marries an engineer from a very traditional family background who believes the wife's place is in the home. Conflict seems inevitable.

Stemming also from America's heterogeneity is the higher incidence of mixed marriages. People of differing marital and family values and philosophies are more apt to marry·in America simply because they are here and freedom of marital choice is encouraged. When such persons marry, building a successful and enduring marriage is more difficult because of their many differences.

In listing the general reasons for marital failure, I would be remiss if I failed to include social upheaval, economic problems, and the general state of health of the society. Certainly the stresses and strains brought on by the Vietnam war took their toll of marriage. Spouses were separated, children disagreed with their parents about the war, and there were periods of riot and social disorganization, all of which strained the family institution.

Continuing economic worries triggered by the unusual inflation-recession economy of the past few years have brought failure to many American marriages. Living in a minority group, living in poverty (Mott & Moore, 1979), and being in a society during turmoil are all factors accounting for marital instability.

Marital failure is highest among the poor, becoming progressively lower as status rises. Some data show divorce rates five times higher for low-status husbands as compared to high-status husbands, though the gap lessened during the 1960s and 1970s (Burchinal and Chancellor, 1962; Glick, 1975).

Acceptance of divorce by Americans is certainly an important factor in the rising divorce rates. The stigma of divorce has largely vanished over the past thirty years. In fact, a forty-year-old divorceé is probably less stigmatized than a forty-year-old woman who has never been married. General social acceptance is also noticeable in the trend toward more lenient divorce laws.

Last but not least and certainly emphasized throughout this book are the personal inadequacies, failures, and problems that contribute to each individual divorce. Regardless of the magnitude of social problems and pressures that disrupt marriage, the ultimate decision to end a relationship is made by one or both spouses.

Paul Glick (1975), after a thorough review of American marriage and divorce statistics, lists a number of steps that might reduce divorce. He suggests first that more effective marriage and family training be given at home and in the schools. Certainly such courses in the schools are increasingly popular, and hopefully such an interest on the part of young persons will lead to a sounder choice of partner and improved marriage.

Reducing Divorce Rates

He also advocates more scientific methods of mate selection than the current haphazard system based only on emotion. Periodic marital checkups through visits to highly trained marriage counselors should be encouraged. As pointed out in Chapter 6, by the time most couples in difficulty seek help, their marriage is beyond help. Facing problems before they are insoluble, building problem-solving techniques into marriage, heading off divorce with help, if necessary, are needed elements in American marriage. Changing marriage laws to encourage couples to take their entry into marriage much more seriously would also help to reduce the necessity of divorce.

California took a step in the direction of stricter marriage laws in Assembly Bill 402 (Civil Code Section 4101), which became effective November 23, 1970. This law, the first of its kind, empowers the courts to require premarital counseling of any couple applying for a marriage license if either party is under eighteen years of age and if the court deems such counseling necessary. In Los Angeles County, the courts acted to make such counseling mandatory (Elkin, 1977, p. 429).

Child care centers would help give couples with young children more time for one another and more time to work positively on their marriage. Many couples simply do not have time for their marriage in the early childrearing — work-oriented years. Later, when they have time because the children are finally capable of independence and economic stability has been achieved, there is often not enough left of the marriage to be salvageable, much less improved.

Certainly we need to give at least as much time to the good aspects of marriage as we do to the negative aspects. Giving publicity to ways in which marriage can be improved, to successfully married couples, and concentrating on relationship improvement will help those who desire to make a go of their marriage more than exaggerating all of the problems inherent in marriage.

Summary   A means of dissolving marriage has existed in almost every society. Divorce is America's mode of ending unsatisfactory marriages. The divorce rate has increased drastically during this century, probably reflecting Americans' high expectations for marriage and tolerance of change. But even during these years, the divorce laws in the books and the divorce laws in practice have been quite different from each other. In general, fairly strict laws are in the books, while the law in practice is quite permissive, and getting more so.

Generally, divorce is arrived at after a long period of gradually deteriorating relations. Indeed, long before legal divorce and perhaps long after it as well, a couple will go through the suffering of an emotional divorce. Divorce is, of course, complicated by the presence of children and/or considerable property.

In the past few years almost all states have instituted some form of no-fault divorce. In these proceedings, neither party has to be proved guilty of breaking some rule leading to grounds (a legal reason) for divorce. The only thing that must be proved is that the marriage has suffered an irremediable breakdown. Property is divided equally. By doing away with fault finding, divorce procedures have been considerably simplified.

Divorce does not necessarily mean the end of a relationship, especially if children are involved. Visitation and financial obligations usually mean that the man and wife must have considerable contact even after divorce. Such contact is usually difficult. Divorce counseling prior to as well as after the divorce can help couples make satisfactory adjustments to the change in their life.

Although divorce to most persons is traumatic, more people are beginning to look to the positive things that can be gained. Getting on with one's life, having a new start, growth, and the learning of new insights into oneself are all possible advantages of divorce, as painful as it may be.

Single Again

My first reaction when I realized my marriage was really over, after more than twenty years, was fear, rage, and despair. Even though we'd never really gotten along well together, he was all I knew. I was engaged at fifteen and couldn't wait to get out of high school to get married. I was a mother at eighteen and spent the next twenty years doing what I'd always wanted most to do — care for a home, a husband, and children.

Then along came a young woman who wasn't tied to a house and children. She made him feel unique and young. I had no car, very little money, almost no experience at getting along in the outside world. I decided it was best to leave the big, comfortable home I'd been so proud of. I couldn't see a way to make the payments on it, and everyone in town knew I had been put aside for a younger model. My ego was shattered, my children's world torn apart. I moved back to my old home town. It was a small place, and my mother and sisters were there. I could find a job I could walk to until I could do better. My family had no money, but I needed their moral support badly.

My seventeen-year-old daughter dropped out of high school and moved into an apart-ment with an older girlfriend. My nineteen-year-old son had an apartment with a friend, and wanted to stay where he was. Neither of them wanted to take sides. My fifteen-year-old tried it with me for a few weeks, but was unhappy without the friends he'd known all his life. I let him move back with his father.

Now I was really heartsick. I felt so terribly old and worn out. I had two little boys who had not run out on me — one was seven and one twelve. I had to move to a tiny four-room house in bad repair, and for a few weeks all I could do was to feel sorry for myself, for the boys…and pray. I looked for work, but I was so limited in what I could do. No car, no training, no experience, no longer young…I put up a good front for my boys and for the rest of my family. I had one sister, who'd been divorced shortly before me, and she was a great morale-booster.

There was a period when I tried to figure out what I'd done wrong. Finally, I decided that whatever mistakes I'd made, I had been loyal to him and had really tried in every way I knew to make him happy. . . . I went to the library and checked out every book I could dealing with overcoming self-doubt and fail-ure. Did you know that every really successful person has only found success after apparent failure? Even Jesus appeared to have failed in his work. Realizing this helped me to pick up the pieces of my life and begin again.

I made friends in the same boat that I was. There were plenty of them in my small home town. Too many men and women had been left behind because someone more interesting had come along. I came to know some of them well, and reached the conclusion that the one who is left is not necessarily the failure. The most common complaint seemed to be that they had been poor bed partners. But I think that's because it's one skill that no one else can comment on. Other people can observe how you dress, whether you're a good cook and keep a clean house, but if someone else does know how you are in that department, they're not likely to admit it. Sex is supposed to be the one most important ingredient in holding a marriage together. I don't agree with that, but that's another story.

After a few months that seemed much longer, I found a job within walking distance and a larger, better house. My boys made some new friends and things began looking up. I decided that we could make a great life for ourselves. I knew I had to learn to make decisions for myself, and if the older children had been with us I would have leaned on them too much. They were doing well where they were and they came to see me often.

So I sat down and talked things over with myself. "You're young, not yet forty, intelligent, attractive. You always knew that someday the kids would no longer need you. Now you can do what you planned on doing when they were older." As I recovered from the blow to my ego, I was actually glad to be rid of a husband who had never seemed satisfied with me. I can laugh again. I can leave the dirty dishes in the sink; it's fun to flirt again. There's always someone around to make me feel that I'm interesting and fun.

With five children to take care of, it wasn't anything new to have to face problems and

to make decisions. But in the past, if things went wrong, I had had someone else to share the blame. I don't now. I laughed when I first realized that I, and only I, was responsible for my own mistakes. I faced the fact that to be happy I had to avoid blaming my ex-husband or anyone else for my unhappiness.

I studied and thought about what I really wanted out of life. This took some doing, because all my life I'd tried to be what I thought someone else wanted me to be. It's not easy to look at yourself objectively. I'm still learning how. I've found that even though some ugly things come to the surface of my mind, letting them surface is the only way to deal with them. It's a tremendous feeling to get rid of negative feelings that you've been burying for years. Each time I got rid of one, I'd feel lighter, freer. My ex-husband had had such different ideas from mine that I couldn't accept them, or even understand how he could believe as he did. I wanted to spend our free time with a quiet group at home most of the time. He liked partying. Our ideas about raising the kids were different and so many other things that I wonder how we lived together for twenty years — and why we did. Even the children are all better satisfied now that we're apart.

Yesterday is dead and gone. I can't do anything to change it, but I can do something about today and tomorrow. It wasn't easy, but the hardest thing was deciding that I could do it. It's hard to face a completely different life style that you didn't choose, and then try to make it the greatest thing that ever happened. It can be done. . . .

I tried hobbies I'd thought about but never really tried. I looked for ego-boosters. I played a game with friends called "Make me feel good about myself." I listened to other people and their problems. I tried to encourage them to look up, not give up. Days went by, then weeks. I got used to taking care of myself and my two sons, and decided I liked it. I found there are a lot of fun things to do, and a lot of great people to know. . . .

I've learned a lot of things about myself

that I like knowing. I'm good at math. Isn't that great? I've learned how to look for a job. I've learned how to say no to a date I don't want, and how to encourage a date I do. All those years while I was cooking, cleaning, sewing, doing PTA and Cub Scout work my mind wasn't dead — just resting. It took only a short time for it to wake up and get moving. I'm not looking for a replacement for my ex-husband. I'm not the same person I was even two years ago. I'm more self-confident, more comfortable around people, a bit slimmer, and I walk taller now. I like men, in fact, I love them. But if and when I do remarry, it'll be a whole new ballgame. He won't have to live with the ghost of an unhappy marriage....

Feel sorry for myself? Not any more. A couple of months ago, I did something I wouldn't have dreamed of doing two years ago.... I was in a dead-end job with no chance for advancement. There was little social life in the small town and few eligible men. I went to Brazoria County, looked around, asked some questions and went back home to turn in my resignation. I put my furniture up for sale and we moved. I work at the newspaper now — a job I've always dreamed of. The pay is better, the hours are better, there's a great PWP (Parents Without Partners) group and lots of other opportunities to meet people and lead an even fuller life.

There's an exciting new life to be lived when you learn to trust yourself, trust God, trust life, trust your kids, and handle your problems one at a time. It's great.

TINCY LACON

Chapter 16 ⁓

Contents

Remarriage:
A Growing Way
of American Life

"It seems to me that John and Helen were just divorced and here's an invitation to Helen's wedding."

"Not only that, but I met John and his new girlfriend at lunch yesterday and from the way they were acting, I'll bet we'll soon get an invitation to their wedding."

"It's hard to understand. They were so eager to escape their marriage and now it seems they can hardly wait to get back into another marriage."

Divorced people as a group are not against marriage. For every age group, remarriage rates are higher than first marriage rates, remarriage rates for men are higher than for women, and remarriage rates for the divorced are higher than for those widowed.

In any given year, for every 1000 single women between the ages of twenty-five and twenty-nine, 140 will marry. For every 1000 divorced women in that age range, 319 will remarry (Duberman, 1974, p. 199).

Actually there are statistically few single divorced people in America's population. Not only do divorced persons remarry in large numbers but they tend to remarry quickly. Approximately 50 percent of the people who get divorced remarry within three years (Glick & Norton, 1977, p. 8). Also, about one in every four marriages (28 percent) is a remarriage for at least one of the mates (U.S. National Center for Health Statistics, 1978). Close to one-half of all remarriages after divorce occur within three years, and two-thirds within five years (U.S. Bureau of the Census, 1977).

From these statistics it is safe to conclude that remarriage is certainly an important aspect of marriage in the United States. Considering the rise in divorce rates, the lengthening life span, and the younger ages at which Americans divorce (about 30 percent of divorcing husbands and 60 percent of the wives are in their twenties at the time of divorce), it would appear that the incidence of remarriage will remain high in the future. What Americans experience is not monogamy, but "serial monogamy," that is, several spouses over a lifetime but only one at a time. "Reconstituted family" is another useful term to describe this trend in marriage (see Duberman, 1974, p. 17, 1975).

Historically, remarriage is not new or novel. But the early death of one spouse has been the reason for remarriage in the past. Today it is divorce. Although the widowed do continue to remarry, they stay single longer than the divorced.

The statistics on divorce and subsequent remarriage indicate that the reconstituted family will continue to increase as a percentage of all American families. Yet to date, this type of family has been little studied and few marriage and family texts devote much space to the subject (Furstenberg, 1979). We will try to correct this deficiency.

Returning to the Single Life

Many people married for some time, burdened with the responsibilities of a growing family and missing the flush of romance that brought them together with their mate, feel pangs of envy when their friends divorce and reenter the single world. Remembering their dating and courting days, the nostalgic memories are of the excitement of the new date and the boundless energies that one expended as a young person pursuing and being pursued. Unfortunately, except for a lucky few, such dreams on the part of the married person are just that, dreams.

Both for men and women, and especially for those married and faithful for some years, the return to the single world is frightening. "Can I again be successful as a single person?" is a question that cannot at first be answered. Most people have experienced a severe blow to their self-esteem with the divorce and they are afraid to face the potential rejections involved with meeting new people. Indeed, for some, the idea may be so threatening that they don't return to the single life, but remain hidden in the safety of their own aloneness. But

Table 16-1 Number and Rate of First Marriages, Divorces, and Remarriages for Women, U.S., Three-Year Averages

Period	First Marriages		Divorces		Remarriages	
	Thousands	Rate[1]	Thousands	Rate[2]	Thousands	Rate[3]
1921 – 23	990	99	158	10	186	98
1924 – 26	992	95	177	11	200	99
1927 – 29	1025	94	201	12	181	84
1930 – 32	919	81	183	10	138	61
1933 – 35	1081	92	196	11	162	69
1936 – 38	1183	98	243	13	201	83
1939 – 41	1312	106	269	14	254	103
1942 – 44	1247	108	360	17	354	139
1945 – 47	1540	143	526	24	425	163
1948 – 50	1326	134	397	17	360	135
1951 – 53	1190	122	388	16	370	136
1954 – 56	1182	120	379	15	353	129
1957 – 59	1128	112	381	15	359	129
1960 – 62	1177	116	407	16	372	133
1963 – 65	1323	110	452	17	404	139
1966 – 68	1488	110	535	20	463	150
1969 – 71	1604	107	702	26	569	168
1975		99		34		150
1977		84		36		145

Source: P. Glick and A. Norton, "Perspectives on Recent Upturn in Divorce and Remarriage." *Demography 10*: August 1973, p. 306. 1975 and 1977 figures from P. Glick and A. Norton, "Marrying, Divorcing, and Living Together in the U.S. Today," *Population Bulletin*. October 1977, **32**, No. 5, p. 5.
[1]First marriages per 1000 women 14 – 44 years old.
[2]Divorce rates per 1000 married women.
[3]Remarriages per 1000 widowed and divorced women 14 – 54 years old.

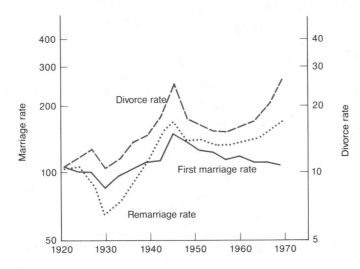

Figure 16-1
First marriage rates per 1000 single women, divorce rates per 1000 married women, and remarriage rates per 1000 widowed or divorced women in the United States, 1921-1971 (a three-year average).

then, remaining alone the rest of their life appears to be even more threatening, and so most divorced persons do eventually venture out into the single world.

Just when they are ready to return to the single life varies greatly. For most, it seems that it takes about one year after divorce to get themselves emotionally back together again (Weiss, 1975). Those who had an ongoing extramarital relationship are in a different position, however. They usually remarry as soon as legally possible.

Learning to date and relate to the opposite sex as a single person is especially difficult for anyone who has been married for a long time because his or her self-image has for so long been that of a married person, part of a couple. However, once the divorced (or widowed) persons reenter the social world, they are often surprised at the number who share their newly single status. Except for the very young divorced, most actually reenter a world of single but formerly married people rather than one of the never married. This helps to ease the transition since those they meet have also experienced marital collapse. There is a certain empathy, which helps newly divorced people feel more acceptable. They often quickly feel much better by simply realizing they aren't alone. In fact, the discovery that they can meet and relate to people of the opposite sex in their new single role is often exciting and certainly heartening. "Maybe I'm not such a failure after all" is often their reaction.

The newly divorced do have the problem of meeting new people. Sometimes friends, relatives, and business associates supply new contacts. Organizations such as Parents without Partners and We Care become meeting places. Actually, their lofty educational and helping goals are often secondary to their social functions. However, the lofty goals make it easier for people to enter the groups without appearing to be simply "people hunting."

There are also many singles clubs that make introductions to others their major purpose. Yet such clubs often frighten and intimidate those just recuperating from marital failure. Too often, the official singles fetes have a "meat market" atmosphere where rejects gather to frantically seek out a new partner.

Although long used in Europe, the newspaper advertisement is just beginning to catch on in the United States. Discounting the ads for sexual partners in underground newspapers, there is a growing use of legitimate classified advertising to seek desirable companions and would-be mates, especially by divorced persons. Inserting an ad like those below in a moderately large metropolitan newspaper will bring forty to fifty replies to females and a dozen to males.

ATTRACTIVE refined widow seeks real gentleman, 60s, home loving, likes music, trips, books, gardening, financially secure & who wants to enjoy lasting companionship.

EXPERIENCED sailboat skipper, fifties, single, yacht club member, wants to meet compatible outdoor gal who would like to go sailing with me.

MALE 39, desires pleasant, attractive easy-going female. Enjoys good home life, occasional outdoor activities, flying, fishing, ghost towning, photo & phone.

RETIRED lady loves nature, fine music, sincere, kind, honest, sense of humor, wants same as bus travel companion or share your trans. No smoking.

MAN seeking intelligent, independent, intuitive female companion (21–35) for social events. Send photo.

Technology has found a place in the formerly marrieds' new single life in the form of computer dating. For a small fee, information is fed into a large bank of personal information on many single clients and a match is made from stated interests, hobbies, habits, education, age, and so on. The pair then meet. Some agencies estimate that about 25 percent of their clients eventually marry someone they met through the computer's selection. Other agencies make a videotape interview with each client. Questions are asked about background, interests, feelings about sexual relations, and the qualities they are looking for in the people they date. The client then has the opportunity to look at videotapes of people who share interests and/or meet the qualifications. An obvious advantage here is that the videotape gives a feeling of the person and also, of course, the client knows what his or her date looks like before they meet.

Of course, there are many other ways to meet new people. The major factor in meeting new people is the active participation of the newly divorced in the single's world. Unless you are out in society,

meeting new people is difficult. Probably the newly divorced in the American small town setting stand the poorest chance of meeting someone new.

Regardless of how it is done, though, remarriage rates indicate that meeting new prospective mates is accomplished by most people who divorce. And the new mate tends to be in the same situation; that is, divorced people marry divorced people. Weiss (1975) also points out that dates often come from the person's present groups of acquaintances.

High remarriage rates among divorced people indicate, as noted earlier, that the divorced are still interested in marriage and the role of "being married." The fact is that most activities in the American culture, for better or worse, revolve around the married pair, the couple. High remarriage rates seem to suggest that it is important to have someone with whom to share, feel intimacy, feel closeness, and to feel a part of something larger than oneself.

To love and be loved are important to most Americans. As unhappy as a marriage may have been, for most there was a time when love and closeness were experienced. Indeed, perhaps loss of this intimacy during the marriage was a major factor in the decision to leave the marriage. Certainly, finding intimacy is a factor in most remarriages just as it was in the first marriage.

The route to marriage for young unmarried Americans is fairly clear (see Chapters 3 and 4). You date, you fall in love, you become engaged, you marry. But in contemplating a second marriage, the simplicity of ignorance has been replaced by the knowledge and, for the divorced, the anxiety, of past experience. Some formerly married people may rush quickly into a new marriage but for many it is a cautious, uneasy road to remarriage. The divorced usually have many

**Remarriage —
Will I Make the
Same Mistake Again?**

negative emotions attached to marriage because of their past marital problems. Often they have prior commitments, children, and perhaps economic responsibilities for the prior spouse, which must be maintained along with the new marriage.

The partners in a remarriage must deal with all of the problems any newly married pair face. But, in addition, they must deal with attitudes and sensitivities within themselves that were fostered by their first marriage. They start their remarriage with many prejudices for and against the marital relationship. They have to divest themselves of these if they are to face their new partner freely and build a new relationship that is appropriate to them. In a remarriage, the mate is new and must be responded to as the individual she or he is, not in light of what the past spouse was. An additional task in every remarriage, then, is the effort each partner must make to free themselves from inappropriate attitudes and behaviors stemming from the first marriage. In essence, second marriages are built on top of first marriages (Furstenberg, 1979, p. 16).

Bob and Carol, Ted and Alice:
Are You Still Married to Your Ex-mate?

Bob had been married for twelve years to Alice, had two children by the marriage, and was established economically when his marriage ended in divorce. Two years later he married Carol, eight years his junior, who had one child by her previous husband, Ted.

Bob and Carol both approached their marriage carefully, giving much thought to their relationship. Both agreed that their new marriage was a big improvement over their past marriages. They find that their biggest problem is making sure they react to one another as individuals rather than on the basis of their past relationships. This is not always easy.

Bob's past wife, Alice, is emotionally volatile and this both attracted and repulsed him. He liked it when Alice showed happiness and enthusiasm but hated her temper fits and general unhappiness.

Carol is placid and even-tempered. In fact it was, in part, these personality characteristics that drew him to her. However, whenever they do things together, he keeps asking her if she is having fun, is she enjoying it? He asks her so often that Carol is bugged by what she considers to be his harassment of her. One day she blew up at him over this. He reacted strongly to her negative emotional display. Once everything was calm again, they both discovered that the problem grew out of his past marriage. Bob simply expected Carol to show her enjoyment in the same way Alice had. He was not relating to Carol as a new and unique individual but rather was reacting in light of his past experiences with Alice. Of course, when Carol blew up at him, his reaction was much larger than necessary. Her emotional blast activated all of his past dislike of Alice's temper fits.

Since most divorced persons marry other divorced persons, the story above clearly shows that another couple is involved in such remarriages, namely, the ex-spouses. This phantom couple often dictates to the newly remarried pair, if not directly through the courts and divorce settlements, then indirectly via years of previous interaction. For example, both Bob and Carol are reacting to one another but in addition they are reacting in light of their interactions with their past spouses.

A remarriage between divorced persons is more difficult than a first marriage for a number of reasons besides the influence, often negative, of past spouses.

First, each mate has problems of lowered self-esteem with which to cope. Second, the divorced are less apt to tolerate a poor second marriage. They have been through divorce and know that they have survived. Life after divorce is not a complete unknown any longer and is therefore less threatening than before. Divorced persons may end a problematic remarriage more quickly than they did the first time.

Third, the past relationship described earlier is never really over. Even if the Bob and Carol, Ted and Alice kind of dynamics are successfully overcome, the past marriage can still directly affect the new marriage. For example, payments to an ex-spouse may be resented by the new spouse of the remarried person, especially if it seems the current marriage is being shortchanged monetarily. Children keep many ex-spouses interacting (also see page 486).

Last, the society around the remarrying person tends to expect another failure. "He (she) couldn't make it the first time, so he'll (she'll) probably fail this time, too." "After all, most divorced persons don't learn, they usually remarry the same kind of person as their earlier spouse." "Once a failure always a failure." These are just some of the folk "wisdoms" about the divorced. This lack of support can create a climate of distrust in the minds of the remarried couple themselves. Community support is almost always present for a first marriage. Indeed, the whole society usually applauds the young couple who announce their plans to marry. "This is the right thing to do," everyone seems to tell them.

Despite such problems, many remarriages do last. Only a small percentage of Americans divorce more than once. What are the statistics on success and failure of second marriages? Unfortunately, the statistics do not present a clear picture. Some studies comparing the divorce rates of first marriages with those of second marriages do report that a remarriage is more likely to break up than a first marriage (see, for example, Monahan, 1952, 1958; Becker, Landes & Michael, 1976; Cherlin, 1977, 1978; Bumpess & Sweet, 1972). However, these studies do not take into account the small group of divorce-prone people who marry and divorce often. Other studies find that remarriages are no more likely to end in divorce or separation than are first marriages (see, for example, Riley & Spreitzer, 1974, p. 67).

Perhaps more important than simple divorce-rate comparisons are the subjective evaluations made by those remarrying. One study reports that three-quarters of the remarrieds surveyed feel their new marriage to be either happy or very happy (Locke, 1951). Another larger study (Bernard, 1956) asked outsiders to evaluate some 2000 remarriages. Seven-eighths of them were rated from satisfactory to extremely satisfactory. More recently, a comparison of the reported marital happiness of divorced and never-divorced white respondents to three national surveys revealed that there is little difference between the two groups. The comparison concluded that remarriages of divorced persons that do not end quickly in divorce are probably, as a whole, almost as successful as intact first marriages (Glenn & Weaver, 1977). Albrecht (1979) also found that remarriages were happy marriages. However, none of the variables that had often been noted in the past as rather good predictors of marital satisfaction among first married couples (presence of children, age at marriage, social class, and similarity of religion) seemed to be strongly related to remarriage satisfaction. Remarriages seem to be judged by different criteria than first marriages, perhaps because they indeed are based on different factors. (Perhaps the romantic illusion is now gone for those remarrying.) Glenn and Weaver (1977) conclude that divorce and remarriage seem to have been effective mechanisms for replacing poor marriages with good ones and for keeping the level of marital happiness fairly high.

So, even though there are mixed statistics on the success of remarriages, it is clear that a great many are successful despite the extra problems facing those remarrying. It just may be that as divorce becomes more prevalent and acceptable, the problems facing those wishing to remarry may diminish. Perhaps social support for remarriage will be greater in the future as more and more people marry more than once during their lifetime.

His, Hers, and Ours   For many years, children in the home precluded the parents divorcing. Everyone "knew" the dire consequences to children if divorce occurred. Many couples stayed together for years after their marriage had failed in order to spare the children the trauma of divorce. In fact, the divorce of their parents as soon as the last child leaves home often comes as a surprise to children who have always thought of their parents as happily married.

But staying together for the children's sake is no longer as prevalent as it once was. Some people are reasoning that intact, strained, and conflict-ridden families are certainly as harmful to children as are divorcing families. "Those persons in discordant marriages who divorce and remarry are often taking positive steps to improve their home situation, and hence may provide a more healthy environment for children than was possible for the original intact family" (Wilson et al, 1975, p. 526). Regardless of one's philosophy on the question of divorce involving children, the number of such divorces is going up dramatically. Since 1922, the number of divorces involving children has increased six times. Just since 1950, the number has doubled. About one million children were involved in divorce proceedings in 1976 (Glick, 1979). It is estimated that about 7 million children live with a stepparent. The proportion of children living with their mother only has doubled since 1960, from 8 percent to 16 percent. Only about 67 percent of all children under 18 live with both natural parents who have only been married once (Glick & Norton, 1977, pp. 27–28).

Many people believe that the divorced person who has custody of the children stands much less chance of remarriage. Actually, if age is held constant, having children does not seem to significantly influence one's chances of remarriage (see Bell, 1975, p. 571). In fact, remarriages may well involve at least three different sets of children. Both spouses may bring their own children into the new marriage and, in addition, they may decide to have children together, hence his, hers, and ours is often a correct description of the children in a remarriage home.

Literature is replete with many examples of the poor treatment accorded stepchildren. The ogre stepparent is a popular stereotype in fairy tales and other children's stories. Yet there is little evidence to support this stereotype in reality. The research on stepchildren is somewhat mixed. Certainly the transition to a new parent is not always easy. In general, the very young child or the grown-up child seems to adapt the easiest (see, for instance, Bowerman & Irish, 1962). Generally, children remain with their biological mother and the stepparent is a new father. Since ties are usually closest to the mother, this is probably an advantage for most children. A frequent impression is that more children are now being placed in the custody of their father. As a matter of fact, more than three times as many children lived with a divorced father in 1978 than in 1960, but the same rate of increase has occurred for children living with a divorced mother. Consequently, a fairly constant 10 percent of all children living with a divorced parent live with their father (Glick, 1979, p. 3).

Several studies report that divorce and remarriage seem to have few detrimental effects on children (for example, Burchinal, 1964; Wilson et al, 1975). One study (Cox, 1960) comparing college students on the Dean's honor role and on probation, controlling for intelligence, found a higher proportion of those on the honor role to be from divorced families.

However, counselors and therapists report that stepchildren and stepparents do have a great deal of trouble in their relationships. Perhaps the reason that the data on stepchildren are mixed is because each situation is unique and one cannot really generalize about the effects of divorce or a stepparent on children. It may well be that if a child is well adjusted and of healthy personality, break-up of her or his family will be coped with successfully and lead to a more mature, independent child. But, if the child is unstable, then divorce will probably cause even greater maladjustment.

To learn what effect divorce and remarriage have on a child, we would need to know the answers to the following questions: What were the preconditions to the divorce (much fighting; calm, quick decision; long, slow decision; emotional; rational; and so on)? How well adjusted was the child? What age was the child? With which parent did the child go? Did the child want to go with that parent? What kind of person is the stepparent? How long was the child given to adjust to the stepparent? How many siblings went with the child into the remarriage? Were other children present from the stepparent? What sort of family atmosphere was created? Did the natural parent support or disrupt the child's adjustment? With so many questions to answer, it is not so surprising that the research findings are mixed. The only valid conclusion is that some children suffer more than others from divorce and remarriage.

But, of course, the divorcing parents want and need to know how to reduce the negative consequences of divorce and remarriage on their children. Probably the single best thing that the parent can do is to maintain a reasonable relationship with the divorced mate. Fighting over children or using them against an ex-spouse will lead to negative consequences for the child.

Stepparents face additional problems beyond those faced by natural parents (Le Masters, 1974, p. 155). To begin with, they must follow a preceding parent. If the child and the natural parent had a positive relationship, the child is apt to feel resentful and hostile to the stepparent. The child may also feel disloyal to the departed parent if a good relationship is established with the stepparent. Often a child feels rejected and unloved by the parent who leaves the household. In this case the child may cling more tightly to the remaining parent as a source of security and continuity. Thus the remaining parent's subsequent marriage can be very threatening to the child. "This stepparent is going to take my last parent away from me." The stepparent may be met with anger and hostility by the child. When the child's relationship with the departed parent was not good, hostility remaining from this prior relationship can be displaced onto the stepparent.

Because of the constant comparison made by children between their real parents and stepparents, many stepparents make the mistake of trying too hard, especially at first. Usually it is better for the stepparent to move slowly, since it takes time for the child to adjust to the new situation and to reevaluate the past parental relationship. It is also important to the child to figure out just what the remaining parent's feelings are toward the new mate. Making this adjustment is even more difficult when the stepparent tries to replace the natural parent, especially if the child is still seeing his or her real parent. Probably the best course for the stepparent is to take on a supplemental role, meeting the needs of the child not met by the previous parent (see, for example, Simon, 1964, for a description of how to take on a supplemental role). In this way the stepparent eases direct competition with the natural parent.

When a remarried family has children of its own, additional problems may arise with stepchildren. The stepchild may feel even more displaced and alienated. The remaining parent may seem to have been taken away first by the new stepparent and now by *their* new child. On the other hand, at least some evidence refutes the above idea. Seventy-eight percent of remarried families who had children together rated their relationships with stepchildren as excellent, while only 53 percent of those who did not have children together rated their stepchildren relationships as excellent (Duberman, 1973, p. 286). Perhaps having brothers or sisters takes the focus off the stepchild, allowing a more natural adjustment for both parent and child.

The role of parent is often difficult. The role of stepparent can even be more difficult, yet an empathic, caring stepparent can give a great deal to a child. The stepparent can be an additional source of love and support for the child. The stepparent can supply friendship and by making the family a two-parent family again, solve some of the child-rearing problems of the single parent. When a stepparent enters a child's life when the child is young, it is possible and often happens that the child comes to look on the stepparent as his or her real parent, thus alleviating the child's feelings of loss when the natural parent left.

Those Who Choose to Remain Single

As we have found, Americans divorce in great numbers, and they also remarry in great numbers. Indeed, the only real solution to marital failure for most is a new marriage. About 80 percent of divorced persons eventually remarry (Glick & Norton, 1977, p. 8). And, as pointed out earlier, if age is held constant, both the widowed and the divorced are more likely to marry than comparable single persons.

Yet, some 20 percent of those divorcing choose not to remarry. There are many reasons for this. For one thing, persons who were married a long time are considerably older than the never married singles. They may wish to remarry but find their choice of prospective mates is quite limited. This is especially true for the older divorced or widowed woman. There simply are not many marriageable men around in later years. Part of this is due to men's shorter life expectancy. In the later years, after sixty, there are far fewer men than women generally.

A few who choose not to remarry may be unable to give up the lost spouse psychologically. This is especially true of the widowed who sometimes feel disloyal to the deceased spouse. Often the children of the widowed spouse discourage marriage as being disloyal to their deceased parent or they are fearful a new stepparent may take what is rightfully theirs.

But probably most who choose to remain single simply do not want to assume the responsibilities of marriage again. They may have adjusted well to single life, enjoy the freedom to do as they please, find meeting new people stimulating, and so on. Or they may not have adjusted to single life but feel that their life is still better than it was when they were married. They may feel so bitter about their previous marriage that they generalize their bitterness to all marriages and perhaps generally to the opposite sex. Of course, there are also those who are simply afraid to take the risk again.

A few may wish to remarry but set such high demands for the second mate, trying to ensure success, that no one can ever meet their high expectations.

Regardless of the reasons that a person remains single after marital failure, he or she may have some difficulties because the

American society remains marriage oriented. Loneliness, loss of previous friends, job discrimination, loan discrimination, and general disapproval of the divorced single person still remain to some degree. It is partially because of these pressures that most people experiencing marital failure seek remarriage as the ultimate solution to their failure.

Summary   High remarriage rates indicate that the high divorce rates do not necessarily mean that Americans are disenchanted with marriage as an institution. Rather, high divorce rates may mean that Americans have high expectations for marriage and the freedom to end their marriages when their expectations are not fulfilled.

The majority of divorced persons remarry and most of them remarry within a few years of their divorce. A few remarry as soon as possible after their divorce, but the rest are usually cast into single life for at least a short period of time. The adjustment to single life is often difficult, especially for those who have been married a long time. Learning to date and interrelate with the opposite sex as a single person after many years of marriage is especially difficult because the newly single person's self-image has for so long been that of a married person, part of a couple. In addition, the newly single person is insecure and suffers from feelings of failure and guilt. These feelings make it hard to relate to a new person of the opposite sex.

Remarriage is sought by most divorced persons. Yet it is often a difficult choice to make since the idea of marriage evokes many negative attitudes in the divorced person due to the negative experience with marriage. People marrying for a second time carry with them attitudes and expectations based in part on their first marital experience. In many cases they also continue to have to cope with their first family. Visiting children, child support, and alimony payments may add to the adjustment problems in the second marriage.

Chidren from prior marriages often add to the responsibilities of a person's second marriage. Becoming a stepparent to the new spouse's children is no easy task. A second family may have children from several sources. Each spouse may have children from his or her previous marriage and in time they may have children together. Children from previous marriages often mean continued contact between the formerly married couple when the ex-mate visits with or takes the children periodically (see Chapter 13). Many remarriages, especially when children from the previous marriage are present, actually become relationships among four adults. The remarried pair naturally have their own relationship but, in addition, each will have some level of relationship with the divorced spouse.

About 20 percent of those divorcing never remarry. For these, single life becomes permanent. However, as divorce rates rise, the likelihood of remarriage rises since there are more potential partners. At present, about one in four American marriages involves at least one person who was formerly married. Remarriage, then, has definitely become a way of life for a significant number of Americans.

Divorce and Remarriage: A Child's Perspective*

Basically, the child faces a number of changed life experiences following divorce. First and foremost, there is a *change in parent-child relations*. Usually *father will be absent* from the home (90 percent of the cases). Thus his role will *be fulfilled by the mother*, the mother's boyfriend, or a step-parent in the case of remarriage. The real father may drop out of his relationship with the child, maintain a partial intermittent relationship, or in a minority of cases, actually improve his relationship with his children. The latter occurs when a divorced father really tries to stay involved and, at times, has the children completely to himself. At such times he must give the children his full attention since mother is not there to attend to them as she was during the marriage. Research suggests that frequent availability of the father is associated with positive adjustment, especially for boys (Hess & Camara, 1979; Hetherington et al, 1978; Wallerstein, 1978).

Another change for the child is often a *downward shift economically* accompanied

*This material has been adapted in part from: E. Mavis Hetherington. "Divorce: A Child's Perspective." *American Psychologist*, Oct., 1979, 851-865.

by practical problems of living. In most cases, divorced mothers are less well off economically than when they were married. There is often a move to more modest housing. The move may involve the loss of friends, neighborhood, and familiar school.

Mother usually must work. If she had not done so before, the child may experience a double loss (of both parents) since now mother is also gone much of the time. Her working, yet being solely responsible for mothering and home duties, contributes to an overload on her and to a *more chaotic life style* (erratic meals, etc.) for the family. This, of course, contributes to the child's feelings of loss of attention and affection. Being tired, feeling harassed, and generally overextended strains the mother's relationship with her children. Also, having a second parent present can serve as a protective buffer between the other parent and the child. When there is only one parent and the parent-child relationship has problems, there is nowhere else to turn.

Children are usually asked to *grow up faster* in one-parent families. They must be more self-sufficient and assume more responsibilities. This can be positive if the child copes successfully or it can lead to feelings of being overwhelmed, of incompetence, and of resentment on the child's part.

Children must cope with *new adults* vying for the parents' attention and affection if the parents date others or remarry. Oftentimes parents beginning to date again find it difficult to deal openly with the subject of their dating and may simply avoid discussing it, assuming the attitude that "this is one thing the children will just have to understand and accept." Therefore, in many instances, it is never really dealt with. The occurrence of parental dating brings a whole new influence into the child's world. Before, the children were the main focus of the custodial parent's affection, time, and energy. Even with the noncustodial parent's dating, visitation time is now often shared with another adult. The person being dated is often viewed as an intruder usurping the time and affection of the parent.

A child's acceptance of the reality of his or her parents' divorce may be impeded by the conscious or unconscious hope for a reconciliation between the parents. Thus, dating is troublesome because it implies that this will not happen. The feelings of abandonment by the absent parent are often carried a step further by parental dating, which arouses fears that the remaining parent will also abandon them.

A child may, on the other hand, feel genuine affection for the dating partner but wonder whether if by liking the new person, he or she is being loyal to the missing parent. This can cause a child a great deal of conflict and guilt.

It is very difficult to measure the effect of divorce on a child's well-being. Parents tend to minimize the effect so as to avoid their own feelings of guilt. Children themselves certainly aren't able to understand, much less describe, the effects they feel. There is no question that a traumatic life change affects children but the exact effects will be unique to a given child. The circumstances of the parental break-up, the age and temperament of the child, the other support systems in the child's life such as grandparents, the sex of the child, and the practical problems that are created by the break-up will all influence the child's reaction to his parents' separation and divorce. Generally, the better the relationship that the parents can maintain, the easier it is for the children.

Chapter 17 ~

Contents

Actively Seeking
Marital Growth
and Fulfillment

The American scenario of marriage has always included "and they lived happily ever after." This meant that once you found the right person, fell truly in love, and married, all your problems would be over. But, of course, this is a fairy tale. We all really know that married couples will certainly face problems.

Yet the persistence of this fairy tale, even at only the unconscious level, hampers many Americans' efforts to realize the fullest possible potentials in their marriages. To find out if this fairy tale influences you, examine your reaction to the following statement: "All married couples should periodically seek to improve their marriage through direct participation in therapy, counseling, or marriage enrichment programs."

What do you think? Following are some typical reactions:

"It might be a good idea if the couple is unhappy or having problems."

"I know couples who need some help, but Jane and I are already getting along pretty well. It wouldn't help us."

"We already know what our problems are. All we need to do is . . ."

"I'd be embarrassed to seek outside help for my marriage. It would mean I was a personal failure."

"We're so busy now, what with work, the children, and social engagements, we wouldn't have time for any of those things."

"John is a good husband [Mary is a good wife]. I really couldn't ask him [her] to participate in anything like that. He [she] would feel I wasn't happy with him [her] or our marriage."

"I could be happier, but overall our marriage is fine."

It is certainly not my opinion that all married couples need to seek counseling. But it is my opinion that marriage needs to be more than just maintained to be successful.

Although it is superficial and a gross oversimplification, the analogy between marriage and the automobile may clarify this point. An unmaintained car quickly malfunctions and wears out. A well-maintained car gives less trouble and lasts longer than an unmaintained one. However, over and beyond maintenance, a car may be modified to run better (faster, smoother, more economically, and so on) and improved (buying better tires, or changing the carburation, exhaust, compression, gearing, etc.).

Most Americans spend most of their adult lives married. Yet they expend little time and energy improving their marriage. At best, they often just maintain it. If the marriage becomes too bad, they leave it to seek a new marriage that will be better. The new marriage (car) may be better for a while but without maintenance and improvement, it, too, will soon malfunction.

Some Americans, as we saw in Chapter 14, expend a fair amount of energy seeking a new mode of marriage. Perhaps communes are the answer. Maybe just living together and avoiding legal marriage is the answer. Yet it seems that many people spend little time or energy trying to make the marriage they have work better.

After all, most of us married the people we did because we loved them, wanted to be with them, wanted to do things for them. We married out of our own decision in most cases. We started out supposedly with the best of all things going for us, "love." Where did it go? Why wasn't it able to conquer all of our problems? Might it be that the fairy tale "and they lived happily ever after," kept us from deliberately setting about to build a better marriage? Did we think that love would automatically take care of everything?

Actually, a number of factors combine to keep most Americans from taking a more active part in improving their marriages. The fairy tale we have been discussing has been called the "myth of naturalism" (see Vincent, 1973). This is the feeling that marriage is "natural," that it will take care of itself if we select the right partner. That is, many people feel that outside forces may support or hinder their marriage, but married couples need do little for marriages to function well, especially when the outside forces are good (full employment, little societal stress, and so on).

Another factor is the general "privatism" that pervades American culture. "It's nobody else's business" is a common attitude we seem to share about our problems in general and our marriage in particular. Marriage is a private affair. Our more intimate and personal lives are not to be shared publicly. That's bad taste. To seek outside activities to improve marriage means sharing personal information about marriage and this is felt as an invasion of privacy.

A third factor is the cynicism that treats marriage as a joke and thus heads off attempts to improve it (Mace & Mace, 1974, pp. 131–135). "You should have known better than to get married. Don't complain to me about your problems." This attitude is, of course, contradictory to the romantic concept of marriage but acts just as strongly to keep people from deliberately seeking to improve their marriage. "Why would anyone want to improve this dumb institution?" Even though American society is marriage oriented, there is still a great deal of ridicule of "being married."

Despite these factors there is a growing trend toward actively seeking marriage improvement, which I strongly support. For example, more than 50,000 couples have participated in the Roman Catholic

Marriage Encounter Program since it started in 1967. Although started for Catholics, it is open to all couples who wish to participate. This hardly indicates a stampede by married Americans to improve their marriages, but it is at least indicative that the idea of marriage improvement is finding a place.

Of course, in order to improve a marriage, it is necessary to believe that relationships can be improved. In other words, the myth of naturalism must be overcome. A marriage will not just naturally take care of itself. In addition, the privatism and cynicism that surround marriage must be reduced if effective steps are to be taken to positively enrich a marriage.

To improve their marriage, a couple must work on three things: themselves as individuals, their relationship, and the economic environment within which the marriage exists. We have already looked at these elements. For example, in Chapter 5 we discussed the Self-Actualized Person in the Fully Functioning Family; in Chapter 7 we examined marriage as an economic institution and found that the economics of one's marriage will drastically affect the marital relationship; in Chapter 6 we looked at ways to improve communication within a relationship.

In this final chapter I wish to stress the idea that every person does have the ability to improve his or her marriage. Marriages tend to get into trouble because many people believe that they can't do much about their marriage and because many of us simply don't take the time to nourish our marriage and make it healthier.

Although this chapter deals specifically with activities designed to improve one's marital relationship, I want to emphasize that a couple must work to improve the other two important influences on marriage, namely, themselves as individuals and their economic situation. Neglect of any one of these influences or emphasis on only one can still lead to marital failure. In fact, a couple can be very successful in one of the three areas and still fail miserably at marriage, as the two following cases demonstrate.

Bill and Susan both worked in order to buy the many things they wanted, a house, fine furnishings, nice clothing, a fancy car, and so on. Bill even held two jobs for a while. Certainly no one could fault their industriousness and hard work. In time, their marital affluence became the envy of all who knew them. Then, after seven years of marriage, they divorced. Their friends were surprised. "They had everything, why should they divorce?" Unfortunately, they didn't have much of a relationship other than to say hello and goodby as each went off to work. In addition, each worked so hard that neither had time for self-improvement. No self-improvement usually means eventual boredom and this often portends failure.

Bill and Susan were successful with their marital economic environment but did not pay enough attention to improving themselves as individuals or to improving their relationship.

Jack and Mary believed that the key to successful marriage was self-improvement. Both took extension classes in areas of their own interest. They attended sensitivity training groups and personal expansion workshops. Unfortunately, they could seldom attend these functions together because of conflicting work schedules. Soon they were so busy improving themselves that they had little time for one another. The house was a shambles, the yard was weeds, and their relationship disappeared under a maze of "do your own thing" self-improvements.

After seven years, they divorced. Their friends were surprised. "After all, they're so dynamic and interesting, why should they divorce?" Unfortunately, they became so self-oriented that their relationship disappeared and their living environment became un-important.

Jack and Mary worked so hard to improve themselves individually that they had no time for each other or for their home.

Both of these scenarios happen every day. And the second is becoming more prevalent with the growing interest in the human potential movement. The very terms used in this book such as self-actualization, self-fulfillment, and human growth orientation can all be taken to such an individual extreme that marriage is disrupted. Thus,

A possible fallacy of the human potential movement is making self-fulfillment the central goal, while seemingly ignoring the fact that the human being is essentially a relationship-oriented and interactional creature. If an educational or therapeutic goal is to unlock human potential, there must be a corresponding focus on marriage and family relationships (Cromwell & Thomas, 1976).

In other words, to make marriage as rewarding and fulfilling as possible, a couple must be committed first to the idea that "effective family relationships do not just happen, they are the result of deliberate efforts by members of the family unit" (Cromwell & Thomas, 1976). Then they must be prepared to work on all three facets of marriage: to improve themselves as individuals, to improve their interactional relationship, and to improve their marital environment.

Such a commitment helps a couple to anticipate problems before they arise rather than simply reacting to them. When there is commitment to active management and creative guidance of a marriage, the marriage can become richly fulfilling and growth enhancing.

Recently researchers have begun to study strong, healthy, successful families. Those doing the research point out that volumes have been written about what is wrong with the family but little has been written about what is right in the successful family. "We don't learn how to do anything by looking only at how it *shouldn't* be done. We learn most effectively by examining how to do something correctly and by studying a positive model" (Stinnett, 1979, p. 24). Such research suggests six qualities shared by all strong and successful families.

Qualities of Strong Families*

1. *Appreciation.* This first quality is one of the most important. It emerged from the research in many ways and seemed to permeate the family. The family members give each other many positive psychological reinforcements and make each other feel good about themselves. Each of us likes to be with people who make us feel good about ourselves, yet many families fall into interactional patterns where they make each other feel bad. One general difficulty we have about expressing appreciation is that we fear that others will take it as empty flattery, that we are not sincere. However, in strong families, members are able to find good qualities in one another and to express appreciation for them.

2. *Spending Time Together.* A second quality found among strong families is that they do a lot of things together. It is not a "false" togetherness; it is not a "smothering" type of togetherness. They genuinely enjoy being together. Another important point here is that these families structure their life styles so that they can spend time together. They make it happen. And this togetherness exists in all areas of their lives — eating meals, recreation, and work.

3. *Good Communication Patterns.* The third quality was not a surprise. The strong families have very good communication patterns. They spend time talking with each other. This is closely related to the fact that they spend a lot of time together. It's hard for people to communicate if they do not spend time with each other. Dr. Virginia Satir, a prominent family therapist, has stated that

*Some of this material has been adapted from "In Search of Strong Families," by Nick Stinnett. In Stinnett, et al (Eds.) *Building Family Strengths*. Lincoln, Nebraska: U. of Nebraska Press, 1979, pp. 23 – 30.

often families are so fragmented, so busy, and spend such little time together that they communicate with each other through rumor.

Another important aspect of communication is that these families also listen well. By being good listeners, they are saying to one another "You respect me enough to listen to what I have to say. I'm interested enough to listen too."

Another factor related to communication is that these families do fight. They get mad at each other, but they get conflict out in the open and are able to discuss the problem. They share their feelings about alternative ways to deal with the problem and in selecting a solution that is best for everybody.

4. *Commitment.* A fourth quality characteristic of these strong families was a high degree of commitment. They are deeply committed to promoting each others' happiness and welfare. They are also very committed to the family group, as reflected by the fact that they invest much of their time and energies into the family.

Some of the best research on commitment has been done in communes. One of the main differences found between successful and unsuccessful groups was commitment. Those communes that are the most successful, that last the longest, that are the most satisfying in terms of the relationships, are those in which there is a great deal of commitment — to each other and to the group. Again, commitment in the communes was reflected in the amount of time the members spent together. The same is true with strong families.

All of us are busy and sometimes feel that we are being pulled in a thousand different directions at the same time. The strong families experience the same problem. One interesting action that these families expressed was that when life got too hectic — to the extent that they were not spending as much time with their families as they wanted — they would sit down and make a list of the different activities in which they were involved. They would go over that list critically and inevitably there were some things that they really did not want to be doing, or that did not give much happiness, or that really were not very important to them. So they would scratch those activities and involvements off their lists. This would free time for their families, would relieve some of the pressure. As a result they were happier with their lives in general and more satisfied with their family relationships.

This sounds very simple, but how many of us do it? We too often get involved and it's not always because we want to be. We act so often as if we cannot change the situation, but we do have a choice. An important point about these families is that they take the initiative in structuring their life style in a way that enhances the quality of their family relationships and their satisfaction. They are on the "offensive." They do not just react; they make things happen. There is a great deal that families can do to make life more enjoyable. These strong families exercise that ability.

5. *High Degree of Religious Orientation.*   The fifth quality that these families expressed was a high degree of religious orientation. This agrees with research from the past forty years, which shows a positive relationship between religion, marriage happiness, and successful family relationships. Of course, we know that there are persons who are not religious who have very happy marriages and good family relationships. Nevertheless, these strong families went to church together often and participated in religious activities together. Most of them, although not all of them, were members of organized churches.

6. *Ability to Deal with Crises in a Positive Manner.*   The final quality that these families had was the ability to deal with crises and problems in a positive way. Not that they enjoyed crises, but they were able to deal with them in a constructive way. They managed, even in the darkest of situations, to look at the situation and to see some positive element, no matter how tiny, and to focus on it. It may have been, for example, that in a particular crisis they simply had to rely to a greater extent on each other and a developed trust that they had in each other. They were able to unite in dealing with the crisis instead of being fragmented by it. They dealt with the problem and were supportive of each other.

It does not seem unreasonable that family members exhibit such characteristics as we have listed. We usually start our family with mutual appreciation, wanting to spend time together, feeling committed, and trying to communicate well. Yet many families seem to lose these characteristics as time passes. How can a family keep these characteristics? How can they get them back if they start to lose them? The first step is certainly awareness. A second step is to consciously work to maintain and improve them. And there are beginning to be techniques available to families to help them to work toward stronger and more satisfying family lives.

A Short Overview of Marriage Improvement Programs

There are now many helping techniques available to families. Some aim at solving existing problems, others aim at general family improvement. We will briefly examine some of these techniques. Hopefully this will accomplish two goals. First, it may help families seek out experiences that may benefit them. Second, it may alert families to some of the possible dangers involved in unselective, nondiscriminative participation in some of the popular techniques.

Help for family problems in the past has usually come from relatives, friends, ministers, and family doctors. The idea of enriching family life and of improving already adequate marriages simply did not occur to most married people. Marriage traditionally was an institution for child rearing, economic support, and proper fulfillment of marital duties defined in terms of masculine and feminine roles. If there were problems in these areas, help might be sought. If not, the marriage was fine.

However, marriage in modern America has more and more become responsible for individual happiness and emotional fulfillment. The criteria used to judge a marriage have gradually shifted from how well each member fulfills roles and performs proper marital functions to the personal contentment, fulfillment, and happiness each individual in the marriage feels.

Marital complaints now concern sex-role dissatisfaction, unequal growth and personal fulfillment opportunities, feelings of personal unhappiness, and feelings that the marriage is shortchanging the individual partners. That is, more and more marriage problems center around personal dissatisfactions than around traditional marital functioning. The "me" in marriage seems to have become more important than the "us" or the marriage as an entity in itself. Perhaps there is too much "me" in modern American marriages.

Emphasis on emotional fulfillment as the most important aspect of marriage makes an enduring marital union much more difficult to attain. According to one authority, "Emotional fulfillment has always occurred in the family; probably more so in the past than is usual today. But it was never before seen as the primary function of the family. It was a lucky "by-product" (Putney, 1972). For example, when Australia was first colonized by male convicts, there was a brisk trade in mail-order wives since there were no available women in the country. Most of these marriages seem to have been successful for the simple reason

> that the prospective husband and wife expected things of each other that the other could provide. The man needed assistance and companionship of a woman in the arduous task of making a farm, and he wanted sons to help him. He expected certain skills in his wife, but all girls raised in rural England were likely to have them. Her expectations were similarly pragmatic. She expected him to know farming, to work hard, and to protect her. Neither thought of the other as a happiness machine. If they found happiness together more often than American couples do, it may have been they were not looking so hard for it. They fulfilled each other because they shared a life; they did not share a life in the hope of being fulfilled (Putney, 1972).

The search for emotional fulfillment has led to many new methods to gain this end. For example, sensitivity training, encounter groups, family enrichment weekends, sex therapy, sexuality workshops, communication improvement groups, massage and bodily awareness training, psychodrama, feminine and masculine liberation groups, and many many more experiential activities have sprung up in recent years to help Americans enrich their lives.

Although I cannot hope to do justice to the many marriage improvement techniques that are emerging, let's take a brief look at some typical ones before we examine marriage enrichment in more detail.

1. *Courses on marriage and the family* These are offered by most institutions of higher learning. The courses aim to help people better understand the institution of marriage. Many schools offer

even more specialized courses, often in the evening, on marital communication, economics of marriage, child rearing, and so on.

2. *Encounter groups* These consist of group interactions, usually with strangers, where the masks and games used by the marital partners to manipulate one another and conceal real feelings that may be unpleasant to one or both are stripped away. The group actively confronts the person, forcing him or her to examine some of his or her problems and the faulty methods that might have been used to solve or deny problems. There is a great deal of emotion released by such groups. Couples contemplating attending an encounter group should carefully consider the guidelines suggested on page 504.

3. *Family enrichment weekends* These involve the entire family in a retreat type setting where they work together to improve their family life. The family may concentrate on learning some new activities that can be shared. They may listen to lectures, see films, and share other learning experiences. They may interact with other families, learning through the experiences of others. They may participate in exercises designed to improve family communication or general family functioning.

4. *Female and male liberation groups* These groups center their discussions and exercises around helping people escape from stereotypical sex roles and attempting to liberate the parts of their personalities that have been submerged to the sex role. For example, women may work to become more assertive, feeling that the typical feminine role has always been too passive. Men, on the other hand, may work to be more expressive of feeling, since the typical masculine role has repressed emotional display and worked against the man being communicative of his feelings.

5. *Married couple's communication workshops* These workshops may be ongoing groups or weekend workshops in which communication is the center of attention. Role playing, learning how to fight fairly, understanding communication processes, and actively practicing in front of the group all help the couple toward better communication. An important aspect of this is the critique made by the group after a couple communicates about something that causes a problem for them.

6. *Massage and bodily awareness training* This training is often a part of sexuality workshops. It is aimed at developing the couple's awareness of their own bodies as well as teaching each the techniques involved in physically pleasuring the other through massage. The art of physical relaxation is part of bodily awareness training.

7. *Psychodrama* This is a form of psychotherapy developed by J. L. Moreno. It is used to dramatize problems by acting them out with other group members as the players. In the case of marriage enrichment, it is used to help individuals in the family better understand the roles of other family members. This is accomplished mainly through timely changes of role by the individuals participating in the drama under the direction of the group leader.

Shifting roles also helps each player understand how the other person in the drama feels and sees the situation.

8. *Sensitivity training* This training consists of exercises in touching, concentrating and heightening awareness, and empathy for the feelings of one's mate, which increase each mate's sensitivity for the other as well as increasing self-awareness.

9. *Sex therapy and sexuality workshops* These focus on a couple's sexual relationship. Sex therapy is used to overcome sexual problems. Sexuality workshops are designed more to help couples improve this aspect of their relationship than to cure severe problems. Such a workshop assumes that there are no major sexual problems. The goal is to heighten sexual awareness so that the couple's sexual relations may be enriched. Films, discussion, mutual exploration, sensitivity, and massage and bodily awareness techniques are all used to reduce inhibitions and expand the couple's sexual awareness.

There are many other techniques, but these at least give you an idea of what is available.

Suggested Guidelines for Choosing Marriage Improvement Programs

Unfortunately, with popularity comes misuse. The large demand has brought untrained and, occasionally, unscrupulous people into the fields of marriage counseling and marriage enrichment. For example, it is relatively simple as well as monetarily rewarding to run a weekend encounter group of some kind. All you need is a place where the people can meet. Some participants have also found that not all such experiences are beneficial nor do they always accomplish what is claimed for them. In a minority of cases, unexpected repercussions such as divorce, job change, and even hospitalization for mental disturbance have occurred after some supposedly beneficial group experience. Consider what happened to the following couple because one partner could not tolerate the intensity of the group experience.

John and Mary have been married for eleven years and have two children. He has always been shy and uncomfortable among people, but despite this he has worked out a stable, satisfying relationship with Mary. She is much more socially oriented than John. She began to attend a series of group encounter sessions out of curiosity. As her interest increased, she decided that John would benefit from a group experience. She prevailed on him to attend a weekend marathon. Unfortunately, the group turned its attention too strongly on John's shyness, causing him acute discomfort that finally resulted in his fleeing from the group. He remained away from his home and work for ten days. Upon returning, he demanded a divorce because he felt he was an inadequate husband. Fortunately, psychotherapeutic help was available and John was able to work out the problems raised by the group encounter.

Couples seeking marital enrichment or help for marital problems are well advised to check out carefully the people offering such services. They should also discuss the kind of experiences they want and make sure that the agreed on experiences are indeed what is offered. For example, if a couple decides that they would like to improve their sexual relations and can do so by seeking some general sensitivity training (learning to feel more comfortable with their bodies, to be more aware, to give and accept bodily pleasure) it might come as a rude shock if the group leader has a nude encounter group where the leader's goal is to examine closely each person's emotional hangups about sex.

Assuming that the couple has a reasonably satisfactory marriage, the following may serve as minimal guidelines in choosing a marriage enrichment activity:

1. Choose the activity together and participate together if possible.
2. If only one mate can participate, do it with the consent of the other mate and bring the other mate into it as much as possible by sharing your experiences.
3. In general, avoid the one-shot weekend group as it is often too intense and no follow-up is available if needed.
4. Never jump into a group experience on impulse. Give it a lot of thought, understanding that such experiences may be painful in the course of leading to growth.
5. Do not participate in groups where the people are friends and associates if the group's goal is total openness and emotional expression. What occurs in a group session should be privileged information.
6. Don't remain with a group that seems to have an ax to grind, that insists that everybody be a certain type of person or that all *must* participate in every activity.
7. Participate in groups that have a formal connection with a local professional on whom you can check. The local professional is also a source of follow-up if necessary.
8. A group of six to sixteen members is optimum size. Too small a group may result in scapegoating whereas too large a group cannot operate effectively. (Some of these guidelines come from Shostrom, 1967.)

Such cautions are not meant to dissuade couples from trying to improve their marriages. They are simply meant to help couples select experiences that are beneficial and supportive rather than threatening and disruptive. Legitimate marriage counselors throughout the United States are working to upgrade their profession and tighten the rules guiding counseling practices. Many states now have licensing provisions for marriage and family counseling.

The foremost organization in the nation for accrediting and certifying marriage counselors is The American Association of Marriage and Family Counselors, 225 Yale Avenue, Claremont, California 91711.

It will supply you with a list of three or more accredited marriage counselors in your area at no charge. Psychologists are also very active in marital counseling and enrichment training. Membership in the American Psychological Association (APA) indicates that the member has met minimum training requirements and has agreed to abide by a strict set of ethics in her or his client relationships. The American Association of Sex Educators and Counselors has recently established certification standards for sex therapists. You can receive a copy of these standards and a list of certified sex therapists by writing to Sex Therapy Certification Committee, American Association of Sex Educators and Counselors, Suite 304, 5010 Wisconsin Avenue, N.W., Washington, D.C. 20016. In addition, more than 350 marriage and family oriented nonprofit social service organizations throughout the nation are affiliated with the Family Service Association of America, 44 East 23rd Street, New York, New York 10010 and the National Association of Social Workers, Suite 600, 1425 H Street, N.W., Washington, D.C. 20005. Many churches also offer family counseling and enrichment programs. In fact, some churches have been pioneers in the marriage enrichment movement.

An Ounce of Prevention Is Worth a Pound of Cure: Marriage Enrichment

It has only been recently that some people working in the field of marriage and family counseling have turned their attention away from marital problems and focused on marriage enrichment. "What we are now seeking to do, late in the day when the scene is already strewn with marital wrecks, is to equip married couples with the insight and training that will keep their marriages in such good order that the danger of going on the rocks will be as far as possible avoided" (Mace & Mace, 1975, p. 133).

Past marital services have been remedial in nature. When a couple had a marital problem, they could seek help from numerous sources. However, marriage enrichment places the emphasis on the preventative concept of facilitating positive growth. In other words, the goal is to help couples with "good" marriages further improve their relationship.

> Marriage enrichment programs are for couples who have what they perceive to be a fairly well functioning marriage and who wish to make their marriage even more mutually satisfying.
>
> Such programs are generally concerned with enhancing the couple's communication, emotional life, or sexual relationship, fostering marriage strengths and developing marriage potential while maintaining a consistent and primary focus on the relationship of the couple (Otto, 1975, p. 137).

Some people in the field make a distinction between marriage enrichment and family-life enrichment programs. The latter involve not only the primary couple, but the entire family in the program. Again, they are designed for the family without severe problems.

If couples are to direct and improve their marriage, they must increase their awareness. You can't improve anything unless you recognize what is taking place. It is helpful to organize awareness into four subcategories (see Hill, 1961): topical, self, partner, and relationship. Marriage enrichment programs usually spend a great deal of time helping couples or families to become more aware in each of these categories.

For example, sensitivity training exercises help you focus on your internal sensory, thinking, and emotional processes. A realistic picture of yourself, openness to your feelings, minimal defensiveness, and eliminating some emotional hang-ups are goals sought by enrichment programs in the category of self-awareness.

Partner awareness involves knowing accurately what it is your partner is experiencing in terms of his or her own self-awareness (see Miller et al, 1975, p. 145). For example, how does this behavior affect my partner? Is my partner happy, sad, or indifferent? How can I best communicate with my partner? What does my partner think or feel about this? Answering such questions accurately is the goal of partner awareness training.

Relationship awareness shifts the focus from the behavior of one individual to the interactional patterns of the couple or the entire family. For example, who starts an argument, who continues it, and who ends the interaction? Does each individual contribute self-disclosures, feeling inputs, negative and positive communications? Does the couple play games such as those described in the Scenes from Marriage in Chapter 6? If so, who initiates the game?

What are the rules by which the family interacts?

> Every interrelationship has boundaries, constraints that either encourage or discourage certain types of awareness and various types of behavior. These rules are usually outside our direct awareness and operate to create and maintain meaning and order.
>
> We like to conceptualize rules in terms of who can do what, where, when, and how, for what length of time. This can be applied to any issue in a relationship (Miller, et al, 1975, p. 147).

For example, is personal criticism allowed in a family? Who is allowed to criticize, when, and to what degree? What is a family's mode of handling conflicts? Some talk directly about issues and try actively to solve them. Other families pretend that conflicts don't exist and ignore them, hoping they will go away. Others deal with the issue in some stereotypical manner that usually fails to solve the conflict but allows the ventilation of hostility.

Topical awareness is less important than the three we have just discussed. Topical awareness encompasses references to events, objects, ideas, places, and people, topics that constitute most of everyday conversation. By increasing topical awareness, the couple can focus on their interests, where they differ, where they coincide. They can find areas in which they can work and play together. They can recognize and tolerate those areas of their spouse's interests that they don't share.

Another purpose of marriage enrichment programs is to help couples and families develop a game plan for handling disputes and

Mr. and Mrs. Smith have been married for fifteen years. They have two children, Colin, thirteen, and Beth, ten. Their church recently started a series of family retreat weekends at a nearby mountain camp. After some discussion, the family agreed that it would be fun and rewarding to go on one of the weekends.

Early Saturday morning they arrive at the camp and move into one of the cabins. Since nothing is scheduled until lunch, the family explores the camp and surroundings. There is a small lake with boating and fishing, a tennis court, volleyball court, and plenty of hiking trails.

At noon, the twenty families gather in the cafeteria-meeting hall for lunch. Everyone is given a name tag and the leaders are introduced. After lunch, each family introduces themselves. Much to the children's delight, there are many other children present. The leaders assign each family to one of five family subgroups. After lunch the family groups meet and the four families become better acquainted. The group leader then introduces the first work session entitled "Becoming More Aware." There are exercises in identification of feelings and attention is given to feelings the participants

would like to have more of and those they would like to experience less.

After a break, the group leader discusses methods the families might use to reduce unwanted feelings and increase desired feelings. Each family then practices some of these methods while the others observe. After a family finishes, there is a general critique of their experience.

The families are free after the work session until dinner. After dinner, short movies on various developmental problems are shown to the children. At the same time, the parents attend a sexuality workshop. The parents are shown massage techniques designed to relax and give physical pleasure. They are asked to practice the techniques in their individual cabins. They are assured of privacy since the children will be occupied for at least another hour. The children meanwhile are asked to form small groups and discuss how the children shown in the films can be helped to meet the developmental problems portrayed.

Next morning, the first work session is devoted to the theme, "Being Free." This involves learning openness to experiencing each other. The children of the four families talk to one another about things

they like and don't like while the parents sit and listen. Then the roles are reversed. Afterwards, each family exchanges children. They are then given a hypothetical problem to work out. Each newly constituted family has a half hour to work on the problem while the other families observe.

At noon, each family group eats together and then uses the hour recreational period to do something together, such as hiking, boating, fishing, or whatever they agreed on.

The afternoon work session again separates the parents and children. In each case, the assignment is the same. The children are asked to form into family groups where some children play the parents' roles. They are given problems to work out as a family unit. The parents also form into family groups with some parents taking children's roles.

In the final dinner meeting all of the families come together. Both the families and the leaders try to summarize the experiences of the weekend and their significance. Then the leaders outline several homework assignments, one of which each family has to choose and promise to work on at home.

conflicts. What are the rules, how are they clarified, and what procedure can change them? For example, "If you haven't a set of rules before the game starts, the game is likely to degenerate into a series of arguments and squabbles, and so it is with relationships" (Miller et al, 1975, p. 147). Thus most marriage enrichment programs spend a great deal of time on the development of communication skills. For example, identifying problem ownership, self-assertion, empathic listening, negotiation, and problem solving are all emphasized. Generally, the kinds of skills discussed in Chapter 6 are taught and practiced in enrichment programs.

Esteem building is another area of concern in enrichment programs. Better communication can equip a person to be more destructive as well as constructive. We sometimes forget this when lauding the improvement of communication skills. By emphasizing esteem building, by making the intent or spirit with which something is said positive, by valuing both the self and the partner, communication becomes constructive and growth enhancing. Esteem building is particularly difficult for a partner who feels devalued and inferior, thus enrichment programs stress the importance of building a relationship that acts to negate such feelings, that supports valued, positive, high-esteem feelings in family members.

The fact that a family is interested in and open to the idea of marriage enrichment is an extremely important strength. Certainly the kinds of goals sought in the marriage enrichment movement are lofty and worthwhile. These goals, however, are not as important as the general attitude toward marriage taken by a family. The family that takes an active role in guiding, building, improving, and working on better family relations is the family that stands the greatest chance of leading a long, happy, and meaningful life.

WHAT DO YOU THINK?

What do you see as the major benefits such an experience could provide a family?

Would you be willing to participate with your family in such an experience? Why or why not?

Do you have any friends who have participated in any kind of marriage enrichment experience? How did they react to it?

Marriage with Purpose: Effective Management

As pointed out earlier, popular lore has it that the love marriage simply happens (the myth of naturalism). If we are in love, then the other factors necessary to a successful relationship and marriage will fall into place automatically, magically. There is no reason to worry about problems ahead of time. Of course, there will be differences but they can be worked out successfully by any couple truly "in love."

Indeed, it is almost a sacrilege to suggest that people entering love relationships should make a conscious effort to guide and build their relationship. In fact, many will argue that it is the attempted guidance and control of a relationship that ruins it. Their advice tends to be "relax and let it happen." This attitude implies a great tolerance on the part of each individual because what happens may not be something the other wants. How tolerant are we? Does love mean that we must never judge our mate? Are we to accept any behavior from our mate in an effort to just "let it happen"?

Actually, most people are tolerant only up to some given point, after which certain behavior becomes unacceptable. Most of us are quite tolerant in some areas of our life and intolerant in other areas. Of course, everyone can learn to be more tolerant but total tolerance of all things is probably impossible for most people. People have many and varying standards. The point is that when we simply let the relationship happen, it usually isn't long before we and our partner discover some of our intolerances. Then we try to make changes in our mate and in our relationship. Conflict usually follows because our mate may not want to change nor have the relationship change in the direction we desire. Without agreed upon ways of handling conflict, unconscious games and strategies may take over, and soon meaningful communication is lost (see Chapters 5 and 6).

Marriage and family implies the necessity of management skills. Work, leisure, economics, emotions, interests, sex, children, eating, and the household generally all require effective management in the fully functioning family. We have discussed most of these matters elsewhere in the book but it seems a proper ending to tie them all together under the concept of effective management.

"Surely you can't be serious? Effective management belongs in business, not in my marriage." But every married couple, especially if they have children, are running a business. For example, just planning what the family will eat for the next week, buying it, preparing it, and cleaning up afterward requires a great deal of management and organizational skill, especially if money is in short supply. There are also recurrent personal and family crises that throw off schedules and plans.

In addition to day to day management there is the planning necessary to achieve long-range goals. Some families seem to move from catastrophe to calamity and back again. Other families seem to move smoothly through life despite the crises that arise periodically. What is the difference? Often it is one of efficient planning and management versus lack of planning and management. Look at the different attitudes toward money of the following two couples:

Jim and Marge went to college with Bill and Sally. They remained close friends after college since both Jim and Bill got jobs with the same company. Each couple has two children. Marge works periodically and the money she earns is always saved or used to achieve some specific goal such as a trip to Europe or an addition to the house. Sally works most of the time also but she and Bill don't care much about things like budgeting. As long as there is enough to pay the bills, nothing much else matters.

"You and Jim are always so lucky. Bill and I have wanted to add an extra master bedroom for ourselves so we could have a retreat away from the children. But we'll never be able to afford it," complains Sally.

"Luck has nothing to do with it. Jim and I have planned to add the bedroom for a number of years. We always budget carefully so our monthly expenses are covered by Jim's salary. That way all of the money I earn less child care costs goes into savings. The new bedroom represents my last three years of work. I'd hardly call it luck."

Naturally Sally isn't very interested in hearing Marge's response. "Luck" is a much easier way to explain her friend's new bedroom.

Besides, what Marge is telling her is "Be a better money manager and you, too, can add a new bedroom." This will only make her feel guilty and inadequate. "It isn't worth all the trouble to budget money and be tightwads to get a new bedroom," Sally will probably think to herself.

Creative family management in all areas helps to make the family run smoothly and achieve the desired goals. This reduces frustrations and conflicts because there is a feeling of success on the part of the family members. Careful planning also helps a family maintain the flexibility necessary to cope with unforeseen emergencies. Such flexibility gives family members a feeling of freedom, a feeling of being able to make real choices rather than having most choices forced on them by events beyond their control.

The feeling of entrapment that many marrieds express occurs in some cases because they do not take the initiative to plan and guide their lives. Rather, they simply react to circumstances. Of course, there are times and situations when one can do nothing but react. The poor in particular often have so little control over their lives that they give up planning altogether and live by luck and fate.

Family control and rational planning become more difficult as social institutions multiply and infringe on family responsibilities.

> The external stresses on the family have emerged out of necessity. When society begins to develop beyond a primitive level, its members soon find that many tasks are better performed by agencies other than the family. Priests take over the job of interceding with the supernatural; police forces, armies, and fire brigades take over that of protecting the family from physical harm; schools undertake to educate children. And, in the complex modern world, the family often has little voice in what kind of work its members will perform, or where, or for how long; all these matters are decided by impersonal forces of the marketplace or by distant corporations, unions, or government bureaus (Wernick, 1974, p. 112).

It becomes even more important that planning and foresight and management be an integral part of family life in order to cope with such outside pressures successfully. The family that actively takes control of its destiny is most often the family that grows and prospers thereby helping every member of the family toward self-fulfillment.

The Family Will Remain and Diversify

Many try to predict the future of the American family. Their predictions vary from an early death to visualizing new and improved families that will be havens of fulfillment for their members. I don't believe families will disappear or that there is any ideal single family structure. All families face problems, both external environmental pressures as well as internal stresses and strains. Older generations will probably always see family deterioration because their children may choose different life styles from their own. Yet difference in life style and in family structure does not necessarily mean deterioration. Perhaps with in-

Good family management leads to smooth family functioning.

creased affluence and freedom each individual will be able to choose from a wider acceptable variety of life styles, thereby increasing the chances that the family will be satisfying and fulfilling to its members.

The family has always been with us and always will be. And it will also change. The family is flexible and changes with societies. This flexibility allows it to survive. It is flexible because humans are flexible and build institutions that meet their purposes at a given time. When we forget the basic flexibility of humans, we then see changes in human institutions as threatening, even when they may in fact be changes that help people to meet their needs.

The idea of family has always been a concept over which people have had conflicts. There are many cultures, times change, yet the idea of family has always been one of the central concepts wherever people congregate into a society. Change is an integral part of the concept of family.

The Eternal Family

Human history, according to Judeo-Christian theology, began with a family in crisis: the marital discord of Adam and Eve, the sibling rivalry of Cain and Abel. In the mythology of the classical Greeks, the principal crisis was the revolt of Zeus and his brothers against the tyrannical rule of their father Cronus; while in legends of North Australia's Stone Age Wulamba, the crucial episode was the theft of tribal secrets by brothers from their sisters. In modern times, Freud has described the primal human event as the banding together of brothers in a savage horde whose members killed and ate their father in order to possess their mother.

At the base of all these disparate systems of thought, there is a sense of the family as something primordial, essential to the existence of man, and at the same time a sense of instability, conflict and change and crisis.

The crisis can indeed be called eternal. There has probably never been a generation from Adam's to the present that did not, in some way, feel certain that the family as an institution was breaking down and that the good old customs were being drowned in laxity and in permissiveness. It is very easy

to understand why. People form their idea of what a family should be when they are very young and impressionable. By the time they have grown up, the world has changed, and the family, that most adaptable of human institutions, has changed with it; things are no longer the way they were in grandpa's day.

The world changes at different rates at different times. Most people think of the present century as the one that has most radically changed the human condition. It is debatable whether other centuries have not seen changes just as drastic, but it is beyond dispute that change these days is more nearly universal than ever before: all corners of the globe are caught up in the process. Industrialization, urbanization, the deification of the nation-state, the breakdown of traditional religious and moral codes, the spread of secularism, the consumer-oriented economy — everything combines to put old family structures under strain on a global scale. Relationships basic to family life — between young and old, between men and women — are undergoing transformation. The African chief sees his sons go off to work in a new city and set up housekeeping with girls from other tribes who do not speak the ancestral language and who will bring up their children unaware of ancestral gods and customs. The elderly Japanese gentleman chokes as he sees women sitting down at the same table with their husbands and even getting into the bath ahead of them. The aging immigrant in America sees his grandchildren choosing wives and husbands without consulting their elders, much less letting them make the preliminary negotiations. It is only natural for older generations to conclude that the family is sick unto death....

The enduring power of family bonds suggests the way the family may be evolving. It adapts to life in a technological age by taking advantage of the freedom of choice that technology offers. There is less emphasis on formal structure dictating who is to do what to whom and for whom. The distinctions between male and female roles blur. People visit their relatives on the basis of which ones they get along with best, not on the basis of a technical tie of genealogy. There is often a conscious effort to avoid anything that might smack of compulsion — parents may make costly, even extravagant gifts to grown children on birthdays or Christmas, but they avoid sending weekly or monthly checks.

These changes do not weaken the ancient strengths of the family. In all its forms, it remains the support of its members, the essential institution for the survival of the human race. It is still, in Robert Frost's (1914) words, the "place where, when you go there, they have to take you in." (Robert Frost, "The Death of the Hired Man.")

From *The Family*, a title in the Human Behavior series by Robert Wernick and the Editors of Time-Life Books, 1974.

⌒ Glossary

Abortion The deliberate removal of a fetus from the uterus in early pregnancy before it can survive on its own.

Abstinence One of several premarital sexual values, based on the belief that sexual intercourse between unmarried men and women is wrong.

Agape The Greek term for spiritual love.

Ambivalence Simultaneous liking and disliking of an object or person.

Amniocentesis An important prenatal diagnostic tool. A long hollow needle is inserted through the mother's abdomen and into the amniotic sac, where a sample of the amniotic fluid is drawn off. This fluid contains sloughed-off cells from the fetus that may be examined microscopically for signs of disease or birth defects, enabling early treatment to be instituted. This technique may also determine the baby's gender.

Alienation A feeling of not being a part of a society or group.

Androgen The dominant male hormone, which is thought to have an effect on aggression.

Androgynous The quality of having both masculine and feminine characteristics.

Aphrodisiacs Chemicals that induce erotic arousal or relieve impotence or infertility.

Areola The pigmented area surrounding the nipples of the breasts, a significant erogenous zone for about half of the male and female population.

Bigamy Being married to two people at the same time.

Bisexuality Having sexual relationships with partners of the same and opposite sex.

Caesarean section The delivery of a baby by means of a surgical incision through the mother's abdominal and uterine walls. Caesareans are generally performed when the physical condition of the mother or the fetus is such that one or both might not survive the stress of vaginal delivery.

Cluster family An artificially contrived family group that meets for companionship, recreation, and other meaningful experiences without the members actually living together.

Clitoris The small organ situated just under the upper portion of the labia minora of the female genitalia. It is the homologue of the male penis, consists of a shaft and a glans, and becomes erect with sexual arousal.

It is also the chief organ for erotic arousal in most women.

Cohabitation A man and woman living together in an intimate relationship without the benefit of legal marriage.

Common-law marriage A marriage that becomes legally recognized after the woman and man have lived together for some time as though they were wife and husband. About one third of the states recognize common-law marriage.

Commune A group of people who live together by choice rather than because of blood or legal ties. Also referred to as an intentional community.

Condom Also known as a "rubber" or "prophylactic," the condom is a thin sheath, usually made of rubber, which is rolled over and down the shaft of the erect penis prior to intercourse. While used primarily as a method of contraception, it also protects against venereal disease.

Congenital A condition existing at birth or before birth but not by heredity.

Consumer Price Index (C.P.I.) A sample of costs of goods and services collected periodically by the Bureau of Labor Statistics; the costs then are compared to some arbitrarily set base period (now set at 1967).

Contraception A deliberate action to prevent fertilization of the ovum as a result of copulation.

Cunnilingus Oral contact with female genitalia.

D&C (dilatation and curettage) A procedure usually used to induce an abortion during the first twelve weeks of pregnancy. It involves dilating (stretching) the cervix and scraping away the contents of the uterus with a sharp instrument (curette). The operation requires no incision, recovery is usually rapid, and most patients are in the hospital only overnight. (Used as a diagnostic procedure, a D&C is performed to determine the cause of abnormal menstrual bleeding or to determine the cause of bleeding after the menopause.)

DES Abbreviation for diethylstilbestrol, known as the morning-after pill. It contains high doses of estrogen and terminates a pregnancy if taken within twenty-four hours of intercourse.

Diaphragm A contraceptive device consisting of a circular piece of thin rubber that is fitted by a physician so that it spans the back of the vagina and covers the cervix. Spermicidal jelly often is used in conjunction with the diaphragm.

Double standard Different standards of appropriate sexual behavior for men and women. It means that it is more acceptable for men to engage in all types of sexual behavior than for women to do so.

Douche Flushing the vagina with water or with a spermicidal agent after intercourse. A relatively unreliable method of contraception.

Embryo The developing organism from the second to the eighth week of pregnancy. During the embryonic period, the second stage of pregnancy, all the organs and tissues are differentiated into their human form.

Empty nest Also known as the postparentel stage of the family life cycle, this period begins when the last child leaves home and continues until the husband retires or either spouse dies.

Enculturation Learning the mores, rules, ways, and manners of a given culture.

Endogamy The inclination or the necessity to marry within a particular group.

Episiotomy A surgical incision made in the mother's perineum during childbirth in order to prevent tearing of the vaginal tissues.

Eros The physical, sexual side of love. Romans called Eros "Cupid."

Estrogen Often called the "female hormone," it is active in many important ways, such as directing the differentiation of embryonic tissue into female genitalia, directing the differentiation of prenatal brain tissue that governs various female physiological functions, and directing the development of female secondary sexual characteristics at puberty. It is produced chiefly in the ovaries and adrenal cortex of the female and, to a lesser extent, in the testicles and adrenal cortex of the male.

Exogamy The inclination or the necessity to marry outside a particular group.

Extended family A nuclear or polygamous family and the parental generation. The typical extended family includes the husband, wife, their children, and the parents (or aunts/uncles) of the spouses.

Fallopian tubes The two tubes in the female reproductive system which link the ovaries to the uterus. Eggs released from the ovaries move down these tubes to the uterus.

Family A group of two or more persons who are related by blood, marriage, or adoption (U.S. Census definition). The term usually implies the presence of children, a common residence, and economic co-operation.

Family enrichment programs Groups of three to five families who meet together regularly for mutual care and support and for the development of family potential.

Family life cycle A model designed to explain the behavior patterns of married couples. It divides marriage into various stages according to the number, age, and health of a married couple's children.

Family of orientation The family into which an individual is born or adopted.

Family planning Controlling the number and spacing of children through systematic use of contraceptive methods.

Family of procreation The family which one begins by marrying and having one's own children.

Fellatio Oral contact with male genitalia.

Fetus The name given to the developing human organism from eight weeks after conception until birth.

Genes The subcellular structures within the chromosomes in the cell nucleus that contain the DNA molecules and determine the traits of the differentiating cells of the organism.

Genitalia The external reproductive organs.

Genotype An underlying genetic trait that, in contrast to the *phenotype*, is not readily observable.

Gonorrhea A venereal disease caused by gonococci. Unlike syphilis, which typically involves the entire body, gonorrhea usually remains localized in the genitalia and is self-limiting, although it may persist and cause serious and permanent damage, including sterility. Symptoms are common in men, but the disease is often asymptomatic in women and difficult to detect.

Gross National Product (G.N.P.) Total value of a nation's annual output of goods and services.

Halo effect The tendency for a first impression to influence subsequent judgments about something.

Hermaphrodite A person who has both male and female organs, or organs that are indeterminant (such as a clitoris that resembles a penis).

Heterogamy The mutual attraction and compatibility of persons with opposite and complementary personality traits — for example, dominance-submission, nurturance-dependence, achievement-vicarious.

Homogamy The strongly practical attraction of persons who share similar objective characteristics, such as race, religion, ethnic group, intelligence, education, social class, age, and interests and skills.

Hysterectomy A surgical procedure which removes a woman's uterus. While hysterectomies result in sterility for the woman, they are usually conducted because of a malignancy.

Impotence The inability of a man to experience erection. It may be caused by either physical or psychological factors and is usually temporary.

Incest Copulation between closely blood-tied relatives. The degree of closeness that is considered incestuous depends on social attitudes, but all societies proscribe sexual relations between parents and children and between siblings.

Infanticide The deliberate killing of infants as a measure to control population or for some other socially accepted purpose.

Intrauterine device Known as the IUD, it is a small object that a physician inserts into a woman's uterus to prevent conception from occurring.

Laparoscopy A two-step sterilization procedure for women. A telescopelike instrument (laparoscope) inserted into the abdominal wall is used to locate the fallopian tubes. A special pair of forceps that carries electricity is then used to burn the tubes closed.

Legal separation A legal decree that forbids cohabitation by husband and wife and provides for separate maintenance and support of the wife and children by the husband. A legally separated couple is still bound by the marital contract and may not remarry.

Masturbation Any voluntary erotic activity that involves self-stimulation.

Menopause The cessation of ovulation, menstruation, and fertility in the woman. It usually occurs between ages forty-five and fifty.

Middlesence A term used to refer to a second adolescence that many people experience in middle age. It usually involves a reevaluation of one's life.

Midwife Usually a woman, trained to assist in childbirth. In some countries, midwives, rather than medical doctors, deliver the majority of children.

Miscarriage A spontaneous abortion.

Monogamy The state of being married to one person at a time.

Naturalism, myth of The belief that two people will naturally get along in marriage if they love each other.

Nuclear family A group of persons, consisting of a married couple and their children, who live by themselves. The children may be natural or adopted by the couple.

Open marriage A relationship which emphasizes role equality and the freedom for each partner to maximize his or her own potential. While extramarital sexual relationships may be involved, they are not necessary for a marriage to be regarded as open.

Oral contraceptive Hormonal materials (in pill form) that suspend ovulation and therefore prevent conception.

Ovulation The regular monthly process in the fertile woman whereby an ovarian follicle ruptures and releases a mature ovum.

Paracervical anesthesia Injection of a pain killer, such as novacain, into the cervix to reduce pain during childbirth.

Philos The Greek term for the kind of love found in deep and enduring friendships; a general love of mankind.

Placenta The organ, developing from the chorionic villi, that joins the fetus to the uterine tissue. The placenta serves as the medium for the metabolic exchange between the mother and the fetus.

Polyandry A form of marriage in which one woman has more than one husband.

Polygamy Marriage with multiple spouses (as opposed to *monogamy*, with one spouse).

Polygyny A form of marriage in which one man has more than one wife.

Postpartum depression Also known as the blues, it is a feeling of depression, after giving birth, characterized by irritability, crying, loss of appetite, and difficulty in sleeping. Such feelings are thought to be a result of numerous physiological and psychological changes that occur as a result of pregnancy, labor and delivery.

Premature ejaculation The inability to delay ejaculation as long as the male or his partner wishes.

Reconstituted family The family that is formed by remarriage after a divorce or the death of a spouse.

Rhythm method A birth-control method involving avoidance of sexual intercourse when the egg is in the fallopian tubes. The "calendar method" and the "temperature method" are used to predict this time. The rhythm method is a relatively unreliable contraceptive technique.

Romantic love A view of love based on the idea that there is love at first sight, that there is only one true love, and that love is the most important criterion for marriage.

Rooming-in The practice of placing the neonate in the mother's room a few hours after delivery, so that the mother (and father) can care for and relate to the baby.

Saline abortion Destruction of the fetus by insertion of a concentrated salt solution into the amniotic sac. In six to forty-eight hours after the fetus is dead, the uterus contracts, pushing the fetus out of the vagina. This method is used after the twelfth or thirteenth week of pregnancy.

Self-actualization The process of developing one's cognitive, emotional, social, and physical potential.

Sensitivity training Training in learning to understand and be more aware of one's body, its feelings and functioning.

Serial marriage The process of having a series of marriages, one after the other.

Socialization The process of a person's learning—from parents, peers, social institutions, and other sources—the skills, knowledge, and roles necessary for competent and socially acceptable behavior in the society.

Spermaticides The chemical substances that destroy or immobilize sperm and are used as contraceptives.

Sterility The permanent inability to reproduce.

Syphilis A venereal disease caused by a microorganism called a *spirochete*. Syphilis goes through four stages, each with separate and distinct characteristics, and can involve every part of the body. It is transmitted by contact of mucous membrane or broken skin with an infectious syphilitic lesion.

Testosterone An important component of the male sex hormone androgen. It is responsible for inducing and maintaining the male secondary sexual characteristics.

Transsexualism A compulsion or obsession to become a member of the opposite sex through surgical changes.

Transvestism A sexual deviation characterized by a compulsive desire to wear garments of the opposite sex.

Trial marriages Cohabitation between two people who intend to marry.

Ultrasound A technique using sound waves to view a person internally; used to view a fetus inside a mother without using x-ray.

Vacuum aspiration A suction procedure usually used to induce an abortion during the first twelve weeks of pregnancy. It requires no anesthesia, can be done without cervical dilation, and can be done in a doctor's office.

Vasectomy A sterilization procedure for males. The vas deferens is cut and tied so that sperm cannot be carried to the penis.

Withdrawal Removing the penis from the vagina before ejaculation. A relatively unreliable method of contraception.

～ Bibliography

Adams, D., Alice Gold, and Anne Burt. "Rise in Female-Initiated Sexual Activity at Ovulation and Its Suppression by Oral Contraceptives." *New England Journal of Medicine*. November 23, 1978, pp. 1145–1150.

Albrecht, Stan. "Correlates of Marital Happiness among the Remarried." *Journal of Marriage and Family*. November 1979, pp. 857–867.

———. "Reactions and Adjustments to Divorce: Differences in the Experiences of Males and Females." *Family Relations*. January 1980, pp. 59–68.

American Friends Service Committee. *Who Shall Live?* New York: Hill and Wang, 1970.

American Psychological Association. "Child Abuse Called Epidemic." *Monitor*, January 1976.

American Social Health Association. *Today's V.D. Control Problem: 1972*. New York: American Social Health Association, Committee on the Joint Statement, 1972, p. 11.

Amundsen, K. *The Silenced Majority*. Englewood Cliffs, N.J.: Prentice-Hall, 1971, pp. 26–27.

Angrist, S., and J. Love. "Issues Surrounding Day Care." *Family Coordinator* 22 (October 1973): 457–464.

Apgar, V., and J. Beck. *Is My Baby All Right?* New York: Trident, 1973.

Bach, G., and R. Deutsch. *Pairing*. New York: Avon, 1970.

———, and P. Wyden. *The Intimate Enemy*. New York: Avon, 1968.

Bane, Mary Jo. *Here to Stay: American Families in the Twentieth Century*. New York: Basic Books, 1976.

Barclay, A. M. "Bio-psychological Perspectives on Sexual Behavior." In D. Grummon and A. Barclay (eds.), *Sexuality: A Search for Perspective*. New York: Van Nostrand Reinhold, 1971, pp. 54–66.

Bardwick, J. *Psychology of Woman: A Study of Biocultural Conflicts*. New York: Harper & Row, 1971.

———. "The Sex Hormones, The Central Nervous System, and Effect Variability in Humans." In V. Bertle and V. Franks (eds.), *Women in Therapy*. New York: Bruner-Mazel, 1974.

Barnhill, L., and G. Rubenstein, and N. Rocklin. "From Generation to Generation: Fathers-to-Be in Transition." *Family Coordinator*. April 1979, pp. 229–235.

Barocas, R., and P. Karoly. "Effects of Physical Appearance on Social Responsiveness." *Psychology Report* 31 (1972): 495–500.

Barrett, C., and H. Noble. "Mother's Anxieties versus the Effects of Long Distance Move on Children." *Journal of Marriage and the Family* 35. (May 1973): 181–188.

Barrett, Nancy S. "Women in the Job Market: Unemployment and Work Schedules." In R. E. Smith, (ed.), *The Subtle Revolution: Women at Work*. Washington, D.C.: The Urban Institute, 1979.

Bartell, G. D. *Group Sex*. New York: Peter Wyden, 1971.

Becker, G., E. Landes, and R. Michael. "Economics of Marital Instability." Working paper #153. Stanford, Calif.: Bureau of Economic Research, 1976.

Bell, R. R. *Marriage and Family Interaction*. Homewood, Ill.: Dorsey, 1975.

———. *Premarital Sex in a Changing Society*. Englewood Cliffs, N.J.: Prentice-Hall, 1966.

———, and J. B. Chaskes Jr. "Premarital Sexual Experience among Coeds, 1958 and 1968." *Journal of Marriage and the Family*, February 1970, pp. 81–84.

Bell, Robert, and Kathleen Coughey. "Premarital Sexual Experience among College Females, 1958, 1968, and 1978." *Family Relations*. July 1980, pp. 353–357.

Berelson, B. *The Population Council Annual Report*. New York: Population Council, 1972.

———, and G. Steiner. *Human Behavior: An Inventory of Scientific Findings*. New York: Harcourt Brace Jovanovich, 1964.

Bernard, J. *The Future of Marriage*. New York: World, 1972.

———. *Remarriage: A Study of Marriage*. New York: The Dryden Press, 1956.

Berne, E. *Games People Play*. New York: Grove Press, 1964.

———. *Sex in Human Loving*. New York: Pocket Books, 1971.

Bianchi, S., and R. Farley. "Racial Differences in Family Living Arrangements and Economic Well Being: An Analysis of Recent Trends." *Journal of Marriage and Family*. August 1979, pp. 537–551.

Biddle, B. J. *Role Theory: Expectations, Identities, and Behaviors*. Chicago: The Dryden Press, 1976.

Bienvenu, M. J. "Measurement of Marital Communication. *The Family Coordinator* 19 (January 1970): 26–31.

Bird, C. Essay. In H. Hart et al. (eds.), *Marriage: For and Against*. New York: Hart, 1972, pp. 168–187.

Bird J., and L. Bird. *Marriage Is For Grownups*. Garden City, N.Y.: Image Books, 1971.

Blake, Judith. "Is Zero Preferred? American Attitudes Toward Childlessness in the 1970s." *Journal of Marriage and Family*. May 1979, pp. 245–257.

Bohannan, P. *Divorce and After*. Garden City, N.Y.: Doubleday, 1970.

Boolootian, R. A. *Elements of Human Anatomy and Physiology*. St. Paul, Minn.: West Publishing, 1976.

Borland, D. M. "An Alternative Model of the Wheel Theory." *Family Coordinator*. **24** (1975): 289–292.

Bossard, J. H. "Residential Propinquity as a Factor in Marriage Selection." *American Journal of Sociology* **38** (1931): 219–224.

Boston Women's Health Book Collective, The. *Our Bodies, Ourselves*. New York: Simon & Schuster, 1973; rev. & expanded ed., 1976.

Bower, D. W., and V. A. Christopherson. "University Student Cohabitation: A Regional Comparison of Selected Attitudes and Behavior." *Journal of Marriage and the Family* **39** No. 3, (August 1977).

Bowerman, C., and D. Irish. "Some Relationships of Stepchildren to Their Parents." *Marriage and Family Living* **24** (May 1962): 113–121.

Bowes, W. A., et al. "The Effects of Obstetrical Medication on Fetus and Infant." *Monographs of the Society for Research in Child Development* **35** (1970): 1–55.

Bowman, H. A. *Marriage for Moderns*. New York: McGraw-Hill, 1974.

Brayshaw, A. J. "Middle-aged Marriage: Idealism, Realism and the Search for Meaning." *Marriage and Family Living*. **24** (1962): 358–364.

"British Birth Survey. 1970." London: William Heinemann Medical Books, Ltd. 1975.

Broderick, C. "Going Steady: The Beginning of the End." In S. Farber and R. Wilson (eds.), *Teenage Marriage and Divorce*. Berkeley, Calif.: Diablo Press, 1967, pp. 21–24.

Brody, Jane E. "Vasectomy Procedure Gains Favor among American Men." *Santa Barbara News-Press*, November 19, 1979, p. F-20.

Broverman, Inge et al. "Sex Roles Stereotypes: A Current Appraisal." *Journal of Social Issues*. **28** (1972): 59–78.

Budd, L. S. "Problems Disclosure, and Commitment of Cohabiting and Married Couples." Unpublished Doctoral dissertation. University of Minnesota, 1976.

Bumpass, L., and A. Sweet. "Differentials in Marital Instability: 1970." *American Society Review*, December 1977, pp. 754–766.

Burchinal, L. "Characteristics of Adolescents from Unbroken, Broken, and Reconstituted Families." *Journal of Marriage and the Family* **26** (January 1964): 44–50.

———, and L. Chancellor. "Survival Rates among Types of Religiously Homogamous and Inter-religious Marriages, Iowa, 1953–1959, Religious Bulletin." Iowa State University: Iowa Agricultural and Home Economics Station, 1962.

Burgess, E., and P. Wallin. *Engagement and Marriage*. Philadelphia: Lippincott, 1953.

Business Week. "The High Cost of Divorce in Money and Emotions." February 10, 1975, pp. 83–90.

Butler, R. N. "How to Grow Old and Poor in an Affluent Society." Public Interest Report No. 9. *International Journal of Aging and Human Development*, 1973.

Calderone, M. "An Interview with Mary Calderone, M.D." *Medical Aspects of Human Sexuality* **2** (August 1968): 46.

Calhoun, L., and S. Selby. "Voluntary Childlessness, Involuntary Childlessness, and Having Children: A Study of Social Perceptions." *The Family Coordinator*, April 1980, pp. 181–183.

Canfield, Elizabeth K. "On the Sex Education Frontiers." Talk given at the California Council on Family Relations Annual Conference. Anaheim, Calif., October 18–20, 1979.

Carlson v. Olson. 256 N.W. 2d 249 (1977).

Carter, H., and P. Glick. *Marriage and Divorce*. Cambridge, Mass.: Harvard, 1975.

Casler, L. *Is Marriage Necessary?* New York: Human Sciences Press, 1974.

———. "This Thing Called Love." *Psychology Today*, December 1969.

CBS *CBS Reports*. "Boys and Girls Together." Harry Reasoner, February 8, 1980.

Chadwick, B. A., et al. "Marital and Family Role Satisfaction." *Journal of Marriage and the Family* **38** (August 1976): 431–440.

Chafetz, J. *Masculine/Feminine or Human?* Itasca, Ill.: F. E. Peacock, 1974.

Cherlin, A. "The Effects of Children on Marital Dissolution." *Demography*, August 1977, pp. 265–272.

———. "Remarriage as an Incomplete Institution." *American Journal of Sociology* **84**, No. 3. (1978): 634–650.

Christensen, H. T., and C. Gregg. "Changing Sex Norms in America and Scandinavia." *Journal of Marriage and the Family* **32** (November 1970): 621–633.

Clatworthy, N., and L. Scheid. "A Comparison of Married Couples: Premarital Cohabitants with Non-premarital Cohabitants." Unpublished manuscript. Ohio State University, 1977.

Close, H. "To the Child: On Parenting." *Voices*, Spring 1968.

Coogler, O. S., Ruth Weber, and P. McKenry. "Divorce Mediation: A Means of Facilitating Divorce and Adjustment." *Family Coordinator*, April 1979, pp. 255–259.

Cox, F. *Psychology*. Dubuque, Iowa: Wm. C. Brown Company, 1973.

———. *Youth, Marriage, and the Seductive Society*, Dubuque, Iowa: Wm. C. Brown Company, 1974.

Cozby, P. W. "Self-Disclosure: A Literature Review." *Psychological Bulletin* **79** (July 1973): 73–91.

Crane, J. A. "The Meaning of Community: Being with

People You Know." Unitarian Church sermon, Santa Barbara, Calif.: January 6, 1974.

Croak, J. W., and B. James. "A Four Year Comparison of Premarital Sexual Attitudes." *Journal of Sex Research* **9** (May 1973): 91–96.

Cromwell, R. E., and V. Thomas. "Developing Resources for Family Potential: A Family Action Model." *The Family Coordinator* **25** (January 1976): 13–20.

Crosby, J. F. "A Critique of Divorce Statistics and Their Interpretation." *Family Relations*, January 1980, pp. 51–58.

————. "The Death of the Family Revisited." *The Humanist*, May-June 1975, pp. 12–14.

Cutler, B. R., and W. G. Dyer. "Initial Adjustment Process in Young Married Couples." *Social Forces* **44** (December 1965): 195–201.

Danzinger, C., and M. Greenwald. *Alternatives: A Look at Unmarried Couples and Communes*. New York: Institute of Life Insurance, Research Services, 1973.

Darnley, Fred. "Adjustment to Retirement: Integrity or Despair." *The Family Coordinator*, April 1975.

David, H., and Wendy Baldwin. "Childbearing and Child Development: Demographic and Psychosocial Trends." *American Psychologist* **34** (October 1979): 866–871.

Davis, K. "Sex on Campus: Is There a Revolution?" *Medical Aspects of Human Sexuality* **5** (1971): 128–142.

Denfield, D. "Dropouts from Swinging." *Family Coordinator* **23** (January 1974): 45–49.

Dibsie, P. "Computer Tracks Down Errant Parents." *San Diego Evening Tribune*, August 25, 1975, p. B-1.

Dick-Read, G. *Childbirth without Fear*, 4th ed. New York: Harper & Row, 1972.

Dienhart, C. M. *Basic Human Anatomy and Physiology*. Philadelphia: Saunders, 1967.

Dillon, T. F., et al. "Midwifery." *American Journal of Obstetrics and Gynecology* **130** (April 15, 1978) (8): 917–926.

Dion, K., E. Berscheid, and E. Walster. "What is Beautiful is Good." *Journal of Personality and Social Psychology* **24** (1972): 285–290.

Dixon, Ruth, and Lenore Weitzman. "Evaluating the Impact of No-Fault Divorce in California." *Family Relations*, July 1980, pp. 297–307.

Duberman, L. *Gender and Sex in Society*. New York: Praeger, 1975.

————. *Marriage and Its Alternatives*. New York: Praeger, 1974.

————. *The Reconstituted Family: A Study of Remarried Couples and Their Children*. Chicago: Nelson-Hall, 1975.

————. "Step-Kin Relationships." *Journal of Marriage and the Family* **35** (May 1973): 283–292.

Easley, E. B. "Sexual Effect of Female Sterilization." *Medical Aspects of Human Sexuality* **6** (February 1972).

Edmiston, S. "How to Write Your Own Marriage Contract." *Ms.*, Spring 1972.

Ehrlich, H. J., et al. *Women and Men: A Socioeconomic Factbook*. Baltimore: Research Group 1, 1975.

Elkin, M. "Conciliation Courts: The Reintegration of Disintegrating Families." *The Family Coordinator*, January 1973, p. 63.

————. "Premarital Counseling for Minors: The Los Angeles Experience." *The Family Coordinator* (October 1977): 429–443.

Erikson, E. H. *Childhood and Society*, 2nd ed. New York: Norton, 1963.

Etzioni, A. "The Family: Is it Obsolete?" *Journal of Current Social Issues*, Winter 1977.

Family Coordinator, The. October 1976 (fatherhood issue).

Feldberg, R., and J. Kohen. "Family Life in an Anti-Family Setting: A Critique of Marriage and Divorce." *The Family Coordinator* **25** (April 1976): 151–159.

Ferris, A. L. *Indicators of Trends in the Status of American Women*. New York: Russell Sage Foundation, 1971.

Figley, C. "Child Density and the Marital Relationship." *Journal of Marriage and the Family* **35** (May 1973): 272–281.

Fisher, E. "A Guide to Divorce Counseling." *The Family Coordinator* **22** (January 1973): 55–62.

Foresman, H., and I. Thuwe. "One Hundred and Twenty Children Born after Application for Therapeutic Abortion Refused." *Acta Psychiatrica. Scandinavia.* **42** (1966): 71–88.

Frieze, Irene H., et al. *Women and Sex Roles*. New York: Norton, 1978.

Fromm, E. *The Art of Loving*. New York: Harper & Row, 1956.

Fullerton, G. *Survival in Marriage*, 2d ed. New York: Holt, 1977.

Furstenberg, F. "Recycling the Family." *Marriage and Family Review*. New York: Haworth Press. Vol. 2 No. 3, 1979.

Gagon, J., and B. Henderson. *Human Sexuality: An Age of Ambiguity*. Boston: Little, Brown, 1975.

Galbraith, J. K. *The Affluent Society*. Boston: Houghton Mifflin, 1958.

Gallop, G. Gallop Poll. *Santa Barbara News-Press*, September 14, 1969, A-7.

————. Gallop Poll. *San Diego Evening Tribune*, April 8, 1974, Sec. D. *a*

————. Gallop Poll. *Santa Barbara News-Press*, April 18, 1974, A-9. *b*

Garfinkel, H. "Trust and Stable Action." In O. Harvey (ed.), *Motivation and Social Interaction*. New York: Ronald Press, 1963, pp. 187–238.

General Mills. "Raising Children in a Changing Society." *The General Mills American Family Report* 1976–1977. Minneapolis: General Mills, 1977.

Gilbert, S. J. "Self-Disclosure, Intimacy and Communication in Families." *The Family Coordinator* **25** (July 1976): 221–231.

Gillman, E. "Is Dating Outdated? *Seventeen* **32** (March 1973): 106.

Gilmartin, B. C. "Swinging: Who Gets Involved and How?" In R. Libby and R. Whitehurst (eds.), *Marriage and Alternatives: Exploring Intimate Relationships*. Glendview, Ill.: Scott, Foresman, 1977, pp. 161–185.

Glenn, N. D., and C. Weaver. "The Marital Happiness of Remarried Divorced Persons." *Journal of Marriage and the Family* **39** (May 1977): 331–337.

Glick, Paul. "The Life Cycle of the Family." *Marriage and Family Living* **17** (1955): 3–9.

———. "A Demographer Looks at American Families." *Journal of Marriage and the Family* **37** (February 1975): 15–27.

———. "Updating the Life Cycle of the Family." *Journal of Marriage and Family* **39** (February 1977): 5–13.

———. "Future American Families." In *The Washington COFO Memo: A Publication of the Coalition of Family Organizations*. Washington, D.C. Vol. II, No. 3 Summer/Fall 1979.

———. "The Future Marital Status and Living Arrangements of the Elderly." *The Gerontologist* **19** (1979): 3.

———. "Divorce and Child Custody and Support." Unpublished paper, 1979.

———. "Social Change and the American Family." *The Social Welfare Forum*. Columbia University Press, 1977.

———, and A. Norton. "Perspectives on Recent Upturn in Divorce and Remarriage." *Demography* **10** (August 1973): 301–314.

———, and A. Norton. *Marrying, Divorcing, and Living Together in the U.S. Today*. Washington, D.C.: Population Reference Bureau **32** (October 1977): 5.

Goertzel, V., and M. Goertzel. *Cradles of Eminence*. Boston: Little, Brown, 1962.

Goleman, D. "Special Abilities of the Sexes: Do They Begin in the Brain?" *Psychology Today*, November 1978.

Goode, W. J. *The Contemporary American Family*. New York: New York Times, 1971, chap. 2.

Gordon, T. *Parental Effectiveness Training*. New York: Peter Wyden, 1970.

Greer, G. Interview. *Penthouse*, September 1971.

Gribbin, A. "The Family Is Not 'Dying.'" *The National Observer*, March 5, 1977.

Grossman, A. "The Labor Force Patterns of Divorced and Separated Women." *Monthly Labor Review*, January 1977, pp. 48–53.

Gunter, B. G. "Notes on Divorce Filing as Role Behavior." *Journal of Marriage and Family*, February 1977, pp. 95–98.

———, and D. T. Johnson. "Divorce Filing as Role Behavior: Effect of No-Fault Law on Divorce Filing

Patterns." *Journal of Marriage and Family*, August 1978, pp. 571–574.

Guttmacher, A. F. *Abortion: A Woman's Guide*. New York: Abelard-Schuman, 1973.

———. *Birth Control and Love*. New York: Macmillan, 1969.

———. *Birth Control, Pregnancy, Birth and Family Planning: A Guide for Expectant Parents in the 1970s*. New York: Viking, 1973.

Hannan, M. T., and Nancy B. Tuma. "Income and Marital Events: Evidence from an Income-Maintenance Experiment." *American Journal of Sociology*. **82**: (May 1977): 1186–1211.

Hardin, G. "Abortion and Human Dignity." Lecture at the University of California, Berkeley, April 29, 1964.

Harlow, H. F., and M. K. Harlow. "Social Deprivation in Monkeys." *Scientific American* **54** (1962): 244–272.

Hart, T. M. "Legalized Abortion in Japan." *California Medicine* **107** (October 1967): 334–337.

Havemann, E. *Birth Control*, New York: Time-Life, 1967.

Havighurst, R. J., B. L. Neugarten, and S. S. Tobin. "Disengagement and Patterns of Aging." In B. L. Neugarten (ed.), *Middle Age and Aging: a Reader in Social Psychology*. Chicago: University of Chicago Press, 1968.

Hawkins, J., and K. Johnson. "Perceptions of Behavioral Conformity, Imputation of Census, and Marital Status." *Journal of Marriage and the Family* **31** (August 1969): 507–511.

Hecht, Annabel. "DES: The Drug with Unexpected Legacies." *FDA Consumer*, May 1979, pp. 14–17.

Helfer, R., and C. Kempe (eds.). *The Battered Child*. Chicago: University of Chicago Press, 1974.

Henry, J. *Culture against Man*. New York: Vintage Books, 1965.

Hess, R., and D. Camara. "Post-divorce Family Relations as Mediating Factors in the Consequences of Divorce for Children." *Journal of Social Issues*, 1979.

Hetherington, E. Mavis. "Divorce: A Child's Perspective." *American Psychologist*. October 1979, pp. 851–865.

Hetherington, M., M. Cox, and R. Cox. "Divorced Fathers." *The Family Coordinator* **25** (October 1976): 417–428.

———. "The Aftermath of Divorce." In J. H. Stevens, Jr. and M. Matthews (eds.), *Mother-Child, Father-Child Relations*. Washington, D.C.: National Association for the Education of Young Children, 1978.

Hicks, M., and M. Platt. "Marital Happiness and Stability: A Review of the Research in the Sixties." *Journal of Marriage and the Family* **32** (November 1970): 553–574.

Hill, C., Z. Rubin, and L. Peplau. "Breakups Before Marriage: The End of 103 Affairs." *Journal of Social Issues* **32** (1976): 147–168.

Hill, W. F. *Hill Interaction Matrix Scoring Manual*. Los

Angeles: University of Southern California, Youth Studies Center, 1961.

Hiltz, S. Roxanne. "Helping Widows: Group Discussions as Therapeutic Technique." *The Family Coordinator*, July 1975, pp. 331–336.

Himes, N. E. *Medical History of Contraception*. New York: Gamut, 1963.

Hirsh, Barbara. *Living Together: A Guide to the Law for Unmarried Couples*. Boston: Houghton Mifflin, 1976.

Hobbins, John C. (ed.). *Diagnostic Ultrasound in Obstetrics*. New York: Church and Liningstone, 1979.

Hoffman, S., and J. Holmes. "Husbands, Wives, and Divorce." In G. Duncan and J. Morgan (eds.), *Five Thousand Families*. Ann Arbor: Institute for Social Research, University of Michigan, 1976.

Hogoboom, W. "Premarital Marriage Counseling for Teenagers—One Year's Experience in California." *Conciliation Courts Review* **9** (1971): 1–10.

Hollander, X. *The Best Part of Man*. New York: Signet Books, 1975.

"Home Tests for Pregnancy." *Newsweek*, September 3, 1979, p. 69.

Honig, Alice S. "What We Need to Know to Help the Teenage Parent." *Family Coordinator*, April 1978, pp. 113–119.

Hoppe, A. "Wife for Hire." *San Francisco Chronicle*, March 24, 1974.

Houseknecht, Sharon. "Childlessness and Marital Adjustment." *Journal of Marriage and Family*, May 1979, pp. 259–265.

Hunt, M. "Maybe Divorce Was Good for You." *True*, November 1969, p. 5.

———. *The Natural History of Love*. New York: Knopf, 1959.

———. "Sexual Behavior in the 1970s; Part II: Premarital Sex." *Playboy*, November 1973, pp. 74–75.

———. *The World of the Formerly Married*. New York: McGraw-Hill, 1966.

Hunt, R., and E. Rydman. *Creative Marriage*. Boston: Holbrook, 1976.

Hurlock, E. *Child Development*, 5th ed. New York: McGraw-Hill, 1972.

Huston, T., and G. Levinger. "Interpersonal Attraction and Relationships." *Annual Review of Psychology, 1978*. Annual Reviews: Palo Alto, Calif., 1978.

Insel, P. M., and W. T. Roth. *Health in a Changing Society*. Palo Alto, Calif.: Mayfield, 1976.

Ivey, M., and J. Bardwick. "Her Body, the Battleground." *Psychology Today*, February 1972, pp. 50–54.

Jacques, J., and Karen Chason. "Cohabitation: Its Impact on Marital Success." *The Family Coordinator*, January 1979, pp. 35–39.

Jensen, G. D., and R. H. Babbitt. "Monkeying with the Mother Myth." *Psychology Today*, May 1968.

Johns Hopkins University. Study prepared for Population Information Program at the Hopkin's Hygiene and Public Health School. As reported in the *Santa Barbara News-Press*, January 23, 1979.

Johnson, M. P. "Commitment: A Conceptual Structure and Empirical Application." *Sociological Quarterly* **14** (1973): 395–406.

Jones, E. E., and C. Wortman. *Ingratiation: An Attributional Approach*. Morristown, N.J.: General Learning, 1973.

Jourard, S. M. *Personal Adjustment*. New York: Macmillan, 1963.

Jursnich, D. Paper, marriage and family class, Santa Barbara City College, Calif., 1974.

Kaats, G., and K. Davies. "The Dynamics of Sexual Behavior of College Students." *Journal of Marriage and the Family* **32** (August 1970): 390–399.

Kahn, H., and A. Wiener. "The Future Meanings of Work: Some 'Surprise-Free' Observations." In F. Best (ed.), *The Future of Work*. Englewood Cliffs, N.J.: Prentice-Hall (Spectrum), 1973.

Kane, F. J., et al. "Emotional and Cognitive Disturbance in Early Puerperium." *British Journal of Psychiatry* **114** (1968): 99–102.

Kanter, R. "Commitment and Social Organization: A Study of Commitment Mechanisms in Utopian Communities." *Sociological Review* **33** (1968): 499–518.

———. "Women in Organizations: Sex Roles, Group Dynamics, and Change Strategies." In Alice Sargent, *Beyond Sex Roles*. St. Paul, Minn.: West, 1977, pp. 371–386.

———, et al. "Coupling, Parenting, and the Presence of Others: Intimate Relationships in Communal Households." *The Family Coordinator* **24** (October 1975): 433–452.

Kapecky, G. "Unmarried—But Living Together." *The Ladies Home Journal*, July 1972, p. 66.

Kaplan, H. *New Sex Therapy: Active Treatment of Sexual Dysfunction*. New York: Brunner-Mazel, 1974.

Katchadourian, H. A., and D. T. Lunde. *Fundamentals of Human Sexuality*. New York: Holt, 1972.

Kephart, W. M. *Extraordinary Groups: The Sociology of Unconventional Life-Styles*. New York: St. Martin's, 1976.

———. *The Family, Society and the Individual*, 2nd ed. Boston: Houghton Mifflin, 1977.

Kerckhoff, A. "More of the Same." *Contemporary Psychology* **22** (1977): 189–190.

Kerckhoff, A. C., and K. E. Davis. "Value Consensus and Need Complementarity in Mate Selection." *American Social Review* **27** (1962): 295–303.

Kerckhoff, Richard. "Marriage and Middle Age." *The Family Coordinator*, January 1976, pp. 5–11.

Kieffer, C. M. "Consensual Cohabitation: A Descriptive Study of the Relationships and the Sociocultural Characteristics of Eighty Couples in Settings of Two Florida Universities." Unpublished Master's thesis, Florida State University, 1972.

———. "New Depths in Intimacy." In R. Libby and R. Whitehurst (eds.), *Marriage and Alternatives: Exploring Intimate Relationships.* Glenview, Ill.: Scott, Foresman, 1977, pp. 267–293.

King, D., J. Balswick, and I. Robinson. "The Continuing Premarital Sexual Revolution Among College Females." *Journal of Marriage and Family*, August 1977, pp. 455–459.

Kinsey, A., et al. *Sexual Behavior in the Human Female.* Philadelphia: W. B. Saunders, 1953.

———. *Sexual Behavior in the Human Male.* Philadelphia: W. B. Saunders, 1948.

Kinsey, Alfred. Institute for Sex Research. "1978 Report on American Sexual Attitudes." Reported in the *Los Angeles Times*, June 18, 1978. Part 1, page 2 in an article by John Barbour, "New Kinsey Report Detects Conservative Sex Trend."

Klaus, M., et al. "Maternal Attachment." *New England Journal of Medicine* **286** (March 2, 1972): 460–463.

Kogan, B. A. *Human Sexual Expression.* New York: Harcourt Brace Jovanovich, 1973.

Krantzler, M. *Creative Divorce.* New York: Evans, 1973.

Kreps, J. "The Occupations: Wider Economic Opportunity." In M. L. McBee and K. A. Blake (eds.), *The American Woman: Who Will She Be?* Beverly Hills, Calif.: Glencoe Press, 1974, pp. 67–80.

Lair, J. *I Ain't Much, Baby — But I'm All I've Got.* Garden City, N.Y.: Doubleday, 1972.

Lancon, T. "Single Again." *The Single Parent*, March 1976, pp. 26–27.

Landes, C., et al. *Sex in Development.* New York: Hoeber-Harper, 1940.

Landis, P. H. *Making the Most of Marriage*, 5th ed. Englewood Cliffs, N.J.: Prentice-Hall, 1970, 1975.

Lasswell, Marcia E. "Looking Ahead in Aging: Love after Fifty." In M. Lasswell and T. Lasswell (eds.), *Love, Marriage, Family.* Glenview, Ill.: Scott, Foresman, 1973.

———, and Norman Lobsenz. *Styles of Loving.* Garden City, N.Y.: Doubleday, 1980.

Latham v. Latham. 274 Ore. 421, 541 P. 2d 144 (1976).

Lavori, N. *Living Together, Married or Single: Your Legal Rights.* New York: Harper and Row, 1976.

Laws, J. L. "A Feminist Review of Marital Adjustment Literature: The Rape of the Locke." *Journal of Marriage and the Family* **33** (August 1971): 483–516.

Lear, H. "Vasectomy—A Note of Concern." In *Vasectomy: Follow-up of 1000 Cases, Simon Population Trust-Sterilization Project.* Cambridge, Eng.: Simon Population Trust, 1969.

Leboyer, Frederick. *Birth without Violence.* New York: Knopf, 1975.

Lederer, W. J., and D. D. Jackson. *The Mirages of Marriage.* New York: Norton, 1968.

Lee, J. A. "Styles of Loving." *Psychology Today* **8** (1974): 44–51.

Leff, Laurel. "You, Living Together, and the Law." *Cosmopolitan*, December 1978, pp. 194–220.

Le Masters, E. E. *Parents in Modern America.* Homewood, Ill.: Dorsey, 1974.

Lessard, S. "Aborting a Fetus: The Legal Right, the Personal Choice." *The Washington Monthly* **4** (August 1972): 29–37.

Le Shan, E. J. *The Wonderful Crisis of Middle Age.* New York: David McKay, 1973.

Leslie, Gerald. "Personal Values, Professional Idealogies and Family Specialists. A New Look." *The Family Coordinator*, April 1979, pp. 157–162.

Levin, R. J., and A. Levin. "Sexual Pleasure: The Surprising Preferences of 100,000 Women." *Redbook*, September 1975.

Levinger, G., D. Senn, and B. Jorgensen. "Progress toward Permanence in Courtship: A Test of the Kerckhoff-Davis Hypotheses." *Sociometry*, 1970, pp. 427–443.

Lewis, R., G. Spanier, V. Storm, and C. Lettecka. "Commitment in Married and Unmarried Cohabitation." Paper presented at the Annual Meeting of the American Sociological Association, San Francisco, 1975.

Libby, R. W. "Creative Singlehood as a Sexual Life-Style: Beyond Marriage as a Rite of Passage." In R. Libby and R. Whitehurst (eds.), *Marriage and Alternatives: Exploring Intimate Relationships.* Glenview, Ill.: Scott, Foresman, 1977, pp. 37–60.

Lindemann, B. "The Sex Role Revolution." In F. Cox, *American Marriage: A Changing Scene?* Dubuque, Iowa: Wm. C. Brown Company, 1976, pp. 175–188.

Lin-Fu, J. S. "New Hope for Babies of Rh-Negative Mothers." *Children* **16** (1969): 23–27.

Linner, B. *Sex and Society in Sweden.* New York: Random House, 1967.

Linton, R. *The Study of Man.* New York: Appleton, 1936.

Locke, H. J. *Predicting Adjustment in Marriage.* New York: Holt, 1951.

Lopata, Helena Z. *Women as Widows.* New York: Elsevier, 1979.

Lucky, E., and G. Nass. "A Comparison of Sexual Attitudes and Behavior in an International Sample." *Journal of Marriage and the Family* **31** (May 1969): 364–379.

Lyness, J. L., et al. "Living Together: An Alternative to Marriage." *Journal of Marriage and the Family* **34** (May 1972): 305–311.

Lynn, D. B. *The Father: His Role in Child Development.* Monterey, Calif.: Brooks/Cole, 1974.

McBee, M. L., and K. A. Blake. *The American Woman: Who Will She Be?* Beverly Hills, Calif.: Glencoe Press, 1974.

McCary, J. *Human Sexuality.* New York: Van Nostrand Reinhold, 1967.

McGuiness, Diane, and Karl Pribram. "The Origins of Sensory Bias in the Development of Gender Differences in Perception and Cognition." In Morton Bortner (ed.), *Cognitive Growth and Development*

—*Essays in Honor of Herbert G. Birch.* New York: Brunner/Mazel, 1979.

McMorrow, F. *Middlescence: The Dangerous Years.* New York: Strawberry Hill, 1974.

Maccoby, Eleanor E., and Carol N. Jacklin. *The Psychology of Sex Differences.* Palo Alto, Calif.: Stanford University Press, 1974.

Mace, D., and V. Mace. "Counter-Epilogue." In R. Libby and R. Whitehurst (eds.), *Marriage and Alternatives: Exploring Intimate Relationships.* Glenview, Ill.: Scott, Foresman, 1977, pp. 390–396.

———. *Marriage: East and West.* Garden City, N.Y.: Doubleday, 1949.

———. *We Can Have Better Marriages.* Nashville, Tenn.: Abingdon, 1974.

Macklin, E. D. "Review of Research on Nonmarital Cohabitation in the United States." In B. I. Murstein (ed.), *Exploring Intimate Life Styles.* New York: Springer, 1978.

———. "Heterosexual Cohabitation among Unmarried College Students." *Family Coordinator* 21 (1972): 463–472.

———. "Nonmarital Cohabitation." *Marriage and Family Review,* March/April 1978, pp. 1–12.

MacLeod, J. S. "How to Hold a Wife: A Bridegroom's Guide." *The Village Voice,* February 11, 1971.

Magrab, Phyllis R. "For the Sake of the Children: A Review of the Psychological Effects of Divorce." *Journal of Divorce* 1 (1978): 1424–1432.

Maher, Charles. "No-fault Divorce—No Rush to End Marriage." *Los Angeles Times,* January 16, 1979.

Marotz-Baden, Ramona, et al. "Family Form or Family Process? Reconsidering the Deficit Family Model Approach." *Family Coordinator,* January 1979, pp. 5–14.

Marvin v. Marvin. 18 Cal. 3d 660, 134 *California Reporter* 815, 557 P. 2d 106 (1976).

———. *Family Law Reporter* 5 (1979): 3109.

Maslow, A. H. *The Farther Reaches of Human Nature.* New York: Viking, 1971.

———. *Motivation and Personality,* 2nd ed. New York: Harper & Row, 1970.

———. *Toward a Psychology of Being,* 2nd ed. Princeton, N.J.: Van Nostrand, 1968.

Masters, W. H., and V. E. Johnson. *Human Sexual Response.* Boston: Little, Brown, 1966.

Matêjcêk, Z., Z. Dytrych, and V. Schüller. "The Prague Study of Children Born from Unwanted Pregnancies." *International Journal of Mental Health* 7 (1979): 63–74.

May, R. *Love and Will.* New York: Norton, 1970.

Mead, M. "Personal Communication." *Redbook,* November 25, 1966.

———. *Sex and Temperament in Three Primitive Societies.* New York: Morrow, 1935, 1961.

Miller, H. L., and P. S. Siegel. *Loving: A Psychological Approach.* New York: Wiley, 1972.

Miller, M., and W. Revinbark. "Sexual Differences in Physical Attractiveness as a Determinent of Heterosexual Liking." *Psychology Report* 27 (1970): 701–702.

Miller, R. L. *Economic Issues for Consumers.* St. Paul, Minn.: West, 1975.

———. *Personal Finance Today.* St. Paul, Minn.: West, 1979.

Miller, S., et al. "Recent Progress in Understanding and Facilitating Marital Communication." *The Family Coordinator* 24 (April 1975): 143–152.

Mischel, W. *Introduction to Personality.* New York: Holt, 1971.

Monahan, T. P. "The Changing Nature of and Instability of Remarriages." *Eugenics Quarterly* 5 (1958).

———. "How Stable Are Remarriages?" *American Journal of Sociology* 58 (November 1952).

———. "National Divorce Legislation: The Problem and Some Suggestions." *The Family Coordinator* 22 (July 1973): 353–358.

Money, F., and R. Athanasion. "Eve First, or Adam?" *Contemporary Psychology* 18 (December 1973): 593–599.

Money, J., and A. A. Ehrhardt. *Man and Woman, Boy and Girl: The Differentiation and Dimorphism of Gender Identity from Conception to Maturity.* Baltimore: Johns Hopkins University Press, 1972.

Montagu, A. *Touching: The Human Significance of Skin.* New York: Harper & Row, 1972.

Montague, M. F. A. *Prenatal Influences.* Springfield, Ill.: Charles C Thomas, 1962.

Moore, Kristin A., and Sandra L. Hofferth. "Effects of Women's Employment on Marriage: Formation, Stability and Roles." In *Marriage and Family Review.* Vol. 2, No. 2. New York: Haworth Press, 1979.

Morgan, R. "Goodbye to All That." *Rat: Subterranean News,* February 6, 1970.

Morris, D. *Intimate Behavior.* New York: Random House, 1971.

———. *The Naked Ape.* New York: McGraw-Hill, 1967.

Morris, J. *Conundrum.* New York: Harcourt Brace Jovanovich, 1974.

Mott, F. L., and Sylvia Moore. "The Causes of Marital Disruption among Young American Women: An Interdisciplinary Perspective." *Journal of Marriage and Family,* May 1979, pp. 355–365.

Murdock, G. "Sexual Behavior: What Is Acceptable?" *Journal of Social Hygiene* 36 (1950): 1–31.

Murstein, B. I. *Love, Sex, and Marriage through the Ages.* New York: Springer, 1974.

Myricks, Noel. " 'Palimony': The Impact of Marvin v. Marvin." *The Family Coordinator,* April 1980, pp. 210–215.

National Center for Health Statistics. *Children of Divorced Couples: United States, Selected Years.* Washington, D.C.: Government Printing Office, 1970.

National Center for Health Statistics. "Final Natality Statistics, 1977." *Monthly Vital Statistics Report, 1979.* 27 (12) (Supplement).

Neubardt, S. "Observations of a Practicing Gynecologist." In D. Grummon and A. Barclay (eds.), *Sexuality: A Search for Perspective*. New York: Van Nostrand Reinhold, 1971, pp. 2–17.

Neugarten, Bernice L., and Karol K. Weinstein. "The Changing American Grandparent." *Journal of Marriage and the Family* **26** (May 1973).

Newsweek. "All About that Baby." August 7, 1978, pp. 66–72.

———. "Legal Battle of the Sexes." April 30, 1979, pp. 68–74.

———. "The Parent Gap." September 22, 1975, p. 48.

New York Times, The. December 12, 1974.

Nye, F. "Emerging and Declining Family Roles." *Journal of Marriage and the Family* **36** (1974): 238–244.

———, and L. Hoffman (eds.). *The Employed Mother in America*. Chicago: Rand McNally, 1963.

Oakley, M. A. "Test Tube Babies." *Family Law Quarterly*, Winter 1974, pp. 385–400.

O'Neill, G., and N. O'Neill. *Open Marriage*. New York: Avon, 1972.

Oppenheimer, V. K. "Divorce, Remarriage and Wive's Labor Force Participation." Paper presented at the annual meeting of the American Sociological Society, Chicago, 1977.

Orlinsky, D. E. "Love Relationships in the Life Cycle: A Developmental Interpersonal Perspective." In H. A. Otto (ed.), *Love Today: A New Exploration*. New York: Dell, 1972, pp. 135–150.

Otto, H. "Marriage and Family Enrichment Programs. Report and Analysis." *The Family Coordinator* **24** (April 1975): 137–142.

Packard, V. *The Hidden Persuaders*. New York: Pocket Books, 1958.

Pahlman, E. "Childlessness, Intentional and Unintentional: Psychological and Social Aspects." *Journal of Nervous and Mental Disease* **151** (1970): 2–11.

Paige, K. "Women Learn to Sing the Menstrual Blues." *Psychology Today*, September 1973.

Pantelakis, S., et al. "Influence of Induced and Spontaneous Abortions on the Outcome of Subsequent Pregnancies." *American Journal of Obstetrics and Gynecology*, July 15, 1973, pp. 799–805.

Peck, E. *The Baby Trap*. New York: Bernard Geis, 1971.

Peel, J., and M. Potts. *Textbook of Contraceptive Practice*. Cambridge, Eng.: Cambridge University Press, 1970.

Peele, S., and A. Brodsky. "Interpersonal Heroin: Love Can Be an Addiction." *Psychology Today*, August 1974.

Page, R., and A. Brown. "The Effects of Physical Attraction and Evaluation on Effort Expenditure and Work Output." *Represent. Res. Soc. Psychol.* **2** (1971): 19–25.

Peplau, L. A., Z. Rubin, and C. T. Hill. "Sexual Intimacy in Dating Relationships." *Journal of Social Issues*, 1977.

Perlman, D. "Self-Esteem and Sexual Permissiveness." *Journal of Marriage and the Family* **36** (August 1974): 470–473.

Peterman, D. J., et al. "A Comparison of Cohabiting and Noncohabiting Students." *Journal of Marriage and the Family* **36** (May 1974): 344–355.

Peterson, E. "The Impact of Maternal Employment on the Mother-Daughter Relationship." *Marriage and Family Living* **23** (1961): 355–361.

Pfeiffer, V. E., and G. Davis. "Sexual Behavior in Middle Age." In *Normal Aging II.*, E. Palmore (ed.). Durham, N.C.: Duke University Press, 1974.

Pierce, C., and J. Sanfaco. "Man/Woman Dynamics: Some Typical Communication Patterns." In A. Sargent (ed.), *Beyond Sex Roles*. St. Paul, Minn.: West, 1977, pp. 97–108.

Pierson, E., and W. D'Antonio. *Female and Male: Dimensions of Sexuality*. Philadelphia: Lippincott, 1974.

Planned Parenthood-World Population. *The ABC's of Birth Control*. New York: Planned Parenthood, 1969.

Popenoe, P. *Family Life*. Washington, D.C.: George Washington University Medical Center, 1974.

Population Reports. "Oral Contraceptives." Dept. of Medical & Public Affairs, The George Washington University Medical Center, Washington, D.C. Series A, No. 2, March 1975.

Porter, Sylvia. *Money Book*. New York: Doubleday, 1975.

Pringle, B. M. "Family Clusters as a Means of Reducing Isolation among Urbanites." *Family Coordinator* **23** (April 1974).

Proulx, Cynthia. "Sex as Athletics in the Singles Complex." *Saturday Review*, May 1973.

Psychology Today. "The Freshmen, 1979." *Psychology Today*, September 1979, pp. 79–87.

Putney, S. *The Conquest of Society*. Belmont, Calif.: Wadsworth, 1972.

Queen, S. A., and R. W. Habenstein. *The Family in Various Cultures*. Philadelphia: Lippincott, 1974.

Ramey, J. W. "Intimate Groups and Networks: Frequent Consequences of Sexually Open Marriage. *The Family Coordinator*, October 24, 1975.

Ramsay, N. R. "Assortative Mating and the Structure of Cities." *American Journal of Sociology* **31** (1966): 773–786.

Rapaport, R., and R. Rapaport. "Men, Women and Equity." *The Family Coordinator* **24** (October 1975): 421–432.

Reiss, I. L. *The Family System in America*. New York: Holt, 1971.

———. Essay. In H. Hart et al. (eds.), *Marriage: For and Against*. New York: Hart, 1972, pp. 234–251.

———. "The Family in the 80's." Talk given at the National Council on Family Relations Winter Board

Meeting in San Diego, California on February 29, 1980.

———. "Toward a Sociology of the Heterosexual Love Relationship." *Marriage and Family Living*, May 1960.

Report from the White House Conference on Families. U.S. Department of Health, Education, and Welfare, 330 Independence Ave. S.W., Washington, D.C., May 1980.

Rheinstein, M. *Marriage Stability, Divorce and the Law.* Chicago: University of Chicago Press, 1972.

Ridley, C., D. Peterman, and A. Avery. "Cohabitation: Does It Make a Better Marriage?" *The Family Coordinator*, April 1978, pp. 129–136.

Riesen, A. "Stimulation as a Requirement for Growth and Function in Behavioral Development." In D. Fiske and S. Maddi (eds.), *Functions of Varied Experience.* Homewood, Ill.: Dorsey, 1961, pp. 57–80.

Riley, L. E., and E. A. Spreitzer. "A Model for the Analysis of Lifetime Marriage Patterns." *Journal of Marriage and the Family* **36** (February 1974): 64–71.

Rimmer, R. H. *The Harrad Experiment.* Los Angeles: Sherbourne, 1966.

Robbins, N. "End of Divorce—Beginning of Legal Problems." *The Family Coordinator* **23** (April 1974): 185–188.

———. "Have We Found Fault in No-Fault Divorce?" *The Family Coordinator* **22** (1973): 359–362.

Robinson, I. E., et al. "The Premarital Sexual Revolution among College Females." *The Family Coordinator* **21** (April 1972): 189–194.

Rogers, C. *Becoming Partners: Marriage and Its Alternatives.* New York: Delacorte Press, 1972.

———. "Communication: Its Blocking and Facilitation." Paper read at Centennial Conference on Communications, October 11, 1951, Northwestern University.

Rollin, B. "Motherhood: Who Needs It?" *Look*, September 22, 1970.

Rollins, B. C., and K. L. Cannon. "Marital Satisfaction over the Family Life Cycle: A Reevaluation." *Journal of Marriage and the Family* **36** (May 1974): 271–283.

———, and H. Feldman. "Marital Satisfaction over the Family Life Cycle." *Journal of Marriage and the Family* **32** (January 1970): 27.

Roncek, D., R. Bell, and H. Chaldin. "Female-headed Families: An Ecological Model of Residential Concentration in a Small City." *Journal of Marriage and Family*, February 1980, pp. 157–169.

Roper, E. "American Woman's Opinion Poll." *Santa Barbara News-Press*, October 3, 1974.

Rorvik, D. M. *Brave New Baby: Promise and Peril of Biological Revolution.* Garden City, N.Y.: Doubleday, 1971.

———. "The Test Tube Is Coming." *Look*, May 18, 1971, pp. 83–88.

Rosaldo, M. Z. "Women, Culture and Society: A Theoretical Overview." In M. Z. Rosaldo and L. Lamphere (eds.), *Women, Culture and Society.* Palo Alto, Calif.: Stanford University Press, 1974.

Rosenberg, B. G., and N. Sutton-Smith. *Sex and Identity.* New York: Holt, 1972.

Rosenthal, R., and L. Jacobson. *Pygmalion in the Classroom.* New York: Holt, 1968.

Rossi, A. "Why Seek Equality Between the Sexes: An Immodest Proposal." *Daedalus*, Spring 1964.

Rougemont, D. "The Crises of the Modern Couple." In R. N. Anshen (ed.), *The Family: Its Function and Destiny.* New York: Harper & Row, 1949.

Roy, R., and D. Roy. Essay. In H. Hart et al. (eds.), *Marriage: For and Against.* New York: Hart, 1971, pp. 60–77.

Rubin, Lillian B. *Worlds of Pain: Life in the Working Class Family.* New York: Basic Books, 1976.

Rubin, Z. *Liking and Loving.* New York: Holt, 1973.

———. "Seeking a Cure for Loneliness." *Psychology Today*, October 1979, pp. 82–90.

———, and G. Levinger. "Theory and Data Badly Mated: A Critic of Murstein's SVR and Lewis's PDF Models of Mate Selection." *Journal of Marriage and Family* **36** (1974): 226–231.

———. "Disclosing Oneself to a Stranger: Reciprocity and Its Limits." *Journal of Experimental Psychology* **11** (1975): 233–260.

———. "Naturalistic Studies of Self-Disclosure." *Personality, Sociology, and Psychology Bulletin* **2** (1976): 260–263.

Russ-Eft, Darlene, Marlene Sprenger, and Anne Beever. "Antecedents of Adolescent Parenthood and Consequences at Age Thirty." *Family Coordinator*, April 1979, pp. 173–179.

Russell, B. "Our Sexual Ethics." In *Why I Am Not a Christian.* New York: Simon & Shuster, 1957, pp. 171–172.

Russell, C. "Transition to Parenthood: Problems and Gratifications." *Journal of Marriage and the Family* **36** (May 1974): 294–301.

Rutlege, A. L. *Premarital Counseling.* Cambridge, Mass.: Schenkman, 1966.

Sabalis, R. F., and G. W. Ayers. "Emotional Aspects of Divorce and Their Effects on the Legal Process." *The Family Coordinator* (October 1977): 391–394.

San Francisco Chronicle. "Device May Pinpoint Fertile Days." December 24, 1976.

Santa Barbara News-Press. October 27, 1974.

———. March 19, 1975.

———. October 25, 1976.

———. November 29, 1976.

———. January 23, 1977, D-12.

———. March 20, 1977, B-4.

———. "America's Skyrocketing Debts." June 6, 1977, A-1.

———. "Living Out of Wedlock." February 9, 1977, B-8.

———. "Pills Taken Off Market." March 1976.

———. November 7, 1979.

Sargent, A. G. *Beyond Sex Roles*. St. Paul, Minn.: West, 1977.

Satir, V. *Peoplemaking*. Palo Alto, Calif.: Science and Behavior Books, 1972.

Saxton, L. *The Individual, Marriage and the Family*. Belmont, Calif.: Wadsworth, 1977.

Schachter, S. "The Interaction of Cognitive and Physiological Determinants in Emotional State." In Leonard Berkowitz (ed.), *Advances in Experimental Social Psychology*, vol. 1. New York: Academic Press, 1964.

Schauble, P., and C. Hill. "A Laboratory Approach to Treatment in Marriage Counseling: Training in Communication Skills." *The Family Coordinator* **25** (July 1976): 277–284.

Schulz, David. *Human Sexuality*. Englewood Cliffs, N.J.: Prentice-Hall, 1979.

Schultz, D. A., and S. F. Rodgers. *Marriage, the Family and Personal Fulfillment*. Englewood Cliffs, N.J.: Prentice-Hall, 1975.

Scoresby, A. L. *The Marriage Dialogue*. Reading, Mass.: Addison-Wesley, 1977.

Scott, J. *Early Experience and the Organization of Behavior*. Belmont, Calif.: Brooks/Cole, 1968.

Seats, R. "Dependency Motivation." In M. R. Jones (ed.), *Nebraska Symposium on Motivation*. Lincoln: University of Nebraska Press, 1963, pp. 25–64.

———. "Development of Gender Role." In F. R. Beach (ed.), *Sex and Behavior*. New York: Wiley, 1965, pp. 133–163.

———. "Identification as a Form of Behavior Development." In R. B. Harris (ed.), *The Concept of Development*. Minneapolis: University of Minnesota Press, 1957, pp. 149–161.

Seebach, Wayne C., and Charles J. Hansen. "Satisfaction with Family Relations among the Elderly." *Family Relations*, January 1980, p. 91.

Segal, S. J. "Prospects for Future Development on Contraception." *Proceedings of International Population Conference*. London: 1969.

Seligman, C., N. Paschall, and G. Takata. "Effects of Physical Attractiveness on Attribution of Responsibility." *Canadian Journal of Behavioral Science* **6** (1974): 290–296.

Sheehy, Gail. *Passages: Predictable Crises of Adult Life*. New York: Bantam Books, 1977.

Sheresky, N., and M. Mannes. *Uncoupling: The Art of Coming Apart*. New York: Viking, 1972.

Sherfey, M. J. *The Nature and Evaluation of Female Sexuality*. New York: Random House, 1972.

Shettles, L. B. "Predetermining "Children's Sex." *Medical Aspects of Human Sexuality* **5** (June 6, 1972): 178–185.

Shostrom, E. L. "Group Therapy: Let the Buyer Beware." *Psychology Today*, May 1969.

Sidel, R. *Families of Fengsheng*. Baltimore: Penguin, 1974.

Sigall, H., and E. Aronson. "Liking for an Evaluator as a Function of Her Physical Attractiveness and the Nature of the Evaluations." *Journal of Experimental Social Psychology* **5** (1969): 93–100.

Silverman, A., and A. Silverman. *The Case against Having Children*. New York: McKay, 1971.

Silverman, Phylis. "The Widow as a Care Giver in a Program of Preventative Intervention with other Widows." *Mental Hygiene* **54** (1970).

Simmons, J. I., and B. Winograd. *It's Happening*. Santa Barbara, Calif.: Marc-Laird, 1966.

Simon, A. W. *Stepchild in the Family*. New York: Odyssey, 1964.

Skolnick, A., and J. Skolnick. *Family in Transition*. 3rd ed. Boston: Little, Brown, 1980.

———. *The Intimate Environment: Exploring Marriage and the Family*. Boston: Little, Brown, 1973.

Skolnick, A. S., and J. H. Skolnick. *Family in Transition*. Boston: Little, Brown, 1971; 1976.

Smart, M. S., and L. S. Smart. *Families Developing Relationships*. New York: Macmillan, 1976.

Smith, M. J. "The Social Consequences of Single Parenthood: A Longitudinal Perspective." *Family Coordinator*, January 1980, pp. 75–81.

Smith, Ralph E. (ed.). *The Subtle Revolution: Women at Work*. Washington, D.C.: The Urban Institute, 1979.

Society for the Scientific Study of Sex, The. Western Regional Meeting. San Diego, Calif.: June 28-30, 1974.

Solanis, V. "SCUM Manifesto (Society for Cutting Up Men)." In R. Morgan (ed.), *Sisterhood Is Powerful*. New York: Random House, 1970, p. 519.

Sorokin, P. *Social and Cultural Dynamics*. New York: Harper & Row, 1937.

Spanier, Graham, et al. "Marital Adjustment Over the Family Life Cycle: The Issue of Curvilinearity." *Journal of Marriage and Family*, May 1975, pp. 263–275.

Stambul, H., and H. Kelly. "Conflict in the Development of Close Relationships." In R. Burgess and T. Huston, (eds.), *Social Exchange in Developing Relationships*. New York: Academic, 1978.

Starr, Raymond H. "Child Abuse." *American Psychologist*, October 1979, pp. 872–878.

———, and D. E. Carns. "Singles in the City." In H. Z. Lopata (ed.), *Marriage and Families: A Transaction/Society Reader*. New York: Van Nostrand, 1973.

Statistical Abstract of the United States. Washington, D.C.: Government Printing Office, 1974, p. 340.

Statistical Abstract of the United States. Washington, D.C.: Government Printing Office, 1976, pp. 38, 51.

Stein, P. J. "Singlehood: An Alternative to Marriage." *The Family Coordinator* **24** (October 1975): 489–503.

Steiner, G. "Family Stability and Income Guarantees." *The Washington Cofo Memo*. Winter 1979. Washington, D.C. Coalition of Family Organizations.

Steinmetz, Suzanne K. "The Use of Force for Resolving Family Conflict: The Training Ground for Abuse." *Family Coordinator*, January 1977(a).

———. *The Cycle of Violence: Assertive, Aggressive*

and *Abusive Family Interaction*. New York: Praeger, 1977(b).

———. "Violence Between Family Members." *Marriage and Family Review* **1** (1978) 1–16.

Stephens, W. L. *The Family in Cross-Cultural Perspective*. New York: Holt, 1963.

Stetson, D., and G. Wright. "The Effects of Laws on Divorce in American States." *Journal of Marriage and the Family* **37** (August 1975): 537–547.

Stinnett, Nick. "In Search of Strong Families." In N. Stinnett, B. Chesser and J. Defrain (eds.), *Building Family Strengths*. Lincoln, Neb.: University of Nebraska Press, 1979, pp. 23–30.

Stone, L. J., and J. Church. *Childhood and Adolescence*. New York: Random House, 1973.

Straus, Murray. "Leveling, Civility and Violence in the Family." *Journal of Marriage and Family* **36** (1974): 13–29.

Streib, Gordon F. "Older Families and Their Troubles: Familial and Social Responses." *Family Coordinator* **21** (January 1972).

Suelzle, M. "Women in Labor." *Trans-action* **8** (November-December 1970): 50–58.

Sugimoto, E. *A Daughter of the Samurai*. Garden City, N.Y.: Doubleday, 1935.

Terman, L. *Psychological Factors in Marital Happiness*. New York: McGraw-Hill, 1938.

Tillich, P. *Dynamics of Faith*. New York: Harper & Row, 1957.

Time, "The New Morality." November 21, 1977, p. 111.

———. "Women of the Year." January 5, 1976, p. 8.

———. "Abortion: The Edelin Shock Wave." March 3, 1975, pp. 54–55.

———. "The American Family: Future Uncertain." December 28, 1970.

———. "Doubts about I.U.D.s." July 15, 1974, p. 81.

———. "Those Missing Babies." September 16, 1974, pp. 54–63.

———. "The New Morality." November 21, 1977, p. 111.

———. "Superkids? A Sperm Bank for Nobelists." March 10, 1980.

Todres, R. "Runaway Wives: An Increasing North American Phenomenon." *Family Coordinator*, January 1978, pp. 17–21.

Toynbee, A. "The Continuing Effect of the American Revolution." Speech, June 10, 1961, Williamsburg, Va.

Trainer, J. *Physiologic Functions for Marriage Counseling*. St. Louis: Mosby, 1965.

Udry, J. R. *The Social Context of Marriage*, 3rd ed. Philadelphia: Lippincott, 1974.

Udry, R. "Marital Instability by Race and Income Based on 1960 Census Data." *American Journal of Sociology* **72** (May 1976): 673–674.

Ullian, D. Z. "The Development of Conceptions of Masculinity and Femininity." In B. Lloyd and J. Archer (eds.), *Exloring Sex Differences*. London: Academic Press, 1976.

U.S. Bureau of the Census. *Current Population Reports: Marital Status and Living Arrangements*, ser. P-20, no. 271, March 1974.

——— *Current Population Reports: The Social and Economic Status of the Black Population of the United States*, ser. P-23, no. 42. Washington, D.C.: Government Printing Office, 1972.

——— *Current Population Reports*, ser. P-20, no. 271. Washington, D.C.: Government Printing Office, 1975.

———. *Current Population Reports: Population Profile of the United States: 1976*, ser. P-20, no. 307. Washington, D.C.: Government Printing Office, 1977.

———. *Historical Statistics of the United States 1789–1945*. Washington, D.C.: Government Printing Office, 1949, p. 63.

———. *Current Population Reports: Marital Status and Living Arrangements, 1977*, ser. P-20, no. 323. Washington, D.C.: Government Printing Office, 1978.

———. *Statistical Abstracts*. Table 44. Washington, D.C.: Government Printing Office, 1976.

———. *Current Population Reports: Projections of the Population of the United States, 1977 to 2050*, ser. P-25, no. 704. Washington, D.C.: Government Printing Office, 1977.

U.S. Department of Commerce. *Monthly Labor Review*, 1977, 1978.

U.S. National Center for Health Statistics. *Monthly Vital Statistics Report, Provisional Statistics, Annual Summary for the United States*, 1970.

———. *Vital Statistics of the United States, Special Report*. December 1975.

———. *Vital Statistics, Special Reports 37*, 1975.

———. *Monthly Vital Statistics Report*. Vol. 27, no. 3. Washington, D.C.: Government Printing Office, June 1978.

U.S. News & World Report. "The American Family: Can It Survive Today's Shocks?" October 27, 1975, pp. 30–32.

———. "Is the American Family in Danger?" April 16, 1973, pp. 71–74.

———. "The Plight of America's Two Million Widowers." April 1974, pp. 59–60.

———. "Throwaway Marriages—Threat to American Family." January 13, 1975, pp. 43–46.

———. "Today's Marriages Wrenching Experience or Key to Happiness?" October 27, 1975.

U.S. Office of Human Development. Administration on Aging. Publication No. (OHD) 77–2006, 1976.

U.S. Public Health Services Center for Disease Control. *Morbidity and Mortality Weekly Report*. Vol. 13, no. 54, 1966 and Vol. 22, no. 53, 1975.

Veevers, J. E. "The Moral Careers of Voluntarily Childless Wives: Notes on the Defense of a Variant World View." *The Family Coordinator* **24** (October 1975): 473–488.

————. "Voluntary Childlessness: A Neglected Area of Family Study." *The Family Coordinator* **22** (April 1973): 199–206.

Verbrugge, Lois. "Marital Status and Health." *Journal of Marriage and Family*, May 1979, pp. 267–285.

Vickery, Clair. "Women's Economic Contribution to the Family." In R. E. Smith (ed), *The Subtle Revolution: Women at Work*. Washington, D.C.: The Urban Institute, 1979.

Vincent, C. E. "Familia Spongia: The Adaptive Function." *Journal of Marriage and the Family* **28** (1966): 29–36.

————. *Sexual and Mental Health*, New York: McGraw-Hill, 1973.

Waldron, I. "Household Work Time: Its Implications for Family Decisions." *Journal of Home Economics* **65** (1973): 7–11.

Walker, Kathryn E., and Margaret E. Woods. *Time Use: A Measure of Household Production of Family Goods and Services*. American Home Economic Association, 1976.

Waller, W. *The Old Love and the New: Divorce and Readjustment*. Carbondale, Ill.: Southern Illinois University Press, 1967.

Wallerstein, J. "Children and Parents 18 Months After Parental Separation: Factors Related to Differential Outcome." Paper presented at the National Institute of Mental Health Conference on Divorce. Washington, D.C., February 1978.

Wallerstein, Judith, and Joan Kelley. "California's Children of Divorce." *Psychology Today*, January 1980, pp. 67–76.

Walster, E., and E. Berscheid. "Adrenaline Makes the Heart Grow Fonder." *Psychology Today*, June 1971, pp. 46–50, 62.

Wattenberg, B., and R. Scammon. *This U.S.A.* Garden City, N.Y.: Doubleday, 1965.

Wedeck, H. *Love Potions through the Ages*. New York, 1962.

Weinberg, Richard. "Early Childhood Education and Intervention." *American Psychologist*, October 1979, pp. 912–916.

Weiss, R. *Marital Separation*. New York: Basic Books, 1975.

Weitzman, L. J. "To Love, Honor and Obey? Traditional Legal Marriage and Alternative Family Forms." *The Family Coordinator* **24** (October 1975a): 531–548.

————. "Sex-Role Socialization." In J. Freeman (ed.), *Women: A Feminist Perspective*. Palo Alto, Calif.: Mayfield, 1975b, pp. 105–144.

Wernick, R., and Editors of Time-Life Books. *The Family*. New York: Little, Brown, 1974.

Westhoff, L. A., and C. F. Westhoff. *From Now to Zero*. Boston: Little, Brown, 1971.

Whelan, E. *A Baby . . . Maybe?* New York: Bobbs-Merrill, 1976.

Whitehurst, R. N. "Sex Role Equality and Changing Meanings of Cohabitation." Paper presented at the annual meeting of the North Central Sociological Association, Windsor, Canada, May 1974.

Whiting, Beatrice. "Folk Wisdom and Child Rearing." *Merril-Palmer Quarterly* **20** (1974): 9–19.

————. "Work and the Family: Cross-cultural Perspectives." Paper presented at *Women: Resource for a Changing World*. Conference held at Radcliffe Institute, Radcliffe College, Cambridge, Mass.: April 17-18, 1972.

Williams, R. "Alimony: The Short Goodby." *Psychology Today*, July 1977, p. 71.

Wilson, K. L., et al. "Stepfathers and Stepchildren: An Exploratory Analysis from Two National Surveys." *Journal of Marriage and the Family* **37** (August 1975): 526–536.

Winch, Robert F. *The Modern Family*. New York: Holt, 1971.

Wolfe, Linda. "The Sexual Profile of that Cosmopolitan Girl." *Cosmopolitan*, September 1980.

Wolfers, H. "Psychological Aspects of Vasectomy." *British Medical Journal* **4** (October 31, 1970): 297, 300.

Yankelovich Organization, The. *Public Attitudes toward the Family*. New York: Institute of Life Insurance, 1974.

Young, W. C. "The Mammalian Ovary." In W. C. Young (ed.), *Sex and Internal Secretions*, 3rd ed. Baltimore: Williams & Wilkins, 1961, chap. 7.

Zablocki, B. *The Joyful Community. An Account of the Bruderhof, a Communist Movement Now in Its Third Generation*. Baltimore: Penguin, 1971.

Zelnik, M., and J. Kantner. "Sexual and Contraceptive Experience of Young Unmarried Women in the U.S. 1976 and 1971." *Family Planning Perspectives* **9** (1977) 2. pp. 55–71.

Zilbergeld, B., and M. Evans. "The Inadequacy of Masters and Johnson." *Psychology Today*, August 1980, pp. 29–43.

Author Index

Albrecht, S. 464
Amundsen, K. 56
Apgar, V. 340
Aron, A. P. 105
Avery, A. 440
Ayers, G. W. 456

Babbitt, R. H. 11
Bach, G. R. 144, 149, 184, 191, 192,
    193, 387
Baker, R. 442
Baldwin, W. 292, 362
Bane, M. J. 7, 8, 28, 30
Barclay, A. M. 265, 281
Bardwick, J. 48
Barnhill, L. 372
Barocas, R. 131
Barrett, C. 367
Barrett, N. 55, 245
Bartell, G. D. 429
Beck, J. 340
Becker, G. 485
Beiswinger, G. 138
Bell, R. R. 120, 371, 487
Berelson, B. 363, 365
Bernard, J. 380, 486
Berscheid, E. 89, 131
Bienchi, S. 24
Bienvenu, M. J. 176
Biddle, B. J. 12
Blake, J. 427
Blau, P. M. 107
Bohannan, P. 462
Bombeck, E. 226
Borland, D. M. 85, 86
Bortner, M. 49
Bower, D. W. 436
Bowerman, C. 487
Bowes, W. A. 338
Bowman, H. A. 149
Brayshaw, A. J. 397
Broderick, C. 113
Brody, S. E. 305
Bronfenbrenner, U. 29
Broverman, I. 248
Burgess, E. 135
Budd, L. S. 438

Bumpass, L. 485
Burchinal, L. 471, 487
Butler, R. N. 407

Calhoun, L. 427
Camara, D. 491
Cannon, K. L. 154
Canfield, E. K. 264
Casler, L. 11, 83, 84
Chadwick, B. A. 154
Chafetz, J. 52, 56, 66
Chancellor, L. 439
Chason, K. 439
Christopherson, V. A. 436
Church, J. 112
Cherlin, A. 845
Close, H. 364
Clark, J. R. 87–88
Chatworthy, N. 439
Coogler, O. S. 465
Coughay, K. 120
Cox, F. D. 159, 162, 369, 487
Cozby, P. W. 176
Crane, J. A. 434
Cromwell, R. E. 498
Crosby, J. F. 21, 451
Cutler, B. R. 176

Danziger, C. 437
Darnley, F. 395, 404
David, H. 292, 362
David, K. 128
Denfield, D. 429
Deutsch, R. M. 144, 193
Devey, G. 341
Dick-Read, G. 347
Dillon, T. F. 351
Dion, K. 131
Duberman, L. 17, 410, 479, 489
Dixon, R. 460
Dutton, D. L. 105
Dyer, W. G. 176
Dytrych, Z. 292

Easley, E. B. 306
Edmiston, S. 148
Elkin, M. 457, 472

Ehrhardt, A. A. 47
Erikson, E. 96, 351, 374
Etzioni, A. 34
Evans, M. 278

Farley, R. 24
Feldberg, R. 175
Fisher, E. 466
Freud, S. 96
Frieze, I. H. 49
Fromm, E. 12, 82, 83, 88, 97, 102
Furstenberg, F. 480, 484

Gagon, J. 44
Galbraith, J. K. 213, 214
Goleman, D. 48, 49
Gilbert, S. J. 176
Gilmartin, B. C. 429
Glenn, N. D. 486
Glick, P. C. 7, 32, 143, 238, 240,
    362, 383, 395, 396, 406, 408, 410,
    424, 425, 438, 449, 460, 463, 471,
    479, 487
Goertzel, V. 302
Gordon, T. 179
Greenwald, M. 437
Gribbin, A. 31
Grossman, A. 449
Gunter, B. G. 461
Gurdon, J. B. 5
Guttmacher, A. F. 295, 305, 315,
    334

Habenstein, R. W. 23
Hansen, C. J. 409
Hannan, M. T. 242
Harlow, H. F. 10, 104
Harlow, M. K. 10
Hardin, G. 310
Hart, T. M. 309
Hawkins, J. 154
Havighurst, R. J. 404
Hecht, A. 335
Helfer, R. 388
Henderson, B. 44
Hess, R. 491
Hetherington, E. M. 373, 491, 492

531

Hicks, M. 154, 371
Hill, C. T. 107, 133, 190, 443
Hill, W. F. 507
Hiltz, R. S. 410
Hobbins, J. C. 341
Hochschild, A. R. 395
Hofferth, S. L. 210, 241, 244, 246, 247
Hoffman, S. 241, 242
Hoffman, L. 373
Holmes, J. 242
Honig, A. S. 385
Houseknecht, S. 428
Huesmann, L. R. 107
Hunt, M. 31, 79, 121, 145, 466
Hunt, R. 178
Huston, T. L. 131

Insel, P. M. 305, 306, 308
Irish, D. 487
Ivey, M. 48

Jacklin, C. N. 49
Jackson, D. D. 161, 197
Jacobs, C. N. 143, 173
Jacobson, L. 161
Jacques, J. 439
Jensen, G. D. 11
Johnson, D. T. 461
Johnson, M. P. 438
Johnson, K. 154, 278, 280, 319
Johnson, V. 125
Jones, E. E. 132
Jourard, S. 164
Jursnich, D. 361

Kahn, H. 249
Kanter, R. 63, 433
Kanter, J. 120
Kane, F. J. 353
Kapecky, G. 436
Kaplan, H. 319
Karoly, P. 131
Katchadourian, H. A. 328, 330
Keller, S. 350
Kelley, H. 132, 467
Kelly, J. B. 466
Kempe, C. 388
Kephart, W. 105, 106
Kerckhoff, A. 128, 129
Kerckhoff, R. 397
Kieffer, C. M. 12, 13, 14, 438
King, D. 120
Kinsey, A. 119, 278, 281
Klaus, M. 354
Kogan, B. 279, 282, 305, 316, 318, 339, 344
Kohen, J. 175
Krantzler, M. 467

Lacon, T. 474, 476
Landers, A. 87
Landis, P. 203, 208
Landes, E. 485
Lasswell, M. E. 91, 410, 411
Lavori, N. 445
Laws, J. L. 154
Lear, H. 305
Leboyer, F. 356
Lederer, W. J. 161, 197
Le Masters, E. E. 488
Le Shan, E. J. 397
Leslie, G. 437, 461
Lessard, S. 313
Levinger, G. 107, 129, 131, 132
Lewis, R. 438
Libby, R. 13, 425
Lindemann, B. 52, 58, 69
Lindsey, B. 4
Linner, B. 50
Linton, R. 79
Lobsenz, N. 91
Locke, H. J. 486
Lopata, H. Z. 409, 415
Lunde, D. T. 328, 330
Lyness, J. L. 438
Lynn, D. B. 373

Maccoby, E. E. 49
Mace, D. 5, 6, 80, 496, 506
MacLeod, J. S. 74
Macklin, E. D. 4, 117, 436, 439, 445
Magrab, P. R. 467
Maher, C. 460
Mannes, M. 467
Marotz-Baden, R. 384
Maslow, A. 12, 13, 50, 108, 163
Masters, W. H. 125, 278, 280, 319, 341
Matêjcék, Z. 292
May, R. 102
McCary, J. 273, 341
McGuiness, D. 49
McMorrow, F. 397
Mead, M. 4, 46
Michael, R. 485
Miller, R. L. 210, 211, 220, 231
Miller, M. 131
Miller, H. L. 102
Miller, S. 507
Mischel, W. 47
Monahan, T. P. 454, 485
Money, F. 43, 47
Montique, A. 96, 97, 340, 351, 352
Moore, K. A. 240, 241, 244, 246, 247
Moore, S. 471
Moreno, J. L. 503
Morris, D. 12, 265
Morris, J. 44

Mott, F. L. 471
Murdock, G. 111
Murstein, B. I. 12
Myricks, N. 445

Neubardt, S. 267
Neugarten, B. L. 411
Noble, H. 367
Norton, A. 143, 424, 449, 463, 479, 487
Nye, F. I. 21, 291, 373

Oakley, M. A. 317
O'Neill, G. 14, 64
O'Neil, N. 14, 64
Oppenheimer, V. K. 239, 240
Orlinsky, D. 100, 101
Otto, H. 506

Pachard, V. 29, 215
Pahlman, E. 427
Paige, K. 48
Pantelakis, S. 313
Peel, J. 294
Peplau, L. A. 107, 127, 133, 443
Peterman, D. J. 436, 440
Peterson, E. 373
Pfeiffer, V. E. 411
Pierce, C. 185
Platt, M. 154, 371
Popenoe, P. 31
Porter, S. 407
Potts, M. 294
Pribram, K. 49
Pringle, B. M. 435
Proulx, C. 426
Putney, S. 502

Queen, S. A. 23

Ramey, J. W. 430
Rapaport, R. 38
Reiss, I. 84, 85, 262, 362, 384, 421, 433, 443
Revinbark, W. 131
Rheinstein, M. 458
Ridley, C. 440
Riley, L. E. 485
Robbins, N. 461
Rodgers, S. F. 90
Rogers, C. 15, 19, 430, 432
Roiphe, A. 139
Rollins, B. C. 154
Roncek, D. 384
Rorvik, D. M. 5
Rosaldo, M. Z. 41
Rosenblatt, P. 107
Rosenberg, B. G. 48
Rosenthal, R. 161

Subject Index

Polygyny 410
Postpartum problems 353–354
Possessive love 94
Pregnancy 331–342
    and drugs 335–338
    and infectious diseases 338
    and radiation 338–339
    and smoking 340
    and intercourse 341
Pregnancy tests 332–334
Premarital medical examination
    136
Premarital sexuality 118–119
Private Freedom Cult 197–198
Privatism 496
Problem solving 192–194
Psychodrama 503
Puberty 111–112, 378–379
Punishment 369

Reconstituted family 479
Rehabilitative alimony 60
RELATE 106
Remarriage 479–492
Reproduction 327–357
Retirement 395, 402–406
Rh blood disease 339–340
Rhythm 302
Role 39–41
Role equity 38
Romantic love 86–87, 94–95, 158
Rooming-in 349–350

Saline procedure 314
Scientific method 193–194
Second mortgage 254
Self-actualization 50
Self-actualized person 161–165
Self-assertion 184–188
Self-disclosure 132

Self-fulfilling prophecy 161
Self-love 96–97
Semen 271
Sensitivity training 504
Serial marriage 449, 479
Sex identity 42, 52
Sex knowledge inventory 266
"Sex-not-sex" 119
Sex role development 51
Sex role differences 49
Sex role problems 52–62
Sex role stereotypes 52, 62–72
Sex therapy 318–320, 504
Sexual anatomy 267–278
    male 269–273
    female 273–276
Sexual harassment 61–62
Sexual health 263–264
Sexual regulation 21–23
Sexual response 278–281
    female 279–280
    male 280
Sexual revolution 119–122
Sexual stress 111–112
Sexuality 261–287
    teenage 138–139
Sibling abuse 389
Single parent family 383–384
Socialization 9
Sperm 269–327
Sperm banks 317–318
Spermicides 294, 302–303
Sterilization 304–306
Stock 256
    preferred 256
    common 256
    blue chip 256
Summary dissolution 457–458
Swinging 429
Syndicates 254
Syphilis 283

Teenage sexuality 138–139
Test tube baby 322–324
Testicles 269
Testosterone 43, 271
Thalidomide 338
"Throwaway marriage" 449
Togetherness 428–429
Transexual 44–45
Transvestite 45
Trophoblast 329
Truth in lending 210
Tubal ligation 305–306
Twins 330

Ultrasound in obstetrics 341
Unselfish love 95
Unwanted pregnancy 123–124

Vacuum asperation 312
Vasectomy 304–305
Venereal disease 123, 283–284
"Vicious circle" 176
Visitation rights 457

We Care 468–481
Weekend family 252
Whitehouse Conference on Families
    24–25
Widowhood 395
Withdrawal (coitus interruptus)
    304
Women and the economy 52–59
    and the law 60–62
    and credit 59
Working wife 237–252
    and divorce 241–243
    and household activities 243–244
    and marital satisfaction 246–248

Young adulthood 379–380

Photo Credits

Chapter 1 **1** Frank Siteman, Stock, Boston, Inc.; **11** Wayne Miller, Magnum; **18** Rose Skytta, © 1977 Jeroboam, Inc.; **20** Arthur Tress, © 1973 Magnum; **28** (left) Tom Carter, © 1977 Jeroboam, Inc.; (right) Anne Dorfmann, © 1980 Jeroboam, Inc.

Chapter 2 **35** Rick Grosse, © 1980/Ekm-Nepenthe; **40** James R. Holland, Stock, Boston, Inc.; **57** Elizabeth Hamlin, Stock, Boston, Inc.; **74** (left) Jean-Claude Lejeune, Stock, Boston, Inc.; (middle) Frank Siteman, Stock, Boston, Inc.; (right) John Maher, Ekm-Nepenthe.

Chapter 3 **77** Steve Malone; **100** Mitchell Payne, © 1978 Jeroboam, Inc.; **104** (left) Lyn Gardiner, Stock, Boston, Inc.; (middle) Steve Malone; (right) Richard Kalvar, Magnum.

Chapter 4 **109** Steve Malone; **113** Owen Franken, Stock, Boston, Inc.; **119** Steve Malone; **130** Susan Ylvisaker, © 1979 Jeroboam, Inc.; **138** (left) Ekm-Nepenthe; (middle) Donald Dietz, Stock, Boston, Inc.; (right) Emilio Mercado/Jeroboam, Inc., © 1977.

Chapter 5 **141** Susan Ylvisaker, © 1979 Jeroboam, Inc.; **144** (right) Stock, Boston, Inc.; (left) Laurie Cameron, © 1980 Jeroboam, Inc.; **145** Bob Adelman, Magnum; **150** Steve Malone; **156** Jean Boughton, Stock, Boston, Inc.; **168** (left) Gilles Peress, Magnum; (middle) Ellis Herwig, Stock, Boston, Inc.; (right) Suzanne Wu, © 1980 Jeroboam, Inc.

Chapter 6 **171** Joyce McKinney, © 1980 Jeroboam, Inc.; **174** Optic Nerve, © 1978, Jeroboam, Inc.; **194** Ed Buryn, © 1979 Jeroboam, Inc.; **196** (left) Mark Chester; (middle) Paul Fortin, Stock, Boston, Inc.; (right) Rick Smolan, Stock, Boston, Inc.

Chapter 7 **199** Steve Malone; **211** Jean-Claude Lejeune, Stock, Boston, Inc.; **213** Mark Chester; **231** (left) David S. Strickler, Monkmeyer Press Photo Service; (middle) Mimi Forsyth, Monkmeyer Press Photo Service; (right) Frank Siteman, Stock, Boston, Inc.

Chapter 8 **235** Barbara Alper, Stock, Boston, Inc.; **249** Abigail Heyman, Magnum; **253** (left) Steve Malone; (middle) Mike Mazzaschi, Stock, Boston, Inc.; (right) Burk Uzzle, Magnum.

Chapter 9 **259** Jim Ritscher, Stock, Boston, Inc.; **286** (left) Harold Chapman, © 1980 Jeroboam, Inc.; (middle) Patricia Hollander Gross, Stock, Boston, Inc.; (right) Charles Gatewood, Stock, Boston, Inc.

Chapter 10 **289** Frederick D. Brolin, Stock, Boston, Inc.; **293** © Erika Stone 1978, Peter Arnold, Inc.; **309** (top) Mark Chester; (bottom) Daniel S. Brody, Stock, Boston, Inc.; **314** Carnegie Institution of Washington, Department of Embryology; **319** Elizabeth Crews; **322** (left and right) © Erika Stone, Peter Arnold, Inc.; (middle) © 1978 Lanna W. Schreiber, Photo Researchers, Inc.

Chapter 11 **325** Andy Mercado, © Jeroboam, Inc.; **339** Carnegie Institution of Washington, Department of Embryology; **348** Suzanne Arms, © Jeroboam, Inc.; **353** Elizabeth Crews; **354** Vicki Lawrence, Stock, Boston, Inc.; **356** (left, middle) Suzanne Arms, © Jeroboam, Inc.; (right) Steve Malone.

Chapter 12 **359** Anna Kaufman Moon, Stock, Boston, Inc.; **363** Mark Chester; **382** Steve Hansen, Stock, Boston, Inc.; **387** (left) Charles Harbutt, Magnum; (middle) James R. Holland, Stock, Boston, Inc.; (right) Jeff Albertson, Stock, Boston, Inc.

Chapter 13 **391** Charles Gatewood, Stock, Boston, Inc.; **398** Suzanne Szasz, Photo Researchers, Inc.; **402** Ellis Herwig, Stock, Boston, Inc.; **410** Robert V. Eckert, Ekm-Nepenthe; **412** Mark Chester; **414** (left) Rick Smolan, Stock, Boston, Inc.; (middle) Constantine Manos, Magnum; (right) Anestis Diakopoulos, Stock, Boston, Inc.

Chapter 14 **419** Tim Carlson, Stock, Boston, Inc.; **430** Roger Lubin, © Jeroboam, Inc.; **433** (top) Kay Lawson, © 1978 Jeroboam, Inc.; (bottom) Dennis Stock, Magnum; **445** (left) Ed Buryn, © 1979 Jeroboam, Inc.; (right) Rohdan Hrynewych, Stock, Boston, Inc.

Chapter 15 **447** Cary Wolinsky, Stock, Boston, Inc.; **455** Mark Chester; **461** Mark Chester; **465** Rick Smolan, Stock, Boston, Inc.; **474** (left) Steve Malone; (middle) Clay Templin, © 1977 Jeroboam, Inc.; (right) Owen Franken, Stock, Boston, Inc.

Chapter 16 **477** Mark Chester; **483** Michael Malyszko, Stock, Boston, Inc.; **491** (left) Jean Gaumy, Magnum; (middle) Charles Harbutt, Magnum; (right) Ellis Herwig, Stock, Boston, Inc.

Chapter 17 **493** Abigail Heyman, Magnum; **498** John R. Maher, Ekm-Nepenthe; **512** Cary Wolinsky, Stock, Boston, Inc.; **513** (left) Steve Malone; (right) Peter Menzel, Stock, Boston, Inc.